BUDDHIST GODDESSES OF INDIA

Buddhist Goddesses of India

Miranda Shaw

Princeton University Press
Princeton ■ Oxford

Published by Princeton University Press, 41 William Street, Princeton,
New Jersey 08540

In the United Kingdom: Princeton University Press, 3 Market Place,
Woodstock, Oxfordshire OX20 1SY

Library of Congress Cataloging-in-Publication Data

Shaw, Miranda Eberle, 1954–
Buddhist goddesses of India / Miranda Shaw.
p. cm.
Includes bibliographical references and index.
ISBN-10: 0-691-12758-1 (cloth : alk. paper)
ISBN-13: 978-0-691-12758-3 (cloth : alk. paper)
1. Buddhist goddesses—India. 2. South Asia—Religious life and customs. I. Title.

BQ4630.S43 2006
294.3'421140954—dc22 2005054533

British Library Cataloging-in-Publication Data is available

This book has been composed in Adobe Garamond and Snell Roundhand

Printed on acid-free paper. ∞

pup.princeton.edu

Printed in Canada

1 3 5 7 9 10 8 6 4 2

TO MY BEAUTIFUL FAMILY,
MAMA (MERRY)
PAPA JOHN
BROTHER TODD
SISTER ROSEMERRY

Contents

Part Three Tantric Female Buddhas

Acknowledgments

I would like to thank Ann Wald, former editor-in-chief of Princeton University Press, for her interest and confidence in this project from the outset. I am equally grateful to my current editor, Fred Appel, and the inestimable Sara Lerner for graciously and skillfully shepherding the manuscript to completion.

Numerous people assisted me over the decade of research and writing of this book. Deep appreciation is due to Sanskritist Abhijit Ghosh of Jadavpur University, Calcutta, for bringing his immense philological expertise to bear on difficult passages in the *Mañjuśrīmūlakalpa* and *Sādhanamālā*. Gautama Vajracharya merits acknowledgment for his meticulous reading of the final manuscript for Sanskrit accuracy and for a range of helpful comments.

For interviews on Tibetan texts, practices, and iconography, I am grateful to Śridar Rana of Kathmandu and the Sakya scholars and masters Khenpo Abbe, Chogay Trichen Rinpoche, Ngorchen Rinpoche, Ngawang Jorden, and Jampa Losel. The Nyingma scholar and master Tulku Thondup Rinpoche provided invaluable bibliographic resources. The Drikung Kagyu master Sonam Jorphel Rinpoche opened his archives to me and spent many hours patiently elucidating technical aspects of Kriyā and Anuttara Yoga Tantra practices. Stateside, Nawang Thogmey, Tibetan archivist of the University of Virginia, was extremely helpful as a guide to the university's Tibetan holdings and an adept procurer of relevant texts.

For interviews on Newar practice, I am profoundly indebted to the late Ratnakaji Vajracharya, who is greatly missed, not only for his rare erudition but for the generosity, patience, and pleasure with which he shared his knowledge. His son, Prajwal Ratna Vajracharya, has also been and remains an invaluable guide to his tradition. Prajwal spent countless hours translating interviews and escorting me to temples, museums, and libraries in Nepal and, now that he has relocated to the United States, responding to my ongoing inquiries with the grace of a true bodhisattva.

I am tremendously indebted to those who brought an expert eye to aspects or parts of my study that fall within their purview. For reading and commenting on portions of the manuscript, improving its accuracy, content, and style in numerous ways, I am immensely grateful to Paula Kane Arai, Constantina Rhodes Bailley, Elisabeth Benard, Jane Casey, Richard S. Cohen, Thomas Donaldson, Joseph Dye III, Francesca Fremantle, William Harman, John Holt, Susan Huntington, Roger Jackson, Susan Landesman, Miriam Levering, Joseph Loizzo, Frédérique Marglin, Ellen Pearlman, Tracy Pintchman, Graham Schweig, John Strong, Bradley Tindall, and Jonathan Walters. Rebecca Nicholls Louick refined and clarified large portions of the manuscript with rare editorial flair. At the finish, Kim Hastings brought her supernally keen talents to bear, providing many touches of precision and polish.

Among the many museums and archives that supplied photographs, all of which deserve thanks and receive credit herein, I would especially like to recognize the individuals who generously made their considerable institutional resources available to me: Dina Bangdel of the Huntington Archive of the Ohio State University, Joseph Dye III of the Virginia Museum of Fine Arts, Stephen Markel of the Los Angeles County Museum of Art, and Jeff Watt of the Rubin Museum of Art. I am also indebted to those who unstintingly provided photographs from their personal collections: Frederick Asher, Lokesh Chandra, Mr. and Mrs. Willard G. Clark, Janice Leoshko, Ulrich von Schroeder, John Bigelow Taylor, and Mr. and Mrs. Jack Zimmerman.

For funding of crucial field research and time for writing, I am indebted to the National Endowment for the Humanities, the University of Richmond, and the American Academy of Religion. For financial assistance with the many illustrations that enhance this volume, I am grateful to the Provost Office of the University of Richmond. I also want to express appreciation to the University Seminars at Columbia University for their help in publication. The ideas presented have benefited from discussions in the University Seminar on Buddhist Studies.

Special appreciation goes to my dear friend, colleague, and editor extraordinaire, Theodore A. Bergren. Ted spent many hours discussing the contours of the manuscript and providing intellectual counsel and emotional support. Moreover, his lucent editing honed the work into a more elegant and conceptually coherent one. I could not have completed this project without his unfailing help.

I owe deep thanks to Helen Appell for invaluable inspiration and assistance in bringing the book to fruition.

For easing my arduous hours of labor, thanks to Jerry for a stream of lattes and ripostes and to Daisy, gentle canine muse.

Finally, for sustaining me with lavish support, encouragement, and wisdom, all gratitude to my mother, Merry Gant Norris; magnanimous Papa John; cherished sister, Rosemerry; beloved brother, Todd; superb sister-in-law, Kathy; sterling sister-scholar, Paula; and nonpareil best friend, Robin.

Note on Transliteration

This work covers a range of historical periods and geographical regions, and hence the deity names, proper nouns, and Buddhist terms differ in the various languages of the sources consulted, namely, Pali, Sanskrit, Tibetan, and Newar. Because Sanskrit serves as the lingua franca of the South Asian and Himalayan Buddhist world, I generally use Sanskrit names and terms rather than what would otherwise be a constantly shifting terminology. I follow the standard system of Sanskrit transcription, except for words that have come into common usage and may be found in an English dictionary (e.g., yoga, mandala, mantra, stupa, Shakyamuni).

Tibetan names and terms are given in phoneticized form in the body of my study to enhance its readability and aid in use of the index. Thus, for example, bsTan-'gyur is rendered as Tanjur so that readers unfamiliar with Tibetan may easily subvocalize and so there is no ambiguity regarding where the term appears in the index. In some cases, however, particularly in the endnotes and in parentheses, Tibetan orthography is followed, using the Wylie system of transliteration. The glossary of Tibetan provides Tibetan orthography for words that are phoneticized in the text as well as Tibetan versions of names of deities and other technical terms.

There is as yet no standardized method for transcribing the Newar script into English lettering. Therefore, I have whenever possible selected common transliterations that readers are likely to find in other sources. In addition, I use the term "Newar" both nominally and adjectivally throughout my study, although the current practice in scholarly writing is to use "Newari" to designate the Newar (*newāḥ*) language and as an adjective for things Newar. My decision defers to Newar political and scholarly efforts to eliminate usage of "Newari," a neologism apparently introduced into scholarly usage by Brian Hodgson in the late nineteenth century. The term "Newari," rendered in Nepali script as *nevārī*, has been so applied and imposed in a range of legal, legislative, and academic contexts that it has come for some Newars to symbolize Nepali political, social, and academic hegemony.

BUDDHIST GODDESSES OF INDIA

Introduction

The Buddhist pantheon of India features a fascinating and diverse array of female divinities. The pantheon is dazzling in its breadth, encompassing voluptuous tree spirits, maternal nurturers, exalted wisdom figures, compassionate healers, powerful protectors, cosmic mothers of liberation, and dancing female Buddhas. Goddesses preside over childbirth, agriculture, prosperity, longevity, art, music, learning, love magic, and occult practices. There are goddesses who offer protection from epidemics, snakebite, demons, curses, untimely death, and every mortal danger. There are also goddesses who support practitioners in their pursuit of knowledge, mental purification, a higher rebirth, and full spiritual awakening.

Female deities occupy every echelon of the divine hierarchy, from nature spirits embedded in the landscape to cosmic figures representing the highest truths and attainments of the tradition. Variously beatific and wrathful, tender and fearsome, serene and ecstatic, they represent the energies, powers, and beings that surround and suffuse human life. They also reflect the inner depths of the human spirit, embodying qualities that may be awakened through spiritual practice. Thus, they are envisioned at once as supernal beings who minister to those enmeshed in worldly existence, as potent forces that may be invoked through ritual and meditation, and as models of human aspiration.

For these female divinities, I use the term "goddess." These goddesses are not marginal to Buddhist thought and practice but play an integral and often prominent role in their varied religious settings. Despite their tremendous importance in living Buddhism and pervasive presence in Buddhist texts and art, relatively little scholarly attention has been devoted to the female deities of the tradition. The last decade has, however, witnessed a dramatic upsurge of interest in the topic and the appearance of numerous substantive articles and several major monographs. This rapidly expanding field of inquiry makes evident the need for a comprehensive survey of the Buddhist goddesses of India that documents the forms, attributes, and roles of the main divinities and traces the historical development of the pantheon.

Although Buddhist goddesses regularly find mention in publications spanning the last century, their treatment has been concentrated in works on Indian and Buddhist art. These include art historical surveys and catalogs of museum collections and exhibitions. Such writings are primarily concerned with issues of iconography, provenance, and style rather than religious meaning and history. Therefore, although Buddhist goddesses appear frequently in print, one finds the same core of basic information with little advance in interpretation. Moreover, because female deities have long been of marginal interest to the field of Buddhist studies at large, knowledge of the female pantheon has not kept pace or been integrated with other advances in scholarship. The information presently available about most of these goddesses is limited to brief iconographic descriptions and thumbnail sketches of their religious meaning.

The present volume provides a fuller portrait of the individual divinities and identifies broader thematic and historical trends in the pantheon. I present a comprehensive overview of each goddess, including the dates of her emergence in literary and artistic sources, her iconographic evolution and range of epiphanies, the types of practices in which she figures, and original and evolving ideas of her nature and religious roles. The historical development of each figure unfolds not simply on a Buddhist stage but also against the backdrop of Indic culture at large. In many cases I identify deities, mythic themes, and symbolic motifs from the surrounding cultural landscape that influenced the character of a given goddess. This aspect of my study brings a new perspective to attributes that might otherwise seem to be Buddhist innovations, revealing the degree to which the pantheon is rooted in broader Indic cosmological, mythological, and symbolic patterns.

This study primarily features the major goddesses that appear in Indian Buddhist literature, visual arts, and practice traditions. In addition, several chapters are devoted to a class of divinity, a significant text, or human figures relevant to the goddess theme. Minor deities that serve only as attendants or mandala retinue figures are not included.[1] In historical scope, the volume covers Indian Buddhism in its entirety, from the earliest traceable origins to the twelfth century C.E., documenting the female pantheon as it evolved through the early, Mahayana, and Tantric movements.[2] The deities introduced in India constituted the core pantheon that was adopted, modified, and expanded as Buddhism spread throughout Asia. This volume also addresses the transmission of these goddesses to Tibet and Nepal, charting continuities and changes in their iconography and practice in the different cultural spheres and examining their ongoing roles in contemporary settings.

One reason for covering such a vast array of divinities is the vantage point this affords for identifying broad regional and historical trends. As later goddesses inherit traits from, expand on, and replace earlier ones, a sequential pattern emerges, making it possible to locate each figure within the developmental trajectory of the pantheon. Furthermore, this study provides a vital perspective on the Buddhist tradition as a whole, for the pantheon reflects changes in theory and soteriology and deepens our understanding of Buddhist devotional and ritual life.

My research is based largely on primary textual and artistic sources. I have consulted a wide range of literary genres, such as meditation manuals, devotional poetry, chanted liturgies, ritual texts, scriptures, and biographies. Many of the Sanskrit, Tibetan, and Newar writings that I use have not previously been translated. For these, I have relied on and present here my own translations. These sources are drawn from such compendia as the *Sādhanamālā*, Derge edition of the Tibetan canon, Sakya *sGrub thabs kun btus* and *rGyud sde kun btus*, and Newar anthologies of hymns and ritual songs, as well as Tibetan visualization manuals and liturgies in current usage.

Archaeological remains and artistic images are also central to my analyses and constitute primary documents equal in value to literary works. Indeed, the visual record significantly complements and supplements the evidence provided by written texts. Because so many works of art are inscribed or datable on stylistic grounds, they often provide more specific evidence of the historical origins and evolution of the goddesses than do the literary sources. When works of art survive from regions or periods that are not well attested in textual sources, the material record provides crucial evidence for establishing the geographic and temporal compass of a particular goddess. Thus, images are invaluable for documenting the evolution of specific divinities and the pantheon as a whole.

Iconographic analysis plays an important part in my interpretations. Traits such as body color, stance, hairstyle, clothing, jewelry, hand gestures, and handheld objects help communicate the religious import and roles of each goddess. Moreover, artistic treatments of a given figure may include iconographic features that do not appear in written descriptions, providing an eloquent "visual text" of her qualities and character. In many cases, iconographic motifs shared with figures other than Buddhist goddesses help reconstruct the influences—within Buddhism and beyond—that shaped the evolution of a divinity. I also address iconographic preferences and innovations that emerged when a deity migrated from India to Tibet or Nepal.

I conducted extensive field research in preparation for this volume, making four trips to India and Nepal between 1995 and 2000. My research in India was primarily historical. I searched photographic archives, libraries, and museums for publications and works of art relevant to my study and consulted Indian scholars and Sanskritists. In Nepal, I conducted research in Tibetan and Newar

Buddhist communities in order to explore the goddesses' roles in contemporary settings. I visited Tibetan and Newar temples and manuscript collections and interviewed Newar priests and scholars and Tibetan masters representing different lineages within the Kagyu, Sakya, Gelug, and Nyingma schools. My time in the field also afforded opportunities to examine works of art in context and to observe rituals, dances, processions, and initiations. These investigations yielded significant historical insights and enhanced my understanding of the roles of the goddesses in the living tradition.

While consulting secondary sources, I regularly encountered errors regarding the identification, iconographic manifestations, and attributes of a given deity. Many of these inaccuracies are traceable to the exploratory efforts of pioneering scholars and have simply been repeated over the decades without reassessment. I directly address such misconceptions when they have a strong bearing on identification or interpretation. In other instances, I simply refer in passing to a common error or misidentification. However, because such mistakes are so numerous and pervasive I have not found it feasible to mention and cite them in every case. To do so would unduly lengthen my study without enhancing its usefulness. Therefore, I offer my references to primary sources in the stead of detailed explanations of discrepancies with information published elsewhere.

This volume is designed to serve a broad range of scholars and educators as a reference, research, and instructional tool. Therefore, each chapter is written as a complete unit that may be read independently as a source of reference on a given goddess. Each chapter opens with a brief portrait of the goddess. The content and organization of the chapters are then shaped by the types of evidence that emerged and the interpretive issues they raised. In some instances, a mythic narrative warrants close attention; in others, questions of historical origins, iconographic analysis, artistic treatments, or distinctive practice traditions come to the fore. Regardless of the differing emphases, readers may expect to find attention to the origins, iconography, and religious roles of each goddess and discussion of her place in Buddhist history and practice.

One of my aims in this work is to redress the unidimensional way in which Buddhist goddesses are customarily described in western scholarship. It is common practice simply to define a given deity by a philosophical concept that he or she represents or a benefaction that he or she confers. This formulaic approach conveys the impression that the deities are abstract entities interchangeable with or reducible to doctrinal categories or functions. I have found, however, that the divinities are typically envisioned as dynamic and complex entities with intricately drawn personae, powers, and numinous qualities. Thus, I have tried to provide fuller and more multifaceted portraits of "who" the goddesses are. This approach accords with their treatment in Buddhist sources, in which the goddesses emerge as living presences with multiple divine bodies, glorious environments, and attributes that proclaim their fabulous powers and spheres of mastery.

Historical Overview

The book is divided into three sections, documenting the female pantheon as it evolved through the early, Mahayana, and Tantric periods.[3] The most ancient phases of Buddhism are not preserved in the historical record. Not until around the third century B.C.E. is early Buddhism evinced in archaeological sources. The same century saw the beginning of a textual canonization process, although the early literary productions survive in later recensions. The Mahayana movement gained momentum in the first and second centuries C.E. and remained on the forefront of intellectual innovation and an expanding practice repertoire until the seventh century, when Tantric elements came to the fore and were forged into a significantly new pattern of theory and practice. The metaphysics and soteriology of each movement are reflected in the deities it advanced and the status and roles accorded to those deities. I place each goddess in the section that covers the movement, or period, during which she was introduced and her central features defined, although I address her survival in later periods and any alterations to her character that occurred.

Part One, titled "Ascent of the Sacred Female in Early Buddhism," chronicles the goddesses who appear in the earliest sources and iconographic programs. A variety of supernatural beings participated in the career of Shakyamuni Buddha and offered various forms of assistance to his followers. Among them are several female figures and figural types that are drawn directly from Indic cosmology and receive little elaboration beyond their incorporation into Buddhist narratives and works of art. Thus, we find Pṛthivī, mother earth, an important figure in Vedic religiosity, playing a pivotal role in the enlightenment of Shakyamuni, defending him against the assault of the demon king Māra and granting him the throne of earthly sovereignty. Another figure of Vedic origin, Śrī Lakṣmī, the goddess of abundance and good fortune, also found an honored place in early Buddhist worship and iconography. The ancient cult of female nature spirits and local guardians known as *yakṣiṇīs* flourished and found unparalleled artistic expression in Buddhist settings. Hārītī rose from the ranks of the yakṣiṇīs to become the yakṣiṇī queen and the focus of a distinctively Buddhist cultus, with an elaborate mythology and shrines in monasteries across the Buddhist world.

Two human figures are also featured in this section. Māyādevī, the mother of Shakyamuni Buddha, is included as an exalted female whose character has supernatural aspects. The section concludes with an examination of Gotamī, the foster mother of Shakyamuni and founder of the female monastic order, whose career and attainment of enlightenment provides the nascent concept of female Buddhahood.

Goddesses receive substantial attention in Mahayana literature, practice, and iconography. This emphasis is already evident in the earliest Mahayana writings, dating to the first and second centuries C.E. Part Two, "Mahayana Mothers of Liberation," opens with a chapter on one such opus, the *Flower Ornament Scripture*, whose narrative of the pilgrim Sudhana reveals the expanded role of female divinities in Mahayana soteriology. Another foundational work, the *8000-Line Perfect Wisdom Scripture*, introduces Prajñāpāramitā, the first cosmic female of the Buddhist pantheon, whose embodiment of transcendent wisdom becomes a hallmark of the conception of female divinity.

Whereas the earlier pantheon was drawn largely from preexisting figures and figural types, the Mahayana movement engendered the rise of female saviors and protectors that embody explicitly Buddhist ideals and attainments. Their benefactions, which aid practitioners both materially and spiritually, flow from their Buddhist virtues of wisdom and compassion. While Mahayana writers and iconographers introduced divinities of recognizably Buddhist provenance, they often drew attributes from earlier figures and Hindu deities, adding their own distinctive stamp through an innovative combination of classical iconographic elements, a Buddhist origin myth, and salvific activities of a decidedly Buddhist cast.

The Mahayana pantheon features several powerful protectors, such as Mārīcī, goddess of the dawn; Sitātapatrā, guardian against supernatural dangers; and Jāṅgulī, protectress against harm by snakes and poison. A range of divinities address specific areas of human need. The most important among them are Parṇaśavarī, a healing deity; Vasudhārā, bestower of wealth and abundance; Sarasvatī, patroness of learning and the arts; Uṣṇīṣavijayā, who confers long life and a fortunate rebirth; and Cundā, who inspires and supports spiritual practice. Tārā, the subject of the last chapter in this section, is the most beloved goddess of the Mahayana pantheon and a savioress of unlimited powers. She is the focus of an immense theological enterprise proclaiming her metaphysical supremacy and, uniquely among the Mahayana cohort, her Buddhahood.

In Mahayana writings, these female divinities are routinely accorded the same titles they have in the Hindu setting, namely, *devī* and *devatā*, synonymous terms that mean "goddess." Interestingly, they are rarely described as bodhisattvas, the term customarily applied to analogous male figures, such as Avalokiteśvara and Mañjuśrī. The female figures display the defining bodhisattva attributes of wisdom, compassion, and commitment to the liberation of all living beings. Instead of "bodhisattva," however, the female divinities are customarily designated by the grammatically feminine terms *dhāraṇī* and *vidyā*.

Dhāraṇī, a noun derived from the verbal root *dhṛ*, meaning "to carry" or "to bear," refers to mantras, the sounds that "carry" the essence, or energy, of a deity. The intonation of the dhāraṇī makes contact with the goddess on her plane of reality, invoking her presence and activating her liberating functions. The term *dhāraṇī* is used to refer to the mantras that invoke female deities as well as the deities themselves.[4] The origin story of Uṣṇīṣavijayā underscores her character as a dhāraṇī goddess by describing her materialization from the light rays with which Shakyamuni Buddha etched her dhāraṇī in the sky. In other accounts, the introduction of a goddess is concurrent with the revelation of her dhāraṇī and its powers.

One less often encounters the term *vidyā*, a feminine noun derived from the verbal root *vid*, "to know." *Vidyā*, too, is synonymous with "mantra," although *vidyā* typically refers to the mantric invocation of a female deity. When used with reference to a deity, *vidyā*, translatable as "incantation lady," designates a female who wields knowledge of magical rites and lore. As in the case of *dhāraṇī*, the term *vidyā* is used to refer both to the deity and to her mantric invocation. A variation on the term, *mahāvidyārājñī*, "great queen of incantations," is used most often with reference to Sitātapatrā but occasionally found in association with other figures.

A dhāraṇī deity is a great savior, protector, and liberator. As such, these Mahayana goddesses occupy a distinctive salvational niche. Their status in the pantheon neither presumes nor precludes their attainment of full enlightenment. The Mahayana theological framework conceives spiritually advanced and fully enlightened beings who can adopt numerous guises—male, female, animal, human, divine—in order to minister to diverse beings throughout the universe. The lofty realizations and powers of such advanced beings are virtually beyond human reckoning, and many complexities arise in efforts to typologize the forms and bodies they may assume.[5] Significant for the present discussion is that fact that the different forms of embodiment are what receive classification. For example, if a fully enlightened Buddha manifests as a demigod (*asura*) in order to appear among and liberate demigods, that embodiment would be identified as an asura rather than a Buddha. Similarly, if a fully enlightened being manifests as a dhāraṇī deity, that embodiment is classified as a dhāraṇī deity rather than a Buddha. This status is assigned on the basis of the form and purpose of the embodiment rather than the level of attainment of the divinity. The explicit and elected purpose of dhāraṇī deities is not to embody full enlightenment but rather to display distinct qualities, exercise particular powers, and confer specific benefactions.

Also important to the understanding and classification of Buddhist divinities is the practices associated with them. The dhāraṇī goddesses do not as a rule figure in practices directly devoted to supreme enlightenment. Rather, their practices devolve upon the invocation of their powers to accomplish a range of practical and magical aims, with an emphasis on immediate efficacy, although the meritorious and purificatory aspects of the practices are understood to create favorable conditions for a positive rebirth and to promote gradual progress toward enlightenment. Deities and practices of this genre began to be introduced as early as the second century C.E. under the Mahayana rubric but were eventually incorporated into the Tantric repertoire. They were largely placed in the categories of Action (Kriyā) Tantra and Discipline (Caryā) Tantra, which entail deity visualization, mantra recitation, and ritual procedures rather than the esoteric yogic practices that lead to Buddhahood.[6]

The final goddess of this section, Tārā, is an exceptional figure with respect to the Mahayana typology. Tārā stands on the cusp of the Mahayana and Tantric traditions because her persona and iconography reflect the Mahayana idiom, while her status as a Buddha—unique in this grouping—brings her into alignment with emerging Tantric themes.

Part Three, "Tantric Female Buddhas," examines the figures introduced in the fully developed Tantric paradigm. Tantric texts use the term "goddess" (*devī*) with reference to these figures but also introduce new nomenclature, such as *ḍākinī* and *yoginī*. Furthermore, the Tantric goddesses are recognized and explicitly designated as Buddhas, for they embody supreme enlightenment, and the goal of practices dedicated to them is Buddhahood during the present lifetime of the practitioner. These practices fall within the Highest Yoga (Anuttara Yoga) Tantra category and entail the cultivation of transcendent bliss (*mahāsukha*) and realization of emptiness (*śūnyatā*), the two qualities whose perfection culminates in Buddhahood.[7] Thus, the iconographic traits of the Tantric goddesses differ markedly from those characteristic of Mahayana goddesses, in accordance with their contrasting roles and status. Whereas the features of the Mahayana figures reflect their powers and benefactions, Tantric iconographic motifs make reference to bliss, emptiness, subtle metaphysical principles, and esoteric yogic and ritual practices.

Each Tantric figure covered in this section embodies supreme Buddhahood. The distinctive personae of the female Buddhas evoke different dimensions of enlightenment. This section opens with Vajrayoginī, the "Adamantine Yogini," who is inarguably the supreme deity of the Tantric pantheon. No male Buddha, including her divine consort, Heruka-Cakrasaṃvara, approaches her in metaphysical or practical import. In this section we also find Nairātmyā, the blue female Buddha, whose persona evokes the spaciousness and selflessness of enlightened awareness. Chinnamuṇḍā, who waves aloft her own severed head, provides a startling portrait of advanced yogic practices and realizations. Lion-headed Siṃhamukhā offers a primal vision of untamable power. The voluptuous Kurukullā, with her flowered adornments, extends an enticing invitation into the realm of spiritual transformation. The female Buddhas are regarded as ultimately inseparable from one another, for the sphere of nondual awareness they inhabit admits no distinctions.

Why "Goddess"?

The use of the term "goddess" to refer to the female divinities of Buddhism is not a widespread practice in western scholarship on the tradition. One finds instead a preference for "female deity," "female divinity," and even "female myth-model."[8] The lexical meaning of "goddess" is precisely "female deity," or "female divinity." Definitional equivalence alone, however, has not been sufficient to establish the term in the scholarly lexicon. Indian scholars have never been hesitant to use "goddess," but western scholars eschew the term, motivated in large part by a desire to discourage facile comparison of Buddhist divinities with those of other traditions. Debate regarding the appropriateness of "goddess" has recently arisen in the context of studies on Tantric deities. Judith Simmer-Brown holds that use of the term would belie the sophisticated, relativistic ontology underlying Tantric conceptions of deity.[9] Anne Klein has voiced a concern that the feminine resonance of "goddess" may be misleading, insofar as the asserted "femaleness" may be incommensurate with western understandings of gender.[10]

Although it is important to be attentive to distinctive Buddhist perspectives on divinity and gender, the fact remains that Buddhist writings have used the term "goddess" for the female deities of the tradition from the early through the Tantric periods. Thus, we find usage of the Pali term *devatā*, Sanskrit *devatā* and *devī*, and Tibetan *lha-mo*, all meaning "goddess," alongside more specific designations for different classes of divinities introduced over the centuries.

The meaning of this nomenclature, however, changed in accordance with evolving Buddhist theological views. Early Buddhism shared the cosmology of the broader South Asian populace, which envisioned a universe inhabited by gods (*deva*), goddesses (*devī, devatā*), and other supernatural beings. Buddhists recognized the existence of a panoply of divine beings but did not accord them moral or spiritual superiority. Rather, Buddhists simply counted the divine beings among the followers and supporters of the Buddha. In this context, use of the term "goddess" is nonproblematic with reference to the divine females drawn from the preexisting pantheon, such as the earth goddess Pṛthivī, the goddess Lakṣmī, and the numerous yakṣiṇīs of the Indian landscape. At the same time, early Buddhism cannot accurately be characterized as a theistic tradition, for it centers on and derives its teachings from an enlightened human being rather than a supreme divinity. Therefore, the theological speculations that arose in this context pertained to the person and career of Shakyamuni and other historical Buddhas.

Mahayana Buddhism entered more classically theistic terrain with the introduction of an array of divine beings whose lofty status was attributable to their Buddhist virtues and advancement along the path to Buddhahood. This newly emerging theism, however, took shape alongside the central Mahayana principle of emptiness, which holds that reality is in perpetual flux and there are no independently or permanently real objects or entities. The doctrine of emptiness precludes the attribution of absolute or eternal existence to the many Buddhas, celestial bodhisattvas, and dhāraṇī deities of the Mahayana pantheon.

The Tantric movement retained many of the earlier divinities and introduced a continuously expanding repertoire of deities with multiple attendants and extensive mandala retinues. The doctrine of emptiness remained operative as the underlying principle of the pantheon. The Tantric practice of deity yoga (*deva-yoga*), which culminates in identification and merging with the envisioned deity, further dispels any view of the deities as concrete entities essentially "separate" or "different" from humans.

The emptiness of the deities, like the concept of emptiness itself, is a nuanced metaphysical view that easily lends itself to misinterpretation. This subtle teaching regarding the impermanence and interdependence of all phenomena is commonly mistaken for nihilism, a denial of any existence whatsoever. Thus, some western thinkers conclude that the deities are "unreal" or "nonexistent" in an absolute sense, interpreting their emptiness as nonreality. According to this view, the deities do not exist in any sense, except as human inventions or useful tools for spiritual development.

Seeking to redress this rather crude absolutism, Bokar Rinpoche, a contemporary Tibetan teacher, clarifies the ontological status of the deities. He explains that the deities are not illusions produced by the human mind. However, human envisionments of deities are mental fabrications that do not correspond precisely to the forms of those deities. In that sense, Bokar Rinpoche concedes, a deity can be said to be a creation of the human psyche.[11] This illusory status, however, holds true only of the human concept and image of a deity, not of the deity himself or herself. The deities are realities that transcend this world and "spontaneously assume . . . various forms . . . to benefit beings."[12] Religious practice, he holds, is an interaction between deity and devotee that invokes the protection, assistance, blessings, and revelation of the deity.[13]

Human envisionments of deity, as in the practice of deity yoga, offer a means to approach the deity and eventually to attain a direct vision of the deity's divine form in all its glory and living reality.[14] When deity and practitioner merge in the culmination of deity yoga, and their identities dissolve into one, it is not because the deity was unreal all along but because the practitioner has entered the radiant, blissful realm of nondual awareness the deity inhabits. Moreover, the practitioner comes to recognize that the qualities of the deity were already present in a dormant state in his or her own being, waiting to be awakened.[15]

Bokar Rinpoche thus clarifies the Buddhist perspective that the deities are not simply the products of human intellect and imagination, although their appearance is molded in accordance with human aesthetic preferences, conceptual categories, and spiritual capacities. Rather, the deities are spiritually advanced and enlightened beings who command an array of supernormal abilities and insights into reality that they employ in order to liberate others. Further, these deities are not merely "symbols" of the qualities they embody, nor are they inventions of human imagination or convenient fictions or tools for human spiritual growth. The powers they grant, protection they offer, and blessings they bestow are tangibly real. The practices associated with them—mantra recitation, ritual, meditation, deity yoga—are regarded as genuinely efficacious and transformative.

Moreover, it is not enough simply to concede that the deities are "just as real as humans," for deities are supernal beings of immense temporal duration whose existence is not subject to the ordinary laws of cause and effect. They will themselves into existence and operate from transcendent planes of bliss and awareness for as long as their presence may benefit living beings. Thus, there is a sense in which the deities are "more real" than humans, for the illusions and suffering that characterize human life are ephemeral phenomena, whereas the wisdom and compassion impelling the deities are irreducible elements of reality.

It was important for early western scholars to distinguish between Buddhism and the forms of theism and monotheism with which they were familiar. However, religious scholarship now recognizes a broad spectrum of views of divinity. Contemporary readers typically have a broader comparative base that includes traditions with ontologically and psychologically nuanced views of deity that are in many respects comparable to those of Buddhism. Many traditions espouse metaphysically subtle understandings of deities as dynamic forces and energies that impinge on human experience in complex ways rather than as "divine persons" narrowly conceived. Moreover, many traditions around the globe recognize the symbolic nature of human conceptions, images, and names for the divine and cast the human-divine relationship in nondual terms. Diverse traditions—from the shamanic to the mystical—envision the possibility of a merging with deity in which human subjectivity is replaced by divine awareness. In view of our more advanced stage of cross-cultural awareness, I have chosen to adopt the term "goddess" in part to include Buddhism in the ongoing conversation regarding the many forms that theism may take.

I have also opted to use the term "goddess" in order to situate my work within the field of goddess studies, which is emerging as a serious branch of academic inquiry. Scholars have documented significant historical and contemporary goddess traditions throughout the world and developed increasingly sophisticated theoretical approaches to this burgeoning body of research. An ever-growing number of universities include goddess courses in their curricula in a variety of departments. Buddhist goddesses, however, are all but absent from the growing corpus of cross-cultural goddess studies, anthologies, and encyclopedias. Providing a source book on Buddhist goddesses is of timely importance so that Buddhist scholarship can begin to inform and benefit from advances taking place in related fields and so that those who teach about Buddhism, goddesses, or religion and gender may gain access to this crucial body of knowledge.

Primarily, however, I use the term "goddess" to draw attention to the ongoing and lively engagement of the Buddhist tradition with the feminine divine. In this respect, Buddhism shares a largely unrecognized commonality with other religious traditions born on Indian soil. The female pantheon of Buddhism often mirrors developments in the Indic divine landscape at large, historically and thematically. Thus, the spectrum of Buddhist goddesses is similar in scope and type to that found in pan-Indic and Hindu religiosity. For example, Buddhism shares the broader Indian tendency to cast nature divinities as female. Indeed, Buddhist goddesses fill many roles similar to those held by goddesses in the surrounding traditions, encompassing an array of benefactions and forms of protection. Finally, there are goddesses of cosmic magnitude, identified with the primary forces of creation and energies of reality, capable of bestowing supreme liberation.

Readers of this volume will find here the sweeping panorama of the feminine divine in the Buddhist imaginal world. Nature divinities abound: mother earth, the grove goddess of Shakyamuni's birthplace, lotus goddesses, mother nature figures, star and planet goddesses, goddesses of the dawn and night sky, grain goddesses, mountain goddesses, tree goddesses, and snake goddesses. We find Buddhist goddesses presiding over human fertility, the health of infants and children, wealth, agricultural abundance, healing, longevity, artistic inspiration, learning, music, love magic, and occult practices. There are goddesses who specialize in protection from fevers, epidemics, snakebite, demons, curses, astrological influences, and untimely death, as well as versatile goddesses with encompassing powers to rescue the worshipper from any danger or mortal peril.

Other Buddhist goddesses have more explicitly salvific ministrations, supporting practitioners in the pursuit of renunciation, discipline, mental purification, wisdom, a fortunate rebirth, and progress on the path to enlightenment. There are goddesses who preside over heavenly paradises where votaries may join them after death and dwell in their enlightening presence. Moreover, Buddhism has exalted female deities to the pinnacle of the pantheon, to embody the loftiest metaphysical principles and goals of the tradition, including Buddhahood. Having documented this remarkably diverse female pantheon, I use the term "goddess" because I believe Buddhism merits a place among the goddess traditions of the world.

Part One

ASCENT OF THE SACRED FEMALE IN EARLY BUDDHISM

CHAPTER I

Pṛthivī

Mother Earth

The goddess of the earth . . .
Surrounded by a retinue of a hundred times
ten million earth goddesses . . .
Revealed the upper half of her body
Adorned with all its ornaments,
And bowing with joined palms,
Spoke thus to the Bodhisattva:
"Just so, Great Being.
It is indeed as you have declared! . . .
In truth, you are the purest of all beings."
—*Lalitavistara*[1]

The honor of being the first goddess to appear in Buddhism belongs to Pṛthivī (pronounced *PRI thi VEE*), "Vast One," mother earth. She was present at the moment the tradition began, if one marks as its beginning Shakyamuni Buddha's attainment of enlightenment. The beneficent earth goddess rejoices in anything that enhances the well-being of life upon her surface. When Māra, the king of demons, challenged Siddhārtha to provide a witness to his worthiness to attain enlightenment, the Bodhisattva stretched forth his golden hand and touched the earth, invoking the one who observes and remembers every event that transpires on her vast body. Responding to his summons, the earth goddess rendered her testimony in world-shaking tones and personally dispersed Māra's armies. In so doing, she created the environment of peace necessary for the Buddha-to-be to enter the subtlest spheres of meditation and attain full spiritual awakening. So crucial was her intervention that she is said to perform the same role in the enlightenment of every Buddha throughout the ages.

Pṛthivī's commendation shows that Shakyamuni's progress toward liberation was not wholly a contemplative achievement but was profoundly rooted in the quality of his earthly journey over many lifetimes. Only by one who has shown compassion for all that lives may the truth be won. Acts of kindness, gratitude, and generosity, as much as yogic prowess and meditative mastery, constitute the path to enlightenment, and those deeds are vigilantly observed and unerringly remembered by mother earth. The earth-touching gesture, one of the most popular renderings of the Buddha, proclaims that he had won Pṛthivī's approval by the way he had lived upon her surface in not one but hundreds of lifetimes.

Mythic Conceptions of Mother Earth

The earth goddess is a complex figure in Indic myth and symbolism. She is, as one might expect, a motherly figure, a source of life, fertility, and abundance as she succors the world with milk from her golden breasts and produces all things from her womb. She provides the material matrix of life in her roles as Bhūmi ("Soil"), Viśvagarbhā ("Womb of the World"), Medinī ("Fertile One"), Janitrā ("Birthplace"), Viśvasvaṃ ("Source of Everything"), Viśvaṃśu ("Producer of Everything"), Dhātrī ("Nursing Mother"), Dhāritrī ("Nurturer"), Viśvadhāyā ("All-Nourishing"), Pṛśṇī ("Mother of Plants"), and Vanaspatīnāṃ Gṛbhir Oṣadhīnāṃ ("Womb of Forest Trees and Herbs"). An enduring, sustaining presence, she is proclaimed as Sthāvarā ("Stable One"), Dṛḍhā ("Steady One"), Kṣamā ("Patient One"), Dharā ("Upholder"), Viśvadhā ("All-Preserving"), Viśvambharā ("All-Bearing"), and Viśvadhāriṇī ("All-Supporting"). Because her subterranean caverns are an inexhaustible reservoir of wealth in the form of precious stones, minerals, and gold, she is known as Ratnagarbhā ("Repository of Gems"), Ratnavatī ("Abounding in Jewels"), and Vasundharā ("Bearer of Treasure").

Pṛthivī has an explicitly ethical dimension as well. She is closely allied with divine law and truth, as well as truth-telling. The *Ṛg Veda* refers to "mother earth, free from deceit."[2] Similarly, the *Atharva Veda* proclaims her to be "founded on truth," "sustained by great truth," and "upheld by eternal law."[3] Another Vedic work goes as far as to declare that "this earth is established on truth; hence truth is this earth."[4] The earth goddess, "founded on truth," cannot be deceived. Thus, she presides over oaths and ratifies words that are spoken in honesty. Giuseppe Tucci elaborates on her role as patron of moral uprightness and veracity:

> As a defender or preserver of the cosmic order she is distressed by unlawfulness and mischief. She cannot stand lies (*mithyāvādin*); false witnesses (*mithyāsākṣin*); those who betray friends (*mitradrohin*) or offend living beings (*jīvaghātin*); those who betray the confidence reposed in them (*viśvāsaghna*); those who do not accomplish their own duties or do not support their own parents, children, masters.[5]

Although primarily benevolent and nurturing, mother earth may evince ferocity in her protection of life and moral virtue. Vedic works laud Pṛthivī as a "mighty guardian," invoking her to drive off demons, grant protection from thieves and evildoers, and deliver victory over enemies and rivals.[6] Capable of tremendous heaving and quaking, at times she shakes the wicked from her surface.[7] Even in India today an earthquake may be viewed as mother earth's protestation against unbearable injustice or immorality.[8] In a similar vein, early Buddhist chronicles tell of the earth swallowing persons who were no longer sustainable because of heinous behavior or dishonesty.[9] All of these aspects of the earth goddess—her maternal bounty, constancy, absolute truthfulness, and potential ferocity—found expression in Buddhist literary and artistic sources.

Role in the Victory over Māra

In the life story of Shakyamuni Buddha, Pṛthivī figures in an event known as the Māravijaya, or "victory over Māra." When the Bodhisattva was on the verge of enlightenment, Māra descended with his armies to attempt to prevent Siddhārtha from attaining his goal. The biographies agree that the earth goddess interceded to drive back Māra's demonic hordes, but the precise manner of her intervention differs in varying accounts. It is important to consider the divergent narratives not only for the role assigned to Pṛthivī but because they have a bearing on artistic representations of the goddess.

In the *Nidānakathā*, Pṛthivī verbally bears witness to the Bodhisattva's virtues. Māra boasted that his army could attest to his superlative acts of generosity and charged that Siddhārtha, on the contrary, could not produce a single witness to his own meritorious acts. The Bodhisattva replied, "Let this great and solid earth . . . be witness of the seven hundredfold great alms I gave," touching his hand to the earth. The earth goddess first quaked in response and then spoke, offering her testimony. Her thunderous voice overwhelmed Māra's troops, forcing them to retreat.[10]

In the *Mahāvastu*, it is the quaking and roaring of the earth that dispel Māra's forces. The event is set in motion when Māra asks Shakyamuni "by whose power" he could hope to vanquish Māra's hosts, given that the sage was sitting alone under a tree. The Bodhisattva confidently asserted that since he had exerted himself in generosity, patience, diligence, meditation, love, and compassion, Māra could not overpower him. Shakyamuni touched the ground with his right hand, and "the whole world quaked six times and there was a fearful roar." The sound terrified the hosts of Māra and sent them fleeing in all directions; the heaving earth dashed their chariots to pieces, crushed their weapons, and threw them to the ground, helpless.[11] These accounts are consistent with Vedic portrayals of the earth goddess as one who knows and allies herself with the truth and actively intercedes to vanquish demonic forces.

The *Lalitavistara* offers a more elaborate narrative in which the earth goddess quakes, roars, speaks, and appears in bodily form. In this account, too, Māra demands, "Through what merit will you gain deliverance?" Siddhārtha responds, "I have freely made hundreds of millions of offerings. . . . [A]rdently desiring the deliverance of beings, I distributed houses, riches, seeds, beds, garments, gardens, and parks to all who asked." Challenged by Māra to produce a witness to this claim, Siddhārtha lightly touched his right hand to the ground and replied, "This earth is my witness." In answer to his invocation, the earth trembled and loudly resounded. The earth goddess, called Sthāvarā, "Stable One," in this work, then appeared with her retinue of ten hundred thousand earth goddesses from around the globe and shook the entire world. The upper half of her body emerged from the earth, and she bowed to the Bodhisattva with joined palms. She ratified his statement, attesting that he was the purest of beings. Māra and his army, terrified by her roaring voice, fled.

As the *Lalitavistara* continues, Māra sent his beautiful daughters to seduce the Buddha-to-be, but the savant met their enticing dance with a discourse on detachment from worldly desires, and they honored and praised him. Māra then rallied his troops for a more violent assault, attacking the Bodhisattva with mountains, uprooted trees, spears, flames, iron balls, and gigantic swords. The Bodhisattva again claimed the earth as his witness, touching the ground a second time. The earth reverberated like a gigantic bell. The thundering sound forced Māra to the ground, unconscious and drained of power. His armies, seeing that their leader had fallen, could not rally. The Bodhisattva, at last left undisturbed beneath the bodhi tree, entered his final meditation and attained full awakening.[12]

Pṛthivī's Navel as the Throne of Enlightenment

The earth goddess also played a role in the Buddha's enlightenment by providing the throne upon which Shakyamuni attained liberation. Her throne, located at the symbolic center of the world, is known as the "navel of the earth" (*pṛthivī-nābhi*) and "seat of wisdom" (*bodhi-maṇḍa*).[13] Ananda Coomaraswamy has demonstrated that here, as in many instances, Buddhist mythographers drew upon established motifs and concepts. Beliefs about the navel of the earth found early expression in the *Ṛg Veda*, wherein it is described as the axis of the universe, supreme sacrificial altar, and seat of planetary sovereignty.[14] The term translated here as "navel" also means "center," "nave," and "hub." Like the hub of a wheel, the earth's navel is the still point in a spinning world. This motif was incorporated directly into Buddhist narratives. The *Nidānakathā* relates that when Shakyamuni circled the bodhi tree to select the seat for his final attempt at enlightenment, he felt the ground undulating beneath his feet like the rim of a wheel until he reached the eastern side of the tree. Only there was the earth stationary, confirming that he had arrived at the precise center of the bodhi-maṇḍa.[15] In Mahayana Buddhism, the spot also came to be known as the *vajrāsana*, or "adamantine throne," in reference to its unshakable stability.

The significance of the place where the Buddha attained enlightenment is elaborated in a range of sources. The *Kāliṅgabodhi Jātaka* celebrates the earth's navel as the victory throne of all Buddhas. In the same work, the Buddha explains that "there is no other place that can support me, if I sit there."[16] The *Lalitavistara* avows that "of all places in the three thousand worlds, only this place is as indestructible as a diamond."[17] Hsuan-tsang, an avid student of Buddhist legendry, recorded in his seventh-century memoirs the belief that the vajrāsana was the first thing to arise when the world came into being and is the one spot that would remain unmoved even if the earth were shaken to its foundations.[18]

According to these accounts, Shakyamuni took his seat upon the most sacred and stable spot on earth, indeed, the only place where he could realize his goal. The *Buddhacarita* completes the picture by explaining that the adamantine stability of the earth's navel is uniquely capable of sustaining the world-shaking power of the Buddha's concentration:

> For this is the navel of the earth's surface, entirely possessed of the highest power, for there is no other spot on earth which can bear the force of his concentrated thought.[19]

Interestingly, in the *Buddhacarita* account Siddhārtha does not call the earth to witness. Rather, his assumption of the seat at the center of the earth is the pivotal event that sends Māra's forces fleeing.[20] Pṛthivī thunders to herald his approach to the seat but does not make an appearance or verbally attest to the Bodhisattva's virtues. Rather, she implicitly supports his right to attain enlightenment by allowing him to occupy the powerful spot at the center of creation, the center of her power.

These accounts add another dimension to the contest between Māra and Shakyamuni. Lowell Bloss has demonstrated that what is at stake is not only spiritual emancipation but also assumption of the throne of the earth goddess, the seat of worldly sovereignty.[21] In the *Nidānakathā*, Māra demands that the Bodhisattva remove himself from what the demon king regards to be his own rightful seat as the ruler of the earth.[22] Similarly, the *Mahāvastu* finds Māra lamenting that he will lose his earthly dominion if he cannot remove Siddhārtha from the throne beneath the bodhi tree. Māra attempted to deflect Shakyamuni from his goal by offering him a secular kingdom in its stead.[23] The Bodhisattva declined this offer, declaring, "I shall become a king of the whole world when I have awakened to the enlightenment. . . . And when I have . . . attained the all-knowing truths, I shall be triumphant over the regions of the world."[24] The Bodhisattva recognizes that his efforts will be crowned not only with the status of "awakened one" (*buddha*) but also that of world ruler (*cakravartin*).

Thus, the earth goddess not only authenticated the Buddha's worthiness of enlightenment but also accepted him as the legitimate claimant to her throne, which she reserves for a "righteous king" (*dharma-rāja*) who has acted in accordance with the universal order, lived in harmony with all creatures, selflessly served others, and, above all, demonstrated the generosity that is the primary qualification of a virtuous ruler.[25]

Developing this line of analysis of the Māravijaya, Bloss adduces an Indic belief that "nature responds to a righteous king with order and abundance," allowing rain to fall and crops to grow in season, and adds that the Buddha's assumption of the earth's throne signals that the earth will now be secure and abundant under a new reign.[26] Indeed, the *Nidānakathā* describes the blossoming of nature that accompanied the enlightenment event:

> Throughout the universe flowering trees put forth their blossoms, and fruit-bearing trees were loaded with clusters of fruit; the trunks and branches of trees, and even the creepers, were covered with bloom; lotus wreaths hung from the sky; and lilies by sevens sprang, one above another, even from the very rocks. . . . The sea became sweet water down to its profoundest depths; and the rivers were stayed in their course.[27]

In this new era, humanity, too, will thrive, as the selfishness, greed, and pride personified by Māra no longer tyrannize the human heart and the wisdom, virtue, and compassion promulgated by the Buddha inaugurate an age of social harmony and spiritual renewal.[28] Thus, it was in the best interest of all her children that mother earth should welcome a ruler worthy to sit upon her throne.

Divine Forms and Symbolic Attributes

The earliest portrayals of the earth goddess are found among the Gāndhāran reliefs illustrating the life of Shakyamuni Buddha. In these reliefs, which date from the Kuṣāṇa period (first through third centuries C.E.), Pṛthivī appears in a number of scenes relating to the enlightenment event. Many of the carvings are now dispersed in far-flung collections, making it difficult to pinpoint the original location of a relief in the narrative sequence and to ascertain whether the earth goddess appeared in multiple scenes in a given frieze.

1.1 Shakyamuni Approaching Throne of Enlightenment, Gāndhāran region (Pakistan/Afghanistan), Kuṣāṇa period, ca. second or third century C.E. Narrative frieze, detail. Schist, height 16.5 in. (42 cm). Chandigarh, Government Museum and Art Gallery, 87. Photo: American Institute of Indian Studies. *Pṛthivī provides the stable throne of enlightenment.*

The extant Gāndhāran examples consistently portray Pṛthivī with her head and upper torso emerging from the earth, surrounded by foliage, at the base of the bodhi throne. One such scene shows the Bodhisattva approaching the throne, preparing to take his seat.[29] Pṛthivī's hands are not usually depicted, but one relief adds the detail of Pṛthivī stabilizing the throne with her upraised hands (Fig. 1.1) as Shakyamuni approaches and receives welcome from the spirit indwelling the

1.2 Conquest of Māra, Gāndhāran region (Pakistan/Afghanistan), Kuṣāṇa period, third century C.E. Schist, height 20.7 in. (52.6 cm). Museum fuer Indische Kunst, Berlin, MIK I 10198. Photo: Bildarchiv Preussischer Kulturbesitz/Art Resource, N.Y. *Pṛthivī emerges from the earth to champion the Buddha on the verge of his enlightenment.*

bodhi tree. In another narrative moment, he stands beside the throne, which bears Pṛthivī's image, as Māra's daughters attempt to distract him from his goal.[30] Yet another scene shows Pṛthivī on the bodhi throne beneath a meditating Buddha.[31]

Pṛthivī was not customarily included in Gāndhāran illustrations of the conquest of Māra, which focused instead on the demonic hordes that Māra unleashed on the Buddha-to-be on the verge of his enlightenment. There are, however, apparently rare renditions of the moment when the Buddha summoned the earth goddess by touching the fingertips of his right hand to the earth, displaying what is known as the "earth-touching gesture" (*bhūmisparśa mudrā*), and Pṛthivī responding to his summons (Fig. 1.2). She is shown in the customary fashion, with the upper half of her body above the ground, but in addition her hands are pressed together in a devotional gesture.[32] This accords with the *Lalitavistara* account, which states that the goddess emerged halfway from the earth, fully adorned, with her palms joined in devotion. This lone description may have guided early depictions of the event.

Buddhist sculptors endowed the earth goddess with a readily recognizable iconographic form. Leaving a portion of her body embedded in the earth perfectly expresses the understanding that her body is the earth itself, a visual motif later revived in Hindu portrayals of the goddess.[33] Moreover, carving her image directly beneath Shakyamuni, on the pedestal of his dais, visually evokes her identity with the throne of enlightenment. Buddhists viewing this scene would be reminded not only of Pṛthivī's role in the narrative but also that she provided the stable platform for Shakyamuni's powerful concentration and, equally importantly, yielded to him the throne of earthly and spiritual sovereignty. In the Gāndhāran works, the base of the throne intersects her womb, or navel, offering a clear-cut visual equation of the throne and her navel, placing the enlightenment event at the literal and symbolic "center" of mother earth.

Beginning in the fourth century, when illustrations of the Buddha's life were condensed into several episodes, portrayals of the Māravijaya featured the pivotal moment when the Buddha invoked the earth goddess as his witness. The Buddha touches his right hand to the earth, and Pṛthivī, as a key figure in this event, is often incorporated in the composition. Pṛthivī's placement on the pedestal of the throne of enlightenment remained a constant in the Indian sculptural tradition. We no longer find foliage framing her body, but the practice of portraying Pṛthivī with part of her body—if only the lower legs or even a single foot—submerged within the earth, continued through the Gupta era (fourth to fifth centuries) and into the Pāla period (eighth through twelfth centuries).[34]

Alongside this convention, however, other iconographic types emerged. Beginning in the late fifth century, representations in which the goddess kneels on one or both knees began to appear, although it is not clear what prompted this innovation. In addition, apparently beginning in the Gupta period, the reverential hand gesture was largely replaced by the display of a spherical vessel in her outstretched hands (Fig. 1.3).[35] The reason for the coincidence of these two developments is not difficult to imagine. If the goddess were portrayed in a kneeling posture with her hands in a reverential gesture, she would be indistinguishable from a human worshipper. Thus, the introduction of another iconographic attribute was warranted.

The vessel borne by Pṛthivī is not explicitly mentioned in literary accounts of the Māravijaya. Art historian Janice Leoshko suggests that the motif appears as an emblem of the goddess rather than as a narrative element, referring to Pṛthivī's character as the bearer of all treasure rather than to a specific action she

1.3 Buddha Summoning Earth Goddess, Sārnāth, Uttar Pradesh, India, Gupta period, late fifth century. Stele, detail. Beige sandstone, height 27.5 in. (70 cm). National Museum, New Delhi. Used by permission. Photo: Janice Leoshko. *Pṛthivī appears twice, bearing a treasure vessel and actively repelling the forces of Māra.*

performed.[36] The full vessel or "vase of plenty" (*bhadra-ghaṭa* or *pūrṇa-kalaśa*), a widespread symbol for abundance and fertility in Indian art, is implicitly understood to be overflowing with treasure—whether water, nectar, plant sap, or jewels.[37] When the contents of the bowl are illustrated, they may include lotus buds and flowers, gems, and pearl garlands. The vessel displayed by Pṛthivī is indeed brimming with riches. This accords with the *Atharva Veda* praise of mother earth as "she who bears her treasure stored up in many a place, gold, gems, and riches, giver of opulence."[38] In Buddhist literature, the *Mahāvastu* refers to the "jewel-strewn earth, rich in varied treasure and wealth," while centuries later the *Hevajra Tantra* describes the earth goddess as the "bearer of many kinds of gems."[39]

Thus, a treasure vase is an appropriate attribute for mother earth, reappearing in later Hindu conceptions of the goddess. The *Padma Purāṇa* describes her as holding two pots of grain, whereas a nineteenth-century iconographic compendium envisions her with three bowls, variously brimming with jewels, rice, and herbs, confirming that the Buddhist attribution of a vessel to Pṛthivī fits squarely within the framework of her pan-Indic conception.[40]

The vessel Pṛthivī bears may also implicitly allude to her role in the Māravijaya. Since the Bodhisattva had invoked the earth goddess to testify to his virtues, it is possible that her container overflows with the treasury of merit he had accumulated over many lifetimes. This interpretation finds support in an episode in the *Flower Ornament Scripture.* When the earth goddess declared to the pilgrim Sudhana that she had witnessed his virtuous deeds and could show him the results, she struck the earth with her foot, causing countless jewels to surface. She imparted that the gems had been produced by his meritorious actions.[41]

Similarly, in a Southeast Asian version of the Māravijaya narrative, Pṛthivī begins her testimonial on behalf of Shakyamuni with the words "I know the magnitude of thy (spiritual) riches."[42] In this account, too, she produces a visible sign of his merit, twisting her hair to wring out the lustral water that had accompanied his donative gifts over the centuries. Each drop represented a gift made by the Buddha in a former life; the torrential flood swept away Māra and his army.[43] The belief that the earth is the receptacle of religious merit is also reflected in the Tibetan Buddhist explanation for the practice of making full-body prostrations on the ground, namely, so the earth will absorb and retain one's merit. Indeed, it is not a long step, conceptually, from sowing a crop to planting the seeds of merit in the body of mother earth.

As artistic depictions of the Māravijaya evolved, a second female figure was introduced in the fifth century. The combative stance of this second figure suggests that she is repelling the forces of Māra. She is typically shown in a dynamic lunging or flying pose, as if rushing into the fray. She waves one arm outstretched in a gesture of warning or expulsion and curls the fingers of her other hand at her mouth (see Fig. 1.3). Leoshko has drawn attention to this second Māra-defeating female, suggesting that she may be a second goddess who appears to assist Shakyamuni.[44] Although scriptural sources do not mention two goddesses, Hsuan-tsang, a seventh-century Chinese pilgrim to India, cites a tradition that one earth goddess arose to help the Bodhisattva resist Māra, while a second, summoned by his fingers touching the earth, came to bear witness on his behalf.[45] That both figures are indeed understood to be earth goddesses is evinced by reliefs in which both are shown emerging from the ground (Fig. 1.4).[46] In other instances, they remain close to but not submerged in the earth (Fig. 1.5).

It is possible, however, that Hsuan-tsang was reporting not something he had heard or read, but rather something he had observed in artistic representations, particularly since his remark appears among comments on a statue at

1.4 Pedestal, Bodhgayā, Gaya District, Bihar, India, late sixth century. Stone, height 11 in. (27.9 cm). Indian Museum, Calcutta. Used by permission. Photo: Janice Leoshko. *When Pṛthivī is submerged in the earth, her womb/navel merges into both earth and throne base.*

Bodhgayā that included the two figures under discussion. If this is the case, an alternate explanation is that the paired divinities in these Māravijaya scenes represent Pṛthivī in a narrative sequence.[47] I suggest that this pictorial convention is a synoptic rendition of the event as recounted in the *Lalitavistara*, according to which the Bodhisattva touched his hand to the earth two times, twice summoning the earth goddess to his assistance. At her first appearance, she bore witness to his virtues and scattered Māra's hordes to the ends of the earth. When they rallied for another onslaught, she came forth again and, with her thunderous voice and mighty quaking, decisively vanquished Māra and his troops.[48] The two figures could well be intended to reflect the role of the goddess on each occasion. The proffered vessel of treasure would represent her initial attestation to the Bodhisattva's treasury of merit, whereas the martial guise would accord with the more physical nature of her second intervention. Following this interpretation, the flying scarves and upraised arm of the latter figure could indicate the quaking she set in motion, while the hand curled at her mouth could represent her thunderous roar (see Figs. 1.3, 1.4).

Janice Leoshko has traced the iconographic evolution of this second Māra-defeating female, documenting that the figure gradually acquired a wrathful visage and the explicit "threatening gesture," as her left hand makes a *tarjanī mudrā* at her breast (Figs. 1.6, 1.7). She came to be depicted in an exaggerated crouching pose, conveying intense physical dynamism, as well as the more traditional lunging pose of conquest. She typically pinions or tramples underfoot her vanquished enemies, represented by an elephant (Fig. 1.7).[49] The elephant may be the mount of Māra, as prescribed in the *Nidānakathā*, or an

1.5 Buddha Summoning Earth Goddess, Mahābodhi temple compound, Bodhgayā, Gaya District, Bihar, India, Pāla period, late eighth century. Gray stone, height 26.4 in. (67 cm). Photo: Janice Leoshko. *Pṛthivī, shown twice in synoptic narrative, remains close to but not submerged in the earth.*

elephant among Māra's forces. In a tenth-century stele, she is actively engaged in battle amidst the troops of Māra.[50] In a Ratnagiri relief, the dejected Māra himself retreats from her advance.[51] The militant stance of this figure is consistent with the role of the earth goddess in the Māravijaya, wherein her defeat of Māra's armies is often described as a martial victory, as she hurls, crushes, and disperses them, pulverizing their chariots and weapons.

1.6 Buddha Summoning Earth Goddess, Kurkihār, Gaya District, Bihar, India, Pāla period, ninth century. Stone, height 38.6 in. (98 cm). Indian Museum, Calcutta. Used by permission. Photo: Janice Leoshko. *The enlightenment event, depicted in this manner, was a popular subject during the Pāla period, especially in the vicinity of Bodhgayā.*

1.7 Detail of Fig. 1.6. Photo: Janice Leoshko.

Evolution into Aparājitā

This Māra-defeating female, or martial manifestation of Pṛthivī, apparently attracted attention in her own right and underwent elaboration as an independent figure, emerging as the goddess Aparājitā, "Unconquerable Lady." When Aparājitā made her independent debut, possibly in the seventh but definitively in the eighth century, she closely resembled her predecessor, the female present at the Māravijaya. Aparājitā displays the same lunging pose and upraised right hand, a gesture designated as a "slapping motion" (*capeṭādānā-abhināya*) in texts on Aparājitā. The fingers of her left hand, too, are held at her breast in the threatening tarjanī mudrā, in some cases clasping a noose (Fig. 1.8).

Moreover, Aparājitā consistently takes her stand upon an elephant-headed creature. This figure resembles and in scholarly works is generally assumed to be a popular Hindu deity, the elephant-headed Gaṇeśa, an identification that suggests a theme of sectarian triumphalism. However, the occurrence of a fallen and trampled elephant in the precedent Māravijaya scenes suggests a different interpretation, namely, the use of an elephant-headed figure to metonymize Māra's army. Literary descriptions of the conquest of Māra variously make mention of his elephant mount or include an elephant or elephant-faced demon among his theriomorphic minions. Moreover, earlier representations of the Māravijaya may depict Māra atop an elephant or feature a rearing elephant in his entourage.[52] The existence of a class of demons known as *gaṇapati*, found in the trains of Śiva and Gaṇeśa in Hindu contexts, may also have influenced the choice of an elephant-headed figure to epitomize Māra's demonic army.[53] Gouriswar Bhattacharya observes in this regard that the elephantine figure depicted as the object of Aparājitā's conquest does not as a rule display the handheld attributes of the Hindu god Gaṇeśa but rather a sword or dagger and in some instances a shield, confirming that the fallen figure represents vanquished obstacles and demonic forces.[54]

The single text devoted to Aparājitā in the *Sādhanamālā* describes her as six-armed and characterizes her as a "destroyer of all *māras*."[55] Tibetan canonical sources similarly typify her as a defeater and crusher of māras or "pulverizer of all demons," showing that her earlier role shaped her vocation as an independent goddess.[56] The name Aparājitā, "She Who Cannot Be Conquered," befits a goddess who began her career helping the Buddha-to-be overcome the forces of Māra. The golden hue of Aparājitā, too, affirms her evolution from Pṛthivī. Distinctive to Aparājitā, however, is the addition of a parasol, which is raised by one or more Hindu deities to form an honorary canopy above her head (see Fig. 1.8).

Stone reliefs of Aparājitā portray her with two, four, or six arms. Her added implements include a bow, arrow, elephant goad, discus or Dharma-wheel, and vajra scepter. The corpus of statuary dates largely from the eighth through tenth centuries, identifying this period as the heyday of her worship, while the concentration of find-sites in Orissa and Bihar reveal these to be the centers of her cultus.[57] That her worship flourished in Bihar, home to Bodhgayā, accords with her original association with the enlightenment event.

Ongoing Roles and Worship

Although Pṛthivī's main role in Buddhist mythology is her legitimation of the Buddha's enlightenment at Bodhgayā, she also finds mention in other contexts. According to a Vinaya tradition, Shakyamuni instructed his chief disciple, Ānanda, that monastic robes should be pieced together in a patchwork pattern to resemble the furrows of ploughed fields, in honor of Pṛthivī.[58] Moreover, each stitch should be the length of a grain of rice, as a reminder of her gift of sustenance.[59] As mentioned above, she appears as one of Sudhana's spiritual guides in the *Flower Ornament Scripture*, wherein she predicts Sudhana's future Buddhahood, imparting that she witnesses the enlightenment of every Buddha.

An entire chapter of the *Golden Radiance Scripture* (ca. late fourth or early fifth century C.E.) invokes the fecundating powers of Pṛthivī in support of the

1.8 Aparājitā, Pachār, Gaya District, Bihar, India, Pāla period, ca. late seventh or early eighth century. Schist, height 31.5 in. (80 cm). Patna Museum, Arch. 10650. Photo: American Institute of Indian Studies. *Aparājitā, a subduer of demons, appears to have evolved from the martial aspect of Pṛthivī.*

teaching and practice of the scripture. She appears here under the name Dṛḍhā, "Steady One," a popular sobriquet for the earth mother. Her awareness of what takes place on her surface is expressed in her charming reminder that "I will lean with my head upon the soles of the feet of the monk who is preaching the Law."[60] Addressing Shakyamuni, Dṛḍhā promises to appear wherever the text is read, studied, or taught and to transform the environment into a lush natural paradise:

> I will make this great earth stronger so that . . . grasses, bushes, plants and trees will grow stronger. All the trees in parks and groves and all the various leaves, flowers, fruits and crops will be stronger, will be more fragrant, more moist, more tasty, will be more beautiful, greater. And . . . beings . . . will enjoy an increase in longevity, strength, complexion and senses . . . will be blessed, will enjoy a variety of pleasure.[61]

Although the primary theme of the *Golden Radiance Scripture* is the glorification of the text itself, the chapter on Dṛḍhā recognizes her as the source of all well-being, enjoyment, and prosperity. The bounty of the earth allows humans to enjoy robust health and to create the dwellings and amenities that enhance the comfort and aesthetic pleasure of the environment, as Dṛḍhā herself proclaims:

> Beings will enjoy the various enjoyments and pleasures on earth and will experience blessings. And may they enjoy all the various foods, drinks, nourishment, clothes, beds, seats, dwellings, residences, palaces, parks, rivers, ponds, springs, lakes, pools and tanks, these and similar varieties of aids and blessings existing on the earth, manifest on the earth and dependent upon the earth.[62]

The benefits humans receive from the fruits of the earth are highlighted here, but the converse is also true, for humankind can nourish the natural order. Any increase in wisdom or virtue replenishes the natural environment, magnifying its abundance. Hence, the earth goddess and her retinue draw sustenance from the teaching of the *Golden Radiance Scripture*. That is why she supports and delights in its exposition, declaring, "I will satisfy myself with that hearing of the Dharma, with the nectar juice of the Dharma. I will do homage, I will rejoice."[63] Fed by the nectar of Dharma, she in turn pours forth the nectar of her blessings, and life on earth flourishes.

Pṛthivī occasionally appears in a Tantric context, but not as a major meditational deity. The *Sarvadurgatipariśodhana Tantra* includes a mantra for summoning Pṛthivī, while the *Hevajra Tantra* declares that she is to be invoked to witness the establishment of a mandala.[64] In the Tibetan corpus, Pṛthivī is

1.9 Pṛthivī, Thailand, ca. nineteenth century. Bronze, lacquer, gold leaf, inset with colored glass. Private collection. Photo after Alfred Salmony, *Die Plastik in Siam* (Hellerau: Avalun-Verlag, 1926), pl. 68. *In Southeast Asia, Pṛthivī is shown wringing water from her tresses.*

commonly envisioned with two arms, holding a treasure vessel.[65] In painted representations of the Māravijaya, she may be shown with the upper portion of her body emerging from the ground, her torso naked except for flowing scarves, her hands pressed together in a gesture of homage.[66]

In Southeast Asia, the earth goddess, known as Wathundaye or Visundhari (= Vasundharā), gained importance over the centuries, becoming the focus of the ritual consecration of religious donations and a favored subject of artistic representations, in which she is shown wringing from her tresses the water gathered from the Buddha's merits (Fig. 1.9).[67] She is depicted in this manner beneath the Buddha making the earth-touching gesture and in Māravijaya scenes, in which the water flowing from her hair may be shown drowning Māra and his troops. She is also a popular subject of temple wall paintings and large statues in public spaces, and one finds shrines devoted to the goddess and fountains charmingly designed so that the water perpetually flows from her upgathered, luxuriantly long hair.[68]

In the Mahayana pantheon, the major attributes of Pṛthivī were incorporated into two goddesses who attained independent importance: Vasudhārā and Aparājitā. Vasudhārā, "Stream of Treasure," is a golden goddess of abundance, whereas Aparājitā specializes in protection from demons. Interestingly, these two figures correspond to the two guises of the earth goddess represented in the later Māravijaya scenes. The vessel-bearing form of Pṛthivī corresponds to Vasudhārā, whose attributes include a vase of plenty, while the martial figure (or aspect of Pṛthivī), active in the conquest of Māra and his demonic forces, evolved into the demon-slayer Aparājitā, as discussed above. Her transformation into Vasudhārā is addressed further in the chapter on that goddess.

Enthroning the World Sovereign

Pṛthivī's role in the enlightenment of Shakyamuni and other Buddhas is a rich and complex motif that resonated on many levels for Buddhist audiences over the centuries. Her appearance as the supporter and champion of Shakyamuni in his contest with Māra shows that the Bodhisattva's path to deliverance was traced out upon the earth on a journey of many lifetimes, which she alone witnessed. Freedom from illusion and suffering cannot be won without profound concern for the suffering of others and concrete actions to secure their welfare. As a guardian of eternal truths and moral order, Pṛthivī would naturally come to the aid of a savant who was on the verge of discovering these truths for himself.

Moreover, the concept that the seat of enlightenment rests upon the navel—and, by extension, the womb or lap—of a female divinity reflects a widespread South Asian belief in the female as the generator of the power essential to kingship, whether temporal or religious. Many dynasties have identified their throne with Lakṣmī or Durgā, while the throne of creation itself remains in the possession of the earth goddess. Sovereignty on earth may not be attained without the assent of mother earth, who grants her approval only to one who has lived in accordance with her desire for the well-being of all creatures. Thus, when the Buddha is shown touching his fingers to the earth, it is at once an invocation of the ultimate judge of honor as well as a triumphal gesture that he has won the right to assume the throne of earthly and spiritual regnancy, the seat of power at the literal and figurative center of creation. Pṛthivī, as the guardian of all life upon her surface, was unerring in her judgment that Shakyamuni was worthy to occupy her primordial throne, in view of the legacy of humaneness and compassion that his teachings have entailed.

CHAPTER 2

Māyādevī

The Buddha's Wondrous Mother and Her Sacred Grove

From the palms of her hands to the soles of her feet,
Her face and her body are exquisite, more than divine.
Indeed, we cannot gaze upon her long enough,
For she brings increasing joy to heart and mind.
Like the moon in the sky glows her beautiful face;
Like the light from the sun her body shines;
Her beauty sparkles like a nugget of pure gold.
She has perfumed curls like the large black bee,
Eyes like lotus petals, teeth like the stars in the heavens.
. . . .
Clearly she could only be the daughter of the gods.

—*Lalitavistara*[1]

Māyādevī (pronounced *mah yah* DAY VEE), the mother of Shakyamuni Buddha, naturally captivated the imagination of Buddhist hagiographers, artists, and poets over the centuries. She offered the irresistible subject of a woman in the bloom of youth, giving birth amidst the splendors of nature to a wondrous child destined for greatness. One finds lavish eulogies of the divinely beautiful mother, the pastoral setting, and, of course, Māyādevī's singular gift to humanity. The queen delivered her charming infant when the moon was full and the flowering of nature was at its height. When the time for the birth drew near, Māyādevī and her female attendants proceeded to the Lumbinī grove. The woodland was a fragrant mass of fruits and flowers, birds and bees, from the forest floor to the topmost branches. As Māyādevī grasped the limb of a tree, the fruit-laden woman and the blossoming tree mirrored one another in an ecstatic moment of creativity as the Buddha emerged from his mother's right side.

Over the millennia, Lumbinī, located in southern Nepal, has served as an international site of pilgrimage and local mother goddess shrine. After the site's association with the Buddha's nativity was forgotten, some time following the thirteenth century, women from surrounding villages continued to venerate the images of the holy mother for aid in childbirth and for the gift of healthy children. Thus, in their own way, local women preserved the memory of Māyādevī until archaeological excavations uncovered an inscribed Aśokan pillar at the site and restored Lumbinī to the Buddhist world at the close of the nineteenth century.

Mother of Shakyamuni Buddha

The relationship between Māyādevī (also known as Māyā or Mahāmāyā) and Shakyamuni began even before his birth as her son at Kapilavastu in the sixth century B.C.E. Stories of the Buddha's former lives include a number of lifetimes in which Māyādevī was the mother of the Bodhisattva, extending their karmic connection as mother and child over many centuries.[2]

Biographies of Shakyamuni often relate his conception and delivery and Māyādevī's pregnancy in great detail. The accounts share a common narrative thread to which various interpretations and levels of poetic embellishment have been added. The following discussion elicits the common story line and some of the salient variations, although an examination of the primary sources would provide additional details and points of comparison.[3]

In his final lifetime, the uniqueness of the Buddha-to-be, or Bodhisattva, was apparent from the moment of his conception. The Bodhisattva, gazing down from Tuṣita Heaven, had decided that it was time to descend into the realm of mortals and consciously entered the womb of the exemplary woman he had chosen to be his mother. Queen Māyādevī, sleeping alone in her royal chamber, dreamt that a wondrous elephant, whiter than snow, with golden tusks, passed through her right side into her womb (Fig. 2.1). When the queen awakened, she knew that she was with child and shared her dream and its portent with King Śuddhodana.[4]

The couple consulted court priests and the sage Asita, who confirmed the good tidings that a son would be born to them (in accordance with the belief that a male child inhabits the right side of the womb). The Bodhisattva did not begin as an ordinary embryo but was "endowed with limbs and fully formed."[5] He settled himself on the right side of Māyādevī's womb and remained there, fully conscious, seated in a meditative posture, for the duration of the pregnancy. When gods came to inquire after his well-being, he raised his right hand in greeting, taking care not to harm his mother in the process. She could see the

2.1 Māyādevī's Dream, Great Stupa, Bhārhut, Satna District, Madhya Pradesh, India, Śuṅga period, ca. 100–80 B.C.E. Sandstone. Indian Museum, Calcutta, 93. Used by permission. Photo: American Institute of Indian Studies. *Māyādevī was sleeping alone in her royal bedchamber when she conceived the Bodhisattva, dreaming that a white elephant entered her womb.*

child in her womb as clearly as if she were looking into a transparent gem, and he in turn could see his mother.[6]

Māyādevī's pregnancy was extraordinarily pleasant. One of the signs of a Bodhisattva is that "his mother experiences no pain, as other women do."[7] Accordingly, Māyādevī did not experience a single moment of discomfort, illness, fatigue, or distress. The *Lalitavistara* and *Mahāvastu* elaborate that she enjoyed a sense of lightness and well-being whether she was sitting, standing, or lying down. Her mood remained buoyant and joyful; she was not afflicted by negative emotions, disturbing dreams, internal discomfort, hunger, thirst, indigestion, or extremes of temperature.[8] Heavenly maidens sprinkled her with sandalwood powder, saffron, and celestial flowers and fanned her with coral leaves as she slept. Divine nymphs bathed, massaged, and anointed her body.[9] Several sources extol the healing powers of the pregnant Māyādevī. According to the *Lalitavistara*, she could heal with the touch of her hand and dispensed medicinal herbs with remarkable curative properties. The very sight of Māyādevī healed every disease known to humankind, and all the women and children in the realm who were tormented by demonic possession were restored to sanity.[10]

Although the earliest literary sources are silent regarding the location of the birth, biographers reached virtual unanimity that the event took place at Lumbinī, a grove situated about halfway between Kapilavastu and Māyādevī's ancestral home in Devadaha. According to the *Buddhacarita*, Māyādevī sought out the natural setting because its spiritual purity matched her own. She proceeded there with a thousand ladies-in-waiting and delivered her child while lying on a couch amidst the trees.[11] Other accounts, however, agree that she gave birth in a standing position while grasping a tree branch overhead. According to one tradition in the *Mahāvastu*, Māyādevī announced, as the time for the birth drew near, that she desired to go to the park. King Śuddhodana ordered that the Lumbinī grove be cleared of debris, adorned with flowers, and decked with banners and carpets of silk. Gods and divine maidens contributed gems, flower garlands, and clouds of perfume. The queen was conveyed to the grove on a luxuriously outfitted palanquin, accompanied by a royal cortege. After entering the copse with her female retinue, Māyādevī, "coming to it in play, leant with her arm on a branch of the wavy-leafed fig-tree, and playfully stretched herself at the moment of giving birth to the Glorious One."[12]

The *Nidānakathā*, voicing a different tradition, states that Māyādevī's destination was her ancestral home in Devadaha, but as her chariot passed Lumbinī she was enchanted by the woodland with its profusion of flowers, fruits, vines, bees, and sweetly singing birds and disembarked to besport herself in the inviting glade. Once there, she was drawn to the most stately *śāla* tree and desired to take hold of one of its branches. The tall tree bent down one of its limbs of its own accord to come within her reach. No sooner had she taken hold of the branch than she delivered her child.[13]

The *Lalitavistara,* the most poetically ornate biography, is particularly rich in narrative detail. According to this account, Lumbinī was Māyādevī's site of choice for the birth. She knew that the śāla trees would be in full bloom, the air would be golden with pollen, and the cuckoos and peacocks would be sweetening the glade with song. King Śuddhodana arranged for the woodland to be adorned with golden ornaments, pearls, and red banners, and the gods assured that all the trees were bearing fruit, even out of season.[14] When Māyādevī entered the grove with her female attendants, she searched among the trees until she found a fig tree (*plākṣa*) of surpassing beauty, elaborately adorned:

> Its well-proportioned branches were covered with bright leaves and buds, as well as with flowers found both in heaven and earth. This tree gave off the sweetest perfumes, and its branches were draped with streamers of many colors. The plākṣa shone with precious stones; jewels adorned it entirely—the roots, the trunk, the graceful branches, and even the leaves. Where the tree stood rooted, the earth was as level as the palm of the hand, and carpeted with grass green as a peacock's neck, soft to the touch.[15]

As Māyādevī approached, the tree bowed in greeting. The queen "raised her right arm, shining like a lightning flash in the sky," and grasped a branch to support her weight; she was standing thus, gazing into the sky, when the Bodhisattva was born.[16] The *Lalitavistara,* magnifying the mythic overtones of the event, asserts that all preceding Buddhas had been born under the same tree and moreover that Māyādevī had been the mother of the Bodhisattva in his previous five hundred lives.[17]

Clearly, the Buddha's nativity was unlike that of other human beings. Indian sages and gods are generally attributed with a distinctive manner of entering the world, such as emergence from a part of the body other than the birth canal, and the Buddha's hagiography reflects this pattern. As the *Mahāvastu* proclaims, it is impossible to find, among gods or humans, "one whose birth was like his, whose conception was like his."[18] Siddhārtha was born precisely ten lunar months after being conceived, and his mother delivered him in a standing position:

> Other women give birth, some before, some after, the completion of the tenth month, some sitting, and some lying down. Not so the mother of the Bodisat. She gives birth to the Bodisat, standing, after she has cherished him in her womb for exactly ten months.[19]

Another distinctive feature of the birth was that Siddhārtha was born from his mother's right side. Moreover, the delivery, like the pregnancy, was painless and noninjurious to the mother. He was born in the twinkling of an eye, without labor pains or travail: "The Bodhisattva, mindful and thoughtful, issues from his mother's right side without doing her any harm."[20] He emerged without piercing his mother's side, and "immediately after the Sugata was born, the mother . . . was without hurt or scar. The womb . . . was unscathed and at ease."[21] Thus, the birth was free from the forms of suffering usually attendant upon birth (*janma-duḥkha*) for both mother and child.[22]

The birth was followed by marvelous occurrences. The gods Indra and Brahmā wrapped the Bodhisattva in his swaddling clothes. The infant was born with full knowledge and memory and immediately began to walk and speak (Fig. 2.2). The grove lacked a source of water for the infant's first bath, but supernatural beings (serpents in some accounts, gods or celestial spirits in others) lustrated him from the sky. Several stream-fed wells and ponds of perfumed oils spontaneously emerged nearby, providing water and oil for the after-birth rites. At the same time, a tank of clear water miraculously appeared on the palace grounds and was immediately put to ceremonial use.[23] Divine beings throughout the universe rejoiced, and a purifying light diminished the suffering of creatures in every realm of existence.

The mythic dimensions and supernatural elements of the nativity were elaborated to differing degrees in different traditions. The *Mahāvastu* universalizes each element, making it characteristic of every Buddha in his final lifetime. Some schools of thought advance the perspective that the event and indeed the entire life of the Buddha was an illusory display staged for the benefit of sentient beings. The *Flower Ornament Scripture*, in keeping with its cosmically expansive outlook, envisions Māyādevī as the mother of all Buddhas in the billions of worlds throughout the universe.[24]

In the *Flower Ornament Scripture*, Māyādevī relates her journey toward this role, beginning with a former life in the distant past in another world system, when she presided over an enlightenment site as the goddess Netraśrī ("Radiant Eyes"). She helped the Buddha of that world attain enlightenment by fighting off the demonic army that assails every Bodhisattva on the verge of complete awakening. She vowed that she would give birth to the ruler of that kingdom in all of his subsequent lifetimes, until he attained perfect Buddhahood. After fulfilling that aspiration, Māyādevī undertook to become the mother of all Buddhas in whatever worlds and forms they might be born. She revealed that, in fulfillment of her vow, she was the mother of Krakucchanda, Kanakamuni, Kāśyapa, and all the former Buddhas of this age and will be the mother of Maitreya Buddha in the future.[25]

Indeed, in the *Flower Ornament Scripture*, Māyādevī fulfills the meaning of her name as "Goddess of Magical Creation," for she employs the art of

2.2 Nativity Scene, Prem Man Chitrakar, Kathmandu, Nepal, last decade of twentieth century. Pigment and gold on cloth, height ca. 16 in. (40 cm). Photo: Author. *This means of portraying Māyādevī and her precocious newborn is popular in contemporary Newar painting.*

miraculous manifestation (*māyā*) to emanate an infinite number of bodies so that she can simultaneously appear as the mother of every Buddha in world systems throughout the cosmos. She declares, "I was the mother of infinite buddhas of the past, and I am mother to the infinite buddhas of the ten directions in the present."[26] Moreover, in this scripture Māyādevī is not only the universal mother of all Buddhas but a cosmic figure whose womb encompasses all existence. She reveals that during pregnancy her womb attained cosmic proportions:

> My body outreached all worlds, and my belly became as vast as space, and yet did not go beyond the human physical size. . . . The enlightening being, together with as many enlightening beings as atoms in ten buddha-lands . . . entered my belly. Once all of them were in my belly, they walked around in strides as big as a billion-world universe, even as big as worlds as numerous as atoms in untold buddha-lands. . . . Yet even though it took in all those multitudes, my belly was not enlarged, nor did this body of mine become any more than a human body.[27]

The work describes Māyādevī in divine and cosmic terms: "Everything in this universe was seen reflected in the womb of Lady Maya," and all the universes, worlds, and Buddhas were visible in every pore of her skin.[28] Here Māyādevī is envisioned as a cosmic world mother, containing all worlds and all Buddhas within her being.

Death and Rebirth in Heaven

The *Flower Ornament* envisions an eternal continuity for Māyādevī as she endlessly re-creates herself throughout the universe wherever a Buddha is to be born. The question of her earthly fate is not addressed. Biographical works, however, cannot evade the vexed issue of the early demise of Shakyamuni's mother. Māyādevī did not live to raise her son; she died shortly after the Bodhisattva was born, and he was raised by her sister and co-wife, Mahāpajāpatī Gotamī. The sources are in general agreement that Māyādevī died seven days after giving birth. The *Lalitavistara* holds that this took place at Lumbinī.[29] Most traditions agree, however, that she returned with her infant to the palace amid great fanfare and was present to hear the lofty predictions regarding her child's destiny.[30] The *Buddhacarita*, too, places Māyādevī at the palace after the birth but holds that the procession to Kapilavastu took place on the tenth postpartum day and that she died at an unspecified time thereafter.[31]

The seemingly momentous event of Māyādevī's passing is a topic on which the biographies are uncharacteristically reticent, perhaps because of the distressing implication that giving birth to the future Buddha did indeed result in harm to Māyādevī. The idea that the Bodhisattva, whose purpose on earth was to relieve suffering, should have caused injury to his own mother casts a shadow on an otherwise joyful occurrence.[32] Various explanations for her early decease are offered. The *Buddhacarita* explains that she was unable to bear the joy of witnessing her son's extraordinary powers; the *Nidānakathā* less charitably avows that "a womb in which a future Buddha has dwelt, like a sacred relic shrine, can never be occupied by another."[33] The *Lalitavistara* confronts the uncomfortable implications head-on:

> If you think that Māyādevī's death was due to the birth of the Bodhisattva, you are wrong. That is truly not the way to see it. And why not? Because she had reached the end of her life.[34]

The work then offers the sympathetic observation that had she lived to see her son leave home, her heart would have been broken. For the same reason, the mothers of all the previous Buddhas also died seven days after giving birth.[35]

The consensus of these works is that Māyādevī's death was preordained even before the Bodhisattva was conceived. When the future Buddha was selecting a mother, he sought a woman who was virtuous and pure and who had ten months and seven days remaining in her life span. According to the *Nidānakathā*, he looked for a woman whose life expectancy was at least that long.[36] According to the *Mahāvastu*, however, his criterion was that the remaining life span should be only that long, for "it is not fitting that she who bears a Peerless One . . . should afterwards indulge in love."[37] Although their reasoning differs, these works agree that Māyādevī's death was not caused by giving birth. The biographies are also in accord that, immediately following her death, Māyādevī ascended directly to Trāyastriṃśa Heaven and dwelt among the gods.[38]

Māyādevī continued to watch over her son from the heavens. When Siddhārtha was perilously close to death as a result of his extreme ascetical disciplines, Māyādevī went with her angelic retinue to the Nairañjanā River, where the Bodhisattva was meditating. When she saw his weak and emaciated condition, she wept in the sky above him, lamenting that he was going to die before he had fulfilled his destiny to attain deliverance. Her tears stirred him, and the Bodhisattva assured her, "I will return to you your fruitful labor. . . . The time is not far distant when you will see the enlightenment of a Buddha." Consoled, Māyādevī blanketed her son with coral-red blossoms from a heavenly tree and then returned to her divine abode.[39]

Following the enlightenment event, the relationship between mother and son endured. Shortly after he attained spiritual awakening, she again came into his presence, and he imparted to her some of his newly discovered truths.[40] During one rainy season, the Buddha ascended to Trāyastriṃśa Heaven and, assuming the golden throne at the pinnacle of heaven, with his mother seated on his right side, preached the Dharma for her sake.[41] Remaining there for three months, he revealed a major body of teachings, the metaphysical Abhidharma discourses, in a single, uninterrupted sitting. His return from Trāyastriṃśa, at the close of the rainy season, was attended by great fanfare; a stairway materialized for his descent, and the gods escorted him with honorific banners, parasols, and clouds of heavenly perfumes.[42]

Māyādevī herself descended from the celestial realm immediately after her son died. She wept over his robe and begging bowl, lamenting that the world was now deprived of his guiding light. The Buddha, moved by her journey from afar to be by his side, sat up in his bier with his hands pressed together in homage to his mother and delivered a final sermon in her honor. When his closest disciple asked the Buddha how he would like this event to be remembered, he replied, "You may say that after the Buddha's Nirvana, his compassionate mother came down from the heavenly palace to the Twin Trees. As a lesson to unfilial people, the Tathāgata sat up in the golden coffin and preached the Dharma [for his mother] with his hands joined palm to palm."[43]

Artistic Representations

Representations of Māyādevī appear on the earliest Buddhist monuments. We meet first with depictions of the conception of the Buddha, or Māyādevī's dream of the white elephant, at Bhārhut (see Fig. 2.1) and Sāñcī.[44] The Sāñcī relief includes, directly below the conception, an elaborate procession bearing mother and child through the streets of Kapilavastu after the birth.[45] These examples are, however, isolated ones among the copious carvings adorning these monuments.

Illustrations of the life of Shakyamuni later became a standard feature of stupa iconographic programs, from the first century C.E. onward, in the Greco-Bactrian region, where images of Māyādevī are found in profusion. The detailed bas-relief narratives of the Buddha's life on Gāndhāran votive stupas include several scenes in which Māyādevī appears. The narration generally begins with the conception, followed by the consultation of the court priests regarding Māyādevī's dream, in which scene the king alone or the royal couple may be shown. The queen setting forth for Lumbinī in her palanquin may also be depicted.[46]

The pivotal event, the nativity, is invariably included, sometimes in elaborate detail (Fig. 2.3). Shown in a woodland setting, Māyādevī may wear a midriff-baring sari or diaphanous garment, as pictured here, in visual accord with the manner of birth. In other instances, owing to Greco-Roman stylistic influences, Māyādevī is heavily swathed in voluminous robes from which it is

2.3 Nativity Scene, Gāndhāran region (Pakistan/Afghanistan), Kuṣāṇa period, late second or early third century C.E. Gray stone, height 26.3 in. (67 cm). Photo: Freer Gallery of Art, Smithsonian Institution, Washington, D.C.: Purchase, F1949.9. *Māyādevī is attended by male gods on the left and human ladies-in-waiting on the right as her infant issues from her side.*

difficult to imagine an infant finding egress. The female figures portrayed on the right side of the reliefs are members of Māyādevī's human entourage. In this finely carved example from the Freer Gallery, one woman lends the queen a steadying shoulder and comforting hand. A woman bearing a mirror converses with a lady carrying a casket or water pot and a bundle of leaves for an afterbirth ritual. The males appearing on the left are gods who attended the birth. Indra receives the infant in a pure cloth from heaven while Brahmā renders homage and a third deity twirls his scarf and whistles in celebration. In the more detailed compositions, such as the frieze illustrated here, celestial beings offer worship and adoration in the heavens above.[47]

In Gāndhāran portrayals of the infant's return to the palace on a festooned chariot, the princeling is borne on the lap of a royal woman—presumably Māyādevī, in accordance with the prevalent view that she returned to Kapilavastu with her son.[48] Similarly, in illustrations of the consultation of the sage Asita and royal soothsayers regarding the destiny of the child upon their return, Māyādevī is in all likelihood the woman enthroned next to the king or standing and presenting the infant, in keeping with her inclusion in descriptions of this event.[49]

The life of Shakyamuni is also frequently illustrated in the narrative friezes adorning the bases and platforms of the monumental stupas of Nāgārjunakoṇḍa and Amarāvatī in Andhra Pradesh, dating mainly from the second and third centuries C.E. It is most common to find the series opening with the nativity, but in some cases it commences with Māyādevī's dream, followed by the consultation with royal priests regarding the import of the dream, in which scene the queen is present but featured less prominently than the king.[50] Additional scenes may be depicted, such as the lustration of Māyādevī with water from a lotus pond, an event that figured in her conception dream as described in the *Nidānakathā*.[51] We also find portrayals of Śuddhodana joining the queen in the *aśoka* grove to which she summoned him after the conception to inform him of her dream.[52] Interestingly, however, the return to Kapilavastu and Asita's predication after the birth have not been identified in the Amarāvatī and Nāgārjunakoṇḍa repertoire and apparently were not included when artists selected episodes to represent the many events surrounding Shakyamuni's birth.

In art of the Gupta period, the illustration of the Buddha's life was condensed into fewer episodes for representation on freestanding stelae. Māyādevī generally appears only in the scenes of the conception and nativity.[53] During the Pāla period, when the portrayal of the Buddha's life was formulated into eight events, Māyādevī's representation was limited to the birth vignette.[54] However, the birth scene remained a favored subject in Bihar and was featured in freestanding stone and metal statuary.[55] Paintings and tinted xylographs of the nativity were produced in a Tibetan context through the twentieth century, as a prominent scene within pictorial narratives of the life of Shakyamuni.[56] The popularity of paintings of the birth in contemporary Newar art (see Fig. 2.2) reflects not only the subject's ongoing artistic appeal but also Nepal's pride in claiming the Buddha's birthplace.

Representations of the nativity follow a readily recognizable visual format. Māyādevī is shown standing beside a tree, enhaloed by a canopy of foliage, with one arm raised to grasp a flowering branch. In many cases, the leg farthest from the tree is bent so that the sole of the foot rests against the trunk. The aesthetic charm of these portrayals varies according to the gracefulness of her posture, the degree of skill in the execution of ornamental detail, and the subtlety of interplay between her figure and the sheltering tree. In one of the most striking depictions, a stone sculpture from Nepal (Fig. 2.4), Māyādevī's body is elegantly elongated, her smooth limbs resemble those of the tree, and one upraised arm wraps around a branch while the other cups a blossom overhead. The tree

2.4 Nativity Scene, Deopatan, Nepal, possibly Licchavi period. Stone, height 33 in. (83.8 cm). National Museum, Kathmandu. Photo: The Huntington Archive, The Ohio State University. *An elegantly posed Māyādeví clasps a tree that bears mangos, aśoka blossoms, and a lotus.*

itself, a paragon of nature's bounty, bears aśoka leaves and flowers, ripe mangos, and a lotus blossom.[57]

The manner of portraying Māyādevī in the nativity scene follows a pattern established in earlier Buddhist depictions of tree spirits (*yakṣiṇī* or *vṛkṣakā*), later codified in architectural terminology as the *śālabhañjikā*, or beautiful women entwined with a tree.[58] In this genre of artistic representation, the tree-dwelling spirit is entwined with her resident tree, expressing their shared life essence and fruitfulness.[59] Ananda Coomaraswamy suggests that, when seeking a visual model for the nativity, "the sculptor had ready to hand a composition almost exactly fulfilling the requirements of the text."[60] The underlying reason for this seemingly providential coincidence may be that literary descriptions of the event were themselves patterned on the dryad motif.

Why Māyādevī is said to have given birth beneath a tree is undoubtedly a complex question. It is interesting, however, that whereas her purpose for going to the grove and the Bodhisattva's issuance from her side are addressed, the fact that she grasped a tree branch receives little comment. The theme of a woman giving birth beneath a tree may have struck a resonant chord in the Indian religious imagination, evoking a long-standing association between fecund women and flowering trees. Thus, when Māyādevī's iconography was modeled on that of the yakṣiṇīs, her visual persona inherited their rich symbolic connotations of fertility, auspiciousness, and abundance, with the difference that the "fruit" she bore was a gift to the entire world, a son whose influence would endure for millennia.

A similar but distinctive manner of portraying Māyādevī was introduced in Nepal. Māyādevī stands beneath a tree, grasping a branch in the customary manner, but the tree is a heavenly *kalpa-vṛkṣa*, the wish-fulfilling tree that generates a fabulous profusion of gems, flowers, fruit, and whatever the heart desires (Pl. 1). This development was foreshadowed by the Newar relief discussed above (see Fig. 2.4), which departs from naturalistic depiction of the natal tree by endowing it with a supernal yield of mangos and two types of flowers. That imaginative flourish, found on a statue originally installed at the Māyādevī temple in Deopatan—a prominent location—may have prompted the innovation of depicting Māyādevī with the celestial tree, a configuration in place by the fifteenth century.

The wish-granting tree receives an array of creative treatments. The large, ovate leaves are standard, but their embellishment is open to artistic interpretation. In our example, jewels represent the riches and objects of desire produced by the heavenly tree. The foliage is sumptuously inlaid with coral, pearls, blue and green turquoise, and amethyst, ruby, and sapphire gemstones, as are Māyādevī's ornaments and lower garment. Additional features move this vignette beyond a simple birth scene. The infant emerging from Māyādevī's side is typically miniaturized—barely discernible beneath her right arm in the statue illustrated in Plate 1—making Māyādevī the focus of the composition. Māyādevī's crown is more elaborate than her customary aristocratic turban, coiffure, or chaplet. Not simply a crown of royalty, it is a standard Buddhist crown of divinity. Her left hand exhibits *nidhi-darśana mudrā*, the "gesture of displaying treasure," signifying bestowal of wealth and abundance.

Such portrayals of Māyādevī became very popular. They are often five or six feet in height and cast in bronze or carved in wood and enhanced with paint or gilding. The portraits were frequently paired with those of Cintāmaṇi Lokeśvara, a wealth-granting form of Avalokiteśvara unique to Nepal whose iconography appears to have been patterned on that of Māyādevī in order to create a counterpart that could be paired with her effigy in temple settings.[61] It is not clear whether the freestanding bronze pictured here, presently held by the Musée Guimet, was once part of a pair, as would assuredly be the case were it designed for installation on an architectural facade. However, the wealth expended on the statue suggests that it was commissioned for a temple altar rather than a private home. Dating from the early nineteenth century, it is a stunning, exquisitely crafted example of the distinctively Newar rendition of Māyādevī.

Such statues render homage to Māyādevī by depicting her as a figure of rapturous, otherworldly beauty. Moreover, by placing her next to a celestial tree blossoming with gems, they enlarge on her role as mother of the Buddha and enrich her association with abundance. She is shown to be not only a human mother but a numinously bounteous figure whose gift to humanity was so precious that it flowed from an unearthly realm of wonder. Therefore, it seems fitting that she would be shown, at the moment of the birth and in perpetuity, standing beside a paradisal wish-fulfilling tree that figures in the Buddhist imagination as a miraculous source of bounty, riches, and treasure.

Commemorative Sites

Chinese Buddhist pilgrims to India encountered a number of structures and memorials associated with Māyādevī among the palace remains and religious monuments in the vicinity of Kapilavastu, the Buddha's natal home. Hsuantsang, who toured the area circa 638–39 C.E., reported seeing the remains of the queen's bedchamber, marked by a shrine installed with her image. Nearby stood a shrine bearing an illustration of the Bodhisattva's descent into her womb. In the vicinity of the bodhi tree was a stupa on the spot where the Buddha preached to his mother shortly after he attained enlightenment and, near the place where Shakyamuni died, a stupa was erected to commemorate Māyādevī's descent to weep over his body. The pilgrim also encountered a temple dedicated to Māyādevī in which her image was enshrined.[62]

The archaeological remains of Tilaurakot (the ancient Kapilavastu region) include a structure built upon what could well be the foundation of the Māyādevī shrine mentioned by Hsuan-tsang. It is currently known as the temple of Samai-ma.[63] Near the building, installed on a lotus pedestal at the base of a tree, is the effigy of "Samai-ma," the fertility goddess in active worship at the site. Despite its advanced state of erosion, the image is recognizable as Māyādevī grasping a tree branch. Smaller reliefs of the infant Buddha and other figures are arrayed around her. The customary offerings to this mother goddess are small burnt-clay horses, elephants, and goats. The former practices of scraping the image (to use the rubbings in a fertility potion), smearing it with vermilion, and sacrificing animals were discontinued several decades ago.[64]

Lumbinī Grove and Its Religious Significance

The main site of pilgrimage associated with Māyādevī was naturally the grove of Lumbinī. In the *Mahāparinibbāna Sutta*, which records Shakyamuni's final teachings, his birthplace is designated as one of the four main pilgrimage sites, along with Bodhgayā, the site of his enlightenment; Sārnāth, where he gave his first teaching; and Kuśinagara, where he passed into nirvana.[65] As pilgrimage gained importance in early Buddhist devotionalism, these sites dominated a route well traversed by laypersons, monastics, and royalty. Lumbinī, in the Himalayan foothills within the present borders of Nepal, was the most remote and least accessible of the four.

Emperor Aśoka journeyed in his twentieth regnal year (ca. 245 B.C.E.) to Lumbinī, where he distributed gold coins to area inhabitants, exempted the village from its rice tax, and established a commemorative pillar surmounted by a horse capital. A Brahmi inscription specifies that the pillar marks the site of the Buddha's birth, a fortuity later of immense historical significance.[66] Several Chinese pilgrims reported on their visits to Lumbinī over the centuries, including Fa-hsien in the fourth century and Hsuan-tsang in the seventh. Fa-hsien mentioned seeing the tank where Māyādevī bathed; Hsuan-tsang noted in addition the natal tree (an aśoka in his account), several stupas, the Aśoka pillar, and a stream of water flowing at the spot where a pool had magically appeared near Māyādevī after the birth.[67] The last documented pilgrimage to Lumbinī before the modern era was that of Ripumalla, a Nepalese ruler who visited the site in 1312 C.E. and recorded his visit on the pillar.[68]

At some point during the ensuing centuries, the location of the Buddha's birthplace was forgotten, perhaps due to its remoteness from the other sacred sites in the Buddhist heartland of Magadha. The site was rediscovered in 1896 by Khadga Shumsher, a government archaeologist, when area inhabitants guided him to the buried Aśokan pillar. The fortuitous presence of the site's name in the pillar inscription restored Lumbinī to the Buddhist world.[69] Further excavations revealed a rectangular bathing tank, five stupas near the tank, sixteen votive stupas along the walkway to a large temple plinth, and assorted Buddhist and Hindu statuary. The oily stream noted by travelers in centuries past still flowed nearby.[70] The grove, about five acres in extent, had presumably dwindled from its former size owing to the encroachment of surrounding farm land. The legendary aśoka and śāla trees were no longer in evidence, although the modest woodland still boasted pipal trees, many fruit trees (bel, tamarind, and guava), and flowering jasmine.[71]

Today the thicket is known in local parlance as Rummindeī. Villagers honor Rummindeī not as the site of the Buddha's birth but as the sacred grove of Rummin-deī, or Rummin-devī, the "goddess of Rummin."[72] Jarl Charpentier suggests that "Rummin" is a colloquial rendition of Lumbinī.[73] Damodar Kosambi, in contrast, suggests that Rummini was the original name of the grove and its indwelling goddess and that Buddhist authors rendered the name as Lumbinī, which simply means "grove": "There is an excellent chance of the name Luṃbini having originally been the adjective *rummini* for some dread goddess, gruesome and beautiful at the same time, like so many tribal Mothers."[74] Visitors to Lumbinī have also been apprised that the grove goddess is known as Rūpādevī ("Beautiful Goddess"), Rupandeī Bhagavatī, or even Tathāgatā, a name preserving the Buddhist associations of the site.[75] Today, two images are in worship there, both effigies of Māyādevī with her arm entwined with a tree and her infant at her feet. One is a heavily eroded, life-sized relief carved in sandstone; the other is a recent copy, executed in marble on a smaller scale (Fig. 2.5).[76]

Women from surrounding villages have come here over the centuries to seek protection in childbirth and healthy children, customarily coating the images with a red paste made from vermilion mixed with oil. The ingestion of stone particles from the statuary is believed to cure infertility, a practice that accounts for the advanced state of erosion of the images. The worship included animal sacrifice until this was outlawed in the 1920s.[77] These practices have been replaced by offerings of red sandal powder and seasonal flowers. An archaeological record dating back thousands of years preserves offerings of beads (perhaps once strung together into jewelry), copper coins, potsherds, human figurines, and terracotta animals.[78]

The annual week-long festival held in honor of Rummindeī in the spring coincides with the celebration of the Buddha's birth on the Vaiśākha (April–May) full moon. The timing of the event may be a vestige of former Buddhist

2.5 Nativity Scene, Chandra Man Maskey, Lumbinī, Nepal, ca. 1956. Marble. Photo: Paula Kane Arai. *This marble statue of Māyādevī, currently worshipped at Lumbinī, is adorned with vermilion powder and flower offerings.*

observances at the site, although the festival itself traditionally centered on animal sacrifices and offerings of miniature baked clay horses.[79] Animal sacrifice and lustration with vermilion (*sindūra*) are common expressions of goddess worship throughout the Indian subcontinent, as is the offering of clay horses. Votive offerings of horse effigies (variously of cloth, stone, or burnt clay) are documented in various village and tribal venues throughout India. In some cases the horse is a customary offering given in thanks for the conception, birth, or cure of a child.[80] Indeed, the horse has a long-standing association with fertility in Indic religions, and, as Francesco Brighenti explains, is a popular offering at open-air goddess shrines in some regions:

> Rough votive figures of a horse made of stone, clay or metal (*mātāghoṛās*) are deposited in hundreds in the popular Devī [goddess] shrines of Bengal and Orissa, lying either under a sacred tree in the jungle or in towns and villages.... The Oriyā villagers believe that when the Devī is invoked for some aid ... she comes to the worshipper's house riding the horse that has been dedicated to her under a sacred tree or in a shrine. The horse, thus, acts as the "magical" carrier of the Goddess when her help is invoked.[81]

It is possible, then, that a long-standing local custom of offering terracotta horses to the divine mother of Lumbinī grove, evinced among the early remains at the site and consistent with broader patterns of goddess worship, was reinforced by the equine capital on the Aśokan pillar, confirming for area residents that the horse was the vehicle (*vāhana*, animal mount and companion) of the fertility goddess, in accordance with the Hindu custom of displaying the vāhana of a deity on a pillar outside the shrine.

The archaeological evidence and ongoing tradition of mother goddess worship at Lumbinī raise the question of the antiquity of this phenomenon. One possibility is that, after Lumbinī became a Buddhist site of pilgrimage, local villagers who were not Buddhist began to worship the image of Māyādevī in their own fashion and that the two forms of worship coexisted until the area ceased to draw Buddhist pilgrims. Another possibility is that the site was already a goddess shrine or even a sacred birthing grove—perhaps centering on a tree deity known to assist childbirth—during Queen Māyādevī's time and that, after its Buddhist association was forgotten, the site reverted to its earlier character. Kosambi proposes that the area had long been revered as Rummindeī's grove and that Māyādevī herself went there to pay respects to the goddess and invoke her protection for a safe delivery.[82]

Indeed, several features of the Buddhist accounts suggest that Māyādevī's visit to the woodland had religious significance. According to the Sanskrit narratives, the grove was Māyādevī's intended destination when the time for the birth drew near. Surely a definite purpose drew her away from the comforts and amenities of the palace at such a time. The *Buddhacarita*, for example, avows that it was "not for a pleasure excursion."[83] Kosambi suggests that the queen was following a custom of her clanswomen at a time normally surrounded by ritual—namely, the rite of passage of giving birth—and notes that the grove in question was near Devadaha, her natal home, and thus may have been sacred to her matriline.[84] The king accepted Māyādevī's plan without question, evincing that the request was unexceptional, and ordered that the grove be carpeted and festooned with banners and garlands. He may simply have been beautifying the grove for the royal birth, or the adornments may have been intended as offerings to the sylvan deities.

Lumbinī's topography is consistent with that of a sacred grove, for, according to Kosambi, "the most primitive mother-goddesses . . . have a *rāna*, literally 'forest', about the aniconic image," and stands of śāla trees find mention in this regard.[85] The sacrality of the grove would help explain why only women entered the glade with Māyādevī.[86] Her female retinue accords with a general Indic tradition that women preside in the sphere of childbirth. Kosambi proposes, however, that the all-female retinue also met a restriction associated with the grove itself, on the principle that "such jungle groves were primeval, originally never to be entered by men."[87]

The belief that Lumbinī was a sacred woodland with a resident "grove goddess" (*vana-devatā*) is evinced in Buddhist sources. For example, a reference to the goddess of Lumbinī appears in the *Mahāvastu*, not in the context of the birth event but in a later episode, when Siddhārtha had developed an aversion toward worldly pleasures and turned his thoughts toward renunciation. As his father pondered why the prince was so melancholic, the goddess of the Lumbinī grove hovered in the air above the king and advised him that the prince had no taste for sensual delights and would soon depart for the "forest of penance."[88] The *Flower Ornament Scripture*, too, includes an episode centering on the "goddess of Lumbinī grove" (*lumbinī-vana-devatā, lumbinī-devatā*).[89] The goddess, named Sutejomaṇḍalaratiśrī in this work, says that in a former life she was the wet nurse of a Buddha in another world system and that she aspired to become the goddess of Lumbinī because she knew that Shakyamuni would be born there. Moreover, her retinue of sylvan goddesses had waited on the Buddha's mother in that lifetime. Sutejomaṇḍalaratiśrī imparts that in preparing the glade for the birth of the Buddha-to-be, she draped jewels and flower garlands from the trees, made lotuses bloom in all the ponds, and summoned the females of all species to bring offerings to the foot of the tree where the Bodhisattva would be born.[90] Here, the grove goddess facilitates the birth, which is precisely the role one would expect.

If Queen Māyādevī went to the grove to give birth under the care of the grove goddess and invoke her protection for a safe delivery, it is likely that the shrine of the arboreal divinity would be a sacred tree. Worship of tree spirits was (and remains) a widespread practice in India. There is no reason to believe that the Buddha's parents did not participate in this virtually universal form of cultic activity. Moreover, trees and tree deities have long had a close association with human fertility; even today many Indic fertility rites, amulets, and magical and ritual practices to promote conception and ease of delivery center on trees.[91]

Thus, it is not surprising that a tree was the focus of Māyādevī's visit to the grove. The *Nidānakathā* describes it as an "auspicious *śāla*" and moreover as the "monarch" śāla, the largest and hence oldest in the glade, which would naturally be identified as the sacred tree of a given locale.[92] The *Lalitavistara* holds that the queen was drawn to an exceptionally beautiful tree decked with banners and garlands, a motif that may indicate signs of active worship.[93] According to the *Mahāvastu*, when Māyādevī's father sent for her as the time for the birth drew near, King Śuddhodana replied that "she should break the branch of the *sāl* tree," perhaps in reference to a birth custom, similar to collecting leaves to hang over the door of the birthing room, a practice still observed in parts of India.[94] Thus, when Māyādevī grasped the tree branch, this gesture may have been intended to invoke blessings for the impending birth.

Although biographical accounts name the śāla or the plākṣa as the type of tree under which Māyādevī gave birth, it almost invariably appears as an aśoka in artistic representations and other literary sources.[95] The widespread conception that the tree was an aśoka, despite literary traditions to the contrary, may be attributed to the aśoka's association with human fertility and its use in a range of healing rites intended to aid in the conception and safe delivery of a child.[96] The identification of the tree as an aśoka supports the interpretation that her tree-grasping gesture invokes magical arboreal powers.

The belief that the natal tree had an indwelling divinity is seen in the account that the tree lowered a bough of its own accord, for, as Coomaraswamy explains, it was "the spirit of the tree that bent down the branch to meet Māyādevī's hand."[97] The conviction that the tree harbored a goddess is also expressed in the account of the visit of Emperor Aśoka and his saintly preceptor, Upagupta, to Lumbinī. When the pilgrims came into the presence of the sacred tree (in this account unsurprisingly an aśoka), Upagupta extended his hand toward the tree and invoked the indwelling spirit: "Let the divine maiden who resides in this aśoka tree and who witnessed the birth of the Buddha make herself manifest in her own body." In answer to his summons, the tree goddess rendered herself visible and gratified Aśoka with a firsthand description of the nativity.[98]

Artistic representations also give evidence of the belief that the tree was the abode of a sylvan deity. For example, an Amarāvatī relief shows the tree deity's hand emerging from the branches to assist Māyādevī.[99] A Pāla-period manuscript painting of the nativity portrays a voluptuous green woman superimposed on the tree trunk (Pl. 2), while an early Newar painting endows the attending female with the same green hue as the tree foliage.[100] In other compositions, when the figure is golden, like the queen, it may be interpretable as a human attendant or a radiant tree spirit,[101] but I suggest that the vernal figure assuredly represents the spirit of the tree, serving as midwife for the sacred birth.

If Māyādevī went to the grove in order to perform birthing rituals, this could also explain why she was accompanied by an all-female entourage, whether or not it was a restriction associated with the sacred grove. Birth practices and rituals were the exclusive province of women in India and still are in areas untouched by western medical practices. Even if Māyādevī had not expected to give birth in the grove, it would follow that she and her party would remain there to perform after-birth rites to ward off dangers to mother and newborn. In contemporary practice, the most critical of these is performed on the sixth night after childbirth. Women keep lamps burning, sing, and hold vigil through the night to ward off demons believed to prey on mothers and infants at this vulnerable time.[102] In Māyādevī's time, too, women may have propitiated a goddess akin to Ṣaṣṭhī, the divinity invoked (especially in northeastern India) for the protection of newly born infants and who may be worshipped at a tree shrine, in the form of a tree branch, and by religious observances undertaken by groups of women in a forest setting.[103]

If mother and child survive, public celebration of the birth commences on or soon after the seventh day. Kosambi notes that Māyādevī's death on the seventh postpartum day did occur "close to the perilous sixth night."[104] Her son lived to fulfill his destiny, while Māyādevī's memory blended with the identity of the grove goddess, at least for the village women who have worshipped her effigy over the centuries, seeking her divine protection and blessings. Her manner of portrayal, entwined with a flowering tree, would signify to them that she was indeed a fertility goddess, the goddess of the sacred grove.

Lumbinī has now entered a new phase of its history. The blood offerings repugnant to Buddhists were disallowed early in the twentieth century, when the Buddhist significance of the site was rediscovered. The practices of smearing and rubbing the images were suspended, too, in the interests of archaeological preservation. The sandstone relief is protected by a plexiglas screen, and a wooden railing keeps worshippers at arm's length as they make offerings at the base of the marble statue (see Fig. 2.5). Besides the traditional local offerings, one now finds standard Buddhist gifts of incense, butter lamps, and honorary scarves. An effigy of the infant Buddha has been brought into the shrine and placed near those of Māyādevī.[105] In celebration of the Fourth World Buddhist Conference held in Kathmandu in 1956, four Buddha statues (from Nepal, Thailand, Burma, and Japan) were installed at the site, along with a monastery and rest house.

In 1972, a United Nations advisory board drew up plans and raised funds to convert the site into an international center for study and pilgrimage. In fulfillment of the U.N. proposal, the area now houses a library, museum, garden, temples, expanded monastic residence, tourist center, and visitor accommodations. The project has also entailed an improved infrastructure of postal service, electricity, plumbing, reforestation, transportation, housing, and economic development in the nearby village.[106] As these ambitious plans permanently alter the topography and ambiance of the site, it is interesting to reflect on whether Lumbinī's development into an international Buddhist center is truly a restoration of its original sectarian affiliation or yet another priestly appropriation of an ancient goddess grove.

Māyādevī as Goddess

Whether Queen Māyādevī should be included in a study on Buddhist goddesses is perhaps debatable. She may have been a marvelously lovely maiden and a paragon among women, but she was, after all, a human being who gave birth to a human son. She emerges nonetheless as a wondrous figure in Buddhist legend. To some extent her glory is a reflection of the crucial role she played in the drama of the life and accomplishments of Shakyamuni Buddha. Yet she is also illumined by her own aura of divinity. Her name alludes to her numinosity, for "Māyādevī" can be translated as "Goddess of Magical Creation" or "Goddess of Mother Love."[107]

Māyādevī possesses the mythic overtones of an independent mother goddess by virtue of the fact that she conceived Shakyamuni through parthenogenesis, without the help of a male. In that sense, the Buddha was her "magical creation," brought forth in a garden of paradise beneath a veritable tree of life. She has also figured as a "goddess of mother love" insofar as Lumbinī has served as a mother goddess shrine over the centuries. Although one of the world's great religious leaders was born there, the object of reverence and source of comfort and healing for hopeful and expectant mothers at the site has been the mother who gave birth, not the son who was born. Moreover, the Buddhist tradition has officially conferred divine status on Māyādevī by the story of her rebirth as a goddess in Trāyastriṃśa Heaven, where she is envisioned as residing still.

Māyādevī was not only the mother of the Buddha but also in a sense the mother of Buddhism. Insofar as the world has benefited from the presence of a Buddha, gratitude must flow to the mother who made that possible, as many Buddhist texts maintain. Thus, Māyādevī represents, for Buddhism, the irreducible reality of motherhood. Every heroic journey, every spiritual quest, must have as its beginning the ineluctable fact of being born. In the human Māyādevī we find the prototype of the first full-fledged cosmic goddess of Buddhism, Prajñāpāramitā, the embodiment of transcendent wisdom and "Mother of All Buddhas," the goddess who arose out of the realization that, in order for there to be Buddhas, there must be mothers.

CHAPTER 3

Yakṣiṇīs

Voluptuous, Magical Nature Spirits

> Yakṣiṇīs traverse the entire world and ascend to the realm of the gods in a fraction of a moment. Great yakṣiṇīs fight in the battle between gods and demons. They are reverent, compassionate, benevolent toward beings, full of mother love. They roam the surface of the earth for the purpose of doing good to humanity. There is nothing they cannot achieve. They are auspicious ones, accomplishing all activities. They have been directed by the bodhisattva (Mañjuśrī) to increase the happiness of humankind.
>
> —*Mañjuśrīmūlakalpa*[1]

The yakṣiṇī (pronounced *YAHK shee NEE*) figures that grace the railing pillars and gates of the earliest known Buddhist monuments were among the first images to greet devotees as they entered the sacred precinct and circumambulated the stupa mound enshrining the relics of the Buddha. At the stupa sites of Bhārhut, Sanghol, and Bhūteśvara, the yakṣiṇīs were prominently situated on the stone pillars of the stupa balustrade; at Sāñcī their images tower above all who pass through the massive gateways. It is intriguing that worshippers at shrines erected to commemorate the Buddha immediately encountered an array of voluptuous, benign goddesses whose presence and symbolic import there, as has been remarked, bear little discernible relationship to the Buddhist ethos of detachment and who, in the words of Ananda Coomaraswamy, "at first sight . . . seem to be singularly out of place."[2]

The yakṣiṇīs and other spirit beings among which they appear are not specifically or exclusively Buddhist in character. Drawn from a common storehouse of Indian icon, lore, and cultic practice, rooted in open-air religious observances that antedate Buddhism, these figures complement textual evidence regarding the beliefs and worship of early Buddhists. The early stupas were not simply tributes to the Buddha but a full-bodied outpouring of the religious sentiments of those who commissioned and worshipped at the monuments.[3] The yakṣiṇīs adorn them not as decorative elements but as icons with symbolic, talismanic, and protective significance. Their effigies sanctify the shrines with an irenic and yet magically potent feminine presence. Moreover, as a focus of devotion and cultic activity in the areas where the stupas were built, yakṣiṇīs played a ritual and possibly liturgical role in Buddhist worship at the sites.

Yakṣa Worship

In Sanskrit, the term *yakṣa*, when used in plural form, refers collectively to both yakṣiṇīs and their male counterparts, the yakṣas.[4] Together, they represent a populous class of supernatural beings with a long history in India. It is difficult to define them precisely, in part because individual members of the class evince a broad spectrum of character and behavior. The etymology of the term itself is unclear.[5] The term generally denotes a supernatural being that is held in reverence and receives offerings; it is often used interchangeably with *devatā*, "deity," in Sanskrit and Pali literature. In the Vedas, the term may designate an entity who is wonderful, mysterious, numinous, radiant, or awe-inspiring; a being of supernal strength or beauty; a spirit that is normally invisible but may manifest in various forms and take possession of human beings; a dreadful or hostile presence; or even one of the high gods of the Vedic pantheon, such as Indra or Brahmā.[6] Thus, *yakṣa* had already emerged in the Vedas as a versatile term for any supernatural being or object of worship or propitiation, from the demonic to the divine.

Yakṣa worship was a major form of cultic activity when Buddhism and the other sectarian traditions took root. Yakṣas and yakṣiṇīs can to a large extent be characterized as nature spirits. Their presence is generally associated with features of the landscape—most notably, trees and woodlands. The simplest yakṣa shrine (*yakṣa-caitya*, or *yakṣa-sthāna*) was a tree. A simple altar or raised dais complete with throne back, parasol, and balustrade might be erected to honor the arboreal sacra.[7] The tree itself, recognized as the dwelling of a deity, received homage as a natural icon of its resident spirit. The common reference to this practice as "tree worship" is a misnomer, insofar as the honor is directed to the indwelling spirit rather than the tree.

Although yakṣas and yakṣiṇīs are closely associated with trees in Indic religiosity, they might be worshipped in a range of sanctuaries and settings, such as a mountain, lake, river, cave, water tank, city gate, cremation ground, private dwelling, palace compound, or shrine or image established for their habitation.[8] Moreover, yakṣas and yakṣiṇīs are by nature genii loci with a limited and specific range of influence. Because they exert a protective influence on their immediate territory, Ananda Coomaraswamy concludes that in many cases yakṣas and yakṣiṇīs functioned as patron deities, or "guardian angels," of their respective domains, which could be a sylvan area, household, or entire city.[9]

Yakṣa worship was virtually universal during the period under discussion. This type of religious observance was not confined to any particular social class, profession, or geographical region. Votaries included royalty and commoners, urban dwellers and rural villagers, merchants and farmers, men and women.[10] Practices ranged from simple votive offerings at a local shrine to communal celebrations and elaborate festivities at major pilgrimage sites. The benefits of worship encompassed every area of life.

Buddhism inherited belief in yakṣas and yakṣiṇīs as an integral part of the preexisting cosmology and cultic activity of the Indian populace. They figure in the pantheon of beings and powers that constitute the physical and spiritual world, just as much a part of the round of existence as human beings. The Buddha and the generations who followed him did not question their existence or prohibit their worship, nor did they ignore their presence in the landscape and religious lives of the people. On the contrary, this class of beings is a recurrent theme in Buddhist literature and art. Indeed much of the evidence of yakṣa worship during this period is found in Buddhist sources.[11] Yakṣas find frequent mention in narratives of the life and career of Shakyamuni Buddha, figuring among his worshippers and sphere of potential converts. Descriptions of the enlightenment event and audiences of his sermons consistently include yakṣas and yakṣiṇīs in the joyous congregation of homage and worship. Moreover, they frequently appear as supernatural allies of the Buddha and protectors of his followers.

Buddhist legend is replete with instances of the Buddha himself commending this form of cultic activity. When Shakyamuni traveled, he frequently rested and on occasion preached at yakṣa abodes (*yakṣa-sthāna*) and was known to pronounce them to be delightful.[12] In a final discourse to the citizens of Vaiśālī, he advised that they would prosper as long as they continued to honor, respect, worship, and make their customary offerings at the yakṣa shrines throughout the city and countryside.[13] The Buddha also sanctioned the worship of yakṣas on Buddhist premises and even ordered that yakṣa altars be established for this purpose. For example, he directed that every monastery should include a shrine to the great yakṣiṇī Hārītī and that she should receive daily offerings.[14] In another instance, Shakyamuni reportedly instructed the citizens of Mathurā to build a monastery and dedicate it to the yakṣa Gardabha. The faithful of Mathurā then honored thousands of local yakṣas by installing their altars in the same number of newly built Buddhist monasteries.[15] Richard Cohen, analyzing this remarkable, if apocryphal, account, concludes that monasteries were indeed constructed in honor of yakṣas, dedicated to their worship, and installed with a yakṣa image or altar as a focus of devotional activity within the monastic complex.[16] There are additional cases where a yakṣa sanctuary was chosen as the site of a monastery and an occasion when the Buddha invited a yakṣiṇī to reside near his preaching chamber.[17] It has also been argued that the trees beneath which he attained enlightenment and entered parinirvāṇa were yakṣa shrines.[18]

These accounts evince that the devotional cult of the yakṣas flourished under Buddhist auspices and in Buddhist institutions. The Buddha, of course, was the main object of reverence, but it was apparently common practice to have as a patron a being already worshipped in the locale as a way to enlist the devotional sentiments already present in the populace. Cohen contends that hosting yakṣa worship on Buddhist premises was a key factor in the spread and localization of Buddhism: "The Buddha and the *saṅgha* become localized insofar as they share their dwellings with the deities who are indigenous and unique to the sites of the monasteries."[19]

Cohen's analysis clarifies why popular nature divinities such as yakṣiṇīs might be included in a Buddhist iconographic program. In view of the fact that yakṣas and yakṣiṇīs represent genii loci associated with the protection of specific places and peoples, the yakṣiṇīs portrayed on these monuments were probably local deities with a cult following in the region in which a stupa was built, evoking a familiar devotional idiom at the point of entry to the sacred space. Jean Vogel notes in this regard that the names of the Bhārhut yakṣiṇīs are not attested elsewhere, suggesting a local provenance.[20] The yakṣiṇīs from the other known stupa sites are not named in inscriptions, and their depiction follows a general formula, but area residents may have ascribed the names and legends of popular local spirits to the images. Even if the figures were not endowed with this degree of individuality, they no doubt furnished a focal point for folk beliefs and practices. They provided a prism through which the monument's universal import was refracted into a local and actively benefic presence, symbolically anchoring the structure in its specific site by invoking a pantheon that had long been active in the protection and blessing of the area.

Artistic Representations

The yakṣiṇīs that grace the early Buddhist monuments are endowed with every gift of the female form, from voluptuous curves and sinuous pose to lavish adornment. Their breasts are rounded and firm above a slender waist and ample hips accentuated by a broad, jeweled hip belt (Fig. 3.1). The figures are nude or minimally clothed with a diaphanous lower garment, but every part of the body is enhanced by ornamentation. The hair is elaborately dressed and the ears adorned by large pendants, the upper torso is decked with necklaces, and the slim wrists and ankles are encircled by tiers of bangles and anklets. The poses are

3.1 Yakṣiṇī, Bhūteśvara, Mathura District, Uttar Pradesh, India, second century C.E. Stupa railing pillar, detail. Red sandstone, height 48 in. (122 cm). Indian Museum, Calcutta, A24946. Used by permission. Photo: American Institute of Indian Studies. *A voluptuous yakṣiṇī adjusts her necklace and lifts her sash to reveal the auspicious pelvic triangle.*

confident yet relaxed; the limbs are sturdy yet supple; the facial expressions are beatific and otherworldly, lending them a majestic air.

Ranking among the world's greatest achievements in sculptural interpretation of the female form, their artists met the challenge of capturing the legendary beauty of the yakṣiṇīs. These sylvan goddesses are reputed to be enchantingly beautiful, irresistible to mortal men, and coveted by the gods in heaven.[21] The famed loveliness of the yakṣiṇīs is celebrated by Kālidāsa in the *Meghadūta* (possibly fourth century C.E.), wherein the playwright describes their braided hair laced with flowers, faces powdered with pollen, and sashes undone and fluttering wide. Such is their beauty, more dazzling than a lightning flash, that the love god does not bother to unleash his arrows in their presence, for their coquettish glances are darts that always find their mark. A wish-fulfilling tree provides them with cosmetics, colored raiment, jeweled ornaments, blossoms for their hair, eye-brightening wine, and lac to redden their lotuslike feet. Kālidāsa's language accords with the images at Buddhist stupa sites when he praises the yakṣiṇīs' intricate adornments, lissome bodies, thighs as fair as plantain stems, and arms like vines. The yakṣa protagonist extols his beloved yakṣiṇī as slight of waist with generous hips and a delicate body slightly bowed by the weight of her breasts; he fondly remembers how the peacock dances to the jingling of her bracelets as she claps her hands.[22] Clearly the yakṣiṇīs were envisioned as creatures of singular grace who equally inspired the chisels of the carvers of Buddhist monuments and the pen of Kālidāsa.

The initial manner of depicting yakṣiṇīs, found at Bhārhut and Sāñcī, was to portray them as dryads in a sylvan habitat. Their affinity for and tendency to inhabit trees makes them indistinguishable from and virtually synonymous with tree goddesses (*vṛkṣa-devatā*, *vṛkṣakā*) and grove goddesses (*vana-devatā*).[23] Thus, it is not surprising to find the yakṣiṇīs most characteristically portrayed in the form of a woman intertwined with a tree, grasping a branch overhead. As a yakṣiṇī's limbs interlace with those of a tree and pull a branch into a graceful arch above her head, they merge into an organic whole. According to Gustav Roth, "there is really no other pose than this one which could more clearly express the unity of a tree with its deity."[24] The yakṣiṇī may also press her body against the trunk in an amorous manner, invoking the simile that a woman (*latā*, "one who gracefully curves") embracing her lover is like a vine (also *latā*) entwining a tree.[25]

The subtle interfusion of dryad and tree is well exemplified by the image of the yakṣiṇī Candrā from Bhārhut (Fig. 3.2). She embraces a flowering *nāgakesara* tree with her left arm and leg while her right hand grasps a branch overhead. A virtually inexhaustible attentiveness to the details of the figure and ornamentation are apparent here. A blossom from the tree is woven into her braided hair; the tree leaves attached to the floret subtly intermingle with the

3.2 Candrā Yakṣiṇī, Great Stupa, Bhārhut, Satna District, Madhya Pradesh, India, Śuṅga period, ca. 100–80 B.C.E. Sandstone, height ca. 118 in. (300 cm). Indian Museum, Calcutta, 106. Used by permission. Photo: The Huntington Archive, The Ohio State University. *The exquisitely rendered beauty of the goddess and the tree reflect and enhance one another.*

3.3 Detail of Fig. 3.2. Photo: American Institute of Indian Studies. *The yakṣiṇī's adornments and plaited hair are rendered in astounding detail, as are the tree leaves and flowers.*

pattern of the braid (Fig. 3.3). Her face is marked with delicate painted designs, a cosmetic practice akin to the contemporary art of applying henna tracery to the hands and feet.[26] The sculpting articulates the individual beads, pendants, and shapes of her necklaces, earrings, bracelets, anklets, and thumb rings. A berry-shaped pendant dangles from a jeweled sacred thread near her deeply carved navel. The level of detail in her attire is mirrored in the tree overhead, where an eye attuned to fine carving will discern finely wrought leaves endowed with veins and flowers with stamens.

Clearly, the beauty of the goddess and the tree reflect and enhance one another. In a subtle detail noticed by Susan Huntington, the left hand of the yakṣiṇī "points to her genital area while holding a flowering branch from the . . . tree as if it emerges from her womb," a dramatic visual expression of the shared essence of yakṣiṇī and tree.[27]

At Sāñcī, yakṣiṇī reliefs, similar in style to the Bhārhut carvings, abound on the profusely sculpted pillars that surround Stupa II. Yakṣiṇīs are also featured as bracket figures supporting the projecting ends of the architraves of the large gateways (*toraṇa*) that punctuate the stupa railings of Stupas I and III. These figures are carved in the round, allowing for a fuller articulation of bodily form. The masterpiece of Sāñcī is undoubtedly the yakṣiṇī entwined with a mango tree whose figure graces the grand gate on the eastern side of Stupa I (Fig. 3.4). The flowering tree laden with ripe fruit beautifully echoes the abundant charms of the yakṣiṇī. Her braceleted arms are as smooth as the tree limbs, creating a subtle visual simile. Her right hand cradles a mango as if her arm were simply an extension of the tree. Her chignon resembles a cluster of mango leaves. Viewed from the back, her upraised arms literally merge into her sylvan canopy (Fig. 3.5). The deft aesthetic interplay between the dryad and the tree perfectly expresses their unity of spirit.

Because yakṣiṇīs were so often conceived as tree sprites (*vṛkṣakā*), the tree alongside each figure may represent her residence, in which case the compositions offered an anthropomorphic rendition of the arboreal shrines at which the devotees customarily worshipped. It has also been suggested, however, that this manner of portrayal was intended to depict the yakṣiṇīs in their supernal domain, in the fabled gardens of the yakṣa realms.[28] One of their kingdoms is described as replete with perpetually fruiting trees and many kinds of birds, resonant with the cries of peacocks and herons, and graced by a lotus lake.[29]

The *Meghadūta*, although later than the sculptures under discussion, evinces the persistence in popular imagination of a sylvan yakṣa paradise, elaborating on the shining gardens where yakṣiṇīs roam and play among ever-flowering trees, aśoka glades, jasmine vines, and strutting peacocks. The paths are strewn with flower petals and pearls that fall from their adornments as they dart among the trees. The yakṣiṇī featured in this lyrical poem tends a coral-blossomed *mandāra* tree as if it were her own child and dearly loves the plantain grove nearby. The aśoka and *keśara* trees require her touch before they will flower. Such is Kālidāsa's description of the bucolic setting where, sporting among the trees, the yakṣiṇīs, "forever young, enjoy the wonders that the gardens hold."[30] Thus, it may be suggested that the trees included in the compositions represent sacred trees in the human realm, a supernal woodland setting, or a dual reference to both.

The yakṣiṇīs in the Gāndhāran corpus are similarly conceived as dryads but are attired in Greco-Roman garb and stand beneath unidentifiable trees, often in an awkward crossed-ankle pose adopted from Greek portraits of male figures (Fig. 3.6).[31] Their distinctive style lacks the Indic charm of earlier yakṣiṇī imagery. Moreover, in the stupa reliefs of Gāndhāra, the yakṣiṇīs have a less prominent role in the overall iconographic program. Their images appear to serve primarily as decorative elements as they punctuate the sculpted narrative panels that adorn the stupa plinths.[32]

A deemphasis on yakṣiṇī imagery is also discernible in the art of Andhra Pradesh, where stupa carvings are concentrated on the drums and platforms rather than on freestanding balustrades. At Nāgārjunakoṇḍa (second to fourth centuries), yakṣiṇīs routinely serve as framing figures at the ends of the narrative friezes around the outermost tier of the stupa plinth.[33] The yakṣiṇīs receive even less emphasis at Amarāvatī (second and early third centuries), where their images are relegated to service as an occasional decorative accent.[34]

Source of Śālabhañjikā and Aśoka-Dohada Motifs

The manner of depicting yakṣiṇīs with trees on the early Buddhist monuments set the precedent for a compositional type that has been dubbed the "woman and tree motif." Ananda Coomaraswamy contends that "there is no motif more fundamentally characteristic of Indian art from first to last."[35] The image of a woman grasping a tree branch eventually lost its primary association with yakṣiṇīs and became a standard figural type known as a *śālabhañjikā*, literally, "maiden breaking a śāla branch." Jean Vogel traced the history of the śālabhañjikā concept in Sanskrit literature and found the term first used in a Buddhist text, referring to a flower-gathering festival in observance of which women climbed śāla trees to pluck their blossoms.[36] Thereafter, the term was used for several centuries to designate a sculpted representation of a woman grasping a tree branch, a pose highly favored for showing the female figure to good advantage. By the seventh century C.E., *śālabhañjikā* came into architectural usage as a technical term for any image of a woman carved on a pillar or building facade.[37]

3.4 Yakṣiṇī, eastern gateway, Stupa I (Great Stupa), Sāñcī, Raisen District, Madhya Pradesh, India, ca. early first century C.E. Buff sandstone, height 48.8 in. (124 cm). Photo: American Institute of Indian Studies. *This yakṣiṇī entwined with a mango tree is prominently placed on the gate of entry to the main stupa at Sāñcī.*

3.5 Back view of Fig. 3.4. Photo: American Institute of Indian Studies. *The limbs of the yakṣiṇī resemble and merge into the tree in which she resides.*

3.6 Yakṣiṇī, Nathu, Pakistan, Kuṣāṇa period, ca. first or second century C.E. Schist, height 14 in. (35.5 cm). Indian Museum, Calcutta, A23239 N.S. 2567. Used by permission. Photo: American Institute of Indian Studies. *This typical Gāndhāran style yakṣiṇī displays Greco-Roman garb, hairstyling, and jewelry and a crossed-ankle pose.*

Another concept associated with the yakṣiṇī imagery on the early Buddhist monuments is that of *aśoka-dohada*, the "longing of the aśoka tree" for the touch of a woman's foot to awaken it into blossom. In many of the Buddhist reliefs, one leg of the yakṣiṇī is bent so that her foot presses against the trunk of the tree (see Figs. 3.2, 3.4). In classical Indian literature, this gesture took on a life of its own. The motif of a woman's kick causing an aśoka tree to blossom became a favored literary trope from the fourth century onward.[38] The playwright Kālidāsa, who makes liberal use of the theme, devotes an entire act of one of his dramas to the choice and preparation of the heroine to kick a sacred aśoka tree that has failed to flower. When she happens upon the tree, she discerns that "this *aśoka*, awaiting the fulfillment of its delicate longing, and not assuming its robe of flowers, seems to invite me." With her feet and ankles adorned as if for a religious ceremony, led before the tree in the presence of the king and queen, she ceremoniously strikes the tree with her left foot. The king admonishes the tree that if it does not immediately blossom after being "honoured with her foot delicate as a fresh lotus and loud-tinkling with jingling anklets," its longing has been in vain.[39] The aśoka's longing is a pregnant craving. *Dohada*, literally "two hearts," refers to a hunger or yearning brought on by the presence of another life growing within a woman or, in this case, a tree, for something essential to the healthy development and birth of the offspring.

As the dohada motif evolved, the list of trees and their respective cravings was elaborated. The red amaranth (*kurabaka*) hungers for the embrace of a maiden, the *vakula* awaits a sprinkling of wine from a woman's lips, and the *campaka* requires a shower of perfumed water.[40] Yet other types of trees may be brought to blossom by a woman's laughter, song, dance, or even mere glance or breath.[41]

Although it is not clear whether a dohada concept is present in the Buddhist reliefs, it is possible that the theme found expression first in visual and later in literary form. The fact that the aśoka most frequently appears in this regard in both the earlier sculptural and later written media suggests a formal and perhaps thematic continuity between the two artistic conventions. Yakṣiṇīs are regarded as agents of vegetative fertility, and clearly the image of a yakṣiṇī beside her tree draws an association between luscious female and lush vegetation. It remains possible, however, that the nuance that the tree awaits or longs for the fecundating female touch may have been the contribution of the poet's art.

Vāhanas

Yakṣiṇīs are usually shown standing atop a supportive figure or object, a motif that helps identify them as supernatural beings. The figure may be an animal, such as a horse or elephant, or a fabulous creature, such as a sea dragon (*makara*), serpent deity (*nāga*), fish-tailed horse (see Fig. 3.2), finned elephant with a makara tail, gryphon (winged, beaked lion), or addorsed lion-makara. Most in evidence are crouching or kneeling gnomes that appear to be yakṣas or *vāma-yakṣas* ("dwarf yakṣas").

A figure beneath a deity's feet may represent either the vehicle (*vāhana*) of that deity or a negative force that the deity has conquered. In this context, the beings upon which the yakṣiṇīs stand are in all likelihood intended as their supporters, or vāhanas, judging from other uses of the same motifs elsewhere on the monuments. For example, yakṣas frequently appear as atlantids in early Buddhist architecture. Depicted in rows along plinths and pillar bases, they uphold the structure both as weight-bearers and as controllers of chthonic forces, directing their primal strength to support of the edifice. Yakṣa-like figures sprouting vegetation from their mouths or navels serve as emblems of fertility and agrarian abundance. Thus, in this setting yakṣas have positive associations with the energies and bounty of nature.

In view of the fact that dwarfish figures are not always seen as auspicious beings, particularly in later iconography, wherein they might symbolize demonic entities, the crouching dwarf could arguably represent the yakṣiṇī's power to conquer obstacles and hostile yakṣas on behalf of her worshippers. The preeminently positive symbolism of the yakṣas on these monuments, however, casts doubt on this interpretation. Moreover, the yakṣas have a dreamily blissful expression, signaling pleasure at supporting the beauteous feet of a yakṣiṇī, rather than the menacing visage of a demonic figure.

The yakṣas must also be interpreted with reference to other figures that appear as supportive elements. Elephants and horses have positive connotations of royalty and fertility. The makaras and aquatic horses and elephants are surely auspicious in character, for they appear elsewhere on the monuments among a range of propitious images (burgeoning foliage, overflowing vessels, lotuses, conch shells, ducks, turtles, wish-fulfilling vines, and fish-tailed bulls and lions) that convey the symbolism of life-giving waters. A positive significance is also clearly intended when the supportive element upon which a yakṣiṇī stands is a vase of plenty or a lotus blossom.[42] Coomaraswamy maintains the symbolical equivalence and hence interchangeability of full vases, aquatic creatures, lotuses, and yakṣas sprouting vegetation as symbols of "the waters as the source of life."[43] Therefore, by analogy to other uses of the same motifs in the iconographic programs, it appears that a positive meaning, akin to a vāhana, is attached to the vessels, dwarfs, animals, and mythical aquatic creatures upon which the yakṣiṇīs stand, symbolizing their sway over the powers of wealth, fertility, growth, and abundance.

Evolution of Yakṣiṇī Imagery

Two additional bodies of Buddhist yakṣiṇī images—found on railing pillars from the stupa sites of Bhūteśvara in Uttar Pradesh and Sanghol in the Punjab—include a greater variety of poses, attributes, and settings. The basic conception of the yakṣiṇī as a dryad is still much in evidence, for a flowering tree appears in many of the compositions. In some cases, the interaction of the yakṣiṇī with the tree is the focus of the relief; in others, the tree simply provides an arboreal backdrop for another pastime. In other instances, however, an urban setting is represented by a balcony upon which a person or, more often, a couple lounges. The reliefs with an urban ambiance may represent an earthly locale but in my view depict a city in a yakṣa kingdom, such as Alakāpurī, the dazzling, rainbow-gated capital of the yakṣas described in the *Meghadūta*, where yakṣas sport with eternally youthful yakṣiṇīs who have flowers entwined in their braided hair. Upon their palaces with mosaic floors and cloud-wreathed towers are crystal balconies dappled with starlight, where yakṣas and yakṣiṇīs engage in amorous pastimes and sup aphrodisiacal wine.[44] This description accords with the balcony scenes on the railing pillar reliefs, which include couples embracing and drinking together. Sanghol also includes a number of reliefs in which a lone male figure on the balcony gazes with admiration at the alluring yakṣiṇī who stands below.

In the Sanghol and Bhūteśvara reliefs, the yakṣiṇīs are engaged in a variety of activities. Several appear with a child. One carries a toddler on her sturdy hip, one offers her breast to her infant, another dangles a rattle before a child, and yet another playfully raises her child aloft. Several of the yakṣiṇīs are associated with intoxicating beverage and are shown bearing a wine goblet or flask, draining a cup, or proffering wine to the sybarites lounging on their balconies (Fig. 3.7). Some carvings offer an intimate glimpse of a woman at her toilette, enhancing her feminine allures by putting on a necklace, adjusting an ear pendant, applying cosmetics, admiring herself in a mirror, or wringing water from her tresses as a swan drinks the falling droplets. A yakṣiṇī may adopt an unmistakably coquettish pose that draws attention to her womanly charms by cupping her breast or loosening or lifting her sash in a revealing manner (see Fig. 3.1). Two yakṣiṇīs in the Bhūteśvara corpus sport charmingly with their pet parrots. One smiles delightedly as her uncaged bird tugs at the flowers in her hair (Fig. 3.8). The other watches with amusement as her pet nibbles her beaded adornment, ignoring the proffered grape (Fig. 3.9). One also finds, in this diverse oeuvre, yakṣiṇīs bearing a flute, lotus blossoms, fruit, a covered basket of cosmetics, and a floral garland.[45]

The yakṣiṇī figures on the railing pillars of Bhūteśvara and Sanghol date from about the second century C.E. and are rendered in the stylistic idiom of

3.7 Yakṣiṇī, Bhūteśvara, Mathura District, Uttar Pradesh, India, second century C.E. Red sandstone, height 49.7 in. (126 cm). Government Museum, Mathura, 11.151. Photo: American Institute of Indian Studies. *A yakṣiṇī holding a cluster of grapes proffers wine to a couple engaged in love-play on the balcony above.*

3.8 Yakṣiṇī, Bhūteśvara, Mathura District, Uttar Pradesh, India, second century C.E. Red sandstone, height 48 in. (122 cm). Indian Museum, Calcutta, M15a. Used by permission. Photo: American Institute of Indian Studies. *As the yakṣiṇī dangles the cage in one hand, her pet parrot tugs at the flowers in her hair.*

3.9 Yakṣiṇī, Bhūteśvara, Mathurā, Uttar Pradesh, India, second century C.E. Red sandstone, height 48 in. (122 cm). Indian Museum, Calcutta, M15c. Used by permission. Photo: American Institute of Indian Studies. *The yakṣiṇī proffers a grape to her pet parrot, which prefers to nibble on her pearl necklace.*

Mathurā. The images command aesthetic interest because of the harmonious interplay of line, contour, and detail and the exquisite carving of the figures, which emerge from the stone with the appearance of warm, living flesh. Art historically they are significant because they document the evolution and diversification of the yakṣiṇī image as an iconographic type. The activities in which these divine damsels are engaged draw heavily on the repertoire of moments at which a woman's loveliness is heightened by unself-conscious absorption: adoration of a child, dalliance with a pet, reflection on a flower, personal adornment. The bodily postures, jewelry, and scant attire, too, are devised to enhance the glory of the female form. Their confident ease, monumental proportions, and seraphic smiles lend these nature divinities a magisterial presence. The yakṣiṇīs' beauty is womanly beauty, and they might easily be mistaken for mortal women were it not for the yakṣas and other supernatural creatures beneath their feet, indicating their divine rank.[46]

The yakṣiṇī imagery on the Mathurān stupa railings perpetuated the tradition seen first in the early monuments at sites such as Bhārhut and Sāñcī and prefigured an enduring approach to architectural embellishment in India. The limited architectural remains from the post-Kuṣāṇa and Gupta periods give little evidence of the yakṣiṇī motif. Following the Gupta era, however, the yakṣiṇī imagery is visible in another form, namely, the multitudes of female images (*nārī-bandha*) that adorn Hindu temple edifices.[47] In many cases, these figures are women (*nāyikā*) rather than supernatural females, but their direct descent from the yakṣiṇī images is evident from the continuities of figural type and subject matter. Noteworthy in this regard is the ongoing popularity of the woman-and-tree motif and its offshoot, the *gelaba-nārī*, a woman entwined or surrounded by a vine.[48] One also finds, in both the yakṣiṇī corpus and later temple reliefs, the motif of a female canopied by a large lotus blossom that serves for her as a floral parasol.

According to an architectural manual believed to date from the eleventh century, the poses of the women (*nārī*), or "maidens at leisure" (*alasā kanyā*), portrayed on temple facades should include touching a branch, gazing into a mirror, holding a child, smelling a lotus, adorning herself with a flower, touching her ankle bells, and playing with a parrot.[49] The motifs of a woman carrying a wine jar, applying cosmetics, and adjusting her jewelry or sash (Fig. 3.10) remained popular. The term *śālabhañjikā*, originally designating a woman grasping a tree branch, was used in Indic literature from the seventh century onward to refer to any female figure carved on a monument, as discussed above. The retention of the same term with a shift in meaning confirms the lineal descent of this imagery from the earlier corpus of dryads.

The yakṣiṇī images on the early Buddhist monuments in turn display continuities with another tradition of female figures. The Buddhist carvings

3.10 Nāyikā, Parśvanātha temple, Khajurāho, Chhatarpur, Madhya Pradesh, India, Candella period, ca. tenth century. Sandstone, height 37 in. (94 cm). Indian Museum, Calcutta, A24228. Used by permission. Photo: American Institute of Indian Studies. *The beauteous maiden at leisure is a descendant of the yakṣiṇī figural type in later architectural adornment.*

bear formal similarities with uninscribed terracotta figurines of the same periods (Fig. 3.11) and their simpler antecedents in the Indus Valley corpus.[50] The wide hips, slender waists, globular breasts, heavy jewelry, jeweled hip belts, and elaborate hairstyles link these figures visually and perhaps symbolically as well. Even if one grants a rather obvious theme of female procreativity and, by extension, abundance and fertility in general, it is difficult to ascertain whether the terracotta figurines represent yakṣiṇīs, fertility fetishes, local divinities, household deities (*gṛha-devatā*), or manifestations of mother earth or some other type of goddess.

Therefore, despite their visual comparability to and probable symbolic continuities with the terracotta figurines, the inscriptions on the Buddhist images at Bhārhut (184–72 B.C.E.) make them the earliest extant yakṣiṇī images that can firmly be documented as such, as well as the earliest known appearance of yakṣiṇīs on religious monuments. At the same time, the features they share with the terracotta corpus suggest that they may illustrate the same genre of figure and constitute the adoption in a Buddhist context of a figural type already well established in the Indic aesthetic repertoire and religious imagination.

Symbolic Import and Role in Stupa Iconography

Many reasons may be adduced for the appearance of yakṣiṇīs on the railings and gateways of Buddhist stupas. Symbolically, they represent the life-enhancing quality of auspiciousness (*maṅgala*) that confers well-being and sparks nature's creative abundance wherever it is present. Their femaleness, magnified by ornamentation, is the focus of the sculptor's artistry because the female body harbors a concentration of the forces that renew and regenerate life. The religious significance of these female figures has not always been apparent to interpreters, for the imagery is rooted in a cultural context in which the female body itself has an inherent spiritual and magical potency that is an extension of its biological fecundity. Art historian Thomas Donaldson avers the presence in India of a belief in the talismanic power of the female form, a conviction that it "emanates numinous power."[51] Donaldson contends that this is true of the entire female form, for "it is their total being, their femininity, that is auspicious."[52] Insofar as the female images on the monuments are auspicious, they may be deemed to possess talismanic significance. One of the meanings of *maṅgala* is "auspicious ornament, amulet," because auspiciousness by definition entails causal efficacy, the capacity to increase the well-being of whatever it touches, whether a monument, a ritual, or a human life.

The metaphysical potency of such figures is expressed in the circa eleventh-century *Śilpa Prakāśa*, whose architect-author asserts that a temple without the

3.11 Female Figurine, Digh Darwaja, Mathura District, Uttar Pradesh, India, Śuṅga period, ca. second or first century B.C.E. Terracotta. Government Museum, Mathura, 59.4748. Photo: American Institute of Indian Studies. *A molded plaque portraying a yakṣiṇī or artistic prototype of the yakṣiṇī.*

adornment of female figures will be spiritually inert, for, "as a house without a wife, as frolic without a woman, thus without female figures the monument will be of inferior quality and bear no fruit."[53] Therefore, the same interpretation may be advanced for the curvaceous yakṣiṇīs on Buddhist monuments and the beauteous maidens (*nāyikā*) that adorn almost all of the later Hindu temple facades in northern India. Alice Boner elaborates that a religious monument is "a spiritual power-house, a power-dispenser for those who approach it in the right spirit," and through the female figures "this power irradiates in the form of earthly grace and beauty."[54]

The symbolism of auspiciousness helps explain the manner of portrayal of the yakṣiṇīs. They are endowed with abundant physical charms because, as stated by Donaldson, "beauty in itself is auspicious and synonymous with fertility or abundance."[55] The female form, as a hierophany and locus of magical forces, is emphasized by depicting the figures as nude or minimally clothed with the barest hint of a diaphanous garment and perhaps a sash whose draping reveals rather than conceals. Moreover, auspiciousness is more pronounced when the pubic triangle and genitalia are displayed or emphasized by deep carving, an intricately detailed fertility belt, or the positioning of a hand so that it rests near or points toward the thighs or hip.[56] These visual devices are all utilized in Buddhist depictions of yakṣiṇīs.

The jewelry, too, reinforces the symbolic significance of the figures. Bracelets are associated with *śakti*, or life-giving energy, while the broad, ornamental girdle (*mekhalā*) is endowed with magical powers. Apropos is the testimony of a hymn in the *Atharva Veda* that praises the hip girdle for conferring long life, vigor, wisdom, intelligence, and victory and even refers to ritual oblation of the "adored, venerated" girdle.[57] The ornaments of the yakṣiṇīs may incorporate auspicious motifs that denote fertility and life-enhancing energy, such as the *śrīvatsa* and *nandyāvarta* (see the girdle clasp in Fig. 3.1 and necklace pendant design in Fig. 3.3).[58] That the yakṣiṇīs also symbolize or stimulate vegetative fertility and the abundance of nature is expressed by their juxtaposition with trees laden with flowers or fruit. Their association with human fertility is conveyed by their portrayal with children.

The yakṣiṇīs also served as protectors of the monument itself. They guarded the gates and the perimeter of the sacred precinct, just as a yakṣa shrine might be installed at a city gate or village boundary to ward off those with evil intent.[59] Thomas Donaldson explains that the builders of religious monuments in India sought to safeguard the structures from lightning, earthquakes, vandalism, enemy attack, breakage by elephants, and damage by demonic beings. Thus, the decorative program was designed not simply to beautify the edifice but also to assure its security and permanence.[60] The Indian architectural text cited above states that "lovely female figures," along with other motifs, assure that the temple structure will be "forever stable."[61] Donaldson clarifies that the portals to a temple or sacred compound are "the most vulnerable part of the structure and the one that most needs protection from evil forces."[62]

This principle illuminates why yakṣiṇīs are positioned on the gates (*toraṇa*) of the early stupas. Moreover, when they appear in rows on railing pillars, as at Sanghol and Bhūteśvara (Fig. 3.12), they form a talismanic circle that "serves as a magical barrier protecting the precincts."[63] Interestingly, guardian figures need not have a frightening appearance to repel evil influences. Beneficent figures and emblems of auspiciousness serve the same purpose, for, according to Donaldson, such images are at once propitious and apotropaic; their very abundance of life-enhancing energies serves both to increase well-being and to ward off harm and hostile spirits.[64]

Moreover, the yakṣiṇī figures and the sculptural program in which they are embedded not only protect the monument but enhance its energies as a repository of power. A stupa may be said to be a talisman in stone, emanating its beneficial influence on the surrounding region just as an amulet worn on the body protects its wearer. A stupa contains and spreads the power of the Buddha's relics in the cardinal directions toward which it is oriented.[65] The yakṣiṇīs and other figures around the perimeter of the monument generate their own forces, which are more specific in function but operate in harmony with the liberative power of the Buddha to dispense blessings to the worshippers and radiate a protective influence outward to the surrounding territory. This irradiating energy is magnified by a repetition of auspicious motifs: nāgas, faces of glory (*kīrtimukha*), lotus blossoms and rhizomes, conch shells, wish-fulfilling vines (*kalpalatā*), and even the pearl strands and scrollwork.[66]

All of these designs have magico-religious properties with which they imbue the monuments on which they are depicted, for their powers of fertility and abundance can be invoked through not only ritual means but also, according to Coomaraswamy, their representation in art.[67] One of the principles of Indian aesthetics is the belief that certain images and geometric shapes contain and emanate different types of energy. The imagery on these monuments, among which the yakṣiṇīs figure prominently, possesses an enriching quality, the ability to bring about fertility, growth, vigor, longevity, and material and spiritual well-being.[68]

Another purpose of the images of yakṣiṇīs on the balustrades of the early stupas was to serve as objects of worship. Peter Skilling observes that the faithful went to stupas not simply to gaze at the images, as would a modern tourist, but to engage in devotional and contemplative activities.[69] The forms of reverence directed to the yakṣiṇī images installed on Buddhist monuments probably

3.12 Stupa Railing, Bhūteśvara, Mathura District, Uttar Pradesh, India, second century C.E. Red sandstone, height 59 in. (151 cm). Indian Museum, Calcutta, M15a-c. Used by permission. Photo: American Institute of Indian Studies. *Outward-facing yakṣiṇī images encircled Bhūteśvara stupa with protective, auspicious energies and received homage from Buddhist worshippers.*

incorporated a range of the observances attested at yakṣa shrines in general, such as prostration, prayers, vows, and circumambulation. Ritual offerings featured flowers, incense, lamplight, sandalwood paste, and oblations, as well as music, dance, and song, of which yakṣas and yakṣiṇīs are reputed to be especially fond. An image might be bathed, lustrated, perfumed, and decked with garlands and banners. The deity was feasted with the foods she or he preferred, whether honey, yogurt, rice, and grains or *bali* offerings consisting of meat, fish, and spirituous liquors.[70] There is evidence that the Buddha and his followers disapproved of the animal sacrifices sometimes associated with yakṣa worship, and therefore it is unlikely that this practice took place in the vicinity of Buddhist stupas.[71]

The benefits sought through the worship of yakṣiṇīs (and their male counterparts, the yakṣas) at Buddhist monuments were presumably similar if not identical to the purposes of their veneration in general. Foremost among their benefactions is the bestowal and protection of progeny throughout gestation and infancy. A husband or wife might be gained through their auspices,[72] and, as agents of vegetative fertility, they were supplicated to promote agricultural productivity and provide guidance regarding upcoming weather conditions and the sowing of crops.[73] Yakṣas and yakṣiṇīs conferred wealth by guiding their devotees to buried treasure, directly bestowing gold coins and jewels, or increasing or restoring property.[74] They might materialize food and drink, create water tanks, help travelers pass unharmed through dangerous regions, rescue lost or stranded merchants, save the shipwrecked from drowning, or halt epidemics.[75] There are instances in which a yakṣa or yakṣiṇī helped a ruler rise to power or defeat enemies in battle[76] and evidence that entire villages and cities had yakṣa tutelaries.[77] Illustrative is Sāta, the patron of Rājagṛha, who safeguarded the royal family, made the rain fall in season, and assured that the lakes were full and plant life abundant. He saw that there was no famine and protected ascetics, priests, the poor, orphans, and merchants.[78] The yakṣiṇī images on Buddhist monuments may have been venerated for any or all of these benefactions.

Peter Skilling suggests that worshippers at Buddhist stupas may also have engaged in recitation as they circled the monument, uttering verses of homage and invocation to the Buddha and other deities represented around the circumambulatory walkway. He adduces that the configuration of the *pradakṣiṇā* path, which normally commences on the eastern side of the monument and continues in a clockwise direction (to the south, west, and north), corresponds to a recitational formula in which the supernatural beings of the cardinal directions, beginning with the east, are invoked as protectors and allies.[79] For example, the *Āṭānāṭiya Sutta* relates the verses that summon the guardian kings and their retinues of yakṣas and other spirits from the four quarters of the universe—east, south, west, and north in turn—to protect whomever calls upon them, promising that they will rush en masse to their aid and ward off hostile yakṣas and other harmful spirits. The Buddha recommends the recitation of the protective spells for both the laity and monastics: "Through them monks and nuns, male and female lay-followers may dwell guarded, protected, unharmed and at ease."[80]

A similar recitational formula occurs in the *Lalitavistara*, wherein Shakyamuni pronounces a blessing by invoking the supernatural beings who dwell in the four quarters of the universe—beginning with the eastern sector and concluding with the north—to safeguard his followers, protect their health, and grant them wealth and success in all their undertakings, delegating to the spirits in the cardinal directions the task of prospering and protecting his followers.[81] The *Golden Radiance Scripture* (ca. late fourth or early fifth century), which postdates the monuments under discussion, documents an ongoing interest in enlisting yakṣas and yakṣiṇīs as directional guardians. The audience of the scripture is assured that the yakṣiṇīs "Caṇḍā, Caṇḍālikā, . . . Caṇḍikā, Kuntī, and Kūṭadantī . . . possessed of supernatural powers, great strength and prowess, will give them protection everywhere in the four directions."[82]

Stupa design, with the Buddha at the center (represented symbolically or through the presence of relics), surrounded by other ranks of beings, is consistent with the pattern of these teachings, in which the Buddha, situated at the symbolic center of creation amid terrestrial and heavenly hosts, invokes their power to prosper and protect his followers. Thus, if the stupa offers a setting for the recitation of such liturgies, it follows that the yakṣiṇīs and other supernatural figures portrayed around the periphery helped delineate the stupa environs as ritual space. Recitational texts of this genre are sometimes designated as "auspicious verses," or "verses that confer well-being,"[83] linking them thematically with the talismanic aspect of stupa embellishment.

A common explanation for the appearance of yakṣiṇīs and other spirit beings of the indigenous pantheon in stupa iconographic programs is that they represent a concession to the "popular" religious interests of the laity and non-Buddhist populace, in contrast to the philosophical and meditative pursuits of the monastic elite. Thus, we read that such figures were present to "meet the needs of an unlettered laity" and to "make the Buddhist religion popular and broad-based."[84] Étienne Lamotte suggests that the monastics were compelled by popular sentiment to develop a mythology that would "attract the greatest number of devotees" and that spirits, such as yakṣas, appeased the superstitions of the lower castes.[85]

However, Buddhist canonical literature, itself compiled largely by monks, reveals a lively interest in yakṣas and yakṣiṇīs on the part of monastics as well as laypeople. There are quite a few instances in which the Buddha addresses monastics regarding their treatment of yakṣas and yakṣiṇīs, urging a spirit of friendship and cooperation. The literature finds monks and nuns interacting with yakṣas and yakṣiṇīs during wilderness sojourns and retreats, reciting incantations to gain their protection, receiving food and provisions from them, and on occasion benefiting from their counsel.[86] Monastics even provided funds for the creation of their images on Buddhist monuments. Most notably, at Bhārhut, where the names of donors are sometimes attached to specific images, three of the large yakṣiṇī reliefs were commissioned by monks.[87] Thus, there is reason to believe that the yakṣas and yakṣiṇīs portrayed on Buddhist stupas exerted a broad appeal and commanded the reverence of monastics and laity alike. These nature divinities may not have played a direct role in the quest for salvation, but they occupied a secure niche in Buddhist legendry, moral discourse, and devotional and magical practice.[88]

Yakṣiṇīs in Pali Literature

The yakṣiṇīs portrayed on the Buddhist stupas are beneficent guardian figures. They are what is sometimes known as *mahā-yakṣiṇīs*, "great yakṣiṇīs," who are devoted to the Buddha and have vowed to protect and bless those who follow the Buddhist path. They are not representative, however, of the entire class of yakṣiṇīs. Like human beings, yakṣiṇīs are circling in the round of rebirth, and some are less morally evolved than others. Some are kind and benevolent, fond of music and dance, and eager to bestow offspring, abundant crops, and wealth on their supplicants. These yakṣiṇīs, memorialized in Buddhist art, may rightly be characterized as sylphs, sprites, nymphs, fairies, or dryads. Others, however, possess a cruel and violent temperament and a taste for meat, spirituous liquor, and even human flesh and blood that leads them to devour living beings and demand blood sacrifice. These fiendish yakṣiṇīs may inflict disease and madness, waylay travelers, and terrorize entire villages by kidnapping and devouring infants.[89] At this end of the spectrum, the category of yakṣiṇī becomes indistinguishable from those of the *piśācī* (ogress), *rākṣasī* (demoness), and *mātṛkā* ("mother," local spirits of a protective but potentially harmful character). What remains constant for the entire range of yakṣiṇīs is their supernatural power. Thus, as a class they elicit both reverence and fear.

A richer characterization of yakṣiṇīs as a class may be found in Buddhist literary sources, in which we encounter not only benevolent yakṣiṇīs but also their dangerous and cannibalistic sisters.[90] Another aspect of the yakṣiṇīs that emerges in Buddhist legend is their role as temptresses of mortal men. It is not surprising, in view of their wondrous beauty, that yakṣiṇīs would be able to attract human paramours. As supernatural beings, they can render themselves visible at will and choose the form in which they will manifest. Thus, even fearsome yakṣiṇīs can assume the guise of an alluring woman in order to stage a seduction. In some legends, a yakṣiṇī marries a human being and bears children. The Buddha was the offspring of such a union in one of his lives.[91] In most of these legends, however, the yakṣiṇī in question is a predator who seizes men and holds them prisoner, using them for erotic pleasure. The men may enjoy their captivity under such circumstances, but the interludes usually end badly, for yakṣiṇīs of this ilk have a tendency eventually to devour their hapless paramours, leaving only the bones.

One jātaka tells of an entire island of man-eating yakṣiṇīs who lie in wait for shipwrecked sailors and meet them at the shore disguised as young mothers with children on their hips, pretending to be widows of merchants drowned at sea. They invite the men to "marry" them and even conjured an illusory city in order to entice their would-be grooms to remain in their midst.[92] Another jātaka describes how a group of yakṣiṇīs set a snare of unearthly beauty for travelers on a remote forest path. As translated by Gail Sutherland:

> There . . . yakkhinīs make houses appear in the middle of the road and, having prepared a costly bed with a canopy painted overhead with golden stars and enclosed with silken curtains in many colors, they decorate themselves with celestial ornaments and go to sit down in the houses from which they ply men with sweet words, saying: "You seem tired; come here, sit down, and have a drink of water before going." When they have summoned them, they give those who come seats and seduce them with the charm of their wanton beauty. But, having excited their lust, they have intercourse with them and then they kill them and eat them while the blood flows.[93]

An encounter with a voracious yakṣiṇī might also have a propitious outcome, for, regardless of their individual temperaments, yakṣiṇīs command magical gifts and occult powers. The jātaka quoted above ends with the promise that anyone who can resist the temptations of the yakṣiṇīs and refuse to gaze upon them will after seven days become a king.[94] Protective talismans and consecrated thread can counteract the sorcery with which they bind their erstwhile lovers. The *Mahāvaṃsa* relates how Vijaya journeyed to Laṅka and brought the man-eating yakṣiṇī Kuvaṇṇā under his power by binding her in a noose and threatening her at swordpoint. In exchange for her life, she transformed herself into a beautiful woman, became Vijaya's consort, and helped him conquer the local yakṣas and gain the throne of the country.[95] Kuvaṇṇa was not a benevolent yakṣiṇī but nonetheless helped Vijaya establish a dynasty. Thus, although some yakṣiṇīs pose a danger, as a class they are regarded as a source of supernatural assistance, protection, and blessings.

The possibility of sexual union with a yakṣiṇī is even recognized in the monastic code of discipline. Intercourse with a yakṣiṇī is as serious a transgression as intercourse with a human woman and carries the same penalty, that is, expulsion from the order.[96] Other infractions, however, entail a lesser offense if performed with a yakṣiṇī, such as sitting together in a secluded spot, sharing sleeping quarters, traveling together, or touching her for pleasure.[97]

Gail Sutherland concludes that some of the episodes recounting the fiendish behavior of yakṣiṇīs are drawn from folk legend, ghost stories, and popular tales of the supernatural. She suggests that in some cases the cruel and fearsome nature of the yakṣiṇīs may be exaggerated to provide a pretext for a tale of conversion or as a rhetorical device to map the Buddhist ethical domain as one of nonviolence and compassion.[98] The unruly yakṣiṇīs are not irredeemable, however; they are capable of the advances in wisdom, morality, and merit that bring one closer to enlightenment. Once reformed by the Buddha, they might become not only followers but powerful allies and protectors of Buddhist practitioners and monuments, bestowing their blessings and guarding them against other supernatural beings—including yakṣas—of hostile intent.

The Buddhist engagement with yakṣas and especially yakṣiṇīs endured in many forms over the centuries. Although yakṣiṇīs as a class received diminished attention on Buddhist monuments after the second century, the "supreme yakṣiṇī" or "yakṣiṇī queen" (*yakṣeśvarī*) Hārītī came to the fore and offered a single object of worship in their place, garnering a significant devotional cult among monastics and laity. Mahayana iconography was deeply informed by iconographic features associated with yakṣiṇīs, while the yakṣiṇī reemerged in yet another guise in early Buddhist Tantra in Bengal, as an object of ritual invocation and magical practice. Once summoned by mantra recitation and appropriate offerings, a yakṣiṇī would serve as mother, sister, or lover to the practitioner and endow him with lavish wealth, take him on nocturnal flights, and fulfill all his requests and desires.[99]

Art Historical and Religious Significance

The yakṣiṇī imagery on the early Buddhist monuments is an important oeuvre, artistically and historically. As artistic specimens they have evoked admiration and fascination and are widely published as masterpieces of Indian artistry. Although they depict a genre of divine being that figures in the popular religiosity and three major religions of India, the images that appear on these Buddhist monuments must be counted among their most exquisite portrayals. Art historically, the yakṣiṇī images from Buddhist stupa sites are important as the earliest documentable representations of this class of beings. They also warrant art historical attention by virtue of occupying a point of transition between an earlier tradition of terracotta figurines and the later practice of adorning temple facades with female figures.

Understanding the symbolism and religious import of these voluptuous female figures has posed difficulties for scholars who attempt to locate them within the Buddhist ethos of detachment and renunciation. Indeed, the sensuously rendered feminine beauty of the yakṣiṇī images predestined them to misinterpretation by early western interpreters. Albert Grünwedel concluded that the Bhūteśvara images are too "erotically represented" to have graced a Buddhist monument.[100] Echoing this sentiment are Vincent Smith's shocked pronouncement that "these figures are indecently naked and could not be Buddhist" and, slightly later, Jean Vogel's adjudgment of their "lasciviousness combined with grossness," concluding that "it marks a degradation to find the sacred shrines . . . enclosed by railings exhibiting women—that snare of Māra and hindrance to salvation—in the greatest variety of graceful attitudes."[101] Étienne Lamotte, too, succumbed to prurience when he insisted that the donors of the monuments upheld the "strictest morality" but that the artists "were easily led astray and . . . willingly yielded to the temptation to embellish the sacred art with audaciously unveiled nude figures."[102]

This line of interpretation even finds contemporary proponents. S. P. Shukla recently reintroduced the claim that these images "were not portraits of divinities," had no religious significance, and were purposely "lewd and salacious" to "arouse lust and desire."[103] U. N. Roy holds that they symbolize the "external allurements and worldly attractions" that must be renounced in order to win the salvation represented by the stupa.[104]

It is unsurprising that scholars might struggle over the meaning of the yakṣiṇī imagery, not only because it deviates from their expectations regarding the appropriate subject matter of religious art but by virtue of its apparent incompatibility with central tenets of the Buddhist faith. This in itself points to the historical significance of the yakṣiṇī images for the evidence they provide regarding the full spectrum of Buddhist beliefs and observances. Detached contemplation and relinquishment of desire are cornerstones of the Buddha's teachings, but the renunciatory impulse is complemented by a celebration of the natural world as a radiant and embracing presence, rich with blessings, suffused with spirit. It is this world-affirming vision of nature as the harmonious, joyous matrix of human life that gave rise to the richly symbolic carvings embellishing the early stupas. Worshippers, seeing the yakṣiṇīs set amid imagery of the earth burgeoning with life, would certainly behold in this symbolism the hope and promise of profound well-being.

If we grant that the yakṣiṇīs in the early stupa iconography were neither concessional nor coincidental, we cannot fail to allow them to render their eloquent testimony that the Buddhist populations that commissioned and worshipped at the stupas sustained a deep homage for female nature spirits as a source of earthly blessings and, through their gifts and guardianship, as channels of spiritual well-being.

CHAPTER 4

Śrī Lakṣmī

Glorious Good Fortune

> Thousands of millions of beings will be blessed with the supply of every excellent blessing, will have no lack. Those beings will be replete with every provision, with food, drink, wealth, grain, gold, jewels, pearls, beryl, conches, crystal, coral, gold, silver. . . . Those beings the great goddess Śrī will watch over. For them she will create great good fortune.
>
> —*Golden Radiance Scripture*[1]

A divinity who is rarely discussed in association with Buddhism but whose image frequently appears on the earliest Buddhist monuments of India is Śrī Lakṣmī (pronounced *shree* LAHK *shmee*). As the patron goddess of wealth, abundance, and good fortune, Lakṣmī is honored as the bestower of fertility, happiness, beauty, brilliance, longevity, noble rank, and royal sovereignty. Her epithet "Śrī," literally, "Glorious," describes her own splendor as well as her role as the fount of all that crowns human life with richness and enjoyment.

Lakṣmī's benedictions vivify crops, herds, families, communities, and kingdoms. Her emblem, the lotus, proclaims the blessings that blossom at her creative touch. She is present in the fecundity of nature—fertile mud, plant sap, life-bearing rains, milk-giving cows, food, and drink—but her influence extends to the social realms of commerce, nobility, and royalty. Lakṣmī is omnipresent in the Indian cultural landscape, from rural village to imperial court, figuring in local agricultural festivals and royal coronations, garnering universal reverence.[2]

Lakṣmī in Early Buddhist Art

Śrī Lakṣmī's history can be traced to the Vedas and may have earlier roots—perhaps as a figural type rather than as an individual deity—in Harappan religious imagery.[3] The Buddhist depictions of Lakṣmī at Bhārhut and Sāñcī are among the earliest known artistic images of the goddess. Her effigies appear

4.1 Outer face of northern gateway, Stupa I (Great Stupa), Sāñcī, Raisen District, Madhya Pradesh, India, ca. early first century C.E. Buff sandstone. Photo: American Institute of Indian Studies. *Lakṣmī in a variety of poses graces the grand gateways of the Great Stupa at Sāñcī.*

on the stupa gateways and balustrades in a variety of iconographic forms (Fig. 4.1). She may be seated on a lotus with her legs crossed or with one leg pendant (Fig. 4.2). She may stand atop a lotus calyx in a frontal, symmetrical stance or sensuous "thrice-flexed" (*tribhaṅga*) pose with out-thrust hip (Fig. 4.3).

Lakṣmī is immediately recognizable by the lotus she holds in one or both hands and is often surrounded by additional lotus buds and flowers. When only one of her hands displays a lotus, the other typically gathers her sash into a knot at hip level in a symbolic gesture that apparently connotes fertility but is not yet fully understood.[4] In several early reliefs, Lakṣmī presses a heavily braceleted hand to her breast (Fig. 4.4), alluding to her role as a source of nourishment and abundance, for her "breasts like golden jars" are a metonym for her cornucopian nature.[5] She is also shown with her hands joined together at her heart in a devotional attitude, presumably rendering homage to the Buddha.[6]

In early Buddhist art, Lakṣmī most commonly appears in her epiphany as Gaja-Lakṣmī, or "Lakṣmī with Elephants," in which a pair of elephants atop their own lotus pedestals lustrate the goddess from vessels held aloft in their trunks.[7] Other elements, such as couples (*mithuna*), animals, and birds, may be added to the composition. In one example at Sāñcī, her female attendants bear food and drink.[8] The numerous pictorial elements of these reliefs are often rendered in elegant interplay within a gracefully balanced design. Their compositional sophistication does not bespeak an experimental phase in the artistic rendition of the goddess, nor is the variety of types indicative of an embryonic stage of iconographic evolution.

The general iconographic conception of Lakṣmī had taken shape earlier. A late Vedic hymn, the *Śrī Sūkta* (possibly fourth century B.C.E.), foreshadows the attributes that would later appear in her visual iconography. In this song of invocation, Lakṣmī is said to be golden (*hiraṇya-varṇā, suvarṇā*), "sun-hued" (*āditya-varṇā*), "made of gold" (*hiraṇmayī*), "radiant as gold" (*hiraṇya-prākārā*), and "adorned with gold" (*hema-mālinī*). The lotus, a symbol of abundant blessings, figures prominently in her description as "lotus-colored" (*padma-varṇā*), "lotus-eyed" (*padmākṣī*), "lotus-thighed" (*padma-ūrū*), "seated on a lotus" (*padmesthitā*), "garlanded with lotuses" (*padma-mālinī*), "encircled by lotuses" (*padmanemī*), and "abounding in lotuses" (*puṣkariṇī*). Moreover, she "takes delight in the roar of elephants" (*hastināda-pramodinī*).[9] Although the hymn does not provide an iconographic description in the classical sense of specifying a number of arms, implements, and bodily posture, it prefigures the golden color and association with lotuses and elephants that came to characterize the goddess in figural form.

This is not to say that Buddhist iconographers consulted the Vedic hymn as their source or even that they formulated the artistic conception of Lakṣmī. Ancient coinage documents several representational types for Lakṣmī dating from the same period as the earliest known Buddhist images (second and first centuries B.C.E.) and even earlier, from the third century B.C.E.[10] The coins display the same span of seated and standing types that appear on Buddhist monuments, including the Gaja-Lakṣmī motif. In view of her association with both wealth and royalty, it is hardly surprising that Lakṣmī is featured on the currency of numerous dynasties, a trend that continued over the centuries.

This body of earlier and contemporaneous coins indicates that the carvers of Buddhist monuments had a fund of iconographic models on which to draw. Several sandstone reliefs and terracotta plaques of Lakṣmī, roughly contemporaneous with the Bhārhut reliefs, document a tradition of her portrayal in these media as well.[11] Given the various forms that appear on the stupa carvings, coins, and other reliefs, the development of the Lakṣmī image probably included an earlier phase during which effigies were created in perishable media (clay, wood, paint on cloth or plaster) that have not withstood the passage of time.

The inclusion of representations of Lakṣmī on Buddhist monuments may be attributed to her association with abundance. She extends the promise of prosperity and well-being to those who worship at shrines embellished by her image. Moreover, she appears thereon amid an array of symbols of fertility and auspiciousness, including yakṣas and yakṣiṇīs, lotuses, conch shells, makaras (fish-tailed water creatures), and overflowing vases of plenty. Ananda Coomaraswamy finds thematic unity among this panoply of images in their common reference to what he terms a "water cosmology." In contrast to a "space cosmology" that envisions a pantheon of aerial and celestial powers, the water cosmology centers on water as the primordial source and essence of life, vivifying all living things with its metaphysical vitality. In this ideology, which finds expression in the Vedas and Upaniṣads, all life originates in the waters. The earth, too, is produced from and rests upon the waters, making water, rather than earth or space, "the support, both ultimate and physical, of all life."[12]

Coomaraswamy observes that in the iconographic expression of the water cosmology, vegetation always issues from a symbol of water but never directly from a representation of the earth.[13] Gautama Vajracharya adds another dimension to this discussion by drawing attention to the importance of water in a climate punctuated by desiccating drought and life-renewing monsoons. In such a climate, Vajracharya contends, water takes on primary significance as the

4.2 Lakṣmī relief from inner face of Sāñcī gateway pictured in Fig. 4.1. Photo: American Institute of Indian Studies. *The Lotus Lady is readily recognizable by the lotuses that abound in her iconography.*

observable source of sustenance for all living things, for it is during the rainy season that the parched earth and its inhabitants—fields, paddies, orchards, forests, swamps, herds, and humans and other creatures—spring to life.[14] Thus, on Vajracharya's analysis, water in the form of rainfall becomes a primary religious metaphor for abundance, prosperity, and divine blessings.

The lotus in its watery habitat is the preeminent symbol of the aquatic source of life in this metaphorical domain, while Lakṣmī is the presiding divinity.[15] She, like the lotus, is liquid-born, for she arose from the churning of the primordial ocean of milk at the dawn of time.[16] Furthermore, she remains closely identified with the lotus as Kamalā and Padmā, synonymous epithets meaning

4.3 Gaja-Lakṣmī, uppermost architrave of southern gateway, Stupa I (Great Stupa), Sāñcī, Raisen District, Madhya Pradesh, India, ca. early first century C.E. Buff sandstone. Photo: American Institute of Indian Studies. *Lakṣmī inhabits the celestial lotus pond that periodically releases fertilizing rainfall on the earth.*

"Lotus Lady." In visual representations, she rests on a lotus flower and is set amidst a profusion of lotuses (see Fig. 4.3). The lotus pond on which Lakṣmī eternally floats is at once her heavenly home and a prefiguration of the flow of rainfall that will cause the earth to bloom to abundance. In India, the sky is often envisioned as a celestial lotus lake that periodically releases its moisture to enliven the earth below. The lotus that perpetually thrives in paradise then makes its seasonal appearance on earth, becoming, according to Vajracharya, a symbol of "agrarian prosperity," for "immediately after the monsoon the lotus grows together with rice plants and flowers till harvest time in autumn. But it remains dormant during the harsh dry summer season."[17] Vajracharya helps us understand the multivalent significance of the lotus as a visual reference to the blessings that Lakṣmī bestows.

The lotus blossom eventually becomes the support par excellence of all Indian deities and the religious structures associated with them (such as temples and mandalas). During the period under discussion, however, only Lakṣmī was consistently portrayed with a lotus pedestal, as the deity most intimately associated with the fructifying waters of life and abundance.[18] According to Coomaraswamy:

> Śrī-Lakṣmī is essentially . . . the Waters, all the possibilities of existence substantially and maternally personified. The Lotus is preeminently hers, because she *is* the Lotus and the Earth, at once the source and support of all existences . . . Universal Mother, Mother Nature, Aditi, Māyā,

4.4 Gaja-Lakṣmī, Great Stupa, Bhārhut, Satna District, Madhya Pradesh, India, Śuṅga period, ca. 100–80 B.C.E. Sandstone. Indian Museum, Calcutta, 177. Used by permission. Photo: American Institute of Indian Studies. *Lotuses and lustrating elephants express Lakṣmī's association with life-giving waters, understood as her "breast milk."*

> the magical ground or substance of existence, fertilized by heavenly showers.[19]

That the water cosmogony should be represented by a female figure is not surprising, for the waters of creation and regeneration are perceived to be maternal in character, eliciting as they do an inevitable comparison to amniotic fluid, the closest analogy in human experience.[20]

The Gaja-Lakṣmī motif, frequently characterized as the "anointing," or *abhiṣeka*, of Lakṣmī, reinforces the association of Lakṣmī with life-giving rainfall. Coomaraswamy identifies the elephants as cloud elephants (*jalebha*), an Indic conception drawn from the semblance between dark, thundering monsoon clouds heavy with rain and a stampede of trumpeting elephants. The vessels with which the elephants lustrate Lakṣmī are upturned rain pots (*varṣa-sthālī*), another symbol for rain clouds: "There is no question that the waters falling from the inverted jars are those of the life-giving rains . . . this rain, which brings with it the heavenly *soma*, is a source of increase and wealth."[21] Thus, the anointing elephants underscore Lakṣmī's connection with rainfall, which circulates water from the firmament into the earthly life cycle. Om Prakash Singh advances the interpretation that the elephant-Lakṣmī pairing constitutes a male-female dyad in which the female earth is fertilized by monsoon rains in a manner analogous to the masculine role in human procreation.[22] The motif of consecration by lustral water also alludes to royal coronation, with which Lakṣmī is associated as the patron of worldly sovereignty, adding another symbolic layer to the image.[23]

Interestingly, after Lakṣmī's prominent visibility in the iconographic programs of Bhārhut and Sāñcī, she is virtually absent among the extant remains of the succeeding Buddhist monuments. There are two known Lakṣmī images in the Gāndhāran corpus,[24] but she has not been identified among the contemporaneous reliefs of Nāgārjunakoṇḍa and Amarāvatī. The scarcity of Buddhist architectural remains from the Gupta period onward makes it difficult to assess her role on monuments of these later epochs. Several Gaja-Lakṣmī reliefs have been found, however, at the far-flung sites of Aurangabad (ca. sixth century C.E.), Nālandā (ca. sixth or seventh century), and Ratnagiri (eighth century), evincing ongoing use of her image in Buddhist architecture up to the eve of the Pāla period.[25] Additional examples may yet come to light, yielding a fuller understanding of her roles in late Indian Buddhism.

The portrayal of Lakṣmī in architectural adornment, particularly on gateways, became a recurrent feature of Hindu temple design beginning in at least the eighth century. The *Śilpa Prakāśa*, a circa eleventh-century Orissan architectural manual, declares that Lakṣmī, the "giver of all auspicious things" and bestower of fearlessness and happiness, is the deity to be featured at the center of a portal (*toraṇa*) architrave.[26] Architectural historian Alice Boner, addressing the significance of such placement, clarifies that "the most vulnerable part of the temple is the portal, the opening through which inimical influences of the outside world can penetrate into the sanctuary"; in this location, Lakṣmī's "benign and smiling presence wards off all adverse influences that may approach the temple."[27] Thus, the portrayal of Lakṣmī at the entryway to Hindu monuments serves to invoke auspicious forces and repel inauspicious (*alakṣmī*) influences, both from the monuments themselves and from those who enter the sacred precincts.[28] Whether Buddhist architects were innovators or inheritors of this convention, Buddhist monuments offer the earliest evidence of this association between Lakṣmī and the glory and fortunes of a religious edifice.

The fact that Lakṣmī might appear in a similar location and with the same significance on Buddhist and Hindu monuments widely separated by time and geography confirms that she does not embody ideals that are distinctively or exclusively Buddhist. Indeed, her presence in a Buddhist context demonstrates the difficulty of drawing a line between Buddhist observances and popular devotional idioms, revealing the extent to which Buddhists subscribed to beliefs and practices indistinguishable from those of the surrounding populace.

It has been suggested that images of divinities linked to worldly well-being, such as Lakṣmī and yakṣiṇīs, were included in stupa iconography to appeal to the population at large and cater to the religious interests of a laity unconcerned with the purist pursuit of liberation.[29] Vidya Dehejia interrogates this theory by examining donative practices at Bhārhut. She notes that the largest carving of Lakṣmī was donated by a nun and that many of the images of yakṣiṇīs and yakṣas—popular divinities of wealth and abundance—were commissioned by monastic elders and preceptors.[30] That a monastic patron would devote funds to the creation of an image of Lakṣmī or another supernatural being of extra-Buddhist origin suggests that these icons were not merely a concession to popular piety. Moreover, such patronage casts an intriguing perspective on the beliefs of contemporary Buddhism, suggesting a complex interrelationship among the divinities portrayed on the early monuments, the pursuit of merit, and the path to deliverance.

Lakṣmī in Pali Literature

References to Lakṣmī (as Sirī Lakkhī) in the Pali literature compiled during the post-Aśokan period (ca. third century B.C.E.) supplement art historical evidence regarding early Buddhist conceptions of the goddess. Lakṣmī finds mention in these sources as one of the supernatural cast of characters whose existence was taken for granted by the authors and audiences of the texts. The *Dhammapada* refers to her as the goddess who grants good fortune to a kingdom.[31] The *Sudhābhojana Jātaka* faults her for capriciously lavishing favors on those who are greedy, lazy, and foolish while neglecting those who are industrious, virtuous, and wise.[32]

It is more common, however, to find Lakṣmī's blessings linked to ethical virtue. For example, the *Mahāunmagga Jātaka* maintains that Lakṣmī favors the wise and casts off those who are thoughtless, undiscerning, and foolish in speech.[33] The *Tesakuṇa Jātaka* asserts that she grants greatness and victory to a righteous ruler who is bold, energetic, free from envy, and benevolent toward all his subjects.[34] The *Sirī Kālakaṇṇī Jātaka* relates that when the Buddha, in one of his former lives as a merchant, worshipped Lakṣmī, she appeared before him in a blaze of golden light. She imparted to him that she smiles on those who are dutiful, generous, gentle, honest, humble, kind, and soft-spoken but abandons those who grow proud and conceited as a result of her good graces.[35]

In the *Siri Jātaka*, which, as the title indicates, focuses on Śrī Lakṣmī, the Buddha professes that all who gain riches do so by her favor. Addressing the perception that she seems to prosper the undeserving as well as the meritorious, he explains that although some who gain wealth may appear to be unworthy, their fortunes are the fruition of virtuous deeds performed in previous lives. He concludes that the same is true of all the blessings of Lakṣmī, which include happiness, physical beauty, and earthly sovereignty.[36] Here the benefactions of Lakṣmī are deftly intertwined with the workings of karma. Virtuous deeds lay the groundwork of one's destiny, but for one who has planted the seeds of merit, worship of Lakṣmī may spark the flowering of good fortune. This story integrates two explanatory models for wealth, one attributing it to the blessings of a divine figure and the other to the fruition of meritorious actions. The tale endorses the worship of Lakṣmī as long as there is no neglect of the merit-making activities that will lead to positive conditions in future lives.

The frame story of this narrative reinforces its message by providing a principle whereby the worship of a prosperity-bestowing deity such as Lakṣmī may be sanctioned within a Buddhist context. The account centers on the merchant Anāthapiṇḍika (a.k.a. Anāthapiṇḍada), famed as one of the most generous donors of the early community, and the goddess (*devatā*) inhabiting the gate tower of his estate, blessing him with affluence. Anāthapiṇḍika's virtually inexhaustible coffers provided local monastics with a constant supply of rice, ghee (clarified butter), honey, molasses, clothing, and offerings of perfume and garlands. He frequently dined the Buddha and a large retinue of monks in his home. The goddess in the gate tower was inconvenienced by the Buddha's visits, because she and her children had to descend from their dwelling each time he passed, in a show of respect. Therefore, she sought to convince the merchant to cease making offerings to Shakyamuni. Her method was to impoverish Anāthapiṇḍika. Eventually he became so poor that he had only leftover porridge to offer his spiritual master.

The tower goddess appeared before the merchant one night and advised him to forsake the Buddha and devote himself to trade, so that he might regain his wealth. Anāthapiṇḍika refused and turned her away from his estate. The goddess became despondent over her homeless condition and, realizing that Anāthapiṇḍika would not renounce his chosen path, requested his forgiveness. As a token of her good graces, she once again filled his storerooms with gold. The merchant brought her before Shakyamuni in the hope that she might come to appreciate the savant's virtues. She was converted by the Buddha's teachings, repented of her former behavior, and returned to her dwelling in the gate tower. Anāthapiṇḍika in turn received praise for not allowing the goddess to deflect him from his faith and for his persistence in making religious donations.[37]

The surface theme of the story is the tremendous virtue of giving alms. The plot, however, addresses the location of spirits and demigods within the structure of the Buddhist faith. The "displacement" of the goddess is at issue in the story, both literally and figuratively. Her attempt to deflect Anāthapiṇḍika from his worship of the Buddha reflects a potential conflict between traditional cultic practices and the new faith. The goddess is evicted from the tower, just as she is at risk of being dislocated by the Buddhist presence in the religious landscape.

The resolution is harmonious. The conversion of the goddess affirms that divine as well as human beings may follow the Buddha and, safely situated in the community of believers, be propitiated for their customary blessings under the Buddhist aegis. With the provision that long-standing objects of reverence do not displace the Buddha, his teachings can embrace them. Thus, the goddess is "restored" to the gate tower, her original location. At end of the story, as at the beginning, Anāthapiṇḍika has a patron goddess who provides and protects his wealth. The only change is that a hierarchy has been established. The goddess "accepts" her subsidiary role in relation to the supreme object of devotion—the Buddha. She remains securely in place, however, as a dispenser of wealth and may continue to receive her customary worship. The tension is ultimately resolved by the principle that the riches that flow from a "non-Buddhist" deity are acceptable and indeed support the ideal of generosity to the Buddhist community.

Although the tale revolves around a conflict—between the genius loci and the Buddhist ethic—its message is ultimately one of harmony and accommodation. Beneath the surface theme of generosity we may discern a message of rapprochement between Buddhism and the preexisting pantheon of divine beings. There need be no forcible displacement, and followers of Buddhism may continue to pay homage to spirits and deities that had long received their worship. This tale sheds light on the motivation for accepting a tremendously popular wealth-bestowing divinity such as Lakṣmī within the Buddhist fold and illustrates a principle advanced to accomplish this.

Lakṣmī in the Later Tradition

Although Lakṣmī occupied an honored, if not central, position in early Buddhism, her role changed with the rise of the Mahayana movement, as Buddhism began to advance its own female divinities. Although she disappeared almost entirely from the Mahayana mainstream and from architectural adornment, a strand of Lakṣmī worship persisted nonetheless.

A chapter devoted to Śrī Lakṣmī in the *Golden Radiance Scripture* (ca. late fourth or early fifth century C.E.) suggests that there was a faction of the Buddhist community for whom she remained a vital object of reverence. The work articulates the many benefits of her worship. She can provide monastics with clothing, begging bowls, medicines, beds, seats, and other necessities so that they may be sufficiently free of material care to study and teach the scripture. Laypersons who offer her "perfumes, flowers and incense" will have prosperous homes, plentiful crops, and abundant offerings with which to worship the Buddha. Wherever the text is promulgated, Lakṣmī will assure that the area residents will experience no lack and will enjoy a surfeit of food, drink, grain, gems, and gold. She will saturate the earth with her moist nectar, nurturing fruits, crops, trees, and bushes to brilliant luster.[38]

The *Golden Radiance Scripture* imparts that worship of Lakṣmī may be performed in a home, monastery, or forest retreat, thereby indicating that the ritual might be undertaken by laypersons or monastics. The worshipper must purify the site, bathe, and don clean, white, perfumed garments. The ceremony opens with homage to the Buddhas and bodhisattvas and mantra recitation. The mandala into which the goddess will be invoked is a circle of cow dung on which flowers, perfume, and incense have been spread. The text promises that Lakṣmī will enter the sacred space thus prepared and reside there, prospering the worshipper and surrounding community "with the supply of every blessing," fulfilling every desire, as long as the worshipper lives.[39]

Lakṣmī's blessings and those of the recitation and study of the text are subtly intertwined, as the audience of the work is enjoined to worship her. Her benedictions are said to flow by the power of the most excellent of scriptures, the *Golden Radiance*. She in turn creates an opulent environment so that the text may be transmitted, its message may endure, there may be no famine or deprivation, the hell realms may be emptied, and all beings may attain supreme enlightenment.[40] Thus, the text reflects an ongoing attempt, as seen in earlier Pali sources, to accommodate worship of popular divinities such as Lakṣmī within a Buddhist framework.

Apart from her appearance in the *Golden Radiance Scripture*, Lakṣmī rarely appears in later Buddhist artistic or literary sources. As the Mahayana movement gained in strength, however, and divinities of recognizably Buddhist provenance began to emerge, at least two of them assumed Lakṣmī's attributes. It appears that her emblematic lotus was inherited by Tārā, who became for Buddhists the "lotus lady" par excellence, source of every blessing, nurturing beings to spiritual perfection. Lakṣmī's golden hue and wealth-bestowing nature were born anew in the figure of Vasudhārā, the Buddhist goddess of abundance and good fortune.[41] Indeed, the emergence of Vasudhārā and Tārā in the Mahayana pantheon could account for the diminished attention to Lakṣmī.

Although Lakṣmī virtually disappeared from later Buddhist sources, she does make an occasional appearance. The *Mañjuśrīmūlakalpa* (ca. seventh century), a Sanskrit compendium of mantric practices, includes a rite to be performed on a boat or riverbank: "Descending in a river flowing to the sea, offer a hundred thousand lotuses. Śrī will appear and grant a boon, bestowing a kingdom. Now offer three hundred thousand lotuses, and one will become a sovereign king, lord of all Rose-Apple Island" (that is, the Indian subcontinent).[42] Lakṣmī's associations with water, lotuses, and kingship converge in this summarily described but lavish donative rite.

The presence of several short canonical texts evinces the transmission of Lakṣmī practices to Tibet, where she survives in the active pantheon as a minor wealth deity.[43] A Sakya meditation on Mahālakṣmī, "Great Lakṣmī," interestingly envisions her as green and riding a snow lion but displaying her emblematic lotus.[44] The practice is recommended as a complement to that of Sarasvatī, so the knowledge and scholarly prowess bestowed by the latter will not be attended by poverty.[45] We also find a green hierophany of Lakṣmī in the Nyingma pantheon, holding a lotus and making the gesture of protection from fear.[46]

Lakṣmī appears as a retinue figure in a range of Tantric mandalas. In the Durgatipariśodhana and Bhūtaḍāmara mandalas she appears under the name of Śrī; in the Kālacakra both "Śrī" and "Lakṣmī" appear three times.[47] In the

Durgatipariśodhana she holds a vajra, lending her iconography a Buddhist cast.[48] In these and other cases, she is placed in the outer tiers of the mandalas along with other Hindu deities.[49] Interestingly, her appearance on the periphery of the mandalas recalls her earlier placement on stupa railings and gateways, in which locations she serves not as a symbol of enlightened wisdom but as a figure within its orbit who prospers and supports those on the path.

The Fluidic Goddess and the Buddhist Historical Stream

Lakṣmī is in essence the abundance of nature personified, not only in the sense of the natural environment as a source of beauty, pleasure, and nourishment but also as the vitalizing force from which humans derive health, vigor, and luster—the golden elixir of life. The character of Lakṣmī can perhaps better be understood by contrast with that of Pṛthivī, the earth goddess, another important life-giving figure in pan-Indic mythology. Both are regarded as sources of sustenance, wealth, and well-being. Although their roles significantly overlap, they represent different facets of the natural world. Lakṣmī is associated primarily with water and personifies the essence of life, the radiant, fluidic force that gives rise to and animates all living things. Pṛthivī, in contrast, is associated with the soil and represents the physical ground of existence, the material matrix of bodies, nourishment, and shelter. Accordingly, Lakṣmī evinces the dynamic effervescence of creativity, whereas Pṛthivī is known for her constancy and stability. Both are essential to life, although water is generally regarded as the more fundamental element, because the fertility of the earth is observably dependent on moisture.

It is unsurprising that Lakṣmī, as a purely auspicious and beneficent figure, found an honored place in early Buddhist art and devotion. Her association with prosperity and abundance easily accounts for her presence on Buddhist monuments, helping to communicate the well-being that will flow from honoring the Buddha and following the Buddhist path. Moreover, by virtue of her connection with kingship and royal coronation, her effigies reflected the world sovereignty attributed to the Buddha by those who built and worshipped at the stupas. It is intriguing and historically significant, for the study of both Lakṣmī and Buddhism, that Buddhist monuments offer the earliest major artistic corpus of Lakṣmī images. Moreover, her iconography in that context evinces the features that endured in her portrayal over the centuries, permanently defining her iconographic form (Fig. 4.5).

As the Buddhist pantheon expanded, Lakṣmī's attributes were incorporated into explicitly Buddhist figures, such as the lotus-bearing Tārā and the golden

4.5 Gaja-Lakṣmī, India, contemporary. Polychrome print. Author's collection. *Lakṣmī now customarily appears with four arms but retains many features present in her Buddhist iconography.*

bestower of bounty, Vasudhārā. Apparently the glorious goddess of good fortune, whose presence makes the natural world blossom luxuriantly and human lives glow with prosperity, was so fundamental to the religiosity of India's inhabitants, rural and urban, that her characteristics and iconography continued to engage the Buddhist imagination in the Mahayana setting. Śrī Lakṣmī herself, having graced Buddhism with her golden touch, flowed on in her consummately fluidic fashion to bless those who continued to invoke her by her original name.

CHAPTER 5

HĀRĪTĪ

Goddess of Motherly Love

Hārītī, giver of life to the young,
Loving toward her devotees,
Destroyer of pain throughout the universe,
Moved by compassion,
Remover of suffering,
Devoted to the happiness and joy of humankind—
Homage to the yakṣiṇī queen,
Mother of many children!

Her subtle body formed of rays of compassion,
Her mind reveling in the Buddha's teachings,
Her feet honored throughout the universe,
Served by celestial hosts,
I worship the yakṣiṇī queen,
Mother of many children!

—*Invocation for protection of children*[1]

Hārītī (pronounced *HAH REE TEE*) was the first object of an independent goddess cult within Buddhism. She rose from the ranks of the yakṣiṇīs to reign as the "yakṣiṇī queen" (*yakṣeśvarī*), garnering the worship once spread among numerous representatives of this populous class of spirit being. Moreover, yakṣiṇīs received homage at tree altars and stupa railings, whereas images of Hārītī were enshrined on monastic premises, placing her cultus at the center of Buddhist institutional life. Shakyamuni Buddha himself purportedly decreed that she should receive food offerings each day. She consequently received a portion of every monastic meal, and her icons became a significant focus of lay devotion. Reverence for Hārītī gave impetus to an impressive corpus of artistic images spanning the second through eleventh centuries. These depict the goddess as the epitome of maternal grace, a serene and benevolent matron, surrounded by children and cradling an infant at her breast.

Hārītī's immense popularity may be attributed in large part to her reassuring, nurturing persona. Central to her character is an abundance of mother love, once directed to her children, now extended to all humanity through the intervention of Shakyamuni Buddha. Her effigies provided Buddhism with a feminine face, complementing the otherwise masculine coloration lent to the religious symbology by the male gender of the Buddha. Moreover, Shakyamuni had revealed the path to liberation and then departed into the transcendent realm of parinirvāṇa, while Hārītī remained sufficiently immersed in earthly life to attend to the needs of the laity and answer their prayers for healthy children, prosperity, and success. Thus, it may seem ironic from one perspective and yet recognized as symbolically apropos from another that Buddhism in the course of its pan-Asian expansion established in its wake not only the teachings, meditative practices, and monastic regimens of the Buddha but also the devotional cult of the mother goddess Hārītī.

The name of the goddess has various spellings and interpretations. In Indic sources we find her name rendered as Hārītī and Hārītikā.[2] In Nepal the spelling Hāratī is favored. A derivative of the verbal root *hṛ*, "to steal," the name alludes to her former habit of abducting and devouring children, before she was converted by Shakyamuni Buddha and enlisted to protect his monasteries and followers. Another interpretation, current in Nepal, is that she is so named because she "takes away," or relieves, the suffering and illnesses of children.[3] Her name can also designate one who "captivates" the mind with admiration or delight. This meaning is reflected in the Tibetan rendition of her name as Yidrogma, "Enchanting Lady," an appropriate sobriquet for a goddess who, despite her former career as a thief of children, is envisaged as a beatific, regal figure, now surrounded by her cherished offspring.

Conversion from Ogress to Benefactor

The tale of Hārītī is one of transformation, as she turns from a devourer of infants into a bestower and protector of children and benefactor of humans. Among the varied literary sources in which Hārītī finds mention,[4] the *Mūlasarvāstivāda Vinaya* (ca. fourth or fifth century C.E.) offers what is apparently the most detailed account.[5] At the beginning of the saga, the yakṣiṇī Hārītī—known at that time as Abhirati, "Joyful Girl"—was the daughter of Sāta, the patron yakṣa of Rājagṛha. When Sāta died, his duties were to pass to his son and daughter, but Abhirati could not follow in her father's footsteps because she had made a vow in a former life to prey on the children of Rājagṛha.

Abhirati confessed her spiteful intentions to her brother, Sātagiri. When Sātagiri could not dissuade her, he quickly arranged for her marriage to Pāñcika, son of the patron yakṣa of Gāndhāra. Following the nuptials, Abhirati went to live with her husband at a safe remove from her native land. After she gave birth to five hundred offspring, however, the force of her vow could no longer be denied. Impelled to action by her baneful pledge, the yakṣiṇī descended on Rājagṛha with her progeny and terrorized the populace by abducting and consuming infants and children.

The townspeople appealed to the king for assistance, and royal counselors advised that they make choice food offerings accompanied by flowers, music, and banners to appease whatever yakṣa was causing the calamity. The problem did not abate, however, and the suffering of the populace was unbearable. Finally, a yakṣa revealed that Abhirati was preying on the city. The citizens responded that such a malicious yakṣiṇī did not deserve the name "Joyful Girl" and dubbed her Hārītī, "Thief," because she was stealing their children. At the advice of the yakṣa, they turned to Shakyamuni Buddha for protection. Moved by their plight, Shakyamuni concealed the yakṣiṇī's youngest son, Priyaṇkara, under his alms bowl and magically rendered the boy invisible. Hārītī searched far and wide for her missing child, blinded by tears and crazed with grief. Eventually a yakṣa leader advised her to consult Shakyamuni. Hārītī immediately went before the sage and declared that she would end her life that very day if Priyaṇkara were not restored to her. The Buddha urged her to recognize that if the loss of one child among five hundred left her so heartbroken, how much greater must be the suffering of those whose only child she had taken.

Hārītī readily empathized with the parents whose babies she had stolen and promised to desist. Shakyamuni returned her child, and Hārītī accepted the Buddha as her spiritual guide. She agreed to follow his teachings and took the five lay precepts, one of which is to abstain from taking life. The yakṣiṇī expressed concern regarding how she and her children would find nourishment if they abandoned their flesh diet. The Buddha promised that she and her offspring would be fed in all his monasteries. He pledged that whenever his disciples sat down for a meal, a plate for Hārītī would be included at the end of the row, she and her children would be invoked, and sufficient food would be provided that they would never hunger. Shakyamuni then pronounced that Hārītī and her offspring should watch over the monks and nuns and vigilantly guard his monasteries day and night, granting them tranquility and security as long as his community exists. After her conversion, Hārītī offered her children to the monastery, which inspired the women of Rājagṛha to follow suit.

The audience of this discourse wanted to know what karmic conditions had led Hārītī to prey on children. The Buddha imparted that in a former life she had been a herdswoman in Rājagṛha. She went to the marketplace to sell buttermilk on a festival day and there encountered hundreds of people singing and dancing. Although she was pregnant at the time, she couldn't resist their invitation to join the celebration. She danced to the point of exhaustion and suffered a miscarriage, which caused her to become deranged. She proceeded on her way and traded her buttermilk for five hundred mangos.

Shortly thereafter, she encountered a Pratyeka Buddha (solitary Buddha). Impressed by his saintly demeanor, she bowed before him and offered him the five hundred mangos. The Pratyeka Buddha rose into the air and displayed other miraculous powers. The herdswoman was filled with reverence and made a pledge, by the merit of her offering, to wreak revenge for her miscarriage by devouring the children of the citizens of Rājagṛha. (Note that Hārītī's interactions with the Pratyeka Buddha did not entail her conversion or moral instruction. Rather, she was confident that offerings and vows made in his presence would bear fruit, as was indeed the case.) Thus it came to pass, in fulfillment of her vow, that she was reborn in Rājagṛha as a yakṣiṇī, gave birth to five hundred offspring, and had the power to suck vitality from humans and consume children.[6]

Variations on this legend place her career in different regions, such as Kashmir and the Himalayas, giving her story a local coloration.[7] The account in the *Hārītī Sūtra* (ca. late third or early fourth century C.E.), attested only in Chinese, is noteworthy for the more prominent role accorded to her children. The geographic setting of this story is unclear, while the name of Hārītī is rendered as "Holiti, Mother of Demons." This version does not explore the motives for her predations. The families who lost their infants appealed to the Buddhist community for relief, and Ānanda conveyed their plea to Shakyamuni. The Buddha revealed the cause of their plight to be Hārītī, a demoness and mother of one thousand children. He imparted that five hundred of her offspring resided in the sky and five hundred lived on the earth. Each was a powerful demon king with an extensive retinue that terrorized the inhabitants of those regions.

The Buddha instructed his disciples to enter Hārītī's residence when she was away on a marauding expedition and to gather her children and bring them to the monastery. When Hārītī returned and found her children missing, she forgot about the children of others and went in search of her own, scouring heaven and earth. After ten days she returned home, crazed by her loss, ranting and weeping, unable to eat or drink. The Buddha summoned her and, as in the narrative related above, helped Hārītī see the error of her ways, asking her, "Seeing that you are capable of loving your children, how can you rob the children of others every day? They love their children just as you do." He disclosed that her actions would cause her to be reborn in hell. Terrified, Hārītī implored the Buddha to take pity on her. He promised to return her children if she sincerely repented. Hārītī recognized the evil she had committed and promised to follow the Buddha. She took the five lay precepts, and the Buddha restored her children.

Here the narrative takes a novel turn, addressing the malicious nature of Hārītī's progeny. The Buddha expatiated that her five hundred aerial children and their minions preyed on the inhabitants of the sky, while her five hundred terrestrial children and their even more demonic hordes were utterly heinous. Forming enormous troops of tree, earth, water, sea, boat, chariot, house, and night spirits, they feasted on blood sacrifices and tormented humans with nightmares and fatal illnesses and accidents. The Buddha said that, for their murderous ways, they were bound for hell and incapable of protecting human life.

Hārītī repented from the bottom of her heart and obtained the status of a "nonreturner," one who will never regress to a lower level of spiritual progress. She expressed her desire to live near the Buddha and to have her children join her, follow his teachings, and serve the beings who live on and above the earth.[8] Shakyamuni praised her aspirations and promised that in the future she would live near a Buddhist monastery and that what she had spoken would come to pass. He directed that Hārītī should grant progeny to the childless and assigned specific benefactions to four of her children. Maṇibhadra, commander of the sky spirits, was to watch over the oceans and protect merchants traveling by land and sea. Hārītī's daughter Tcheni was to aid pregnant women during their confinement and delivery. Vaiśravaṇa was to guard and increase wealth, while Asura, ruler of the serpent deities (*nāga*) and all poisonous spirits, was to offer protection from venom.[9]

Conversions of demonic beings are often collective in nature. When the Buddha converts a powerful spirit who has a populous train, the conversion of the main figure simultaneously brings under control the legions of spirits under their command. Hārītī's children served as her core retinue and formed a veritable army that joined in her marauding expeditions. This is one reason every account emphasizes that her conversion was immediately followed by that of her children. The *Hārītī Sūtra*, however, expands on this theme. This legend doubles her number of children and endows each with an entourage of exceedingly demonic entities that exercised a broad range of destructive powers on land and sea and in the sky. This magnifies the importance of Hārītī's conversion, expanding the extent of her influence as it filtered through her children to harmful spirits threatening humans everywhere and in myriad ways. Another work voices this aspect of the conversion, declaring that when "Hārītī, with her children, took refuge in the Buddha, she led males and females in great number, hordes of male and female demons and their male and female descendants, like streams and rivers going into the sea."[10]

Moreover, after the conversion Hārītī's children are not simply rendered harmless but undergo reform and become active in the protection of monasteries and Buddhist followers. This theme, present in all the narratives, also finds special attention in the *Hārītī Sūtra*, which singles out four of Hārītī's offspring and assigns them and their retinues specific benefactions. This motif affirms Shakyamuni's power to secure the safety and well-being of his followers, but it also clarifies why Hārītī is such an important convert and supernatural ally of the Buddha.

Interpretation of Conversion Accounts

The legendry of Hārītī's conversion is theologically and historically complex. On the surface, the story serves as a morality tale, expressing key ethical and psychological insights. Shakyamuni's response to Hārītī's heinous actions was neither punitive nor condemnatory. Rather, he demonstrated the cardinal Buddhist virtue of compassion for others, even those engaged in violent and harmful behavior. He recognized the intense suffering at the root of her ghoulish conduct, discerning that her motivation was not indiscriminate cruelty but rather a deep psychic wound incurred during a previous life, when grief over a miscarriage caused her to become demented and vengeful. Such traumas can provoke a psychological disturbance of potentially monstrous proportions. Yet even a being who evinces an extreme deformation of character is not irredeemable. The potential for enlightenment is still present beneath the overlay of negative emotionality and may be awakened by appeal to some vestige of virtue, however faint. The Buddha found Hārītī's remnant of goodness in her love for her children and used this insight to elicit her compassion and moral transformation.

The Buddha's conversion of Hārītī also conveys a psychological lesson regarding the path to freedom from suffering. Hārītī had sought to assuage her pain by inflicting suffering on others. One of the principles of Buddhist psychology is that one who is consumed by misery will inevitably cause suffering to others, either unintentionally or in a spirit of vengeance or cruelty. However, seeking to ease pain by victimizing others is a futile project that garners no inner peace and generates new cycles of suffering. One way to break this dolorous pattern is to use one's own suffering as a basis for empathy with others. Thus, the Buddha prompted Hārītī to recognize the anguish of those whose children she was stealing.

In order fully to reform her behavior and secure for her a lasting source of happiness, Shakyamuni charged her to devote herself to the well-being of others. Hārītī's assigned benefaction was grounded in the one positive quality that had survived her descent into the demonic condition, namely, maternal love. She expanded the feeling once directed exclusively to her own children and adopted a motherly role toward humankind. One text finds Shakyamuni voicing precisely this principle: "Just as Hārītī loved her own children, she extended that love to other humans and forever ceased to kill, for I charged (her), 'O venerable one of great compassion, with your compassion of a mother for a child, extend that compassion to all others.'"[11]

The conversion of Hārītī also provides a classic case study in the process of pantheon formation. The Buddhist pantheon has incorporated supernatural beings of a local character into its lower rungs wherever the tradition spread. The demon-conversion narrative is a mainstay of this geographic and theogonic expansion. In this process, beings of cruel and evil bent, accepting the Buddha's desideratum of helping rather than harming others, direct their powers to good. Gananath Obeyesekere clarifies the cultural logic:

> These beings are already there—available for promotion, so to speak—obviating the need to invent new gods. Consider the case of demons. They are known, felt presences. . . . Like the gods, they have power that has immediacy and relevance for many people. Their power, unlike that of the gods, is directed toward evil, but if it could be harnessed for good then surely its effects must be as profound for good as it was previously in the sphere of evil.[12]

After conversion, the former demon devotes himself or herself to the service of others and, due to the consequent improvement in karma and increase in virtue and merit, gradually attains a more purely benevolent and hence godlike or divine character. The names and mythologies of these prize converts preserve the memory of their former demonic status.[13]

Eliciting the good graces of supernatural beings was integral to the Buddha's role as savior and refuge. He secured the protection and well-being of his followers in part by neutralizing the threat posed by harmful entities and transforming them into agents of compassion. Putting in place a pantheon of supernatural allies in turn helped preserve the Buddha's primary role as revealer of the path to liberation. The idea that the Buddha should directly intervene in mundane affairs is in tension with his transcendence of worldly life, or samsara. His transcendent status demands that he delegate practical concerns to lesser spirits, while "the Buddha is spared from being a conventional intercessionary god through the . . . view that he allocated these powers while he was alive."[14]

Although the conversion of demons is an expression of the Buddha's compassion and transcendence, it is primarily a demonstration of his power, establishing his sovereignty over spirit beings and supernatural forces. He was accorded the title of "god of gods" (*devātideva*), superior to all other deities, capable of converting them through his powers of compassion and wisdom. Conversion narratives establish that "the powers of the gods *ultimately* derive from the founder himself."[15] Shakyamuni remains free from the taint of worldly involvement, but it is *his* power that is refracted through the lower tiers of the pantheon.

The danger posed by Hārītī, as well as her motivation, were familiar in the Buddhist cultural landscape. Her preconversion profile as a devourer of infants was by no means idiosyncratic. Morally unevolved yakṣas and yakṣiṇīs were, and are, believed to prey on humans and even to consume human flesh. The type of yakṣiṇī that devours children elicits considerable fear. The desire to steal and ingest babies generally stems from a past trauma of childlessness, miscarriage, death in childbirth, or the death of a newborn. As in Hārītī's case, a woman or female animal might choose to be reborn as a yakṣiṇī specifically in order to consume children, driven to this extreme by frustrated motherhood or lust for revenge against someone she believed had harmed or killed her offspring.[16] This pattern may become a vicious cycle perpetuated over many lifetimes, with each mother gaining vengeance in turn.[17] Shakyamuni typically pacified child-eating yakṣiṇīs by having a monastery built in their honor or by arranging that they receive regular food offerings.[18] Hārītī was the only one of these who attained a panlocal status and a prominent and permanent place in the Buddhist pantheon.

An association with disease may have been intrinsic to Hārītī's character as well. It is commonly remarked that her consumption of infants and children resembles the scourge of an epidemic that decimates infantile populations. Among the infectious fevers and virulent contagions that "devour" the vulnerable young, smallpox is one of the most feared. As Alfred Foucher observes, "in India, smallpox is so dreaded that children aren't counted as 'living' until they survive it."[19] It is quite common in South Asia for both the origin and cure of febrile epidemics to be attributed to the agency of a type of female divinity characterizable as a "smallpox goddess," "epidemic goddess," or "fever goddess."[20] There is evidence that Hārītī is to be included in this class. The *Avadāna Kalpalatā* explicitly states that when Hārītī descended on Rājagṛha, "an epidemic in the city caused the women to lose their children in the womb."[21] The understanding that Hārītī "seized" children by inflicting disease may also have been implicit in other versions of her legend, in view of the currency of such ideas during the period when her mythology was taking shape.

In the first and second centuries C.E., the role of the fever, or epidemic, goddess was shared by a range of female spirits, local and folkloric in provenance, that threaten the unborn and newly born with smallpox, diphtheria, cholera, and other conditions that cause barrenness, miscarriage, and infant mortality. This type of spirit was variously designated as a *yakṣiṇī*, *rākṣasī* (cannibal demon), *bāla-graha* ("seizer of children"), *jāta-hāriṇī* ("thief of newborns"), *jāta-hārikā* ("captor of infants"), and *mātṛkā* ("mother" spirits of variously protective and predatory nature). Such entities were closely identified with the diseases they inflicted. Unquestionably dangerous, they were also capable of protecting and curing when appeased with offerings.

This genre of child-devouring and pestilential figure was part of the complex of religious ideas that informed and found a focal point in the figure and mythology of Hārītī.[22] On an historical level, then, her legendry records a Buddhist response to this broader cultural phenomenon, namely, offering a single figure to be propitiated in place of a plethora of analogous figures. A similar process was taking place throughout India, as this diffuse array of localized figures coalesced into several divinities of panlocal significance. Among these, Revatī is little in evidence today, but Śītalā, Salabai, and Māriyammān find worship across vast geographic regions and in different sectarian contexts. Hārītī, too, counts among their number.

In keeping with the nature of these pathogenic supernatural females, after her conversion Hārītī became a bestower and protector of children. The fever goddess and purveyor of pestilence typically becomes a prophylactic and curative figure, a divine mother who enhances fertility and childbirth. The area of expertise remains unchanged, becoming the basis for a career as a guardian of children. Such a being is intimately familiar with threats to the health of children and pregnant mothers and thus perfectly placed to guard them from such dangers. Indeed, protection from spirits and diseases that threaten fetuses is a key role attributed to Hārītī:

> Terrifier of spirits who prey on pregnant women,
> Destroyer of smallpox and myriad diseases,
> A mother to her devotees,
> With limbs that cool like white sandalwood,
> I reverently praise the supreme yakṣiṇī,
> Mother of many children.[23]

Hārītī's "cooling" limbs intimate her ability to cool febrile conditions, a necessary feature of divine curers of smallpox, diphtheria, and other feverish afflictions.

In her benevolent aspect, Hārītī also subsumed the role of the auspicious yakṣiṇīs who protected and received worship at early Buddhist stupas dating from the second century B.C.E. through the second century C.E.[24] The devotional cultus of the yakṣiṇīs was directed toward a range of sacred sites and icons of a local character. None of the yakṣiṇīs portrayed on the early stupas emerged with a panlocal identity, reputation, or significance. This cult gained a singular focus when Hārītī was elevated above other members of the yakṣa class, becoming the "supreme yakṣiṇī" (*yakṣeśvarī*). With the introduction of Hārītī, an otherwise diffuse cult without firm canonical status came to be concentrated in a single figure whose worship was sanctioned—indeed, commanded—by the enlightened one himself. This transition is datable to the second century C.E., the period that saw the final florescence of significant artistic activity devoted to the depiction of yakṣiṇīs on stupa railings and the rise of a corpus of votive images of Hārītī.

Hārītī clearly exemplified a whole complex of supernatural females—yakṣiṇīs, fever goddesses, demonic mothers, and child-seizers. She thus provided a point of entry at which a range of such figures could be incorporated into the Buddhist fold. Richard Cohen draws attention to Hārītī's importance in this regard, asserting that she functioned as both a local and a translocal deity. She was translocal insofar as she traveled with Buddhism into new territories and was enshrined in monasteries across the Buddhist domain. As Cohen observes, Hārītī was at the same time "a portable local deity," providing an interface for the absorption of the cults, rites, and roles of similar types of figures—an "immediate point of intersection" between local traditions and the translocal ethos of Buddhism.[25]

Although Hārītī rose from a class of morally ambivalent beings, little remains of her dangerous, demonic overtones. By the time we meet her, as an object of Buddhist worship, she is a nurturing, ostensibly benevolent figure. In Mallar Mitra's analysis, the most significant aspect of her preconversion profile is the intensity of her motherly love. Hārītī was so deeply devoted to her five hundred children that the loss of even one was unbearable, rendering her suicidal. Here we find perhaps her primary qualification for the role of mother goddess and the decisive key to her enduring appeal. In Mitra's view,

> [Hārītī] approaches the ideal of the mother offering her purest affection for her children. . . . [I]t is this motherhood that glorifies her—the mother who is totally at a loss at the disappearance of one child of five hundred; the mother who realizes the suffering of others in the process; the mother who is anxious for the nourishment of the children.[26]

Carnivorous predator she may have been, but Hārītī already flowed with the mother love that would characterize her divine persona and the fertility for which she would be supplicated.

Art and Worship

Literary sources on the ritual observances devoted to Hārītī are limited but sufficient to reveal that she figured in both lay and monastic religiosity. In the detailed version of her legend from the *Mūlasarvāstivāda Vinaya*, related above, Shakyamuni addressed monastic worship of Hārītī, stipulating that she should receive food offerings whenever the monks or nuns take meal, but no mention is made of lay worship. Obligatory monastic worship of a yakṣa or yakṣiṇī was apparently a novel development, warranting textual attention, whereas lay veneration of yakṣas was by then a sufficiently well-established practice to require no comment or justification.

The only firsthand account of worship of Hārītī in India, provided by I-tsing (seventh century), confirms that food offerings were central to her cultus. The Chinese pilgrim relates in brief her conversion tale and the Buddha's promise that the yakṣiṇī and her family would be fed daily in his monasteries, continuing:

> For this reason, an image of Hārītī is found either in the porch or in a corner of the dining-hall of all Indian monasteries, depicting her as holding a babe in her arms, and round her knees three or five children. Every day an abundant offering of food is made before this image.[27]

Although it is doubtful that I-tsing visited "all" the Buddhist monasteries of India, his statement would suggest that he recurrently encountered Hārītī shrines on monastic premises.

Significantly, I-tsing reports that laypersons made their own offerings at these altars and informs us of two of the benefactions they sought:

> [Hārītī] has the power of giving wealth. If those who are childless on account of their bodily weakness (pray to her for children), making offerings of food, their wish is always fulfilled.[28]

The fact that I-tsing mentions only food offerings is telling, for he was a detailed chronicler of Buddhist practices he observed. For instance, in the following passage, he describes an array of offerings (food, incense, lamplight) rendered before another image on the same premises.[29] Therefore, his account indicates that lay worship of Hārītī consisted largely or solely of food offerings, rather than the complement of votive garlands, lamplight, and incense that customarily constituted yakṣa worship. It is likely, however, that food was her primary daily offering, as witnessed by I-tsing, but that worship on festival days was more elaborate, in accordance with a pattern observable in Buddhist communities today.

I-tsing also reports on a bimonthly rite in which the laity feasted monastic residents and Hārītī at the same table. He describes the seating arrangement, with images of Arhats (the Buddha's enlightened disciples) at the head, followed by the row of monks, and ending with Hārītī.[30] Feeding monastics has perennially been a major merit-making activity in Buddhism, but the opportunity of simultaneously propitiating Hārītī may have figured in the motivation of some donors of this lavish meal.

It has been suggested that food offerings were intended to appease Hārītī's appetite and curb her bloodlusting tendencies.[31] In my reading of her legendry, however, Shakyamuni permanently removed the danger posed by Hārītī when he converted her and elicited her oath to abstain from a flesh diet. The decisive nature of this moral transformation is conveyed by her status in varied texts as a "stream-winner" (*śrotāpanna*) or "nonreturner" (*anāgāmin*). Both terms signify an aspirant who is solidly progressing toward enlightenment with no prospect of regression or a lower rebirth, much less a descent or return to a demonic state. Therefore, I believe that food offerings have been made to Hārītī not to control her demonic nature but to elicit her blessings in answer to prayers and to sustain her as she fulfills the benefactory role Shakyamuni entrusted to her in perpetuity. It remains possible, however, that an aura of danger lingered around Hārītī, as it does in contemporary Newar settings.

I-tsing's invaluable reportage indicates that Hārītī was an integral part of Indian Buddhist institutional life. She figured in daily worship and regular ritual events and provided a vital interface between the lay and monastic communities. For monastic residents, she served as a veritable "Dharma-protector" (*dharmapāla*), a being who safeguards Buddhist institutions and teachings and those who follow them. Her effigies also drew laypersons to the monasteries, knowing they could find there not only spiritual guidance but also emotional comfort and hope for more immediate benefits of progeny, prosperity, good health, and success in worldly undertakings. Thus, there is little doubt that her shrines helped make the monasteries more vibrant and multifaceted centers of religious life.

There may also have been temples devoted to Hārītī. The remains of two such temples have been unearthed in Andhra Pradesh and Uttar Pradesh.[32] Hsuan-tsang reported on a stupa erected at Peshawar in Gāndhāra by Aśoka to mark the site of Hārītī's conversion. When the pilgrim visited the area in the seventh century, the stupa was still in worship by local women for its child-bestowing powers.[33] Alfred Foucher located a large tumulus in Peshawar that he believed to be the remains of this stupa. He discovered that Hindu and Muslim women of the area took earth from the mound and placed it in amulets to be worn by their infants to ward off smallpox. Interestingly, no legend was attached to the mound to explain its protective and curative powers. Thus, Foucher surmised that the site's original reputation had endured although its Buddhist character had been forgotten.[34]

Works of art devoted to the goddess provide a fuller portrait of her character and role in Buddhist devotional life than do literary sources. Although Hārītī is classed as a yakṣiṇī, her artistic representations were not based on the yakṣiṇī figural type. Yakṣiṇīs were almost invariably depicted in a standing posture, sensuously posed and scantily clad, generally canopied by a tree or lotus parasol (see Figs. 3.2–3.6). Their association with fertility and abundance was expressed primarily by fruit, flowers, vegetation, vessels, elaborate hip girdles, and aquatic motifs and only rarely by the presence of a child.[35] Hārītī, however, is a stately figure, a mature matron rather than a nubile maiden, dignified in posture, radiating an air of majesty. Her iconographic emblem is the children that sport at her feet and rest on her lap and shoulders.

The earliest surviving depictions of Hārītī date from the Kuṣāṇa period (first through third centuries C.E.), which leaves us a legacy of remarkable statuary of the goddess in the Gāndhāran style of the Greco-Bactrian region. Ambitious in design and impressive in execution, they represent a significant outlay of funds and artistic effort. Indeed, the finest Gāndhāran Hārītī carvings epitomize the zenith of the craftsmanship of their period. If the quality of the artistry is any measure, the reverence for Hārītī rivaled that accorded to the Buddha and the bodhisattva Maitreya, the future Buddha. The elaborately detailed Gāndhāran portrayals of the holy mother are carved from fine gray schist with clear, crisply chiseled lines, rendering their subject with elegant formality softened by touches of affectionate and whimsical detail.

Consider a third-century statue that exhibits this level of artistry and exemplifies the Gāndhāran vision of Hārītī (Fig. 5.1 and Pl. 3). The divine mother is seated on a throne in the frontal *pralambapāda* pose, with her knees spread and feet firmly planted on a small dais, a posture signifying royalty and authority. Her clothing and adornments bear the strong Greco-Roman imprint of the Gāndhāran style. Her beautifully coifed hair, its every wave rendered with loving attention, is drawn into a topknot that rises above her coronet. She is crowned with a laurel wreath that centers on a rosette. Her serene, gently smiling face is spangled with floral designs. She is opulently ornamented with dangling earrings, a torque, a heavy necklace, bracelets (visible beneath her sleeves), and anklets. Her classical-style robes convey a sense of luxury, too, with their sumptuously pooling folds, except where the fabric is stretched smooth over her breasts, and ornately pleated sleeves embellished with embroidery or beading.

Hārītī is depicted with eight children, a convention common to her Gāndhāran portrayals. As is typical, she cradles an infant to her breast. The other

5.1 Hārītī, Gāndhāran region (Pakistan), Kuṣāṇa period, ca. third century C.E. Schist, height 35.8 in. (91 cm). Private collection. Photo courtesy of Mr. and Mrs. Willard G. Clark. *The happily cavorting children and infant pressed to her breast reflect Hārītī's nature as a loving mother goddess. (See Pl. 3)*

children perch on her shoulders and sport at her feet in playful attitudes. The child on her shoulder plays cymbals; the toddler at her feet plucks a grape and bears a piece of fruit or a toy. All the children, displaying the plumpness of the prosperous yakṣa race, wear varied adornments (necklaces, armbands, bracelets), signaling their superhuman status. Two of the youths, more mature in appearance, wrestle in mock combat, serving as a reminder that Hārītī's progeny are powerful spirits who populate their mother's troops.

This statue displays many recurrent features of Gāndhāran artistic treatments of Hārītī. Some works, however, show her in a standing pose, and her outer garment may be draped over one shoulder in the manner of an Indian sari. The coronet may be fashioned from strands of gems or pearls rather than leaves, and the hair and jewelry styles vary (Fig. 5.2). Great inventiveness is displayed in depicting the charming attitudes and antics of Hārītī's children. The babe-in-arms may suckle, press a tiny hand to her breast, or pull at her necklace. The toddlers may suck on their fingers, reach for food, play with a toy or pet, or tussle among themselves. Rosettes and vegetative motifs are creatively integrated into the carvings, subtly alluding to Hārītī's association with earthly fertility and abundance.[36]

These statues eloquently testify to the devotion of those who commissioned and conducted worship before them. Hārītī emerges in the visual record as an unambiguously auspicious and benevolent figure, potent with the energies of life and abundance, fecundity and well-being. Perhaps the faithful identified with the children on the statuary as they derived comfort and security from the reassuring presence of the divine mother.

Seeking to explain the concentration of Hārītī images in the Gāndhāran region, A. Bivar inserts a pragmatic consideration, proposing that the "great and costly . . . output of statues, many in fine style," was a response to a devastating smallpox epidemic that swept through and beyond the Roman Empire via trade routes in the second century. Bivar surmises that Hārītī was not yet as integral to Buddhist worship as she would later become and that these statues were created for a specific purpose, namely, "to avert the threat of infection."[37] Supporting his conjecture is an image, found in the vicinity of a stupa marking the site of Hārītī's conversion, inscribed with a prayer invoking the goddess "to take smallpox away into the sky."[38] Although Hārītī has been propitiated for a range of benefactions, Bivar's claim is important for suggesting that concrete sociohistorical conditions may have stimulated the spread of her cultus at specific times and places.

Hārītī images are also found in conjunction with those of Pāñcika in the Gāndhāran corpus, either combined in a single relief (Fig. 5.3) or in separate reliefs placed in paired niches. Pāñcika plays a minor role in the legendry of

5.2 Hārītī, Sikri, Pakistan, Kuṣāṇa period, ca. second or third century C.E. Schist, height 35.75 in. (90.8 cm). Lahore Museum, 2100. Photo: The Huntington Archive, The Ohio State University. *Hārītī, stately in Greco-Roman garb, interacts lovingly with her children.*

5.3 Hārītī and Pāñcika, Sahrī Bāhlol, Kuṣāṇa period, ca. second or third century C.E. Schist, height 40 in. (101.6 cm). Peshawar Museum, 241. Photo: The Huntington Archive, The Ohio State University. *Hārītī and Pāñcika, accompanied by capering offspring, personify the prosperity and fertility they bestow.*

Hārītī, appearing briefly as the husband with whom she lived for a period before returning to Rājagṛha with her children to torment the populace. Although written accounts do not reunite the couple, it is unsurprising that the converted Hārītī was once again linked with her spouse to form a divine pair. Pāñcika, a powerful yakṣa general (*senāpati*) and supporter of the Buddha, could easily be envisioned as working in concert with his wife in her benefactory role. Thus, we find a Buddhist missionary in the Kuṣāṇa domain requesting both Hārītī and Pāñcika to "do no further harm to the harvests, cherish all beings and let mankind live in peace."[39]

Just as Hārītī came to represent the aggregate of yakṣiṇīs, Pāñcika could stand for the many yakṣas that follow and support the Buddha. Thus, the two emerged as a popular divine couple in devotional contexts. In artistic representations, Pāñcika is a fitting consort of Hārītī. He is a regal figure, mustachioed, turbaned, richly adorned, and prosperously portly (see Fig. 5.3). His identifying attributes are a spear, reflecting his martial aspect, and a bulging coin purse, signifying the granting of wealth. Surrounded by their thriving progeny, Hārītī and Pāñcika are visibly suited for their role as bestowers of prosperity, fertility, health, and agricultural bounty.[40]

Hārītī and Pāñcika find a close parallel in another pair of divinities depicted in the Gāndhāran repertoire. This couple similarly appears on a shared plinth in flowing robes of non-Indic design. Unlike the barefooted Pāñcika and Hārītī, however, the male figure wears leggings and sandals and the female, too, is shod. The male bears a pouch of wealth, while the female displays a cornucopia. In at least one composition they are shown with a smaller figure that could well be a child. Sometimes mistaken for Pāñcika and Hārītī, the couple, which also appears on Kuṣāṇa coinage, has been identified as Pharro and Ardokhsho, Iranian deities imported by a Kuṣāṇa ruler.[41] Although historically and iconographically distinct from Hārītī and Pāñcika, this pair clearly extends the same promise of wealth and well-being. John Rosenfield opines that, in view of the "syncretic atmosphere of the times," the two couples were surely recognized as symbolically equivalent and probably conflated to some degree.[42]

Another important center of Buddhist artistic production during the Kuṣāṇa era was the Mathurā region. The definitive identification of Hārītī images among the Mathurān remains is problematic. Many of the extant reliefs, carved from porous red sandstone, survive in fragmentary or eroded condition. Moreover, "divine mothers" (*mātṛkā*) constitute one of the most popular subjects of the Mathurān repertoire. These bestowers of fertility and protectors of children are typically shown in the frontal pralambapāda pose, knees spread apart (more pronouncedly than in the Gāndhāran idiom), supporting on their lap an infant, typically cradled with the left hand. An additional child or children of the portly yakṣa type may appear at their feet. Thus, many of these maternal figures display attributes that in a purely Buddhist setting would decisively identify them as Hārītī. The pluralistic Mathurān milieu and popularity of the mātṛkās as objects of propitiation, as well as the diffuse and largely nonsectarian nature of the mātṛkā cult during this period, make such attributions difficult.

Fortunately, one Mathurān relief bears an inscription that identifies the donor as a follower of the Buddha. This, as well as its discovery at a Buddhist site, provides a secure basis for identifying the figure as Hārītī. In the portion the relief that has survived, she is seen to support a child on her capacious lap, while a corpulent yakṣa nestles at her feet.[43] Another probable carving of Hārītī is a relief, its head and right hand missing, in which four children are discernible at her feet (Fig. 5.4). The base portrays an array of small figures in poses suggestive of wrestling and mock combat, including two equestrian figures. This closely reproduces the manner of representing Hārītī's children in a Gāndhāran relief illustrated above (see Fig. 5.3) and another at Ajanta, discussed below. Thus, there is evidence that we find here the Mathurān vision of Hārītī, designed in conformity with the prevailing idiom for portraying divine mothers. Similar infant-cradling figures with one or more children at the base may represent Hārītī as well.[44] Moreover, numerous Mathurān reliefs and fragments depict a couple tentatively identifiable as Hārītī and Pāñcika. These carvings—which feature a child-cradling female accompanied by a corpulent, squatting yakṣa—may represent the Mathurān conception of the pair.[45]

Images of Hārītī dating from the Gupta and post-Gupta eras (fourth through seventh centuries C.E.) are found at the Deccan cave sites (Ajanta, Ellora, Aurangabad) and among the Ratnagiri remains in Orissa. The surviving images represent a small portion of the artistic output of this period. Most of the Buddhist monasteries and even large monastic complexes in northern India were laid to ruin by the series of Muslim invasions that finally brought Indian Buddhism to a close in the twelfth century. As a result, much of the artistic legacy of those periods is lost, including the Hārītī images that I-tsing reported seeing at every monastery he visited in the seventh century. Therefore, the extant stone reliefs are invaluable documents of what was assuredly an extensive corpus of Hārītī images.

In these later representations, the clothing, ornaments, figural type, and posture of Hārītī reflect regional stylistic developments and broader Buddhist iconographic trends. At Ajanta, Hārītī and Pāñcika are the focus of an entire shrine in Cave 2 (fifth century). This famous relief records a transitional phase in the artistic conception of Hārītī. Hārītī has an elaborate hairstyle and a

5.4 Hārītī, Tayapur, Mathura District, Uttar Pradesh, India, Kuṣāṇa period, first century C.E. Red sandstone, height 33 in. (84 cm). Government Museum, Mathura, F 30. Photo: American Institute of Indian Studies. *Mathurān portrayals of Hārītī depict her in the same pose as the divine mothers (*mātṛkā*) widely worshipped in the region.*

coronet reminiscent of the Gāndhāran effigies, but she is bare-breasted and wears a diaphanous lower garment, in conformity with Indic artistic conventions. We see here the massive bodily proportions and rotund breasts that characterized her portrayal for several centuries, conveying her character as a prosperous matron. Her torso receives the frontal, straight-backed treatment typical of Ajanta figures. Her legs, departing from the configuration seen in earlier images, are shown here with one folded inward and the other pendant, in the posture of royal ease (*lalitāsana*). Hārītī supports a child with her left hand, while the right bears a partially effaced object that appears to be a cluster of fruit on a long stem. She is accompanied by Pāñcika, who is seated on her left. Eleven children, two of them straddling horses, wrestle and sport across the lower register of the relief, reproducing the pattern seen in the Gāndhāran and Mathurān examples illustrated above (Figs. 5.3, 5.4).

A distinctive aspect of the Ajanta sanctuary is the presence of a pictorial narrative of Hārītī's conversion and worship. The shrine walls are covered with sculpted and painted vignettes illustrating the well-known story, opening with a flailing, wild-eyed Hārītī approaching the Buddha, followed by a peaceful Hārītī kneeling in reverence, and closing with a scene of women and children bringing and piling offerings before Hārītī and bowing at her feet.[46]

The reliefs at Aurangabad (in a sixth-century cave) and Ellora (seventh century) are iconographically and stylistically similar to the Ajanta relief, although Hārītī's ample body receives a more rounded, softly modeled treatment. The presence of offspring remains constant, as her primary identifying attribute, but her many children are now metonymized by a single child perched on her left thigh, supported by her left hand. Hārītī and Pāñcika are flanked by fan-bearing attendants and flying celestials, representing their honor by divine hosts.[47]

A wonderful relief of Hārītī from Ratnagiri, found in an external niche on the rear porch of Monastery 1 (late seventh or early eighth century), represents her mature and somewhat condensed iconographic conception (Fig. 5.5). Hārītī's hairstyle remains elaborate, piled high on her head and held in place by strands of beads, but she now wears a crown rather than a coronet. It is not the five-pointed crown of an enlightened being but a jeweled diadem adorned with a band of flowers, accentuating her divine status. The ample contours of her body and breasts are accented by intricately detailed ornaments, multiple bangles, a hip girdle with a floral clasp, and bell anklets. Her adorable child, chubby and decked with jewelry, gazes up at his mother. Hārītī's upraised right hand holds a stalk of grain with the treasure-displaying mudrā, signaling her association with agricultural fertility, a theme subtly echoed by the floral pattern on her throne.

5.5 Hārītī, eastern wall of Monastery 1, Ratnagiri, Cuttack District, Orissa, India, ca. late seventh or early eighth century. Chlorite, height 28 in. (71 cm). Photo: American Institute of Indian Studies. *Hārītī appears here with a stalk of grain, floral motifs, and a hen, suggesting her association with agricultural abundance.*

The relief includes a chicken or cock beneath her seat, an unusual motif. This may be a naturalistic detail, reflecting the agrarian aspect of the goddess, or an indication that she was supplicated to safeguard and increase the domestic animals crucial to rural subsistence. The bird may also carry symbolic significance, as seen in a later Hindu context, where we find a cock invoked to "protect his own (devotees) . . . whose body colour is golden . . . whose comb is red, who grants success in all matters."[48] This passage, although much later than the image under discussion, suggestively links the capon with divine blessings and protection. Or the spry bird may simply be, as Debala Mitra suggests, a pet of Hārītī's child.[49]

Very few images of Hārītī are known to survive from the Pāla period (eighth through twelfth centuries). One is a ninth-century votive bronze from Nālandā.[50] Hārītī is shown in what had become her standard posture, with her right leg pendant and a child on her left thigh. Hārītī's body is relatively slender, with a narrow rib cage accentuating generous breasts, in keeping with contemporaneous Bihari figural conventions. A floral garland provides the vegetal motif often found in her representations. Unique to this statue is Hārītī's placement on a lotus pedestal and lion throne with an elaborate *vyālaka* throne back that incorporates mythic creatures, a standard throne type in Buddhist iconography.

A Pāla stone carving, dating from the eleventh or twelfth century, shows that the goddess continued to receive a variety of visual interpretations (Fig. 5.6). The iconography resembles that of the Nālandā statue, except that Hārītī's right hand makes the boon-granting gesture, its palm marked by a small jewel, and her pedestal is a simple rocklike structure. The child cradled on her lap presses his palms together in a gesture of devotion, reverencing his mother, while the child standing on her right thigh also adopts hand gestures implying honor. In the upper corners of the relief, two flying figures bearing garlands render homage from heaven, recalling the song of praise (translated at the beginning of this chapter) eulogizing Hārītī as "honored throughout the universe" and "served by celestial hosts." The flying figures in the lower corners of the relief also suggest this theme.

The additional figures in the stele hold special interest. They appear in areas where Hārītī's children would typically be portrayed, but their activities and attitudes are novel. At Hārītī's feet two females churn butter. On the same plinth a female kneels and a male leans against Hārītī's right leg. The lower register includes a female figure playing a drum, which could be a devotional act or a creative pastime. In the adjacent scene, a kneeling female pays homage to a mother supporting a large, adultlike "child" on her lap. It is difficult to tell whether these figures represent human worshippers or Hārītī's children at play. Because the child on her lap also makes a gesture of homage, however, it is

5.6 Hārītī, Silaur, Saran District, Bihar, India, Pāla period, eleventh or twelfth century. Basalt, height 22 in. (56 cm). Patna Museum, Arch. 6362. Photo: American Institute of Indian Studies. *This stele surrounds Hārītī with celestial worshippers (in the four corners) and casts her children in attitudes of homage.*

possible that the image intentionally homologizes human devotees and Hārītī's offspring as recipients of Hārītī's maternal love.

As in the case of the earlier works, the Pāla images are precious survivals of time, the elements, and the iconoclasts' sword. Another Pāla stone stele, identified elsewhere as Hārītī, is not included in my survey. The subject of the relief, housed in the Dacca Museum, is a female divinity with four arms, displaying in her two upper hands a fish and a skull cup.[51] Although the figure cradles an infant, the fish and the skull cup bear no known association with Hārītī. Moreover, Hārītī does not appear in four-armed form in any other known literary or artistic source. Even in the context of Tantric *yakṣiṇī-sādhana*, wherein one might anticipate iconographic innovation, Hārītī is envisioned in the customary, two-armed manner. The same holds true for her iconography in Tibetan and Newar Buddhism to the present day.[52]

Tibetan observances devoted to Hārītī are limited to the monastic setting. In the Sarma sects, Hārītī, known by her Tibetan name Yidrogma (sometimes shortened to Drogma), receives a share of the main repast of the day, the noontime meal. Each monk and nun sets apart a portion of food as an offering to Hārītī and her offspring. The food is collected and deposited outside the monastery.[53] A Gelug mealtime prayer invokes a range of beings to whom the food is offered, beginning with Buddhas and bodhisattvas and concluding with Hārītī and her five hundred children.[54] When monastics take a communal meal, such as during a summer retreat, a table may be set up on which each cenobite places something from his or her own plate for Hārītī, accompanied by a prayer of dedication.[55]

In contemporary Tibetan monasteries, however, one does not find Hārītī shrines or even Hārītī images used in conjunction with votive food offerings. This has apparently long been the case, for few representations of Hārītī are attested in the Tibetan artistic corpus. She may be shown holding a child, but the mongoose, a symbol of wealth, also appears in her iconography in that setting (Fig. 5.7).[56] This painting depicts Hārītī as white, as she is most commonly described, and portrays her as a beatific and benevolent figure. In addition to the mongoose, the fruit and jewel born by her pudgy child, bouquet of jewels in her gift-bestowing hand, treasure vase supporting her foot, and jewels lining the bottom of the painting all suggest the supplication of Hārītī for wealth. In the Sakya pantheon, Hārītī is envisioned as golden in color and bears a mongoose, goad, and noose but supports no child on her lap, although she is described as surrounded by her children.[57] Painted narratives of the life of Shakyamuni Buddha may include the conversion of Hārītī.[58] Independent representations of the goddess, however, seem to be rare in Tibetan settings.

5.7 Hārītī, Sikkim or Tibet, nineteenth century. Pigment on cloth, 14.6 × 10.6 in. (37 × 27 cm). Musée Guimet, P 474. Photo: Réunion des Musées Nationaux/Art Resource, N.Y. *The presence of the mongoose, bouquet of jewels in her right hand, treasure vase beneath her foot, and lower row of jewels cast Hārītī as a granter of prosperity.*

Mantras and Magical Practices

The earliest strand of Buddhist magical practice consisted of the recitation of spells to elicit the aid and protection supernatural beings. Yakṣas and yakṣiṇīs figured prominently among the beings to be so invoked.[59] Thus, it is not surprising that Hārītī, as a yakṣiṇī, would be associated with this type of practice. We find perhaps the earliest reference to Hārītī in this regard in the *Lotus Scripture* (ca. first or second century C.E.). In the chapter devoted to incantations (termed *dhāraṇī* in this work), ten rākṣasīs (female cannibalistic spirits), listed by name, along with Hārītī and her children and retinue, collectively address Shakyamuni and impart their spell. They vow to protect all who study, follow, and teach the scripture. The dangers from which they promise safety feature a range of harmful spirits, with yakṣas and rākṣasas heading the list. Among the many problems that might be caused by demonic predation, they single out fevers, adducing those that last from one to seven days as well as persistent feverish conditions.[60] A later work, possibly dating from the third or fourth century C.E., prescribes lighting seven lamps before a statue of Hārītī and repeating her mantra seven times.[61] Centuries later, the *Sādhanamālā* (late eleventh or early twelfth century) inserted Hārītī mantras into the liturgies of other deities.[62] The temporal range of these texts suggests that mantric invocation retained an ongoing role in the Hārītī cultus.

When the Tantric movement was gaining momentum, in the seventh and eighth centuries, Hārītī became the focus of a full-blown magical corpus. She figures in this role in two texts translated into Chinese by Amoghavajra (eighth century), the *Sādhana of the Great Yakṣiṇī* and *Scripture of the Mantra of Mother Hārītī*.[63] In both of these works, Hārītī reveals her mantra and its ritual applications to Shakyamuni. The rites belong to a branch of magic known as *yakṣiṇī-sādhana*, or ritual invocation of yakṣiṇīs. This type of practice centers on conjuring a yakṣiṇī through a complement of offerings, mantra recitation, and fire offerings. The rendition of a portrait of the yakṣiṇī is a recurrent feature. The goal of yakṣiṇī-sādhana is to compel a yakṣiṇī to appear before the practitioner in bodily form and render service. The manner of the yakṣiṇī's arrival is foretold, and the aspirant is instructed regarding how to address and behave toward her and what gifts and blessings she may bestow.[64] It stands to follow that Hārītī, as the "supreme yakṣiṇī" (*yakṣeśvarī*), would figure in such rites.

The *Sādhana of the Great Yakṣiṇī* opens with the familiar conversion account. Before taking leave of Shakyamuni, however, Hārītī (under her original name, Abhirati, "Joyous One") offers to reveal her mantra: "I possess a heart mantra (*hṛdaya-dhāraṇī*) capable of removing every misfortune and all fear.

I and all my attendants will protect without ceasing whoever possesses this formula and assure their peace." Her spell, recited in Sanskrit, translates as:

> Homage to the Three Jewels! Homage to Hārītī, the great yakṣiṇī! Unfailing! Truthful! Devoted to the Buddha! Loving toward beings! Surrounded by five hundred children! Benevolent! Glorified! Honored by all! I turn my heart to the noble Hārītī, calling on the power of the Buddha to remember these words. Blessed one, you guard the city! Holy one, you rescue the children of others! Ruler of obstacles! Destroyer of adversity! . . . Excellent one! Truly excellent one! Great leader! Accomplisher of all activities! Let it be so![65]

This relatively lengthy mantra is typically recited 21 or 108 times in order to consecrate ritual objects, accompany offerings and burnt oblations, and invoke Hārītī's presence.

Great attention is given to the ritual preparations. The hierophant must first create a portrait of Hārītī on white cotton or silk. She imparts that she is to be portrayed

> as an angelic celestial (*apsaras*) of great beauty, clothed with precious vestments of red or white Indian silk, wearing a crown, earrings, bracelets of white shell, and ornaments of all types adorning my body. I am seated on a jeweled Dharma-throne, the right foot pendant. On each side of the throne, near the knees, depict two children. The mother, with the left hand, holds to her breast the infant Priyaṇkara, elegant in form. The right hand, drawn near the breast, bears a *bilva* fruit (wood-apple). On the right and left, depict servants and followers bearing white fans and assorted finery.[66]

Having completed the portrait, the practitioner bathes, puts on new clothing, and maintains a state of ritual purity. The next step is to erect an altar in a secret room. On a square platform anointed with a mixture of cow dung and perfumes, a circle is formed from a coating of white sandalwood paste. The altar is decked with banners and strewn with seasonal flowers, and the painting of Hārītī is placed on it.

Sitting in the dark, with only an amaranth torch for illumination, the practitioner invokes Hārītī, contemplating her with unwavering attention and reciting the aforementioned mantra unceasingly: "If, following this method, one proceeds with great concentration and in secret, mother Abhirati will surely show herself in corporeal form and accomplish all that the practitioner commands." When Hārītī appears, the practitioner should continue to recite the mantra and make additional offerings. She will return repeatedly: "Eventually, she will demand of the practitioner, 'What would you have me do?' Or she will remove her earrings, bracelets, or precious adornments. If she hands them over, one must accept them. One cannot refuse, but one must not speak to her. In this way, she will gradually become familiar, and one can speak to her. Then one can request that she be one's mother or sister."[67]

The significance of the roles of mother and sister are not addressed but may be elicited from other sources on yakṣiṇī-sādhana. A mainstay of this genre of magic is that, once summoned, a yakṣiṇī may be requested to serve as a mother, sister, or wife. The maternal role is to provide nurture and sustenance in the form of food, shelter, wealth, or any desired object. The sororal role entails bestowal of treasure, whereas a yakṣiṇī wife becomes a divine lover and companion, often bestowing the gift of magical flight. A given yakṣiṇī may eschew or specialize in one of the three roles. It is consistent with her character that Hārītī will serve only as a mother or sister. The practitioner is forbidden to entertain lustful thoughts toward her, as is commonly the case with yakṣiṇī mothers.

Some of the rules surrounding the rites of Hārītī are typical of yakṣiṇī-sādhana. For instance, they are to be carried out in seclusion and complete secrecy. The hierophant must not speak of the practices or their successful outcome, and it is crucial no one overhear or witness the proceedings. Were this to happen, all the benefits would evaporate and the practitioner would incur misfortune. Even a monastery or temple is deemed too public a setting. Moreover, any wealth or goods thus gained must be shared liberally with others. There are some specific stipulations as well. The ritualist should not feel acrimony toward anyone during the rites, or adversity will befall that person. Furthermore, to assure the ongoing protection of Hārītī, the practitioner should set aside a portion of every meal for her, consecrate the food with mantra, and afterward dispose of it in a pure place. Any food offered to Hārītī must be carried by the votary and may not be eaten by anyone else after it has been offered, or it will have no efficacy as an offering, and the mantra will lose its potency. Another distinctive requirement, following the appearance of Hārītī, is the performance of eighty thousand fire offerings to solidify the attainment and guarantee success in all subsequent ritual activities.[68]

The successful invocation of mother Hārītī and the ability to converse with her face-to-face, impressive an achievement as this may be, simply marks the first step into the supernatural realm of magical abilities to which the ritualist has now gained entrée. The *Sādhana of the Great Yakṣiṇī* describes more than twenty-five additional rites that might be undertaken for varying purposes. There are procedures for healing illness, neutralizing poison, release from demonic possession, and cure of diseases caused by evil spirits. A number of rites pertain to familial matters and affairs of the heart, such as those to secure a woman's affection, reunite with a lost love, establish marital harmony, find a husband for one's daughter, and ease a difficult pregnancy. There are assorted rites for gaining the good graces of an official, victory in debate, a strong memory, and success in a lawsuit. One also finds techniques to silence a slanderer, banish ghosts, and gain the goodwill of someone with whom one is in conflict.

Many of the procedures devolve upon the consecration of food, clothing, or other objects with mantra recitation and presenting them to or burying them near the subject of the rite. One of the noteworthy rituals entails the sanctification of a prepubescent girl (*kumārī*), who then serves as an oracle. Following the lines of *kumārī-pūjā*, the girl is to be bathed, dressed in fresh clothing suitable to the occasion, seated next to the altar with flowers in her hands, and anointed eight hundred times with a sprinkling of perfumed vermilion water and an equal number of mantra recitations. The girl will reveal the location of hidden treasure, and any question may be posed to her. She will utter the answer, or the reply may come in the form of a disembodied voice or message in a dream.[69]

Another notable rite requires the procurement of a human skull, preferably that of an able, strong person. The skull is washed with pure water, immersed in perfumed water, placed on the altar in front of the Hārītī icon, and consecrated with eighty thousand mantra recitations: "That same night, the dead person will speak his name or manifest in corporeal form and demand to serve you. After that, any tasks with which that one is charged will be fully successful." This practice is to be undertaken in utmost secrecy, for obvious reasons.[70] The skull rite and oracular child are not standard to yakṣiṇī-sādhana but recur in the Buddhist and broader Indic ritual repertory. The text includes a section on applications of the spell of Priyankara, the son identified as Hārītī's favorite child in some traditions.

The *Scripture of the Mantra of Mother Hārītī* follows a similar pattern, as Hārītī reveals her dhāraṇī and its powers to Shakyamuni. A distinctive feature of this text, however, is that it is addressed specifically to women with fertility problems. The practice is recommended for women who have been unable to conceive, have miscarried, or cannot bear children for any reason, such as a bodily imbalance, demonic interference, past actions, or karma from previous lives. The ritualist begins by creating a portrait of Hārītī almost identical to the one described in the previous text, except that both legs are pendant and rest on the earth. The notion of a woman who longs for a child painting a likeness of Hārītī circled by her five children (two at her knees, two on her lap, one held to her breast) seems a poignant exercise in sympathetic magic. The altar is decked with flowers, perfumed lustral water, pastries, cakes, fruits, rice flour mixed with milk, and other foods. The image is positioned so that it faces west; the votary faces east, gazing at the image.[71]

The central practice is to recite the mantra one thousand times per session for three daily sessions. Then, when the woman prays before the image for what she desires, her wish will be granted. There are also more specific rites. One, to induce conception, is to collect milk from a cow that has recently calved, store the milk in a silver vessel, and stir the milk while incanting the mantra eighty thousand times. After drinking the milk, the woman will conceive within seven days. Another rite pertaining to childbirth is for a pregnant woman to put ghee (clarified butter) in a golden vessel and chant the mantra unceasingly during a lunar eclipse, until the moon emerges. If the expectant mother then offers part of the ghee to Hārītī and drinks the remainder, the child to which she gives birth will be intelligent and blessed by good fortune.[72]

The practices outlined in these proto-Tantric works lay no claim to salvational import. The ritual procedures and their fruits are advanced as ends in themselves, while Hārītī stands at the portal to this realm of magic. Nonetheless, an ethical veneer is provided by the claim that the rites and spells are imparted so that Buddhists and Buddhist institutions may enjoy protection and security. Hārītī places her practices within the larger Buddhist project when she pronounces that "by means of this dhāraṇī and these practices, I will accomplish the benefit of all beings." Hārītī likens her mantra to a wish-fulfilling jewel, for it "has the power to fulfill all desires and to achieve every kind of benefit and happiness." The Buddha commends her motivation and revelations and charges her to protect his followers and institutions:

> I consign all to your care! You all—you and your dependents—through my Dharma, will zealously protect the monasteries, their residents, monks, disciples, and all humankind. You will not allow evil spirits to cause them any trouble, and you will grant tranquility, until my teachings disappear.[73]

Here we see the formula, found also in the first legend discussed above, that guaranteed the longevity of her worship, namely, that Shakyamuni not only entrusted Hārītī with the protection of his institutions but assigned her this role in perpetuity. Moreover, these Tantric works reassert the perennial purpose and rationale for enrolling supernatural beings in the pantheon. That is, they support the central mission of Buddhism to ease suffering and promote peace of mind. They protect the Dharma, too, by configuring Buddhism into a tradition that not only provides resources for the metaphysical quest but also addresses the fundamental needs of humankind for health, security, progeny, and material goods. Toward this end, the Buddha aptly enlisted the service of many supernatural supporters. One of the most enduring and beloved of these allies was the best of yakṣiṇīs, mother Hārītī.

Hārītī as Mother Goddess

Hārītī is arguably the first true "mother goddess" of Buddhism. Other female figures were accorded honor and even veneration in the cultic life that found expression in early stupa iconography and in Pali writings of the third and second centuries B.C.E. and several hundred years thereafter. None of these female figures, however, was the object of a flourishing devotional cult. Pṛthivī, the earth goddess, esteemed for her crucial role in the enlightenment event, was most often celebrated and portrayed in that context. Māyādevī was lauded for her singular role in birthing Shakyamuni, but the devotional feelings she inspired remained intertwined with the veneration of her remarkable son. Worship of yakṣiṇīs was widespread and vibrant but remained local in character. The appeal of Lakṣmī, worshipped for wealth and well-being, was arguably limited by the absence of legendry linking her specifically with the Buddha.

It was Hārītī, then, who emerged from this constellation of divine females to become an independent and canonically sanctioned object of Buddhist worship. It is interesting to consider why the figure selected for this crucial role was not a tree spirit, lotus goddess, or earth mother, or even the human mother of Shakyamuni, but a divine mother envisioned with children clustered around her body and pressed to her breast. Hārītī contributed to the fund of Buddhist iconography the appealing and comforting image of a mother nursing and watching over her children, one of the purest forms of benevolence and nurture in human experience. Moreover, the nurturing mother is one of the most enduring and potent images of divine succor in Indian religious imagery. Alfred Foucher finds in the elevation of Hārītī evidence of a perennial human impulse, observing that "the most universally attractive role will always revert to those figures which incarnate the maternal . . . grace of the eternal feminine."[74] There can be no doubt that Hārītī provided Buddhism with a feminine face that softened the austere sublimity of the renunciatory ideal and complemented the soothingly androgynous but nonetheless masculine object of worship represented by the Buddha.

It is fascinating to find the worship of a mother goddess flourishing within Buddhist monastic institutions. The surface purport of her legendry is the Buddha's conversion of a death-dealing supernatural damsel into a protector of Buddhist establishments and adherents. Yet, read another way, the story records the conversion of Buddhism into an increasingly and explicitly goddess-worshipping tradition. An eminently maternal divinity, a mother of many children, was brought into the Buddhist fold and placed within the institutional centers of the tradition, the monasteries, with the seal of approval of the enlightened one. Including goddess worship under its expanding canopy made Buddhism more relevant and viable to its followers, allowing Indian Buddhists to direct their reverence for divine females to an expressly Buddhist mother goddess.

CHAPTER 6

Female Buddhas

The Case of Gotamī

Know this, O monks, she was most wise,
With wisdom vast and wide.
She was a nun of great renown,
A master of great powers.
She cultivated "divine-ear"
And knew what others thought.
In former births, before this one,
She mastered "divine-eye."
All imperfections were destroyed;
She'll have no more rebirths.

—*Glorious Deeds of Gotamī*[1]

Mahāpajāpatī Gotamī (Skt. Mahāprajāpatī Gautamī), the maternal aunt of Shakyamuni Buddha, is the woman who raised the Buddha from infancy, after her sister, Queen Māyādevī, died.[2] Little mention is made of Gotamī (pronounced *go tah* MEE) in the pre-enlightenment phase of the biographies of Shakyamuni.[3] She appears in the narratives primarily after his attainment of Buddhahood, when she accepted his teachings and embarked on her own quest for liberation. Most significantly, it was she who created a contemplative order for women. It is in this context that Buddhist literature celebrates the achievements of Gotamī—as the first female to seek monastic vows, the founder of the renunciant order for women, and the much beloved preceptor of the original nuns.

The honor Gotamī might arguably deserve for her part in rearing the Bodhisattva was eclipsed by her monumental role in Buddhist institutional history. Gotamī conceived the plan to seek monastic ordination and create a nun's order, so that women could pursue enlightenment with the discipline and single-minded focus afforded by the renunciatory path. The different narratives agree that Gotamī first approached the Buddha alone with her proposal. She

6.1 Narrative frieze, stupa drum, Kāfir-kot, Gāndhāran region (Pakistan/Afghanistan), Kuṣāṇa period. Gray schist, height 9.25 in. (23.5 cm). The British Museum, 1899.0609.21. Photo copyright The British Museum. *Gotamī leads a group of women to request monastic ordination, supported by Ānanda on the Buddha's left.*

then returned with a group of noblewomen of the Śākya clan who shared her aspiration and joined her in taking tonsure and donning monastic robes for the occasion. Ānanda, the Buddha's personal attendant, interceded on the women's behalf.[4] Thus, he is included in sculpted reliefs that are believed to represent this event.

In this recurrent scene in Gāndhāran art (Fig. 6.1), female figures in aristocratic garb are led by a similarly clothed Gotamī, who bears an offering. Floral details suggest that the gift is a bundled garland. Although the women are said to have taken tonsure, they would be indistinguishable from monks if they were portrayed with shaved heads and monastic robes. Therefore, they are presumably shown in lay attire to disclose their gender. The monk immediately flanking the Buddha on the other side could be none other than Ānanda, who supported the women in their successful petition.[5] The symmetry of male and female figures flanking the Buddha signals that two parallel monastic orders would exist after this event.

As the pioneer of female monasticism, Mahāpajāpatī, the "venerable" (*mahā*) "chief queen" (*pajāpatī*), superceded her contribution as foster mother of the Buddha and achieved a greater destiny—whether historical or legendary—as a pivotal contributor to the legacy of her nephew and foster son. It is natural, then, that she should be acclaimed as an exemplary figure, a paragon of female attainment, in the hagiographic literature that took shape in the ensuing centuries. Gotamī provided the inspiring example of a woman who embodied the ideals of renunciation, discipline, leadership, compassion, and enlightenment.

The early Buddhist pantheon included an array of divine females—featuring Pṛthivī, Lakṣmī, and yakṣiṇīs—who supported those on the Buddhist path and in some cases were aspirants themselves. These goddesses might be beautiful, auspicious, and powerful, but they had not reached the pinnacle of spiritual attainment. The goal of ultimate peace (*parinibbāna*, or *parinirvāṇa*) was seen as the fruition of a distinctively human path of renunciation, meditation, and wisdom, and thus its exemplars were human beings who had successfully traversed that path. Female divinities did not suffice as role models for female renunciants and laywomen who sought affirmation of their capacity, as human women, to attain the ultimate fruit of Buddhist practice. In answer to their need for a human exemplar, the legendary life and accomplishments of Gotamī, tailored by the hagiographer's art, rendered her into a model, at once historical and archetypal, whose attainments matched those of Shakyamuni Buddha.

Whether Gotamī, as a human figure, should be included in a book on goddesses might be questioned. Any consideration of divinities in the Buddhist context must, however, take into account the category of Buddhahood, which, as the supreme spiritual state envisioned by the tradition, has divine and cosmic overtones. Therefore, the present chapter is devoted to Gotamī, the female figure who most closely approaches the status of Buddhahood in early Buddhism.

Biography of Gotamī

A biography of Mahāpajāpatī Gotamī appears in a collection of forty "moral biographies" of enlightened women (*Therī Apadāna*) composed in Pali in the second or first century B.C.E. The *Glorious Deeds of Gotamī* (*Gotamī Apadāna*) is the longest and most elaborate piece in the anthology. Written in poetic verse and a dramatic format centering on dialogue rather than narration, the work was intended for recitation and public performance as a vehicle of religious edification and inspiration.[6] The *Glorious Deeds of Gotamī* reveals what the illustrious foster mother of the Buddha and foremost nun meant for the composers and contemporary audience of the work.

Jonathan Walters has translated Gotamī's poetic biography in full and extensively analyzed its historical context, thematic content, and religious significance. He demonstrates that the text emerges from a period of strong female participation in Buddhism. Epigraphic sources reveal that, from the first century B.C.E. through the first century C.E., nuns wielded substantial political, economic, and social power through their patronage practices and imperial influence, while their literary efforts and participation in public festivals and dramatic performances signal their cultural and civic prominence.[7]

The internal evidence of the *Glorious Deeds of Gotamī* is consistent with such a setting, delivering an unambiguous proclamation and "vindication of woman's religiosity."[8] Assessing the tone of the work as a "voice of leadership and certainty," Walters characterizes it as "the product of women who strove to realize the egalitarian ideal of early Buddhism in a world that listened to their voices, in which they were empowered to represent one half, the woman's half, of the universal Path."[9] Through the composition and public oration of texts such as the *Glorious Deeds of Gotamī*, nuns celebrated their accomplishments and encouraged other women to strive for religious excellence.

Further explicating the religious setting of Gotamī's biography and the internal Buddhist dynamics that gave it rise, Walters emphasizes the strict gender separatism of Theravada institutions, practice, and ideology. Men and women were considered to be on "parallel but separate" paths. This gendered approach to soteriology meant that the religious paradigms available for men, including the biography and past life accounts of the Buddha himself, were not directly applicable as religious models for women.[10] In the irreducibly gendered discourse of Theravada Buddhism, women required female exemplars to model and reflect their religious capacities. It was in this context that Gotamī's biography was articulated as the "supreme religious paradigm for religious women."[11]

What follows is a synopsis of the biography of Mahāpajāpatī Gotamī, drawn from and quoting Jonathan Walters's translation of the *Glorious Deeds of Gotamī*, cited by verse.[12] The events take place in Vaiśālī, where Gotamī established and presided over a female monastic center. Hsuan-tsang, who visited Vaiśālī in the seventh century, reported on a stupa marking the place where Gotamī and her congregation of nuns realized enlightenment.[13] The entire *Glorious Deeds* transpires on the final day of Gotamī's life, which occasions the narration of her past lives, accomplishments, death, funeral, and imminent destiny.

Gotamī was dwelling in Vaiśālī as the leader of a community of five hundred nuns and an unspecified number of resident laywomen when she decided that her time to depart the world had come. Her ability to make this decision is the first textual indication of her spiritual attainments. To choose the exact time and manner of one's death requires supreme detachment from life, conquest of the fear of death, and thorough self-mastery. Gotamī proceeded to prepare her followers for her departure from their midst. She announced her decision and delivered a final sermon to her lay followers, exhorting them to embrace the renunciatory path with fervent dedication and sealing her farewell with the advice, "If you love me, be like me" (vv. 28–29). When the laywomen were nonetheless overcome by grief, she urged them to view her leave-taking as a joyous event: "Today's a day to laugh!" (v. 20). She then set out with her coterie of nuns to secure the Buddha's approval for her decision.

In her addresses to the nuns, monks, and Shakyamuni, Gotamī explained the timing of her final departure by pronouncing that she had attained her earthly and spiritual goals and was satisfied with her accomplishments. She boasted that she gained ordination for women and "taught and instructed nuns" (vv. 45–46), referred to herself as "one who's done the work" (v. 91), and expressed contentment with her life: "The existential desert's crossed; the Dharma makes me shine" (v. 54). She reviewed the stages of realization that she had traversed: "Defilements gone I've abolished existence . . . breaking every single fetter . . . I attained the three special knowledges . . . the four analytic knowledges, the eight deliverances, the six higher knowledges. . . . The Buddha's teaching is achieved!" (vv. 76–78). Gotamī also pointed out that she had reached the ripe old age of 120 years and remarked, "That much is old enough . . . I'll now go out!" (v. 93). (Regardless of her vaunted age, she was assuredly older than the Buddha, who was soon to pass away at the age of eighty.)

Gotamī acknowledged her supreme debt to the Buddha, whose shining example sent her forth on her own spiritual journey. Not satisfied merely to bask in his illuminated presence, she became determined to quest for liberation herself. She exulted, "Now that I've become perfect, my mind is quenched by dharma-taste" (v. 50). She announced that the Buddha, too, would soon depart and reflected that even the presence of a Buddha in the world is not reason enough to remain, since all things are impermanent: "Who needs your face and body . . . ? Everything conditioned changes; it provides no comfort" (v. 138). Gotamī dispelled any tendency that others may have to interpret her decision as an expression of distress or melancholy. Her calm resolve and triumphal attitude ring in her words: "This is the time for drums of joy!" (v. 27) and "The time to laugh has come!" (v. 64). Hers was a spirit empowered by nonattachment to the impermanent body and the world surrounding her.

On her final day, Gotamī also exhibited her supernatural powers (*ṛddhi*). Although such powers are a natural concomitant of spiritual advancement, any display of magical abilities without a specific heuristic or salvific intent is discouraged in the Buddhist context. However, in order to dispel the skepticism of "fools who doubt that women too can grasp the truth," the Buddha encouraged her to perform supernatural feats: "Show miracles, that they might give up their false views" (v. 79). Gotamī proceeded to leap into the sky, multiply her body, disappear, walk through walls, sink into the earth, walk on water, fly, use the cosmic pillar as the handle of her parasol, cup mountains and oceans in the palm of her hand, wreathe the earth in flames, cause rain to pour from her hand, conceal the sun and moon with her fingertips, garland herself with suns and moons, and magically generate and then dissolve a vast array of nuns (vv. 80–90).

At this juncture in the narrative, the five hundred nuns who accompanied Gotamī to the dwelling place of the Buddha rose into the air: "Just like stars, those great women then shone" (v. 120). They proceeded to display their own supernormal powers (vv. 120–23). The women addressed the Buddha on their attainments and announced that, thanks to Gotamī's compassion in founding a nun's order, they too had abolished all defilements, attained perfect knowledge, and realized the Buddha's teachings (vv. 124–28). The nuns' words evoke an image of an erudite female congregation: "We understand meanings and doctrinal things, etymology and how to preach" (v. 130). The nuns proclaimed that they, too, would take their leave of existence and accompany Gotamī into the realm of ultimate quiescence: "With every imperfection gone, we won't be born again" (v. 129).

Thus having announced her imminent departure to Shakyamuni, paid her respects to him one last time, and fulfilled his last request of her, Gotamī returned to the nunnery and arranged herself in a meditative posture, sitting upright with her legs crossed, preparing herself to cross the threshold of death in a state of mindful awakeness. The laywomen, weeping and crying out in distress, begged the foremost nun, their refuge, not to abandon them (vv. 142–43). Gotamī's parting words echo the Buddha's farewell speech in the *Mahāparinibbāna Sutta*. Addressing her final message to a foremost lay disciple, she instructed her not to grieve but to remember that all things are impermanent and to strive for liberation from the bonds of existence (vv. 143–44). Gotamī then commenced to traverse a series of higher states of consciousness (infinite space, pure perception, and nothingness whatsoever) and, "rising up, she went out like a fuelless lamp's flame" (v. 148).

The authors of the *Glorious Deeds* leave no doubt that Gotamī has attained ultimate liberation. Hers was not an ordinary death that led to rebirth but a passage into parinirvāṇa, the great, mysterious, unconditioned beyond. She had exhausted the fuel of existence, karma, and thus carried with her no vestige of personal consciousness or attachment that would ensnare her in the round of earthly existence. The text regularly returns to this theme: "This one now is all dissolved" (v. 151), "Gotamī . . . is now gone out completely" (v. 180), "She now is cool, she's well gone out" (v. 182). In keeping with the indescribability of that state, "it's not known where she went" (v. 187), "even the Buddha . . . cannot see where she went" (v. 159), but, in any case, "those with solid happiness do not get born again" (v. 188).

Gotamī's decease was an event of global and cosmic proportions, for the entire world shakes at the passing of a great soul. Thus, when Gotamī passed away, the earth quaked, lightning flashed, flowers rained from the sky, Mount Meru trembled, and the ocean wept in distress. Her funeral was a magnificent event, staged by humans and divine beings. A golden, gabled pavilion was erected to shelter her body. Four gods lifted the bier, which was covered by a canopy decorated with gold stars, sun, and moon. A carpet of flowers was spread, and the real moon and stars shone at midday. Human mourners bore incense and banners of tribute; gods offered garlands, dance, and song; supernatural hosts paid homage. Surrounding the funereal shrine of Gotamī were the biers of the five hundred nuns who followed her into the sorrowless realm. The narrator of the text eulogizes:

> The Buddha's great nirvāṇa, good,
> but not as good as this one:
> Gotamī's great going out
> was positively stellar. (v. 173)

Because five hundred nuns also figure in Gotamī's legend, Walters regards it as a collective biography.[14] The nuns explained that they chose to depart the world with Gotamī just as she had devoted herself to and remained close to them during life. Thanks to her guidance, their level of spiritual attainment matched hers, making it possible for them to make such a decision:

> Along with us you left your home
> and also left the world.
> Again together all of us
> to the great nirvāṇa city go! (v. 11)

There is also an implication that the nuns did not wish to remain after the decease of their beloved teacher and mentor, just as Gotamī chose not to witness the Buddha's demise. The inclusion of a large congregation of female disciples in Gotamī's story forecloses on the inference that she is a uniquely accomplished woman and makes it clear that she is not an anomaly, token, or isolated case. The writers of this text offer an unambiguous portrait of women's capabilities and deliver their proclamation in clarion, victorious tones that would surely encourage others to emulate the lofty example they set forth.

The Buddhahood of Gotamī

The *Glorious Deeds of Gotamī* is patterned on the *Mahāparinibbāna Sutta*, which describes the final day and demise of Shakyamuni Buddha. Jonathan Walters delineates numerous structural and thematic parallels between the two works, arguing that both the literary structure and the content of Gotamī's biography are designed to present her as a female counterpart to the Buddha.[15] The text does not directly refer to her as a Buddha, nor would Theravada doctrine permit the bestowal of this title on more than one person at a time. Nonetheless, Gotamī's spiritual path, accomplishments, and death are explicitly presented as analogous and equal to those of the Buddha. Walters maintains that the authors of the text chose to highlight the intended analogy by referring to the Buddha's foster mother as Gotamī, the clan name that she shares with the Buddha and a female version of his appellation Gotama, rather than by using her given name, Mahāpajāpatī.[16]

Gotamī also fulfilled the role of a Buddha by winning liberation not only for herself but for many others as well,[17] as highlighted by the repeated reference to the five hundred nuns. Walters explains that "her Buddhahood is important precisely because it verifies the goal of female monastic practice" and concludes that "Gotamī is the Buddha for women."[18] He elaborates that her biography

> provided an independent ontological basis for the female Path, a female Buddha. Thus the arhatship of women is not dependent on Gotama, but on Gotamī: it was she who founded the nuns' order, it was her *parinibbāna* that cleared the way for nuns to reach the goal.[19]

Although Shakyamuni Buddha bodied forth the fruition of human potential, his male gender lent a potential qualification and exclusivity to his attainment in the irreducibly gendered discourse of Theravada Buddhism. One result was the Theravada doctrine that a female could not become a Buddha. Although this tenet, mentioned only twice in the voluminous Pali canon, appears not to have been a central one, its presence records one possible reply to the question of whether it is possible to attain the level of Buddhahood in a female lifetime.[20] A different response is recorded in the *Glorious Deeds of Gotamī*, which adopts the unequivocal stance that women can indeed follow the spiritual path to its ultimate conclusion and hence attain a state equivalent to Buddhahood.

Walters argues that although Theravadin women could theoretically have elected to promote an androgynous ideal and assert the irrelevance of gender to spiritual attainment (a doctrinal turn taken in the Mahayana movement), they remained within the gendered parameters of Theravada thought and affirmed women's spiritual potential *as women.*[21] Although the authors could not honor Gotamī with the title of "Buddha," they could maintain that her achievements exceeded those of Shakyamuni in one area, for the Buddha was not followed into parinirvāṇa by any of his disciples, whereas five hundred of Gotamī's congregation of nuns were so intensely devoted and highly accomplished that they accompanied her on her final journey.

Contending Views

The *Glorious Deeds of Gotamī*, as its title signifies, glorifies Gotamī's accomplishments and concedes no limitations on her institution-building efforts or spiritual attainments. Her career is presented as a paradigm for women who would undertake the disciplines of monasticism or pursue the fruits of Buddhist practice in the context of lay life. The celebratory and affirmational message of the biography is, however, by no means univocal in the tradition as a whole. As is well documented in western scholarship, a different and less appreciative assessment of Gotamī and the extent of her achievements appears in Pali literature compiled and canonized by male monastics. The qualified portrayal of her success in founding a nun's order and prescribed restrictions on female independence and leadership in the organizational structure reflect the androcentric bias and at times misogynistic tenor of that literature.[22]

In view of the fact that women's religious roles and status have been contested and constantly reconfigured in Buddhist institutional and doctrinal history, it is not surprising to encounter passages in the *Glorious Deeds of Gotamī* that seem to address and refute opposing viewpoints. For example, when the nuns voice their gratitude for Gotamī's concern for them and recount their achievements—including the attainment of enlightenment—under her leadership and tutelage, one may discern a subtle rebuke of members of the community who would discourage female monasticism. In its emphasis on Gotamī's compassion, the text may intend to imply a lack of this trait—the core ethical value of Buddhist morality—in those who would limit women's access to religious training and its fruits. Indeed, the rhetorical intentions of the text are unmistakable when Shakyamuni directs Gotamī to display her supernatural powers so that "fools who doubt that women too can grasp the truth . . . might give up their false views" (v. 79).

Another dispute that the text may be addressing is an issue ancillary to women's attainment of Buddhahood, namely, whether a woman can advance toward Buddhahood in a series of *female* lifetimes as a Bodhisattva.[23] That all the former lives of significant progress recounted by Gotamī are female incarnations (vv. 95–114), just as Shakyamuni and accomplished monks cite primarily male rebirths, further supports the work's affirmation of women's religious capacities by positing that women, as women, may progress along the path to Buddhahood, in a single lifetime or over the course of many female lifetimes.

Regardless of the degree to which the authors crafted the *Glorious Deeds of Gotamī* with self-conscious ideological intent, divergences among extant texts demonstrate that documents emanating from particular factions may not speak for the entire tradition. Moreover, Gotamī's biography exemplifies that Buddhist women have not universally conceded to men the right to define or delimit their spirituality. The history of Buddhism includes groups of women who developed their own sources of inspiration, celebrated their own role models, and forged a tradition that was meaningful and empowering to them.

Later generations would turn their attention to divine archetypes, but Theravada women chose a human exemplar. In the centuries following the founding of Buddhism, Theravadin women took the initiative to select and honor their own enlightened role model: Gotamī, the first nun and female teacher—the woman who for them embodies the ideals of detachment from worldly life, dedication to contemplation, fearless leadership, compassionate concern for others, and supreme spiritual awakening.

Part Two

MAHAYANA MOTHERS OF LIBERATION

CHAPTER 7

Goddesses in the *Flower Ornament Scripture*

> Then Sudhana, having seen the night goddess's enlightening liberation, prostrated himself before her, enraptured: "I have seen your immense body, beautified as the sky is by stars. Your aura of light pervades everywhere endlessly. Myriad pure suns emerge from your mouth; your sunlight shines. Pure moon and star lights radiate from your eyes and pervade the ten directions, illumining the world and destroying darkness. Your body appears before all beings everywhere, creating joy."
>
> —*Flower Ornament Scripture*[1]

India's divine landscape has perennially been populated with multitudes of female divinities: village goddesses, household goddesses, goddesses of twilight and crossroads, mountains and hills, rivers and ponds, groves and trees, dusk and dawn, stars and sky—goddesses, in fact, indwelling virtually every aspect of the phenomenal world. Evidenced in ancient terracotta and stone images and sites of prehistoric antiquity, these pervasive goddesses received limited attention in textual traditions before the first century of the common era, when their worship began to percolate in the classical salvific systems. This cultural trend, well documented in scholarship on Hindu texts, is also manifest in Buddhist works.

An important document of the ascent of goddesses in a Mahayana context is the *Avataṃsaka Sūtra*, or *Flower Ornament Scripture* (first or second century C.E.). An extensive galaxy of goddesses appears in the *Gaṇḍavyūha* portion of the work, which relates the journey of the lay pilgrim Sudhana on his quest for enlightenment. Each teacher describes his or her own spiritual odyssey, bequeaths a lesson or vision, and then directs the seeker to another guide for more advanced instruction. Sudhana traverses northeastern and southern India and sojourns in celestial realms. His diverse preceptors include monastics and laity, royalty and commoners, adults and children, priests and courtesans. He also encounters a range of divine beings who appear before him in visionary splendor. This wide spectrum of teachers powerfully evokes the Mahayana ethos as one in which all beings—human and divine, Buddhist and not explicitly Buddhist—are involved in the grand drama of universal awakening.

The *Gaṇḍavyūha*, a classical source on Mahayana thought and practice, also serves as a cosmological atlas, revealing that Sudhana inhabited a religious world replete with divine females. Not only are goddesses (*devatā*) included among his preceptors but, remarkably, they form the most populous group by far. Twelve of his major teachers were goddesses, and some of these were accompanied by retinues of hundreds of thousands of goddesses.[2] Additional goddesses find mention as teachers of Sudhana's guides and as transitional figures that prepare him for the next stage of his journey. By contrast, Sudhana had only one brief meeting with a god, Mahādeva, who appeared without attendants. This encounter spans less than two pages of the printed Sanskrit text, whereas the episodes centering on goddesses occupy 143 pages, a number that would be increased were the discussions of all the female divinities he met along the way included. This dramatic contrast surely reflects the religious preferences of the authors and immediate audience of the work.

Predication of Enlightenment by the Earth Goddess

The first goddess who assisted Sudhana in his quest was the earth goddess, designated here as Sthāvarā, "Steadfast," and by her popular appellation Pṛthivī. Sudhana found her residing at Bodhgayā in Magadha, where she witnessed Shakyamuni's enlightenment and remains to oversee the enlightenment of all Buddhas. Sthāvarā proclaimed, "I have seen the spiritual transformations of all those buddhas when they came to the site of enlightenment."[3] She and her entourage of ten hundred thousand earth goddesses heralded the pilgrim's advent, prophesying that he would attain liberation and become a refuge for all living beings. The fertile powers of the earth goddesses sparked an exuberant blossoming of nature:

> Those earth goddesses, led by Sthavara . . . emerged from the surface of the earth, with all tree sprouts growing, all flowering trees blooming, all rivers flowing, all lakes and ponds rising, fragrant rains showering, great winds bearing flowers . . . and hundreds of billions of treasuries surfacing.[4]

Here the role of mother earth parallels the one she played in the enlightenment of Shakyamuni. On the eve of his complete awakening, the Buddha-to-be called on her to attest to his right to attain enlightenment, for she alone had witnessed the many lifetimes he spent on her surface pursuing truth and virtue.[5] Serving again as witness and legitimator, the earth goddess predicted Sudhana's enlightenment, certifying that "this is a spot of ground where you have planted roots of goodness, which I have witnessed."[6]

Sudhana paid his respects to Sthāvarā, heartened by her assurance that he would reach his goal. She then touched the earth with the sole of her foot, causing countless jewels to appear, a visual symbol of Sudhana's treasury of merit. This reflects an Indic belief that the touch of a woman's foot can cause trees to bear fruit, vines to blossom, and buried treasures to surface. For Buddhists, Sthāvarā reigns supreme among the legions of earth goddesses because she presides over the site of the ultimate treasure, Buddhahood. It is appropriate that Sudhana should honor her and receive her blessings.

Sudhana met the earth goddess more than halfway through his pilgrimage, as the thirtieth of his fifty-three teachers. This location in the progressive sequence of the journey is purposive. It is a common motif in Mahayana narratives that, after a period of struggle and progress, a prediction of enlightenment fortifies the seeker for the remainder of the quest. When full awakening will take place in a future life, a Buddha makes the pronouncement. When the goal is imminent in the present lifetime, the earth goddess issues the proclamation, as seen in this account. Meeting the earth goddess and receiving her prophecy was a decisive turning point in Sudhana's journey, an infallible sign of his impending enlightenment.

Goddesses of the Night Sky

After leaving Sthāvarā, Sudhana commenced to visit nine "night goddesses" (*rātri-devatā*) in turn—the only long series of a single type of teacher in the *Gaṇḍavyūha*. Some of the most exquisite illustrations of the surviving palm-leaf manuscripts of the text, executed in Nepal, depict Sudhana's meetings with these nocturnal divinities. Against the background of a starlit night sky, a graceful blue goddess lightly clad in gossamer garments as diaphanous as clouds delivers a discourse to Sudhana, who kneels at her feet with hands pressed together in homage and prayerful attention (Fig. 7.1).[7]

The meetings with the night goddesses clearly inspired the imaginations of the readers and illustrators of this scripture. The lengthy treatment of this series of teachers renders tribute to a common type of divinity in India, where deities of the night sky, planets, stars, moon, and lunar phases are often feminine in gender.[8] These as well as myriad other female divinities preside over the darkness and become active and tangible to the worshipper at night in the form of visions, dreams, and temple visitations. The nocturnal goddesses would be

7.1 Night Goddess Instructing Sudhana, Nepal, twelfth century. *Gaṇḍavyūha* manuscript folio, detail. Ink and color on palm leaf, height 2 in. (5 cm). Los Angeles County Museum of Art, From the Nasli and Alice Heeramaneck Collection, Museum Associates purchase, M.71.1.1f. Photo copyright 2004 Museum Associates/ LACMA. *Sudhana kneels before the night goddess in a devotional attitude as he receives her teachings.*

found among the deities worshipped in a given region by Buddhists and Hindus alike. Further, the celestial goddesses naturally appealed to the authors of the *Flower Ornament Scripture* as exemplars of the spacious awareness, purity, and expansiveness of being sought by Mahayana bodhisattvas.

Vāsantī, "Lady of Springtime," was the first night goddess to be visited by Sudhana.[9] He found her inhabiting the sky above Kapilavastu, the capital of the Śākya clan into which Shakyamuni Buddha was born. In order to invoke Vāsantī, Sudhana stood in the middle of a crossroads at twilight, concentrated on his longing to see her, and generated a strong desire for a vision. This reflects a widespread Indic belief that primeval goddesses preside over crossroads, or places where three roads meet. It was and is the practice of local worshippers as well as merchants, nomads, and other travelers to salute the goddesses as they pass and make offerings to them there at nightfall.[10] Sudhana was clearly following that custom. As a young Indian man it was natural for Sudhana to go to a crossroads to invoke a goddess, while as a Mahayana seeker it was suitable for him to respect a being with a non-Buddhist pedigree as a "spiritual benefactor" and "abode of knowledge."

As Sudhana gazed into the night sky, Vāsantī revealed herself in all her glory:

> He saw the night goddess Vasanti in the sky over Kapilavastu, in a tower of brilliant, incomparable jewels, sitting on a great jewel lion throne in the calyx of a lotus of all the finest fragrances. She was beautiful, with a golden complexion, soft, rich black hair, and dark eyes. Her body was adorned with all kinds of ornaments, and she was wearing a red robe. She wore a sacred crest adorned with the orb of the moon, and her body showed reflections of all the stars and constellations. He also saw in her pores all the sentient beings who had been liberated by her from the calamities of unfavorable circumstances, evils, and miserable conditions.[11]

Sudhana was enraptured by the stunning vision of a goddess clothed in the red robe of the sunset sky. With her crown adorned by the moon and body ornamented by stars and constellations, she displayed the awe-inspiring splendor of the starry firmament.

Vāsantī described her religious practices, spiritual odyssey, and versatile saving powers. She revealed that she always takes female embodiment and had incarnated as a goddess in numerous lifetimes. She imparted that other night goddesses had assisted her on her own religious path and that she now uses celestial phenomena as instruments of her compassion:

> For those on land on a dark night, where there are thickets and brambles, gravel and grit, on uneven terrain, battered by vicious wind and rain, painfully cold or hot, where savage beasts lurk, where killers and bandits roam, I save those who have lost their way on the earth, by means of the forms of the sun, the risen moon, meteoric showers, planets, the light of the stars, celestial beings, and enlightening beings.[12]

Vāsantī's powers are akin to those of Rātri, Vedic goddess of the night. Rātri was glorified for safeguarding nocturnal wayfarers from the natural and human dangers of the night and for illumining the darkness.[13]

Clearly, then, Vāsantī reflects a long-held belief that the illumination of the night by heavenly bodies is a great blessing and divine gift. In defining her character, however, the traditional vocations of a night goddess are recast as the ministrations of a bodhisattva who uses every resource at her command to assist and liberate others. Sudhana's song of praise conveys the devotional ecstasy that Vāsantī inspired, extolling those qualities of the goddess of the night sky that reflect his religious ideals: her transcendent purity, her illumination of the world and the human spirit, the vastness of her all-pervading mind, and the clouds of enlightening displays that flow from her heavenly body.[14]

Impressed by the astronomical virtues of the first nocturnal goddess he encountered, Sudhana sought and received teachings from the eight night goddesses illuminating the sky above the site of enlightenment in Magadha. These meetings constitute a lengthy portion of the *Gaṇḍavyūha*.[15] The goddesses are endowed with explicitly Buddhist names, such as Samantagambhīraśrīvimalaprabhā ("Universally Profound and Stainless Radiance") and Sarvanagara-rakṣāsaṃbhava-tejaḥśrīḥ ("Glorious One Whose Brilliance Protects All Cities"). Such lengthy Sanskrit compounds are unlikely sobriquets for Indic goddesses of the night, twilight, and crossroads, who usually possess names in local dialects. Providing these divinities with Buddhist epithets integrates them into the Mahayana salvational scheme and commends them as advanced beings well on their way to enlightenment, worthy of reverence and discipleship.

Teachings on Birth by the Goddess of Lumbinī Grove

Along with goddess figures, a range of female motifs and symbols receive attention and elaboration in the *Flower Ornament*. Motherhood, the womb, gestation, and birth are celebrated as the epitome of purity and the miracle of manifestation. This imagery reflects a sophisticated understanding of phenomenal appearance refined through centuries of metaphysical inquiry, namely, that a concrete agent or principle of causality can never be found and therefore that all phenomenal arising is miraculous, spontaneous, and illusory. All things are born out of emptiness, take form in empty space like clouds coalescing in the sky, shimmer momentarily like a magician's illusion, and then dissolve back into the cosmic source. In this prevalent Mahayana view, the world of appearances shares in the purity and ultimate meaningfulness of its ontological matrix, emptiness, the womb of reality.

The symbolism of the womb, motherhood, and a Buddha's birth are elaborated in the account of Sudhana's meeting with Sutejomaṇḍalaratiśrī, the "grove goddess" (*vana-devatā*) of Lumbinī, where Shakyamuni was born. She explained that she chose to preside over this woodland because she foresaw that a Buddha would be born there. Under her auspices, the grove transformed itself into a fitting environment for a Buddha's birth, providing smooth terrain strewn with gems, trees laced with jewels and flower garlands, and blossoming lotuses in the ponds. Females of various classes of being heaped offerings under the tree where the holy birth would take place and gathered reverently in the arbor to await the arrival of Māyādevī.[16]

Sudhana interrogated the goddess of the Lumbinī grove about how to be born into the lineage of Buddhas, a topic on which she is expert by virtue of having sheltered the births of many Buddhas with the lush, twining vegetation of her body.[17] As presiding goddess of the sacred grove where Shakyamuni was born, Sutejomaṇḍalaratiśrī can describe the conditions of such a birth, as well as the nativity itself. In a poetic stream of visionary ecstasy, the grove goddess eulogized the miracles and cosmic events that took place in Māyādevī's body, beginning with an outpouring of healing light:

> As Lady Maya leaned against the holy fig tree, all the world rulers, the gods and goddesses of the realm of desire . . . and all the other beings who had gathered there to make offerings to the enlightening being were bathed in the glorious radiance of Maya's body . . . and all the lights in the billion-world universe were eclipsed by Maya's light. The lights emanating from all her pores . . . pervaded everywhere, extinguished all the pains of the . . . beings in all states of existence, then remained, shining, illuminating.[18]

Sutejomaṇḍalaratiśrī expressed her wonderment at Queen Māyā's cosmic womb and body. Māyādevī became a veritable world mother as universes streamed from her body. She in turn appeared simultaneously in each universe, standing in a sacred grove, about to give birth.[19] The name Māyādevī, translatable as "Goddess of Magical Creation," fittingly describes her as a mistress of illusory manifestation. Her ability to multiply her physical form and appear in many universes is a magical power enjoyed by highly realized beings. Just as the Buddha performed this miracle when he revealed the *Lotus Scripture*, Māyādevī manifested this supernatural display on the eve of the Buddha's birth. According to the goddess of Lumbinī, to see Māyādevī on this occasion was to recognize her body as the cosmos, for everything in the universe was visible within her womb and indeed in each of her pores.[20]

Innumerable mansions, diamond nets, fragrances, ornaments, and statues cascaded from Māyādevī's womb, followed by millions of bodhisattvas, to herald the birth. Finally the Buddha-to-be was born, a birth described in language that explicitly evokes the miraculous nonproduction and uncaused nature of all phenomena: "Thus did the enlightening being manifest emergence from the abdomen of Lady Maya, by the nature of manifestation of illusory form, by the nature of noncoming, by the nature of manifestation of appearance to the world without origin or extinction."[21] No stigma attaches here to the process of birth, and Māyādevī's womb is glorified without reservation.

Although the *Flower Ornament* devotes little attention to sexuality, it dwells on the natural yet miraculous processes of birth and creation. In dualistic philosophies that separate mind and body, or pure spirit and impure matter, the female body and especially the womb are often maligned as the gateway into the prison of matter. In the nondualistic Mahayana ethos, however, birth, like all phenomenal arising, is miraculous and illusory. All things are born out of emptiness, shimmer momentarily in empty space, and then dissolve back into the cosmic source. Emptiness is the fertile matrix of reality, and, as the grove goddess revealed, the womb possesses the same wondrous power of manifestation.

Final Meetings with Goddesses

After his stirring meeting with Sutejomaṇḍalaratiśrī at the grove where Shakyamuni was born, Sudhana returned to Kapilavastu, the city where the Buddha grew up as a prince in the ruling clan. There the pilgrim encountered a goddess named Aśokaśrī ("Sorrowless Glory"). She was not one of his major teachers but rather a transitional figure who welcomed Sudhana into the presence of his next guide. Aśokaśrī presided over a bodhisattva meeting hall, indicating that a Buddhist place of assembly might have a tutelary goddess, just as would a familial residence. Aśokaśrī was accompanied by ten thousand "house goddesses" (*gṛha-devatā*), a populous genre in India. The house goddesses welcomed Sudhana, praising his aspiration and honoring him with magically emanated jewels, perfumes, and garlands.[22]

Within the meeting hall, Sudhana encountered his next teacher, Gopā, the wife of Shakyamuni. Gopā told of a former lifetime in which, as the daughter of a courtesan and trained in all the arts of a courtesan herself, she had married the Bodhisattva, who was a prince in that lifetime. Together they worshipped the Buddha of that age. Gopā advised Sudhana on how to maintain purity of motivation and aspiration while participating fully in worldly life and then directed him to seek out Māyādevī.[23]

Along the way, the pilgrim met two goddesses who prepared him for that momentous meeting. The first was Ratnanetrā ("Jewel Eyes"), the "city goddess" (*nagara-devatā*) of Kapilavastu. As a city goddess, Ratnanetrā represents a type of divinity found throughout India, in many variations, as the patron mother of a particular village or town.[24] The jewel-eyed goddess appeared in the sky above her city, surrounded by "sky goddesses" (*gagana-devatā*), bearing a basket of celestial flowers. She showered blossoms on Sudhana while she discoursed on the need to guard, expand, and illuminate the citadel of the mind.[25]

The goddess Dharmapadma-śrīkuśalā ("Auspicious Glory of the Lotus of Truth") then advanced with her retinue to fill the seeker with light in preparation for Māyādevī's resplendent presence. These goddesses surrounded him with rainbow webs of luminosity and poured light beams into his body, illuminating him with supernal radiance.[26] Their mistress praised Queen Māyādevī, heightening Sudhana's anticipation to behold her glory.

Thus prepared by several goddesses and their retinues, as well as by Gopā, Sudhana came at last into the exalted presence of Māyādevī, enthroned on a magnificent, gem-laden lotus in a jeweled golden tower. She proceeded to reveal the infinite dimensions of her womb, which had expanded during her pregnancy to encompass the universe itself:

> My body outreached all worlds, and my belly became as vast as space, and yet did not go beyond the human physical size. The supernal manifestations of the enlightening beings' abode in the womb everywhere in the ten directions all appeared in my body. . . . Once all of them were in my belly, they walked around in strides as big as a billion-world universe, even as big as worlds as numerous as atoms in untold buddha-lands. Also all the untold congregations of enlightening beings . . . in all worlds in the ten directions entered my belly. . . . Yet even though it took in all those multitudes, my belly was not enlarged, nor did this body of mine become any more than a human body.[27]

These disorienting visions of mind-expanding vastness, with their astronomically large numbers of light rays, beings, and worlds emerging from a single atom or pore of skin, express a key insight of Hua-yen philosophy, namely, that enlightenment unveils a realm of unlimited possibilities. Normally humans operate in one dimension of reality, whereas enlightenment reveals infinite experiential realms that encompass and interpenetrate one another. As a Hua-yen text, the *Flower Ornament Scripture* envisions the universe as a womb of infinite possibilities and a web so intricately interwoven that every single event, from the flapping of a butterfly's wing to the birth of a Buddha, reverberates simultaneously in every world throughout the cosmos. This is expressed doctrinally as the mutual interpenetration and nonobstruction of all phenomena. Sudhana's pivotal meeting with Queen Māyādevī revealed this truth.

Māyādevī sent Sudhana to the final goddess among his major teachers. In order to meet her, Sudhana sojourned to Trāyastriṃśa Heaven, abode of the gods. His ability to visit a celestial realm after encountering so many goddesses on the earth demonstrates the immense progress that he had made under their tutelage. There he met Surendrābhā, a "divine maiden" (*deva-kanyā*) who had mastered the art of "unimpeded recollection." She charged him to remember all the Buddhas and the entirety of the teachings he had received.[28]

Goddesses in the Expanding Mahayana Cosmology

Sudhana's meetings with the goddesses may be said to represent the apogee of his journey. The literary structure of the *Gaṇḍavyūha* highlights these encounters in several ways. Compositionally, they receive emphasis by virtue of their occurrence as a series, the only example of a lengthy sequence of the same type of figure.[29] In terms of numerical representation, the goddesses constitute a high percentage of his teachers, that is, more than one-fifth of his guides. Proportionately, the goddesses constitute a major focus of the scripture and vehicle of its message. Nearly 40 percent of the text is devoted to their description and teachings.[30] Moreover, they are attributed with some of the pivotal revelations, such as the prediction of Sudhana's enlightenment and the discourse on the birth of a Buddha. The denouement is arguably the encounter with Māyādevī, for she revealed within her universal womb a vision of reality in which all things harmoniously coexist and interpenetrate one another, the key doctrine of Hua-yen metaphysics.

After leaving the goddesses, Sudhana had seven brief meetings, each described in several lines of text, and a relatively short interview with two children. He then proceeded to his culminating encounters with Mañjuśrī, Maitreya, and Samantabhadra, the celestial bodhisattvas who unveiled enlightenment in its cosmic totality, bringing Sudhana's quest to fruition.

Judging from the content and literary structure of the *Flower Ornament Scripture*, Sudhana's religious world was vibrantly alive with goddesses. These female divinities inhabit the earth and pervade the sky, sacralizing the physical setting of his journey with their spiritual presence. They are said to convey their compassion through trees, fruit, flowers, ponds, caves, rivers, medicinal herbs, moonlight, stars, and clouds. They voice their wisdom through the sounds of water, fire, wind, ocean wave, and birdsong.[31] Among them we find genres of goddesses that appear to have been widely revered in the Indic setting: earth goddesses, night goddesses, house goddesses, and city goddesses. When Sudhana gazed into the night sky, arrived at a crossroads, entered a city or dwelling, or visited the sites of the birth, upbringing, and enlightenment of Shakyamuni Buddha, the pilgrim received spiritual sustenance and guidance from the female deities inhabiting those locales.

Every preceptor he encountered is implicitly a bodhisattva, and thus the goddesses too are cast in this role, as beings aspiring to complete awakening for themselves and others, motivated by compassion, replete with insight about the path to enlightenment. They revealed their beauty and imparted their knowledge to Sudhana, inspiring his devotional rapture and poetic eulogies, deepening his wisdom.

Buddhism was caught up in the rising current of goddess worship that swept through India during the first and second centuries C.E. The *Gaṇḍavyūha* portion of the *Flower Ornament Scripture* substantiates this trend. Buddhism has continuously incorporated into its fold spirit beings and divinities of vital interest to the populace at large. This ongoing creative recasting of the pantheon has helped secure the relevance of Buddhism in varying cultural settings. For an historian, then, the pantheon provides vital insights into the environments to which Buddhism has adapted over the centuries. The Mahayana movement, in its attempt to universalize its mission and message, could not fail to address current trends in the broader religious landscape. Therefore, the prominence of goddesses in the *Flower Ornament Scripture* reveals the importance of female divinities in the imaginal world of the text's immediate audience. The scripture exalts goddesses by advancing them as Mahayana preceptors and in return is elevated by them, gaining relevance, credibility, and appeal by tapping into the rising stream of devotion to the goddesses who indwell and enliven India's divine landscape, infusing it with their spirituality and feminine presence.

CHAPTER 8

Prajñāpāramitā

Luminous Mother of Perfect Wisdom

She is the Perfect Wisdom that never comes into being
And therefore never goes out of being.
She is known as the Great Mother. . . .
She is the Perfect Wisdom who gives birthless birth to all Buddhas.
And through these sublimely Awakened Ones,
It is Mother Prajnaparamita alone
Who turns the wheel of true teaching.

—*8000-Line Perfect Wisdom Scripture*[1]

In the foundational body of Mahayana literature known as the Prajñāpāramitā or Perfection of Wisdom texts, the highest metaphysical principle—the energy, glory, and radiance of enlightened wisdom—is envisioned as a cosmic female, the mother of knowledge, the source of all Buddhas. This goddess, known as Prajñāpāramitā (pronounced *prahj nyah* PAH RAH *mee* TAH), is regarded as the "mother" of all beings who attain enlightenment, for it is her wisdom that engenders liberation. She is the supreme teacher and eternal font of revelation. All who seek illumination must sit at her feet and drink from the stream of teachings that flow from her presence. Thus, Prajñāpāramitā is the ultimate source of refuge and object of reverence, for only those who prize wisdom above all else may attain it. Even Buddhas and bodhisattvas pay homage to her, because to her they owe their omniscience. To worship a Buddha, the relics of a Buddha, or a stupa is to honor what she has brought into being; to revere her is directly to worship the source.

Just as philosophy is the queen of sciences, Prajñāpāramitā is the *philosophiae regina*, the Buddhist Sophia, a dazzling figure who represents the transcendent wisdom that crowns the intellectual and spiritual quest. In the wake of the contending schools of Abhidharma philosophy, mother Prajñāpāramitā arose to cast her serene, clear-sighted gaze of nondual wisdom over all disputants. Her luminous, golden persona draws her devotees away from worldly attachments and into the encompassing splendor of her mystical mother light.

Origins

Prajñāpāramitā shares her name with the literature in which she appears, the philosophy with which she is associated, and the knowledge she personifies. The text that introduces both the philosophy and the goddess, the *Aṣṭasāhasrikā Prajñāpāramitā Sūtra*, or *8000-Line Perfect Wisdom Scripture*, took shape during the first two centuries of the common era, although portions of the work evince earlier origins. In the traditional Buddhist view, this scripture is an abridgment of a much lengthier work revealed by Shakyamuni Buddha. Nonetheless, as the earliest known textual expression of the philosophy, this volume marks the historical emergence of Prajñāpāramitā. Although the work advances a systematic philosophical viewpoint, its language is redolent with poesy, devotion, and emotional fervor as it celebrates the goddess and her namesake wisdom.

The central importance and cosmic status of the wisdom mother at her earliest appearance are surprising given the apparent swiftness with which she rose on the Mahayana horizon. Nothing in the female figures who preceded her would foreshadow such a development. Her female forebears were divinities associated with nature and its fecundating powers, such as tree spirits (*yakṣiṇī*), Pṛthivī, and Lakṣmī. There is little in these goddesses of earthly provenance, however benevolent and auspicious they might be, to foretell the radiant entity of pure spirit and wisdom that is Prajñāpāramitā. Even Edward Conze's suggestion that she represents the "irruption" into Buddhism of the Paleolithic and Dravidian mother goddess does not explain the sudden transformation of the chthonic, fertile earth mother into the metaphysically sublime mother of wisdom.[2] The goddess, like the philosophy with which she is associated, appears to represent a revolutionary shift in Buddhist consciousness.

Although Prajñāpāramitā, like her namesake wisdom, is said to transcend all categories and to be beyond form, she has the trait of gender, and femaleness is central to her character.[3] She hypostasizes the wisdom that is most often designated in this literature by the feminine noun *prajñā*. Her femaleness, however, has an internal logic that goes beyond mere linguistic coincidence. There are deep metaphorical resonances between motherhood and the matrix of wisdom and reality she represents. If gender is to be assigned to a generative principle, the feminine gender is a logical choice, for the womb is the most tangible source of generation in human experience. Just as male bodies derive biologically from female ones, it stands to follow in the religious sphere that male Buddhas would have a female source. Thus, the femaleness of Prajñāpāramitā carries the force of logic and observation.

Mother of All Buddhas

One of the main titles and roles of Prajñāpāramitā is that of "Mother of All Buddhas" (*sarva-buddha-mātā, sarva-jina-mātā*). This theme, one of the guiding principles of the scripture, is introduced in an opening verse:

> The Buddhas in the world-systems in the ten directions
> Bring to mind this Perfection of Wisdom as their mother.
> The Saviours of the world who were in the past,
> And also those that are now in the ten directions,
> Have issued from her, and so will the future ones be.
> She is the one who reveals reality,
> She is the genetrix, the mother of the victorious ones.[4]

The work restates in numerous ways that Prajñāpāramitā is the begetter of all Buddhas because she is the source of the omniscience that qualifies them as Buddhas, or Tathāgatas, "those who have gone to reality": "The all-knowledge of the Tathagatas has come forth from her. . . . It is in this sense that the Perfection of Wisdom generates the Tathagatas."[5]

As the wisdom that makes possible the attainment of Buddhahood, Prajñāpāramitā is an enduring reality, whereas her children, the Buddhas and bodhisattvas, are ephemeral and illusory: "Prajnaparamita, Mother of the Buddhas, is the . . . sole reality. The emanation-bodies of Buddhas and bodhisattvas appear and disappear, whereas the wisdom light of Mother Prajnaparamita is always shining."[6] The *8000-Line Perfect Wisdom Scripture* emphasizes the theme that Buddhas cannot bring themselves into being but "owe their existence" to her.[7] Thus, this philosophy accords primacy to the source—the metaphorical birth-giver—rather than to its fruits, extending the reassurance that even if a given Buddha and his teachings pass away, the mother abides and will birth more illumined children.

The text develops the metaphor of motherhood at length. Just as mothers extend comfort and safety to their children, Prajñāpāramitā is the "shelter, defence and protection" of the seeker of wisdom.[8] Just as parents guide their children in morality, she is the source of all virtues, or perfections of character.[9] She nurtures her progeny by providing the knowledge they require to fulfill their highest destiny, namely, to understand the nature of reality and dedicate themselves to the welfare and liberation of all beings. Children naturally adore such a mother, seek to protect her from harm, and strive to bring her happiness:

> They would therefore look well after her, give her everything that can make her happy, protect her well, make much of her. . . . In just this same

> way . . . fond are the Tathagatas of this Perfection of Wisdom, so much do they cherish and protect it. For she is their mother and begetter, she showed them this all-knowledge, she instructed them in the ways of the world.[10]

It is incumbent on the offspring of such a mother not only to honor and cherish her but to remember and transmit what she has taught them.

Prajñāpāramitā's motherhood devolves upon her role as the source of the wisdom that generates Buddhas. Therefore, she is celebrated as the ultimate teacher—the beacon, torch, and instructor of those who seek liberating insight.[11] She reveals the world as it is, the end goal of all religious instruction. Thus, she is the teacher of teachers, the guide of the Buddhas and bodhisattvas as they lead others.[12] She is the "inexhaustible storehouse" of truth that is given voice by all Buddhas of the past, present, and future.[13] When Buddhas teach, Prajñāpāramitā is the source and content of their teachings. As the fount of all truth, it is she who sets in motion the wheel of Dharma.[14] Thus, a Buddha may teach for the duration of a single lifetime, or even in myriad worlds and aeons, but the teachings of mother Prajñāpāramitā flow for all eternity. Because she is eternal, the Buddhas and bodhisattvas will always have guidance and assistance.[15] This is why, even in the absence of a human teacher, or in a world or era not graced by the presence of Buddhism, a questing spirit may discover the truth and reveal the path to freedom anew.

Ultimate Object of Worship

Perfection of Wisdom literature exalts Prajñāpāramitā as the highest object of refuge and worship, not only for aspirants on the path to enlightenment but also for Buddhas. Because she brought them into being and nurtured them to omniscience, they owe her infinite gratitude.[16] If Buddhas honor and revere her, it stands to follow that she is equally or more worthy of reverence than a Buddha, Buddha relics, or a stupa. The *8000-Line Perfect Wisdom Scripture* weighs the relative merits of these objects of reverence and proclaims worship of Prajñāpāramitā to be superior in every case. Most dramatic is the claim that veneration of Prajñāpāramitā supersedes that of Buddhas because she is the "real eminent cause and condition" of the Buddhas' omniscience. Therefore, if one honors Prajñāpāramitā, one has worshipped all Buddhas of the past, present, and future throughout the universe.[17]

It follows, then, that worship of relics should be subordinated to veneration of Prajñāpāramitā. Relics include a Buddha's teeth, hair, bones, cremation ashes, turban, robes, staff, and begging bowl. Treasured artifacts such as these, enshrined in an ornate casket or stupa, are prized by the communities that possess them and honored with devotional offerings, pilgrimage, processions, and festivals. Reliquary objects, by virtue of their physical contact with the living Buddha, are traditionally believed to be imbued with a trace of his presence, rendering them worthy of homage.

According to the analysis found in the *8000-Line Perfect Wisdom Scripture*, however, it is the presence of the Perfection of Wisdom that confers sanctity on Buddha relics. Subhuti, a foremost Mahayana disciple, voices this principle:

> The relics of the Tathagata have come forth from the Perfection of Wisdom. . . . That Tathagata-body should be seen as brought about by the supreme reality, i.e., by Perfection of Wisdom. It is not, O Lord, that I lack in respect for the relics of the Tathagata. . . . I have real respect for them. They, however, are worshipped because they have come forth from this Perfection of Wisdom and are pervaded by it.[18]

Here the work argues that relics are venerable because she brought them into being, and thus they are saturated with her energy. Therefore, the worship of relics is indirect; worship of Prajñāpāramitā is direct. One who renders homage to her

> is directly venerating, absorbing and radiating Perfect Wisdom, which is the very power of sanctification, while the other person is venerating relics which have become infused with the power of Prajnaparamita and thereby sanctified.[19]

In sum, relics *possess* sanctity; she *confers* sanctity.

Similarly, the merit of worshipping Prajñāpāramitā exceeds that of building stupas to enshrine Buddha relics. With characteristic hyperbolic flair, the text contends that even the merit of filling India with stupas, or the merit that would be generated if every person in the world built a stupa and honored it for thousands of years, does not approach the supreme and immeasurable virtue of honoring Prajñāpāramitā.[20] She is to be recognized, then, as the source of sacredness. Her "power of sanctification" is boundless, for any spot on earth where she is honored becomes "a true shrine for beings, worthy of being worshipped and adored . . . a shelter for beings who come to it, a refuge, a place of rest and final relief."[21]

The Perfection of Wisdom philosophy does not, however, eschew all physical modes of worship. It advances as a material object of veneration the manuscripts that record the Buddha's teachings on transcendent wisdom. Worship of a single Prajñāpāramitā manuscript is said to be more meritorious than worship of a continent piled high with Buddha relics.[22] The way to honor the text is to read, study, recite, contemplate, analyze, teach, explain, copy, distribute, and preserve it.[23] Moreover, because of its sacredness, a manuscript merits ritual worship:

> When . . . it has been well written, in very distinct letters, in a great book, one should honour, revere, adore and worship it, with flowers, incense, scents, wreaths, unguents, aromatic powders, strips of cloth, parasols, banners, bells, flags and with rows of lamps all round, and with manifold kinds of worship.[24]

Shakyamuni asserts that the text is worthy of the same reverence as a living Buddha and avows that, after he has departed from the world, those who treasure and revere a Prajñāpāramitā text may be confident that they have seen a Tathāgata face-to-face and dwell in his presence.[25]

Divine Forms and Symbolic Attributes

Prajñāpāramitā was personified before she was cast into iconographic form. The Perfection of Wisdom literature characterizes her as a female being and describes her as the mother, teacher, and guide of seekers of spiritual awakening. There is, however, no attempt to envision her as a deity with specific bodily attributes, such as color, posture, gestures, attire, and ornaments.

Several reasons can be adduced for this initial lack of iconographic delineation. The primary reason may be that Prajñāpāramitā by nature transcends symbolic representation. She is identical to highest wisdom and represents a vision of reality that lies beyond all conceptual, linguistic, and symbolic constructs. The *8000-Line Perfect Wisdom Scripture* emphasizes that the nondual wisdom she personifies is inconceivable and indescribable, and she shares these qualities:

> Perfection of Wisdom cannot be expounded, or learned, or distinguished, or considered, or stated, or reflected upon by means of the sense organs, mental faculties, or sense objects. . . . Where there is no perception, appellation, conception, or conventional expression, there one speaks of "Perfection of Wisdom."[26]

Perfect wisdom and the goddess who shares its name cannot be apprehended by the discursive mind or the senses. She is, however, omnipresent as the essence of all phenomena; thus, she may be encountered in the midst of any experience or activity.[27] To see the world as it is—a dynamic, fluidic, open horizon of meaning—is to gaze upon her divine body and holy face.[28] Hence, there is no theoretical impetus within the philosophy to cloak the wisdom mother in a figural form that might disavow her transcendence.

Supplementing this philosophical reason is an historical one. The literature in which Prajñāpāramitā makes her debut predates the worship of votive images as a major Mahayana practice.[29] Buddhist art of the same period (first and second centuries C.E.) features supernatural beings more worldly in nature (e.g., yakṣiṇīs, nāgas, Hārītī, Kubera), illustrations of the Buddha's life, vignettes of lay worship, and a range of auspicious symbols (e.g., lotuses, vases of plenty, Dharma-wheels). No significant trend of image worship of Buddhas and bodhisattvas is discernible. Moreover, the Perfection of Wisdom literature promotes manuscripts, rather than effigies of the goddess, as objects of ritual devotion, giving rise to what Gregory Schopen terms the "cult of the book."[30] Therefore, on both theological and historical grounds, it is unsurprising that Prajñāpāramitā is not vested with bodily attributes in this literature.

It is not until the eve of the Pāla period that we find effigies of Prajñāpāramitā and written descriptions of her iconography.[31] The earliest known image dates from the seventh century and is found at the cave site of Ellora. She is portrayed in a standing posture, with one hand displaying the boon-granting gesture (*varada mudrā*) and the other grasping a lotus supporting a manuscript.[32] The earliest datable literary description of the goddess, from about the same period, describes her as golden in color, seated on a white lotus, with one hand displaying a teaching gesture and the other bearing a scripture.[33]

The ensuing centuries saw a range of visual interpretations of the wisdom goddess. These appear in statuary, manuscript illuminations, and literary sources. The sculptures may have been created for votive purposes or to support the Tantric practice of deity visualization, which gained impetus in the eighth century and stimulated image production as well as the introduction of various epiphanies. Tantric texts describe several epiphanies of the goddess, along with the mantras that invoke her presence. The main Indic source in this regard is the *Sādhanamālā* (late eleventh or early twelfth century), which includes nine such descriptions.[34]

Prajñāpāramitā is envisioned most often as golden in color and alternately as white. She appears with either two arms or four. As is typical of Mahayana goddesses, Prajñāpāramitā is decked in divine raiment, gems, and a jeweled diadem. Her tiara is sometimes described as a five-Buddha crown, signifying that she encompasses all aspects of enlightened knowledge.[35] She sits in the cross-legged posture of meditative equipoise. Her hands are typically brought together at her heart in a teaching gesture known as *vyākhyāna mudrā*. The thumb and forefinger of her left hand form a circle, representing the wheel of Dharma. Some portion of her right hand touches the wheel, signifying its

8.1 Prajñāpāramitā, Bihar, possibly Nālandā, India, Pāla period, ca. mid-ninth century. Schist, height 28.74 in. (73 cm). Asian Art Museum of San Francisco, The Avery Brundage Collection, B62S32+. Photo copyright Asian Art Museum of San Francisco. Used by permission. *Prajñāpāramitā displays a teaching gesture, signaling the endless stream of wisdom that flows from her presence.*

turning and thus symbolizing the revelation of religious truths. Her identifying attribute is the Perfection of Wisdom text that she bears, supported on a lotus or clasped in an upraised hand.

A popular manner of envisioning and portraying the goddess, in India and beyond, is the two-armed form in which she makes a teaching gesture and clasps the stem of a lotus in each hand (Fig. 8.1).[36] The lotuses blossom above her shoulders and support a pair of Perfection of Wisdom scriptures.[37] This formal symmetry, unusual in the iconography of Buddhist deities, beautifully conveys the mental quiescence and stability afforded by nondual wisdom. Her downcast eyes bespeak deep meditative calm, a theme reinforced by her legs crossed in the traditional posture of contemplation. This two-armed epiphany prevails in the Indic sculptural tradition, finding expression in large stone reliefs created for public worship spaces and small metal statuary most likely commissioned for personal use in a domestic or monastic shrine (Fig. 8.2).[38]

In the four-armed manifestations, her central pair of hands may rest on her lap in the meditation gesture (Fig. 8.3).[39] This positioning of the hands reinforces the theme, conveyed by her cross-legged posture, that contemplation is the path to perfect wisdom. One or both of her handheld lotuses support a scripture recording that wisdom. Four-armed effigies alternately show her central pair of hands brought together at her heart in a teaching gesture, signaling the endless stream of wisdom that flows from her illumined presence. The pair of lotuses blossoming above her shoulders preserve an element of symmetry, but one of her hands may rest on her knee in the gift-giving gesture, bestowing wisdom and its fruits. An irenically smiling effigy from Orissa beautifully portrays this conception of the goddess (Pl. 4).[40] In another variation, discussed below, four-armed Prajñāpāramitā displays a rosary, in reference to the practices of contemplation and mantra recitation.

In Nepal, the two-armed epiphany in which Prajñāpāramitā exhibits the teaching gesture and holds two lotuses is widely attested. A manuscript of her namesake literature may appear on one or both lotuses or be omitted altogether.[41] Most prevalent in that setting, however, is a four-armed configuration in which the central pair of hands forms a teaching gesture, the upraised left hand displays a manuscript, and the upraised right hand bears a rosary (Fig. 8.4).[42] Prajñāpāramitā bears the text and rosary directly in her hands; the supporting lotuses are no longer present. The earliest known appearance of this iconography is a Pāla-period manuscript illustration dating from the eleventh century.[43] This specific rosary-bearing form of the goddess is not otherwise attested in an Indic context but gained currency in Nepal, where it is featured in independent portrayals and in Newar representations of the Three Jewels—

8.2 Prajñāpāramitā, Nālandā, Patna District, Bihar, India, Pāla period, ca. ninth century. Bronze. Nalanda Museum. Photo: The Huntington Archive, The Ohio State University. *Prajñāpāramitā's pair of lotuses support scriptures that express the wisdom she personifies.*

8.3 Prajñāpāramitā, Nālandā, Patna District, Bihar, Pāla period, ca. ninth century. Stone. Indian Museum, Calcutta. Photo after *Archaeological Survey of India, Annual Reports*, 1930–34, pl. 127a. *Prajñāpāramitā with her central pair of hands in the meditation gesture.*

Buddha, Dharma, and Sangha—in figural form. In this triad, centering on the Buddha, Avalokiteśvara represents the Sangha and four-armed Prajñāpāramitā displaying a rosary represents the Dharma.[44]

Various forms of the goddess are attested in Tibetan settings. For instance, we find preserved the two-armed epiphany exhibiting the teaching gesture and symmetrical lotuses supporting manuscripts.[45] We also find a four-armed configuration, with Kashmiri precedent, in which Prajñāpāramitā makes both

8.4 Prajñāpāramitā, pillar on western side of Svayambhū Stupa, Kathmandu, Nepal, eighteenth century. Gilt bronze. Photo: Dina Bangdel. *The prevalent Newar epiphany of Prajñāpāramitā, displaying a rosary and manuscript in her upraised hands.*

the teaching and meditation gestures with her central pair of hands, combining her characteristic mudrās.[46] An iconographic preference that emerged in Tibetan portrayals is the inclusion of a vajra as one of her handheld attributes, generally displayed in her upraised right hand. The vajra attribute is a rarity in Indian and Newar iconography.[47] However, the vajra was widely adopted in Tibetan representations and is assigned to diverse epiphanies, including four-armed forms with the central pair of hands in the teaching gesture or,

8.5 Prajñāpāramitā, Tibet, ca. fourteenth century. Gilt copper inset with turquoise and other precious stones, painted with cold gold and blue pigment, height 8.5 in. (21.5 cm). Jokhang/gTsug Lag khang Collection (Lhasa, Central Tibet), 96. Photo after Ulrich von Schroeder, 2001, *Buddhist Sculptures in Tibet*, vol. 2, pl. 261E. *In Tibetan settings, Prajñāpāramitā often displays a vajra as one of her handheld attributes.*

alternately, resting on her lap in meditation (Fig. 8.5).[48] Indeed, the vajra came to be characteristic of Prajñāpāramitā in the Tibetan context. As a symbol of emptiness (*śūnyatā*), the central tenet of Perfection of Wisdom philosophy, the vajra is a fitting attribute for the wisdom mother, although I found no textual sources for this widespread iconographic motif.

In Indian, Tibetan, and Newar iconography, Prajñāpāramitā appears most often with two or four arms. There are several isolated six-armed versions that, judging from their rarity, did not find wide circulation.[49] Images with six or more arms identified as Prajñāpāramitā in many publications are actually effigies of Cundā, who also has as one her attributes a lotus supporting a scripture.[50]

It is intriguing that the iconography of Prajñāpāramitā in India and the Himalayas does not evince the ongoing proliferation of arms and handheld implements that so often characterizes the historical evolution of Mahayana divinities. Deities display emblems to signal their powers and ministrations. Prajñāpāramitā, who inhabits the pinnacle of metaphysical ultimacy, suffuses the spiritual journey as its starting point, content, and goal. She performs no specific function, apart from bestowing perfect wisdom, and thus she arguably requires no implements beyond the attributes symbolic of wisdom. On this principle, it appears that her relative iconographic simplicity reflects her singular character.

Similarly, one finds few mandalas centering on Prajñāpāramitā. These are historically obscure and not encountered in artistic representations.[51] Instead, one finds her effigies surrounded by numerous Buddhas and bodhisattvas. This is seen in some painted representations and well exemplified by two chapels at Gyantse, which customarily depict the mandalas of the deity to which a chapel is dedicated.[52] This motif finds expression in a twelfth-century liturgy that describes the goddess as "golden and beautiful, her entire body adorned with effigies of Buddhas . . . displaying the five Buddhas on her crown and surrounded by Buddhas and bodhisattvas."[53] This conception explains the otherwise puzzling paucity of mandalas devoted to the revered wisdom mother. All Buddhas and bodhisattvas, as her creations and emanations, constitute her mandala retinue, obviating the need for specific mandalic diagrams.

A similar principle is at work in the illumination of Prajñāpāramitā manuscripts. In addition to portraits of Prajñāpāramitā, the covers and pages are embellished with scenes from the former and final lifetimes of Shakyamuni Buddha and with Buddhas, celestial bodhisattvas, dhāraṇī goddesses, and even Tantric deities. These images do not illustrate specific contents of the text but rather celebrate Prajñāpāramitā's motherhood by picturing her fruits and offspring: the stages of spiritual awakening and array of enlightened beings that stream from her presence. The same principle may be discerned in

Prajñāpāramitā's placement at the center of mandalas devoted to the Medicine Buddha, Bhaiṣajyaguru. The tiers of the mandala feature the eight healing Buddhas, their sixteen bodhisattva attendants, and sundry guardian figures. Glenn Mullin clarifies that Prajñāpāramitā appears at the center of the assembly because she "represents the healing wisdom of all enlightened beings of the past, present, and future."[54] Thus, one finds Prajñāpāramitā in visual configurations that reflect her perennial role as the source of Buddhahood.

Most of the earliest surviving images of the goddess are manuscript illustrations executed in northeastern India and Nepal.[55] An Indic sculptural tradition is also attested, as discussed above. The relatively modest number of extant votive images is somewhat surprising in view of the centrality of Perfection of Wisdom thought to Mahayana Buddhism. It could well be that manuscripts, rather than sculpted images, have long constituted the primary icons associated with Prajñāpāramitā veneration, as they do in contemporary practice.

Mantra and Protective Power

Prajñāpāramitā is also embodied by a mantra, or magical incantation that invokes her divine energies. Mantra recitation establishes a relationship with the goddess and awakens transcendent wisdom within the practitioner's mindstream. The *8000-Line Perfect Wisdom Scripture* does not impart her mantra but lauds its powers. The omission of the mantra itself suggests that the potent syllables were held in reserve and imparted orally to serious practitioners. Thus, it is no longer ascertainable whether the incantation under discussion in the work is the root mantra later revealed in the *Heart Sūtra*, namely, *Oṃ gate gate pāragate pārasaṃgate bodhi svāhā*, translatable as "*Oṃ* gone, gone, gone beyond, gone beyond beyond, hail awakening!"[56]

The Prajñāpāramitā mantra—like the goddess and wisdom that share its essence—provides protection from an array of tangible dangers. For example, disciples of the philosophy "cannot be hurt by men or ghosts" and will enjoy freedom from fear wherever they may be, on land or at sea, even if under armed attack.[57] Wisdom offers a protective mantle against all harm:

> Those who are devoted to the perfection of wisdom should expect therefrom many advantages here and now. . . . Those devotees will not die an untimely death, nor from poison, or sword, or fire, or water, or staff, or violence. . . . The calamities which threaten them from kings and princes, from king's counsellors and king's ministers, will not take place.[58]

The protective power of wisdom, described here, and divine energy of Prajñāpāramitā are concentrated in the mantra and invoked by its recitation.

Those who intone the mantra, the scripture promises, will be free from disease, will not die a violent death, and are assured of an auspicious rebirth.[59] The mantra carries not only the protective force of wisdom but also its liberating power. Thus, the mantra confers all virtues, all spiritual perfections, and full awakening.[60]

The Prajñāpāramitā mantra is clearly attributed with tremendous practical and metaphysical efficacy. The material and spiritual benefits of its recitation are inseparable, for the apotropaic power of the mantra ultimately derives from wisdom itself. Realizations associated with growth in wisdom confer a protective mantle of psychological insight, an inner sense of security and safety. Wisdom unveils the illusory nature of the world and of the self, revealing that in reality there is no "self" to be harmed.[61] One who attains nondual insight will transcend the self-referential viewpoint that generates dualistic dramas of victimization, conflict, and adversity, thereby removing its possessor from harm's way.

The themes of protection and nondual wisdom are linked in contemporary Tibetan practice of Prajñāpāramitā deity yoga. Geshe Kelsang Gyatso translates and comments on a visualization of four-armed Prajñāpāramitā that, in his words, "can be used to avert or overcome hindrances and obstacles."[62] An accompanying prayer requests protection from disease, interferences, demonic possession, and unfavorable circumstances. Gyatso echoes the early scripture when he avers that while reciting the mantra, the meditator should "contemplate that we, all that harms us, and the harm itself are all empty of inherent existence."[63] Here, too, the protective power of the mantra devolves on the wisdom its recitation engenders.

Additional mantras appear in various Perfection of Wisdom scriptures.[64] Yet another Prajñāpāramitā mantra was inscribed on clay seals produced by Indian monks to serve as protective talismans. These small amulets, dating from the eighth through tenth centuries, contain a lengthy mantra meticulously rendered in tiny script. According to Simon Lawson, who has translated the mantra, the seals would have been "carried in a pocket or bag or kept on an altar or shelf in a [monastic] cell" and "were credited with irresistible magical power" to protect and empower the possessor.[65] Spells used to invoke specific manifestations of the goddess, as part of the process of deity visualization, are related in the *Sādhanamālā*, compiled near the close of Indian Buddhism.[66]

A Prajñāpāramitā mantra revealed in a short and rather late (ca. eighth century) scripture offers a portrait of the goddess while invoking her wisdom spirit:

> *Oṃ*! May you conquer! May you be victorious, Lotus-like one! One who is close to me, close to me! O path we traverse! Wise one, wise one! Goddess! Protectress! Rescuer from strife! Repeller of evil actions of

> others! Lovely lady! Hope of all! Cleanse my karmic impurities and those of all beings! Dweller in Buddhas! *Svāhā*![67]

This mantra, the text avows, accomplishes the benefits of all other mantras. In it, the saving powers of the goddess are concentrated, and "even all the Buddhas cannot express in words her advantages, even after hundreds of millions of aeons."[68]

Contemporary Practice

Meditation and ritual practices centering on Prajñāpāramitā are current in both Tibetan and Newar Buddhism, in accordance with the enduring importance of Perfection of Wisdom thought in those settings. In Tibet she is known by the Tibetan translation of her name or simply as Sherchinma, "Wisdom Mother," or Yum Chenmo, "Great Mother." Many visualization practices and associated initiation rites are maintained by the Sarma sects. In the Nyingma order her practice is largely replaced by that of Yeshe Tsogyal, whose name means "Victorious Ocean of Primordial Wisdom." Yeshe Tsogyal, a Tibetan woman who attained enlightenment and renown as a guru, was transfigured into a deity whose womb is recognized as the source of Buddhas and matrix of phenomenal reality. Meditation on Yeshe Tsogyal fosters the transcendent wisdom personified in other contexts by Prajñāpāramitā.[69]

A Tibetan woman regarded as a living embodiment of Prajñāpāramitā is Machig Labdron (1055–1153). After reading and studying Perfection of Wisdom texts with her mother and sister from a very young age, the adolescent Machig gained renown as a peerlessly rapid and faultless reciter of the texts. She so perfectly mastered the philosophy that she consistently bested learned monks and lamas in debate. Machig introduced a practice known as Chöd, "Cutting Off," so called because the practitioner envisions his or her own dismemberment and consumption by bloodthirsting demons as a means of cutting the bonds of ego. Chöd practice cultivates the realization of such Perfection of Wisdom insights as nonduality, emptiness, and selfless generosity through a ritual that incorporates Tantric, shamanic, and exorcistic elements. Prajñāpāramitā herself does not figure in the visualization but appears at the head of many Chöd lineages as the divine revealer of the system, while Machig Labdron is commonly recognized as the first human guru.[70]

Machig herself is regarded as an emanation of many female deities, foremost among them the great wisdom mother, as Tārā revealed to her:

> You are a mind emanation of the Great Mother Yum Chenmo [Prajñāpāramitā]. . . . She is the pure expanse of emptiness, the knowledge of

the non-self. She is the matrix which gives birth to all the Buddhas of the three times. However, so as to enable all sentient beings to accumulate merit, the Great Mother appears as an object of veneration . . . golden in color, with one face and four hands . . . her body beautiful with all the major and minor marks of a Buddha, surrounded by . . . the Buddhas and bodhisattvas of the ten directions. . . . Finally she took birth in Tibet. She is no other than yourself, Shining Light of Lab.[71]

Thus, the wisdom goddess, working through the illustrious Machig Labdron, is recognized as the divine inspiration behind a practice that remains important in all Tibetan sects to the present day.

In Nepal, worship of Prajñāpāramitā devolves on the ritual reading of and rendering of votive offerings to a Perfection of Wisdom text. Recitation and veneration of the scripture, largely undertaken by priests on behalf of parishioners, are the primary methods of gaining the blessings of the goddess. These observances may be directed to any Prajñāpāramitā manuscript or text. The foremost object of such devotions, however, is a large and lavishly produced thirteenth-century copy of the *8000-Line Perfect Wisdom Scripture* with a gold-gilt cover, held by the Golden Temple (Kwā Bāhā) in Patan (Fig. 8.6). The manuscript is displayed in the temple courtyard on major ritual occasions, including five annual ceremonies devoted to the text, and receives ongoing worship throughout the year. The potency of the text is attributed to the presence of the goddess it contains and channels. David Gellner, who conducted extensive field research at Kwā Bāhā, was advised that "the goddess herself is present" in the text and observes that the text is revered "as a goddess in the minds of her devotees."[72]

Rites focusing on the manuscript are requested by members of the Kwā Bahā parish and other Newar Buddhists drawn by its reputation for powerful efficacy. Gellner reports that such rites are most often initiated for the cure of illness, for which the text is especially famed, but also to gain success in an educational or business venture, assure a safe journey, solve family problems, facilitate purchase of property, or gain religious merit. Stories abound of remarkable cures and divine interventions secured through the ritual reading or worship of the text or even through a vow to undertake such an observance. Gellner relates:

> One member of the *guthi* [parish] told me that the very moment one vows to have the text read, the ill person begins to get better. He listed various cases, including one of diabetes, where people had recovered thanks to the goddess. Another local had the text read three days in a row, he said, when he had won a court case. Another was trading in Tibet in the old days and got a lot of gold which it was forbidden to bring out of the country. He

8.6 *8000-Line Perfect Wisdom Scripture,* Kwā Bāhā, Patan, Nepal, thirteenth century. Ink on handmade paper with a gold-gilt cover. Photo: Ashok Vajracharya. *The blessings of Prajñāpāramitā, when invoked through worship of this famed manuscript, are credited with remarkable curative powers and divine interventions.*

vowed to the Perfection of Wisdom; somehow the border guards forgot to check his luggage at the frontier.[73]

Even with no specific need in mind, a family might sponsor the reading of the text periodically, perhaps once every ten years, or, funds allowing, several times a year, to secure the ongoing protection and blessings of the goddess.[74] Water that has been offered to the text is distributed at the site and saved by its recipients to be ingested for healing from an illness or sprinkled in the home to remedy a problem concerning the family or property.[75]

One also finds in Nepal a monthly Amoghapāśa Vrata observance that includes ritual worship of the Buddha, Dharma, and Sangha in the form of sand mandalas. The Dharma mandala consists of nine Mahayana scriptures (the *navagrantha*, "nine texts") that constitute the core canon of Newar Buddhism. At the head of the canon and center of the mandala is a Prajñāpāramitā text, as the font of all Mahayana teachings. The accompanying recitations include homage to mother Prajñāpāramitā as the embodiment of the Dharma.[76]

Prototypical Mahayana Goddess and Wisdom Figure

Following Prajñāpāramitā's appearance in the Mahayana pantheon, many female divinities arose in her wake. The historical precedence of Prajñāpāramitā cast her in the role of ancestress and prototype of all the ensuing dhāraṇī goddesses and female Buddhas. Consequently, the titles "Prajñāpāramitā" and "Mother of All Buddhas" invariably appear among the epithets of female deities of the Mahayana pantheon, expressing the recognition that, as her descendants, they partake of her essence.

Unlike Prajñāpāramitā, however, other Mahayana goddesses have areas of specialization, or specific needs to which they respond. Their ministrations fall broadly into the categories of nurturance—providing the necessities of life and spiritual practice—and protection from human, natural, and supernatural dangers. Therefore, the association with wisdom in most cases remains a minor theme in the persona and salvific career of a given goddess. Nonetheless, the gift of wisdom and hence of liberation is implicitly present as the ultimate fruition and goal of their diverse saving activities. Similarly, every female deity, regardless of how she assists practitioners and devotees, thereby helps them progress toward Buddhahood and is thus a "mother of Buddhas."

The personification of wisdom as a female figure also shaped Mahayana doctrine in various ways. One is the adoption of the feminine term *vidyā* (literally, "knowledge") for female deities and their mantras and the related term *vidyā-dhāraṇī* for the mantras themselves. In the Mahayana formulation of the two aspects of enlightenment, the active force of liberating wisdom (*prajñā*) is assigned a female gender, whereas the male gender is attributed to the complementary quality of compassion (*karuṇā*), alternately expressed as skill in liberating others (*upāya*).

Moreover, Mahayana literature introduced a number of female figures who voice profound philosophical insights and subtle understandings of nondual wisdom. Queen Śrīmālā, the main speaker in the scripture that bears her name, is a preeminent example of this trend, as is the goddess who delivers the pivotal lessons on nonduality in the *Vimalakīrtinirdeśa Sūtra*.[77] That the Mahayana movement did not regard wisdom as a male quality or the cultivation of wisdom as an exclusively male pursuit is arguably another legacy of the envisagement of wisdom as a goddess.

To Prajñāpāramitā may be traced the ongoing association of female figures with liberating wisdom in Tantric Buddhist symbology. Tantric female Buddhas share with their Mahayana sisters the epithets "Prajñāpāramitā" and "Mother of All Buddhas." They are accorded these titles simply by virtue of their femaleness. That is, male and female Buddhas are by definition fully enlightened beings who have realized perfect wisdom, but male Buddhas are not accorded these titles. In Tantric discourse, the term "wisdom" (*prajñā*) is used to refer to female deities when they appear as consorts of male deities and to the human partners of male Tantric practitioners. In the Tantric formulation of enlightenment as a male-female equation, bliss, the experiential dimension, is assigned a male gender, whereas the realization of emptiness, the sapiential component, is assigned a female gender. On the same principle, Tantric scriptures and biographies feature female figures known as ḍākinīs—a broad category encompassing female deities, enlightening spirits, and women—who are closely associated with the awakening of nondual insight and wisdom.

In sum, Prajñāpāramitā set the precedent for a perennial association between wisdom and female figures that lent a unifying principle to the ensuing female pantheon and a structuring principle to symbolic dyads expressed in terms of gender polarity.

Exalting the Wisdom Mother

Prajñāpāramitā represents a fascinating development in the history of the Buddhist pantheon. With no discernible precedent or evolutionary trajectory, she emerged on the Buddhist horizon with stunning swiftness. While the question of whether there could be a female Buddha was taking shape in the theoretical arena, Prajñāpāramitā herself outleapt the debate and was enthroned at the pinnacle of the pantheon as the overarching wisdom and cosmic, womblike reality that gives rise to all Buddhas. She personifies the liberating wisdom that is the content, active force, and final destination of the spiritual quest. Thus, with the appearance of Prajñāpāramitā, the history of the divine female in Buddhism took a dramatic turn, rising from the supporting cast to the apex of the pantheon in a single, definitive leap.

The entire edifice of Prajñāpāramitā philosophy is based on the premise that the birth-giver is greater than the one who is born. The Buddhas receded in importance as devotion was directed to the maternal matrix of their omniscience—the inconceivably vast, magnificent, dazzling mother who brought them into being. The birthing of Buddhas is qualified as a "birthless birth," for all that is born from emptiness is a transitory display. That which brings them into being, however, is intrinsic to the structure of reality, namely, the creative fecundity of emptiness, conceived as an oceanic mother-reality. Buddhas are like jewels arising in the ocean depths, while Prajñāpāramitā is likened to the ocean, the inexhaustible treasury of gems.[78] Just as the earth produces trees, fruit, and flowers without end, Prajñāpāramitā generates saviors and teachers in infinite array.[79]

With these and other metaphors, Perfection of Wisdom literature eulogizes the transformative and generative power of the Mother of All Buddhas, celebrating her unlimited capacity to give birth to her exquisite creations: the awakened beings who liberate the world from suffering and lead beings to enlightenment. Thus, she is "the most precious thing in the world."[80] As long as there is a mother of Buddhas, there will be more Buddhas, and she endures when they pass away. For proponents of Perfection of Wisdom philosophy, Buddhas may *attain* liberation, but mother Prajñāpāramitā *is* liberation.[81]

That Prajñāpāramitā is female lends inviting warmth and softness to the concept of wisdom. Wisdom might well be conceived as sharp and cold, a merciless cutting away of false beliefs, an exposure of all sentiments and cherished illusions to the steely glare of harsh clarity. But such is not the case. Wisdom is warm and embracing, a comforting, nurturing presence. It glows with golden radiance. Wisdom reaches out to enfold, cherish, and protect her seekers. Wisdom is the truth that gives us birth and awaits us at journey's end. Wisdom is a mother.

CHAPTER 9

Parṇaśavarī

Healing Goddess Clothed in Leaves

Pacifier of all intense pain,
Destroyer of all sickness . . .
Mistress of all well-being,
You deserve universal honor.
As long as there is suffering,
Do not abandon the world!

—Drikung ritual prayer[1]

Parṇaśavarī (pronounced *PAR na sha va REE*) dwells in a forest glade high on a mountainside. Her beauty reflects the allure of the forest. Her skin glistens with emerald light; the healing sap of trees flows in her veins; her limbs are robust and supple as saplings. Parṇaśavarī adorns herself with nature's finery: feathers, flowers, fruit, and berries. A skirt made of leaves sways around her hips as she dances in her primeval bower. Thus arrayed in tribal splendor, she wanders in a state of joyous, primal rapture, alive to the colors, fragrances, and textures of the forest. Her woodland home is a treasure trove of botanical riches and medicinal secrets. Tutored in the unwritten lore of the forest, she is mistress of its healing mysteries, a goddess with the power to cure the most drastic illnesses and epidemics. Parṇaśavarī embodies the close relationship with nature that must be maintained if the healing arts are to flourish. Even when Parṇaśavarī is invoked in ritual, the environment created for her is not the standard jeweled mansion of a deity but a gem-laden mountain dense with groves of magical trees and carpeted with flowers of every hue.[2] Thus, the goddess need not leave her verdant wildwood paradise to manifest at the ritual.

Divine Forms and Symbolic Attributes

Parṇaśavarī, whose name means "Tribal Woman Clothed in Leaves," was an important goddess of healing in Indian Buddhism and continues to serve in this role in the Tibetan pantheon. Her clothing and attributes express the connection with nature from which her healing powers derive. Her leaf skirt blends harmoniously with sylvan surroundings and offers a ready supply of herbaceous remedies. Her skirt is festooned with fruit, flowers, and feathers. She is necklaced by a white snake, crowned with flowers, and has small snakes as hair ribbons.

Parṇaśavarī carries the equipage of one who lives in the wilds. She wields a small axe (*paraśu*) that would be invaluable to anyone subsisting in a forest, with its long handle and small blade ideal for harvesting fruit, herbs, and medicinal plants. Parṇaśavarī brandishes a bow and arrow, tools befitting a huntress, and waves aloft a tree branch laden with fruits, flowers, and fresh young leaves, exhibiting the abundance of nature with which she is so closely attuned. The mountain goddess also sports a noose that could serve a number of practical purposes, such as snaring small game and bundling botanical harvests.

In the Buddhist view, everything in the universe has healing power under some circumstance, and a healer knows how to channel this omnipresent force. Parṇaśavarī personifies the magical healing properties of nature that can be tapped through dance, trance, and incantation. Because Parṇaśavarī's curative powers are channeled through meditation, ritual, and mantra, the objects that she bears also serve a ritual purpose. For example, tree leaves are used in assorted healing rites in India. A healer may fan the patient with leaves, tie a leaf garland around the patient's neck or waist, or apply leaves or leaf rinse water to the affected area.[3] Freshly cut leaves must be used for these purposes, and texts on Parṇaśavarī specify that the leaves on her skirt and wand are "fresh."[4] Thus, her emblematic leaves have at once rustic, medicinal, and ritual associations.

Her implements also serve in the ritual capture and binding of diseases. In South Asian and Himalayan medical theory, diseases are not only bodily conditions, but entities—invisible to the eye but nonetheless tangible—that can be banished or destroyed. When Parṇaśavarī is ritually invoked to perform this function, she uses her vajra-tipped noose to lasso the disease demons. She clasps the noose with a threatening hand gesture (*tarjanī mudrā*), signaling the imminent entrapment of harmful spirits. After she has extracted the disease demons, she uses her axe to chop them or her bow and arrow to pierce their hearts, rendering them impotent.

The ritual dimension of Parṇaśavarī's healing activity is most directly indicated by the vajra (bronze scepter) she bears. The vajra symbolizes her indestructibility as well as her adamantine insight into the illusory nature of all phenomena. A healer, to be effective, must have the wisdom to recognize the ultimate insubstantiality of a disease if she or he is to envision its absence and accomplish its removal. Moreover, in Tantric ritual a vajra is flourished with sacred hand gestures to channel energy. Thus, the vajra conveys that the healer works with the patient's energy. The physical symptoms are understood as a tangible manifestation of a negative energy embedded in the patient's psyche or a disturbance of the patient's energies due to toxic substances, harmful psychological forces, or malevolent supernatural agency. A healer must discern the nature of the disease as a blockage in the energy flow and intervene to restore a balanced, healthy pattern. The vajra, as a tool for directing energy, addresses this metaphysical level of healing work. The scepter strikes through the physical manifestation to the core of the problem.

The epiphany of Parṇaśavarī most common in India and later in Tibet has six arms and wields the implements described above. In her three right hands she holds, in varying order, the vajra, axe, and arrow; in her left, the noose, bow, and freshly cut tree branch (Fig. 9.1). Her body color differs according to various meditation manuals. In some cases she is green, a natural hue for a forest deity. She is most commonly envisioned as yellow, radiant with the golden glow of supernal well-being.[5] Additional forms of the goddess appear as ancillary figures in meditations centering on her yellow, six-armed epiphany. These have varying numbers of arms (two, four, eight), implements (peacock feathers, bowl of medicines, double vajra), and bodily hues (red, blue, black).[6]

Parṇaśavarī is the picture of robust vitality. She is said to be youthful, vibrant, and muscular, with a plump, firm body.[7] Her plumpness, sometimes represented visually by a stocky, rotund form, is a sign of good health in India and reflects Parṇaśavarī's capacity to trample disease demons.

The following song of praise, from a Tibetan meditation manual, artfully invokes the rustic associations of the goddess and her healing potency:

> Goddess whose practice pacifies every illness
> And all disease-causing demons,
> I bow before you, divine mother.
>
> Manifesting in every field and village,
> Especially appearing in forested places . . .
> Homage to you, powerful mountain lady. . . .
> Homage to you, playful goddess.
>
> You know all the methods of taming,
> Adorned with clothing of fresh tree leaves,
> Ornamented by many fruits and flowers,
> Homage to you, goddess wearing leaves.

9.1 Parṇaśavarī, Tibet, sixteenth century. Gilt copper inset with precious stones, height 8.3 in. (21 cm). Private collection. Photo after Ulrich von Schroeder, 1981, *Indo-Tibetan Bronzes*, pl. 114C. *The healing goddess, caped with leaves, raises the leaf wand she uses to fan away disease and exorcise disease demons.*

With the roar of peaceful mantras,
You pacify epidemics and suffering;
With the thunder of wrathful mantras,
You destroy poisonous spirits;
Homage to your holy speech.

Your peaceful heart soothes living beings;
With deep affection and delight,
You magnify life and glory;
O goddess whose mind is spacious and free,
I worship you![8]

The composer of this paean writes as one for whom the goddess is a living presence. With poetic flair, the hymnist extols a figure implacable in pursuit of disease yet merrily at play in her woodland roaming, affectionate toward living beings, and joyful in the exercise of her healing art. The author also draws attention to Parṇaśavarī's mastery of the four modes of ritual activity in her cure of diseases, as she pacifies and subjugates all illness and causes of illness, destroys harmful spirits, and enriches life and good health.

In the Indian artistic corpus, Parṇaśavarī may be shown in a cross-legged meditative posture.[9] Most evident, however, is the lunging pose that conveys kinesthetic intensity and physical prowess in confronting an adversary (see Fig. 9.1). Fundamentally an archer's stance, the pose represents the end of a vigorous leaping motion and is a codified dance movement for unleashing weapons. This mode of representation casts the goddess in a spirited dance, flourishing her implements and leaf wand to drive away illness.

The dance motif in her iconography may reflect the role of dance in Indic healing rituals. For example, in the Nenaveli ritual of Kerala, the dancer wears a skirt of leaves and waves tree branches to ward off the demon of smallpox. In the Karagam dance of Tamilnadu, the main dancer balances a pot of leaves on his head and holds leaf clusters in both hands as he dances to appease the epidemic goddess. In a shamanic ceremony of the same region, the healer shakes a drum decked with leaves as he dances in trance to exorcise disease demons.[10] Indeed, there are many instances of this type of healing dance, in which the dancer waves a branch or peacock feather to sweep away pathogenic spirits.[11] Especially relevant are Śavara ritual dances, variously performed by priestly specialists and communal assemblies, to invoke their epidemic goddess, drive away smallpox, prevent snakebite, and effect individual cures, as discussed below.

Parṇaśavarī's dancelike lunging pose is also attested in Tibet (see Fig. 9.1).[12] Tibetan artistic representations and meditation manuals, however, introduce

9.2 Parṇaśavarī, China or Mongolia, ca. 1850. Mineral pigment and gold over woodblock print on paper, height 3.54 in. (9 cm). Ethnographic Museum of the University of Zurich. Photo after Willson and Brauen, *Deities of Tibetan Buddhism*, no. 218. *Parṇaśavarī often appears in this yogic pose in Tibetan iconography.*

a posture not evidenced in the Indic corpus, namely, a kneeling stance in which one leg is bent up so that the heel of the foot presses against the pelvis.[13] In artistic portrayals, the foot may be shown in front of the skirt to reveal its position (Fig. 9.2), but texts stipulate that it is pressed against the pelvis.[14] Parṇaśavarī may also be depicted in a seated variation on the pose.[15] In both versions, the heel is positioned to stimulate the flow of energy in the pelvic area for the purpose of sending it upward along the spine and directing it to desired ends, such as creativity, healing, or heightened states of awareness. Tibetan interpretations of the goddess favor this yogic posture over the lunging pose. As the goddess migrated from her Indian venue, where ritual dance was a cultural commonplace, into Tibet, yogic aspects of the goddess and her practice thus came to the fore. Furthermore, in Tibetan, which has no lexical equivalent of the tribal designation "Śavara," her name was rendered as Ritrö Lomagyunma, "Leaf-Clad Mountain-Dweller."

Healing Methods

Buddhist practitioners can gain access to the healing powers of Parṇaśavarī in several ways. All of these techniques begin with the creation of a vivid mental image of the goddess. The meditator absorbs the image and then works with her divine healing energies in a state of unity with her. One method is to transmit colored light from the meditator's body to specific persons (as described below) or to whole towns or areas that are threatened by contagious diseases or epidemics. Another method is to make amulets that are imbued with her presence by dhāraṇī recitation. Such an amulet is worn to protect the wearer against infectious disease and other misfortunes.[16] A healing practitioner may compound medicinal pellets from powdered herbs, foods, and gemstones according to instructions provided in a Parṇaśavarī text and then, in the ritual context, generate a clear image of the goddess, envision her dissolving into the pills, and further vivify them with mantra recitations.[17] The pills may be administered to sick persons or distributed in areas at risk of epidemic.[18] Moreover, public teachings and initiation ceremonies were staged in Tibet and, now, in Tibetan communities in Nepal to disseminate Parṇaśavarī's curative influence to the populace at large.[19]

Although the process of healing associated with Parṇaśavarī involves physical substances and ritual acts, it is ultimately seen as a process of spiritual purification. The inner dimension of healing operates on the most subtle levels of a person's being, eliminating the underlying causes of illness by clearing blockages in the normal flow of energy and infusing the recipient's spirit with sufficient radiance and resilience to prevent a recurrence of the disease.

A Tibetan text on Parṇaśavarī describes a healing meditation that operates on this subtle level. The healer focuses on five energy centers in the yogic anatomy of his or her body. These five centers, known as chakras, are located at the crown of the head, throat, heart, navel, and sexual organ. The healer creates a mental image of Parṇaśavarī in each chakra: a white goddess at the crown, red at the throat, blue at the heart, yellow at the navel, and green at the pelvis. These small figures emit streams of light that the healer mentally transmits to the corresponding bodily sites in the patient. The patient consciously absorbs the energy and visualizes it flooding the energy centers, removing energy blockages and regenerating the body at the etheric level.[20]

A person who is sufficiently self-aware can prolong the benefits by refraining from pathogenic patterns of thought and emotion in the future. This technique is most effective for those who can use their own proficiency in meditation to complete the process by establishing three protective shields of light around the body. The outer layer is formed from white light generated from the crown of the head, the next from red light emanated from the throat, and the innermost from blue light radiated from the heart. These protective barriers consist of many images of Parṇaśavarī densely packed together. Her luminous effigies protect the body, speech, and mind of the meditator and stand guard against any negative energies or contagions that arise in the future.[21]

Parṇaśavarī is attributed with virtually limitless healing powers. A Sakya manual in current usage declares that she is effective against "all illness and demons causing illness" and provides a detailed list of diseases she can cure, including those that are otherwise incurable or resistant to treatment, are of short or long duration, disrupt the body on the elemental level (of earth, air, fire, water, and space), involve the humors (wind, bile, phlegm), attack any part of the body, cause fatigue or fever, are caused by demons or harmful astrological influences, and afflict domestic and wild animals. She even wards off nightmares and injurious accidents.[22] Although Parṇaśavarī's curative powers are comprehensive, she is regarded as a specialist in the cure of contagious diseases, plagues, and epidemics in human and animal populations.[23] In these cases, Parṇaśavarī's healing energies may be invoked—by means of a public ceremony in the area at risk and the distribution of consecrated pills (described above)—to prevent the spread of the contagion to a community, grant individual immunity once a plague has begun, or hasten the end of an epidemic in progress.[24]

As Epidemic Goddess

Parṇaśavarī shares her role as a healer of epidemics with many non-Buddhist figures. In South Asia, this function has long been attributed to female deities, particularly the divine mothers, or "village goddesses" (*grāma-devatā*), around whom revolves much of agrarian India's religious life. Each village protectress watches over her immediate domain and includes in her purview control over virulent diseases and fevers, such as cholera and smallpox. This genre, which scholarly works variously term "epidemic goddess," "smallpox goddess," and "fever goddess," probably inspired the inclusion of an analogous deity in the Buddhist pantheon. There are numerous instances in which the festivals and rites of such goddesses involve wearing leaves, especially those of the margosa tree. Leaves may be worn by all the villagers, certain groups, the leader of a ritual procession, or a person to be possessed by the goddess.[25] The donning of leaves in public worship of these goddesses sheds further light on Parṇaśavarī's leaf-clad persona.

The numerous local epidemic goddesses have tended to merge over the centuries and coalesce into panregional divinities, such as Śītalā, Salabai, and Māriyammān.[26] Foremost among them in northern and eastern India is Śītalā, who governs smallpox and childhood fevers, inflicting disease when she is displeased and removing it when she is pacified. Bengal, where worship of Śītalā is prevalent, was also the epicenter of the cultus of Parṇaśavarī in late Indian Buddhism. The leaves and leaf wand in Parṇaśavarī's iconography may in part have been inspired by cultic attributes of her counterpart. Śītalā is known as a goddess of the forest and is often worshipped in a woodland setting or beneath a sacred tree.[27] Also apropos is the practice associated with Śītalā of fanning a fever or pox victim with margosa leaves.[28] Moreover, dance figures in contemporary worship of Śītalā in Bengal and presumably played a role in centuries past as well. Subrata Mukhopadhyay describes several such ritual dances, including the communal nocturnal Changu dance performed in the forest to drive away smallpox.[29] The fact that these dances are current among Śavara groups draws an even richer network of associations between the two goddesses.

Buddhists were aware of the affinities between Śītalā and Parṇaśavarī. Two large stone stelae from northeastern India, dating from the tenth or eleventh century, show the Buddhist goddess trampling a pair of pustulated figures that personify vanquished diseases (Fig. 9.3). At the base of both statues, beneath the lotus pedestal, is an elephant-headed figure in a sprawling posture indicative of defeat, representing obstacles overcome by Parṇaśavarī.[30] These lithic reliefs include, to Parṇaśavarī's left, a small effigy of Śītalā, riding a donkey and bearing the broom and winnowing basket with which she brushes and fans away fevers and disease.[31] On the other side is Hayagrīva (alias Jvarāsura), a horse-headed god of fever. It has been suggested that these two figures are fleeing "in terror to escape the wrath of the principal goddess" and that their presence here is an expression of sectarian animosity.[32] I suggest, rather, that Śītalā and Hayagrīva—both curers of fevers and other epidemics—are cast here as emissaries working in concert with Parṇaśavarī to banish pestilential threats to human well-being. This interpretation is consonant with the long-standing artistic practice, traceable to the earliest Buddhist art, of portraying Hindu divinities as attendants of Buddhist figures.

Although Parṇaśavarī's healing activities overlap those of Śītalā and other epidemic goddesses, the associated practices differ. Śītalā is generally propitiated either by whole communities or by family members of the afflicted. Her worship

9.3 Parṇaśavarī, Naynanda, Tangibari, Vikramapura, Dacca District, Bengal, India, Pāla period, ca. eleventh century. Black stone, height ca. 44 in. (112 cm). Dacca Museum, 67.319. Photo: The Huntington Archive, The Ohio State University. *Parṇaśavarī tramples pustulated figures representing vanquished fevers and smallpox.*

centers on "cooling" offerings (yogurt, sweets, honey, tamarind, sandalwood paste), public procession of her images, devotional singing, and the trances of human mediums—usually women—who convey her presence, instructions, and prophecies. The process of healing is understood to be one in which the goddess herself, having become overheated and inflicted with the disease, is subsequently cooled, thus quelling the illness.[33] In contrast, Parṇaśavarī's healing power is invoked through visualization and mantra recitation rather than worship. Her energies are wielded by healers in a state of identification with her and through amulets, medicines, and mantra-blessed water infused with her presence. Prayer and devotion to Parṇaśavarī may also be effective, but ultimately she is an object of contemplation rather than supplication.

Tribal Attributes and Associations

Although the concept of a female divinity who cures fevers and epidemics is pan-Indic, Parṇaśavarī assumed a distinctive iconographic form that was not patterned on that of Śītalā or other goddesses of the genre. Rather, the Buddhists rendered their healer in the guise of a tribal woman. The word *śavarī* in her name, meaning "tribal woman," is used both as a generic term and with specific reference to the Śavara tribe.[34] Śavaras are known to wear skirts made of leaves or peacock tail feathers and to hunt with a bow and arrow.[35] These cultural traits have left an imprint on Indic iconography at large. For example, the Hindu pantheon includes Śavarī-Durgā, who is adorned with peacock feathers and bears a bow and arrow.[36] In the Hindu Tantric repertoire one finds both Śavareśvarī, a goddess similar in iconic type, clad in leaves, and Śavarī, who bears a bow and arrow and wears a bark skirt, a garland of *guñjā* berries, and peacock feathers in her hair.[37] Moreover, a Śavara woman skirted with peacock feathers and sporting with snakes in a vernal setting typically represents the Āśavarī-rāginī in paintings of the "garland of musical modes" (*rāga-mālā*), in which different female figures are selected to illustrate varying moods and styles of music. The Aśavarī-rāginī paintings exemplify music with an enchanting or hypnotic quality akin to the melodies of a snake charmer.[38]

Although the Śavara woman recurs as a figural type in Indian culture, it is open to interpretation why such a figure would serve as prototype for a divine healer. By virtue of their rural habitat and nature-based material culture, Śavaras would fittingly be attributed with knowledge of the medicinal and magical healing properties of plants. Moreover, female Śavaras may have inspired the iconography of Parṇaśavarī by their practice of ritual healing trance. Śavara women outnumber men in the shamanic role, and dance is integral to their healing ceremonies, which find them engaging in vigorous lunging

9.4 Kuranboi, probably 1940s. Photo after Verrier Elwin, "Saora Priestess," pl. 18. *A Śavarī healer dancing and lunging in trance to dispel disease offers a striking visual analogue to Parnaśavarī.*

movements to ward off pathogenic spirits (Fig. 9.4).[39] Their healing implements include a bow and arrow to diagnose and treat illness and bundles of leaves to diagnose, fan, and brush the patient and sprinkle medicated water.[40]

Verrier Elwin, who conducted his fieldwork in Orissa, provides an ethnographic account of female Śavara healers, known as Kuranboi. He reports the great honor accorded to the Kuranboi and vividly describes a group of women who impressed him with their dedication to the healing profession:

> Here is a body of women dedicated to the public service and fulfilling that dedication with grace and energy. Here are women, believed to be vitally in touch with supernatural affairs, on whom one can rely, women who respond to the needs of the sick and anxious with professional thoroughness and affectionate concern. . . . The Kuranboi is indeed an impressive and honorable figure. She lives a dedicated life on the boundary between two worlds. . . . The Kuranboi is the nurse and friend, the guide, the analyst . . . using her priceless gift of intuition to reassure and heal.[41]

Elwin also remarks on Śavara women's festive enjoyment of their natural environs: "They move freely about their lovely hills; gay and happy, their laughter and their singing echoes at all hours among the palm trees."[42]

Elwin's descriptions, although far removed in time from the sources under discussion, are intriguingly consonant with Parṇaśavarī's persona. If we may assume any degree of continuity in the healing offices of Śavara women over the centuries, Elwin's characterization helps explain why such women would serve as fitting prototypes for a divine healer. Clearly, Parṇaśavarī, in her vigorous, dancelike stance, waving aloft her bow, arrow, and stalk of leaves, could well offer a portrait of such a woman in the midst of a healing trance.

The fact that Śītalā is a chief deity of Śavaras in Bengal and Orissa provides a link between the two aspects of Parṇaśavarī, namely, her role as an epidemic goddess and the reference in both her name and attributes to the Śavara tribe.

Tantric Associations

Textual and artistic evidence of Parṇaśavarī first appear in sources dating from the tenth and eleventh centuries, rather late in the dhāraṇī trajectory, when Tantra was well under way.[43] This would account for her Tantric attributes. For example, Parṇaśavarī may wear a tiger skin, a prerogative of yogic adepts. The snakes that serve as her hair ribbon, necklace, and belt also have Tantric connotations, for the energy that is made to rise in the body through inner yogic practices is often likened to the uncoiling of a snake. One who has mastered this serpentine force becomes a mistress of snakes. Snakes, attracted by her intensified energy field, are compelled to wrap around her body and content to serve as her ornaments, a visible sign of her yogic mastery.

The snakes and tiger skin suggest that Parṇaśavarī is envisioned as a tribal woman who is also a Tantric yogini. This confluence may have a concrete basis. Suggestive in this regard are two Tantric Buddhist songs extolling a highly realized Śavara yogini. One describes the practice and realizations of a Śavara couple.[44] The other dwells on a Śavara woman named Sahajasundarī, "Beauty of Spontaneous Enlightenment":

> High and lofty is the mountain;
> There dwells the Śavarī.
> She is decked with colorful peacock feathers
> And a garland of *guñjā* berries around her neck,
> (Singing) "O intoxicated Śavara, O mad Śavara,
> Do not revel in worldly pleasure!
> I am your consort, Sahajasundarī!"
> Many trees are in bloom,
> Their branches touch the sky;
> The Śavarī girl, decked with earrings and a vajra,
> Plays alone in the forest.[45]

This song well evokes the Śavarī's delight in mountain solitude, her natural adornments, and the purity of her consciousness, which plumbs the subtle levels of reality just as tree branches "touch the sky." She has realized the truth of emptiness and, passing the night in erotic play with her yogic consort, experiences transcendent bliss. By virtue of her metaphysical attainments, the poet likens her to the female Buddha Nairātmyā.[46]

It is possible that the Śavarī, portrayed in these songs as a fully enlightened Tantric adept, functions as a poetic metaphor, for Śavaras often serve as a literary trope for that which is beyond the pale of civilization. This symbolic meaning would well express the Tantric ideals of freedom from social convention and ecstatic immersion in the immediacy of life. Potential poetic allusions of the imagery, however, do not obviate the possibility that the songs make literal reference to women known to the authors or offer a general paean to Śavara women in Tantric circles.

Tantric annals celebrate two female gurus, described as mountain-dwelling tribal huntresses, who resided with a Tantric master named Śavara (a.k.a. Śavarīpā). They clothed themselves with skirts of bark and leaves (and may be portrayed as wearing peacock feathers) and kept their bows and arrows at the ready. These yoginis, Padmalocanā and Jñānalocanā by name, were sufficiently rustic in appearance that the yogi Maitrīpā failed to recognize them as Tantrics when he met them, even though they were living with a renowned Śavara yogi. The women later used their hunting expeditions to enlighten Maitrīpā with key religious insights, becoming his gurus.[47] The evidence of this account, combined with the songs discussed above, strongly suggests the inclusion of Śavara women among the Tantric constituency. The presence of such women in Buddhist circles would have provided a ready source of inspiration for iconographic design. Their presence in Tantric groups may also have prompted the introduction of a divine yogini named Śavarī in the Hevajra, Nairātmyā, and Pañcaḍāka mandala retinues.[48]

The Buddhist tradition of magico-religious dhāraṇī practice that gave rise to Parṇaśavarī drew inspiration from diverse quarters. Local trance healers, sorceresses, and other magical specialists would be a natural source of incantations and ritual techniques, which could then be aligned with Buddhist metaphysics. It has been suggested that Parṇaśavarī's tribal persona was designed to draw Śavaras into the Buddhist fold.[49] I contend, however, that Buddhist iconographers recognized the healing powers and ritual expertise of Śavara women and chose them as the human models for their healing goddess. Moreover, when Śavara women embarked on Buddhist practice, as Tantric history chronicles, they could well have transmitted their healing knowledge to the Tantric circles they joined. Thus, on my view, Parṇaśavarī offers a compelling and evocative portrait of homage to India's tribal women and their ritual healing arts. This portrait is advanced not that the goddess herself may receive worship but because of the healing powers she evokes within the Buddhist practitioner for whom she serves as an object of ritual invocation and meditation.

CHAPTER 10

Mārīcī

Lady of Sunrise Splendor

> There is a goddess who travels before the sun and moon.
> She is invisible, indestructible, unbindable,
> Unstoppable, inescapable, unerring,
> Unpunishable, unburnable, and unassailable by weapons.
> Her name is Mārīcī.
> Hearing her name, one attains these qualities.
> —*Mārīcīnāma Dhāraṇī*[1]

Mārīcī (pronounced *mah* REE CHEE), "Lady of Brilliant Light Rays," rises on the horizon as the dawn each day. At first blush she appears to be a delicate, gentle maiden, but on approach she reveals her full glory as a dazzling battle queen, brandishing flashing weapons, riding astride her golden chariot in a blaze of sunrise brilliance. With a shining visage and triumphant smile, she is a glory to behold. Her skin is golden; jewels sparkle like stars in her glistening black hair; her silken robes wave across the sky as streaks of red, white, and yellow light. Mārīcī is a celestial warrior, armed for combat. Relentless and invincible, she advances on her chariot drawn by fierce wild boars, unleashing arrows of light, raising her golden victory banner on the horizon each morning. Like the dawn, she perpetually circles the earth, pursuing all that threatens well-being—destructive demons and humans, aggressive foes, and mortal perils of every kind.

Inexorable as the sunrise, clearing away the darkness on her victory march, Mārīcī is an unfailing source of protection from danger and harm. Shakyamuni Buddha himself took recourse to her saving powers. According to the Mahayana literature that introduces Mārīcī, the Buddha revealed her mantra at Śrāvastī, a city where Shakyamuni displayed his own miraculous powers, henceforth named as the site of many of his teachings on magic, ritual, and mantra. There the Buddha professed his reliance on the unconquerable goddess:

> There is a goddess known as Mārīcī. She travels in front of the sun and moon. It is impossible to see, hold, bind, obstruct, oppose, deceive, punish, behead, rob, burn, or overpower her as an enemy. Monks, anyone who knows the name of Mārīcī will also attain these qualities. . . . I, myself, because I know her name, cannot be seen, held, bound, obstructed, out-argued, deceived, punished, beheaded, robbed, burned, or overpowered by an enemy.[2]

As the Buddha's testimony would suggest, Mārīcī is most often invoked for protection from immediate mortal threats and dangers. She grants invincibility to her supplicants in the face of attackers, thieves, rulers, wild animals, snakes, supernatural serpents, poison, fire, drowning, imprisonment, execution, and enemy armies.[3] As a dhāraṇī (incantation) goddess, Mārīcī is an emanation and embodiment of her mantra, which includes invocations and requests along with untranslatable syllables of magical potency:

> *Parākramasi, udayamasi, vairamasi, arkamasi, markamasi, vanamasi, antarddhānamasi.* On my path guard me! On the wrong path guard me! From man and from thief guard me! From king and from lion, from tiger, from snake, and from serpent, guard me from all! Guard me and all beings from all fears and from all troubles in every event! Hail! . . . Glory to the divine Mārīcī![4]

Mantra recitation is necessary to establish a relationship with the goddess and to be granted a vision of her radiant form. Dawn is a favored time for her daily invocation.[5] During times of danger, simply calling her to mind will elicit her protective powers. The following song of praise extends this assurance and reveals how resplendently beautiful Mārīcī is envisioned to be:

> One who merely remembers your name
> Will be protected from all fears.
> I revere the goddess Mārīcī,
> Granter of supreme, stainless bliss.
>
> You ride a jeweled chariot drawn by seven wild boars,
> Seated gracefully on a lotus and moon seat,
> With one face and two hands, dazzlingly golden,
> I pay homage to you, lady Mārīcī.
>
> With your right hand in the gesture of blessing
> And your left bearing an aśoka tree,

Draped with jewelry and enjoying every opulence,
Adoration to you, glorious Mārīcī.[6]

Mārīcī is envisioned here as a figure of dazzling beauty, "draped with jewelry" and devoid of weaponry, but nonetheless regarded as a powerful protectress.

Another way to invoke Mārīcī's protection, in addition to reciting her invocation and "remembering her name," was to inscribe her image on a small amulet that could be worn as a protective talisman.[7] Such amulets were typically molded from clay and imprinted with the dhāraṇī and effigy of the deity.

Lady of the Aśoka Tree

Mārīcī underwent several dramatic transformations in the course of her iconographic evolution. The simplest and from all evidence original form, described in the preceding song of praise, is the two-armed epiphany known as Aśokakāntā. She holds an aśoka tree, branch, or flower in her left hand and extends her right hand with the palm outward in the gesture of divine munificence. She sits with her legs crossed in a meditative pose or with one leg outstretched, ready to spring into action. Her lotus pedestal rests on her animal mount, a boar of golden hue.[8] The aśoka wand remained her emblem in all of her manifestations.

The name Aśokakāntā, "Aśoka Maiden," or "Beautiful Lady of the Aśoka Tree," evokes her close connection or spiritual affinity with the aśoka. Thus, the inspiration behind this goddess may be sought in the cultural significance of this type of tree. The aśoka, which blossoms with magnificent clusters of coral-red flowers, is attributed with magical and healing properties relating to female fertility and amorous desire. Women may invoke the indwelling spirit of a tree for the gift of a child or use its bark to induce menstruation or aid in conception.[9] The aśoka in turn feels a longing, or pregnant craving (*dohada*), for the touch of a woman's foot and may refuse to unfurl its flowers until it has received the fecundating kick.[10] The affinity between the flowering tree and fruitful women was once celebrated in a springtime festival in which maidens decked in holiday finery gathered the colorful blossoms, wove them into their hair, and danced around the trees beneath the canopy of scarlet-laden branches.[11] Merely being in the presence of a tree in bloom may arouse erotic longings, as it did for Emperor Aśoka.[12] Aśoka wands and flowers figure in Buddhist love magic intended to attract or compel a lover[13] and in Tantric rites of yakṣiṇī propitiation.[14] An exceptionally large and august aśoka might attract pilgrims and receive a full range of ritual worship.[15]

The aśoka tree was also significant in Buddhism prior to its association with Mārīcī. The tree under which Queen Māyādevī gave birth to Shakyamuni is recurrently identified as an aśoka.[16] In the sculptural program of Bhārhut (second and first centuries B.C.E.), the flowering aśoka abounds as a tree that graces the gardens of heaven and earth. One stone roundel depicts worship of a sacred aśoka with an altarlike dais around its base. Lay worshippers kneel before the tree in prayerful reverence, offer flower garlands, and wave blossoms in their upraised hands.[17] In ensuing centuries, the tree most frequently portrayed in the Mathurā school of Buddhist art is the aśoka.[18]

In early Buddhist stupa reliefs, aśoka trees are often depicted with an indwelling goddess (*yakṣiṇī*), or tree spirit. A Bhārhut pillar portrays such a dryad entwined with her resident aśoka tree (Fig. 10.1). One arm embraces the tree while the other bends a branch into an arch over her head, her left leg is wrapped around the trunk, and her left hand points to her pelvic area, which is accentuated by an intricate hip girdle and knotted sash. The interlacing of blossom-laden tree and voluptuous sprite beautifully illustrates their shared fecundity, as the same sap of life circulates between them. The motif of a yakṣiṇī or tree spirit (*vṛkṣa-devatā*) intertwined with an aśoka tree also appears at Sāñcī and Nāgārjunakoṇḍa.[19] Perhaps most definitive in this regard are the stupa railings of Sanghol, where all of the arboreal yakṣiṇīs are shown beneath a flowering canopy of aśoka boughs.[20] Moreover, Buddhist and Jain writings introduce several yakṣiṇīs named Aśokā after their resident trees.[21]

In view of the recurrent association between yakṣiṇīs and aśoka trees, Aśokakāntā Mārīcī appears to be a metamorphosis of a popular type of sylvan spirit into a Mahayana goddess, whose persona thus reflects the enduring Buddhist veneration for tree spirits. Several meditation manuals state that Mārīcī "arises from the luster of the aśoka tree," signifying that she derives her essence from her tutelary tree.[22] Yakṣiṇīs are commonly envisaged as radiant and golden, which may account for the original attribution of this color to Aśokakāntā. The aśoka wand—pictured as a branch or entire tree—that she displays may well have been inspired by the characteristic stance of a dryad grasping a tree bough. There are even artistic representations in which aśoka branches blossom above Mārīcī or she stands beside a flowering tree in the manner of a yakṣiṇī.[23]

Aśokakāntā Mārīcī occurs both as an independent goddess and as an attendant of Tārā (see Fig. 17.4).[24] The earliest known representations, in stone reliefs at Ratnagiri, depict her in both roles, although primarily as an independent figure.[25] She also appears in both capacities in the *Sādhanamālā*, representing the latest phase of Buddhist iconography in India.[26] In Tibet, too, she retains both offices, figuring as the focus of a range of meditations and as an acolyte of Tārā in her tremendously popular Khadiravaṇī form (Pl. 10).

10.1 Culakoka Devatā, Great Stupa, Bhārhut, Satna District, Madhya Pradesh, India, Śuṅga period, ca. 100–80 B.C.E. Sandstone. Indian Museum, Calcutta. Photo: American Institute of Indian Studies. *The tree spirit of the flowering aśoka prefigures Mārīcī in her Aśokakāntā, or "Aśoka Maiden," epiphany.*

Warrior Goddess of the Dawn

The next stage in Mārīcī's evolution was her incarnation as warrior goddess of the dawn, brandishing weapons and mounted in a militant pose on a golden chariot. There are no identifiable phases of transition between Mārīcī as the lady of the aśoka tree and her emergence as a multiarmed warrior, and thus the link between these epiphanies is unclear. Both hold an aśoka branch, flower, or tree, but here the similarity ends. Mārīcī in her martial manifestation, as goddess of the dawn, is usually described as golden but may also be envisioned as red or white. Her raiment is similarly drawn from the sunrise palette of yellow, red, and white. A female charioteer steers her chariot in constant pursuit of her foes—the dangers that beset her worshippers. Along with beams of light, her arsenal includes an aśoka flower or branch, bow, arrow, scepter (vajra), elephant goad, noose, needle, and thread.

Addressing the use of her implements, a Sanskrit meditation manual explains that she uses her bow and arrow to pierce her foes, noose to capture them, goad to strike their hearts, thunderbolt scepter to shatter their hearts, needle and thread to bind their eyes and mouths, and aśoka branch to sprinkle them.[27] Sprinkling water from a branch is an exorcistic motif, referencing the expulsion of demonic forces. This description leaves no doubt regarding Mārīcī's primary function.

Whatever prompted Mārīcī's dramatic transformation from tree goddess to warrioress of the dawn, the latter became her most prevalent form in India. This martial hierophany appears first with six arms, bearing an array of the implements described above. The presence of the needle, thread, and aśoka wand generally allows a definitive identification (Fig. 10.2). In the most common configuration, pictured here, Mārīcī wields a vajra, arrow, and needle in her right hands and a bow, aśoka bough, and thread in her left. One does, however, occasionally encounter a rearrangement of these attributes or the replacement of one or two by a goad or a noose. Her chariot may be drawn by galloping pigs, her customary steed, but about two-fifths of the reliefs show horses in their stead, as seen here.[28]

The six-armed version of the iconography prevails at Ratnagiri and Bodhgayā and is amply attested at other Buddhist sites in Bihar, Bengal, and Orissa.[29] Despite its obvious popularity, the six-armed epiphany receives scant attention in extant written sources of Indian origin.[30] The Sakya pantheon, however, includes a six-armed form with a horse-drawn chariot, discussed below.

The six-armed form apparently evolved into and was largely supplanted by the eight-armed form, which predominates in artistic representations from the tenth century onward. Accordingly, it is the eight-armed variety, with differing

10.2 Mārīcī, Bodhgayā, Gaya District, Bihar, India, Pāla period, ca. ninth or tenth century. Sandstone, height 21.65 in. (55 cm). Museum fuer Indische Kunst, Berlin, MIK I 380. Photo: Bildarchiv Preussischer Kulturbesitz/Art Resource, N.Y. *Mārīcī with her needle and thread clearly visible in her lowermost pair of hands and an aśoka blossom beside her left shoulder. Rampant horses draw her chariot.*

combinations and configurations of implements, that is recorded in the *Sādhanamālā*.[31] Thomas Donaldson observes that these liturgies reflect the final and most elaborate phase of Mārīcī's iconographic evolution as an auroral warrior, including such late-appearing elements as her chaitya (stupa) residence, diadem ornament, sow head, and fourfold mandala entourage.[32] The eight-armed form is also well represented in the Tibetan Tanjur.[33]

There are numerous stone stelae of this conception of the goddess, from ateliers spanning northeastern and eastern India.[34] A circa eleventh-century relief from Bihar crisply delineates her boar face, formidable needle and thread, and mandala retinue (Fig. 10.3). Seven rampant boars draw her chariot, while the flames carved into her aureole and deeply incised flowing lines in her lower garment convey her brilliance and dynamism. Many comparable large-scale statues herald the importance of this vision of Mārīcī in late Indian Buddhism. This impressive corpus, elaborate in conception and exquisite in workmanship, reflects intense devotion to the goddess and ardent faith in her saving powers. In addition to large images intended for public worship spaces, one finds smaller-scale bronze votive images.[35] Such statues are known to have been commissioned for private use in a home shrine or monastic cell, but they might also be found on a temple altar or placed on a mandala platform during an initiation ritual, as seen in Himalayan settings today.

Additional iconographic forms of Mārīcī attest to the degree that she stimulated the religious imagination over the centuries.[36] These rarely encountered epiphanies are eclipsed in popularity by her six- and especially eight-armed manifestation as warrioress of the dawn.

Mārīcī's powers are ultimately those of enlightened mind; her light is the radiance of spiritual illumination. A mind that has discovered the truth becomes in essence a light to the world, a source of inspiration and guidance for others, dispelling the shadows of delusion and moral torpor. In the form of Mārīcī, this light is apotheosized as a dynamic, all-conquering warrioress who protects and liberates. Mārīcī is described as "residing in a chaitya" and as one "whose hair is ornamented by a chaitya."[37] The chaitya, or stupa, is a mound-shaped, pinnacled structure that symbolizes enlightenment. In artistic images, she may be framed by a chaitya or shown with one or more chaityas floating above her or displayed on her crown, signaling that the light she bears is the radiance of truth. Moreover, her stelae may be endowed with a flame pattern or deeply incised light rays to convey her brilliance (see Fig. 10.3).

The dawn motif associated with Mārīcī also alludes to enlightenment, for Shakyamuni Buddha attained complete awakening with the appearance of the first rays of morning light. Janice Leoshko attributes the popularity of Mārīcī at Bodhgayā, evinced by the concentration of stelae found there, to her association

10.3 Mārīcī, Bihar, India, Pāla period, ca. eleventh century. Black basalt, height 22 in. (56 cm). Indian Museum, Calcutta, A25192 N.S. 4614. Used by permission. Photo: American Institute of Indian Studies. *Mārīcī as warrioress of the dawn, fiery and dynamic, her left face that of a fierce boar.*

with the "dawning" of enlightenment.[38] Suggestive in this regard, too, is the Sakya inclusion of several forms of Mārīcī in the "Vajrāsana" series, so named with reference to the "adamantine throne" (*vajrāsana*) beneath the bodhi tree, where Shakyamuni attained illumination. The stated purpose of the series is the destruction of all outer and inner obstacles to enlightenment.[39]

Mārīcī's porcine mount and chariot steed is portrayed in some cases as a pig but more often as a boar. Texts may refer to the creature simply as *śūkara*, "pig," without stipulating whether the domestic pig (*gṛha-śūkara*) or wild boar (*vana-śūkara*, or *varāha*) is intended. In artistic representations, her chariot sometimes appears to be drawn by the domesticated variety, while in other cases the sleek, tusked wild boar is depicted. When Mārīcī herself gains the attribute of a sow head, however, in the mature phase of her iconographic evolution, it is designated and rendered as that of a wild boar (*varāha*), with its characteristic tusks and long snout (see Fig. 10.3). Texts may specify that the face is wrathful and snarling, with bared fangs and lolling tongue.[40] Her theriomorphic attendants similarly have boar rather than pig heads.

The association of the pig and boar with Mārīcī has given rise to several lines of speculation.[41] I propose that the boar primarily reflects her character as a warrioress and protector. In Indian symbology, the boar always connotes power, whether it represents intransigent negativity, conquering might, or royalty. Thus we may understand why the Hindu gods Viṣṇu, Kṛṣṇa, and Brahmā all assumed the form of a boar in order to rescue the earth.[42] Similarly, we find a boar-headed Vārāhī, "She-Boar," among the fierce "mothers" (*mātṛkā*) who offer protection to their worshippers.[43] The ferocious boar, a formidable predator, is also associated with divine huntresses in India.[44] The creature is armed with lethal tusks and is by temperament a swift and vicious fighter and undeterrable attacker of prey. A boar will fearlessly charge even a potentially deadly quarry. Therefore, the boar is an appropriate emblem and chariot steed for a huntress and warrior goddess. One meditation manual confirms that, as Mārīcī advances, "obstacles are trampled down by the boars."[45] Others elaborate that the seven boars apply their aggressiveness to her service by crushing underfoot the nine planets (*navagraha*), malefactors, famine, disease, and death.[46]

The boar steeds also have an astronomical aspect. We find precedence for this in a Vedic reference to the morning star, the celestial herald of the dawn, as a fiery boar of heaven.[47] The golden color of the boars pulling Mārīcī's chariot would accord with their representation of shining planetary bodies or rays of light. Typically numbered as seven, the boars match the number of planets governing the days of the week in Indic astronomy. Thus, the boars appear to be analogous to the chariot mounts of Sūrya, the Indic sun god, which are explicitly understood to represent planetary bodies.[48] Bolstering this interpretation is the appearance of another heavenly figure, Rāhu (the eclipse deity and ascending lunar node, regarded as a planet), as the prow ornament of Mārīcī's chariot.[49] Moreover, Mārīcī may be described as holding the sun and moon, which are also counted as planetary bodies (*graha*), and the sun and moon may appear in her crown or shining above her.[50]

It may seem incongruous that Mārīcī should be credited with the power to defeat the planets and yet display them in her armory. However, the planets themselves receive worship in India for their power to overcome enemies and protect from danger, including perils of which they have been the origin.[51] Therefore, the constellation of such luminaries in the portraiture of Mārīcī would magnify her celestial splendor and proclaim the forces at her command as she soars through the firmament.

Tantric Manifestations and Mandalas

Like many dhāraṇī goddesses, Mārīcī has explicitly Tantric hierophanies that represent the latest phase in her iconographic evolution. In these forms she is red, the prototypical color of Tantric goddesses, and has one or more boar heads. She displays a fierce demeanor and wears Tantric regalia, such as a tiger skin around her hips, snake adornments, and a necklace of skulls. In her twelve hands she holds weaponry and a skull bowl. The various Tantric forms of Mārīcī differ only in minor variations among the hand implements.[52] Several names of her Tantric manifestation make reference to Oḍḍiyāna,[53] perhaps to identify or claim its place of origin as Oḍḍiyāna (or Uḍḍiyāna), a region in northwestern India and present-day Pakistan that was a major center of Tantric practice and innovation.

Representations of Mārīcī in Tantric, twelve-armed form are relatively rare, although a small selection of manuscript paintings and stone sculptures have been documented. One of the stone reliefs was discovered in an Orissan village aptly named Mārīcīpur, "City of Mārīcī."[54]

Even in her Tantric manifestations, Mārīcī is primarily envisioned as an independent deity who is rarely paired with a consort. In her non-Tantric forms, Mārīcī is linked with Vairocana, the Buddha of infinite luminosity, whose effigy may appear on her diadem or at the pinnacle of her chaitya, particularly toward the close of the Pāla period. Therefore, it is unsurprising that Vairocana is cast as her consort in an isolated Tantric meditation on Mārīcī.[55] I have not, however, encountered a text in which she appears as *his* consort or an artistic representation of the pair as a couple in sexual embrace. When Vairocana is envisioned with a consort, he is typically coupled with Tārā, Cakravartinī, or an unnamed partner.[56] Therefore, the relationship between Vairocana and Mārīcī appears to be an association based on the luminous essence they share rather than a Tantric conception of the two as a divine couple.

Mārīcī mandalas are characterized by an all-female retinue. The simplest consists of five deities: Mārīcī at the center and an emissary posted in each of the cardinal directions. Her four attendants are red Vartālī, with a boar face; yellow Vadālī; white Varālī; and red Varāhamukhī, optionally with a boar face. These goddesses have two or four hands and hold varying implements drawn from Mārīcī's standard arsenal.[57] It is appropriate that they share her colors and attributes, for they are emanations she sends forth to accomplish her purposes. When this mandala is depicted in sculptural form, the four subsidiary goddesses may be carved wherever there is available space (see Fig. 10.3), although the viewer understands them to be arrayed in a circular mandala pattern. Thomas Donaldson has identified an independent relief of Varāhamukhī, raising the intriguing possibility that the four retinue figures might be carved separately and arranged into a massive, truly impressive tableau.[58]

A more elaborate mandala, with twenty-five deities, is also well attested. Here Mārīcī has six arms and assumes a lunging stance but may be portrayed in the dancing pose characteristic of Tantric goddesses. She has three faces; the left one is that of a dark blue, fierce wild boar. Each of her twenty-four emissaries has a boar head and two arms and dances atop a lotus pedestal supported on the back of a boar.[59] Lokesh Chandra notes that the names of most of the retinue deities reflect phenomena associated with the dawn. For instance, the designations of the four innermost goddesses describe the sun just before it crests the horizon, namely, "invisible," "concealed," "dimly visible," and "glowing."[60]

Uṣas and Durgā as Divine Prototypes

While Aśokakāntā Mārīcī appears to be a natural evolution of a sylvan deity (*yakṣiṇī*) popular in earlier Buddhism, it is not clear what propelled her metamorphic leap into a queen of battle and goddess of the dawn. The most widely accepted explanation is that Mārīcī in her martial mode was patterned on the Hindu sun god, Sūrya, a chariot-borne warrior of fiery splendor.[61] It is unnecessary, however, to link Mārīcī with a male solar deity when she has a direct female forebear in Uṣas, the goddess of the dawn celebrated in the Vedas (second and first millennia B.C.E.).

Mārīcī shares many features with the Vedic dawn goddess. Hymns of the *Ṛg Veda* invoke Uṣas as a lovely, radiant young woman clothed in sunrise hues. She is golden, wears jewelry and white raiment, and bares her gleaming breasts. Smiling as though to invite a lover, Uṣas is friendly, benevolent, a joy to behold, gladdening to the heart, inspiring praise.[62] Blushingly beautiful and enticingly nubile as she may be, this alluring maiden has battle rather than love on her mind. She sends forth her beams of light like "heroes preparing their weapons for war" and "troops arrayed for battle."[63] Advancing swiftly in her chariot drawn by red horses, Uṣas drives back evil, dispersing demons in her wake and protecting her worshippers from their enemies.[64] A warrioress and a huntress, "she chases the foes like a valiant archer; like a swift warrior she repels darkness."[65] Mārīcī shares all of these characteristics with Uṣas. The Buddhist goddess even has a popular hierophany, discussed below, in which her chariot is drawn by roan horses, like that of her Vedic ancestress.[66]

The Hindu goddess Durgā, in her all-conquering Mahiṣāsuramardinī form, may also have inspired Mārīcī's transformation into a battle queen. This epiphany of Durgā, tremendously popular throughout India from the late Gupta period (fourth through fifth centuries C.E.) onward, rescued the universe from annihilation when she killed the buffalo demon Mahiṣa. She is usually portrayed at her moment of supreme victory, in the act of slaying the demon. With many arms (typically eight or ten, but ranging from four to twenty or more), holding numerous weapons, she takes a triumphal lunge with her sword raised high, having just decapitated Mahiṣa, and delivers the fatal spear thrust to the demon who had threatened the universe with the darkness of total destruction.

Mārīcī bears a striking visual semblance to the Hindu goddess. Like Durgā, she is arrayed for battle, brandishing weaponry in her many arms. Mārīcī stands in the same militant pose but usually faces right, whereas Durgā typically lunges to the left. In their most commonly depicted, eight-armed forms, both goddesses wield a bow and arrow, thunderbolt scepter, and noose. Interestingly, in a number of stone reliefs of eight-armed Mārīcī, her uppermost right hand brandishes a sword (Fig. 10.4), although the sword is not prescribed in textual descriptions.[67] Mārīcī raises the sword above her head in the manner typical of Durgā (Fig. 10.5), heightening the similarity to her Hindu counterpart.

As Mārīcī's arms were multiplied to ten, twelve, and sixteen, she acquired a shield, spear, staff, sword, trident, severed head of Brahmā, water pot, mace, club, and discus.[68] All of these appear in Durgā's arsenal, narrowing the iconographic gap between the two figures. Unlike Durgā, who pinions Mahiṣa with one of her feet, Mārīcī does not typically trample an antagonist. In some forms, however, Mārīcī is described as treading upon several Hindu gods, including Indra, Śiva, Viṣṇu, and Brahmā, thereby sharing Durgā's ascendancy over these male deities.[69]

There is also a close correspondence in the activities of Mārīcī and Durgā on behalf of their petitioners. After Durgā performed her act of cosmic salvation, she assured her devotees that she would come to their rescue in times of distress

10.4 Mārīcī, Bihar, possibly Nālandā, India, Pāla period, ca. ninth or tenth century. Black basalt, height 43.7 in. (111 cm). Indian Museum, Calcutta, A25131 N.S. 3827. Used by permission. Photo: American Institute of Indian Studies. *In addition to her customary weaponry and aśoka wand, Mārīcī raises a sword.*

10.5 Durgā Mahiṣāsuramardinī, Backerganj District, Bengal, India, Pāla period, ca. early eleventh century. Black stone, height 42 in. (107 cm). Dacca Museum. Photo: The Huntington Archive, The Ohio State University. *Durgā at her moment of supreme triumph, sword raised, slaying the buffalo demon Mahiṣa.*

and danger, promising to save them from thieves, assault, fire, lions, tigers, elephants, demons, enemies, imprisonment, execution, shipwreck, and invading armies.[70] These closely dovetail the perils from which Mārīcī offers protection, although admittedly they represent a rather standard litany of the dangers from which a great savior would be expected to provide rescue.[71] Both Avalokiteśvara and Tārā, for example, are invoked to save their petitioners from "eight great fears" that overlap this list. Avalokiteśvara and Tārā, however, are envisioned as peaceful rather than martial figures in this role. Significant for the present argument, then, is that Mārīcī in her militant aspect approximates Durgā in both activity and iconographic form and even incorporates some of her attributes.

Therefore, it seems likely that this hierophany of Mārīcī—armed for battle against demons, dangers, and delusion—was a Buddhist response to the strong appeal of Durgā Mahiṣāsuramardinī as a radiant, all-conquering warrioress. In the Hindu context, the power that Durgā personifies is known as *śakti*, a potent force, female in essence, dynamic as electricity, whose movement through the phenomenal world bestows life, creativity, genius, military prowess, and royal sovereignty. Although Indian Buddhists would call Mārīcī's power by another name, it is possible that by virtue of their cultural background they envisioned her as an embodiment of a fiery, commanding, conquering force that is essentially feminine in nature and thus finds its most powerful and direct expression in female deities.

Mārīcī in Tibet and Nepal

The many manifestations of Mārīcī were transmitted to Tibet, and she retains a presence in the active pantheon in a range of forms. The six- and eight-armed varieties gained some currency, although the lunging pose was largely supplanted by a seated posture (Fig. 10.6).[72] The white, ten-armed form found a place in the Tibetan canon but is not otherwise attested.[73] The more explicitly Tantric versions—red with twelve arms—were transmitted to Tibet but are less frequently encountered in art or active practice traditions.[74]

The manifestation now prevalent in the Tibetan pantheon is two-armed Aśokakāntā Mārīcī, who appears both as an attendant of Tārā and as an independent deity. Meditations on Aśokakāntā envision her divine essence first in the form of an aśoka branch whose golden radiance then gives rise to the goddess in figural form. Her visualization is to be performed at dawn while facing the rising sun or at twilight while facing the setting sun. A distinctive feature of her practice is the creation of a protective halo of light rays around the meditator in the shape of a stupa. Moreover, the shining golden boars that draw her chariot

10.6 Mārīcī, Tibet, nineteenth century. Thang-ka, detail. Mineral pigment on cotton, 34 × 19 in. (86.4 × 48.3 cm). Shelley and Donald Rubin Collection, P1996.3.1. Photo: Shelley and Donald Rubin Collection. *In Tibet, Mārīcī came to be shown in a seated posture rather than the lunging stance favored in India.*

send forth countless emanations that scavenge among the remains of her conquests, devouring vanquished evildoers and then coalescing into a protective shield made of their menacing, snarling faces.[75] A feature seen in Tibetan statuary of Aśokakāntā—stipulated in some Sanskrit liturgies but not encountered in known Indic images—is that she sits on a lotus atop a large boar rather than a chariot.[76] One also finds more elaborate effigies in which her chariot and boar steeds are cast separately, creating a dramatic tableau of a goddess in perpetual pursuit of threats to her petitioners (Fig. 10.7).[77]

Other forms practiced in Tibetan Buddhism include a two-armed hierophany bearing a needle and thread. The violent application of these seemingly innocuous implements becomes apparent when she is invoked to "bind, bind the eyes and mouth of all the wicked and corrupt, and when their mouth is bound, crush, paralyze, and confuse them." She sends forth countless emanations, identical to herself, to capture and render impotent all beings bent on inflicting harm.[78]

A six-armed manifestation riding a horse-drawn chariot figures in a meditation in which each of her weapons is multiplied to form concentric protective

10.7 Mārīcī, Tibet, possibly seventeenth century. Bronze. American Museum of Natural History. Photo: Library Services, American Museum of Natural History. *A lively tableau of a goddess in perpetual pursuit of dangers to her supplicants.*

barriers of scepters, threaded needles, bows, arrows, nooses, and aśoka trees around the meditator.[79] Interestingly, the same six-armed epiphany, with horses as the chariot steed, is well attested in Indic statuary (see Fig. 10.2) but not in extant textual sources,[80] alerting us that the Tibetan pantheon may preserve the record of Indian deities whose memory would otherwise be lost.

Although Mārīcī is primarily envisioned in the Tibetan pantheon as a celestial queen in seated repose (Fig. 10.8), rather than as the lunging, Durgā-like warrioress revered in India, she is nonetheless deemed to be a powerful and fearsome protector. Even when she wields only a seemingly innocuous aśoka branch, or needle and thread, she is a formidable champion, capable of warding off enemies and serious evildoers, and the predominant deity of choice for protection from robbery and criminal assault.[81] On the metaphysical level, Mārīcī's power may be attributable to the force of wisdom, but in the realm of ritual performance her ability to protect her supplicants from harm is the predominant concern.

The dictum that Mārīcī be invoked at dawn also remained in force, although it is not clear how widespread the custom may have been. L. Austine Waddell reported that during his visit to the Gelug Namgyal monastery in Tibet, in the late nineteenth century, the monks invoked Mārīcī each morning by saluting the rising sun with raised right hand and reciting her mantra seven times, declaring, "Whenever I recall your name I am protected from all fear. . . . Protect me, O Goddess, from all the eight fears of foes, robbers, wild beasts, snakes and poisons, weapons, fire, water, and high precipices."[82] The danger of imprisonment in the Indic formula is replaced here by that of high precipices, a peril endemic to the Tibetan landscape, but the emphasis on her protective powers remains. I did not investigate the continuance of the sunrise salutation in contemporary Tibetan monastic life in diaspora, a question I leave for others to pursue.

There is little evidence of the practice of Mārīcī in Nepal today, although her mantra figured in the dhāraṇī repertoire for many centuries. An historical chronicle reports that King Aṃśuvarman (seventh century) used her mantra to slay a nāga king and claim his crest jewel, which the ruler donated to be placed at the pinnacle of Svayambhū Stupa.[83] Paintings of Tantric forms of Mārīcī illustrate two Prajñāpāramitā manuscripts dating from the eleventh century.[84] Mārīcī appears in *Saptavāra Dhāraṇī* texts as one of the seven (*sapta*) goddesses whose mantras are to be recited on their respective days (*vāra*) of the week to invoke their varied benefactions and forms of protection. Evidence of this sevenfold group spans the fifteenth through nineteenth centuries.[85] Mārīcī also finds inclusion in the *Dhāraṇī Saṃgraha*, a mantra compendium once important in Nepal that, like the *Saptavāra*, has largely fallen into disuse.[86] Newar sources primarily envision Mārīcī in pacific six- and eight-armed forms.[87]

Although she retained a long-standing presence in Newar Buddhism, Mārīcī did not emerge as a major deity in that setting and at present plays no discernible role in the pantheon. There are no active sites or venues of her worship in Nepal, and she figures in contemporary art only in the form of statuary crafted for Tibetan patrons. I observed many exquisite effigies of Mārīcī in the shops of Patan, the metal-working center of Nepal, during a series of research trips in the late 1990s and 2000. Mārīcī was represented in various iconographic

10.8 Mārīcī, China, Ming Dynasty, Yongle period (1403–1424). Gilt brass painted with cold gold and blue and pigments, height 11.4 in. (29 cm). Potala Collection (Lhasa, Central Tibet), Lima Lhakhang, 950. Photo after Ulrich von Schroeder, 2001, *Buddhist Sculptures in Tibet*, vol. 2, pl. 357B. *Even in seated repose, atop a single boar, the warrioress of the dawn is an imposing figure.*

forms, but, regardless of the epiphany, the prevailing convention was to depict her seated atop a large boar, in the manner illustrated here (see Fig. 10.8).

Therefore, Mārīcī's presence has been most strongly felt in India and Tibet, where Buddhists have turned to her for protection from enemies, thieves, mortal dangers, and invading armies. Medieval Indian devotion to the goddess produced a legacy of magnificent paeans in stone that render eloquent testimony to the saving powers vested the unconquerable warrioress of the dawn, and she yet remains a living force in Tibetan Buddhism. It is not difficult to understand the tremendous appeal of the dazzling goddess who reveals herself in the rays of early morning light, rising each day to renew the promise of safety from the terrors that crowd the dark recesses of the human heart. Her luminosity is the brilliance of enlightened mind. She personifies the liberative power of its effulgence to reassure and protect those beset by danger, clear shadows and doubts from the paths of those who have lost their way, and illuminate the minds of those who long for spiritual awakening.

CHAPTER 11

Jāṅgulī

The Buddhist Snake Goddess

She is canopied by seven yellow serpents
And adorned with flaming jewels.
She . . . is blazing with the qualities of a young girl,
Fiercely smiling, girdled by an encircling serpent. . . .
Her right hands bear a vajra-scepter, sword, and
Māra-terrifying arrow raised with a dancing motion;
In her left are a noose grasped with a threatening gesture,
A poisonous flower, and a bow.
Her mantle is decorated with flowers,
Her lotus-seat is golden, her luster is red. . . .
From the moon-pitcher in her hand
She sprinkles waves of the Buddha-ocean
On those rendered unconscious by poison.

—*Sādhanamālā*[1]

Jāṅgulī (pronounced *JAHN goo LEE*) is arguably the most specialized deity of the Mahayana pantheon. Her sole function is to offer protection from snakebite and immunity to poison. The appearance of Jāṅgulī in the dhāraṇī repertoire perpetuated a long-standing form of supernatural intervention by Buddhist clerics. As Buddhists incorporated magical spells into their faith, it is natural that they would address so pernicious a danger as the lethally venomous snakes inhabiting India's forests and rural areas. Indeed, the earliest and largest body of spells attributed to the Buddha, found in the Pali canon and early Buddhist Sanskrit literature, protect against snakebite and commend a spirit of friendship toward the serpentine races.[2] In the accompanying stories, the occasion of the revelation of an incantation is usually the death or imminent demise of a monk who has been bitten by a snake. Killing snakes was not permitted; the Buddhist prohibition against taking life necessitated recourse to ritual measures.

When verbal incantations were transformed into deities in the dhāraṇī corpus, it stood to follow that the evolving pantheon would include a deity who embodied this crucial form of magical intervention. The introduction of Jāṅgulī augmented the magically apotropaic methodologies by which Buddhist clerics safeguarded themselves against snakebite and extended this form of protection to the laity. These formulas met the needs of Buddhist renunciants who traveled and meditated in wilderness areas and afforded them a way to serve their lay supporters. Supplementing the recitations and methods of amulet preparation already in circulation, Jāṅgulī offered a deity who could be visualized and deployed against this ever-present threat to human well-being.

Serpentine Powers

With the introduction of Jāṅgulī, Buddhists tapped into a preexisting stratum of snake worship. Before the ninth century, the female snake divinities of India were represented by earthen pots and by stone and clay effigies of snakes, rather than being rendered in anthropomorphic form. In the ninth or tenth century, the major sectarian traditions introduced personified versions of the snake goddess: Manasā appeared in the Hindu pantheon, Padmāvatī in the Jain, and Jāṅgulī in the Buddhist.[3] All three offer immunity from snakebite and display serpentine elements in their iconography. Divine yoginis displaying a serpent staff or snake head in Śākta temple reliefs during the same period represent other efforts to cast the serpent lady in iconographic form, as seen in a circa tenth-century effigy still worshipped at its original temple site in Orissa (Fig. 11.1).[4]

The name Jāṅgulī, meaning "Snake Charmer," denotes a goddess who counteracts "venom" (*jāṅgula*), possesses "knowledge of poisons" (*jāṅgulā*), and "lives in the jungle" (*jāṅgala*).[5] Although her function is to provide protection from snakes, she holds a snake as one of her emblems, for she participates in the serpentine world over which she holds sway. Snakes and their supernatural counterparts, the nāgas, are widely revered in Indian culture. They are believed to possess jewels, guard treasures beneath the earth, and harbor wisdom gleaned during their subterranean wanderings. Snakes and nāgas are also associated with life-giving rain and human fertility, in which role they are the objects of women's rituals in contemporary Bengal.[6] Consequently, transgressions against snakes and nāgas are linked to poverty, drought, and disease. Although snakes are held in fear, it is believed that they inflict harm not out of malice or aggressive instinct but because they have been disturbed and provoked to defensiveness. Therefore, snakes have a numinous aura that extends to the deities who share in their powers in order to offer protection from them.

11.1 Divine Yogini, Hirapur, Puri District, Orissa, India, ca. tenth century. Gray chlorite, height ca. 24 in. (61 cm). Photo: Archaeological Survey of India. *This divine yogini displays a snake scepter to proclaim her serpentine powers.*

Jāṅgulī is said to have a "poisonous kiss," a trait she shares with venomous snakes, and a "poisonous glance," a feature that recalls Manasā, who keeps her malignant eye closed until she desires to release venom. Moreover, one of Jāṅgulī's handheld attributes is a "poisonous flower."[7] Jāṅgulī would never inflict harm, but she has poisonous properties because she holds the secrets of the primal elixir of life, which manifests both as healing nectar and as its inverse, poison. Jāṅgulī must be intimately acquainted with both of these properties in order to exercise her curative powers. Her poisonous attributes proclaim her immunity to poison, a quality she transmits to others when invoked by mantra. The nectar she pours from her pitcher signifies her ability to nullify fiery snake venom and may allude to the sprinkling of mantrified water that typically accompanies magical snakebite cures. Indeed, the Chinese repertoire of Jāṅgulī practices includes two applications for water consecrated by her spell. In one case the water is swallowed by the poison victim; in the other the hierophant flings the water at the victim's heart.[8]

Although the prevention and cure of snakebite remain Jāṅgulī's primary roles, one finds in connection with her a rite for magically traversing bodies of water.[9] This could well stem from the association of snakes with rainfall and watery habitats, in which they maneuver as easily as on land, and thus may be an extension of her serpentine powers.

Origin Account

One of the earliest references to Jāṅgulī in Buddhist literature is a passage in the *Śikṣāsamuccaya* (ca. seventh century) wherein her name appears in conjunction with an incantatory poison antidote.[10] Jāṅgulī, like all dhāraṇī goddesses, is endowed with the sterling pedigree of having been imparted by Shakyamuni Buddha himself. In the following account, Ānanda, the Buddha's closest disciple, recounts the revelation of her practice and mantras:

> At one time, lord Buddha was traveling through Śrāvastī and staying with Anāthapiṇḍika at Jetavana, with hosts of monastics, bodhisattvas, great beings, gods, nature spirits, supernatural serpents, spirit-eagles, celestial satyrs, and demigods.
>
> Lord Buddha addressed the monastics: "Once, when I was a Bodhisattva, I traversed Gandhamādana, north of the Himalayas. Near that great mountain was a prepubescent girl (*kumārī*) with hundreds of auspicious signs, clad in deerskin, her girdle embellished by snakes, with a poisonous kiss and poisonous glance, wearing a crown, eating poisonous flowers, munching on a *mālutā* [a creeper that chokes its host].
>
> (She said:)

'Come, dear child, listen to me! I am Jāṅgulī, a magical lady most excellent, a destroyer of poison. All poisons are destroyed by my name. *Oṃ ilimitte tilimitte ilitilimitte dumbe dumbālīe dumme dummālīe karkke tarkke tarkkaraṇe marmme marmmaraṇe kaśmīre kaśmīramukte aghe aghane aghanāghane ili ilīe milīe ilimilīe akyāie apyaīe śvete śvetatuṇḍe ananurakte svāhā!*'

"O monastics, this is our incantation-lady (*vidyā*), all white and generous. One who hears this incantation (*vidyā*) just once will not be bitten by a snake for seven years, and poison will not spread in that person's body. Anyone who wears this incantation on the body (as a talisman) will not be bitten by a snake during their lifetime, and poison will not spread in that person's body. If a snake bites that person, its head will split into seven pieces, like a basil (*arjaka*) branch.

"These mantras should not be spoken in the presence of a snake, lest the snake die. [Several mantras follow.]

"O beggars, I have pronounced, spoken, stated, and declared, precisely and in entirety, what is unalterably, incontrovertibly, and utterly true: the great incantation of Jāṅgulī, in the presence of all the assembled gods, demigods, supernatural serpents, nature spirits, and beings.

"So remember the truth of the Buddha, remember the truth of the Dharma, remember the truth of the Sangha, remember the truth of speakers of truth. By this truth, by this truthful speech, let poison be nonpoisonous! Let it return to the giver of it! Let it go to the one that bites! Let it go into fire, earth, water, and pillar! Let it come to an end! Let it be pacified! Let it go to a pacification rite! Let it be so!"

Thus spoke the venerable Ānanda, and the entire assembly took delight in the discourse of the Holy One.[11]

This origin story of Jāṅgulī is interesting on several counts. The setting is Śrāvastī, a favored site for Shakyamuni's teachings on mantra recitation. The Buddha says that he met Jāṅgulī during a sojourn in the Himalayas, a region sufficiently remote to explain why the audience had not previously heard of this wondrous goddess. Furthermore, a mountain is a customary and hence credible abode for a deity. The Buddha refers to Jāṅgulī as a *vidyā*, a female who possesses knowledge of magical rites and lore, and also uses the term *vidyā* to refer to her incantation, reflecting the unity of deity (divine body) and incantation (sacred sound) in this context.

Jāṅgulī is described as a *kumārī*, a girl who has not yet experienced the onset of menstruation. The prepubescent female is accorded sanctity and magically efficacious qualities in many parts of India and the Himalayas and thus worshipped in a range of ritual settings.[12] Although Buddhist deities are commonly characterized as youthful, casting Jāṅgulī as a kumārī may have enhanced her numinosity for some factions of the audience.

Another noteworthy aspect of the origin story is the "profession of truth," a recurrent theme in dhāraṇī literature. The audience is enjoined to "remember the truth of speakers of truth," adducing a widely held Indic belief that the words of truth-speakers—such as the Buddha—have inherent supernatural power. Their "words of truth" (*satya-vāda*) carry a metaphysical potency, or "truth-magic," that can accomplish supernatural feats such as bringing rain, extinguishing fire, and counteracting poison.[13] Thus, the effectiveness of the mantras is guaranteed by the fact that they were spoken by one whose words are imbued with the miracle-working power of truthfulness. This principle underlies the mantric utterance: "By this truth, by this truthful speech, let poison be nonpoisonous!"

The narrative also includes an escape clause. The Buddha promises that a snake will not bite anyone who hears or wears the Jāṅgulī mantra, but if perchance a bite occurs, the poison will not spread. Such provisions are not uncommon, for even the most effective spell can work only in the absence of countervailing karmic forces.[14] Moreover, the snake who renders the bite will in consequence have its head split apart like a seven-pronged basil branch, a formulaic retribution in the dhāraṇī repertory.[15]

Divine Forms and Symbolic Attributes

Jāṅgulī has two arms when she appears as an attendant or retinue figure.[16] She displays her emblematic snake as her handheld attribute. Jāṅgulī sometimes appears thus in artistic representations as one of two flanking attendants of Green Tārā, although I am not aware of a textual source that prescribes this placement.[17] Jāṅgulī is, however, named as a member of the fourfold entourage of Mahāśrī Tārā, and when she appears in the fourfold retinue of Varada Tārā, she bears a fly whisk in her right hand and a snake in her left.[18]

As an independent figure, Jāṅgulī variously appears with four or six arms and as white, golden, or green in color. Three epiphanies are described in the *Sādhanamālā*. In one she is white, has four arms, and wears white snakes as ornaments. She also holds a white snake, displays the gesture that dispels fear, and with her central pair of hands strums a vina (Fig. 11.2).[19] The vina probably alludes to her influence over snakes, on the belief they are mesmerized by music, and may signal her association with nāgas, whose musical accomplishments include lute-playing.[20]

A second form of Jāṅgulī is green and her four hands display a snake, peacock feather, trident, and gesture granting freedom from fear.[21] The feather

11.2 Jāṅgulī. Drawing by Asif Sikder after Waddell, "'Dhāraṇī' Cult," fig. 6; iconography amended to that of *Sādhanamālā* nos. 106, 122. *Jāṅgulī makes a gesture of reassurance as she strums an instrument that pacifies snakes.*

reflects her role as a curer of snakebite, for the peacock is regarded in India as an enemy of the snake and is credited with the ability to ingest venom and poison without harm. A third form of the goddess is yellow and six-armed, displaying a sword, vajra, noose, bow, arrow, and "poisonous flower" (*viṣa-puṣpa*, blue lotus). She is girt by a snake and shielded by the hoods of seven serpent kings, fulfilling the requisite presence of this creature in her iconography.[22] A yellow, six-armed epiphany of Jāṅgulī is also described in the *Kṛṣṇayamāri Tantra*. This work, however, specifies only one of her handheld attributes—her emblematic snake—although it provides a peacock as her vehicle and endows her with a fourfold retinue.[23]

The iconographic variations described in literary sources imply the existence of multiple practice lineages, each with its own manner of envisioning the goddess. From this evidence, one would predict that numerous images of Jāṅgulī would have been commissioned to serve as protective talismans and ritual icons. It is perplexing, then, that so few images of Jāṅgulī appear in the known corpus of Indian Buddhist art. A large relief carving of the goddess, found at Ellora in a set of twelve dhāraṇī goddesses, all shown with two arms, portrays her with her emblematic snake scepter.[24] Another rare survival is an impressive bronze statue, crafted in Kashmir and recently discovered in the Potala collection by Ulrich von Schroeder, which depicts Jāṅgulī with six arms (fig. 11.3). Five of her handheld attributes match those assigned to her six-armed epiphany in the *Sādhanamālā*, namely, the bow and arrow in her upraised hands, vajra and poisonous flower in the middle pair, and at her heart the threatening gesture, a common visual reference to a noose grasped with a menacing flourish. The sword is not present, replaced here by the gesture of blessing. An interesting feature is the inclusion of miniature effigies of the mythical bird Garuḍa, devourer of snakes, supporting Jāṅgulī's lotus throne. Shown at the base of the sculpture are the donors who wished to secure her perpetual protection.

Additional effigies may be unearthed or ascertained in the future. Several images of snake-bearing deities found in an Orissan village have tentatively been identified as Jāṅgulī.[25] A stone sculpture from Nālandā, misidentified as Manasā, could well be Jāṅgulī. The figure is shaded by a five-serpent canopy and holds a sword, noose, varada mudrā, and axe, the first three of which are attributes of Jāṅgulī.[26] Although this iconographic configuration does not precisely match written descriptions, a discrepancy between extant Pāla-period textual and artistic sources is not uncommon.

The fact remains, however, that effigies of Jāṅgulī are conspicuously few among the extensive artistic remains of Indian Buddhism, for reasons that remain unclear. Monastics and yogic practitioners may have favored painted representations, which are unlikely to survive because of the ephemerality of the medium. It is also conceivable that small talismans were preferred because they could be worn as amulets, offering protection wherever the wearer might be. Such talismans are generally made of bark, paper, cloth, or clay and disintegrate over time. Metal images, although more durable, are vulnerable to destruction by those who desire the metal for other purposes. Therefore, the impressive Kashmiri bronze

11.3 Jāṅgulī, Kashmir, India, tenth or eleventh century. Brass, painted with cold gold and blue pigment, height 8.2 in. (20.8 cm). Potala Collection (Lhasa, Central Tibet), Lima Lhakhang, 71. Photo after Ulrich von Schroeder, 2001, *Buddhist Sculptures in Tibet*, vol. 1, pl. 65A. *Jāṅgulī's lotus pedestal is supported by miniature effigies of the mythical bird Garuḍa, devourer of snakes.*

pictured above (Fig. 11.3) may be a rare survival of a more extensive sculptural repertoire. Stone effigies created for public worship spaces are more likely to endure. The absence of such stelae may indicate that Buddhists propitiated their local snake divinity under the name of Jāṅgulī, obviating the need for explicitly Buddhist icons and shrines. Such worship of different divinities at common shrines is attested in the Buddhist world today, for example, in Nepal.

Jāṅgulī in Tibet and Nepal

Jāṅgulī was transmitted to Tibet, where her name was rendered as Dukselma, "Poison Remover."[27] Her practice, however, did not take permanent hold. The narrowness of specialization that recommended Jāṅgulī in the Indic context may have limited her appeal in the new venue, while her serpentine features may not have held the same numinosity for a populace less beset and awed by snakes. Tibetologist Stephan Beyer concludes that the snake goddess "evoked almost no response in the hearts of any but the most scrupulously studious Tibetans," for he could find no artist familiar with her iconography or scholar who knew of a text devoted to her, even among his most learned informants.[28]

Although Tibetans pursue supernatural protection from snakebite and affliction by nāgas, they turn for this service to other deities, such as Mārīcī and especially Tārā, the most beloved goddess of Tibet. One of the "eight great fears" from which Tārā offers rescue is snakes and indeed every type of poison, from snake venom, rabid dogs, and tainted food and drink to the poison of wrong views.[29] The most popular Tibetan hymn to Tārā hails her as the "dispeller of all poison" and claims for its recitation the power to counteract any poison ingested by oneself or another.[30] This litany, recited daily by monastics and laity, keeps this aspect of Tārā in the forefront of awareness, arguably rendering a deity with Jāṅgulī's specialization superfluous. Thus, when Jāṅgulī appears in this context as an attendant of Tārā, she becomes in essence an emanation of that goddess, personifying one of Tārā's capacities. Apropos is an early (ca. 1100) Tibetan painting that pairs Jāṅgulī and Mahāmāyūrī, another protector against snakebite, as Tārā's acolytes.[31] This configuration, unique among known representations, signals recognition of Jāṅgulī while intimating her absorption by the Tārā cultus, which eventually brought to a close her independent career in that setting.

Neither is there evidence that the worship or mantra practice of Jāṅgulī has survived in Nepal, where the widespread propitiation of snakes and nāgas is directed to supernatural serpent kings that are supplicated throughout the year and during their annual festival, Nāga Pañcamī. The need for a specialist such as Jāṅgulī was obviated by the popularity in the Newar pantheon of the Pañcarakṣā goddesses, who offer protection from snakebite among their diverse benefactions. One may predict that, had Buddhism survived in India, Jāṅgulī would have retained there her honored position in the magico-medicinal repertoire. Although Jāṅgulī has receded into the mists of history, she bears witness to a time when Indian Buddhists held snakes in awe and took refuge in a deity who wielded her influence over them by sharing in their serpentine powers.

CHAPTER 12

Sarasvatī

Divine Muse

I pay homage to you, vibrant, youthful maiden,
Your beauty equal in splendor to Mount Kailash,
Your face a hundred times more exquisite than the autumn moon,
Your entrancing eyes as delightful as a cluster of blue lotuses.

I pay homage to you, elegant in your cross-legged pose,
As your hands draw forth sweet harmonies of celestial musicians;
Your voice is a honey-sweet stream,
An abundant elixir for all who hear.

I pay homage to you, Sarasvatī, for you bestow
Perfect skill in oratory, debate, and composition. . . .
Lucid expression thrills every sharp mind, so I beseech you:
Grant me wisdom in writing, debate, and teaching.

—The Second Dalai Lama[1]

Sarasvatī (pronounced *sah RAS wah TEE*) is the patroness of art, culture, and all the fruits of the intellect. She floats in a sonorous cloud of music, rustling silk, and tinkling ornaments as she glides, graceful and serene, on her celestial swan, alighting in heavenly lotus pools. Her moonlike radiance quickens intelligence and discernment; her calm smile fosters lucid reflection and creative inspiration. Sarasvatī continuously strums an instrument that fills the universe with ethereal song. Her delicately tapered fingers clasp a crystal rosary, for she inspires contemplation and sacred speech of every kind: hymns of praise, scriptural recitation, prayers, and mantras. The Buddhist muse also bears a palm-leaf manuscript, for she grants fluency and elegance of expression to poets, scholars, playwrights, philosophers, and teachers. Worshippers invite her into their hearts in the hope that she will reside there, bestowing a stream of eloquence and a blossoming of literary and artistic creativity.

Early History and General Character

Sarasvatī predates Buddhism by many centuries, having first been introduced in Vedic hymns in the second millennium B.C.E. Her name means "Lady of the Waters," or "Flowing One." The goddess originally derived her name from the river Sarasvatī, no longer extant, along which the composers of the Vedas settled and performed their rituals. It has been conjectured that the river was attributed with powers of inspiration because many Vedic hymns were composed on its banks, resulting in the deification of the river as a goddess who vivifies sacred utterance. Sarasvatī came to be honored as the divine force underlying ritual chants, the "tongue" of the sacrificial fire that conveys human communications to the gods, and indeed as the essence of sound itself. She created the art of music and imparted it to the angelic *gandharvas*, who henceforth became the musicians of heaven.[2] The *Ṛg Veda* praises her intellectually refining presence: "Inciter of all pleasant songs, inspirer of all gracious thought, Sarasvatī . . . with her light illuminates, she brightens every pious thought."[3]

In early epic and Purāṇic mythology, Sarasvatī was associated with several male deities, most notably as the daughter of Brahmā and wife of Viṣṇu, but she gradually resumed autonomous status in Purāṇic theologies and came to be worshipped independently. As her roles were elaborated, Sarasvatī became the patroness of learning, giver of intelligence to the newborn, source of the Sanskrit alphabet, bestower of poetic skill, and granter of knowledge and wisdom. She taught the art of music to the supernatural serpents (*nāgas*) as well as to humans. She is also associated with the moon, whose phases are linked to human creativity. The moon, once a jewel in her possession, became a heavenly body when she tossed it from her toiletry case.[4] The goddess eventually lost her association with a particular river but retained her role as queen of the waters with a riverine capacity to sweep away mental obstacles, refresh the intellect, and give rise to a torrent of speech.[5]

In appearance, Sarasvatī is the portrait of grace and refinement, in keeping with her role as bearer of culture and all the civilizing arts. As her appearance is delineated in Purāṇic sources, white predominates in her iconography as the color of her complexion, silken garments, and flower garland. She is as brilliant as the light of ten million moons, and a crescent moon adorns her tiara. She rides a *haṃsa*, a heavenly bird that graces the lotus lakes of paradise according to Indic cosmology. This celestial creature, variously termed "swan" and "goose" in English writings, may be rendered as a large, swanlike bird or small water fowl in artistic representations. In Hindu iconography, Sarasvatī most commonly has four arms and holds a vina, rosary, book, and consecratory vessel. The vina (*vīṇā*), as the first musical instrument according to Indic mythology, reflects Sarasvatī's role as originator and inspirer of the musical arts. The book contains "all knowledge," while the flask dispenses the "nectar of all the scholarly treatises."[6]

Sarasvatī is envisioned as a solitary goddess who is content to spend hours making music in blissful solitude; her introspective smile exudes the serenity of one who derives complete fulfillment from the inner life. Her purity and chastity are often praised; she is never associated with motherhood, fertility, or sexuality. As David Kinsley explains:

> Her presence is therefore not usually sought in the home. She is not a domestic goddess. Nor is her presence sought in the fields, where fertility is crucial, or in the forests and mountains, where isolation from culture is desired in the quest for *mokṣa.* Her presence is sought in libraries and schools, by those who create and bear culture in the ongoing task of transforming the natural world into a refined and civilized habitation for human beings.[7]

Throughout her history, Sarasvatī has been associated with intellectual and artistic pursuits and invoked by those who seek knowledge or strive through education or sacred arts to transmit the cultural values that ennoble and embellish life.

Adoption into the Buddhist Pantheon

Sarasvatī's association with the intellectual sphere assured that she would find favor among Buddhists, who highly value wisdom and its servants: mental clarity, reasoning ability, memorization, and oratorical skill. Sarasvatī thus has an affinity with Prajñāpāramitā, the goddess of perfect wisdom. They may be invoked by the same mantra, reflecting the kinship between the wisdom goddess and the patroness of learning.[8]

Sarasvatī is the only Hindu goddess adopted into the Mahayana pantheon without a change in name or significant alteration of divine persona. This continuity is reflected in her epithets in Buddhist literature as "Emanation of Viṣṇu," "Gandharva Maiden," "Swan Child," "Daughter of Brahmā" (Tshangs-pa Sras-mo), "Lady of the Lake" (mTsho-ldan-ma), "Sister of the Moon" (Zla-ba'i sring-mo), "Goddess of Speech" (Smra lha-mo), "Divine Lady Who Empowers Enlightened Speech" (Ngag-dbang lha-mo), "Goddess Rich with the Power of Adamantine Speech" (rDo-rje dbyangs kyi dbang-phyug-ma), "Bestower of Understanding" (bLo yi gter), "Goddess of Knowledge" (Rig-pa'i lha-mo), and "Wisdom Goddess" (Shes-rab kyi lha-mo).[9] Her association with speech is emphasized in the Tibetan translation of her name as Yangchenma, "Goddess of Melodious Voice." Buddhist texts acknowledge that she is worshipped by "all scholars in India, Hindus and Buddhists alike, without contention."[10] The *Kāraṇḍavyūha* (ca. sixth century), however, endows her with an explicitly Buddhist origin, holding that she emerged from the eyetooth of Avalokiteśvara when different parts of his body gave rise to the Hindu gods.[11]

There is little evidence of Buddhist worship of Sarasvatī before the fourth century C.E. She apparently finds no mention in Pali literature, and her effigies are absent from the known corpus of early Buddhist art. A female figure playing a stringed instrument, carved on a Bhārhut railing pillar (second century B.C.E.), has been accepted by some as the earliest effigy of Sarasvatī.[12] This image, however, predates iconographic descriptions and other known images of the goddess by several centuries and thus appears to be a celestial musician (*apsaras*), a type of figure often described as rejoicing in the presence of the Buddha and his relics. The same is true of several lute-bearing females in the Gāndhāran repertoire (first and second centuries C.E.).[13] Sarasvatī finds passing mention in the *Buddhacarita* (second century C.E.) among Hindu deities who helped bring forth the Vedas, according her no special Buddhist significance or reverence.[14]

The *Golden Radiance Scripture* (ca. late fourth or early fifth century) marks a transition in Buddhist conceptions of Sarasvatī. Her name appears throughout the work among the pan-Indic, rather than specifically Buddhist, divinities whose blessings are promised to listeners and reciters of the text. The non-Buddhist origin of Sarasvatī is acknowledged by her inclusion in these passages, but she is favored with placement at or near the head of these lists as the "foremost" (*pramukhā*) of the assembly and is repeatedly lauded as a "great goddess" (*mahādevī* and *mahādevatā*).[15] Moreover, Sarasvatī is the focus of one of the few chapters devoted to individual divinities. This portion of the work is the earliest known document of her explicit incorporation into the Buddhist pantheon, advancing her as an object of Buddhist invocation, ritual, and worship. She is praised as "supremely, extremely beautiful" and, among all divine females, as "the supreme, chief, excellent goddess," brilliant and pure, "a mine of knowledge," "endowed with profound wisdom."[16]

As the chapter opens, Sarasvatī pays homage to the Buddha and promises that she will grace the preachers of the scripture with eloquence, oratorical power, perfect memory, inconceivable knowledge, penetrating wisdom, illumination, skill in liberating others, scholarly expertise in every field, proficiency in all the arts, merit, prosperity, and long life.[17] Several Sarasvatī mantras (termed *dhāraṇī* in the work) for different purposes are given in the chapter, including a special recitation for memory retention. In the following mantra, translatable phrases alternate with syllables of evocatory power:

> May my insight be unobstructed! May my knowledge prosper in textbooks, verses, magic books, doctrinal books, and poems! So be it: *mahāprabhāve hili hili mili mili*. May it go forth for me by the power of the blessed goddess Sarasvatī! *karaṭe keyūre keyūrabati hili mili hili mili hili hili*.[18]

The *Golden Radiance Scripture* outlines a role for Sarasvatī that far exceeds begetting wisdom. The text proclaims that she frees her devotees from unfavorable planetary influences, human discord, nightmares, and persecution by supernatural beings—negative conditions that fall within her purview as disruptions to the tranquil, harmonious environment necessary for intellectual and creative pursuits. These obstacles and adversities are to be removed by an elaborate ablution rite. More than thirty herbs and medicinal plants must be powdered, consecrated with mantras, and added to the purifying ablution water. A Sarasvatī mandala is then constructed out of flowers, gold and silver vessels, mirrors, banners, and incense, to the accompaniment of five kinds of musical instruments. Sarasvatī is to be envisioned in eight-armed form, but her attributes are not described. The goddess promises that she will appear at the ritual site and, in addition to the aforementioned benefits, remove "every disease from that village, city, district, or dwelling," so that all who reside there may gain relief from suffering and rapidly attain enlightenment.[19]

Divine Forms and Symbolic Attributes

Buddhist envisionments of Sarasvatī took Hindu conceptions of the goddess as a point of departure. A favored Buddhist form, known as Vajravīṇā, "Lady of the Adamantine Lute," is a white, two-armed epiphany in which she plays her supernal lute, or vina. The instrument is made of lapis lazuli and has a thousand strings capable of eliciting every musical note. Sarasvatī's melodies pervade the universe and delight all types of beings in accordance with whatever is most pleasing to their ears.[20] She sits with ankles crossed and knees raised in a distinctive posture suitable for balancing a musical instrument (Fig. 12.1).[21]

Writers expend themselves to describe the patroness of poesy with literary flourish, as seen in a passage from a Sakya meditation manual:

> On the tremulous corolla of a pure white lotus, sitting charmingly on a moon-disc with upraised knees . . . she strums a celestial lute, producing melodious sounds that satisfy the hearts of the diverse beings in the three

12.1 Sarasvatī, China or Mongolia, ca. 1850. Mineral pigment and gold over woodblock print on paper, height 3.54 in. (9 cm). Ethnographic Museum of the University of Zurich. Photo after Willson and Brauen, *Deities of Tibetan Buddhism*, no. 8. *Sarasvatī assumes a musician's crossed-ankle pose for balancing a stringed instrument.*

realms, each in their own idiom. Her long hair, soft and black as bees, is twisted into a chignon, with soft curls hanging down on the right and left, and tresses streaming down her back. Her head is circled by a garland of white flowers; her diadem is ornamented by a crescent moon. Her face is lovely and smiling, with comely cheeks framed by dangling golden earrings. . . . She wears a crystal necklace and is wreathed with a garland of white lotuses. Her hands and wrists are adorned with strands of jewels and tinkling bells. The sight of the youthful, enchanting goddess inspires wonder in all beings.[22]

Another two-armed, white manifestation known as Mahā-Sarasvatī displays a white lotus (often supporting a book) and the gesture of divine blessing. She has a retinue of four goddesses, identical in appearance to herself, whose names reflect the gifts they bestow as her emanations: "Wisdom" (Prajñā), "Insight" (Matī), "Intelligence" (Medhā), and "Recollection" (Smṛtī).[23] This form of the goddess appears in the art of Nālandā and Ratnagiri.[24] Additional two-armed, white forms are described in the *Sādhanamālā*.[25] Sarasvatī may be depicted in a range of poses. The crossed-ankle *utkuṭakāsana* posture is most characteristic, but she may appear in a cross-legged meditative posture, seated with one leg pendant, or standing in a variety of stances. A four-armed, white epiphany in the Sakya pantheon bears, along with a lotus and musical instrument, a sword of wisdom (Fig. 12.2).[26] Buddhist texts rarely mention Sarasvatī's swan mount, but the bird may be included in artistic portrayals, adopting the Hindu convention.[27] The swan may be shown as her vehicle, her companion, or even her downy footrest.

Red forms of the goddess were introduced in the Buddhist pantheon. One two-armed form, actively practiced in Tibet, holds a wish-fulfilling gem in her right hand and a mirror of wisdom in her left.[28] She is invoked to quicken intelligence, but the miraculous jewel, source of bounty, is present to offset the poverty often attendant on intellectual pursuits. A red, six-armed manifestation known as Vajra Sarasvatī, attested in both India and Tibet, has Tantric attributes, such as a flaying knife and skull cup.[29]

The most explicitly Tantric epiphany of Sarasvatī is the red form in which she appears in union with her consort, Mañjuśrī, a male embodiment of wisdom and thus a fitting counterpart for the knowledge-bestowing goddess. Both have four arms—two for embracing one another and two left free to hold their implements. Sarasvatī strums her vina, filling the universe with an ocean of song, while Mañjuśrī bears aloft his effulgent sword and a blue lotus supporting a Prajñāpāramitā text. As he sits on her lap, their legs intertwine amidst the petals of their lotus throne. Attended by Sarasvatī's retinue of four goddesses, the divine couple is "wondrous to behold, adorned with arrays of jewels, seated within a glorious blaze of light."[30]

In Tibet, the wrathful Dharma protector Palden Lhamo is sometimes regarded as a fierce emanation of Sarasvatī.[31] To express this relationship, the lute-playing goddess may float above Palden Lhamo in paintings of the latter.[32] This association between divine protectress and muse, on surface a puzzling one, is traceable to Indic connections between Sarasvatī and Durgā, a Hindu

12.2 Sarasvatī, China or Mongolia, ca. 1850. Mineral pigment and gold over woodblock print on paper, height 3.54 in. (9 cm). Ethnographic Museum of the University of Zurich. Photo after Willson and Brauen, *Deities of Tibetan Buddhism*, no. 193. *Four-armed Sarasvatī strums her instrument yet has one arm free to raise a sword of wisdom, signifying bestowal of knowledge.*

warrior goddess. In Hindu mythology, Sarasvatī is sometimes cast as the knowledge aspect or speech aspect of the battle queen Durgā.[33] In the Buddhist context, too, Sarasvatī is linked with Durgā in the *Golden Radiance Scripture*. Although this work makes no mention of Durgā, its description of Sarasvatī draws on liturgies and iconographic conceptions of Durgā in her buffalo-demon-slaying mode.[34] Although the connection between Sarasvatī and Durgā is not a prominent theme in literature on either goddess, it is apparently one of many aspects of Durgā that left a stamp on Palden Lhamo.[35]

Patroness of Learning and Scholars

The range of blessings for which Sarasvatī is invoked in Buddhism has remained the same as in Hinduism. Even when the goddess migrated into a new cultural venue in Tibet, her character was not significantly redefined, as seen in a Drikung text extolling the benefits of meditating on a white form of Sarasvatī:

> One will become learned in all scholarly treatises.
> One will have no problem writing, debating, or teaching. . . .
> Anyone who pursues the five sciences (grammar, logic, art, medicine, and metaphysics),
> Clarity of mind, mental stability,
> A pleasant voice, and the ability to gladden others
> Should practice Sarasvatī.[36]

Rituals of white Sarasvatī may be performed by monastic or yogic specialists on behalf of lay petitioners, while the practice of red Sarasvatī, reserved for serious contemplatives and yogic practitioners,[37] yields similar benefits with greater rapidity:

> A yoga practitioner, in six months, can attain perfect wisdom;
> In six days, the meaning of all treatises will become clear;
> With a hundred thousand recitations,
> One will be able to compose one hundred verses daily
> And effortlessly memorize one hundred treatises. . . .
> Every day you can memorize a hundred verses,
> And you will achieve the power of eloquence.[38]

Because many conditions can interfere with the pursuit of knowledge, Sarasvatī has the power to remove any potential impediment. The same work promises that "one who contemplates (her) diligently and intensely will become free from all obstacles in the present lifetime. . . . The benefits are inconceivable."[39]

In Tibetan Buddhism, the practice of Sarasvatī is less widespread than that of Mañjuśrī, the male bodhisattva of wisdom, but her practice is deemed to be more powerfully and swiftly effective.[40] Her greater potency, however, carries an element of risk. Initiation into her practice is customarily followed by an intensive retreat lasting about a week, during which her mantra is recited many thousands of times, to establish a strong connection with her divine energies. The rules of the retreat include dietary restrictions, rules of food preparation, and scrupulous hygiene.[41] If the retreatant does not adhere to all the requirements, the practice may have the reverse effect and cause mental instability and derangement.[42] There is also a concern that desired mental powers may be accompanied by poverty. This belief apparently springs from a Hindu conception that Sarasvatī and Lakṣmī, the goddess of wealth, have an antagonistic relationship, a view that Upendra Nath Dhal attributes to the fact that affluence and learning rarely accompany one another.[43]

Signs of success in the practice of Sarasvatī include, according to a Gelug text:

> an improved memory, the ability to recite mantras rapidly and clearly, an understanding into the import of many scriptural texts, and even a wish to write poetry. You may also have dreams of being offered curd, milk or butter by beguiling maidens wearing much jewelry; of eating or being given fruit or the best of medicines; of being offered chalk, rare and valuable wood, or jewel and flower garlands; of seeing the sun or moon rise; of picking flowers; or of constantly bathing in pure, clean water.[44]

Among these dream signs, the color white and images of sweetness, beauty, and purity predominate, in accordance with the persona of the goddess herself.

The most definitive sign of Sarasvatī's blessings, however, is heightened intellectual powers. Many such instances may be gleaned from biographical literature. For example, when Nāgārjuna defeated a Hindu scholar in a debate on the Vedas, the latter converted to Buddhism and wanted to know the secret of Nāgārjuna's superior knowledge of a subject to which the pundit had devoted a lifetime of study. Nāgārjuna taught him the mantra of Sarasvatī, whereby the brahman gained the ability to copy an entire hundred-thousand-stanza Perfection of Wisdom scripture in just a few days. He used this gift to produce and distribute numerous copies of the manuscript to monastic libraries.[45] It was through the blessings of Sarasvatī that the Second Dalai Lama could memorize a hundred verses of scripture during a tea break and spontaneously mastered the art of poetic composition without formal training.[46] The renowned scholar Bodong became both brilliant and prolific after beholding Sarasvatī in a vision; her inspiration enabled him to compose a hundred volumes.[47] There is even report of a Hindu brahman who consistently defeated Buddhist pundits in debate because the goddess granted him expertise in logic.[48]

Scholars intent on success in intellectual pursuits continue to invoke Sarasvatī as divine muse. The possibility of attendant poverty mentioned above may be offset by augmenting her ritual with offerings to a wealth deity,[49] combining the practice of white Sarasvatī with that of Lakṣmī, or invoking red Sarasvatī.[50] The desire to avoid the proverbial genteel poverty of the scholar may help account for the prevalence in Tibet of the red form of Sarasvatī in which she bears a mirror on a lotus, symbolizing knowledge, as well as a wish-granting gem, signifying material prosperity.[51]

Worship in Nepal

Sarasvatī does not figure in the meditative and yogic practices of Newar Buddhism, a role generally reserved for esoteric Tantric deities. She is, however, important in popular devotional practices observed by Buddhists and Hindus alike. Children write the alphabet for the first time in a ritual that takes place at a Sarasvatī shrine. The chosen shrines are festooned for the occasion and surrounded with children in holiday attire. The children receive sweets and pastries and are guided by a parent or teacher in writing the letters of the alphabet in the presence of the mother of language. The goddess's roadside temples are frequented by students as they pass on their way to and from school, seeking her blessings on their studies and examinations. The annual festival of Sarasvatī, Vasant Pañcamī, is also nationally observed. During this celebration, which marks the beginning of spring, Sarasvatī is fêted with holiday repast, music, and song at her temples, while implements of art and study—pens, writing tablets, books, paintbrushes, musical instruments, and weaving tools—are honored in the home.[52] Some Buddhists undertake to make offerings at one hundred Sarasvatī shrines to observe the holiday.[53]

Although Sarasvatī retains a place in popular piety, her role in priestly liturgy and ritual is overshadowed by that of the male bodhisattva of wisdom, Mañjuśrī, who enjoys pride of place in the Newar pantheon by virtue of his role in creating the Kathmandu Valley. Indeed, in Nepal the worship of Sarasvatī is largely conflated with that of her male counterpart.[54] They share the same name, Sasudyaḥ, and Mañjuśrī temples inhabit several sites devoted to Sarasvatī.[55] Sarasvatī Mahāmañjuśrī Vihāra (New. Sasu Nanī) in Kathmandu enshrines an image of Mañjuśrī, but its Sanskrit name evinces that both deities have been honored here.[56]

Sarasvatī's main place of worship, on Svayambhū Hill, is also dedicated to Mañjuśrī. This site, a level outcropping on the hillside, is paved with a flagstone terrace and studded with stupas and trees strung with prayer flags. The focal point is a modest shrine boasting Mañjuśrī's footprints embedded in stone. The only visual reference to female divinity is the crossed-triangle *yantra* design in the metalwork gate framing the shrine. Buddhists congregate here to celebrate Sarasvatī's annual festival on the first day of spring. Hundreds of celebrants converge to make offerings to the goddess and picnic on the verdant hillside. However, even the legendry surrounding Vasant Pañcamī has begun to yield to Mañjuśrī, for some maintain that the festival marks the day he first visited Nepal or the day he cut the gorge to drain the valley for habitation, while others recognize it as the day he paid homage to Sarasvatī.[57]

12.3 Sarasvatī, Amrit Karmacharya, Patan, Nepal, last decade of twentieth century. Paubhā, detail. Pigment and gold on cloth, 15.5 × 13.5 in. (39.4 × 34.3 cm). Author's collection. *This four-armed epiphany of Sarasvatī, riding a swan, is shared by Hindus and Buddhists in Nepal. (See Pl. 5)*

Although Sarasvatī is now closely identified with Mañjuśrī in Nepal, images and sites dedicated to the goddess, many dating from the eleventh through fifteenth centuries, show that she has received her share of homage over the centuries.[58] Iconographically, four-armed manifestations of Sarasvatī, rarely encountered in the Buddhist pantheons of India and Tibet, predominate in

Nepal. She is most commonly envisioned as white, bearing a rosary and manuscript, and strumming a vina.[59] She may be seated, standing, or riding a swan (Fig. 12.3, Pl. 5). The same four-armed epiphany is favored in Hindu images, making it difficult in some cases to tell whether an icon was originally commissioned for Buddhist or Hindu use.

This iconographic convergence may stem from festivals and places of worship that Hindus and Buddhists in Nepal have held in common while maintaining their distinctive beliefs and practices. Thus, Sarasvatī's earlier worship by Hindus and Buddhists in concord has continued in Nepal. The following verse by a Nepali poet certainly expresses a widespread sentiment:

> She rides the quick and magical swan
> Which dives and plays in our hearts' deep lake,
> And she brings to life the world's games and their glory:
> May I never forget, the whole of my life,
> The goddess Saraswatī.[60]

Sarasvatī's presence in the Buddhist pantheon shows that the western dualism which assigns maleness to the superior sphere of culture while relegating femaleness to the realm of nature does not apply in the cultural setting that gave rise to Sarasvatī. The Indian ethos on the whole attributes to women and goddesses the power to give life, but "life" in this context is not understood as a merely biological or material phenomenon. Female life-giving power (*śakti*) nourishes, inspires, and empowers on every level. Without it, no goal of human life can be achieved, whether material, social, intellectual, creative, or religious. The Buddhist pantheon reflects this principle. Female divinities may be allied with the procreative forces of nature and the earth, as in the case of Vasudhārā, but they serve equally to embody wisdom, as does Prajñāpāramitā, or the animating forces of culture, as epitomized by Sarasvatī, the lady of the waters who pours forth the nectar of knowledge and artistic inspiration, nourishing the mind and spirit.

CHAPTER 13

Vasudhārā

Lady Bountiful

Holy lady, source of all blessings and well-being,
Queen of riches and glory, Vasudhārā,
Bestower of all desired good fortune,
I bow to you, noble lady, wish-fulfilling mandala.

Font of cloudlike heaps of possessions and all desirable objects,
Sporting on a water-crystal mandala,
Resting on the corolla of a many-hued lotus,
I render homage to you, holy Vasudhārā.

Beautiful as a golden mountain,
Adorned by two hands—wisdom and skillfulness,
Bestower of endless treasure to living beings,
I worship you, sublime Vasudhārā.

—Sakya ritual prayer[1]

Vasudhārā (pronounced *vah soo* DAH RAH) is a bestower of sustenance, abundance, and lavish well-being. Her name means "Stream of Treasure," "Flow of Wealth," or "Shower of Gold." She is a rich, warm harvest gold, the color of the sun as it crests the horizon, ripening grain and fruit, and the glitter of jewelry and coins. She is as bountiful as the earth as she pours forth her treasures in whatever form her devotees require, be it agricultural fertility, wealth, or wisdom. Her golden color signifies her enriching, nourishing, and ultimately enlightening presence. Vasudhārā is the doorkeeper to an invisible realm that can magically materialize riches for those who know the incantations and rites of propitiation. Her compassionate heart, overflowing with love for all beings, gives rise to an endless stream of generosity. Thus, it cannot be a mystery why, once introduced, the lady of plenty occupied a permanent place in the hearts of lay devotees and the repertoire of monastic and yogic specialists.

Vasudhārā was evidently a popular deity in late Indian Buddhism, judging from the numbers of statuary and manuscript paintings that have survived and their geographic distribution, emanating from ateliers concentrated in the Buddhist heartland of Bihar but also as far afield as Bengal, Orissa, and the Chola domain in southern India.

Origin Account

As in the case of other dhāraṇī goddesses, the introduction of Vasudhārā is attributed to Shakyamuni Buddha. What follows is the origin narrative from the *Vasudhārā Dhāraṇī*, also known as *The Inquiry of Layman Sucandra*. Sucandra approached Shakyamuni in the Kantaka grove in Kauśāmbī and, confiding that he was impoverished and had many mouths to feed, requested a method whereby he could amass stores of grain, gold, silver, and gems in order to support his family and servants and engage in philanthropy. Shakyamuni disclosed that he had learned a mantra for precisely this purpose from another Buddha in an age distant past and proceeded to reveal the incantation, promising that Vasudhārā will appear in person to shower a rain of wealth and grain on anyone who memorizes, recites, writes, or simply listens to the sacred syllables. The incantation is to be accompanied by worship of Buddhas, bodhisattvas, and Vasudhārā and a mandaḷa rite. Those who undertake the invocation will attain great merit and good fortune, while places where the mantra is recited will be prospered and blessed by its enriching influence.

Sucandra was elated with the instructions and, promising to teach others what he had learned, departed to commence the practice. Soon thereafter, Shakyamuni sent his disciple Ānanda to visit Sucandra. The monk, having seen Sucandra's overflowing storehouses, wanted to know how the layman had prospered so rapidly. The Buddha instructed Ānanda regarding the Vasudhārā dhāraṇī and extolled its powers, claiming that no god, demon, or human can impede its efficacy. He directed his disciple to practice the mantra and impart it to others "for the good of many, for the happiness of many."[2]

This origin story advocates both lay and monastic practice of Vasudhārā. Interestingly, in his discourse to Ānanda (who represents here the monastic community), the Buddha did not emphasize the material benefits of the practice, although they are implicit in the circumstances of the teaching. Rather, he commended it as a means to alleviate suffering. Perhaps anticipating those who might wonder why a teacher of renunciation would furnish a means of attaining material prosperity, Shakyamuni declared that not only he but all Buddhas teach the Vasudhārā dhāraṇī "for the well-being of all poor people and for the removal of all fears, obstructions and calamities."[3]

13.1 Vasudhārā, Kurkihār, Gaya District, Bihar, India, Pāla period, ca. mid-tenth century. Metal, with copper and silver inlay on face, height 8.4 in. (21.2 cm). Patna Museum, 9738. Photo: The Huntington Archive, The Ohio State University. *Vasudhārā displays a stalk of grain and a jewel or seed, treasures generated by the earth.*

13.2 Vasudhārā, southern wall of Monastery 1, Ratnagiri, Cuttack District, Orissa, India, possibly eighth century. Chlorite. Photo: American Institute of Indian Studies. *This stone carving evokes the primal maternal fecundity of the agrarian goddess.*

Gifts and Powers

Vasudhārā's name is rendered in some contexts as Vasundharā ("Bearer of Treasure").[4] Her primary role as a bestower of bounty is seen in her epithets as "Wish-Fulfilling Tree" (Kalpa-vṛkṣā), "Perfectly Generous One" (Dāna-pāramitā), "Giver of Wealth" (Dhanaṃ-dadā), "Dispenser of Riches" (Ratnadhātā), "Lady Who Rains" (Varṣaṇī), "Maker of Good Fortune" (Śrīkarī), "Great Wish-Granting Jewel Goddess" (Cintāmaṇi-mahādevī), "Lady Who Delights in Currency and Storehouses of Rice" (Dhānyāgāradhana-priyā), and "Supreme Ruler of the Realm of Opulence" (Ratnadhātvīśvareśvarī).[5]

Vasudhārā's gifts are not limited to material prosperity, for she bestows both outer and inner riches. Knowledge is included among life's greatest treasures in the sapiential tradition of Buddhism, wherein wisdom is the key to spiritual liberation. Therefore, the goddess who bestows all that is precious is also endowed with the names "Bearer of Knowledge" (Vidyādharī), "Embodiment of Perfect Wisdom" (Prajñā), "Bearer of Truth" (Dharma-dhāriṇī), "Foremost among Bestowers of Knowledge" (Vidyādāna-īśvareśvarī), "Knowledge Incarnate" (Jñānamurtī), "Glorious Increaser of Enlightened Ones" (Śrī Buddhavardhinī), and "Revealer of Buddhist Paths" (Darśanī Buddha-margāṇāṃ).[6] There is no inherent conflict between wealth and gnosis in the Buddhist worldview, for prosperity may well serve the persons and institutions engaged in the pursuit of wisdom.

Tāranātha's history of Buddhism in India includes several stories of the wealth that was bestowed by Vasudhārā and the uses to which it was dedicated. Buddhajñāna, a Tantric preceptor at Vikramaśīla monastery, received three hundred pearl necklaces from Vasudhārā each day, and every morning a buyer came through her auspices to purchase them. Buddhajñāna used the funds to support monks and other students, purchase worship and ritual supplies, install large votive lamps in various temples, and make a steady stream of pious donations. Because he expended the revenue for the benefit of others and didn't seek to amass a personal fortune, the flow of riches continued throughout his life. Similarly, when Supramadhu devoted himself to practice of the mantra, he used his resultant wealth to support hundreds of Mahayana teachers and monks, build temples, and benefit other living creatures.[7]

Tāranātha also tells of Yamāri, a philosopher who was too poor to support his wife and child until a wandering yogi taught him the rites of Vasudhārā. Within a year, Yamāri received a sizable tract of land from the king and was awarded a distinguished teaching post at Vikramaśīla. He wrote a hymn in praise of his divine benefactor and transmitted a method for visualizing Vasudhārā to future generations.[8] Although the prosperity bestowed by Vasudhārā might be expended in myriad ways, these stories highlight the connection between her benefactions and the support of Buddhist teachers and institutions.

Divine Forms and Symbolic Attributes

In the basic iconographic conception of Vasudhārā, which appears most consistently in the extant Indic images and *Sādhanamālā*, Vasudhārā is yellow and has two arms.[9] Her right hand displays varada mudrā, the open-palmed gesture denoting the pouring forth of divine blessings. In order to signify a bestowal of material riches, a symbol of wealth appears on her palm in the form of a small gem or a larger oval object that may be a large jewel or piece of fruit, analogous to the wood-apple (*bilva*) and citron displayed by other wealth deities. *Sādhanamālā* liturgies mention only the gesture of blessing, but the visualization system emanating from Yamāri specifies that she bears a purple, plumlike fruit.[10] On the whole, however, this feature was not standardized, presumably because the fruit and gem are interchangeable symbols of abundance. Some images also include a small figure reaching into a vessel brimming with jewels, positioned beneath her right hand to collect the treasure that pours forth (Fig. 13.1).[11]

Most emblematic of Vasudhārā is the sheaf of grain (*dhānya-mañjarī*) she displays in her left hand. This iconographic feature reveals her agricultural aspect, showing the provision of crops to be central to her character. In an agrarian setting, an abundant harvest is not only a source of sustenance but a primary source of wealth. The plant displayed by Vasudhārā may be grain in general or rice in particular, for both are designated as *dhānya*. Its presence proclaims that Vasudhārā's gifts include an abundant harvest. The grain-bearing goddess is eulogized as the "mother of all beings" (*bhūta-mātā*), "one who has mother love for her worshippers" (*bhakta-vatsalā*), and "universal mother" (*sarvatra mātṛkā*),[12] who fulfills her maternal role in part by fecundating crops to nourish and prosper her offspring.

The grain that Vasudhārā displays is subject to a wide variety of visual interpretations.[13] It may be stylized as a single long stem (see Fig. 13.1) or shown as a fanned spray, as seen in a Ratnagiri relief (Fig. 13.2). The stalk may be rendered as a large cluster bursting with ripe grains, dramatizing the agrarian powers of the Buddhist patron of the harvest (Fig. 13.3). Interestingly, the plant rarely resembles an ear of corn, as it is erroneously identified in many scholarly studies.[14] Iconographic sources often describe the attribute in her left hand as a "vessel raining grains and varied gems."[15] In artistic representations, this cornucopian vase, sprouting foliage, may rest on her uplifted palm or on a lotus that blossoms beside her left shoulder.

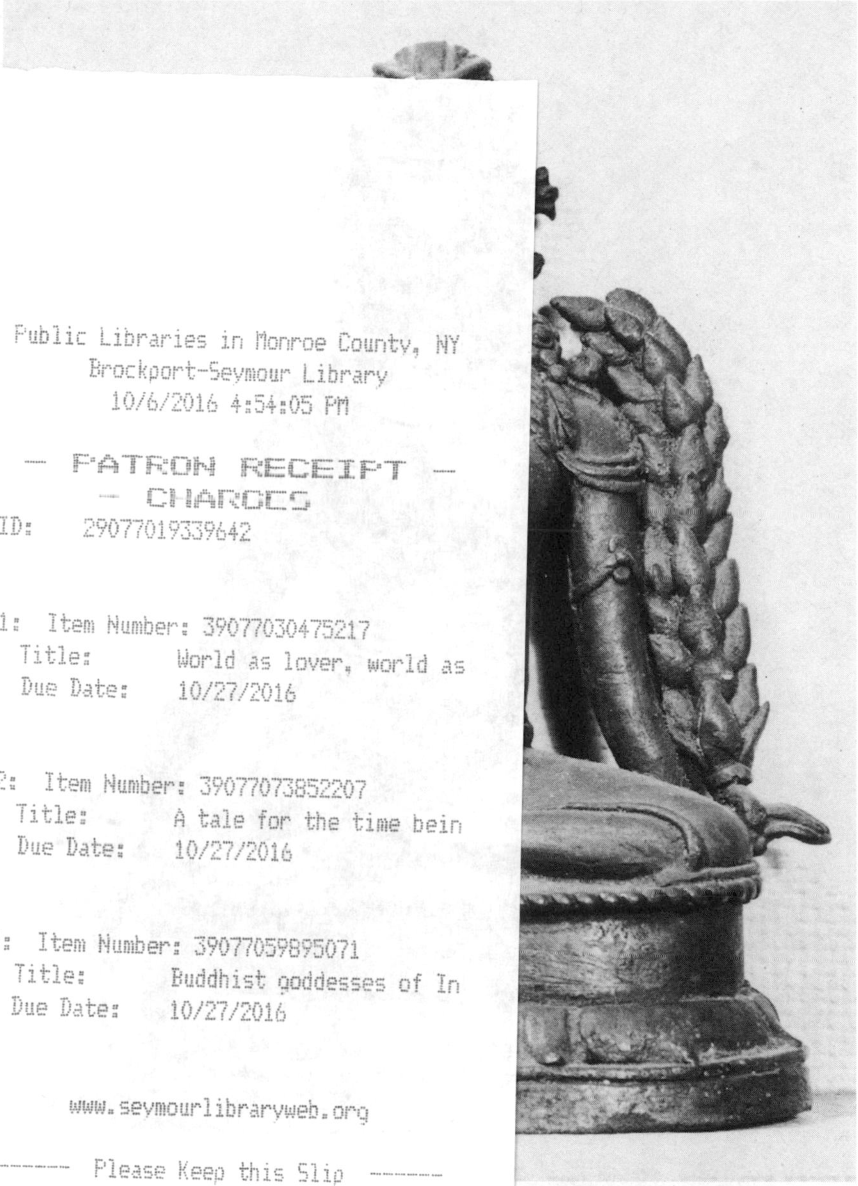

gal, India, Pāla period, ca. mid-
ian Museum, Calcutta, A24347
Institute of Indian Studies. *The gigantic stalk of rice proclaims the bountiful agrarian powers of the goddess in this image from rural Bengal.*

13.4 Vasudhārā, Site 1, Nālandā, Patna District, Bihar, India, Pāla period, ca. tenth century. Gray basalt, height 13.8 in. (35 cm). Nalanda Museum, 1-459. Photo: American Institute of Indian Studies. *The cornucopian nature of the goddess finds expression in a vase of plenty sprouting foliage and upturned vessels raining jewels.*

Vasudhārā's golden hue is the color associated with opulence, fertile earth, the harvest season, precious metals, and the luster of spiritual vitality. Indeed, one of the meanings of *vasu* is "gold." In Tantric symbology, yellow remained appropriate for Vasudhārā as the color of the earth element and as the color associated with generosity, one of the five primary qualities of Buddhahood, the result of the transformation of greed into infinite charity. Her bodily posture is not specified in the *Sādhanamālā*. She may be shown standing or seated in meditation but is most commonly portrayed in the posture of royal ease (*lalitāsana*), with her outstretched right foot resting on an upturned vessel raining treasure.[16] The "rain vessel" (*varṣa-ghaṭa*) is a complex visual reference to rainfall, abundant harvest, and wealth.[17] When Vasudhārā is depicted in a standing pose, an upright vase may appear below each foot.[18] Treasure vessels line the pedestal of several images from Ratnagiri and Sārnāth, enhancing the mood of abundance.[19] A Nālandā stele (Fig. 13.4) adds another flourish, arraying the gem-filled vessels in the upturned "raining" position, ready to pour forth their contents, extending a promise of divine largess. Stylized florets on Vasudhārā's lower garment lend a subtle botanical accent to the relief.

Iconographic Evolution and Mandalas

Several four-armed images of Vasudhārā, dating from the ninth through twelfth centuries, have survived. It appears, however, that a standard version of her four-armed iconography did not emerge, for no textual description has yet been found and the extant images differ iconographically. The stone relief in the Indian Museum, attributable on stylistic grounds to ninth-century Bihar, displays, in her two left hands, a cluster of grain stalks and a vessel surmounted by a jewel (Fig. 13.5). The grain and vase of plenty, formerly combined into a single motif, are here separated to provide an attribute for the additional arm. The right hand resting on her knee grasps a large oval object resembling a dimpled piece of fruit. In the fourth hand, a new element is introduced, namely, a rosary, signifying the knowledge-bestowing aspect of the goddess. Three additional four-armed examples, with differing combinations of attributes, are also attested.[20] These disparate images may represent experimental attempts to introduce a four-armed epiphany or local variations that did not gain currency.

There are isolated examples of a six-armed form of Vasudhārā in the Indian artistic corpus. One illuminates a manuscript dating from the twelfth century.[21] Another, a metal statue, recently surfaced among the consecration materials removed from a seventh-century Newar stupa in Kathmandu during its reconsecration.[22] The six-armed manifestation of Vasudhārā appears to have

13.5 Vasudhārā, Gaya District, Bihar, India, Pāla period, ca. ninth century. Gray basalt, height 35 in. (89 cm). Indian Museum, Calcutta, A25138 N.S. 3822. Photo: Indian Museum, Calcutta. *This four-armed image shows Vasudhārā with a rosary, signaling her bestowal of knowledge.*

enjoyed little currency in Indian Buddhism, for it is little attested among the texts transmitted to Tibet.[23] It did, however, become the primary epiphany in Nepal.

Vasudhārā is sometimes paired with Jambhala, a male wealth deity. Several Indic images portray the two as a couple, seated or standing side by side on a plinth.[24] Three liturgies in the *Sādhanamālā* describe mandalas that center on the pair, surrounded by eight couples identical to themselves. Their retinues consist of yakṣas and yakṣiṇīs, supernatural beings associated with fertility and abundance.[25] Vasudhārā may also appear with Jambhala at the center of his mandala.[26] Pratapaditya Pal notes the semblance between Vasudhārā and Jambhala and a couple widely worshipped in Buddhist contexts during the Kuṣāṇa and Gupta periods, namely, Hārītī and Kubera.[27] Kubera (alias Pāñcika) and Jambhala are closely related and even equatable with one another. Hārītī and Kubera were supplicated for wealth, progeny, and other forms of prosperity. Thus, Vasudhārā and Jambhala appear to have replaced the earlier couple in the evolving Mahayana pantheon, a shift discernible around the eighth or ninth century.

Vasudhārā also appears independently as the center of her own mandalas. The simplest is a fivefold configuration in which she has four emanations identical in appearance to herself: Śrī Vasudhārā, Vasuśrī, Vasumukhī, and Vasumatīśrī.[28] There is also a nine-deity version with an all-female retinue.[29] This, in combination with the ninefold mandala of Jambhala, forms the shared mandala, discussed above, in which the females of Vasudhārā's entourage are coupled with the males in Jambhala's cohort.

As Mother Earth

Vasudhārā carried a rich array of symbolic resonances on the Indian soil that gave her birth, for her iconography and divine persona incorporated features of figures prominent in Indic mythology. For example, she is a later permutation of an iconic type found at the protohistorical site of Harappa, the so-called *śākambharī*, or "lady of plants," shown with vegetation growing from her womb. This agrarian figure appears upside down with her legs spread apart to allow for the egress of the plants, expressing that her body is the maternal earth, delivering forth crops from her own body.[30] Although this is an isolated motif among extant Indus seals, it represents the genesis of a figural type in which the plant mother is portrayed with her legs splayed in a birthing position, a lotus blossom in place of her head, and lotus buds in her upraised hands.[31] This enduring theme later found literary expression in the *Mārkaṇḍeya Purāṇa*, wherein Durgā declares: "I shall support the whole world with the life-sustaining vegetables that shall grow out of my own body during a period of heavy rain; I shall gain fame on the earth then as Śākambharī."[32] The Buddhist lady of plenty, displaying a sheaf of grain in her hand, represents another epiphany of the fertile, plant-bearing earth mother.

Foremost among divine prototypes of Vasudhārā is the earth goddess, most commonly known as Bhūmidevī or Pṛthivī.[33] Vasudhārā inherits the mantle of mother earth as a "bearer of treasure" (*vasundharā*) and font of maternal sustenance. Vasudhārā's role as a provider of bounty recalls the nature of the earth goddess as a "repository of gems" (*ratnagarbhā*), "source of riches" (*vasudhā*), "bestower of wealth" (*vasudā*), and "treasure store" (*vasumatī*). A hymn to Pṛthivī in the *Atharva Veda* could well be addressed to Vasudhārā when it eulogizes:

> May Earth the Goddess,
> who bears her treasure stored up in many a place,
> gold, gems, and riches, giver of opulence,
> grant great possessions to us,
> bestowing them with love and favor. . . .
> Pour . . . a thousand streams of treasure to enrich me![34]

The conception of Vasudhārā as a "stream of wealth" (*vasudhārā*) and as the "lady who rains" (*varṣanī*), showering grain and gems from her vase of plenty, dovetails with descriptions of the earth goddess as one who rains, flows, and pours forth her bounty.[35] The *Atharva Veda* invokes mother earth, as the "lady of many streams" (*bhūridhārā*), to "pour out for us honey," "lustrate us with splendor," and "yield a thousand streams of treasure."[36]

Vasudhārā's color further evinces her association with Bhūmidevī, who is known as the "golden-breasted one" (*hiraṇya-vakṣā*), possessor of nutritive soil, giver of gold, and one who makes humans glow golden with well-being.[37] The earth goddess, too, is the "mother of plants" (*mātaraṃ oṣadhīnāṃ*), the one who is ploughed, the source of grain and food.[38] Vasudhārā retains the agricultural resonance of her namesake through her association with cultivated plant life.

The earth goddess herself, under the name Pṛthivī, appeared in earlier Buddhist art and literature as a participant in Shakyamuni's enlightenment. In artistic representations of the event, Pṛthivī commonly displays a vessel as her identifying attribute.[39] Therefore, Vasudhārā's treasure vase can be traced to the Buddhist iconographic conception of the earth goddess. The association between Pṛthivī and Vasudhārā is explicitly invoked in the *Vajrāvalī*, which tells us that Vasudhārā and Pṛthivī "are one and the same" and that, just as Pṛthivī averted Māra's attack on Shakyamuni, Vasudhārā intervened on behalf of Śākyasiṃha Buddha, on which occasion she displayed her vessel of jewels and the gesture that dispels fear as she vanquished Māra's forces.[40]

Associations with Lakṣmī

Vasudhārā is closely analogous to the Hindu goddess Lakṣmī, for both are bestowers of wealth, good fortune, and agricultural abundance. Lakṣmī, like Vasudhārā, is a golden-hued lady bountiful, a source of riches, nourishment, and vegetative fertility. She, too, is praised as *śākambharī,* the "lady of plants" who provides the world with food and drink.[41] Like Vasudhārā, Lakṣmī is worshipped for an abundant harvest and is specifically a patroness of rice cultivation.[42] Vasudhārā's namesake "shower of wealth," or "shower of gold" (*vasudhārā*), recalls Lakṣmī, who is invoked to bestow a "stream of gold" and is commonly envisioned as raining gold coins from her palm (see Fig. 4.5).[43] Lakṣmī also bears much in common with the earth goddess, resulting in significant similarities among the three figures as variations on the archetype of the *magna mater* who offers both fertility and prosperity.

Although the main emblem of Lakṣmī, the lotus, is not a major attribute of Vasudhārā, the goddesses bear other iconographic affinities. They share in common the gesture of bestowing divine blessings. Lakṣmī is described as holding a "wood-apple" or citron or may alternately display a jewel on her palm in the same manner as Vasudhārā. Portrayals of both goddesses may include figures or jars, collecting the treasure that flows from the divine hand. When Lakṣmī is described or depicted in four-armed form, she often displays a vessel of nectar (*amṛta-ghaṭa*) or golden pitcher (*kanaka-kalaśa*), which is also an emblem of Vasudhārā, as well as a rosary,[44] which appeared as an attribute of four-armed images of Vasudhārā (described above).

Another iconographic motif that Vasudhārā shares with Lakṣmī is the appearance of vessels beneath her feet or along the base of her pedestal. Although pots of treasure may be included in depictions of other wealth deities, such as yakṣas, yakṣiṇīs, and Jambhala, it seems likely that the use of vessels to support Vasudhārā's feet was adopted from representations of Lakṣmī, who often sits or stands atop a vessel that is sprouting lotuses (see Fig. 4.4). Similarly, the overturned vessels that sometimes appear along the base of sculptures of Vasudhārā recall the upturned vessels that recur in association with Lakṣmī, either held above her head in the trunks of two elephants (see Figs. 4.1–4.5) or supported by a pair of dwarfish yakṣas at her feet.[45] Moreover, the occasional pairing of Lakṣmī with the male wealth deity Kubera,[46] the Hindu counterpart of Jambhala, offers a couple that is virtually interchangeable, visually and symbolically, with Vasudhārā and Jambhala.

Tibetan Conceptions and Practices

Vasudhārā remained important in Tibet, where she is a primary "Wealth Deity" (Nor-lha), a status she shares with Jambhala and, to a lesser extent, Vaiśravaṇa. The Kagyu, Sakya, and Gelug schools include Vasudhārā in their repertoire of initiations and visualization practices and offer sacerdotal rites of propitiation, largely on behalf of lay patrons. A Sakya lama informed me that monks and nuns generally rely on Tārā to meet all their needs, while Vasudhārā is regarded as a benefactor of the laity. An individual practitioner may choose Vasudhārā as a personal meditation deity and undertake her visualization, but on the whole her rites are performed at the behest of laypersons.[47] Even so, in this role Vasudhārā is a constant presence in monastic institutional life. A given patron may request that the rites be performed daily, weekly, or monthly for a set period. Therefore, the rites are conducted on a regular basis, although their frequency and scale vary.[48]

In Tibetan iconography, Vasudhārā frequently appears in the form that prevailed in India, namely, the golden, two-armed epiphany in which she displays the gesture of generosity and a sheaf of grain or, alternately, a vase of plenty. She may be standing or seated in the meditative posture or lalitāsana. One or more treasure vessels beneath her lotus throne carry forward the motif found in Indian images.[49] This is the form in which Vasudhārā is most often encountered in Tibetan texts and art, although some variations, also with two arms, are documented. Gopāla Vasudhārā, "Cowherd Vasudhārā," elicits a pastoral rather than agrarian theme as she stands on vessels raining gems amid grazing wish-granting cows.[50] Manohara Vasudhārā, "Enchanting Vasudhārā," red and portly, supports a mongoose-skin pouch spewing jewels with her left arm and raises a scepter in her right.[51] Rakta Vasudhārā, a Tantric version of the goddess practiced in the Sakya sect, is red in color, with upward-streaming hair and bone ornaments, displaying a jeweled sheaf of grain in one hand and a skull cup full of blood in the other.[52]

Six-armed manifestations of Vasudhārā also appear in Tibetan contexts, as an independent deity and with a mandala retinue. The iconography generally conforms to the six-armed epiphany favored in Nepal since at least the tenth century, that is, displaying a rosary, jewel cluster, and varada mudrā in her right hands and a scripture, sheaf of rice, and vase of plenty in her left (Fig. 13.6, Pl. 6).[53] The relatively late appearance of this iconography in a Tibetan setting and its virtual absence from written sources raises the possibility of its transmission to Tibet from Nepal rather than India. Newar artists were brought to Tibet for major commissions, especially between the twelfth through sixteenth centuries, under Sakya patronage. It is telling, then, that the earliest known representation of six-armed Vasudhārā in a Tibetan context appears in a late

13.6 Vasudhārā, Amrit Karmacharya, Patan, Nepal, last decade of twentieth century. Paubhā, detail. Pigment and gold on cloth, 16 × 12 in. (40.6 × 30.5 cm). Author's collection. *This epiphany, popular in Nepal, displays a text, rice paddy, treasure vase, gesture of generosity, jewel bouquet, and rosary. (See Pl. 6)*

fourteenth-century painting in a Sakya *Vajrāvalī* series.[54] The nineteen-deity Vasudhārā mandala illustrated in the composition is not found in the original *Vajrāvalī* compilation but was appended in Tibet.[55] This version of the mandala is popular in Nepal,[56] supporting conjecture that both the six-armed form of Vasudhārā and her nineteenfold mandala were transmitted to Tibet from Nepal.

It is unusual to encounter Vasudhārā as the main subject of a painting in Tibet.[57] She usually appears as a subsidiary figure in paintings of other deities or sectarian hierarchs. When the subject of the work is another divinity, Vasudhārā's presence indicates that she figures in the practice of the person who commissioned the painting. When the work portrays a historical personage, she may be included as a patron of the lama or his lineage.[58]

Artistic representations of Vasudhārā are, however, found in a range of other contexts. Freestanding bronze statues are attested, including several stunning examples of Newar craftsmanship.[59] She is customarily included whenever an extensive pantheon is illustrated, for example, in the elaborate murals that grace temple walls, surrounding worshippers with a colorful cosmos of divine beings and adepts. The stupa of Gyantse (fifteenth century), a multistoreyed monument that houses a vast Sakya pantheon in painted and sculpted form, includes a chapel devoted to Vasudhārā. On the right side, her fivefold mandala is represented by freestanding sculptures. Vasudhārā and her retinue display *nidhi-darśana mudrā*, or *bindu mudrā*, in which the upraised left hand exhibits a small jewel or seed between the thumb and forefinger, signifying bestowal of wealth. The main shrine mural features six-armed Vasudhārā and her nineteen-deity mandala. The left wall illustrates the mandala of Vasudhārā and Jambhala and their retinue of eight couples.[60] Because the chapel is dedicated to Vasudhārā, she is shown as the primary figure. Jambhala is seated on her lap as her consort (Fig. 13.7), a pattern replicated in the depiction of their entourage.

The combined mandala of Vasudhārā and Jambhala may also serve as a protection wheel (*'khor-lo*) to be placed inside a statue as part of its consecration by relics and other magically propitious objects. Gennady Leonov, examining the contents of more than a hundred images, frequently found among them the eighteenfold mandala of Vasudhārā and Jambhala. Their respective mandalas were separately drawn or printed in mantric form and then placed or folded together, bringing Vasudhārā and her female retinue of eight yakṣiṇīs into juxtaposition with Jambhala and his male retinue of eight yakṣas.[61] Leonov observed that in some cases Jambhala and his entourage are placed on the bottom, making him the principle deity; in others, Vasudhārā and her retinue form the base, according her primacy, as in the Gyantse

13.7 Vasudhārā Embracing Jambhala. Drawing by Gautam Vajracharya after Gyantse mural (Tibet, fifteenth century). *Vasudhārā embraces her consort, the wealth deity Jambhala, as he sits on her lap.*

mural described above. The coupled mandala diagrams are carefully placed inside the image so that the deities inhabit their appointed cardinal directions.[62]

The popularity of the Vasudhārā-Jambhala mandala as a consecratory medium demonstrates that Vasudhārā's benefactions have been sought not only for the laity but also to prosper the monasteries and temples in which these statuary were to be housed.

Bestowal of Wealth in a Buddhist Context

It may seem incongruous to have a wealth-bestowing deity such as Vasudhārā in the Buddhist pantheon, for the Buddha identified the cause of all suffering as desire, which in turn stems from false belief in a self. Nevertheless, from its inception, Buddhism has perennially recognized the need for laypersons to support their families and promoted the ideals of charity and philanthropy. Many Buddhist legends celebrate the *dānapati*, or "master of generosity," a donor who endows religious teachers and institutions on a lavish scale and funds projects of communal welfare, such as the establishment of rest houses, wells, public gardens, medical dispensaries, and other humanitarian ventures. In Mahayana Buddhism, generosity is elevated to one of the six perfections of character that lead to Buddhahood, while spiritually advanced beings are expected to provide living beings with material and spiritual sustenance. Indeed, Buddhism has never drawn a clear line between spirit and matter and has always recognized that it is dauntingly difficult to pursue religious goals unless the basic requirements of survival—food, clothing, shelter, and medicine—are met. Moreover, in the Tantric model of psychological transformation, one whose heart has been purified of pride and avarice attains infinite generosity, the aspiration to provide all beings with every form of abundance.

Therefore, the divine role of Vasudhārā finds ample support in Buddhist doctrine. It is doubtful, however, that the majority of worshippers over the centuries required philosophical justification for their veneration. Rather, as the Mahayana pantheon evolved, Buddhists surely turned to Vasudhārā for the same reasons they had propitiated yakṣas, yakṣiṇīs, Lakṣmī, Hārītī, and Kubera in earlier eras. For many she was in all likelihood a manifestation of mother earth, a nurturing figure whose compassionate heart responded to their prayers and whose munificent, cornucopian nature enabled her to provide whatever they might require. Whether they entreated her for wealth, bountiful crops, or enlightenment, they have found in her a divinity dedicated to the nourishment and enrichment of the human spirit on every level.

Pl. 1 Māyādevī, Nepal, early nineteenth century. Gilt bronze inset with turquoise, coral, and other precious stones, height 22 in. (56 cm). Musée Guimet, MA 1779. Photo: Réunion des Musées Nationaux/Art Resource, N.Y. *Māyādevī, standing beside a gem-laden wish-granting tree, is a figure of supernal bounty and blessings.*

Pl. 2 Nativity Scene, Bihar, India, ca. 1150. Prajñāpāramitā manuscript folio, detail. Opaque watercolor on palm leaf, height 2.5 in. (6.35 cm). Los Angeles County Museum of Art, From the Nasli and Alice Heeramaneck Collection, Museum Associates Purchase, M72.1.23. Photo copyright 2004 Museum Associates/LACMA. *Māyādevī, giving birth in the sacred grove, is supported by the tree goddess (the green figure) as the infant emerges effortlessly from her side.*

Pl. 3 Color plate of Fig. 5.1. Photo courtesy of Mr. and Mrs. Willard G. Clark.
This Gāndhāran masterpiece, carved in a warm-toned schist, portrays Hārītī as the epitome of maternal grace, a regal yet tender figure.

Pl. 4 Prajñāpāramitā, Chauduar, Cuttack District, Orissa, India, Eastern Gaṅga Dynasty, ca. twelfth century. Stone, height 23.6 in. (60 cm). National Gallery of Australia, 90.531. Photo: National Gallery of Australia. *In this irenic image of Prajñāpāramitā, a scripture appears on the (visual) right lotus, while her lower right hand dispenses the blessings of wisdom.*

Pl. 5 Color plate of Fig. 12.3. *The blue palette of the painting reflects Sarasvatī's watery environment and the riverine flow of creativity she inspires.*

Pl. 6 Color plate of Fig. 13.6. *Vasudhārā's warm golden hue reflects her enriching nature as she bestows sustenance, wealth, and wisdom.*

Pl. 7 Color plate of Fig. 15.3. Photo: The Rose Art Museum, Brandeis University. *Sitātapatrā's body is covered with eyes, representing the all-seeing wisdom with which she protects her petitioners.*

Pl. 8 Color plate of Fig. 15.6. Photo copyright John Bigelow Taylor. *This lavishly gilt statue beautifully evokes the supernal brilliance of the indomitable protector Sitātapatrā.*

Pl. 9 Commemoration Thang-ka for Bhīmaratha Rite, Tashilumpo Monastery, Central Tibet, nineteenth century. Opaque watercolor on cloth, 28.25 × 22 in. (71.7 × 56 cm). Los Angeles County Museum of Art, Gift of Christian Humann, M.71.98.1. Photo copyright 2004 Museum Associates/LACMA. *Uṣṇīṣavijayā in a long-life stupa casts her gaze over a Bhīmaratha ritual, performed for the longevity and fortunate rebirth of the honorees.*

Pl. 10 Paradise of Khadiravaṇī Tārā, Tibet, nineteenth century. Pigment and gold on cloth, 35.6 × 26.8 in. (90.5 × 68 cm). Musée Guimet, MG 16546. Photo: Réunion des Musées Nationaux/Art Resource, N.Y. *Khadiravaṇī Tārā in her Buddha paradise, where the fortunate join her after death and dwell in her enlightening presence.*

Pl. 11 Color plate of Fig. 18.5. *Nāroḍākinī's red body and rippling hair are illumined by her aureole of yogic fire and adorned with gleaming bone ornaments.*

Pl. 12 Color plate of Fig. 18.6. Photo after Ulrich von Schroeder, 2001, *Buddhist Sculptures in Tibet*, vol. 2, pl. 266D. *The penetrating gaze and golden luster of this remarkable statue of Vajravārāhī superbly express her transcendent wisdom and shimmering, dynamic presence.*

Pl. 13 Nairātmyā, Central Tibet, sixteenth century. Gilt copper inset with turquoise, painted with red pigment, height 9.25 in. (23.5 cm). Los Angeles County Museum of Art, From the Nasli and Alice Heeramaneck Collection, Museum Associates Purchase, M.70.1.4. Photo copyright 2004 Museum Associates/LACMA. *Nairātmyā represented as a seated yogini, her face ablaze with all-seeing wisdom.*

Pl. 14 Color plate of Fig. 20.1. *The crimson blood streaming from Chinnamuṇḍā's neck is a dramatic symbol of spiritual sustenance and immortality.*

Pl. 15 Siṃhamukhā, Amdo region, Tibet, nineteenth century. Pigment and gold on cloth, 18.25 × 13 in. (46.35 × 33 cm). The Newark Museum, Holton Collection, 1936; 36.518. Photo: Newark Museum/Art Resource N.Y. *Roaring exultantly, Siṃhamukhā personifies pure, untamable power.*

Pl. 16 Color plate of Fig. 22.2. *Kurukullā's roseate hue reflects her ability to awaken love, desire, and spiritual aspiration with the release of her flowery arrow.*

CHAPTER 14

Cundā

Saving Grace

> Cundā quickly ripens all spiritual powers;
> She motivates Buddhas and bodhisattvas to help living beings,
> Induces beings to embark on the Buddhist path, and
> Inspires renouncers and solitary achievers to follow the bodhisattva way. . . .
> Shakyamuni proclaimed that her mantras shake the Buddha-worlds,
> Defeat all demons, and bestow many miraculous powers. . . .
> Through the recitation of her mantra,
> All diseases are purified and Buddhahood is quickly attained.
> Even a tenth-level bodhisattva does not surpass her in brilliance.
> All worldly and spiritual perfections are attained through her mantra.
>
> —Drikung meditation manual[1]

Cundā (pronounced *chun* DAH), was one of the most important dhāraṇī goddesses of late Indian Buddhism (ca. ninth to twelfth centuries C.E.). She was invoked as a powerful savior who could grant any boon and remove any form of adversity. Her specializations were purification of negative karma and support of spiritual practice. Her popularity during her heyday may have approached that of Tārā in some regions, judging from the large numbers of extant images of Cundā and their widespread geographic and temporal distribution. Effigies of Cundā have been found, in some cases in profusion, at sites spanning western, northern, eastern, and southeastern India.

These artistic representations attest that Cundā figured prominently in the devotional and meditative practices of the Buddhists of Pāla-period India, from whose domain her cult spread to Tibet, Nepal, Java, Thailand, and East Asia. The worship of Cundā subsequently receded into obscurity in Himalayan Buddhism but flourishes in China and Japan.[2] The widely varying reception of Cundā in different cultural settings bears witness to the dynamism of the pantheon as it is reconfigured for new audiences.

Patron of the First Pāla Ruler

Cundā's origins are intertwined with her role as divine patron of the first Pāla ruler, Gopāla I (reigned ca. 750–775 C.E.), after whom the dynasty was named. The earliest known record of this chapter in her history appears in the writings of Tāranātha (sixteenth century). According to the Tibetan historian, Gopāla was born in Bengal as the son of an aristocratic mother and a tree deity father. The youth discovered a valuable gem among the roots of his paternal tree and offered the jewel to a religious teacher in exchange for instruction. The preceptor, unnamed in the account, initiated Gopāla into the practice of Cundā. She became his patron deity and appeared to him in a dream, assuring him of her blessings and support. The goddess also empowered a small club that he might use for his protection.

At that time, a Bengali queen who was a supernatural serpent (*nāginī*) in disguise killed anyone who ascended the throne. A new ruler was elected each day, only to die mysteriously during the night. Gopāla arrived in the area and volunteered to serve as king, an offer that was readily accepted. When the nāginī approached to attack him, he subdued her with his magical club. Thus, to everyone's surprise, he survived his first night as ruler. When he remained alive for seven days, the people recognized him as their destined king and elected him as their sovereign. After Cundā helped place him on the throne, Gopāla added new territories to his kingdom and established many monasteries and temples.[3]

The Pāla dynasty, founded by Gopāla, endured for more than four centuries (ca. eighth through twelfth centuries C.E.). It is not clear whether Cundā was already a prominent deity whose well-attested powers were invoked by the aspiring ruler or whether she was a relatively obscure deity who rose to prominence under the auspices of her royal devotee. In either case, her role as Gopāla's patron no doubt promoted her reputation and helped spread her cultus. Gopāla would not have failed to lavish honor on the goddess to whom he owed his throne, and he assuredly included images of his divine benefactor among his numerous religious donations. Art historical evidence confirms that the goddess's popularity rose in the ninth century and remained strong for several centuries thereafter.

Saving Powers

Cundā now poses an historical conundrum. Despite her former prominence, it is a challenge to reconstruct the religious niche she once occupied. The name "Cundā" itself sheds little light on her character, for its etymology and meaning are unclear.[4] Textual descriptions of her salvific roles are meager. The earliest datable reference to Cundā is probably the passage in the *Śikṣāsamuccaya* (ca. seventh century C.E.) that recommends her dhāraṇī for the purification of negative karma. The practitioner is instructed to recite the mantra until she or he has a dream that confirms the destruction of impurities in the mindstream. Such dream signs include a bull, a blazing fire, elephants, mountains, thrones, boats, and the acts of drinking milk, climbing a milk tree, listening to Buddhist teachings, and gazing at the sun and moon.[5]

The inscription on a circa thirteenth-century metal talisman, designed to confer the protection of the goddess on its wearer, attributes encompassing benefits to the Cundā mantra. If chanted 108, 1080, or many thousands of times, it will ward off misfortune and attract blessings; bestow health, wealth, and progeny; and restore affection between husband and wife. Moreover, the incantation offers protection against snakebite, insect bites, water-dwelling dragons, drowning, enemies in battle, and demonic possession.[6] Although the amulet was produced in a Chinese context, the inscription is reproduced in a Newar script, suggesting that this conception of the goddess was culturally widespread.

These literary sources evince that the beneficent and protective powers attributed to Cundā were extensive. A more recent Drikung text, dating from the eighteenth century, outlines an even broader spectrum of roles. She is said to defeat all "demons" (*māra*), remove all diseases, bestow miraculous powers, and purify those who recite her mantra so that they may quickly attain Buddhahood. She is lauded in superlatives. Her mantra has the power to shake the Buddha-worlds, and her brilliance exceeds that of a tenth-stage bodhisattva. The work concludes that there is nothing Cundā cannot accomplish, for her practice bestows all worldly and spiritual perfections (*siddhi*).[7]

Amid this range of benefactions, one specialization emerges. Cundā is credited with motivating beings to increase their religious efforts, regardless of their level of attainment. She inspires ordinary persons to undertake spiritual practice, induces Pratyeka Buddhas (solitary Buddhas) to follow the bodhisattva path of universal service, and even encourages Buddhas and bodhisattvas in their liberative activities.[8] This role apparently emerged as Cundā's distinctive function over time, for it is reflected in the Tibetan rendition of her name as Kulchayma, which means "Motivator" or "Inciter." The Tibetan appellation of a deity is usually a direct translation of the Sanskrit version, but in this case the etymological relationship appears to be indirect.[9]

Divine Forms and Symbolic Attributes

Cundā most commonly appears in four-armed form. The three visualization guides in the *Sādhanamālā* describe her as displaying an alms bowl, the boon-granting gesture (*varada mudrā*), and a book resting on a lotus.[10] Many Indic sculptures conform closely to this description. The liturgies make no mention, however, of the rosary she typically displays in her upraised right hand in artistic representations. A metal votive image from Kurkihār portrays a widely represented epiphany (Fig. 14.1), with her lower right hand in the open-palmed gesture of blessing and generosity. One also finds effigies in which her lower two hands rest on her lap in the gesture of contemplation (Fig. 14.2).

Cundā's most characteristic attribute is the vessel she displays, resting on the open palm of a hand on her lap or brandished by an upraised hand. The vessel may be portrayed as a large and prominently visible alms bowl (as in Fig. 14.2), a flat and barely discernible dish (as in Fig. 14.1), or a water flask (*kamaṇḍalu*). The implement born in her upper left hand, although described as a book on a lotus, may be depicted as a lotus, book, water flask, lotus supporting a book, or lotus and water flask. Her posture, unspecified in the liturgies, is almost invariably represented as the seated, cross-legged pose of meditative equipoise.

Many four-armed images, dating primarily from the ninth and tenth centuries, have been found at the far-flung sites of Ellora in western India, Nālandā and Bodhgayā in the north, Maināmatī in the northeast (present-day Bangladesh), and Ratnagiri and Achutrajpur on the eastern seaboard.[11] Broad regional trends in Cundā's iconography are discernible, as well as individual variations at a given locale.

The iconography of Cundā sheds further light on her character, with an emphasis on her munificence. Most emblematic is the alms bowl (*pātra*) she holds. This type of begging bowl is frequently seen in the iconography of Shakyamuni Buddha and other mendicants as a sign of renunciation. Its presence may signify Cundā's role as a patron of monastics and supporter of the contemplative life. Possibly it is also regarded as an inexhaustible bowl, a magical vessel that appears in Indian and Buddhist lore, generally used to nourish and prosper others with its ever-flowing elixir.[12] This interpretation is supported by a manuscript painting in which Cundā's bowl is shown as a brimming vessel heaped full of a white substance.[13] The water flask (*kamaṇḍalu*) that may appear in place of or in addition to the bowl suggests her ability to shower a rain of blessings, quench spiritual thirst, and bestow purifying nectar.

Another recurrent attribute of Cundā is a rosary of mantra beads (*akṣamālā*), alluding to the practice of dhāraṇī recitation to evoke her saving powers and purify the meditator's mindstream. Her white hue in most of her manifestations signifies her purifying influence. The lotus she bears also alludes to inner purity and the blossoming of enlightenment, while the rectangular palm-leaf manuscript, a Mahayana scripture, extends the promise of wisdom to those who engage in her practice. At least one text specifies that the book is a

14.1 Cundā, Kurkihār, Gaya District, Bihar, India, Pāla period, ca. early eleventh century. Metal. Patna Museum, 9696. Photo: The Huntington Archive, The Ohio State University. *This image exalts Cundā by placing her on an elaborate throne surmounted by a parasol of spiritual victory.*

14.2 Cundā, Nālandā, Patna District, Bihar, India, Pāla period, ca. ninth or tenth century. Stone. National Museum, New Delhi, 47.31. Used by permission. Photo: National Museum, New Delhi. *Cundā is shown with her hands in meditation and an alms bowl, expressing her support of renunciants and the contemplative life.*

Prajñāpāramitā, or Perfection of Wisdom, text.[14] It is natural that wisdom, the fruit of mental purification, would be one of her gifts.

Care must be taken to distinguish between Cundā and other female deities appearing in four-armed form. For example, Bhṛkuṭī frequently displays a rosary and water pot in her four-armed epiphany. When Bhṛkuṭī is depicted in a seated meditative posture she may easily be mistaken for Cundā without careful attention to other identifying traits, such as Bhṛkuṭī's pronounced topknot and renunciant's staff (*tridaṇḍaka*).[15] The Hindu goddess Pārvatī in her four-armed form also carries a water pot and rosary and displays varada mudrā. Pārvatī is usually distinguishable from Cundā, however, by her ascetic's topknot of matted hair and other iconographic attributes, such as a trident or staff, lion vehicle, and iguana companion.[16]

The potential confusion is greatest in the case of Prajñāpāramitā, who, like Cundā, frequently appears in four-armed form, seated in the meditative posture. A text on a lotus (*padma-pustaka*), displayed in an raised right hand, is an emblem of both goddesses, as is a rosary in the raised right hand. Although Prajñāpāramitā most characteristically displays the Dharma-teaching gesture, she may on occasion, like Cundā, be shown with her central pair of hands resting on her lap (see Fig. 8.3) or with one hand extended in the gift-bestowing gesture (Pl. 4).

These shared traits have not infrequently led to the misidentification of Cundā effigies as Prajñāpāramitā.[17] However, the presence of a vessel in Cundā's iconography decisively differentiates between the two figures. When Cundā bears a large bowl, her identity is readily ascertainable (see Fig. 14.2), but scholars may overlook the vessel when it is rendered as a flat dish that is barely visible in her cupped palm (see Fig. 14.1). The rosary also helps distinguish the iconography of Cundā in the Indic corpus. Although a rosary is a recurrent attribute of Prajñāpāramitā in the Tibetan and Newar pantheons, it appears only in one late Indic representation of the goddess. Nonetheless, the shared traits of Cundā and Prajñāpāramitā have given rise to a persistent confusion between the two.[18] Images of Cundā with six or more arms are commonly misidentified as Prajñāpāramitā as well.

Six-armed effigies of Cundā have been found in Bodhgayā, Chittagong (in present-day Bangladesh), and Orissa.[19] Evidence for an eight-armed epiphany in the Indic pantheon is not conclusive.[20] However, twelve-armed images of the goddess were found at Achutrajpur (Fig. 14.3) and Nālandā.[21] In representations with twelve or more arms, the central pair of hands may display the meditative gesture (as in Fig. 14.3) or the gesture of teaching. There are several isolated images of Cundā in sixteen-armed form.[22] More prevalent is her eighteen-armed manifestation, of which many examples have been found (Fig. 14.4).[23] The votive

14.3 Cundā, Achutrajpur, Puri District, Orissa, India, ca. ninth century. Chlorite, height 56.7 in. (144 cm). Patna Museum, Arch 6500. Photo: American Institute of Indian Studies. *Cundā received ongoing iconographic elaboration, appearing here with twelve arms and Tārā and Bhṛkuṭī as attendants (in lower corners of pedestal).*

14.4 Cundā, Nālandā, Patna District, Bihar, India, Pāla period, ca. late ninth century. Bronze, height 12 in. (30.5 cm). National Museum, New Delhi, 47.34. Used by permission. Photo: American Institute of Indian Studies. *Cundā popularly appears with eighteen arms. Her emblematic vessel is present here as the water flask held at her left knee.*

bronze pictured here, from Nālandā, features the teaching gesture exhibited by her central pair of hands. In these many-armed configurations, her emblematic vessel typically appears in the form of a water flask grasped in the lower left hand as it rests on her left knee (see Figs. 14.3, 14.4). An epiphany with twenty-six arms is also attested.[24]

Cundā's iconography displays the multiplicity of variations that often characterizes major deities. The proliferation of forms signifies vitality of worship, for new features often emerge as a deity migrates from one region or context to another. Iconographic innovation also arises from adepts who receive visions of a deity and initiate practice lineages centering on the newly revealed forms, a process that generates a lively diversity of meditation practices and modes of representation. Therefore, both the number of surviving images and their iconographic diversity evince the former renown of Cundā. At the same time, it is puzzling, in view of her many epiphanies, that there appears to be no mandala centering on Cundā, although she figures in the mandala retinues of other deities.[25]

It is possible that Cundā garnered shrines of panregional repute. The existence of such temples is suggested by an eleventh-century manuscript that purportedly illustrates several famous Buddhist sanctuaries throughout India. A painting of a sixteen-armed form of Cundā identifies the image as "Cundā of the glorious Cundā temple in Paṭṭikerā," naming a kingdom that once centered on the Tippera district of Bangladesh.[26] Archaeological excavations in the area have unearthed remains of several large religious monuments, affirming that a major temple was located there.[27] Another painting in the same manuscript is labeled as "Cundā of Vuṃkarā city in Lāṭadeśa," a former toponym of Gujarat.[28] The inclusion of these Cundā shrines in a Newar manuscript suggests that she was sufficiently renowned to be attributed with major temples, although it is unclear whether the specific shrines depicted in this manuscript actually existed. Nonetheless, the fact that the other temples named in the manuscript are those of the illustrious Tārā, Avalokiteśvara, and Vasudhārā places Cundā among the most celebrated deities of late Indian Buddhism.

Wane in Himalayan Buddhism

This intriguing array of historical evidence leaves no doubt that Cundā was once a popular goddess honored as a powerful benefactor of laypeople, monastics, and even the founder of one of India's greatest dynasties. It is surprising, in retrospect, that a goddess of such prominence during the Pāla period disappeared almost entirely from view in Himalayan Buddhism.

The illuminated manuscript and amulet discussed above show that Cundā was once known in Nepal, but I found no evidence of her presence in Newar

Buddhism today. Meditations on Cundā were also transmitted to Tibet.[29] They are nonetheless little in vogue in the contemporary tradition. Evidence of her ongoing role may be found in her occasional inclusion as a subsidiary figure in painted compositions.[30] Her appearance in this context signals that she was important to the person who commissioned the painting or, if the painting centers on a hierarch, to the master portrayed. The relative rarity of this occurrence, however, confirms how limited interest in the goddess had become.

Cundā's versatility may be the key to her once-flourishing worship as well as its eventual demise. By all evidence she was revered as a powerful savior who served her votaries in assorted ways, whatever their needs might have been. In Nepal, the diversity of Cundā's ministrations may have limited her appeal as more specialized deities came to the fore. In Tibet, Tārā, who offers an even greater breadth of benefactions, garnered universal reverence while the worship of Cundā virtually disappeared. The significant overlap in salvific roles between the two figures may explain why one languished as the other thrived in the new cultural venue. One Tibetan text notes that Cundā is "the same as Tārā."[31] Moreover, Tārā's importance as the divine patron of Atīśa, a key figure in the transmission of Buddhism to Tibet, secured her reputation in the land of snows, whereas Cundā did not enjoy the benefit of such an influential proponent. A form of Tārā known as Cundā-Tārā suggests an assimilation between the two.[32] This epiphany is red, however, and bears no salient resemblance to Cundā and so, apart from the name, does not truly preserve her presence in the Tibetan pantheon. The dramatic trajectory of Cundā reveals the extent to which the history of a given deity may be shaped by cultural, social, and even political forces.

CHAPTER 15

Sitātapatrā

Invincible Goddess with a Thousand Heads and Hands

I salute you, exalted one!
Only mother of all Buddhas, past, present, and future,
Your glory pervades the three worlds.

Homage to you, savioress from the evil influence of demons
and planets,
From untimely death and evil dreams,
From the dangers of poison, arms, fire, and water.

The mandala of your being is exceedingly vast.
You have a thousand heads full of innumerable mindstates,
A thousand hands holding flaming attributes.

Queen of all the mandalas of the three worlds . . .
Ever-present in the work of taming evil ones,
I salute you, goddess of magical spells, turning demons into dust!

—Gelug ritual prayer[1]

Sitātapatrā (pronounced *see* TAH *tah pah* TRAH), "Goddess of the White Parasol," is regarded as an invincible protector against every form of supernatural danger, such as demons, black magic, and astrologically ordained mishaps. The parasol after which she is named is not an ordinary umbrella but a large, white silken canopy that serves as a symbol of high rank—a sign of royalty and divinity—in Indian culture. As an emblem of kingship, the white umbrella shelters the ruler from the sun's rays, with which he must never come into direct contact lest they diminish his own luster.[2] In Buddhist symbology, the parasol proclaims the spiritual sovereignty of the Buddha and his dominion over all worldly appearances and suffering.

Just as the goddess Lakṣmī personifies the royal sunshade in the Hindu context,[3] a female divinity hypostasizes the silken canopy of the Buddha and, by extension, his universal mantle of protective power. Sitātapatrā's delicate beauty belies her indomitability. Moreover, although Sitātapatrā represents an invincible force, the method of invoking her is relatively simple, a fortuitous combination that has commended her practice to Buddhists throughout Asia and established her in the repertoire of every Tibetan Buddhist sect.

Sitātapatrā's mantra is known as the "queen of magical spells" (*mahāvidyārājñī*) and the "invincible incantation," or "incantation of the unconquerable goddess" (*aparājitā-dhāraṇī*).[4] Numerous texts of the spell survive in the Sanskrit, Newar, Tibetan, Tokharian, Khotanese, and Chinese scripts, documenting the diffusion of the practice across Central and East Asia and the Himalayas, beginning in at least the seventh century, the date of the earliest extant manuscript.[5] Judging from the widespread adoption of her practice, it is clear that Sitātapatrā once enjoyed renown throughout the Buddhist world as the powerful protectress she remains to the present day in Tibetan Buddhism. The appeal of this goddess is summed up by the promise that "one who does this practice cannot be defeated by anyone."[6]

Origin Story and Mythic Prototypes

According to the Buddhist origin account, Shakyamuni Buddha materialized the goddess from the crown of his head (*uṣṇīṣa*, literally, "crown protrusion") when he was in Trāyastriṃśa Heaven. The Buddha entered a meditative state known as "perfect vision of the diadem" and emitted the holy syllables of her dhāraṇī from his crown in the form of letters etched in light. Next her voice was heard, greeting the Buddha and assembled bodhisattvas, deities, and spirits. Finally, the light of the Buddha's mind, streaming from the top of his head, crystallized into the sparkling white body and sunshade of Sitātapatrā. The Buddha pronounced her role to be "to cut asunder completely all malignant demons, to cut asunder all the spells of others . . . to turn aside all enemies and dangers and hatred."[7] Lest her seraphic persona mislead the congregation, he asserted that Sitātapatrā is a fierce, terrifying goddess, garlanded by flames, a pulverizer of enemies and demons, who manifests in the form of a graceful, beauteous maiden.[8]

This genesis is reflected in a longer version of her name, Uṣṇīṣasitātapatrā, meaning "White Parasol Lady Who Emerged from the Buddha's Crown of Light," of which Sitātapatrā is the commonly used abbreviation. Interestingly, the origin story does not address her relationship to the Buddha's sunshade.

Only her name evinces her personification of the saving energy inherent in the white (*sita*) parasol (*ātapatra*), while the story traces the source of this energy to the Buddha's cosmic awareness and supernal brilliance.

Sitātapatrā represents a Mahayana version of a figural type already present in Buddhist mythology, namely, a female spirit that indwells a royal parasol and acts as a royal patron. The *Mahāunmagga Jātaka* treats just such a figure. This story, recounting the Buddha's former life as Prince Mahoṣadha, has as a pivotal character the goddess who "dwelt in the royal parasol." One night she emerged from the center of the parasol and posed four riddles to the king. When the foremost wise men in the realm could not solve the riddles, the goddess, enraged, threatened that if the king did not produce the answers she would sever his head with her "fiery blade." She upbraided him for seeking out the famous wise men but overlooking his own son Mahoṣadha: "What do they know? Like fireflies are they, like a great flaming fire is Mahoṣadha blazing with wisdom. If you do not find out this question, you are a dead man."

Prince Mahoṣadha, who had been wandering in self-imposed exile, was promptly summoned to the palace. The king accorded his son the honor of sitting on the throne in the shade of the white parasol. Mahoṣadha reassured his father: "Sire, be it the deity of the white parasol, or be they the four great kings . . . let who will ask a question and I will answer it." When Mahoṣadha solved the first riddle, the goddess rose from the parasol, revealing the upper half of her body, and rewarded him with a casket of heavenly perfumes and flowers. She praised him in sweet tones. As he unraveled each successive conundrum, she emerged and presented him with scent and blossoms. When he solved the final riddle, she gifted him with coral, ivory, and other precious objects befitting a king.

Mahoṣadha remained at the palace and proceeded to restore order to the kingdom, revealing treasonous plots and advising the king how to repel an invasion. Thus, it transpired that the goddess's riddles had been a stratagem to bring Mahoṣadha to his father's assistance and establish the security of the realm. Interestingly, the story also uses "white umbrella" as a metaphor for royal protection, when the prince announces, "I am indeed the king's white umbrella," in reference to his success in securing the safety of the throne.[9]

A royal parasol goddess also figures in the *Mūgapakkha Jātaka*. In this former lifetime, again as a prince, the Buddha-to-be decided in infancy that he did not want to assume the throne when he grew older. The king was an unrighteous ruler, and the Bodhisattva feared that he would amass negative karma if he followed in his father's footsteps. The goddess of the white parasol under which the princeling was shaded advised that he could escape this fate if he pretended to be deaf and showed no signs of intelligence. Recognizing her as a well-wisher

15.1 Sitātapatrā. Polychrome print, contemporary. Author's collection. *Sitātapatrā displays her namesake white parasol, symbolizing her protective powers and victory over negative forces.*

and ally, he followed her advice, feigning inability to rule for sixteen years, until he was finally released to pursue a life of asceticism as a forest hermit. Inspired by his example, the king and queen decided to become ascetics themselves and attempted to relinquish the throne and royal umbrella to the Bodhisattva. The Bodhisattva's indifference to worldly sovereignty inspired everyone in the realm to embrace the renunciatory lifestyle. An invading ruler from an adjoining territory was similarly converted and withdrew his troops.[10] In this case, too, the intervention of the parasol goddess benefited the royal family and kingdom at large.

In these stories, the "white parasol goddess" is not a single figure but rather a genre of goddesses believed to inhabit royal umbrellas. This type of goddess is associated with sovereignty and intercedes to protect and preserve the possessor of the honorary umbrella. Indeed, it stands to follow that, just as the umbrella itself shelters the ruler from harsh sunlight, the deity inhabiting the protective canopy would be a guardian figure who safeguards his reign. Thus, these narratives reveal the idea underlying the personification of the Buddha's sunshade as a female deity. The generic goddess of the white parasol, like her Mahayana counterpart, is envisioned as a benevolent figure with a dulcet voice who manifests a wrathful demeanor and wields a sword when occasion demands. Sitātapatrā thus inherited from her mythic prototype her association with the royal umbrella, protective function, and beatific yet fearsome nature.

Divine Forms and Symbolic Attributes

Sitātapatrā has several iconographic manifestations. Her body is invariably white, reflecting her emergence from the purifying brilliance of the crown protrusion of the Buddha. The simplest version of her iconography is a two-armed form in which she gracefully sports her white, ribbon-festooned parasol in her left hand (Fig. 15.1). Her right hand typically hovers above her knee in what appears to be a gesture of expulsion of the evils and dangers from which she protects her devotees.[11] In some instances, the standard boon-granting gesture (*varada mudrā*) appears in its stead. The contemporary painting pictured here, however, places in her slightly upraised right hand a Dharma-wheel (*dharma-cakra*), symbolizing truth, the ultimate source of victory and protection. This apparently recent innovation lends specificity to an historical gesture that never received codification in Buddhist iconographic sources.

Sitātapatrā also manifests in six- and eight-armed forms, brandishing an array of weapons that typically include a Dharma-wheel, vajra, bow, arrow, sword, noose, elephant goad, and parasol.[12] She may display, in addition to the parasol, a victory banner (*dhvaja*), symbolizing triumph over demonic forces (Fig. 15.2).

15.2 Sitātapatrā. Woodblock print. Photo after Chandra, *Buddhist Iconography*, no. 43. *Eight-armed Sitātapatrā, displaying a parasol and victory banner in her central pair of hands.*

15.3 Sitātapatrā, Central Tibet, eighteenth century. Colors and gold on cotton, 28.12 × 19.5 in. (71.4 × 49.5 cm). The Rose Art Museum, Brandeis University, Waltham, Mass.; gift of N. and L. Horch to the Riverside Museum Collection, 1971.194R. Photo: The Rose Art Museum, Brandeis University. *Sitātapatrā with a thousand heads, a thousand arms, and a thousand legs is an awesome sight.* *(See Pl. 7)*

In some instances, the parasol is replaced by the victory banner or is absent altogether. When Sitātapatrā has more than one face, the central face may be portrayed as either tranquil or wrathful, for she may adopt either persona at will.

In her most prevalent form, Sitātapatrā has a thousand heads, arms, and legs (Fig. 15.3, Pl. 7). This vision of the goddess represents an iconic type known in India as a *viśva-rūpa*, or "universal form." In her viśva-rūpa mode, Sitātapatrā displays her omnipotence and omnipresence by appearing with the thousands of faces, eyes, mouths, hands, feet, implements, and weapons with which she rescues her supplicants. The viśva-rūpa motif accentuates the theme of unconquerability, for no evildoer could escape, much less defeat, such an all-seeing, multilimbed, infinitely mobile being.

The following song of praise, used in ritual invocation, delineates her thousandfold iconography:

> Born from the crown protrusion of the Buddha, out of compassion,
> You combat those who would harm the Buddhist teachings, the source
> of happiness,
> And bestow the fruit of well-being;
> I praise and pay homage to you, supremely blissful Sitātapatrā.
>
> Displaying many sacred gestures, such as granting refuge;
> Holding scepters, wheels, jewels, lotuses,
> Swords, arrows, bows, and lassos,
> I pay homage to you, with your thousand arms.
>
> Your body is white, red, blue, yellow, and green;
> You are graceful, heroic, and terrifying;
> You appear tranquil, angry, and mirthful;
> I pay homage to you, lady with a thousand heads.
>
> On your multiform body, with your many heads and arms,
> Your wide-open eyes look to the sides,
> Flashing with lightninglike anger.
> Homage to you, lady with a hundred thousand million eyes.
>
> Your body is unbreakable as diamond,
> Flaming like a mountain of apocalyptic fire,
> Destroying all obstacles, bestowing all miraculous powers,
> I pay homage to you, blazing, indestructible.[13]

The thousandfold form of Sitātapatrā is widely depicted in Tibetan art. Five colors of heads are shown in a towerlike formation; each head has three eyes and one of the three expressions (tranquil, angry, or mirthful) she assumes as

15.4 Detail of Fig. 15.3. Photo: The Rose Art Museum, Brandeis University.
The eyes on her body represent the all-seeing wisdom that guides her actions.

15.5 Detail of Fig. 15.3. Photo: The Rose Art Museum, Brandeis University. *Sitātapatrā's feet trample legions of malefactors and evildoers.*

occasion demands in order to perform her saving activities. The central face, like her body, is white. Her hands, arranged in concentric layers, form a fanlike aureole (Fig. 15.4). Distributed among them are her implements and weapons: vajras, Dharma-wheels, jewels, lotuses, swords, bows, arrows, lassos, goads, and crossed vajras. Each hand has an open eye on its palm, for Sitātapatrā offers her divine protection with all-seeing wisdom. The artist may mark her body and limbs with additional eyes to symbolize the omniscience that guides her movements.

The medium of painting is ideally suited to rendering Sitātapatrā's thousandfold iconography in its astonishing minuteness of detail.[14] It is difficult to imagine the artistic finesse and patience required to render her exquisite hands, the diminutive eye on each palm, and the tiny tools of liberation clasped in her delicate fingers. The central pair of hands typically brandish a parasol and a Dharma-wheel. A billowing brocade skirt covers her legs, but a thousand feet emerge beneath the hem. Her dainty feet crush the legions of malefactors and

15.6 Sitātapatrā, Tibet, mid-eighteenth century. Gilt bronze inset with turquoise and coral, painted with blue and red pigments, height 40 in. (102 cm). The State Hermitage, Leningrad, Prince Ukhtomsky Collection. Photo copyright John Bigelow Taylor. *This intricate statue of thousand-armed Sitātapatrā is a marvel of sculptural artistry. (See Pl. 8)*

agents of misery that she subdues (Fig. 15.5). The artist may select among an extensive array of figures to conjure a nightmarish league of natural and supernatural dangers: unrighteous kings, cruel ministers, armored generals, military troops, airborne weapons, chains, flying rocks, black-robed sorcerers, demons and ogres in garish array, raging fires, crashing waves, sea serpents, wild animals, charging elephants, and birds of prey and eaters of carrion scavenging among the slaughter.

It is less common but not unknown for a sculptural atelier to attempt such a complex design.[15] In a stunning example dating from the eighteenth century, presently in the Hermitage Museum, the artist sculpted some of the heads and feet in a solid mass but cast each of the thousand hands separately (Fig. 15.6, Pl. 8). The result is a technical and artistic marvel.

Sitātapatrā mandalas centering on her thousandfold form appear with configurations of seventeen and twenty-seven deities.[16] There is a third version of her mandala with twenty-nine deities. Sitātapatrā may be represented by a white parasol and the retinue figures by their emblems.[17] Tibetan paintings include a compositional format in which the central image of the goddess is surrounded by eighty miniature replicas, expressing her power to manifest simultaneously in myriad locations.[18]

Savior from Supernatural Dangers

Canonical and liturgical texts devoted to Sitātapatrā detail the many dangers from which she offers protection. Foremost among them are the occult threats posed by black magic, sorcery, and evil curses, against which she is the foremost protector. Also within her purview are inauspicious stellar and planetary configurations and the associated hazards of meteors, lightning, earthquakes, and drought. Sitātapatrā is effective against every kind of potentially harmful spirit: *nāga*, *garuḍa*, *asura*, wind sprite, *kinnara*, *yakṣa*, *rākṣasa*, *preta*, *piśāca*, *bhūta*, *mātṛkā*, malevolent ḍākinī, and the myriad demons that cause memory loss, depression, disturbing dreams, outbursts of temper, and untimely death. Her powers naturally extend to the prevention and cure of illness, including all communicable diseases, epidemics, and sicknesses afflicting every part of the body. She also offers protection against enemies, armies, imprisonment, royal punishment, murder, weapons, poison, quarreling, poverty, famine, wild animals, fire, and water.[19] In sum, she averts "the 84,000 outer hindrances" in their entirety.[20]

Although many of these might sound like "natural" perils, in the Buddhist worldview most of them can be traced to malevolent supernatural agency, which brings them within Sitātapatrā's compass. When occult curses and demonic and negative influences are removed, positive effects automatically follow. These include rainfall, plentiful crops and herds, prosperity, happiness, well-being, an increase in merit and virtue, long life, and rebirth in Sukhāvatī, the "Realm of Bliss."[21]

Practices

There is little evidence of Sitātapatrā practice in Nepal today, although late Newar manuscripts of the mantra and a dated painting indicate that her worship was known there as recently as the early nineteenth century.[22] Presently a virtually identical protective role is filled in Nepal by a pentad of goddesses known as the Pañcarakṣā.[23]

In Tibet, however, Sitātapatrā is important for all the Buddhist sects.[24] The practice is surprisingly simple, in view of her iconographic complexity, and centers on a relatively brief invocation and recitation of the mantra.[25] The meditation is classed in the Action Tantra category and thus may entail visualization of Sitātapatrā and meditative identification with her but not, as a rule, inner yogic techniques, as one would find in Yoga Tantra and Highest Yoga Tantra practices. The associated ritual is unelaborate, and the recitations are brief. This simplicity contrasts with the tremendous efficacy attributed to her practice, a fortuitous combination that makes Sitātapatrā a favored source of refuge. Marcelle Lalou observes that it is rare to encounter in Buddhist texts a mantra credited with such potency that its power is fully activated by recitation, without the accompaniment of visualization or ritual.[26]

Monastics and yogic practitioners can invoke Sitātapatrā on their own behalf and at the behest of lay patrons. Common reasons for requesting the practice are illness, disturbing dreams, and land problems that are attributed to demonic or occult interference. Her ritual is requested often and performed numerous times annually in countless institutions throughout the Tibetan Buddhist world. Despite the frequency of its performance, the ceremony is not undertaken lightly. Because of its tremendous power, it is only to be deployed in cases of extreme need.

Moreover, an amulet made of cloth, birch bark, or paper, inscribed with her mantra and consecrated with incantations, may be worn as a protective talisman.[27] Her mantra may be inscribed on banners to be hung from a roof, fence, or city gate so the wind will spread its mantle of protection over those who reside within.[28] Lalou makes mention of magical dagger (*phur-bu*) rites described in canonical sources on Sitātapatrā,[29] but none of the lamas I consulted noted use of the dagger among current ritual techniques.

Similarities to Aparājitā

Sitātapatrā bears features in common with Aparājitā, whose name means "Unconquerable Lady." The identifying iconographic trait of Sitātapatrā is the white parasol, or large umbrella (*ātapatra*), after which she is named. Aparājitā, too, has as her emblem a parasol, although it is held aloft by a Hindu deity rather than borne in one of her own hands (see Fig. 1.8). In her two-armed form, Sitātapatrā's right hand hovers above her knee in an idiosyncratic gesture resembling the gesture of rebuke and repulsion, or slapping motion, characteristic of Aparājitā. The function of the two goddesses is essentially the same. Aparājitā serves to defeat the *māras* ("devils"), or supernatural beings driven by ignorance, selfishness, and greed to harm others and place obstacles in their path. Sitātapatrā's vocation similarly focuses on protection from demons, although it encompasses a broader range of supernatural dangers. Sitātapatrā is celebrated as an invincible goddess who unfailingly defeats any obstacle against which she is pitted, thus sharing the unconquerability of Aparājita. Sitātapatrā's name reflects this commonality, for a fuller version of her name is Sitātapatrā-Aparājitā, that is, "Invincible Goddess of the White Parasol," and she is often designated simply as Aparājitā.

These parallels and shared epithet raise the question of whether one of these goddesses influenced the conception of the other. The comparative chronology of the two figures, however, does not support this conjecture, for they emerged at about the same time, and each evinces a demonstrably independent historical trajectory. The Sitātapatrā mantra (*dhāraṇī*) was in circulation by the seventh century, while her protective function and association with the honorary sunshade may be traced to a generic white parasol goddess who figures in early Pali accounts of the Buddha's former lives, as related above. Aparājitā made her debut possibly in the seventh but definitively in the eighth century.[30] Therefore, it is improbable that her attributes influenced the developing conception of Sitātapatrā. It is equally unlikely that Sitātapatrā's persona informed that of Aparājitā, for the latter has a well-documented historical evolution traceable to fifth-century depictions of the Māravijaya.[31]

While the commonalities between Sitātapatrā and Aparājitā do not discernibly stem from a historical connection between the two, their shared attributes may explain why Aparājitā did not retain the significant presence in the Tibetan pantheon that her importance in late Indian Buddhism would predict. Her career was arguably eclipsed by that of Sitātapatrā, who similarly vanquishes demons, along with a more impressive array of supernatural threats.[32] The fact that Sitātapatrā is often designated as Aparājitā reflects how fully she has superceded the other goddess, for there is apparently little concern regarding possible confusion between the two figures, which would be the case were Aparājitā still in active worship.

A Beatific Protector

Sitātapatrā's historical origins are complex. As the personification of the honorary canopy (*ātapatra*) of the Buddha, her conception was informed by the belief, expressed in the jātakas, that the sunshade of a sovereign is inhabited by a female deity who has a patron relationship with the possessor of the parasol. The belief that she apotheosizes the brilliance of the Buddha's crown of light lends another dimension to her symbolism and confirms the liberative intent of her mighty saving powers. Because she emanated from mantra syllables and because her mantra contains the totality of her protective powers, she is rightly known as the "Mantra Queen."[33]

Sitātapatrā has a relatively tranquil and irenic appearance. That is, she does not display some of the traits commonly associated with wrathfulness in Buddhist iconography, such as a profoundly menacing visage, flaming hair, heavyset body, animal-hide skirt, or other adornments signaling destructive capabilities. Nonetheless, she is regarded as a fearsome protector against necromancy, demons, and other supernatural dangers. This seeming contradiction highlights the conviction that a powerful destroyer of demons need not manifest an intensely wrathful or martial guise. The destruction of demons, illnesses, and negative forces is an expression of compassion and protectiveness toward living beings, and this benevolence, rather than fearsome martial capacities, may be emphasized in the persona of a given divinity. One is reminded, for example, of Mārīcī, who is disarmingly serene, bearing an aśoka branch, yet astonishingly violent in function. It is on this principle that the delicately feminine, parasol-bearing Sitātapatrā has remained for her votaries over the centuries a reliable and mighty protector against evil.

CHAPTER 16

Uṣṇīṣavijayā

Bestower of Long Life and Immortality

Annihilate my suffering and
Bestow the sublime fruit of bliss, I pray.
Pacify all karmic and emotional impurities
With the *samādhi* of supreme, stainless bliss.
Cleanse and pacify all the defilements
That cause a short life, which I have accumulated
During my previous wanderings in samsara
By taking the lives and property of others . . .
May you wash away and purify all that
With a stream of immortal nectar.

—Sakya ritual prayer[1]

Uṣṇīṣavijayā (pronounced *oosh* NEE *shah vee jah* YAH), "Victorious Queen of Crowning Light," is an effulgent white goddess who bestows long life and grants rebirth in a Buddha paradise. She arose from the brilliant rays of light that crown Shakyamuni Buddha. The flamelike crown of light (*uṣṇīṣa*) is a sign of spiritual mastery, a result of the Buddha's attainment of infinite knowledge, awareness, and vision. The topmost portion of the head is regarded as the seat of inner vision and cosmic consciousness, the "divine eye" that perceives spiritual truths and subtle phenomena beyond the range of the physical senses. Moreover, a yogic concentration of psychic energy in the crown of the head endows the uṣṇīṣa with a supernal luminosity, sometimes likened to the blossoming of a thousand-petaled lotus of light.

This crown of glory after which Uṣṇīṣavijayā is named is invisible to ordinary sight and hence signaled in artistic representations by a diadem, turban, or topknot. The uṣṇīṣa proclaims that its possessor has broken the bonds of earthly existence and opened the doors of perception to the cosmos in its immensity and profundity. As an emblem of the supreme spiritual state, the uṣṇīṣa symbolizes the all-vanquishing power of omniscience, which grants victory even over death. Uṣṇīṣavijayā personifies this victorious force.

Origin Account

A widely circulated story of the origins of Uṣṇīṣavijayā takes place in Trāyastriṃśa Heaven, where Shakyamuni Buddha had sojourned to deliver a sermon before an assembly of gods and goddesses. The divine inhabitants of this heavenly realm enjoy a lengthy life span and cavort in a lighthearted manner, oblivious to the possibility of their eventual death. During Shakyamuni's visit, a carefree young god was distressed by the news, imparted by a voice from the sky, that he was doomed to die in seven days and undergo seven rebirths. Aghast, he consulted Indra, sovereign of the gods, who used his clairvoyant vision to confirm that the godling was indeed destined soon to die and to be reborn as a dog, fox, monkey, snake, vulture, crow, and blind man.

Disturbed by his vision, Indra prostrated before Shakyamuni, spread offerings at his feet, and implored him for release from this form of suffering. The Buddha emanated brilliant rays from his crown of light, purifying all the worlds throughout the billion-world universe, and reabsorbed the cleansing radiance. He commenced to teach the practice of Uṣṇīṣavijayā, whose name most literally means "Victorious Queen of the Crown of Light." Yama, the lord of death and gatekeeper of the afterlife, promised to protect those who do the practice of Uṣṇīṣavijayā. The godling recited the dhāraṇī of Uṣṇīṣavijayā, enjoyed a long life, and never again took a lower rebirth.[2]

Bestower of Long Life

This simple and concise narrative articulates Uṣṇīṣavijayā's primary function, a role that has endured throughout her history. According to Buddhist belief, a person's life span comes to an end when the causal conditions sustaining that life are exhausted. However, Uṣṇīṣavijayā has the power both to prevent untimely death[3] and to extend a life that has reached its natural end. As one text promises, "one who has a short life will live for seven years; one who has seven years to live will live for seventy or even one hundred years, with a sharp memory and freedom from disease."[4] The goddess's powers extend into the afterlife. The incantation of her mantra seals the gates to the lower realms of rebirth (as an animal, hungry ghost, or denizen of hell) and opens the door of Sukhāvatī, the "Realm of Bliss," a Buddha paradise whose inhabitants attain enlightenment without descending again into the realms of suffering.

Uṣṇīṣavijayā prolongs life through karmic purification rather than divine intervention. One of her main mantras, revealed by the Indian master Asaṅga, is *Oṃ amṛtāyur dade svāhā!*, translatable as "Oṃ! Bestower of deathless life! So be it!"[5] The mantra extends life by cleansing the life stream of karmic factors that bring about death, namely, the residue of lifetimes of nonvirtuous behavior and delusion. A Sakya treatise explains that the practice of Uṣṇīṣavijayā "purifies and cleanses the accumulation of karmic impurities that produce a short life" and "deterioration and frailty" by washing away all mental defilements "with a stream of immortal nectar."[6]

In the process of purifying the life stream, the goddess pacifies the emotional and mental impediments that cause "every inner and outer affliction of body and mind" and establishes the meditator in "supreme, stainless bliss."[7] Other benefits include relief from bad dreams,[8] enhanced ability to meditate, and a fortunate rebirth. The ultimate fruition of this purification process is literally a deathless state. According to Buddhist soteriology, ordinary beings die through the force of karma, fueled by misdeeds and ignorance, but it is possible to attain an advanced spiritual state in which one is no longer bound by karma and can choose the time and manner of one's death, as well as the bodies and realms one will inhabit. The practice of Uṣṇīṣavijayā is a favored method of progressing toward this goal.

The benefits of the dhāraṇī of Uṣṇīṣavijayā are seen in the biography of Vasubandhu, a circa fifth-century Indian philosopher who had generated negative karma by contradicting and thereby showing disrespect to his preceptor and brother, Asaṅga. When Vasubandhu proposed to meditate on Maitreya, the patron deity of Asaṅga, the latter advised his brother that he was not ready for this practice and should instead rely on Uṣṇīṣavijayā to purify his negative karma. Vasubandhu recited the mantra one hundred thousand times, activating its supernatural powers. He consequently enjoyed full meditative mastery and attained clear yogic perception on the visionary plane of experience, in addition to longevity. The philosopher lived to a ripe old age of eighty or a hundred years, according to different accounts. Moreover, he overcame the karmic forces that bring an end to life, enabling him to choose the moment of his death. When Vasubandhu was ready to die, he chanted the mantra backwards three times and immediately passed away.[9] The intriguing motif of backward recitation suggests that, just as intonation of the mantra prolongs life, its reversal may repeal its life-sustaining effects and allow death to occur.

Divine Forms and Symbolic Attributes

Uṣṇīṣavijayā's iconography has changed very little over the centuries. She is invariably white, the customary hue of Buddhist long-life deities and a fitting color for a goddess who embodies the purifying luminosity of the Buddha's crown of light. Uṣṇīṣavijayā has three faces. The central visage is white and joyful, the right is yellow and tranquil, the left is blue and slightly wrathful. She sits on a lotus with her legs crossed in the pose of meditative stability.

At her first appearances in Indian art and literature, Uṣṇīṣavijayā already had eight arms and bore her characteristic implements (Fig. 16.1). The handheld emblems have remained constant, although the hands in which they appear may vary, and either one or both of her central pair of hands may be held at her heart. Her four right hands (in varying order) display a double vajra (*viśva-vajra*), a Buddha resting on a lotus, an arrow, and a gesture of divine generosity. The arrow "pierces the heart of the obstacles of the lord of death," that is, conditions that end life.[10] The Buddha held on one of her palms may simply be identified as a Buddha or specified as Amitābha, relaying that she opens the path to Sukhāvatī, the Buddha-land over which he presides.[11] Amitābha may be represented by his seed syllable or depicted in figural form. Her four left hands (in varying order) exhibit a bow, a noose grasped with a threatening gesture, a gesture granting freedom from fear, and a vase of nectar (*amṛta-kalaśa*).[12] The term for "nectar" (*amṛta*) literally means "deathless," for this divine ambrosia bestows immortality.

Uṣṇīṣavijayā dwells in the womb of a chaitya, or stupa, which is both a commemorative funerary monument and a symbol of the Buddha's enlightened mind. Her association with the chaitya is doubly meaningful, for she personifies the conquest of death as well as the victory of enlightenment. Thus, she is often portrayed within a stupa (Fig. 16.2) and is associated with the ritual worship of stupas and Buddha relics in various settings, such as Tibet and Nepal, as discussed below. She may also bear an image of Vairocana, Buddha of universal resplendence, on her crown, alluding to her association with the supernal brilliance of Buddhahood.[13]

The rarity of images of Uṣṇīṣavijayā in the surviving corpus of Indic art is surprising in view of the apparent popularity of her practice. Only three examples, all sculptures, have been documented. Among them, the earliest is most likely the carved plaque found at Ratnagiri.[14] Another is a small votive bronze from Kashmir, datable on stylistic grounds to the tenth century.[15]

The most striking is an exquisite stone stele from Nālandā, probably dating from the tenth century (Fig. 16.1). There are three chaityas along the upper register of the piece rather than a single chaitya framing the whole. The work is masterfully carved in deep relief against a plain ground from which the body of the goddess emerges in lush, bejeweled curves that seem to breathe with the warmth of life and softness of flesh. The sinuous curve of her spine and gentle animation of her limbs convey the artist's vision of a goddess who gracefully accomplishes her purposes without rising from deep meditation. The sure

16.1 Uṣṇīṣavijayā, Nālandā, Patna District, Bihar, India, Pāla period, ca. tenth century. Stone. Indian Museum, Calcutta, 4613. Photo: Indian Museum, Calcutta. *This carving portrays the bestower of immortality as a figure of warmth and grace.*

16.2 Uṣṇīṣavijayā, Western Tibet, ca. early fifteenth century. Mineral pigment on cotton, 20 × 18.75 in. (50.8 × 47.6 cm). Rubin Museum of Art, F1998.17.1. Photo: Rubin Museum of Art. *Uṣṇīṣavijayā in the womb of a long-life stupa with her mandala retinue arrayed around her.*

rendition of the lines and contours suggests a confident approach to this portrayal of Uṣṇīṣavijayā, although it is not clear whether the artist was applying a familiar style to a novel subject or drawing on a well-developed tradition of portraying Uṣṇīṣavijayā. The widespread geographic distribution of these three images—from Kashmir in northwestern India, Bihar in the north, and Orissa on the eastern coast—suggests a broad diffusion of the practice of the goddess that makes the paucity of extant Indic images all the more puzzling.

The mandalas of Uṣṇīṣavijayā, like the goddess herself, figure in practices devoted to long life and a favorable rebirth. Female deities customarily have female retinues, but not so the mandalas of Uṣṇīṣavijayā. Her ninefold mandala has an all-male retinue of four peaceful figures and four wrathful ones. They may encircle her in a classical mandala arrangement.[16] One also finds, however, an unusual mandalic configuration in which the foremost members of her entourage, Avalokiteśvara and Vajrapāṇi, flank Uṣṇīṣavijayā in her stupa niche (see Fig. 16.2). Four wrathful figures stand sentinel in front of the goddess, and the two celestials (*devaputra*) hover above the assembly.[17] This arrangement accommodates the portrayal of Uṣṇīṣavijayā within a stupa dome and was presumably designed with that intent.[18] There is also a thirty-three-deity mandala that includes female deities.[19]

Tibetan Conceptions and Practices

Uṣṇīṣavijayā has remained important in the Tibetan pantheon as a major long-life deity. Her practice falls within the Action Tantra class, which features ritual invocation rather than contemplative and yogic disciplines. She is a member of a popular triad of longevity divinities known as the "Long-Life Trinity," along with Amitāyus and White Tārā. Any of the three may be cast as the primary figure. Thus, Uṣṇīṣavijayā appears as the main figure in some liturgies and artistic representations.[20] The three deities share the role of bestowing long life, but each has a specialization. The esoteric yoga of Amitāyus is performed to attain rebirth in Sukhāvatī. White Tārā figures in a healing practice for curing an array of physical and psychic ailments. Uṣṇīṣavijayā is an emergency reserve system to be used when a person is seriously ill or approaching the end of life through old age. She is also invoked to prevent rebirth in the three lower realms and to assure rebirth as a human being, god, or demigod or in a Buddha-land such as Sukhāvatī. A person may recite the mantra of Uṣṇīṣavijayā on his or her own behalf, whereas a monastic or yogic specialist may perform the recitation and associated rituals for someone else or for personal, communal, or universal well-being.

A large-scale ceremony devoted to Uṣṇīṣavijayā, known as the Thousandfold Worship (rNam-rgyal sTong-mchod), invokes her protection even more dramatically and swiftly than mantra recitation. As the name indicates, the offerings of flowers, sticks of incense, banners, butter lamps, flour sculptures, mantras, and circumambulations are made in sets of one thousand. Uṣṇīṣavijayā is represented by a stupa consecrated for the occasion.[21] The rite may be performed at the behest of one or more sponsors. The ritual is elaborate and costly, requiring many hands and hours; therefore, group rather than individual sponsorship is not uncommon. There is no set time in the ritual calendar for this event; the number of annual performances at a given institution depends on the number of requests. A donor might sponsor the Thousandfold Worship for its life-extending benefits or on behalf of an aged or infirm relative. The ritual is deemed so intensely purifying and powerfully effective that it should only be performed in response to a dire need, serious illness, or impending death.[22]

The eight-armed epiphany that was introduced in India also prevails in Tibet, where it finds expression in many exquisitely painted and sculpted representations. Because such images are commissioned to generate merit for a long life and higher rebirth, the statues are typically lavish, made of precious metals and studded with turquoise and gemstones.[23] The Sakya repertoire includes a two-armed epiphany displaying a double vajra in her right hand and a vase of immortality nectar in the left.[24] This manifestation, however, is less prevalent in active practice than the eight-armed version.

Since Uṣṇīṣavijayā is said to reside in a stupa, she is often depicted within a stupa in artistic representations. She is most typically portrayed within a distinctive long-life form known as an Uṣṇīṣavijayā Stupa, or Namgyal Chorten, characterized by three circular steps between the dome and square plinth. In painted works, the beautifully festooned and garlanded stupa provides a graceful frame for the goddess and a distinctive and dramatic compositional format (see Fig. 16.2).[25] In sculpted versions, the figure of Uṣṇīṣavijayā may appear in a niche recessed into the dome, or "womb," of the structure (Fig. 16.3). Her dhāraṇī, inscribed around the pedestal or written on paper and encased within, imbues the statue with her spiritual presence. The work itself may be several inches or several feet in height.[26]

A long-life stupa is often cast in copper or a malleable bronze that is conducive to intricate detailing and then gilded with silver or gold, like the finely crafted piece pictured in Figure 16.3. As is often the case, this work is further embellished with turquoise, lapis lazuli, pearls, and red gemstones or glass. In other instances one might find coral and other gems. One senses in the sumptuous artistry a fervent desire to enhance the meritorious power of the effort. Such a stupa is generally dedicated to the long life of the person by or for whom it is commissioned. For example, a group of disciples may pool their resources and draw on wealthy lay patrons or a monastic treasury to consecrate an ornate long-life stupa to the longevity of a revered teacher.

Newar Observances and Artistic Representations

Uṣṇīṣavijayā also plays a prominent role in the pantheon of Nepal as a granter of longevity.[27] She presides over the Bhīmaratha (New. Jaṃko) ceremony that

16.3 Namgyal Chorten, Central or Eastern Tibet, ca. seventeenth century. Gilt copper inset with gemstones, height 11.75 in. (30 cm). Virginia Museum of Fine Arts, Gift of Berthe and John Ford, 91.534. Photo copyright Virginia Museum of Fine Arts. *This long-life stupa is intricately crafted, gilded, and inlaid with turquoise and gemstones to increase the meritorious power of the piece.*

is staged when a person reaches the age of seventy-seven years, seven months, and seven days.[28] The celebration may also be held for a couple when either the husband or the wife reaches that age. The Bhīmaratha observance reflects the belief that Uṣṇīṣavijayā can lengthen a life span that approaches its natural end. Vajrācārya priests perform three days of ritual in the home of the honorees or in a temple courtyard. An Uṣṇīṣavijayā painting, commissioned in advance for the occasion, is displayed at the ritual site. The goddess will also be ritually present in the form of a vessel that has been vivified by mantra recitation and filled with liquid representing her nectar of immortality.

At the culmination of the Bhīmaratha festivities, the honored person or couple, dressed in brocade raiment, is paraded through the streets in a chariot (*ratha*) drawn by their children and grandchildren and fêted with music, flowers, blessed water, vermilion powder, and incense. The honorees' ears are pierced for a second time, and their youngest grandchild places new silver earrings in their ears.[29] Henceforth, they are released from religious and ritual obligations, for their sins have been remitted and their karma purified.[30]

As mentioned above, a painting of Uṣṇīṣavijayā is customarily commissioned to commemorate a Bhīmaratha. Elaborate examples from centuries past attest to the expense and effort that might be lavished on the work, and this is still the custom when finances allow. Uṣṇīṣavijayā, enhaloed by a stupa, occupies the center of the painting (Pl. 9). She is attended by her mandala entourage and additional deities fill the surrounding space. The ceremony itself may be depicted, typically in a lower register. The person or couple undergoing the Bhīmaratha, along with family members and priests, will be shown engaging in various rites and festivities in an elaborate visual narrative.[31]

Our nineteenth-century example (Pl. 9) illustrates four scenes, read from right to left. The first shows the couple on a simple pedestal being blessed by a priest as two males who recur in the scenes, one wearing white and the other red—probably sons of the couple—look on. Next, the couple, seated on a more elaborate dais, receives homage from a group of celebrants. The third vignette is the procession, rendered in lively detail. The couple rides a brightly painted, canopied chariot that is festooned with banners and ornately carved with a horse prow, attended by family members of all ages. In the concluding scene on the left, a Vajrācārya priest presides over the closing fire ceremony as the two males dressed in red and white bring offerings. In the bottom register, male and female family members bearing lotus blossoms worship an image of Prajñāpāramitā, apparently a goddess important to the family. These festivities unfold under the gaze of Uṣṇīṣavijayā, bestower of the fortunate afterlife destiny that is the goal of the Bhīmaratha rite.

16.4 Uṣṇīṣavijayā Chaitya, Nepal, dated 1882. Gilt copper, height 8 in. (20.3 cm). Zimmerman Collection. Photo: Mr. and Mrs. Jack Zimmerman. *Uṣṇīṣavijayā in her long-life pavilion blesses an elderly couple, shown riding the chariot that will carry them to a fortunate afterlife destination.*

A long-life stupa, or Uṣṇīṣavijayā Chaitya, might also be produced for the occasion. The stupa has the three circular steps below the dome that also characterize the Tibetan examples (see Fig. 16.3). The Newar design, however, may incorporate an additional element. The honored individual or couple may be included at the stupa base, riding a chariot drawn by flying horses, the magical steeds that will transport them to paradise or to nirvana (Fig. 16.4), the afterlife destinations secured by the Bhīmaratha ceremony.[32] The sculpture may have supplemented or substituted for a painting, but currently commissioning a painting is the standard practice.

Another development that took place in Nepal is to show Uṣṇīṣavijayā as indwelling Svayambhū Stupa (Fig. 16.5). Svayambhū (also known as Svayambhū Mahāchaitya) is an actual edifice in Nepal and indeed the foremost monument of Newar Buddhism. It is regarded as the first stupa of Nepal, primeval in origin, and is recognized as the spiritual generator and prototype of all stupas in the Kathmandu Valley. Therefore, placing Uṣṇīṣavijayā in this primordial monument accords her the status of paramount deity of the stupa in Nepal.

Expressing this theme, we find a Newar genre of painting in which Uṣṇīṣavijayā appears in a composition filled with stupas. She occupies the dome of Svayambhā Stupa in the center of the design, surrounded by smaller stupas (Fig. 16.6). The earliest known painting of this type is datable on stylistic grounds to the fourteenth century.[33] Because the creation of stupas is a preeminent merit-making activity in Mahayana Buddhism, we may assume that the multiplication of stupas was intended to increase the merit generated by such a painting.

It is not clear, however, why Uṣṇīṣavijayā has come to be integrally associated with the stupa in Newar art. She not only is depicted within a stupa but is featured more broadly in stupa portrayals, although Vairocana is officially the presiding divinity of the stupa in Nepal and is invoked in this role during stupa consecration rituals and worship (*caitya-sthāpana* and *caitya-pūjā*). Nonetheless, Uṣṇīṣavijayā rather than Vairocana most typically indwells the stupa dome in paintings dating from the fifteenth century onward. Thus, despite Vairocana's canonical status in this role, it appears that Uṣṇīṣavijayā has become a reigning patron of the stupa in the Newar religious imagination.

Scholars commonly hold that paintings of Uṣṇīṣavijayā within a stupa and surrounded by smaller stupas are associated with a ceremony known as Lakṣachaitya Vrata. This lay observance, held during the holy month of Guṇlā in late summer, centers on the creation of one hundred thousand (*lakṣa*) miniature stupas (chaitya) made of black clay or other material as a lavish votive offering. The connection between the genre of painting in question and the

16.5 Uṣṇīṣavijayā. Drawing by Gautam Vajracharya. *A traditional Newar rendering of Uṣṇīṣavijayā in the dome of Svayambhū Stupa.*

Lakṣachaitya Vrata, however, remains unclear. The only painting known from its inscription to commemorate the Vrata does not depict Uṣṇīṣavijayā or rows of miniature stupas. Rather, the painting portrays the donor family and priests performing the Vrata, a subject unique to this composition.[34] Moreover, the multiplication of mantras, motifs, or effigies is a common manner of generating merit in Buddhist settings. Therefore, the Lakṣachaitya Vrata ritual

16.6 Uṣṇīṣavijayā, Nepal, dated ca. 1510–1519 c.e. (inscription abraded). Pigment on cotton, 28.5 × 22.5 in. (72.4 × 57 cm). Zimmerman Collection. Photo: Mr. and Mrs. Jack Zimmerman. *Uṣṇīṣavijayā in Svayambhū Stupa is surrounded by additional stupas to increase the merit generated by the painting.*

and paintings of Uṣṇīṣavijayā surrounded by stupas could both be instances of this practice and bear no intrinsic relationship to one another. Indeed, during my fieldwork in Nepal I could find no priest who would posit such a connection. Therefore, until confirmation is found in the written or oral tradition, it seems judicious to dispense with the widely published interpretation and to assume that such paintings were commissioned to secure the longevity and favorable afterlife destinations of the donor family.[35]

Whereas the popularity of other dhāraṇī goddesses rose and fell over time and their benefactions and iconography evolved and diversified, Uṣṇīṣavijayā has retained the same iconography and essential role in India, Tibet, and Nepal. Her popularity reflects an ongoing fascination with the Buddha's uṣṇīṣa and the magico-religious powers attributed to its supernal light. Perhaps the story that Shakyamuni generated the goddess from his uṣṇīṣa lent a special sanctity that assured her retention in the Buddhist pantheon as a bestower of long life, or perhaps the perennial appeal of the promise of victory over death has sustained her worship over the centuries. Clearly there is something compelling about the luminous white goddess who emerged, sparkling and translucent, from the Buddha's crown of light and now floats through the universe on her lotus blossom, a heavenly vision of angelic grace, showering nectar of immortality in crystalline streams that wash away lifetimes of karmic sediment, opening the portals of celestial realms of rebirth, quenching the eternal human thirst for illumination and immortality.

CHAPTER 17

Tārā

Mahayana Buddha, Universal Savior

O mother of the world, perfect in understanding,
Endowed with great compassion,
You arose for the world's liberation.

You hold a blue lotus in your hand and say, "Fear not!
I will protect all beings! I will ferry all beings
Across the terrifying ocean of existence!"

O Tārā, you are bright, with beautiful eyes, joy of starlight,
Full of pity for all beings, savior of all beings;
Look down, gaze on all beings as your children.

Your body is emerald green, blazing with splendor, invincible.
If one simply remembers your name, you come forth to save from
any terror.
O mother, savior, protector, remover of every obstacle,
Homage to you!

—*108 Praises of Tārā*[1]

Tārā (pronounced TAH RAH), the "Savioress," is a universal mother who nurtures, assists, and protects all seekers on the spiritual path. She cherishes each being as dearly as an only child and, driven by the fierce commitment of a mother's heart, exerts herself in myriad ways to relieve the suffering of the world. No work of art can capture her luminous, magical beauty. Her translucent body is an exquisite creation of emerald light. Upon her gentle, moonlike face, radiant with the glow of compassion, sparkling black eyes and a blissful smile invite all who behold her to take refuge at her holy feet. Her tranquil countenance bespeaks deep meditative calm, while the swirling scarves and lotus plants that encircle her are borne aloft by her shimmering, dancing energy.

Ethereal yet regal, delicate yet majestic, Tārā exudes supreme confidence that she can answer every prayer and fulfill any need. She sends forth countless manifestations in every color of the rainbow, displaying infinite nuances of liberating power, filling the universe with her nectar of mercy, enveloping living beings in the mantle of her maternal grace. At once a transcendent Buddha queen and tender mother, Tārā is without doubt the most beloved goddess of the Indo-Tibetan pantheon.

Tārā has been the subject of an immense body of scholarship. Two substantial studies appeared in the late nineteenth century.[2] In recent decades the published research and translations have attained voluminous proportions. Moreover, Tārā finds mention in almost any work on Buddhist history or culture in South Asia and the Himalayas, for her presence in the religious landscape is impossible to ignore. Her worship crosses lay and monastic lines and spans devotional, ritual, and Tantric practices. One would be hard pressed to find any need—whether physical welfare, healing, or spiritual salvation—for which Tārā is not supplicated. Hence, many scholars regard her as the "Buddhist Madonna," likening her to the Virgin Mary with regard to her maternal persona, direct accessibility, cultic status, and miracle-working powers.

Origin Accounts

There are many versions of the origins of Tārā. She is variously said to have arisen from a vow made by Amitābha, a ray of blue light streaming from Amitābha's left eye, a light beam issuing from Avalokiteśvara's right eye, and a many-colored lotus.[3] One of the most popular stories tells of her birth from the compassion of Avalokiteśvara. In this account, Avalokiteśvara was overwhelmed by the feeling that his extraordinary efforts had not significantly diminished the seemingly endless miseries of living beings. His tears of mercy gathered into a pool on which a lotus blossomed. From the lotus arose Tārā, exquisite in beauty (Fig. 17.1), lovelier than a million lotuses. She consoled the bodhisattva, assuring him that she would join him in his mission to liberate the world from suffering.[4] As this legend evolved in Tibet, Avalokiteśvara is said to have wept two tears. The left teardrop transformed into Green Tārā, while the right turned into White Tārā.[5]

A substantially different and longer account recorded by Tāranātha commences in another universe in the distant past, when Tārā was a human being, Princess "Moon of Knowledge" (Jñānacandrā). An ardent follower of the Buddha of that world, she made precious and costly devotional offerings for millions of years. When the princess set her aspiration on full enlightenment, some monks urged her to pray to be transformed into a man so she could

17.1 Green Tārā, Nepal, fourteenth century. Gilt copper inset with precious and semiprecious stones, height 20.25 in. (51.4 cm). The Metropolitan Museum of Art, Louis V. Bell Fund, 1966, 66.179. Photo: All rights reserved, The Metropolitan Museum of Art. *This Newar bronze portrays Tārā as an elegant figure of exquisite, luminous beauty.*

progress more quickly toward her goal. The princess responded with the nondualistic insight that everything in the phenomenal realm lacks inherent existence and thus there is in reality no man, woman, self, or person. She issued the rather pointed rejoinder that "this bondage to male and female is hollow: Oh how worldly fools delude themselves!" In the presence of the assembled monks she vowed to remain in a female body until all sentient beings are established in supreme enlightenment.

Princess Moon of Knowledge eventually attained a meditative power known as "Saving All Beings." Every morning before breakfast she released millions of beings from their worldly preoccupations; each evening she repeated the feat. Thus, she became known as Tārā, "Savioress." In the following aeon, Tārā pledged to protect all beings throughout the universe from harm. Through a power called "Defeating All Māras," she established billions of spiritual guides each day and defeated a billion demons each night.

After ninety-five aeons had passed, a spiritually advanced monk received initiation from the Buddhas of the ten directions and became the compassionate lord Avalokiteśvara. The light of all the Buddhas crystallized into a ray of compassion and a ray of wisdom, which united and formed Tārā. She emerged from the heart of Avalokiteśvara and proceeded to protect beings from the eight inner and eight outer perils. She continued to progress and eventually received consecration from the Buddhas of the ten directions—that is, attained Buddhahood—and became the mother of all Buddhas.

Finally, in the present epoch, Avalokiteśvara was born on planet earth on Mount Potala. When Shakyamuni assumed the throne of enlightenment beneath the bodhi tree and the armies of Māra descended to attack him, Tārā manifested and subdued the demonic forces with her laughter, and Shakyamuni revealed her Tantric aspect for the beings of the present era.[6]

Pierre Arènes, comparing the origin stories, observes that Tāranātha confers "historical reality" on Tārā by recounting her former lives, beginning with her human birth as a princess who through her own efforts attained the rank of a bodhisattva and progressed toward Buddhahood over many lifetimes. The inclusion of a human incarnation accords with the Mahayana tenet that all celestial bodhisattvas and Buddhas begin as ordinary humans and that the state of Buddhahood is the fruit of many lifetimes, if not aeons, of exertions on behalf of others. Tāranātha also incorporates the popular story of her apparitional birth from Avalokiteśvara by inserting the episode as one of her appearances in the world. This illusory manifestation is consonant with the Mahayana belief that spiritually advanced beings can generate divine bodies at will. Thus, according to Arènes, Tāranātha's hagiography offers a "double version" of Tārā's origins, endowing her with both human and divine births.

Moreover, Tāranātha addresses her career as a bodhisattva (in her former lives) as well as a Buddha. She attained Buddhahood when she received consecration from the Buddhas of the ten directions and, endowed with the title "Mother of All Buddhas," proceeded to manifest the enlightened activity of all Buddhas. All this took place before the current world age.[7]

Universal Savior and Miracle Worker

Tārā's powers of salvation are indicated by her name, which means both "Star Lady," with reference to a stationary star, and "She Who Carries Across," that is, "Savioress." Tārā, like the northern star, is a guiding light in the spiritual firmament, a lodestar of religious aspiration and a stable point of orientation in the troubled waters of life. Tārā helps her devotees cross the ocean of worldly existence, rescuing them from all dangers and obstacles, delivering them safely to the other shore: spiritual perfection, ultimate peace, Buddhahood. Thus, she is *jagattāriṇī*, "savior of the world," the ultimate provider and protector. Her heart mantra, *Oṃ tāre tuttāre ture svāhā*, is famous throughout the Himalayan Buddhist world as a heartfelt prayer as well as a mystical chant. When a votary in need or distress intones her mantra, Tārā responds as quickly as an echo follows sound.[8] Her invocation has the power even to raise the dead. According to the First Dalai Lama, "if one knows enough to recite her mantra, then, it is said, though one's head be cut off one will live, though one's flesh be hacked to pieces one will live."[9]

Hymns in praise of Tārā convey the fervent tenor of her worship. Hundreds of devotional poems, flowing from the pens of sages and visionaries, express absolute faith that Tārā can relieve the direst circumstances and most extreme forms of misery. An early hymn by Sarvajñamitra (eighth century) epitomizes the hyperbolic flavor of the genre. He writes that one who is consumed by disease and covered with oozing sores may be endowed with a healthy, beautiful body. One who is forced by poverty to wear cremation rags, sleep on the bare ground, and beg for food may attain kingship. One who is bound and starved in captivity, too parched even to utter her name, may suddenly be released. One who is trapped in a burning house may be drenched by a sudden downpour. One who is impaled by an elephant's tusk may be removed to safety in an instant. One who stands paralyzed with fear on the deck of a sinking ship may suddenly be standing on the shore.[10]

Such are Tārā's powers of salvation that at the time of death and even during the afterlife journey, one may call on her and be purified of negative karma and established in the blissful realm of ḍākinīs.[11] Celestial bodhisattvas, too, regardless of their level of attainment, seek assistance from Tārā. The First Dalai Lama explains that "the bodhisattvas of the ten stages, who are completing the ten perfections, must also fully rely upon Tara, for she embodies the utter fulfillment of the ten."[12]

Tārā's status as supreme savior and source of refuge has given rise to an attitude of total reliance and surrender more akin to Hindu Bhakti traditions than to Buddhist devotionalism. Some of the praise poems express an attitude of abject and even exaggerated humility on the part of the worshipper. This is seen, for example, in the hymn of Sarvajñamitra introduced above, wherein he characterizes himself as miserable, evil, ignorant, pretentious, greedy, and arrogant. He likens his verses, "sad and pitiful," to a "howl of lamentation," surrendering himself to her mercy, grateful that she is powerful enough to save even a wretch such as he.[13] Another hymnist adopts a similar tone of self-abasement when he claims that, as a heedless, sinful, and defiled person, he can only hope for her blessings because she is "specially kind to inferior beings."[14]

In the same spirit, Lozang Tenpai Jetsun, in his "Cry of Suffering to Mother Tārā," assumes the attitude of a child, unworthy of her attention, totally dependent on her grace. Lauding her as his guru, patron, protector, refuge, dwelling, wealth, and only friend, the very "essence of love," he declares, "you are all things to me," and offers himself to her completely, urging others to "leave everything to Tārā . . . and you will see her face."[15] Such panegyrics go well beyond the more restrained supplicatory mood one usually encounters in Buddhist hymnodic literature and convey the uniquely fervent devotionalism of Tārā worship.

Tārā is renowned as a worker of miracles. Her powers as a savior find expression in written and oral literature telling of her miraculous interventions and extraordinary benefactions. A collection of such tales, mainly set in India, was compiled by Tāranātha in his *Golden Rosary* anthology.[16] These stories recount her deliverance of devotees from danger, adversity, and illness. Many a fortunate has been snatched from the proverbial jaws of death. She might protect individuals, caravans, armies, or whole villages. Numerous stories devolve upon salvation from the "eight great fears" from which Tārā offers rescue: lions, elephants, fire, snakes, brigands, drowning, captivity, and demons. She calms rampaging beasts, quenches fire, quells floods, turns back thieves, releases from prison, turns poisonous snakes into floral garlands. An interesting aspect of these narratives is that the petitioner in question need not be a devotee of Tārā or even Buddhist. One finds many instances in which a person with no special claim on her attention finds himself or herself in dire straits and simply calls on the holy mother for deliverance, eliciting a miracle.

The basic repertoire of stories gathered by Tāranātha is continuously expanding. This body of legend yields many interesting themes. For instance, Tārā is known to manifest in dreams to impart spiritual guidance or crucial advice.[17] She confers a range of supernatural powers, such as invisibility, location of buried treasure, eternal youth, aerial and subterranean travel, the ability to conjure food and wealth, and command of serpents and spirit beings.[18] Such powers find emphasis in Tantric settings and are elicited by the recitation of her mantra, whose powers are an extension of her own.

The miraculous powers of her statues to interact with devotees is another fascinating theme. Tāranātha tells of one such image from whose hand "a long-life elixir dripped like a perpetual flow of milk," and another whose hand dripped a "liquid-like medicine . . . in an endless stream," curing leprosy and bestowing beauty.[19] A statue in Kashmir, too, was famous far and wide for its ability to cure leprosy.[20] Another statue sprouted a stone vessel that brimmed with wealth sufficient to sustain five hundred monks for thirty years.[21] A painting of Tārā came to life and handed her priceless ornaments to a beggar seeking alms to pay for her daughter's wedding.[22] Several statues changed direction or location, burst apart, or consumed food offerings; a sculpture in Nepal that had fallen into the hands of a smuggler became too heavy to lift at the airport and was recovered.[23]

One also hears of "self-arising" (Tib. *rang-'jung*) images of Tārā, unfashioned by human hands. One such icon—on a solid rock face in Pharping, Nepal—has gradually emerged and observably grown from four to ten inches in height over the past few decades.[24]

Most in evidence are talking statues and paintings, known in India, Nepal, and Tibet.[25] Stephan Beyer observes that such images were numerous but nonetheless prized in Tibet, celebrated for their ability to protect persons, dwellings, and even entire regions. Beyer remarks that many temples boasted such an effigy, complete with local legendry, and that "native Tibetan temple guidebooks are so full of casual references to talking images of the goddess that one gets the impression that they were not even considered unusual."[26]

Tārā's miracle stories warrant further examination for the evidence they provide of Buddhism in practice. The repertoire has continued to grow among Tibetans facing the rigors and perils of exile and diaspora, giving evidence that Tārā is a reliable savior still.[27]

As Mahādevī, "Supreme Goddess"

The forces contributing to Tārā's tremendous renown as a savior stem in part from contemporary developments in Indic religion at large. The period when Tārā was introduced—by all evidence the seventh century—coincides with the ascent of several Hindu goddesses to the rank of supreme deity. Each goddess became for her adherents a cosmic figure of universal import, the supreme savior and source of refuge. The Mahādevī, or "supreme goddess," is all-encompassing in nature, infinite in consciousness and being, worthy of supreme reverence as the source of existence and bestower of liberation. This vision of female godhood was gathering force in India at that time, with an outpouring of devotional theologies to Mahādevīs such as Lalitā of Śrīvidyā Tantra, Mahālakṣmī of the Pāñcarātra tradition, and Durgā of the *Devī Māhātmya*.

This historical development, as much as factors internal to Buddhism, could well provide the key to Tārā's apparently meteoric rise in popularity. The emerging concept of supreme female deity—a creator yet not an earth mother, an omniscient being, at once profoundly maternal and infinitely powerful—surely awakened Buddhists to the possibility of a female divinity of this magnitude. That this ultimate power has an irresistibly beautiful feminine face can only have sealed the triumph of the concept. Franco Ricca and Erberto Lo Bue voice the opinion, shared by a number of scholars, that "it was the deep-rooted Indian mythic theme of the great Mother Goddess which determined [Tārā's] success and put her cult on a firm foundation."[28]

Durgā's impact on the conception of Tārā as savior is most frequently noted in this regard. Durgā emerges as supreme savior and goddess in the *Devī Māhātmya*, whose sixth-century date precedes the casting of Tārā in this role. Durgā's benefactions encompass material assistance, miraculous rescue, and spiritual emancipation. She is addressed as Tārā and Tāriṇī and is known as one who ferries her devotees across the troubled waters of life, delivering them from all dangers.[29] Tārā in one of her forms in turn received the name Durgottāriṇī Tārā, whose specialization, akin to Durgā's lifesaving interventions, is the release of votaries from perils such as imprisonment, execution, and demonic attack.[30] The only epiphany of Tārā with an animal mount has as her steed a lion, the vehicle of Durgā.[31] Other commonalities between Tārā and Durgā include shared epithets, featuring explicitly Hindu concepts and figures, that were adopted into Tārā's litany from that of her Hindu counterpart.[32]

Although the historical framework of Tārā's evolution warrants further examination, her cult is clearly part of a broader stream of Indic goddess worship and must be assessed in that light. Buddhist authors, however, do not use the term "Mahādevī" to describe their goddess supreme. Quite early in her history they began to apply to her the most exalted title possible in a Buddhist context, namely, Buddha.

From Emissary of Avalokiteśvara to Female Buddha

The roots of the concept of Tārā in the Buddhist pantheon may be traced to the sixth century C.E. In reliefs of that date at Nālandā and Kānheri, Avalokiteśvara appears with a pair of female attendants, one of whom bears a lotus, which came to be emblematic of Tārā.[33] Apart from the lotus, however, the females have no identifying traits. Thus, they could well have been generic acolytes at their first appearance, although they may be recognized in retrospect as antecedents of Tārā and Bhṛkuṭī. Another precursor of Tārā appears in Cave 7 at Aurangabad, which dates from the mid-sixth century. There, the entrance to the main shrine, which centers on a Buddha, is flanked by two similar reliefs of a lotus-bearing female with a pair of female attendants. Similar in date, the side walls of the Cave 9 veranda feature a lotus-bearing female with flanking female acoltyes.[34] These female figures, because they display a lotus, are often identified as Tārā; however, the lotus-bearing acolyte, both male and female, was and remains a stock motif in Buddhist art. Therefore, it seems possible that here, too, we find a precursor to Tārā rather than Tārā herself.

When the earliest definitive evidence of Tārā emerges to historical view, in the seventh century, she appears first as an attendant and emissary of Avalokiteśvara in both literary and artistic sources. The earliest firmly identifiable artistic representations of Tārā in this role, paired with Bhṛkuṭī, are early seventh-century reliefs at Nālandā and Ellora.[35] Tārā and Bhṛkuṭī were also named as Avalokiteśvara's attendants in seventh-century writings and continued to appear in that role thereafter.[36] One of the first texts to introduce Tārā attending Avalokiteśvara, the *Mañjuśrīmūlakalpa*, includes a passage instructing that she is to be painted as golden and beautifully adorned, displaying a blue lotus in her left hand and the boon-granting gesture in her right, seated on a couch and looking toward noble Avalokiteśvara, hearkening to a command.[37] Elsewhere the text briefly refers to Tārā as "famous in the world."[38] The *Mahāvairocana Sūtra* similarly casts Tārā as Avalokiteśvara's attendant, describing her as "the goddess Tārā of great fame, virtuous, dispeller of fear, green in color, of many forms. One draws her with . . . palms together holding the *utpala* [blue lotus] flower, surrounded by light rays."[39]

The lotus-bearing attendant of the lord of compassion resonated in the Buddhist imagination and quickly began to acquire an independent identity. Indicative of this development is the concentration of datable shrines at the cave site of Ellora. Beginning in the mid-seventh century, Tārā shed her sole association with Avalokiteśvara and began to appear in other divine groupings and retinues, variously paired with Bhṛkuṭī, Cundā, and Jambhala.[40] Around the turn of the eighth century, she became the center of a divine triad, with her own pair of attendants.[41]

Literary sources, too, trace a rapid expansion of interest in Tārā, first as an associate of Avalokiteśvara and then as an object of reverence in her own right. An important document in this regard is the *Tārāmūlakalpa*, a circa seventh-century work in which Avalokiteśvara as narrator introduces Tārā and a broad array of practices in which she figures. This massive treatise of more than four hundred folios is the subject of a book currently being brought to press by Susan Landesman under the title *The Great Secret of Tārā*. According to Landesman, the text is a compendium of ritual practices such as mantra recitation, mandala construction, painting on cloth, fire offerings, and varied magical rites that largely represent the standard Mahayana and Action (Kriyā) Tantra repertoire. As would be expected of a female deity figuring in practices of this genre, Tārā is most frequently characterized in the work as a *devī* ("goddess") and *mahāvidyārājñī* ("great queen of magical incantations"), as well as the somewhat more generic *bhagavatī* ("holy one") and *āryā* ("praiseworthy one"). The work also introduces an array of iconographic forms in which Tārā may be envisioned.[42]

The *Tārāmūlakalpa* represents an important but little-known chapter in the early history of Tārā. The text casts her as an associate of Avalokiteśvara but at the same time articulates a significant body of methods for her invocation and practices in which she is featured. Yet, absent are the explicit soteriological concerns and devotional theology that would come to define her cultus. Therefore, by virtue of its date and content, the volume appears to represent a formative phase in the conception of Tārā, as Landesman will elucidate.

A fuller assessment of the historical location of the *Tārāmūlakalpa* must await the publication of Landesman's study. There can be little doubt, however, that Tārā's sojourn as a dhāraṇī deity was short-lived. Works roughly contemporaneous with the *Tārāmūlakalpa* evince a rapid evolution of her character and elevation of her status from attendant and dhāraṇī deity (*mahāvidyārājñī*) to female Buddha. Compositions by Candragomin (early seventh century) and Sūryagupta (mid-seventh century) provide primary evidence of this development. The writings of Akṣobhyavajra and Sarvajñamitra (both eighth century) are also sufficiently early to be relevant. In this body of sources, Tārā is attributed with every perfection of character and all enlightened qualities and powers. She is explicitly referred to as a Buddha.[43] Her character encompasses all that Buddhahood entails.[44]

The writings under discussion express Tārā's Buddhahood in myriad ways. Physically, she is said to display the thirty-two major and sixty minor marks of a Buddha.[45] As a Buddha, she possesses the three "Buddha-bodies" (*buddhakāya*). The transcendent *dharma-kāya* is one with ultimate reality and hence formless, imperceptible, and indescribable. The *saṃbhoga-kāya* refers to her manifestation in the divine body of a goddess. This level of embodiment encompasses her many epiphanies and the works of art that represent them. The *nirmāṇa-kāya* is that in which she appears in the human realm.[46] She manifests among humans by adopting the illusory appearance of a woman and by acting through human women of sufficient spiritual attainment to embody her presence.[47]

When Tārā's Buddhahood is expressed in Mahayana terms, invoking the definition of enlightenment as the realization of universal compassion and transcendent wisdom, Tārā is said to embody compassion (*karuṇā*), which impels her to relieve the suffering of the world, and to command every liberative art (*upāya*) in the service of others. She is also attributed with the complementary quality of perfect wisdom (*prajñā*), crowning her character with omniscience.[48] According to the Tantric model of Buddhahood, Tārā has integrated emptiness (*śūnyatā*) and supreme bliss (*mahāsukha*) and manifests the five Buddha wisdoms that comprise the totality of enlightenment.[49] She is proclaimed to be utterly transcendent, immersed in ultimate reality, beyond samsara and nirvana, inconceivable and inexpressible.[50] Her being, universal in compass, envelops all that exists and enfolds all living beings.[51]

By the evidence of these early sources, dating from the seventh and eighth centuries, Buddhahood had become integral to the conception of Tārā within a remarkably short span of her emergence to historical view. Moreover, the early writings under consideration do not simply count her as a Buddha among Buddhas. They exalt her as the embodiment of the very principle of Buddhahood. We find assertions that Tārā encompasses the body, speech, and mind of all Buddhas and is the essence of all past, present, and future Buddhas.[52] Her liberative specialty is expansively conceived as the accomplishment of the enlightened activity of all Buddhas. This declaration, found already in a hymn by Candragomin and repeated throughout her literature, encapsulates the tremendous saving powers vested in Tārā. There is no power or property of Buddhahood that she does not possess and thus, in short, nothing she cannot accomplish. With this range of doctrinal formulations, scholars laid in place the theoretical foundations for a broadly held belief in Tārā as a liberator, protector, and savior without equal.

Mother of Wisdom and Compassion

Motherhood is central to the conception of Tārā. She is frequently invoked in Sanskrit and Tibetan liturgies and prayers as "mother" (*mātā*), "loving mother" (*byams-pa'i yum*), "supreme mother" (*mchog gi ma*), "only mother" (*yum-gcig*), "mother of the world" (*loka-mātā, srid-pa'i yum, 'jig-rten-ma*), and "universal mother" (*viśva-mātā*). Her motherhood has two dimensions, corresponding to her complementary qualities of infinite compassion (*karuṇā*) and transcendent wisdom (*prajñā*).

By virtue of her boundless compassion, Tārā is regarded as the personification of motherly love. Mahayana literature in general maintains that, among the many bonds of affection that sustain and enhance human lives, mother love is supreme, for the mother is the person most fiercely committed to her children's survival and well-being. This valuation of motherhood underlies the concept of Tārā as a divinity who nurtures and protects living beings with maternal constancy and ardor. According to Akṣobhyavajra, she "devotes herself to the three realms in the form of a goddess who loves like a mother."[53] Candrakīrti voices the widespread conviction that she cherishes everyone as her own child, while the First Dalai Lama entreats her to "care for me always as a mother [for] her child."[54]

By virtue of her maternal nature, Tārā is regarded as an unfailing source of refuge who never turns a deaf ear to any prayer. Like a mother, she has intimate knowledge of her devotees, a theme invoked in a famous hymn: "O holy Tārā! You know everything that I have done, my happiness and suffering, my good and evil . . . think lovingly of me, my only mother!" The author urges others to rely fully on Tārā, "knowing that she knows all about you," promising that if they do so, the holy mother, "whose essence is compassion," will fulfill all their desires and see that they come to no harm.[55]

The second aspect of Tārā's motherhood proceeds from her transcendent wisdom. She is lauded as an omniscient being, a possessor of nondual gnosis, equal in insight to all enlightened ones. This quality, too, figures in her ministrations as she helps practitioners advance toward Buddhahood, serving for them as a bearer of knowledge, granter of truth, and shining lamp of insight "blazing with glorious wisdom light-rays," dispelling the darkness of unknowing.[56] Tārā wields the sword of wisdom that delivers beings from ignorance and delusion.[57] She turns the wheel of the Dharma, proclaiming the truth of selflessness, taming unknowing with the lion's roar of ultimate truth.[58] Knowing all words to be empty, she uses vowels and consonants as playthings, ringing her voice as a melodious bell of truth to declare the emptiness of all phenomena.[59]

Because of her maternal role in fostering wisdom, Tārā is known as the "Mother of All Buddhas" (*sarva-buddha-mātā*). This title was originally vested in Prajñāpāramitā, the first Mahayana goddess to personify the transcendent wisdom (*prajñāpāramitā*) that gives birth to Buddhas. Tārā, like Prajñāpāramitā before her, came to be known as the "Only Mother of the Buddhas of the Three Times" and "Mother of All Victorious Ones." Other Mahayana goddesses as a matter of course count "perfection of wisdom" and "mother of Buddhas" among their epithets, but Tārā was more fully identified with Prajñāpāramitā and to a large degree assumed her mantle as the foremost personification of transcendent wisdom and "mother of Buddhas." David Snellgrove explains that because Prajñāpāramitā exerts a more specialized appeal, Tārā, as the object of a broad-based devotional cult, came to outshine her ancestress in the role of wisdom mother and progenitor of Buddhas.[60]

Tārā's succession of Prajñāpāramitā may in part be attributed to the contours of their respective archetypes. Prajñāpāramitā is a sublimely transcendent figure, calmly inhabiting the pinnacle of realization that crowns the spiritual quest. Although Prajñāpāramitā fosters, guides, and instructs seekers of truth, she remains an ethereal figure, reigning over the lofty and rarefied realm of perfect wisdom. Tārā, in contrast, personifies lush maternal compassion as well as liberating wisdom, offering a more complex, dynamic, and hence satisfying "mother of Buddhas" who commands every liberative art and nurtures practitioners at every step along the path to Buddhahood. Therefore, it is evidently because Tārā possesses both compassion and wisdom to a superlative degree that she came to be reverenced as the mother par excellence of all Buddhas and all practitioners.

Liberator from the Eight Great Fears

As Tārā's character was defined, by all evidence in the seventh century C.E., she appeared in what was to remain her enduring role as "Liberator from the Eight Great Fears," or Aṣṭamahābhaya Tārā, so named after the "eight" (*aṣṭa*) "great fears" (*mahābhaya*), or mortal perils, from which she offers protection: lions, elephants, fire, snakes, thieves, drowning, captivity, and evil spirits.[61] The theme of salvation from the eight terrors, introduced in a Buddhist context in the *Lotus Scripture*, was initially associated with the bodhisattva Avalokiteśvara. His popularity in this role is amply attested at Deccan cave sites (Ajanta, Aurangabad, Kānheri) by a corpus of relief carvings dating from the fifth through seventh centuries.[62] Tārā was cast in the role of savior from the eight fears in the seventh century, as documented by literary works of this period.[63] The earliest known artistic representation of this aspect of Tārā probably dates from the seventh century as well. Found at the cave site of Ellora, the relief portrays her in the same manner as Avalokiteśvara, standing between two panels of vignettes (four on each side) depicting the eight perils.[64]

Although the religious and artistic conceptions of Aṣṭamahābhaya Tārā were patterned on those of Avalokiteśvara, her popularity in this role superceded that of the male bodhisattva from the eighth century onward. Surveying extant Indic treatments of the two figures, Debala Mitra concludes that "in the later Indian scultures and texts we find Tārā and not Avalokiteśvara in the role of protector from the Eight Great Perils."[65] Forces promoting Tārā to the fore in a role she initially shared with Avalokiteśvara may have included influences from Indic religion at large. Most notably, the *Devī Māhātmya* (ca. sixth century) celebrates Durgā as protector from a virtually identical range of terrors (albeit not standardized into an eightfold set),[66] establishing a precedent and perhaps for some a preference for a female deity in this salvific role.

Tārā's role as "Liberator from the Eight Great Fears" was further delineated in Tibet. Each fear was endowed with a psychological counterpart, that is, a mental or emotional tendency that imperils a practitioner on the spiritual path. This metaphorical elaboration is attributed to the First Dalai Lama, whose internal correlates of the dangers have remained in place over the centuries, with little variation: the lion of pride, elephant of delusion, fire of anger and hatred, poisonous snake of envy, thieves of false views, chains of greed, floodwaters of desire, and demons of doubt.[67] His dramatic verses reveal the "inner" dangers to be no less terrifying than the external ones. Consider the stanzas on the fire of anger and chains of greed:

> Driven by the wind of wrong attention,
> Amidst a tumult of smoke-clouds of misconduct,
> It has the power to burn down forests of merits,
> The fire of anger—save us from this fear!
>
> In the unbearable prison of *saṃsāra*
> It binds embodied beings, with no freedom,
> Clasped by the lock of craving, hard to open—
> The chain of avarice—save us from this fear![68]

The resultant sixteenfold set—sometimes confusingly designated as the "eight and sixteen great terrors"—remained a popular theme for poetic and theological elaboration and deepened Tārā's significance as a deity who responds to the needs of a broad spectrum of people—lay householders, travelers, monastics, and solitary meditators.

The iconography of Aṣṭamahābhaya Tārā evolved and remained in flux for several centuries. In the earlier reliefs at Ellora and Ratnagiri, dating from the seventh through tenth centuries, she is a peaceful and regal figure, akin to the male bodhisattva of compassion, standing amid panels depicting the eight perils bearing down on terrified devotees who supplicate Tārā for rescue. Each scene includes a small effigy of the goddess, representing an emanation she sends forth to accomplish her saving work.[69]

A Ratnagiri relief that dates from perhaps the late eighth or ninth century has survived with many of its details intact (Fig. 17.2). Each vignette includes a small Tārā seated in meditation calmly floating above the scene on a lotus blossom. In the lowermost left panel one can clearly discern passengers on

17.2 Aṣṭamahābhaya Tārā, Ratnagiri, Cuttack District, Orissa, India, ca. late eighth or ninth century. Stone, height 64.5 in. (164 cm). Photo: Ulrich von Schroeder, 1978. *Aṣṭamahābhaya Tārā stands amid panels illustrating the perils from which she offers deliverance.*

a wave-tossed boat appealing in desperation to Tārā. Immediately above this scene, we find an attack by a brigand armed with bow and arrow. Continuing upward, next is a charging lion and, above this, a menacing snake emerging from a rock ledge. The topmost right panel depicts a charging elephant. Below this, a bound prisoner held at sword-point represents the peril of captivity. Next, a squat demon assails the devotee, while in the lowermost panel is a person engulfed by flames. The other relief from Ratnagiri, also featuring a standing Tārā, portrays the imperiled supplicants and the emanations of their savior rushing to their rescue in a dynamic flying pose.[70]

Aṣṭamahābhaya Tārā is portrayed in a standing pose in the early reliefs and predominantly in a seated posture (alternately *lalitāsana* and *dhyānāsana*) from the tenth century onward. Her left hand displays her emblematic lotus, but her right may exhibit the gesture of blessing (seen in Fig. 17.2) or of granting freedom from fear. In the later Indic reliefs, the eight perils may receive abbreviated treatment, for they are often represented by eight miniature versions of Tārā without accompanying illustrations of the mortal dangers.[71]

Aṣṭamahābhaya Tārā may be green or white in Indic sources.[72] The same remained true in the Tibetan setting, although the role of savioress from the eight fears came to be associated primarily with the Khadiravaṇī form of green Tārā, introduced below.[73] Another iconographic conception of Aṣṭamahābhaya Tārā is green and has eight arms, corresponding to the number of perils from which she offers rescue. She displays an array of implements and gestures. A standing epiphany appears in late Indic iconography, while a seated rendition with substantially different attributes is found in the Sakya pantheon.[74]

Her role as protector from the eight fears also gave rise to eight distinct forms of Tārā. This concept finds precedence in an early work by Sarvajñamitra (eighth century), which envisions her eight emanations as markedly diverse in appearance.[75] The idea of eight epiphanies was crystallized into a set of eight Tārās, each endowed with a name denoting the fear from which she offers deliverance. In these eightfold groupings, of which there are several versions, Tārā exhibits a lotus in her left hand and with her right makes the reassuring gesture of granting freedom from fear (*abhaya mudrā*) or of granting blessings (*varada mudrā*). Variations may be introduced in her clothing, ornamentation, bodily posture, and color of the lotus. What distinguishes the different manifestations is the portrayal, beneath her outstretched hand or at her feet, of the corresponding peril or a devotee in an attitude of supplication.[76]

Aṣṭamahābhaya Tārā is a popular subject in Tibetan art, finding expression in diverse formats and media. The medium of scroll painting (*thang-ka*) provided scope for the artist's imagination in rendering the perils and Tārā's manner of intervention, as her eight emanations float through a mountainous landscape in bubbles of rainbow light, dousing fires, stilling waters, pacifying wild animals and demons, delivering her supplicants from banditry and bondage.[77] One also finds sets of paintings in which one peril is featured in each composition.[78]

Effigies of Aṣṭamahābhaya Tārā also appear in the form of stone relief carvings and small wooden shrines.[79] They may embellish charm boxes (*gau*) made of wood or precious metals, rendered magically efficacious by Tārā mantras, relics, and consecrated medicines secreted within. Such portable talismans, strapped to the hip or back, invoke Tārā's protection against the many dangers that beset travelers.[80] The theme of salvation from the eight great fears also finds expression in metal statuary, intricate in design, in which eight miniature Tārās are portrayed within the scrolling stems of a lotus plant encircling the central effigy.[81]

Tārā as "Bodhisattva"

Tārā has been characterized as a bodhisattva in scholarly works too numerous to cite, from the late nineteenth century to the present day. In order to ascertain the basis of this widely held view, Pierre Arènes surveyed an extensive range of Sanskrit and Tibetan texts and western scholarly writings. Arènes traced the genealogy of the idea in western scholarship but found no support for the assessment of Tārā as a bodhisattva in Buddhist literature itself.[82] Even the *Tārāmūlakalpa*, the seventh-century work that introduces Tārā as an associate of Avalokiteśvara, does not apply the title "bodhisattva" to her.[83] Buddhist sources relegate Tārā's career as a bodhisattva to the distant past, to the many aeons of lifetimes in which she progressed toward Buddhahood. Her efforts culminated in Buddhahood long before the current world age. Locating no body of Buddhist literature that introduces Tārā explicitly as a bodhisattva, Arènes dispenses with the theory that Tārā appeared first in historical sources as a bodhisattva and was later recast as a Buddha.

Two main reasons may be cited for the common misconception that Tārā is a bodhisattva. One is her association with Avalokiteśvara, the bodhisattva of universal compassion, in the popular origin story of her emergence from one of his teardrops and their shared role as savior from the eight perils. Perpetuating this connection, Buddhist sources commonly state that Tārā embodies the compassion of Avalokiteśvara. Arènes clarifies, however, that compassion is naturally and necessarily one of her many attributes and that "to save others from various fears, dangers, and perils is the essential activity of all Buddhas and bodhisattvas."[84] Therefore, to say that Tārā embodies Avalokiteśvara's compassion is a trope for her infinite compassion rather than a delimitation of her qualities or powers. Nonetheless, this explicit and ongoing linkage with the male bodhisattva of compassion does lead reasonably to the conclusion, however erroneous, that Tārā is simply his female counterpart and, as stated in a relatively recent work, that she "is no different from him either conceptually or iconographically."[85]

Another reason Tārā is mistaken for a bodhisattva is her iconographic conformity to Mahayana rather than explicitly Tantric deities. As a regal divinity adorned with silken robes and precious ornaments, her hair twisted into an elegant chignon, serene and benign in her primary manifestations (see Fig. 17.1), Tārā fits the classical mold of the Mahayana goddess, whose divine status is that of dhāraṇī (incantation) deity and the question of whose Buddhahood does not arise. Tārā was introduced first in a Mahayana and proto-Tantric milieu, and her iconography reflects this genesis. When Tārā was recognized as a Buddha, as asserted in some of the earliest known literary sources, she became an anomaly among these visually similar goddesses. Tārā's ascent in the pantheon coincided with the rise of the Tantric movement, when the doctrine of female Buddhahood was taking shape. Although the articulation of her character as a Buddha was clearly informed by this theoretical development, her iconography remained rooted in the Mahayana symbolic idiom, which has apparently contributed to the confusion regarding her spiritual status on the part of western interpreters. If the field of comparison is expanded to include male deities, however, her iconography finds a close parallel in that of the Jina Buddhas, who display a similarly regal, bejeweled, crowned epiphany of Buddhahood.

"Consort" of Avalokiteśvara

Almost invariably encountered in works that discuss Tārā is the statement, usually at her first mention, that she is the "consort" of Avalokiteśvara. This rubric, introduced by L. Austine Waddell in his pioneering article of 1894, "The Indian Buddhist Cult of Avalokita and His Consort Tara," has retained a remarkably tenacious hold on western conceptions of Tārā, although Waddell himself offers no evidence for this characterization.[86] Given the period when he was writing, Waddell apparently assumed that all females—human and divine—must come under the guardianship of a male and are definable by this affiliation. Apart from the influence exerted by Waddell in this regard, it is not clear what has perpetuated this view of Tārā for more than a century, particularly in view of the fact that she is not named as the consort (*prajñā*; Tib. *yum*) of Avalokiteśvara in the *Sādhanamālā* or any known text on either figure.[87]

This assessment of Tārā is presumably an inference drawn from her appearance, paired with Bhṛkuṭī, as an attendant of Avalokiteśvara from the seventh century through the present day.[88] That a consort relationship is implicit in this iconographic configuration, however, has been disputed by a number of scholars, largely on the grounds that there is no evidence that the attendants should in this case be understood differently from any pair of divinities—male or female—who might appear as emissary or acolyte figures.[89] That is, attendants are not as a rule identified as consorts of the main deity; therefore, why Tārā has been singled out in this regard remains unclear. The imputation of a consort relationship is particularly problematic in the case of a celibate divinity such as Avalokiteśvara. Moreover, a consistent application of this interpretation would require that Bhṛkuṭī be identified as a consort as well, in which case the possession of two consorts necessitates the introduction of a rather elaborate theory that dispenses with Avalokiteśvara's explicitly asexual, celibate persona in the Mahayana context. Another consideration is that Tārā is frequently paired with a male deity when she appears in attendance on Avalokiteśvara.[90] In these instances, it is not clear why she would be regarded as the consort of Avalokiteśvara rather than of the male with whom she is paired. For all these reasons, the supposition that Tārā—whether in contrast to or along with Bhṛkuṭī—figures as Avalokiteśvara's consort in these reliefs requires significant revision of the known principles of Mahayana thought and iconography.

In explicitly Tantric contexts, when both Tārā and Avalokiteśvara are endowed with consorts, they are paired with other deities. In his Tantric form as Padmanarteśvara ("Lotus-Dancing Lord"), Avalokiteśvara is variously coupled with Pāṇḍaravāsinī, Guhyajñānā, and Guhyavajravilāsinī.[91] Tārā is coupled with Viśvaḍāka in the Pañcaḍāka mandala.[92] In the Pañca Jina mandala and other contexts, she may be paired with Amoghasiddhi or Vairocana.[93] A Sakya practice features Tārā at the center of her own mandala with her consort Amoghasiddhi seated on her lap in sexual embrace.[94]

There is, however, an exceptional instance in which Tārā and Avalokiteśvara are cast as consorts. A meditation practice introduced by Jamyang Khyentse Wangpo (nineteenth century) features White Tārā as the main deity, accompanied by an eightfold female retinue. Supported on her lap is her consort, Padmanarteśvara, holding a lotus and a vessel of long-life nectar, his face upturned to meet her kiss.[95] Because Avalokiteśvara appears here as *her* consort, this meditation does not provide evidence that she is to be defined as *his* consort. Therefore, although scholars persist in describing Tārā as Avalokiteśvara's consort, concrete evidence has yet to be adduced for this characterization.

Green Tārā as Nature Goddess and "Lady of the Plants"

Tārā is envisioned as green in her original and most enduringly popular form, which came to be known as Green Tārā. This epiphany may be depicted in a standing pose but is most commonly seated on a lotus, with her right foot extended forward, elegantly cushioned by a lotus flower (Fig. 17.3). Her right hand rests on her knee with the palm outward in the gesture of blessing. Her left hand bears the stem of a blue lotus (*utpala*) that blossoms above her left shoulder. In earlier Indic representations, her left hand often languidly rests on her left knee or even behind the knee, hidden from view.[96] Over time, however, it became customary to envision Green Tārā as raising her left hand to the level of her heart, visibly clasping the lotus stalk between her thumb and ring finger (as in Fig. 17.3). This form of Tārā is often designated in Tibetan as sGrol-ljang, "Green Tārā," which translates into Sanskrit as Śyāma Tārā, a name not attested in Sanskrit sources, which introduced this epiphany simply as "Tārā."[97] This epiphany remains the focus of numerous Tibetan liturgies and visualization practices.[98] It also appears as the center of a fivefold mandala.[99] This came to be regarded as her primary manifestation, the emanational source of her diverse forms.

Iconographic descriptions of Green Tārā, intended as a guide to visualization, may lyricize her beauty and adornments, attempting to do justice to her nonpareil beauty:

> She is adorned with ornaments of heavenly precious substances such as gold, rubies, and pearls, her two breasts decorated with hundreds of lovely garlands and necklaces, her two arms wrapped in heavenly bracelets and bangles, her hips adorned with the beautiful splendor of the glittering rows of flawless gems on her girdles, her two feet beautified by golden anklets set with multicolored gems, her lovely matted hair entwined with fragrant wreaths made of flowers. . . . She [presents] a shapely corporeal image, a radiant and most seductive semblance, in the prime of her youth, her eyes [the color] of a spotless blue lotus blossom in autumn.[100]

A major variation on this basic green epiphany is Khadiravaṇī Tārā, "Tāra of the Acacia Forest," distinguishable by her pair of attendants (Fig. 17.4). Her acolytes are Aśokakāntā Mārīcī (golden, serene, waving an aśoka bough or blossom) and Ekajaṭā (dark blue, portly, wrathful, bearing a skull cup and flaying knife or other attribute when she has two arms and additional weaponry when she has four). Another distinctive feature of the iconography of Khadiravaṇī Tārā is the flowers adorning her hair. The floral motif is often but not invariably included in visual portrayals, appearing in the form of a floral diadem or flowers festooning her crown. The earliest literary sources on Khadiravaṇī Tārā may date from the late eighth or early ninth century, while artistic representations survive from the ninth century onward.[101] She is typically shown in a standing posture in reliefs of the ninth and tenth centuries (as in

Fig. 17.4) and continued to be represented in this manner but also came to be portrayed in a seated pose with one leg pendant (Pl. 10).[102]

A genre of Tibetan painting portrays Khadiravaṇī holding court in her Buddha paradise, Yuloku, "Land of Turquoise Leaves," the afterlife destination of devotees who are fortunate enough to be reborn in her presence.[103] The compositions center on Tārā in the courtyard of a many-tiered mansion decked with jewels and banners (Pl. 10). Around the pool that waters her lotus throne are dancers and musicians in perpetual celebration. Her palace is set amid a flourishing woodland of pearl-garlanded trees bearing flowers, fruit, and gems, as pictured here. The sky is filled with celestial hosts bearing victory banners, heralding the arrival of those whose spiritual journey came to such glorious fruition. In this paradisal setting, Tārā's votaries may attain enlightenment without descending again into the realms of rebirth.

Buddhist sources commonly attribute Tārā's green hue to her affiliation with the Action (Karma) family of the green Jina Buddha Amoghasiddhi and the corresponding enlightened quality of all-accomplishing wisdom, or unimpeded liberative power. This explanation accords with her specialization, namely, the accomplishment of all Buddha activities, but does not fully account for her green coloration. Indeed, the origin stories of her emanation from Amitābha and Avalokiteśvara, related above, place her within the Lotus (Padma) family, whose color is red. Moreover, as a fully enlightened being, Tārā encompasses the five Buddha wisdoms and hence all five Buddha families.[104] Thus, she herself generates emanations in all five colors (white, blue, yellow, red, and green), expressing the totality of her powers and modes of activity.

Because Tārā's green coloration cannot be explained solely on the basis of the symbology of the five Buddha families, a different explanation should be sought. Dipak Chandra Bhattacharyya, examining the relationship between bodily color and Buddha family affiliation, rejects this commonly accepted correlation and posits a deeper, more fundamental psychological or intuitive association between the color of a divinity and the qualities and insights the deity personifies.[105] On this principle, it is valid to explore the deeper significance of Tārā's green hue as a key to her symbolic significance and appeal.

Visually, Tārā's green hue evokes an association with nature, trees, and vegetation, raising the possibility that she embodies magical and religious properties connected with plant life. A recurrent theme of Indic culture, well documented elsewhere, is the numinosity attributed to plants and trees, a religious impulse that has taken manifold expressions. Leaves and boughs figure widely in religious life in the adornment of shrines and images and as ritual implements, protective amulets, and ceremonial attire. A plant or tree may receive veneration

17.3 Green Tārā, Central Tibet, ca. fourteenth to seventeenth century. Silver, brass, copper, gold, gilded copper, and gilded silver, height 8.75 in. (22.2 cm). Virginia Museum of Fine Arts, The Adolph D. and Wilkins C. Williams Fund, 84.74. Photo copyright Virginia Museum of Fine Arts. *This resplendent statue portrays what is regarded as the primary form of Tārā, the source of her myriad emanations and epiphanies.*

as the natural icon or altar of its indwelling divinity, while branches or leaves may be fashioned into a divine effigy.[106] This array of observances is partially traceable to the belief, voiced in the Vedas, that plant sap carries the vital elixir of life and thus possesses a range of healing, restorative, and transformative powers. Accordingly, various grasses, plants, and trees are attributed with the capacity to enhance fertility and vitality, banish illness and misfortune, "sweep away" demons and diseases, and increase good fortune. It is not uncommon to encounter divinities—both male and female—who manifest in or through particular plants.[107]

In view of this pervasive theme in Indic culture, it is reasonable to suggest that Tārā's green hue may in part derive its symbolic meaning and communicative power from the sanctity inhering in the plant world. Pupul Jayakar proposes that when goddesses who are closely identified with vegetation are cast into figural form, the "magical sap within the plants" that is "the essence and blood of the goddess" will give rise to vegetal attributes, explaining:

> To perform the magical act of healing and protecting, the female principle of divinity has to undergo the magical processes of transformation. Being a composite of human, animal, and plant, she is potent with energy and charged with a power to heal and transform. In time, in contact with the great tradition, her form once again changes. . . . She appears accompanied by beast or bird. The plant elements within her become manifest in the lotus held by the goddess and in the plants that explode around her and clothe her body.[108]

Tārā's iconography, with her vernal green body surrounded by lushly blooming lotus plants, in some portrayals seated within a forest bower on a lion throne adorned with animals, does in many respects conform to Jayakar's description of divine plant ladies.

The nomen Khadiravaṇī Tārā, or "Tārā of the Acacia Forest," reinforces the sylvan associations of her visual iconography. The *khadira*, or acacia, is a hardwood, fruit-bearing tree with medicinal properties. The tree, like the goddess herself, offers shelter, nourishment, and healing. A song of praise by Nāgārjuna, possibly the earliest known literary treatment of this manifestation, places Tārā in the midst of an earthly paradise:

> Holy Tārā's palace is in the Khadira Forest,
> A grove of glomerous figs, acacias, jujube trees,
> Banyans, sandal, three thousand fruits, nutmeg, and cloves,
> A pleasant leafy place of flowers budding and blossoming.
> Among the close-packed trees and fruit, ripe and unripe,

17.4 Khadiravaṇī Tārā, Gaya District, Bihar, India, Pāla period, ca. eleventh century. Basalt, height 32 in. (81 cm). Patna Museum, Arch. 11103. Photo: American Institute of Indian Studies. *Khadiravaṇī Tārā is identifiable by her pair of attendants, Aśokakāntā Mārīcī (in lower right corner) and Ekajaṭā (lower left).*

> There sweetly trickles water with the eight qualities,
> Sweet, joyous cries of peacocks, parrots, and cuckoos resound;
> Tigers and leopards run, stags frolic, and bears leap.
>
> Jackals sing, monkeys play, and antelope calves suck;
> Youthful heavenly maidens play music in the woods.[109]

Nāgārjuna envisions Tārā as the presiding divinity in her natural "palace," replete with flowering and fruiting trees, bird song, and animals harmoniously at play in her blissful presence. He moreover describes her as a "forest maid," "forest goddess," and one "seen in the forest," endowed with the "fragrance of nutmeg, cloves, and magnolia."[110] Clearly Nāgārjuna associates Tārā with the beauties and harmony of nature.

Tree and nature imagery abound in poetic eulogies of Tārā. An early Sanskrit work describes her earthly residence, Potalaka, as burgeoning with trees, vines, waterfalls, minerals, savory fruits, flowers, wild creatures, bird song, humming bees, and throngs of elephants.[111] An Indian devotee sings of her "arms like tree-trunks" and praises her as the "best vine" on the wish-fulfilling tree that grants all desires.[112] Another likens her to "white sandalwood growing among castor-oil plants in a forest."[113] The First Dalai Lama similarly addresses her as "beauty of the acacia forest" and compares her arm to "an outstretched branch of a heavenly tree of turquoise."[114] The *Mañjuśrīmūlakalpa* envisions her in a vernal bower of "trees, studded with flowers on every branch, abounding with open flowers. . . . Their bending boughs . . . look as if turned toward goddess Tārā."[115]

Effigies of Tārā, too, suggest her kinship with the world of nature. Although her divine body is implicitly fashioned of light, the green hue suggests that plant sap—replete with healing, regenerative, and divine energies—flows in her veins. Her body resembles a curving lotus stalk, beginning with the stem of the lotus beneath her right foot and curling upward along her green leg and through the trunk of her body, continuing as the lotus shoot she holds in her hand, whose flowering blossom appears to be an outgrowth of her own body, nourished to supernal beauty by her vernal life force (see Fig. 17.3). Tārā is adorned with flowers and may display a second lotus in her right hand. In artistic representations, she may be endowed with an aureole of blossoming lotus plants and framed by a canopy of trees burgeoning with fruits, flowers, and even jewels, as nature brings forth its bounty in her presence (Pl. 10). She may also be seated on a throne adorned with lions, elephants, stags, and crocodilian water creatures (*makaras*), incorporating the animal realm into the composition.[116]

An early painting of Tārā, dating from the eleventh century, exuberantly elicits this theme, coloring the goddess a deep forest green echoed in the surrounding foliage. An antelope, panther, and elephants gambol amidst the vines of her lotus pedestal, while above her expands a dense woodland "where haloed, bare-chested figures frolic with lions and elephants" and mountains populated by "humans and animals playing or making offerings."[117] This mode of portrayal casts Tārā in the role of mother nature, sitting at the center of lavish creation as if she were its generative source and personification.

Pierre Arènes rejects any suggestion that Tārā is an earth goddess, or "lady of the plants," on the grounds that she embodies such lofty and inarguably "unearthly" principles as transcendent wisdom, universal compassion, and ultimate liberating power.[118] Yet the theological categories assigned to a given divinity do not necessarily address, much less encompass, the symbolic nuances of the visual imagery. Apropos here is Robert Paul's distinction between "secondary rationalizations" (i.e., intellectual formulations and doctrinal exegeses) of a symbol and the "core generative reality" it expresses.[119] In the case of Tārā, one "core generative reality" may well be the understanding of nature—epitomized by trees, plants, and lotuses—as a feminine matrix that nurtures and sustains human life. Maternal nurturance is central to Tārā's character, and it is difficult to imagine a better way to convey her motherly essence than to align her persona with the nourishing abundance and spiritual potency of nature itself.

Regardless of the complex and indeed magnificent theological edifice that has been constructed around Tārā, her portraits have doubtless communicated to their audiences on a direct and literal level that she is an earth goddess, mother nature personified, enthroned amidst the lush world of her creation. Whether or not Tārā's iconography was elaborated with this conscious intention, it is nonetheless apparent that beliefs fundamental to the Indic worldview shaped her symbolic attributes, enhancing the psychological power and emotional appeal of this supremely beloved goddess.

Associations with Lakṣmī

The lotus, the most characteristic attribute of Tārā, is also the emblem of Lakṣmī, the "Lotus Lady" (Kamalā, Padmā). Long an object of Hindu reverence in India, Lakṣmī also received worship in Buddhist contexts, most notably, from the third century B.C.E. through the second century C.E., as evinced by the profusion of effigies at the stupa sites of Bhārhut and especially Sāñcī.[120]

Iconographic similarities between Lakṣmī and Tārā are unmistakable, although rarely noted. For example, when a bejeweled, elegantly clad Tārā is shown standing atop a lotus, bearing in one upraised hand a lotus that blooms above her shoulder, little distinguishes her from Lakṣmī in a standing pose (compare Figs. 4.4 and 17.4). Similarly, when Tārā sits on a lotus pedestal with her right leg pendant and foot resting on a lotus cushion, she appears virtually identical to Lakṣmī in a seated pose, as seen at the Buddhist sites of Sāñcī and Aurangabad (compare Figs. 4.2 and 17.3). Indeed, their essential iconographic conceptions so closely approximate one another that one could easily mistake some of the Bhārhut and Sāñcī reliefs of Lakṣmī for Tārā were it not for their earlier dating and the fact that Lakṣmī may display her lotus in her right hand and when seated may appear with her left leg pendant.

Similarities between the two goddesses go beyond outward appearance. Their origin stories, for example, are remarkably convergent. One of the most popular accounts of Tārā's genesis, related above, tells of her emergence from a lotus that blossomed on a lake formed from the tears of Avalokiteśvara, recalling Lakṣmī's birth from a lotus that arose from the primordial ocean of milk.[121] Tārā's association with Avalokiteśvara calls to mind Lakṣmī's affiliation with Viṣṇu, the Hindu god of whom Avalokiteśvara is in many respects the Buddhist counterpart. The two goddesses also share a number of symbolic resonances. Lakṣmī is innately associated with water, for she generates and nourishes life with rain, moist soil, milk, and plant sap. Tārā's name refers to the crossing of a body of water as well as to the north star, guide of seafarers. Helping her worshippers traverse the ocean of existence is one of the primary metaphors for her saving activities. She is commonly likened to a sea captain, ferrywoman, and boat, as well as a fisherwoman who pulls beings from the troubled waters of suffering, delivering them to the shore of spiritual awakening.[122] The First Dalai Lama envisions Tārā herself as oceanic, glorifying her as an "ocean-like treasury of qualities" whose "miraculous activities . . . like tides of the ocean . . . spontaneously flow in an endless stream."[123]

The benefactions of the two goddesses, although by no means identical, are nonetheless analogous. Lakṣmī bestows fertility, abundance, and happiness, bringing the natural and human worlds to fruition. This role is not far removed from that of Tārā, who nurtures living beings to their full potential and flowering as Buddhas. In both cases, the lotus that the goddess bears proclaims her nurturing powers and the blessings that blossom at her divine touch. Lakṣmī is closely allied with the fructifying forces of nature; lush vegetation, crops, and rice harvests figure among her gifts to humankind. Although Tārā does not share the same agricultural associations, her affinity with the earth and its nourishing, healing powers are conveyed by her sap-green hue, aureole of lotus plants, and the lavish profusion of nature within which she is often envisioned. Lakṣmī's kinship with Tārā is implicitly recognized by two Tibetan meditations that envisage Lakṣmī as green, rather than her customary golden hue. One of the liturgies expressly invokes Lakṣmī as "Tārā" and summons her presence with Tārā's heart mantra.[124]

These shared features suggest that Tārā's iconography and character bear the imprint of traits inherited from Lakṣmī. This is not surprising. The early Buddhist pantheon drew its cast of supernatural beings from Indic religiosity at large, incorporating such divinities as Pṛthivī, yakṣiṇīs, and Lakṣmī. This trend prevailed until the first century C.E., when distinctively Buddhist divinities began to emerge, as the Mahayana movement introduced an expanded cosmology, proliferation of savior figures, and more explicitly devotional theology. It is natural that figures who already garnered reverence in Buddhist communities would bequeath their iconographic traits and religious roles on the new pantheon.

White Tārā

Second in popularity to Green Tārā is the epiphany most commonly designated as Sita Tārā, which simply means "White Tārā." She has two arms and is seated on a white lotus with her legs crossed in the meditative pose (Fig. 17.5). Her right hand displays the boon-granting gesture; her left hand clasps a lotus plant bearing a bud, an unfurling blossom, and a fully opened flower, indicating that she nurtures beings at every stage of spiritual unfoldment. Another distinctive aspect of her iconography, not seen in Indian sources but now integral to her persona in Tibetan and Newar settings, is the possession of seven eyes. In addition to the third eye of omniscience on her forehead she has four "wisdom eyes" (*jñāna-locana*) on the soles of her feet and palms of her hands. Thus, in Nepal she is known as Saptalocana Tārā ("Seven-Eyed Tārā").[125] Her specializations are healing and prolonging life. Indic sources therefore designate her as Mṛtyuvañcana Tārā ("Tārā Who Cheats Death"), denoting her capacity to avert impending death.[126] In the Tibetan pantheon she serves as a major longevity deity and figures in the "Long-Life Trinity," along with Amitāyus and Uṣṇīṣavijayā.[127]

White Tārā intercedes to prolong life whether its end approaches owing to an accident or natural causes such as waning physical vitality, exhaustion of life-sustaining merits, or fruition of life-shortening karma.[128] So great is her power that, according to the First Dalai Lama, one who "knows how to correctly practice her mantra becomes almost invincible. . . . Even if the most definite signs of death have occurred, such as having received many ostensibly fatal wounds, he or she will easily and fully recover."[129] Atīśa, one of her foremost devotees, wrote that her practice "crushes the lord of death" and that the mere sound of her name "dispels death, sickness and misery and bestows long life."[130] Addressing the therapeutic effects of White Tārā, Beyer explains that her soothing, moonlike energy fills the body with healing nectar, creating a calm condition in which restoration can take place, purifying all latent and active causes of disease and death, cleansing the subtle somatic energies to a sparkling luster, augmenting the recipient's life force with her own.[131]

17.5 White Tārā, Nepal, last decade of twentieth century. Pigment on cloth. Mass-reproduced, sold in photographic form. *White Tārā, encircled by rings of colored light, figures in a range of healing practices that purify karma and prolong life.*

This white form of Tārā became very popular in Tibet and is preserved in several lineages stemming from Vāgīśvarakīrti, the Indian adept who formulated an important healing practice centering on the goddess.[132] In Tibetan contexts she may be designated as Drolma Karmo, "White Tārā," or simply as Drolkar. She is also known as Drolkar Yishinkorlo, "Wish-Fulfilling Wheel White Tārā," rendered into Sanskrit as Cintāmaṇicakra Tārā.[133]

The associated healing meditation commences with the envisionment of White Tārā, supernally beautiful:

> The color of her body is white as an autumn moon, as clear as a crystal gem. . . . Her eyes and earlobes are long, and the whites and blacks of her eyes are sharply differentiated; she is beautiful with eyelashes like those of the finest cow, and with eyebrows slightly curved. The sweet smell of lotuses diffuses from her nose and mouth; the line of her lips is pure and red. . . . Her hair is black as bees or onyx. . . . Her fingers are like the filaments of a lotus, thin and soft, wondrously beautiful. Just by seeing her sensuous manner—one can't have enough of looking at it—she gives inexhaustible bliss. . . . Her whole body, above and below, is tantalizingly adorned with many divine flowers. . . . Behind her back is the full orb of the moon, radiating cool beams of light far off, bright and stainless.[134]

The meditator, identifying fully with White Tārā, emanates white light rays that transform the world into a mandala, then dissolves all appearances, sounds, and himself or herself into white light and finally into the expanse of emptiness.

The "wish-fulfilling wheel" featured in her name refers to a distinctive element of her practice, namely, the envisionment of a series of "protection wheels" or "circles of protection" (*srung-'khor*) made of colored light. The meditator emerges from the state of emptiness, appearing again in the form of White Tārā, effulgent with moonlike radiance. From the heart of the meditator-as-Tārā, crystalline light rays go forth and form an encasing orb of white light. Next, golden rays stream forth and form a yellow orb about six feet beyond the white one. Continuing outward, the meditator envisions successively larger spheres of ruby red, sky blue, emerald green, and finally indigo or purple light. Paintings of White Tārā may portray her with an aureole of colored spheres of light, in reference to this visualization (see Fig. 17.5).

Each hue is attributed with a different healing power. The white light pacifies all illness, negative karmic forces, and causes of timely and untimely death. The golden light increases the life span, merit, glory, fame, mental clarity, and wisdom. The red light bestows conquering power and brings the three worlds under dominion. The sky-blue light grants destructive power, eradicating demonic obstacles, enemies, poisons, and misfortune. The green light bestows magical and supernatural powers, while the deep blue or purple light solidifies these attainments. The meditator is thus ensconced within a pavilion of healing, all-accomplishing light.[135]

If the meditation is performed on behalf of others, the persons and beings to be benefited may be envisioned at the center of the spheres, collectively radiating colored light and enhaloed by its protective aura. Alternately, someone in need of healing may be envisaged as seated on a moon disc, facing the meditator, who generates light from his or her heart, directing it out of the right nostril and into the left nostril of the recipient, removing any disease or obstacle to long life and permeating the body with life-sustaining forces.[136]

For a person who is gravely ill, a lama may be summoned to recite the mantra of White Tārā and perform a daylong ceremony to invoke her potent healing forces. This may effect a cure where other treatments have failed. An associated practice, also recommended in serious cases, is to commission a painting of White Tārā, which ideally should be completed in a single day.[137] The artist should bathe, maintain a state of ritual purity, eschew meat and alcohol, and eat only foods that are white in color. The painting should be executed on the day of a full moon or begun when the moon is waxing and completed on the full moon day, so the representation will absorb the lunar energies at their most potent and transfer these to the patient.[138]

A painting or statue of White Tārā may be offered to a spiritual teacher to evoke blessings for his or her long life. The Tibetan government has been known to commission a painting of White Tārā on a monthly basis to preserve the life of the current Dalai Lama.[139]

Rainbow of Emanations

There are numerous iconographic manifestations of Tārā, in addition to the popular and widely practiced green and white forms discussed above. Whereas other Mahayana goddesses typically have several manifestations, or iconographic variations, Tārā is envisioned in a veritable rainbow of figural forms and broad spectrum of moods. This is not surprising, in view of her tremendous popularity. Theologically, this variety of manifestations reflects her infinite array of enlightened qualities. She is understood to generate endless emanations to express the boundless facets of her nature and accomplish the innumerable modes of liberative work.

An early hymn by Sarvajñamitra (eighth century) celebrates Tārā's all-encompassing and protean nature:

Your form . . . is canopied
with the heavens' splendor;
The triple world is pervaded by
its radiance. . . .

Some perceive you full of anger,
raising shimmering weapons. . . .
Others, in every single hair
of your Body see the expanse of space. . . .

Some see Your form as red like the sun,
with rays that are redder still
than the red of cinnabar or red lac;

Others, as beautiful intense blue
like a powder of splintered fragments
of precious sapphire;

Others again as shining like gold,
or dazzling white, surpassing
the milk when the Ocean of Milk is churned.

It is a universal form,
varied like crystal,
changing according to circumstance.[140]

Sarvajñamitra rhapsodizes that hers is a "universal form" (*viśva-rūpa*), encompassing every living creature, all deities, and infinite space.[141] Her appearance changes in accordance with the needs and preferences of living beings for different aesthetic expressions of divinity.

It would be impossible to offer here more than a sample of Tārā's many iconographic forms, which document the many guises in which sages and mystics have envisioned and invoked her. Some manifestations differ from one another by a single iconographic detail, such as the color of the handheld lotus. Many are green in hue and resemble Green Tārā, with two arms displaying the gesture of blessing (*varada mudrā*) and blue lotus, but also have a distinguishing attribute. For example, Mahattarī Tārā is generally seated in the cross-legged meditative posture.[142] Varada Tārā has a distinctive fourfold retinue.[143] Vaśyādhikāra Tārā is seated in *bhadrāsana*, the royal pose in which both legs are pendant.[144] Kāpālī Tārā stands beneath a tree of celestial fruits.[145]

Other green forms include Mahāśrī Tārā, recognizable by her teaching gesture and pair of lotuses (Fig. 17.6).[146] She is attended here by two members of her fourfold retinue. Durgottāriṇī, a four-armed manifestation, brandishes a

17.6 Mahāśrī Tārā, Lakhi Sarai, Monghyur District, Bihar, India, Pāla period, ca. eleventh or twelfth century. Stone. Indian Museum, Calcutta, 5618. Used by permission. Photo: Indian Museum, Calcutta. *An exceptionally fine carving of Mahāśrī Tārā, shown displaying her characteristic teaching gesture.*

noose and specializes in releasing votaries from fetters, imprisonment, death by hanging, and seizure by demons.[147] Four-armed Dhanada Tārā, bestower of wealth, has a retinue of eight Tārās and four door guardianesses.[148] A Kashmiri bronze of this epiphany, unusual for its standing pose, includes at its base Ujalakantā, the female donor, gazing up at her benefactor in adoration as she offers a flower garland, perhaps thanking the goddess for prosperity she has bestowed.[149]

White forms of Tārā are legion. Most prominent among them is the widely practiced two-armed form introduced above, envisioned primarily as a healing goddess, which has a range of subtle variations. The white manifestations include a four-armed form, also known as Sita Tārā ("White Tārā"), whose central pair of hands are cupped at her heart in the manner of a lotus bud (*utpala mudrā*). Her second pair of hands display a blue lotus and the gesture of granting blessings with a wish-fulfilling jewel in the open palm, denoting that she "fulfills the prayers of all beings." Mārīcī and Mahāmāyūrī attend her.[150] Ṣaḍbhuja-śukla Tārā has three faces, six arms, and an array of attributes, including a bow and arrow. Her yogic topknot of matted hair, skull crown, and cremation ground setting lend a Tantric coloration to her iconography.[151]

Another white epiphany, Svapna Tārā ("Dream Tārā"), is invoked to appear in the dream state and reveal past, present, and future events.[152] Serinity Young explains that Tārā, as the savior from all inner and outer dangers, "is the perfect guide through the possibly treacherous dream realm." Young translates a text describing the invocation of Svapna Tārā. The practice entails elaborate ritual preparations and offerings to be made throughout the day, prayer for the desired revelations before retiring, and mantra recitation while falling asleep.[153]

Tārā appears with a golden hue as Rājaśrī Tārā, who bears a blue lotus.[154] Yellow Cintāmaṇi Tārā ("Wish-Granting Gem Tārā") displays a miraculous jewel and stands beneath a gem-laden tree.[155] A yellow, eight-armed manifestation known as Vajra Tārā gained wide currency. She figures in a range of magical procedures for bewitching, paralyzing, stupefying, enslaving, destroying, and protecting. The extensive ritual repertoire associated with Vajra Tārā apparently garnered considerable interest. Five lengthy works in the *Sādhanamālā* describe the rites, and many stone and metal effigies of this epiphany have survived in the corpus of late Indian Buddhist art.[156] Her tenfold mandala retinue apotheosizes the ten-syllable Tārā heart mantra, *Oṃ tāre tuttāre ture svāhā*.[157]

In the Indic pantheon, the primary red manifestation of Tārā is Pīṭheśvarī, the dancing Tantric form discussed below. In the Tibetan context, the Sakya pantheon features Drolma Marmo, "Red Tārā," bearing an elephant goad and a red lotus whose stem curls into a noose, invoked for her powers of subjugation.[158] Another red epiphany, introduced as a "treasure" (*gter-ma*) hidden by Yeshe Tsogyal and revealed in the twentieth century by Apong Terton, circulates in the Nyingma sect and entered the Sakya repertoire in recent decades. Known as Rigjay Lhamo, "Goddess Who Brings Forth Awareness," she is seated in the posture of royal ease within an aureole of rainbow light. Her right hand, outstretched in the gesture of supreme generosity, holds a long-life vase, while her left clasps the stem of a red lotus whose petals cushion a fully drawn bow and arrow made of tiny lotus blossoms.

The practice of Rigjay Lhamo encompasses a range of advanced Tantric techniques, such as dream yoga and the yoga of the inner winds and veins. In a healing practice centering on Rigjay Lhamo, the meditator envisions rainbow beams of five-colored light emanating from her head, throat, and heart. The rainbow rays purify all beings of the five root poisons (anger, pride, desire, envy, and ignorance) and establish in their place the five aspects of enlightened awareness: mirrorlike clarity, wisdom of equality, recognition of emptiness, all-accomplishing wisdom, and spacelike wisdom. Her visualization is ideally to be performed at sunrise and sunset, when the sky is red.[159]

Most forms of Tārā are pacific (*saumya*) in aspect, but she also has several wrathful (*raudra*) manifestations. Ekajaṭā, or Ugra Tārā ("Fierce Tārā"), is dark blue, portly, and fearsome, with upward-flaming hair and wrathful accoutrements. She appears with two, four, and twenty-four arms.[160] Golden Prasanna Tārā is "terrible to behold," blazing like the sun, with a necklace of bloody heads and sixteen arms holding an array of weapons and Tantric attributes. She "emancipates the universe" and "destroys the veils of ignorance."[161] Pīṭheśvarī, or Uḍḍiyāna Tārā, another wrathful form, is red with four faces (red, blue, green, and yellow) and eight arms. The most pronouncedly Tantric manifestation of Tārā, Pīṭheśvarī is envisioned as a corpulent ḍākinī dancing in a ring of fire. She wears a necklace of skulls and a tiger skin around her hips and displays other wrathful attributes, such as tawny, flamelike hair. Her mandala retinue of twenty-four ḍākinīs corresponds to twenty-four major Tantric pilgrimage sites in India, which, as implied by this sādhana, are inhabited by her ḍākinī emanations. The practice of Pīṭheśvarī encompasses Tantric feasting in cremation grounds, wilderness areas, and red-light districts.[162]

Some of the more unusual manifestations include "Tārā Who Is Peaceful by Day and Wrathful by Night." The daytime form is the ever popular Green Tārā. The nocturnal epiphany is white and corpulent, aggressive in mien, garbed in a leopard-skin vest and snake necklace.[163] Mahāmāyā Vijayavāhinī, a thousand-headed, thousand-armed martial form invoked to "devour the forces of the enemy," is characterized by Dipak Bhattacharyya as a "war-goddess."[164]

In Tibet one also finds a fierce emanation known as "Blue She-Wolf," envisioned as a blue wolf looking back toward her tail. Her mantra is invoked to protect Tārā ritual practitioners and texts. Gotsangpa encountered this hierophany during a pilgrimage to Mount Kailash. Twenty-one blue wolves appeared and led the pilgrim to a mountain pass. The spectral wolves then merged into a single blue wolf, which dissolved into a boulder. Hence, the spot came to be known as Drolmala, "Tārā Pass."[165] It is fitting that Tārā's protective presence should permanently be enshrined at this perilous point of passage onto the Tibetan plateau.

Another function of Tārā's power as a savioress is the ability to send forth innumerable emanations to perform her saving work. To express this theme, one encounters among Tibetan paintings a compositional format in which the central effigy of the goddess is surrounded by 108 or more miniature replicas of herself.[166] There is a triptych format in which each painting portrays 333 emanations, a twofold set in which each depicts five hundred emanations, and even one thousand or more simulacra in a single painting (Fig. 17.7).[167] While increasing the merit generated by the creation of icons, this visual motif expresses Tārā's omnipresence, assuring the worshipper that she is never far away and hence always ready to come to his or her rescue. A composition densely packed with her emanations also makes an ontological statement that Tārā permeates the fabric of the universe, as the essence of phenomenal reality and the infinite expanse of space.

Other female divinities of the Mahayana pantheon, too, came to be linked with Tārā and regarded as her manifestations. To reflect this affiliation, her name might be affixed to theirs (e.g., Jāṅgulī-Tārā, Parṇaśavarī-Tārā, Cundā-Tārā, and Tārā-Kurukullā), or they may appear in her entourage or mandala retinue. For example, Jāṅgulī, Cundā, Mahāmāyūrī, Uṣṇīṣavijayā, and Mārīcī are frequently found in her orbit. This association led some of the pioneering art historians to group and treat all Mahayana goddesses as aspects of Tārā.[168] In most cases, however, it is possible to distinguish between female deities that were introduced into the pantheon explicitly as manifestations of Tārā and those that have an independent historical trajectory. The latter have their own liturgies, mantras, religious roles, artistic representations, attendants, and mandala retinues, whereas figures introduced specifically to populate Tārā mandalas do not appear in other contexts.

Therefore, Buddhist efforts to assimilate other goddesses to Tārā, which were not in any case systematic, must be seen as theological rather than historical in nature. They are part of an evolving Tārā theology in which she reigns as the supreme embodiment and encompassing essence of female divinity. On this principle, Tārā is also said to be the emanational source of all the Tantric ḍākinīs

17.7 Green Tārā, Central or Eastern Tibet, ca. late seventeenth to eighteenth century. Mineral pigment on cotton, 60.5 × 38.5 in. (153.7 × 97.8 cm). Shelley and Donald Rubin Collection, P1994.8.2. Photo: Shelley and Donald Rubin Collection. *Tārā sending forth countless emanations to minister to beings throughout the universe.*

of the five Buddha families and even of the female Buddha Vajravārāhī.[169] Carrying this line of analysis to its logical conclusion, not only female divinities but all Buddhas throughout the universe are envisioned as her magical creations, issuing from her body on infinite rays of light.[170]

Praising the Twenty-One Forms of Tārā

Any discussion of the iconographic manifestations of Tārā must include an extremely popular group known as the "Twenty-One Tārās." The source of this series is a text titled *Twenty-One Praises of Tārā and Their Benefits*, which survives in Sanskrit and Tibetan editions and has generated an immense body of commentarial literature.[171] Stephan Beyer assesses this work to be "the single most important praise of the goddess in the entire literature."[172] The *Twenty-One Praises* is attributed with the invocatory and protective power of mantra and, despite its length, constitutes a popular prayer.[173]

As the title indicates, each verse praises a different aspect of Tārā. The opening phrase, "Homage, Tārā, quick one, heroine, whose eyes flash like lightning," epitomizes the celebratory tone of the composition. The stanzas evoke the familiar imagery of a beauteous goddess, "blissful, virtuous, calm," "whose hand is adorned with a lotus."[174] The canticle dwells at more length, however, on Tārā's might and conquering powers, victory over evil forces and spirits, and universal worship. The periodic intonation of mantra syllables creates a rhythmic cadence that reinforces the triumphal mood of the piece, as seen in the following verses:

> Homage, Lady whose face is filled
> with a hundred autumn moons,
> blazing with the laughing beams
> of the hosts of a thousand stars.
>
> Homage, Lady who fills all quarters of space
> with the sounds of TUTTĀRE and HŪṂ,
> trampling the seven worlds with her feet,
> able to summon all before her.
>
> Homage, Lady whose diadem spreads a garland
> of shining and happy beams,
> subjugating Māra and the world
> with a laughing, mocking TUTTĀRE!
>
> Homage, Lady who strikes the earth with her hand,
> who pounds upon it with her feet,

shattering the seven underworlds
with the sound of HŪṂ made by her frowning brows.[175]

Tārā emerges in the *Twenty-One Praises* as a formidable figure, victorious in every sphere, who, in the language of the text, annihilates, tramples, destroys, shatters, and slays, yet accomplishes these mighty deeds while sitting calmly "in her joyous posture of royal ease." The closing verses, usually omitted from oral recitation, extol the benefits of the prayer and promise that one who recites it faithfully every morning and evening will attain all desires and quickly advance to Buddhahood.[176]

The *Twenty-One Praises* gave rise to the Twenty-One Tārās. Each verse is interpreted as an homage to a manifestation of Tārā. The name and specialized role of each epiphany is suggested by a phrase or theme in the corresponding verse. The prefatory stanza containing the Tārā root mantra is generally taken to refer to Green Tārā or Khadiravaṇī Tārā as the emanator of the other twenty-one forms.

There are three main versions of the Twenty-One Tārās, each with its own set of names and iconography. In the system of Sūryagupta, apparently the earliest, the Tārās differ significantly from one another, appearing in varying poses and moods, with differing numbers of arms and attributes.[177] Currently the most popular, according to Stephan Beyer, is the tradition attributed to Nāgārjuna and Atīśa, in which each Tārā is envisioned in seated, two-armed form, peaceful in countenance, her left hand displaying a lotus blossom and her right resting on her knee in the gift-bestowing gesture, supporting a flask. What differentiates these Tārās iconographically is their bodily hue and the color of the flask. Moreover, each has a separate mantra that is used in her evocation.[178] In the Nyingma version of the Twenty-One Tārās, dating from the fourteenth century, the Tārās are seated in an identical pose, with the right leg pendant, the right hand displaying the gift-bestowing gesture, and the left hand clasping a lotus stalk. They are distinguished by color and by an identifying emblem exhibited on the lotus.[179]

Artistic renderings of the Twenty-One Tārās abound. Painted representations may include them in a single composition or devote a separate canvas to each.[180] The group may be depicted on a small portable shrine that can be carried while traveling.[181] The Twenty-One Tārās also appear in paintings of other forms of Tārā, surrounding the central effigy.[182] A famous Tārā temple known as Drolma Lhakhang, established by Atīśa in the eleventh century, escaped the depredations of the Cultural Revolution and still houses its original set of large gilt statues of the Twenty-One Tārās.[183] It is not uncommon to find statuary of the series in Tibetan monastic chapels. The tremendous popularity of the Twenty-One Tārās may be attributed to the belief that they encapsulate all the modes of saving activity of a goddess whose emanations and powers are infinite in number and diversity.

Holy Mother of Tibet

Although Tārā was clearly an important and popular deity in late Indian Buddhism, it is unlikely that she had yet reached the zenith of adoration she garnered in Tibet, where her worship attained the status of a national cult, unifying the religiosity of laity and monastics of all the sectarian traditions. Stephan Beyer opens his monumental work on Tārā in Tibet with an assessment of her significance:

> The worship of the goddess Tārā is one of the most widespread of Tibetan cults, undifferentiated by sect, education, class, or position; from the highest to the lowest, the Tibetans find with this goddess a personal and enduring relationship unmatched by any other single deity. . . . Thus to understand something of her cult is to understand something of the whole structure of Tibetan culture and religion.[184]

In view of Tārā's prominence in the Tibetan pantheon and pervasive presence in Tibetan cultural life, Terence Day suggests that "it seems more appropriate to refer to Tibet's national religion as 'Tārāism' rather than 'Lāmaism.'"[185]

Although Tārā images and texts were introduced in Tibet as early as the seventh century, the establishment of her worship is credited to Atīśa, a Bengali scholar-adept and devotee of Tārā who came to Tibet in the eleventh century, guided by visions of Tārā herself.[186] Atīśa imported and authored texts devoted to Green Tārā and White Tārā. Upon his works, writes Beyer, "was built almost the entire structure of her Tibetan cult."[187] In the same century, the translation efforts of Darmadra and Bari Lotsawa expanded the available literary corpus. Tārā's adoption by a range of important founding figures in the eleventh and twelfth centuries secured her status across the Sarma sectarian board, and she figures in the Nyingma repertoire as well.[188] The efforts of Tāranātha (sixteenth century), another great devotee, further systematized and promoted her cultus.

The origin myth of the Tibetan people was revised in the fourteenth century to incorporate Tārā as divine progenitress. The legendary monkey demon and rock ogress to whose union the Tibetans traced their descent were identified as incarnations of Avalokiteśvara and Tārā. Thus, the holy mother Tārā was cast as the "mother" of the Tibetan people in a literal sense, as their biological ancestress.[189] Moreover, the two wives of the first Buddhist king of Tibet,

Songtsen Gampo, came to be regarded as emanations of Tārā. Princess Bhṛkuṭī-devī from Nepal and Wen-cheng from China, both devout Buddhists, imported votive images, texts, and artisans and influenced their husband to promote their faith, thereby altering the course of Tibetan history. The Tibetan script and earliest Buddhist architecture, icons, and translation efforts date to their seventh-century reign. The Nepalese princess is recognized as White Tārā (or as Bhṛkuṭī, a white manifestation of Tārā), the Chinese princess as Green Tārā, and Songtsen Gampo as Avalokiteśvara incarnate.[190] Through these apocryphal pieties, the Tibetans express their special relationship with the goddess whose compassion for them has shaped the history of their nation.

One of the distinctive aspects of the cult of Tārā in Tibet, according to Beyer, is the intimate, personal nature of the worship. Contact with deities is customarily mediated by the monastic and yogic elites, while practices centering on wrathful protectors and Highest Yoga Tantra divinities are limited almost exclusively to the advanced and adept among the ranks of religious specialists. In contrast, Tārā is directly approachable and immediately accessible to anyone who calls on her.[191] Tibetan Buddhists rely on her divine support with absolute conviction that she watches over them in life and at death, heeding their cries of distress and sharing their joys.[192] The ten-syllable mantra of Tārā, *Oṃ tāre tuttāre ture svāhā*, is a constant prayer, as often to be found on the lips of a Tibetan as the mantra of Avalokiteśvara.

The most common hymn to Tārā, at least equal in popularity to her ten-syllable mantra, is the *Twenty-One Praises*. The hymn figures in the morning and evening liturgies at monasteries throughout the Tibetan Buddhist world. All Buddhist children memorize the rather lengthy prayer at an early age and subsequently recite it in various contexts, as a private and familial votive practice and at public ceremonies.[193] Prayer flags imprinted with the hymn spread its influence through the atmosphere, carried on the wind.[194] Beyer describes how Tārā's protection is invoked at the beginning of the day by the hearty, nomadic Khampas. After gathering to recite the *Twenty-One Praises*, family members continue its intonation as they perform their morning chores:

> A woman visualizes that Tārā has entered into the turquoise ornament she wears on her head; a man will place upon his head a flower, which he later throws away; or the goddess may enter into a ring or any other ornament. She is seen as holding a green ball, inside of which one sits protected for the remainder of the day.[195]

These charming observances epitomize the direct accessibility of a goddess who requires no sacerdotal mediation.

Worship of the holy mother is woven into the fabric of Tibetan cultural life. Beyer observes that, contrary to what one might expect, Tārā "has no great monastic rituals or dances," although folk traditions abound, such as masked dramas enacting tales of her miraculous interventions, a tradition undergoing revival now in diaspora.[196] There are also priestly rites that may be performed in a monastery or private home on request, to generate merit and invoke Tārā's blessings. Such ceremonies—featuring offerings and recitation of Tārā texts, mantras, or prayers—may last one night or, in the case of the "Hundred Thousand Tārā Prayers," three months. Laypersons often prefer to employ nuns rather than monks, on the belief that the Tārā rites and prayers of female monastics are "more efficacious," with the fortuitous result that Tārā rituals may generate crucial income for a nunnery.[197]

The major festival of Tārā is the Fourfold Mandala Offering, a popular ritual performed to generate merit (most efficaciously on the full moon, new moon, or eighth lunar day), to invoke blessings on a new venture, and to accompany celebrations of Buddha's birth, enlightenment, first sermon, and passage into the great beyond. The second through fourth mandala offerings are devoted to Tārā, accompanied by many recitations of the *Twenty-One Praises* by all present—monastics and laity, young and old. Everyone, too, joins in the tossing of rice and flowers toward an elaborately decked Tārā altar. As formerly performed in Tibet, the ceremony was a festive and colorful occasion when conducted in a flowering meadow during the summer months, as children joined in the gathering of alpine blossoms and families and friends enjoyed conversation, picnics, games, horse races, gambling, and drinking during the breaks in the ritual, which might last as long as eight days.[198]

Special concerns of women, too, fall within Tārā's purview. She figures in protective rites for mothers during and immediately following pregnancy and for newborn infants. Recitation of the Tārā mantra is performed to consecrate water, butter, amulets, and medicinal mixtures for anointing expectant mothers and newborns. So comprehensive are Tārā's powers of blessing that she can help a woman conceive without the assistance of a male.[199] Drolma, "Tārā," is a popular female name in Tibet. Candragomin, one of the great early devotees of Tārā, decreed that it is essential to show respect for women so named:

> If to a woman whose name is Tārā
> One develops respect and pays devout homage,
> The merits of this will cause Buddhahood.[200]

Serious practitioners of Tārā are enjoined to honor and mentally worship women named Drolma, recognizing them as embodiments of the goddess. Interestingly, however, the special rules associated with the Tantric practice of

Tārā include a prohibition against engaging in sexual union or entering matrimony with a woman of that name.[201] Candragomin himself abandoned his royal marriage to a princess named Tārā because she bore the name of his divine patron.[202]

Biographies of female adepts in Tibet often evince the direct guidance, inspiration, and empowerment of Tārā in the woman's spiritual journey. In some cases, the sign of a connection with Tārā appears in infancy. For example, Machig Labdron began to intone the Tārā mantra when she was still at her mother's breast. In some cases, Tārā makes ongoing appearances throughout the woman's life.

A woman's identification with Tārā may also be evinced at the time of death. One such story pertains to Tursi, who spent her time in solitary meditation and renounced all possessions but never joined a nunnery. When a revered teacher passed away, Tursi made a farewell visit to her parents and then slipped away in the night, in the midst of a blizzard. Her father, searching for her the next day, found her discarded clothing in the snow:

> Finally he found his daughter on a windswept knoll in a remote charnel ground, completely naked, seated erect in meditation, her hands in the gesture of the female Buddha Tara. She was dead. . . . For three days Tursi remained in her extraordinary meditative state, sitting in the snow like a lovely, unadorned icon of Tara, her skin imbued with a rosy translucence. . . . After three days . . . all vestiges of heat and life disappeared. . . . In her [cremation] ashes was found a perfectly clear, naturally formed image of White Tara, formed from one of her vertebrae.[203]

Thus, at death, too, a woman may evince signs that she has merged identity with Tārā or will ascend bodily to her Buddha-realm, Yuloku.

Another case in point is Dawa Drolma, "Moonlike Tara," a twentieth-century yogini whose name foretold her close and lifelong relationship with White Tārā. Dawa Drolma's autobiography, a precious survival of the textual holocaust of the Chinese occupation, relates how White Tārā began to intercede early in her life, protecting her from demonic obstacles and once curing her of a life-threatening illness with medicines the goddess administered directly to the young girl. White Tārā instructed the adolescent Dawa Drolma to undertake a visionary journey during which her body would be lifeless. The goddess gave detailed instructions regarding the ritual preparations and precautions to be taken while the girl's consciousness was absent from her body.

Dawa Drolma's religious teachers tried every means of persuasion to discourage her from this perilous undertaking. Against the advice of august lamas many times her senior, at the age of sixteen she undertook the visionary journey, inspired by Tārā's praises and prophecies. Those who watched over her body invoked the long-life deities Tseringma and Uṣṇīṣavijayā to safeguard her life force. White Tārā served as her escort, guiding and conversing with her, revealing the prayers and songs she should voice along the way. She traversed realms of heavenly splendor and hellish torment, encountering scores of female deities, exquisite goddesses, and bone-ornamented ḍākinīs who imparted to her special powers, treasures, and wisdom.

The otherworldly journey culminated in a visit to Yuloku, Tārā's Buddha paradise (Pl. 10), which Dawa Drolma describes in vivid detail:

> The entire country was verdant wherever I looked, beautiful and vividly clear. . . . Pavilions of five-colored rainbow light hovered in the sky. Many kinds of flowers and lotuses grew everywhere. . . . The wish-granting trees were in full leaf, and from them hung small chimes and bells. . . . Birds that were emanations of the Noble Lady—sparrows, ducks, peacocks, cranes, parrots, grouse, cuckoos, and swans—played everywhere. . . . The mountains themselves consisted of gold, silver, turquoise, and precious gems.[204]

In this wondrous land, where beings take birth from lotus buds, every sight, sound, and fragrance delights and liberates. There, resplendent in a mansion made of coral, ruby, emerald, sapphire, quartz crystal, conch shell, pearls, and turquoise, praised by "many thousands of goddesses dressed in green," presides Green Tārā, "more intensely luminous than a mountain of turquoise lit by a thousand suns."[205] Tārā placed her feet on Dawa Drolma's head while receiving her worship and then placed her right hand on the girl's head. Tārā imparted the many ways that she, "while primordially a Buddha," manifests in the world to benefit living beings. She also gave parting advice, assuring her votary that "we will never be separate in any lifetime" and that she would send an emanation to remain with her constantly, "like one person talking to another."[206]

After returning from this extraordinary, five-day journey, Dawa Drolma was recognized as a *delog*, literally, one who has "gone and returned" from the afterlife and can thenceforth teach with the authority that such experiences confer. She gained wide repute in Tibet and, not surprisingly, was recognized as an emanation of White Tārā. Her story, given here in brief, relates numerous ways that White Tārā served as intimate guide, companion, and teacher throughout Dawa Drolma's spiritual journey.

This is not to say that Tārā is not an immensely influential figure in men's spiritual development. Besides her inspirational presence and flow of blessings, she is known to manifest her presence to men in dramatic ways to foster their spiritual progress or direct them to act in a way that will widely benefit living beings. Atīśa immediately comes to mind. Tārā intervened twice to prompt and then convince Atīśa to make the journey to a distant and foreign land, traveling on faith alone, to bring her gospel to the Tibetan people, knowing that to do so would shorten his life by ten years and that he would never return to his native land.[207] Examination of biographical literature would surely yield additional examples. In the literature presently known to me, however, Tārā's direct guidance and empowerment is encountered more consistently in women's biographies, although further studies will reveal whether this is more broadly the case.

Tārā in Nepal

Tārā is also worshipped in Nepal but has a less prominent role there than in Tibetan settings. She appears in two main epiphanies, her two-armed green and white forms (known as Ārya Tārā and Saptalocana Tārā, respectively), rather than in the diverse manifestations seen in Tibet. Her images are ubiquitous, appearing in homes and among the statuary and relief carvings so abundant in Newar shrines and temple complexes. Tārā is a popular subject, too, for Newar painters and sculptors. Indeed, many of the most exquisite representations of Tārā in collections around the world are Newar creations, produced for use in Nepal or for Tibetan patrons. The many works of art evidence her ongoing presence in Newar religiosity over the centuries. At the same time, her role is fairly limited, for she has no annual festivals or chariot processions, and her images are mainly housed in shrines devoted to other deities.

Tārā does, however, have an enduring niche in the Newar pantheon as an object of devotion and invocation. She is recognized as a Buddha and as the consort of Amoghasiddhi, one of the five Buddhas of the Pañca Jina mandala that is a mainstay of Newar iconography and ritual practice. Tārā is regarded as a great being of wisdom and compassion and hence may be invoked and worshipped for any number of reasons. Her presence in Newar Buddhism may definitively be traced to the ninth century,[208] and there is no doubt that her history in that setting has been varied. Her primary role at present, however, is that of healing deity. In cases of serious illnesses or even of mild conditions that have not yielded to medical treatment, it is common for the family of the afflicted to sponsor a Satva Vidhāna Tārā Pūjā.[209] The exceptionally lovely ritual features shining rows of 108, 360, or even 1000 small tapers (*satva*) formed from sweetened flour, bowls of water, flickering butter lamps, and cups filled with rice and a coin. This glittering display is embellished by a colorful and fragrant array of food offerings, jasmine flowers, peacock feathers, greenery, and green vegetables and fruits (such as green apples, melons, bananas, and mangos), accompanied by recitation of the 108 names of Tārā.[210]

Another important observance is the Tārā Vrata. It has no set place in the ritual calendar and is performed on a voluntary basis. The holy month of Guṇlā, when Newar religious and merit-making activity is at its peak, is commonly chosen for its performance.[211] Moreover, a sponsor may organize the staging of a Tārā Vrata every month for a specified period, most typically one or three years. Fliers publicize the event, and anyone can participate in one or more of the Vratas. The Vrata might be undertaken to express piety, purify karma, or fulfill a specific wish or need. In accordance with Tārā's primary role in the Newar context as a healing deity, her Vrata, too, is associated with healing. Todd Lewis reports the Newar belief that the Tārā Vrata can prevent premature death and may be "observed in the name of a person who is seriously ill."[212]

The women who make up a majority of the participants maintain a state of ritual purity for the one-day rite and wear green in honor of Ārya Tārā. Each woman brings the supplies she will need for the ritual, which centers on the creation of a Tārā mandala. The offerings feature the color green. One of the special preparations is hand-molded jewelry made of rice dough. The women fashion beaded necklaces, bracelets, finger rings, and toe rings and paint them green with a homemade vegetable dye.[213] The Vrata may be held in any temple courtyard, but two of the favored sites are Itum Bāhā and Tārā Tīrtha.

The main Tārā temple in Nepal is located on the grounds of Itum Bāhā in Kathmandu. At Itum Bāhā, the Tārā Nani ("Tārā Courtyard") centers on a modest but handsome temple enshrining Nepal's most famous Tārā image, a large bronze statue whose face is painted to identify the epiphany as White Tārā (Fig. 17.8). The temple marks the spot where Tārā descended from the Himalayas to the north (i.e., Tibet) and taught the Dharma. Reference to the miraculous event is preserved in a temple inscription identifying the image as "The Great Peaceful White Tārā Who Turned the Wheel of Dharma."[214] The image was donated in the fourteenth century by Jaitra Lakṣmī, a noblewoman from Banepa whose clan wielded significant political influence. This statue is sufficiently renowned that Tibetans in Nepal frequent the shrine to render homage to the famous icon.

Another sacred place associated with Tārā in Nepal is Tārā Tīrtha, a riverside cremation *ghāṭ* on the bank of the Bāgmati River near the Vajrayoginī Temple at Śānkhu. The *vrata-kathā*, or "Vrata tale," of the Tārā Vrata, translated by Todd Lewis, tells of a pious Hindu woman of priestly caste whose abusive alcoholic husband frequented prostitutes. When he tired of her exhortations to better himself, he cast her out of their home. She wandered in the forest, despairing at her negative karma, and decided to commit suicide. Fortunately, she

17.8 White Tārā, Tārā Nani, Itum Bāhā, Kathmandu, fourteenth century. Bronze with painted detailing on face. Photo mass-reproduced and distributed by Itum Bāhā. *This revered statue of White Tārā in Nepal marks the location where Tārā herself appeared and gave teachings.*

met a sage who counseled her that Tārā could relieve her misery. He directed the woman to pray to Tārā at Tārā Tīrtha, a place where Tārā had formerly appeared in person and performed a great act of salvation.

The woman did as instructed, praying, making devotional offerings, and bathing in the holy waters. Green Tārā appeared, holding a lotus, and showered her votary with blessings. Rather than returning to her abusive husband, the woman remained there for the rest of her life, subsisting on fruit and water, meditating, and performing the Tārā Vrata. Her suffering had indeed come to an end, for upon her death she was reborn in Sukhāvatī, "Land of Bliss," the Buddha paradise of Amitābha.[215] This inspirational story is related at Tārā Vrata ceremonies to emphasize the tremendous benefits of its performance. The story also establishes Tārā Tīrtha as an auspicious place to perform the Vrata.

In sum, although Tārā is not one of the major divinities of the Newar pantheon, she is nonetheless revered in Nepal. Her presence is felt throughout the art, architecture, ritual life, and sacred landscape of the Kathmandu Valley.

From Mother Nature to Mother of All Beings

The goddess Tārā, green in her primary and most popular forms, appears to blossom, delicate as a flower petal, amid her aureole of leaves and lotuses. Her sap-green hue and vernal setting allude to her kinship with the nurturing, healing energies of nature. Her persona is redolent with the richness of the earth as she sits on a lotus throne in a lush, harmonious landscape, the very image of the benevolent face of mother nature. Tārā encompasses the starry heavens, the teeming oceans, the flowering planet. As the Star Lady, she shines in the firmament as a guiding light. As Savioress, she guides her devotees across the perilous seas of life. As the lotus-bearing goddess, she tends the universe as if it were her garden, nurturing beings from the budding of aspiration to the full bloom of enlightenment.

The lavish and indeed nonpareil reverence accorded to Tārā arguably finds its roots in the emotional appeal of her kinship with nature, luminous feminine beauty, and gentle, reassuring persona. This homage in turn gave rise to a complex theological edifice, as she came to be exalted as the Buddha mother par excellence, the emanational source of all Buddhas, an embodiment of the very principle of Buddhahood, and a transcendent figure whose being encompasses all things, all living beings, and infinite space.

Although the many doctrines that establish Tārā's ultimacy no doubt appeal to seekers of philosophical bent, the cornerstone of her character is her role as a liberator who saves her devotees from every peril, be it physical, emotional, or spiritual. This, rather than the lofty philosophical verities she personifies, has enshrined her in the hearts and devotion of millions of South Asian and Himalayan Buddhists over the centuries.

The Buddhist tradition celebrates motherhood in many ways and through a range of female divinities, but nowhere is motherhood more complete or exalted than in Tārā, the ultimate embodiment of mother love. Her maternal tenderness, bolstered by the omniscience and powers of Buddhahood, have made her the supreme and most beloved savior of the Buddhist pantheon. The many dimensions of her saving activities find expression in a remarkably diverse array of epiphanies: the Twenty-One Tārās, Eight Tārās, Tārās of every color and mood, Tārās sending forth countless emanations, filling the cosmos with her beauty like stars adorning the night sky. At the core of this expansive theophany is her amazing grace, her heart of compassion, her divine mother love for all beings.

Part Three

TANTRIC FEMALE BUDDHAS

CHAPTER 18

Vajrayoginī

Her Dance Is Total Freedom

Dancing Vajrayoginī holds a skull bowl in her left hand
And a crescent-shaped knife in her right.
She wears ankle bells and a garland of skulls.
The dancing goddess, Vajrayoginī,
Is crowned with a topknot
And has the third eye of omniscience.
She pervades the universe. . . .
An immense and subtle goddess, a stainless goddess,
Goddess holding a skull bowl of emptiness,
Whose essence is emptiness. . . .
Goddess revealing the path to liberation, homage to you!
Homage to glorious Vajravārāhī,
Embodiment of mantra, Buddha-queen!
Granter of all fruits of yogic practice. . . .
The very image of spontaneously arising bliss,
Granter of knowledge and wisdom,
Homage to glorious Vajrayoginī!

—Newar Tantric song[1]

Vajrayoginī (pronounced *vah jrah* YOH *ghee* NEE) is the mistress of all she surveys, and she surveys the universe in its entirety. She displays Buddhahood in female form and revels in the ultimacy of her attainments. Her glowing red body is ablaze with the heat of yogic fire and circled with flames of wisdom. Her dancing, leaping, and soaring poses proclaim that she is fully alive and joyously free. Her flowing hair and swaying bone ornaments ripple on the currents of her swirling energy field. Vajrayoginī never parts from her brimming skull cup, ever slaking her thirst for primordial ecstasy, which is not ordinary pleasure but the innate bliss that pulses at the core of every being and is the birthright of all living creatures. Her chalice is made from a human skull, for nothing deters her ability to taste and enjoy life—even when life's feast is served in something that looks like death.

Vajrayoginī and the other Tantric female Buddhas mark a radical departure from the female archetypes of the Mahayana movement. The reign of the maternal nurturer gave way to the triumphal sway of the dynamic, fiery ḍākinī ("sky-goer"), whose sole interest is liberation. From her sovereign vantage point of ultimate truth, she recognizes all human concerns as mere bubbles of illusion, the eternal play of primordial bliss. Rather than fulfilling petitioners' needs and desires, Tantric female Buddhas sever the bonds of attachment and dissolve conventional thought, removing all vestiges of duality and delusion. Dancing in the realm of ultimate freedom, they beckon their beholders to leap free of the confines of worldly illusion and soar into a dazzling realm of infinite possibilities.

A clear line of demarcation can be drawn in the categorization of the two classes of female deities. The female divinities featured in Mahayana practice are primarily conceived as divine mothers and dhāraṇī (incantation) goddesses. They are worshipped, supplicated, and invoked as savioresses who are tremendously evolved and have extraordinary powers for helping and liberating beings, but they do not body forth full enlightenment.[2] In the Tantric tradition, the sacred female completed her ascent and attained the highest stature possible in Buddhism, namely, Buddhahood. The introduction of female Buddhas was spurred in part by the Tantric belief that, with intense practice of potent transformative techniques, it is possible to attain Buddhahood in the current lifetime and present body. Since bodies may be male or female, it follows that Buddhas may appear in male or female form. The Tantric female Buddhas rose on the crest of this theoretical advance.

The iconographic conventions of the Mahayana and Tantric movements also reflect their respective emphases. The iconography of Vajrayoginī and indeed all Tantric female Buddhas differs markedly from that of the goddesses characteristic of the Mahayana movement. Mahayana divine females are usually shown in a regal seated posture, modestly and sumptuously clothed in silken raiment, draped with jeweled adornments, and elaborately coifed. Modeled on aristocracy and royalty, their elegant appearance conveys a mood of grandeur, evoking the opulent well-being they aspire to bestow on the world. Their faces glow with maternal warmth and compassion, while their attributes reflect their specific ministrations and liberative activities. The noteworthy exception to this pattern is Tārā, who is explicitly recognized and titled as a Buddha but whose iconography reflects the Mahayana idiom.[3]

In contrast, Tantric Buddhas such as Vajrayoginī have a more dynamic, passionate persona that signals a new stage of Buddhist theory and practice.

Their faces exhibit intense concentration and even ferocity. Their bodies are unclothed, and their hair is unbound in the fashion of female ascetics and yoginis. Their bone ornaments betoken a nondualistic outlook and familiarity with the charnel ground, while their handheld attributes allude to their attainment of supreme bliss and wisdom.

Ḍākinī as Buddha

Vajrayoginī is the original and prototypical female Buddha of the Tantric pantheon. Her name, meaning "Adamantine Yogini," describes her as a female who has attained perfection through the practice of yoga and thus become a divine, or "adamantine," yogini—compassionate, all-knowing, and supremely blissful. "Adamantine" in the Buddhist context refers specifically to the indestructible state of enlightenment she has attained. She is also known as Vajravārāhī, "Adamantine She-Boar," whose significance is discussed below.

Vajrayoginī is characterized as a *ḍākinī*, a Tantric term for female practitioners, adepts, spirits, and deities.[4] Among all ḍākinīs, human and divine, Vajrayoginī reigns supreme as Sarvabuddhaḍākinī, "Ḍākinī Whose Essence Is That of All Buddhas." This title is supremely important in her invocation, appearing in the primary mantra of most forms of the goddess. Her other epithets include "Adamantine Ḍākinī" (Vajraḍākinī), "Glorious Ḍākinī" (Śrīḍākinī), "Ḍākinī of Highest Knowledge" (Jñānaḍākinī), and "Fully Enlightened Ḍākinī" (Buddhaḍākinī). The word *ḍākinī* has a complex range of associations, describing Vajrayoginī as one who flies, moves freely in space, dances in the sky, and sports blissfully in the limitless expanse of emptiness.

Vajrayoginī is, first and foremost, an enlightened being. She has attained full awakening and manifests a divine body that expresses her spiritual realizations, providing a model on which others may meditate in order to achieve the same goal. As an enlightened being, Vajrayoginī has attained both transcendent wisdom (*prajñā*) and supreme bliss (*mahāsukha*). Buddhist writings customarily adduce both qualities, and indeed they are regarded as "arising together" (*sahaja*), for neither may be found in its fullness of perfection without the other. Typical is the statement that "she possesses the five transcendent insights of a Buddha and the essence of spontaneously arising bliss."[5] Liturgies lay equal stress on her compassion and blissfulness alongside her wisdom and realization of emptiness.

As a Buddha, Vajrayoginī has three bodies (*trikāya*), or levels of embodiment. Her ultimate "body" is a formless "truth body" (*dharma-kāya*) of pure radiance and wisdom that is one with all of reality and understands everything as it is. She also manifests in subtle "bliss bodies" (*saṃbhoga-kāya*), the divine forms in which she sports as a deity, enjoying enlightenment and teaching and inspiring others. Celestial bodhisattvas and spiritually advanced humans may perceive her divine forms directly, while works of art make them accessible to ordinary human perception. Third is the "transformation body" or "emanation body" (*nirmāṇa-kāya*) forms in which Vajrayoginī appears among humans in the phenomenal realm. In this mode of embodiment she manifests her presence through female adepts (known in this context as "field-born ḍākinīs") who gather at Tantric pilgrimage sites and through other women, both human and apparitional. Beyond the human sphere, Vajrayoginī generates millions of emanations in countless worlds, suited to the bodily types, levels of understanding, and wishes of their myriad beings.[6]

Vajrayoginī has established and presides over Khecara, a Buddha-land suffused with her enlightening presence. Her residence is located in Akaniṣṭha, the purest and subtlest plane of existence, as are the realms of all Buddhas. Vajrayoginī resides in her paradisal abode in bliss-body form, amidst clouds of enlightened ḍākinīs in rainbow array, accompanied by her consort, Heruka-Cakrasaṃvara. Yogis and yoginis who have sufficiently purified their vision may glimpse her Buddha-land or hold concourse with her ḍākinī emissaries, receiving crucial revelations, guidance, and blessings. Those who have made significant progress in Tantric practice during their lifetime will ascend to her realm at the time of death. Many an advanced adept, both male and female, is said to have left behind a tiny corpse or only hair and fingernails, or the sky was filled with rainbows at the time of cremation, signifying that the body was so luminous that it dissolved into light and was absorbed directly into Khecara in "rainbow body" (Tib. *'ja'-lus*) form.

Passionate Cosmic Female

Each Buddha manifests enlightenment in a unique way, revealing different aspects of the supreme state. Vajrayoginī demonstrates that enlightenment is not a passionless condition but rather a state of wholeness in which one has access to all the energies and capacities of one's being. With her vibrant crimson body, streaming hair, and irrepressible dynamism, Vajrayoginī manifests a state of total awareness in which the passions are fully operative and freely flowing. Her passionate nature affirms that the Tantric path is ideally suited for passionate people, providing powerful meditative tools for the transformation of primal egoic drives (anger, greed, selfish lust) into their enlightened counterparts.

It is commonly said of Vajrayoginī that "her essence is great passion."[7] "Great passion" (*mahārāga*) denotes a rarefied "transcendent passion," or "divine passion," free from self-referentiality and selfish or harmful expression. Having transcended selfishness and illusion, she can tap her passion in its sacred purity and direct it to the liberation of others. Chögyam Trungpa clarifies that what he terms her "cosmic lust and passion" has a compassionate dimension, for, "freed from grasping, it becomes a force of expansion and communication." It "simultaneously nurtures the welfare of beings and blazes to destroy the neurotic tendencies of ego."[8] Trungpa's analysis shows that the intensity of passion embodied by Vajrayoginī is prized in the Tantric setting.

In keeping with her wholeness of being, Vajrayoginī has every emotional modality at her command and can employ them at will. Most deities have one predominant facial expression or multiple faces displaying their repertoire of guises, but Vajrayoginī's countenance registers a complex range of emotions. Her facial expression may be described as blissful, erotically enraptured, or intensely wrathful in varying hierophanies, or she may exhibit a blend of moods, as described in a liturgy stating that "she is imbued with a mixture of wrath and passion, in the fullness of bliss, laughing and baring her fangs."[9] Artistic representations vary accordingly, ranging from tense contortions of anger to supernal alertness to a more tranquil mood of exaltation (Fig. 18.1). Even in a beatific mode, however, she is generally shown with sharp incisors, alluding to her ferocity and the omnivorous quality of the Tantric path, which requires that one confront and transform—"digest," as it were—every experience that arises in the journey to enlightenment.

Tantric Buddhism emerged when female deities had been on the ascent for many centuries and were taking center stage in both Hinduism and Buddhism. During the sixth and seventh centuries, these female divinities attained their full status as cosmic figures, universal mothers, and supreme beings in the classical sense. In Buddhism, Vajrayoginī is one of the goddesses who assumed the role of supreme cosmic female. Several elements of her iconography derive from the pan-Indic symbolic vocabulary of female divinity. Foremost among them is the color of her body, for red is the prototypically female color in India, as the hue of the life force (*śakti*), blood of birth, menstrual blood, and fire of spiritual transformation. The life force is omnipresent in the phenomenal world but flows most strongly in the female body, providing the heat and creative energy for the generation of life. Vajrayoginī's red color signifies that she abounds in this primal female essence, a visual allusion immediately recognizable by those of Indic cultural background. Buddhist writings, however, rarely invoke the concept of śakti explicitly, attributing her ruddy hue to one of its manifestations, the fiery energy accumulated through yogic practice.[10] For this psychic heat, known as *kuṇḍalinī* and *kuṇḍalinī-śakti* in Hindu Tantra, Buddhist sources prefer the term *caṇḍālī*, which denotes both blazing heat and burning passion.

Also drawn from the fund of Indic iconography is the red, downward-pointing triangle or pair of interlocking triangles upon which Vajrayoginī stands and which furnishes the design of her mandala (Fig. 18.2). The

18.1 Nāroḍākinī form of Vajrayoginī, Gobind Danghol, Kathmandu, Nepal, last decade of twentieth century. Paubhā, detail. Pigment on cotton, 9 × 6.75 in. (23 × 17 cm). Author's collection. *Vajrayoginī shown with an enraptured expression as she sups nectar of supreme bliss from her skull bowl.*

downward-pointing triangle is an ancient and widespread symbol of female divinity and generative power in Indian culture. As a geometric rendition of the pubic triangle, the motif represents the birth source of the phenomenal world.[11] In Buddhist writings, the triangular diagram, similarly understood as the cosmic womb, is termed *dharmodayā*, meaning "source of phenomena," or "place where reality arises." The dharmodayā recurs in association with Vajrayoginī as an object of meditation, ritual diagram, and symbolic emblem. Different versions appear in relation to specific visualizations, rites, and epiphanies of the goddess. The triangle may be single, doubled, flat, multidimensional, containing or encircled by a red lotus, combined with a square or circle, or inscribed with seed syllables.[12] Pink or rainbow-hued "bliss whorls" added to the corners of a dharmodayā represent the bliss that Tantra recognizes as the origin and destiny of existence (see Fig. 18.2).[13]

As the universal source, Vajrayoginī emanates and reabsorbs all things, animate and inanimate.[14] Her womb encompasses the "three realms" (i.e., the

18.2 Nārodākinī, *Tantra-samuccaya* illustration, Tibet. After Vira and Chandra, *Tibetan Maṇḍalas*, p. 208. *Nāroḍākinī in a six-pointed dharmodayā, four of its corners marked with bliss whorls.*

universe, comprising the realms of desire, form, and formlessness), and during the "perfection stage" of her yoga, red light rays emanate from her vulva, dissolving all beings and worlds, gathering them back into her womb.[15] This is a Buddhist rendition of the Śākta theme that all beings are born from and return to the womb of the all-compassionate, all-wise cosmic mother. In contemporaneous Śākta metaphysics, the ultimate principle of the universe is understood as pure, infinite consciousness. The same holds true in Buddhism, for it is the "pure and radiant mind" of Vajrayoginī, her luminous wisdom, that emanates and absorbs all things.[16]

The triangular dharmodayā motif and its symbolism as the cosmic womb were easily merged with the Buddhist doctrine of emptiness, which denotes the fecund aspect of reality that gives rise to phenomenal appearances.[17] The marriage of these two themes is beautifully illustrated by an apparatus widely used in Vajrayoginī rituals, namely, a mirror covered with red vermilion powder (*sindūra*) in which her emblematic dharmodayā is traced. The mirror symbolizes the clarity of a mind that cognizes emptiness, whereas the red powder represents the life blood of the universal womb and the passion of the supreme goddess to communicate, participate, and liberate.[18]

Divine Forms and Symbolic Attributes

Vajrayoginī has a range of epiphanies. In India the names Vajrayoginī ("Adamantine Yogini") and Vajravārāhī ("Adamantine She-Boar") were used interchangeably to refer to her variety of manifestations. Thus, one could accurately speak of the goddess as Vajrayoginī-Vajravārāhī, and indeed both names are freely invoked in the same litanies to the present day, along with the more specific designations of different iconographic forms.

Common to all forms of Vajrayoginī is her passionate, dynamic persona. The following description from an Indic meditation manual conveys her powerful presence and core iconographic conception:

> Holy Vajrayoginī emanates brilliant rays of power. She is naked and striding, with two arms. Her breasts are firm and swelling. She is red in color and transcendently passionate by nature. Her three wide-open eyes flash fiercely, with furrowed brows. Her mouth is terrible with tusks. She has a lashing tongue, her reddish hair flames upward, and she treads on a corpse. She is high-spirited, youthful, and wondrous with the resonant clanging of her many necklaces and circlets of bells. Her jeweled anklets jingle, and she is adorned with five bone ornaments. In her left hand is a skull bowl filled with the blood of gods and demigods; in her right is a curved knife grasped with a menacing gesture. She is overwhelmingly awesome, abiding in a cremation ground.[19]

This passage evokes the dynamism of a goddess who churns the air with her yogic heat, streaming hair, and clamoring ornaments. Her red hue proclaims her passionate nature. She wears bone ornaments and strands of bells but is otherwise unencumbered by clothing that would conceal her divine glory. Her youthfulness is not primarily a mark of conventional beauty but rather a sign of yogic perfection, for mastery of the inner yogas regenerates the body, reversing the results of aging and restoring vigor, flexibility, and a smooth and radiant complexion.[20]

A vajra-bearing manifestation of Vajrayoginī, no longer present in the active pantheons, was important in the Indian pantheon. This epiphany is featured in four meditation texts in the *Sādhanamālā* and is also the most prevalent version of the goddess to appear in the *Guhyasamaya Sādhanamālā*, a late twelfth-century Indic compendium of practice manuals devoted to Vajrayoginī.[21] Named as both Vajrayoginī and Vajravārāhī in these works, this epiphany is also the subject of the earliest known image of the goddess (Fig. 18.3), which dates from the ninth or tenth century. The somewhat crude but vigorous carving conveys her vitality and joy as she lunges to her left, gazing skyward, raising her skull bowl with an exuberant flourish. Fangs lend a hint of ferocity to her jubilant countenance. She is, as described, naked, or "clothed with the sky," with unbound hair, "naturally joyous," "terrible with tusks," "drinking the stream of blood" that flows from her skull cup.[22] Grasped in her right hand with a threatening gesture, the vajra is an appropriate emblem for the "vajra yogini" and as a characteristically Buddhist symbol sets her apart from analogous Hindu yoginis of the day.[23]

Her adornments are simple in this early stone carving. Absent are the skull crown and garland of heads (*muṇḍa-mālā*) adduced in written descriptions. However, the artist has taken care to include the bell anklets and a strand of bells around her hips. It is interesting to find in this work of art and associated texts an emphasis on "bell ornaments" (*kiṅkiṇī*), "tinkling anklets" (*kvaṇan-nūpura*), and "buttocks like drums ablaze with jingling ornaments," indicating the tumult of sound generated by the dynamic dancer. A traditional part of dance costuming in India, the bells confirm that she is in motion rather than static. Indeed, one finds her described as "dancing violently, trampling Bhairava and Kālarātri with a lunge."[24] Her Tantric staff—termed a "skull staff" (*kapāla-khaṭvāṅga* or *karoṭa-khaṭvāṅga*)—is decked simply with a vajra and skull above and a half-vajra end piece below, pinioning one of the nefarious figures at her feet.

The back slab of the carving is incised with her characteristic flame aureole but includes some novel elements. The female votary kneeling at her feet is virtually naked, save for a filmy lower garment, suggesting engagement in yogic practices. A yogi in a loincloth renders homage, his spiritual attainments signaled by a lotus pedestal. The pair may represent a Tantric couple who travel and practice together. The seated figure in the lower left corner is a Tantric guru-as-Vajrasattva, the type of master who confers initiation into esoteric deities such as Vajrayoginī. This tableau vividly invokes the realm of Tantric practice. The relief also has a hollowed opening behind the goddess, visually representing the space through which she moves. Depicted in association with Vajrayoginī, the motif refers to the power of flight intrinsic to her character as a ḍākinī and *khecarī*, "female who flies."

18.3 Vajrayoginī, Chauduar, Cuttack District, Orissa, India, ca. ninth or tenth century. Stone. Present location unknown. Photo after *Memoir of the Archaeological Survey of India* 44 (1930), pl. 8, fig. 1. *In the earliest known statue, Vajrayoginī, decked in bells, bears her namesake vajra and joyously raises her skull bowl skyward.*

This form of Vajrayoginī—red, striding, bearing a vajra—no longer appears in the active Tantric pantheons, despite its importance in late Indian Buddhism. However, a similar epiphany, also introduced in India, remains important in contemporary Tibetan practice. Nāroḍākinī, or Nāro Khachöma, is readily recognizable by her lunging posture and raised skull bowl (Fig. 18.4). Her head is uptilted, poised to imbibe the blood that overflows her skull bowl, and her right hand brandishes a curved knife (angled toward the viewer in this carving). Nāroḍākinī is crowned and garlanded with skulls and adorned with bone ornaments. She lunges to her left in a dynamic, heroic pose that displays the suppleness of spine and limb attained through yogic practice. The tangible torsion of her upraised left shoulder conveys her dancing motion and sets her tresses flying. She takes her stand on the prostrate bodies of Bhairava and Kālarātri. Beneath them is a solar cushion, its radiance eclipsed by her own. Her primary support is a dharmodayā, depicted in her case as a pair of crossed triangles but conceived three-dimensionally as intersecting tetrahedrons (see Fig. 18.2).[25]

Nāroḍākinī's physical attributes are interpreted with reference to longstanding Buddhist principles as well as distinctively Tantric concepts. For example, her freely flowing hair is in the Indic setting a mark of a yogic practitioner, especially one who cultivates psychic heat, whereas Buddhist exegetes interpret the unbound tresses as a sign that her mind, free from grasping, is a flowing stream of nonconceptuality.[26] Her crown of five skulls represents her transformation of the five aspects of selfhood into the five transcendental insights of a Buddha. Her garland of fifty severed heads symbolizes her purification of the fifty primary units of language and thought. Her bone ornaments represent five of the six perfections of a bodhisattva. Her body itself represents the sixth perfection, transcendent wisdom (*prajñā*), which all female deities implicitly personify. Patterned on an instrument of butchery, her flaying knife has a vajra handle, indicating that its bearer wields the unfailing power of wisdom to overcome negative mindstates such as anger, hatred, and delusion. Four of the six points of Nāroḍākinī's dharmodayā are marked by bliss whorls (see Fig. 18.2), representing the four states of bliss that arise in the four main chakras during inner yogic practice. Two corners are left empty to represent the unreality of things and of persons.[27]

Nāroḍākinī carries a mystical staff (*khaṭvāṅga*), supported by her left arm or balanced across her left shoulder. The staff indicates that she is not celibate and has integrated eroticism into her spiritual path, mastering the art of transmuting pleasure into transcendent bliss. The staff, also known as a "secret consort," represents Heruka-Cakrasaṃvara, her male partner, with whom she is eternally united in spirit. In earlier representations the staff is a short pole,

18.4 Nāroḍākinī, Rajgir, Patna District, Bihar, India, Pāla period, ca. eleventh century. Schist, height 16.5 in. (42 cm). Patna Museum, Arch. 10540. Photo: American Institute of Indian Studies. *Nāroḍākinī, like all Tantric female Buddhas, is unclothed and her hair unbound, expressing her free spirit and pure vision.*

sturdy and simple in structure, with vajra end pieces and an impaled skull (see Fig. 18.4). In her fully elaborated iconography (Fig. 18.5 and Pl. 11), the staff is elongated and intricate in design, incorporating a *viśva-vajra* (double vajra), nectar vase, two severed heads, and a skull. Ribbons, bells, and a small drum may hang from the upper portion. Each part of the staff receives iconographic exegesis. For example, the pole may be interpreted as Mount Meru and the other features as the realms of existence arrayed along the cosmic axis. The motifs may also be taken to represent spiritual attainments or esoteric yogic practices.[28] One also finds the staff divided into features symbolizing the sixty-two-deity mandala of Cakrasaṃvara and Vajrayoginī.[29]

Western sources commonly misidentify Nāroḍākinī as Sarvabuddhaḍākinī, "Ḍākinī of All Buddhas." This latter term is, however, a general epithet and mantric invocation of Vajrayoginī in her many manifestations rather than a proper name.[30] Nāroḍākinī is so designated because her practice lineages stem from Nāropā, an Indian adept to whom she revealed herself in this form.[31] Nāroḍākinī is also known as Nārokhecarī (Naro Khachöma or simply Khachöma in Tibetan). Khecarī, meaning "female who flies" or "sky-goer," is a synonym for *ḍākinī* but also identifies her as the "Divine Lady of Khecara," her paradisal Buddha-land.[32] She is sometimes designated as Nāḍīḍākinī, evoking her aspect as a ḍākinī who has purified her *nāḍī*, the arterial network that carries the inner breath energy through the subtle yogic anatomy. This version of her name, too, expresses her association with powerful esoteric yogic techniques for cleansing the nāḍī of karmic residues. These methods, which she is said to have transmitted directly to Nāropā, are important in the Sakya and Gelug schools of Tibetan Buddhism.[33]

Although Vajrayoginī is fully enlightened, envisioned as supremely blissful and transcendently wise, she is also attributed with tremendous ferocity. Indic texts, and Tibetan works in their wake, describe her as "fierce" (*ugrā*), "terrible" (*atibhīmā*), "violent" (*pracaṇḍā*), "indomitable" (*aparājita*), and "terrifying" (*trāsanī*). This aspect of her character is not prominent in her visual persona but manifests in such details as bared fangs and the threatening gesture formed by her right hand. A violent streak is also suggested by her bloodthirsty nature, as she "savors the blood" (*rudhira-priyā*) that flows from her skull cup.[34] Her dance, too, is sometimes described in Indic works as a *tāṇḍava*, a wild or violent dance of destruction.[35]

Wrathful qualities have a range of meanings in Buddhist iconology, often signaling powers of protection or subjugation. In the case of Vajrayoginī, these traits are interpreted as signs of her yogic and spiritual attainments. Her conquering power is directed against "demons" (*māra*), a category that includes destructive spirits but features the "inner" demons of anger, hatred, greed, and

18.5 Nāroḍākinī, Amrit Karmacharya, Patan, Nepal, last decade of twentieth century. Paubhā, detail. Pigment and gold on cloth, 16.4 × 13.25 in. (19.4 × 33.65 cm). Author's collection. *Nāroḍākinī raises her brimming skull bowl, ever imbibing the primordial bliss that pulses at the heart of reality. (See Pl. 11)*

all selfish and deluded mindstates. The blood she drinks from her skull cup is often said to be that of demons, expressing that she has deprived them—and all negative appearances—of their life essence, or power. The blood is alternately said to be that of gods and demigods, beings that represent pride and envy in Buddhist symbology. The drinking of blood, a potent image of primal origins, becomes at the hand of Buddhist exegetes a metaphor for insight into emptiness, the realization that negative appearances have no reality.[36] Further, the figures she crushes underfoot, Bhairava and Kālarātri, represent desire, ignorance, and hatred. As an enlightened being, Vajrayoginī has emerged victorious over all such beings and egoic forces, perceiving them to be empty.

Sermey Tharchin further clarifies that her wrathful traits signify the invincibility of bliss and emptiness, which conquer all lesser mindstates. Moreover, Vajrayoginī's wrathfulness represents the intensity of her inner heat, which purifies the subtle nervous system of karmic obscurations, filling the mind and body with inseparable bliss and wisdom. In sum, her wrathfulness expresses "control and mastery of the entire path" to enlightenment.[37] Thus, her forbidding fangs and blood diet signal that she has consumed and digested—that is, mastered—every quality of energy and experience that arose on her spiritual journey.

Vajrayoginī's ferocious aspect is reflected in her designation as Vajravārāhī, "Adamantine She-Boar." "Vajravārāhī" was originally an epithet of Vajrayoginī rather than a distinct iconographic form. Both names appeared interchangeably within a single liturgy, while separate liturgies devoted to "Vajrayoginī" and "Vajravārāhī" might describe identical figures. Very few of her Indian hierophanies count a boar head among their attributes. The goddess in all her forms, however, is typically endowed with the "tusks" (*daṃṣṭrā*) that are the boar's primary weapon. The significance of the epithet "Vajravārāhī" may be found in the character of the creature to which she is thus likened. The boar (*varāha*), a numinous figure in Indic religiosity, has an aura of tremendous power, signifying royalty and the potency of forces at its possessor's command. Too, the wild boar is recognized in Indic myth as "the most wrathful of all animals,"[38] a ferocious aggressor, fearless and indomitable when aroused or on attack. Thus, likening Vajrayoginī to a she-boar expresses her sovereignty and awesome power, her relentless focus on liberation, and her intrepid conquest of all obstacles to enlightenment.

Eventually, the name Vajravārāhī came primarily to denote a specific epiphany, red in color, displaying a curved knife, skull bowl, and Tantric staff. Vajravārāhī is characterized by a dancing pose and the small head of a wild boar that emerges behind her right ear (Fig. 18.6 and Pl. 12) or above her skull crown amid her tawny, upward-streaming tresses.[39] The boar-head appendage

18.6 Vajravārāhī, Tibet, fifteenth century. Gilt copper inset with turquoise, coral, and lapis lazuli; painted with cold gold and blue pigment, height 16.3 in. (41.5 cm). Potala Collection (Lhasa, Central Tibet), Lima Lhakhang, 1680. Photo after Ulrich von Schroeder, 2001, *Buddhist Sculptures in Tibet*, vol. 2, pl. 266D. *This stunning statue of Vajravārāhī beautifully conveys her piercing clarity of awareness and the sow head emerging to the right of her face. (See Pl. 12)*

was added to her iconography by the twelfth century, appearing in a number of artistic representations of that period.[40] Tibetan writings typically interpret the boar head as a sign that she has overcome ignorance, which is represented by a boar in earlier Buddhist symbology.[41] This interpretation appears to be a creative exegesis formulated in Tibet, where the boar is not an indigenous species and carries no symbolic associations.

Therefore, the interpretation of the boar as ignorance, which has now become standard, does not take into account the long-standing Indic significance of the boar as a symbol of wrathfulness, sovereignty, and conquering might. These traits are consistent with Vajrayoginī's character and well explain her original designation as a she-boar and her endowment with tusks or fangs. Therefore, I maintain that she was initially identified with the boar, connoting her power to overcome negativity, and that the boar did not originally symbolize a negative quality she had overcome.

This dancing, red epiphany of the goddess with a sow head emerging from her tresses is the primary form of Vajravārāhī. It is, moreover, one of the preeminent forms in which Vajrayoginī is envisioned in Tibetan Buddhism today. Her practices are of central importance for the Kagyu school but are included in the curriculum of all Tibetan sects. Thus, her artistic representations are ubiquitous, and she is the subject of numerous meditations, canonical texts, and commentaries.

There were many iconographic forms of Vajrayoginī in the late Indian pantheon. Some of these are described in the *Sādhanamālā*. Others have recently been documented by Elizabeth English, including four-, six-, and twelve-armed epiphanies.[42] Also noteworthy is "Flying Vidyādharī Vajrayoginī," a red form shown with both legs upraised in full flight, supping from her skull bowl and adorned only by a red floral garland.[43] English also discovered three novel *yab-yum* (coupled) forms, described in sensuously erotic prose and associated with esoteric sexo-yogic practices. In two of these, the goddess is the forward-facing partner on whose lap the consort is seated.[44] This "reverse *yab-yum*" configuration, a rarity in Tantric iconography, is recurrently found in association with Vajrayoginī (Fig. 18.7).[45] Commenting on this plethora of diverse epiphanies, English observes that "the impressive number of forms in which Vajrayoginī manifests and the variety of her practices together reflect the richness and popularity of her cult in the land of its birth."[46]

The hierophanies of Vajrayoginī in the Tibetan pantheon significantly overlap those known to have been present in the Indic repertoire, but additional forms are attested, and practices devoted to the goddess proliferated over the centuries. Two manifestations in the Tibetan pantheon are actually boar-headed. One is a lunging, red epiphany whose main distinguishing trait is her

18.7 Vajrayoginī with Consort, China or Mongolia, ca. 1850. Mineral pigment and gold over woodblock print on paper, height 3.54 in. (9 cm). Ethnographic Museum of the University of Zurich. Photo after Willson and Brauen, *Deities of Tibetan Buddhism*, no. 88. *Vajrayoginī appears as the forward-facing partner, embracing her male consort in sexual union.*

boar head.[47] Another is Sarvārtha-sādhana Vajravārāhī, "Vajravārāhī Accomplishing All Goals," a red form with four arms, displaying a vajra, vajra-tipped goad, skull cup, and noose (Fig. 18.8). She is invoked to conquer negative forces and is described as "very fierce," with a "terrifying, very wrathful pig's face," a "garland of blood-dripping heads," and a "laugh hard for any vicious being to bear."[48]

White manifestations are much in evidence, including an epiphany with upraised left leg, held in place by her bent arm as she brings her skull chalice to her lips, supping the red and white nectar that flows from the Buddha couples floating around her.[49] Another white manifestation, generally designated as Prajñālokā, "Light of Wisdom," displays a vajra and a skull bowl. Her stance, described as *pratyālīḍha*, may be interpreted as a lunging or dancing pose.[50] Because white is the color most typically associated with deities of healing and longevity, it is not surprising to find a healing practice, which entails the preparation of flower-essence pills, in connection with Prajñālokā.[51]

Two epiphanies that must find mention in any survey are Maitrīḍākinī and Indraḍākinī, so named after Maitrīpā and Indrabhūti, the adepts associated with their revelation. Indraḍākinī has a sow-face appendage and is virtually identical to the classical red, dancing Vajravārāhī described above, except that she holds her curved knife with its blade turned inward, although artistic representations do not invariably follow this convention.[52] The iconography of Maitrīḍākinī, also red in color, has several versions. According to a Sakya liturgy, she bears a vajra in her right hand and a flower garland and skull cup of nectar in her left. Her bodily pose is described as *ūrdhva-pāda*, that is, with raised foot or feet, in the manner of flight.[53] Accordingly, Maitrīḍākinī is often shown with one leg uplifted, flourishing a vajra and a skull bowl (Fig. 18.9). A floral wreath is usually draped over her arms, although this motif may be omitted.[54] In other renditions, Maitrīḍākinī is shown with both legs aloft in a soaring pose, often flying above mountain peaks. Her arms support a floral garland, and she bears a curved knife or a vajra in her right hand.[55]

Nāroḍākinī, Maitrīḍākinī, and Indraḍākinī are grouped in the Sakya pantheon as the "Three Ḍākinīs" (Khachö Korsum), and their initiations are contiguous in the Golden Dharma (Serchö) series.[56] The three may be pictured together, centering on Nāroḍākinī.[57]

One of the most dramatic hierophanies is Tröma Nakmo, "Wrathful Black Lady," also known as Pakmo Trönak, "Wrathful Black Vārāhī." She resembles the red, dancing Vajravārāhī except that her body is midnight blue or black and she is pronouncedly fierce. Her color is appropriate as that associated with wrathfulness and subjugation in Tantric symbolism. Different practice traditions endow her with varying attributes that reflect her wrathful persona (Fig. 18.10).[58] This painting shows her with a necklace of freshly severed heads and a cape of human skin, well conveying her arresting presence.

This form of the goddess appears to have been introduced in Tibet, for it is not attested in Indic sources and is generally envisioned in the distinctively Tibetan practice of Chöd, or "Cutting Off," which is directed against outer demons that cause obstacles and disease and the inner demons of egoic mind-states. One liturgy describes Black Vārāhī's awesome capacity to conquer negative forces, praising her for "crushing opponents throughout the triple world,

18.8 Sarvārtha-sādhana Vajravārāhī, Tibet, ca. 1700. Gilt copper painted with cold gold and red pigment, height 5.4 in. (13.8 cm). Jokhang/gTsug Lag khang Collection (Lhasa, Central Tibet), 99[A]. Photo after Ulrich von Schroeder, 2001, *Buddhist Sculptures in Tibet*, vol. 2, pl. 267A. *This epiphany of Vajravārāhī is unusual for its primary boar head and possession of four arms.*

scarer and confuser, paralyzer!"[59] Although her specialty is slaughter, it is understood that she performs her destructive activities out of compassion and "subjugates all demons for the sake of all sentient beings."[60]

Ultimately a clear boundary cannot be drawn around the manifestations of Vajrayoginī identifiable as Vajravārāhī. Although "Vajravārāhī" properly designates and immediately calls to mind the red, dancing form with the sow-head excrescence, the name continues to be synonymous with Vajrayoginī and to be used as an epithet for all forms of the goddess, whether or not a boar head is present.

Mandalas and Tantric Consort

Many forms of Vajrayoginī are accompanied by extensive mandala retinues that figure in intricate meditative and yogic practices. Documenting their iconography and sources would require a monograph in its own right. Among this plethora of mandalas, however, one finds three configurations that widely recur in association with different epiphanies of the goddess. These mandalas consist of five, thirteen, and thirty-seven deities, all female. The retinue figures are drawn from the sixty-two-deity mandala centering on Vajravārāhī and her consort, Heruka-Cakrasaṃvara, as outlined in the *Cakrasaṃvara Tantra*.[61]

The mandalas of Vajrayoginī typically center on a dharmodayā formation, composed of a pair of interlacing triangles with bliss whorls in the points of the "star" pattern thus formed (see Fig. 18.2). In the fivefold mandala, the retinue consists of the four yoginis that constitute the inner circle of Cakrasaṃvara-Vajravārāhī mandalas: blue Ḍākinī in the east, yellow Rūpiṇī in the south, red Khaṇḍarohā in the west, and green Lāmā in the north. In what appears to be their original conception, the yoginis are lunging and four-armed, bearing a staff and skull bowl in their left hands and a small drum (*ḍamaru*) and curved knife in their right.[62] (This group is not to be confused with the iconographically similar but entirely distinct set of six "armor yoginis" that may appear as or among a Vajrayoginī mandala retinue.)[63] In another, perhaps later, version of the fivefold mandala iconography, again centering on Vajravārāhī, the retinue conforms to a classic mandalic pattern. The four entourage figures retain their standard directional colors but are two-armed and replicate the pose and attributes of the central epiphany.[64]

A thirteen-deity mandala builds on this fivefold version by adding an outer circle of eight directional guardians with the heads of humans, animals, and birds.[65] A mandala of thirty-seven deities surrounds the fivefold core with three rings of eight divine yoginis, a total of twenty-four, encircled by the eight gate guardians.[66] A distinctive fivefold mandala of Vajravārāhī, found in Nepal, casts as her retinue blue Nairātmyā, soaring Vidyeśvarī, Vajrayoginī with one leg upraised, and sword-bearing Khadgayoginī.[67]

Vajrayoginī also appears in art and practice with her male consort, Heruka-Cakrasaṃvara. This Buddha couple, introduced in the *Cakrasaṃvara Tantra* (ca. eighth century), figures in a range of major Highest Yoga Tantra practices of India, Tibet, and Nepal, where one finds many mandalas centering on the pair. The couple appears in myriad iconographic variations, with differing numbers of arms, attributes, and bodily hues and stances. Thus, it is impossible to specify one form of Vajrayoginī as the consort of Cakrasaṃvara. It is the goddess herself, rather than one specific epiphany, who is understood as his partner and female complement.

Reflecting the Tantric ideal of male and female in cosmic harmony and eternal embrace, Cakrasaṃvara and Vajrayoginī are regarded as equal in status and ultimately inseparable. However, the *Cakrasaṃvara Tantra* is classed as a "mother *tantra*," which means, among other things, that the female side of the equation is primary and receives fuller elaboration and emphasis. Indeed, although both figures receive commensurate attention in the text, Vajrayoginī came to surpass her male counterpart in importance. The role of Heruka-Cakrasaṃvara is almost completely limited to the partnering of Vajrayoginī, whereas she became the independent focus of a vast body of meditative, ritual, and yogic techniques. Bringing this development to its logical conclusion, Tibetan practices centering on Vajrayoginī are said to encompass the entire Cakrasaṃvara system and to represent the "quintessence" of all Cakrasaṃvara instruction and practice, bestowing all of its fruits and offering "the quickest and most supreme path for attaining Buddhahood."[68] In Nepal, too, initiations and methodologies centering on Vajrayoginī represent the culmination and completion of all Cakrasaṃvara practices.

Attaining Ḍākinī Paradise

Practices associated with Vajrayoginī are traditionally undertaken by advanced yogis and yoginis who have undertaken disciplines that develop concentration, compassion, philosophical insight, and yogic stability. A similar course of preparation is required for meditation on any Highest Yoga Tantra deity. It is also necessary to receive ritual initiation into the specific practices, which typically entail visualizing oneself as the deity, envisioning the mandala of the deity, and a range of esoteric yogas. Hundreds of texts are devoted to Vajrayoginī, detailing the many rituals, meditations, and yogas in which she figures. Several book-length studies would be required to begin to give account of these complex and metaphysically nuanced methodologies.[69] I focus here on

18.9 Maitrīḍākinī, Gobind Danghol, Kathmandu, Nepal, last decade of twentieth century. Paubhā, detail. Pigment and gold on cloth, 10.75 × 7.5 in. (27 × 19 cm). Author's collection. *Maitrīḍākinī is shown with one or both legs upraised in the manner of flight, soaring in the infinite expanse of ultimate reality.*

18.10 Tröma Nakmo, Tibet, eighteenth century. Mineral pigment and gold on cotton, 15 × 10.5 in. (38 × 26.7 cm). Rubin Museum of Art, F1998.17.1. Photo: Rubin Museum of Art. *Wrathful Black Vārāhī specializes in destruction of demons and demonic mindstates.*

a body of techniques currently important in the Sakya and Gelug orders of Tibetan Buddhism, namely, the Eleven Yogas (Neljor Chuchig), attributed to the Indian adept Nāropā and featuring the Nāroḍākinī form of Vajrayoginī introduced above.

The Eleven Yogas are regarded as a relatively quick path to enlightenment for those who are prepared to perform them. They include many methods for "transforming daily life into the path," using every moment of experience as an opportunity for spiritual practice and insight. Throughout the day, the practitioner envisions all food and drink as offerings to Vajrayoginī, all sounds as her mantra, every living being as her emanation, and the environment as her mandala. Consciously identifying with Vajrayoginī in the course of every activity—waking, sleeping, and dreaming—transforms the body, speech, and mind into those of a Buddha. The Buddhahood envisioned in the form of Vajrayoginī is understood to be intrinsically present in each person as pure, radiant awareness, the essential nature of the mind. Geshe Gyatso explains, "One's own mind is, from the very beginning, Vajrayogini. However, due to ignorance and defilements, one does not realize this."[70] The path to Buddhahood, then, is a process of discovering and uncovering that enlightened essence.

Purifying the body is an essential feature of the Eleven Yogas. This process is premised on the belief that the karmic residue of many lifetimes is lodged in one's subtle anatomical makeup, encoding a pattern of mental and emotional defilements and blocking the free flow of energy and consciousness. In contrast, Vajrayoginī's body has been purified through inner yogic practices, rendering her energy channels and centers luminous and clear and fanning her inner heat into a flame that burns away all worldly perceptions and conceptions, leaving only the spontaneous play of bliss and wisdom. Performing these inner yogic practices confers the somatic dimension of Buddhahood, a purified yogic body.

The Eleven Yogas feature the inner yogic method of visualizing a mandala in the heart chakra. Nāroḍākinī is envisioned at the center of the heart chakra, the seat of consciousness. The radiating veins are envisioned as her retinue of thirty-six female deities: an inner circle of four, a tier of twenty-four, and eight sentinels around the periphery. The thirty-seven divine ḍākinīs thus envisioned are invited to inhabit the mental images the meditator has generated. This draws the energies of bliss and wisdom into the center and branching veins of the heart chakra. From there the energies flow outward into the seventy-two thousand subtle veins throughout the body, filling them with the nectar of bliss, a process understood as receiving the blessings of the ḍākinīs. The goal of this practice, known as a "body mandala," is attaining the purified yogic body of a Buddha.[71]

One who becomes a Buddha lives in the world of a Buddha, and for practitioners of Vajrayoginī that world is Khecara, her Ḍākinī Paradise. Thus, the goal of the Eleven Yogas and of Vajrayoginī practice in general is commonly expressed as the attainment of Khecara. The name Khecara, "Flight" ("moving," *cara*, "in space," *khe*), becomes in Tibetan Khachö, "Enjoyment of Space" or "Sky Pleasure," but may also accurately be rendered as Ḍākinī Paradise and Ḍākinī Land. It is also known as Dakpa Khachö, Pure Ḍākinī Land, for it is generated and perceived by purified awareness. Throughout the Eleven Yogas, Nāroḍākinī is supplicated as "Khecara Queen" (Kachö Wangmo), "Divine Lady of Khecara" (Jetsun Khachöma), and "Joyful Lady of Khecara" (Kachö Gama).[72] Her liturgies are threaded with prayers voicing the aspiration to "reach the supreme state of Khecara" and entreaties to "carry me away to the Blissful Dakini's Kechara city" and "take me and all sentient beings to Kechara Paradise."[73]

Nāroḍākinī's upturned face points to this supernal destination, for "she looks up to space, demonstrating her attainment of outer and inner Pure Dakini Land, and indicating that she leads her followers to these attainments."[74] She may be pictured in her paradise, which centers on the goddess on her hexagonal red pedestal in a many-tiered mansion, surrounded by illumined souls and divine beings. The enveloping sky will be filled with ḍākinīs in flight or, as featured here, goddesses celebrating her presence with music, dance, and offerings (Fig. 18.11).[75]

Khecara occupies the same realm of aesthetic experience as all Buddha-lands, such as Sukhāvatī ("Land of Bliss"), Amitābha's realm, and Abhirati ("World of Pleasure)," Akṣobhya's divine abode. Buddhist cosmology envisions the numerous realms of existence as horizontal planes stacked along the vertical axis of Mount Meru, the symbolic center of the universe. At the bottom are the realms of desire, in the center are the subtler realms of form, and above are the formless realms. Khecara and other Buddha-lands are located in the uppermost and subtlest realm of form, known as Akaniṣṭha (Tib. 'Og-min). The realms are not physical "places" but rather spheres of experience created and sustained by the consciousness of their inhabitants. The desire realms are forged by attachment and delusion, whereas Buddha-lands are spun of compassion and bliss. Enlightened beings create paradises of heavenly splendor and beauty, sustained by their visionary power, as ideal environments for nurturing beings to enlightenment. Such Buddha-lands are also known as Pure Lands because of the purity of intention that gives them rise and the purity of vision required to perceive them.

The belief in Khecara finds authority in the *Cakrasaṃvara Tantra*. The final chapter extends the promise that Heruka and Vajrayoginī, their hands over-

18.11 Nāroḍākinī in Khecara, Central Tibet, Sakya lineage, nineteenth century. Mineral pigment and gold on cotton, 25.5 × 17.25 in. (64.8 × 43.8 cm). Shelley and Donald Rubin Collection, P1998.3.1. Photo: Shelley and Donald Rubin Collection. *Vajrayoginī in a many-tiered mansion of light in her Buddha paradise, a coveted afterlife destination of Tantric practitioners.*

flowing with many kinds of flowers, will come forth to welcome ardent practitioners at the time of death. For such fortunate ones, the passage continues, "death" is a misnomer, for they will be honored with streamers and victory banners, with cymbals and song, as the divine couple escorts them to the land of Khecara.[76]

Khecara also emerges as a common afterlife destination in the biographies of the eighty-four *mahāsiddhas*, or enlightened masters, of Indian Vajrayāna. Several adepts remain on earth in an immortal body, but seventy-five are said to have ascended to Khecara at the end of their earthly existence. The biographies state that they "rose bodily" into Khecara, or "attained Khecara in this very body," indicating that upon death their body dissolved into light and was absorbed directly into the blissful realm of ḍākinīs, leaving behind no corpse. Several (Saraha, Saroruha, Ghaṇṭāpa) went to Khecara in company with their Tantric consort; others were accompanied by hundreds of disciples.[77] Interestingly, very few of these enlightened ones meditated on Vajrayoginī or Cakrasaṃvara. Some meditated on other deities, while many did unique practices designed by their gurus. Nonetheless, Khecara is identified as their afterlife destination, showing that in some settings the Buddha-land of Vajrayoginī has been envisioned as the ultimate destination of Highest Yoga Tantra practitioners, regardless of their specific practices.

Khecara has been divided into two levels of attainment designated as "outer Khecara" and "inner Khecara."[78] Those who make significant progress in Vajrayoginī practice but do not realize full enlightenment during their lifetime attain outer Khecara as their afterlife destination. That is, at the time of death they ascend to the paradise of Vajrayoginī, located in the ethereal upper reaches of the realm of form. She presides there with her consort, Heruka-Cakrasaṃvara, and hosts of ḍākinīs. Those who have attained the status of a Vidyādhara—that is, one advanced in Tantric wisdom and powers—merit rebirth in her pure land and will dwell there in an immortal, eternally youthful body. The beings of this realm know no suffering, and everything that is desired materializes out of thin air. With Vajrayoginī and Cakrasaṃvara as their gurus, the inhabitants receive Tantric teachings and rapidly progress to Buddhahood. From Khecara they can travel freely to other Buddha-lands and send emanation bodies to the realms of desire to minister to the beings still struggling there.[79]

The Eleven Yogas include a preparation for ascent to outer Khecara so that one may accomplish a direct "transfer of consciousness" (*pho-ba*) into the heavenly realm at the time of death. In this intricate visualization, one gathers all the energy of the environment, living beings, and his or her own consciousness into a luminous red Vajrayoginī at the navel chakra. One merges into this miniature Vajrayoginī and shares with her a strong wish to go to her

Buddha-land, drawn by the sounds of drums, bells, and song emanating from that realm. Oneself-as-Vajrayoginī then rises within the hollow core of the central channel, ascending from the navel to the heart chakra and then the crown of the head. From there, one projects one's consciousness to Khecara "like a tiny shooting star" and dissolves into that realm. This visualization purifies the subtle yogic body and rehearses entry into Khecara at the time of death.[80]

Those who master the entire course of Vajrayoginī practice, from the generation through perfection stages, attain Khecara during their present lifetime. This attainment is known as "inner Khecara," or "great Khecara." That is, having become fully enlightened, one discovers this world to be in actuality the blissful realm of Khecara. Thus, the great Khecara is not a "place" but rather a mode of experience that reveals the "inner" or "secret" dimension of ordinary reality to be the Buddha-land of Vajrayoginī. As Geshe Kelsang Gyatso explains, "Pure Dakini Land is not some far-away place, nor is it necessary to disappear from this world to reach it."[81] Inner Khecara is attained by purifying the mind of ordinary conceptuality and attaining the inseparable bliss and wisdom of Buddha Vajrayoginī. Through the process of identifying with Vajrayoginī, one "attains" her paradise by achieving the enlightened awareness that generated and now sustains it. Such a person not only attains Khecara but in essence creates, or re-creates, it anew: "When we achieve full enlightenment . . . we become a newly-born Vajrayogini . . . and our world becomes a newly-developed Pure Dakini Land."[82]

Thus, we find in association with Vajrayoginī the vision and promise of paradise, a wondrous realm whose residents dwell in the presence of Vajrayoginī, Cakrasaṃvara, and hosts of ḍākinīs on the most ethereal plane of existence. At the same time, this paradise is everywhere present. For one who has pure vision, life on earth attains the splendor of paradise.

Soaring in Freedom

The appearance of Vajrayoginī signals the Buddhism participation in an upsurge of goddess worship throughout India and the Himalayas in the seventh and eighth centuries. One of the central insights of this religious revolution was the recognition that the female body is more universal than the male, for it contains, gives birth to, and nurtures all bodies, both male and female, and is therefore more encompassing in nature. Furthermore, the female body contains the mysteries of creation and generation, bringing forth something where there was nothing, providing both the space and substance necessary for existents to take shape. Moreover, śakti, the sacred life force, is most concentrated in the female body, providing the heat and creative force for generation, as well as the energy for spiritual transformation. Therefore, Tantric Buddhism was adding its voice to a chorus of Śākta theologies—Purāṇic, Pāñcarātra, Śrīvidyā, Kaula—proclaiming that ultimate reality may fittingly be envisioned as female, as a cosmic goddess, in its creativity and transcendent nonduality.

One consequence of this gynocentric orientation was an expanded religious role for women in the movements that espoused it. One of the exciting aspects of Vajrayoginī is that her emergence in the pantheon was accompanied by the full participation of women in Tantric Buddhist circles as practitioners, gurus, and formulators of practice and doctrine.[83] Vajrayoginī provided a divine exemplar who mirrored the aspirations of female Tantrics and supported them in their search for enlightenment, offering an archetype of female freedom, wholeness, and Buddhahood.

Vajrayoginī is inarguably the supreme goddess of the Highest Yoga Tantra pantheon. As such, she occupies a subtle and intricate metaphysical domain. One cannot describe her without reference to the loftiest of Mahayana and Vajrayāna philosophical insights that, as a Buddha, she has realized and embodies: egolessness, emptiness, nonduality, primordial mind, clear light, transcendent wisdom, universal compassion, and supreme bliss. At the same time, her persona evokes the more primal, earthier realm of Tantra, with its life-affirming ethos. Sensuously beautiful and vibrantly alive, she blazes with vitality and irrepressible dynamism, reveling in the sheer pleasure of being. Her crimson hue evokes the pulsing river of life that unites all living beings to one another and the world.

Vajrayoginī is a transcendently passionate goddess fully attuned to the richness and intensity of life. Joyful and exuberant, she is ever intoxicated by the dazzling perfection of reality in its luminous immediacy. She reveals the Tantric insight that one who is free from attachment and desire need not turn away from the ever-shifting panoramas of the senses and emotions but may savor them as the magical play of bliss and emptiness, the sacred arena of spiritual awakening. Worldly appearances swirl around her as rainbow clouds of illusion through which she dances and soars in total freedom.

CHAPTER 19

Nairātmyā

Her Body Is the Sky

She is enlightened spontaneity in female form,
A supremely blissful divine yogini.
She is the mansion of enlightened awareness,
Possessor of the five Buddha-wisdoms. . . .
She is pure, universal awareness,
The sovereign of the mandala.
She is Nairātmyā Yogini,
The essence of ultimate reality.

—*Hevajra Tantra*[1]

Nairātmyā (pronounced *nai* RAHT MYAH) is subtle and spacious and vast as the sky. Her body is blue, the color of infinite space, reflecting the limitless expanse of her awareness. Buddhism teaches that what we perceive ourselves to be—namely, independent, separate selves—is an illusion, for in truth we are connected with all that exists in a vast web of communion. Nairātmyā embodies this realization. Her name may be translated as "Lady of Emptiness" or "She Who Has Realized Selflessness." Like the element of space, she flows through the universe without impediment, for she has transcended ego-centered existence. Her eyes blaze with the wisdom of one who understands the mysteries and depths of life. She raises her curved knife skyward, poised to sever negative mindstates wherever they arise. In her skull bowl, she pulverizes illusions and returns them to their original state—a mere play of light, a rainbow of energy, shimmering in empty space. Thus, Nairātmyā perpetually dances, celebrating the bliss that pulses at the heart of reality. Her gleaming bone ornaments sway, glistening like cascading beads of light, illuminating the heavenly expanse of her body with shooting stars and swirling galaxies. To behold Nairātymā is to long to join in her cosmic, eternal dance.

Nairātmyā, like other female Buddhas, embodies the supreme state of Buddhahood. Unlike dhāraṇī goddesses and Dharma-protectors, she has nothing to accomplish. Knowing all that is to be known, she manifests a divine form that expresses this completeness, inviting others to strive for the highest level of spiritual awakening. Accordingly, the goal of her practice is the attainment of full enlightenment, or Buddhahood.

Goddess of Emptiness and Bliss

In Tantric Buddhism, enlightenment is characterized as the realization of emptiness and supreme bliss. Both qualities figure prominently in Nairātmyā's divine persona. One meaning of her name is "Lady of Emptiness." Emptiness (*nirātman,* or *śūnyatā*) denotes the intrinsic insubstantiality of all phenomena. To understand emptiness is to recognize that all beings and phenomenal appearances lack an abiding "self" or "essence." What we perceive as solid, permanent, independent entities are in actuality interconnected patterns of energy without center or boundary. One path to the realization of emptiness is to visualize and identify with a Buddha such as Nairātmyā through the Tantric practice of deity yoga, wherein the meditator envisions himself or herself to have the appearance, qualities, and enlightened awareness of the divinity.

Preparatory to this esoteric meditation, however, the practitioner should master one or more of the Mahayana philosophical techniques for deconstructing the contents of ordinary experience. These analytic methods employ logic to deconstruct the subjective responses that distort reality and give rise to attachment and suffering. For instance, one can logically dismantle the supposed cause of the suffering, recognizing its lack of inherent existence. One can expose the illusory nature of the "self" that is suffering and recognize that such a fictive entity can never truly be harmed or diminished. One can dissect the conceptual, psychological, or sociocultural factors at the root of one's habitual reaction patterns, unmasking the false dualisms at play. Another approach is to realize that the feeling of suffering has emerged in empty space and will dissolve again, and thus penetrate to a deeper level of experience where the emotion is simply a neutral pattern of energy, devoid of negative characteristics.

These sophisticated strategies for deconstructing the contents of ordinary experience, a classical *via negativa*, are then crowned and complemented by the *via positiva* of deity yoga. Envisioning Nairātmyā engages the imagination in the process of replacing conventional self-awareness with a divine archetype, or visual symbol, of emptiness that ushers the practitioner into the subjective realm of enlightened awareness, characterized above all by transcendent bliss, or spiritual ecstasy. The elimination of negative emotions that cause suffering to oneself and others gives rise to a rich emotional repertoire of joy, empathy, humor, and devotion to the liberation of others. Thus, Nairātmyā, as the "Lady of Emptiness," is also celebrated as a "supremely blissful divine yogini," "bestower of bliss," "bliss personified," "source of great bliss," and "font of spontaneous joy."[2]

The bliss that Nairātmyā personifies is beyond the realm of sense experience. Described as "spontaneously arising joy" (*sahajānanda*),[3] it is an intrinsic quality of being that emerges spontaneously—that is, without additional effort—when the illusions that cause suffering have been dispelled. The *Hevajra Tantra*, the main scriptural source on Nairātmyā and her divine consort, identifies bliss as the "supreme essence" of all things, living and unliving, elaborating that

> Great bliss is self-experiencing. . . .
> The five mental poisons cannot prevail against it.
> It is the origin of all that is;
> It is knowledge; it is like space.[4]

Supreme bliss is said to be "self-experiencing" because it transcends the dualism of subject and object. No object or event can produce or prevent its arising, for it is the primordial nature of the mind. The "poison" of negative emotions may temporarily obscure but cannot destroy the blissful essence of the mind, just as mud may conceal but never diminish the brilliance of a diamond. As the same text goes on to say, Nairātmyā "is that bliss . . . she is . . . the unique and highest joy."[5]

In sum, to contemplate Nairātmyā is to behold "the essence of ultimate reality."[6] Ultimate reality, *dharmadhātu*, is the infinite expanse of all that exists. The essence of ultimate reality is emptiness and bliss.

Divine Form and Symbolic Attributes

Iconographic descriptions of Nairātmyā in Sanskrit and Tibetan sources are highly consistent. She is deep blue in color, the indigo of midnight. She displays the Buddha Akṣobhya on her diadem and is draped with a skull necklace, bone ornaments, and a tiger-skin skirt. Bearing a flaying knife, skull bowl, and Tantric staff, she dances on an upward-facing corpse on a moon disc (Fig. 19.1). Interestingly and perhaps somewhat unexpectedly, Nairātmyā has a fierce persona, with furrowed brows, lolling eyes, bared incisors, lashing tongue, and upswept tawny hair.[7] Although she is bliss incarnate, this wrathful mien in part reflects her association with the Vajra family of Akṣobhya, symbolized by the color blue and associated with the transformation of anger into mirrorlike clarity. The ferocity often attributed to female Buddhas also evinces the intensity of one who has faced and conquered all obstacles to enlightenment.

Nairātmyā's bodily hue is central to her symbolic significance. Blue is the color of space, conveying the fathomless depth and infinite expanse of her being

19.1 Nairātmyā, Gobind Danghol, Kathmandu, Nepal, last decade of twentieth century. Paubhā, detail. Pigment and gold on cotton, 9.25 × 6.75 in. (23.5 × 17 cm). Author's collection. *Nairātmyā brandishes a skull bowl and flaying knife, the standard implements of Tantric female Buddhas, representing supreme bliss and wisdom. Though described as fierce, she may appear radiantly serene in artistic representations.*

and awareness. In Buddhist cosmology, space (*ākāśa*) is the subtlest element of the phenomenal world, an all-pervading essence that does not obstruct or displace the more tangible elements (earth, air, fire, and water). By virtue of its omnipresence, space is the matrix of phenomenal reality, for all forms arise and dissolve in its subtle expanse. Space is thus akin to emptiness, the principle that underlies and makes possible all phenomena. Blue, then, is an appropriate hue for the "Lady of Emptiness," expressing not only her selfless quality and realization of emptiness but also her association with space and sky. She is a "sky-goer" (*ḍākinī*) and "one who flies" (*khecarī*), who, having won freedom from conventional dualities, soars freely in the expanse of ultimate reality, reveling in the bliss of emptiness, savoring the joy of freedom from illusion.

Nairātmyā displays the customary adornments of a Tantric female Buddha. Whereas Mahayana goddesses wear silken raiment and luxurious ornaments made of precious metals, gems, and pearls, evoking a mood of sovereignty and grandeur, the insignia of Tantric goddesses elicit a different realm of thought and practice. They wear no clothing, in keeping with the Tantric affirmation of the body as an abode of bliss and vehicle of enlightenment. Their ornaments are made of human bone: a diadem and garland of dried skulls and earrings, armlets, bracelets, anklets, gorget, and filigree skirt fashioned from carved bone beads (Fig. 19.2). These sepulchral adornments convey the radically nondualistic outlook of those who make and wear them. In the mainstream value system of Indian culture, the by-products of death are held to be ritually polluting. Contact with them is feared and avoided and, when it occurs, must be remedied by purification rites. In this setting, ornaments made of human bone proclaim freedom from the conventional dualisms of purity and impurity, of life and death. Human bone, like ivory, can retain its luster for centuries. Viewed without bias, these gleaming adornments epitomize the sacredness and beauty of all things that may be discovered when the veil of duality is lifted.

The bone ornaments, counted as five or six, also have more specific meanings with reference to Buddhist doctrinal categories. Nairātmyā, as is typical of female Buddhas, wears a set of five bone ornaments, termed *pañca-mudrā*. Iconographic writings stipulate that her ornaments represent the five Buddhas and their five transcendental insights. Her earrings signify the discriminating wisdom of Amitābha, which perceives what is appropriate for all situations and beings. Her bracelets, armlets, and anklets together represent the mirrorlike wisdom of Vairocana, the ability to perceive without distortion. Her necklace represents the equal and infinite generosity toward all of Ratnasambhava, and her girdle, or bone apron, the all-accomplishing ability of Amoghasiddhi. Her topknot is fixed in place by a bone "wheel" of beaded strands, representing pure awareness, or omniscience (*dharmadhātu-jñāna*).[8] Thus, Nairātmyā's bone

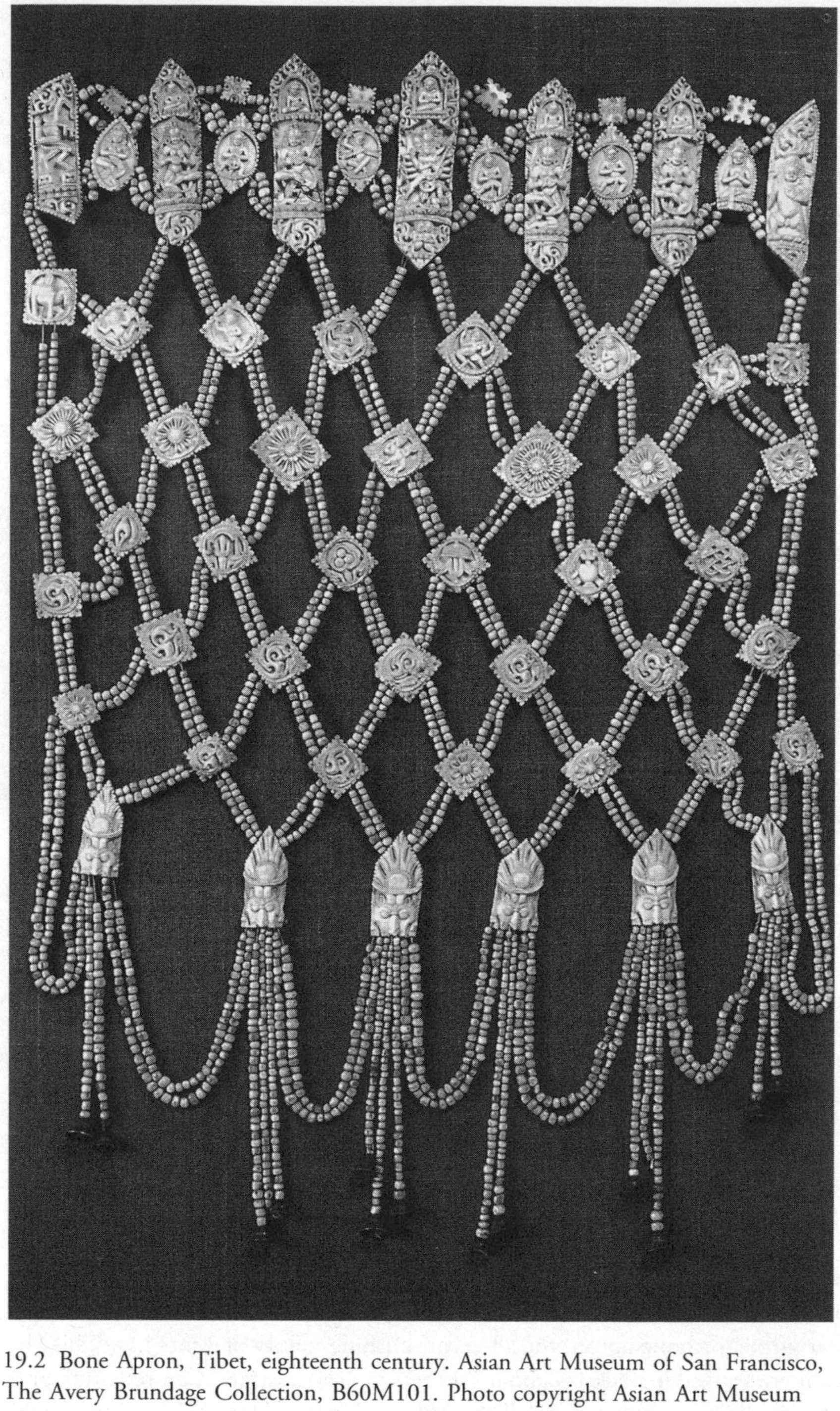

19.2 Bone Apron, Tibet, eighteenth century. Asian Art Museum of San Francisco, The Avery Brundage Collection, B60M101. Photo copyright Asian Art Museum of San Francisco. Used by permission. *A filigree skirt made of bone typically adorns Tantric female Buddhas and appears in the ritual regalia of Tantric practitioners.*

adornments express her status as a Buddha who has attained the five forms of enlightened wisdom. Similarly, her head is marked by OṂ, her throat by ĀḤ, and her heart by HŪṂ, signifying that she has perfected her body, speech, and mind and thus performs the deeds of a Buddha, communicates as a Buddha, and possesses the all-seeing wisdom of a Buddha.

Nairātmyā brandishes in her right hand a small knife with a curved blade, in her left, a bowl made from a human skull. The flaying knife and skull bowl, standard attributes of female Buddhas, are Tantric ritual implements with profound symbolic meaning. In Tantric symbology, the object held in the right hand signifies the male principle of skillful means, or techniques of attaining liberation. The object on the left signifies the female quality of enlightened insight, or realization of emptiness.[9] Accordingly, Nairātmyā's knife represents her power to destroy illusion and negative mindstates. The *Hevajra Tantra* clarifies that her knife severs the "six defects" of pride, ignorance, doubt, greed, hatred, and false views.[10] The knife is used, then, in a metaphorical sense, to remove these root causes of suffering. The usual response to suffering is to polarize the situation, reifying the self and the problem as concrete, opposing forces. The skull cup, emblem of emptiness, represents the absence of such dualistic thought, including the fundamental distinction between existence and nonexistence.[11]

The skull cup, then, is an alchemical vessel in which attachment and illusion are transformed into the gold of emptiness. Wielding her crescent-shaped blade—bringing the force of wisdom to bear on seeming sources of suffering—Nairātmyā perceives that ultimately they are not real. She pulverizes them in her skull bowl, returning them to atoms, meditating that they are simply a dance of energy and awareness that has manifested as anger, pride, or some other threatening or hostile appearance. Recognizing them as mirages, mere figments of imagination—neither real nor unreal—she returns them to pure energy, dissolving pain, attachment, and illusion into the skylike expanse of pure awareness.

Nairātmyā supports in the crook of her left arm a mystical staff (*khaṭvāṅga*) rich with symbolic significance. On one level, the staff represents her male consort, Hevajra. She embraces the staff-pole just as she wraps her arm around his waist when she dances with him in sacred union. Moreover, the staff symbolizes the ultimacy of her attainments. It is elaborate in design, bedecked with a vase of nectar supporting two heads in varying stages of decay and a dry skull, sealed top and bottom with vajra finials, and festooned with streamers. Each element has a range of meanings corresponding to different levels of spiritual practice and insight that in combination represent the totality of qualities constituting Buddhahood.[12]

Beneath Nairātmyā is a corpse. Her foot is positioned on its heart,[13] repository of the life force and seat of the mind and emotions. This motif does not represent her conquest of external beings or forces but rather triumph over negative and self-centered mindstates. Spiritual growth entails death of the selfish and unenlightened aspects of one's being so that the blissful, enlightened essence can emerge. Thus, Nairātmyā dances on the corpse of her former self, which she has left behind in the course of her journey to Buddhahood.

Purifying Awareness through Mandala Meditation

A mandala, also known as a "measureless mansion," represents the enlightened awareness of the central deity, while the entourage personifies aspects and powers of the enlightened state. Nairātmyā mandalas consist solely of female divinities, as is typical of the retinues of female Buddhas. The simplest consists of fifteen deities. Nairātmyā is surrounded by an inner circle of four yoginis in a fivefold configuration symbolizing the five transcendent insights of a Buddha. The outer ring consists of eight yoginis; two goddesses at the apex and nadir complete the assembly.[14]

In this context, Nairātmyā displays her classical iconography but is sometimes designated as Vajra Nairātmyā, "Adamantine Nairātmyā."[15] Each of the retinue yoginis is dark blue and identical in appearance to her mistress, with upswept tawny hair and fierce mien, draped with bone ornaments and a tiger skin, dancing on a corpse. The flaying knife is for cutting off mental and emotional defilements, and the skull bowl is the realization of emptiness, which is beyond being and nonbeing. From their skull cups they drink the blood of the four māra-demons, symbolizing the primary forms of attachment to self.[16]

There is also a twenty-three-deity mandala centering on a four-armed form of Nairātmyā. In her two additional arms she exhibits a vajra and raises her khaṭvāṅga. Fourteen retinue yoginis replicate this iconography. This core group is encircled by eight protectors: four in the semidirections and four theriomorphic gate guardians with the heads of a horse, boar, dog, and lioness.[17]

The mandalas of Nairātmyā figure in a practice of mental purification.[18] The underlying principle is that all we perceive is a creation, or projection, of our own consciousness. Therefore, any faults we detect in the world and any suffering we experience are the products of our own minds. The path to freedom and happiness is to purify the mind of the tendency to attribute concrete reality to its own creations. The mandala deities represent the basic elements of experience, while the mandala itself provides a structure, or template, for the systematic purification of those elements. The ring of guardians forms a protective barrier within which this process of psychic exploration and transformation may be undertaken in safety.

The fifteen deities of the mandala core personify the basic components of each person's mental construction of self and world, encompassing sense experience, objects of perception, and the emotional and motivational drives of the psyche. Following are the fifteen core deities and corresponding aspects of experience:[19]

SENSORY EXPERIENCE	
Gaurī	sight
Caurī	sound
Vetālī	smell
Ghasmarī	taste
Bhūcarī	touch
Khecarī	thought
ELEMENTS OF THE PHENOMENAL WORLD	
Pukkasī	earth
Śavarī	water
Caṇḍālinī	fire
Ḍombī (a.k.a. Ḍombinī)	air
FIVE EMOTIONAL POISONS AND COMPONENTS OF SELFHOOD	
Vajrī	delusion and bodily form
Gaurī (a.k.a. Guptagaurī)	hatred and feeling
Vāriyoginī	lust and perception
Vajraḍākinī	envy and volition
Nairātmyā	anger and consciousness

In the mandala meditation, each deity is envisioned in turn, beginning with the outermost tier (sensory experience) and circling inward. The visualization process purifies the corresponding aspect of experience, culminating in the consummate purity of consciousness represented by Nairātmyā at the center.

This purification process does not eliminate the rich texture of experience or the colorful panorama of the phenomenal world. Rather, a fundamental shift occurs in the practitioner's mind, from a dualistic mode of perception to nondual awareness. What is eradicated is the deeply ingrained tendency to dichotomize experience into inner and outer, self and other, subject and object. The apparent solidity of the world, too, dissolves, giving way to a unitary field of energy, as samsara and nirvana, all realms of existence, and self and other merge into one.[20] This state of awareness, represented by Nairātmyā, is "like the sky, pure and empty . . . it is all-pervading . . . universal consciousness."[21]

Thus, through Nairātmyā mandala practice, all mindstates are discovered to be pure in essence.[22] The same is true of phenomenal appearances and sense experience. Henceforth, sense enjoyments need not be avoided and indeed should be savored and embraced, recognized as the pure essence of Buddhahood manifesting in the world.[23] The experiential quality of this purified awareness is supreme bliss (*paraṃ sukhaṃ*).[24] Thus, Nairātmyā's joyful dance at the center of the mandala represents the bliss that dwells in the heart of every being and is ever-present as the essence of every experience.

The Nairātmyā mandala also represents the process by which phenomenal reality arises in the vast expanse of empty space. Nairātmyā, at the center, represents the source of all that exists. Her body, blue in color, is understood to be all-encompassing, like space. Her seed syllable, the sound that shares her essence, is the letter "A" (pronounced "ah").[25] As the first letter of the Sanskrit alphabet, "A" is regarded as its root and source, because no other letter can be pronounced without an exhalation. The voicing of consonants requires an expiration, while the vowels are variations on "A," produced by shaping the mouth in different positions while exhaling. Nairātmyā and her yogini retinue apotheosize the Sanskrit vowels and personify her root mantra, which consists of the vowels framed by *oṃ* and *svāhā*: *Oṃ a ā i ī u ū ṛ ṝ ḷ ḹ e ai o au aṃ aḥ svāhā*.[26] Because there are sixteen vowels but fifteen deities in the mandala, the sixteenth vowel, *aḥ*, is often omitted.[27] The vowels make possible the voicing of all units of speech, and thus Nairātmyā and her retinue represent the source of language.

The originary role of the vowels is not simply linguistic but ontological as well, for sound operates on the subtlest level of reality as the vibrational waves that underlie and shape phenomenal reality. Just as deities have sounds, or mantras, that evoke their divine energies, all phenomena have corresponding sonic vibrations. Human use of sound in the form of language further shapes reality by molding the processes of perception, labeling, and interpretation. Thus, sound shapes reality ontologically, while language shapes reality psychologically and experientially. Vowels, as the primary and fundamental sounds, are known as *mātṛkās*, "divine mothers," by virtue of their generative role in birthing reality. Vowels provide the material, or maternal matrix, of language, and speech in turn is the "mother" of phenomenal reality. In this respect, Nairātmyā's mandala is a cosmogonic diagram representing sound as an originary force. Nairātmyā at the center is the "A," the primal sound and "source of all things," the primordial creative principle.[28]

Nairātmyā is thus established as the source of emanation of the world, but she is also envisioned as the force of its dissolution. In this latter role,

Nairātmyā is identified with the mystical heat that is kindled in the navel chakra through inner yogic processes. Thus, Nairātmyā is called Caṇḍālī, "Burning One," and described as "dwelling in the navel, source of supreme bliss, glorious, adorned with flames by virtue of her fiery heat."[29] Nairātmyā, as the inner yogic fire, consumes delusion by rising upward along the spine, purifying the chakras of karmic residues of thought and emotion. Upon reaching the crown chakra, the heat causes the nectar of bliss in the crown of the head to melt and flow downward, generating increasing rapture and bliss, culminating in the supreme state of "spontaneous joy" (*sahajānanda*) when the nectar reaches and saturates the navel chakra.

This internal fire is a yogic version of the apocalyptic conflagration that destroys the world at the end of every cosmic cycle so that it may begin anew. In both cases, fire is the consuming element, reducing all things to an undifferentiated state, returning them to their essence. This essence—the one thing remaining at world's end, the irreducible quality of the world that is realized upon enlightenment—is, according to the *Hevajra Tantra*, bliss: "Bliss is the single self-existent . . . perfect and eternal."[30] Bliss gives rise not only to all worldly appearances but to the millions of Buddhas throughout the universe. Thus, when Nairātmyā "blazes up at the navel, she burns the . . . Buddhas," returning them, too, to their original condition and source, pure bliss.[31]

Nairātmyā represents the bliss that gives rise to the world and the liberating display of countless Buddhas. She is the primordial sound that underlies and shapes all phenomena through sonic vibrations. She is also the fire that consumes illusion and reduces all things, including Buddhas, to their original state of unity and eternal essence, bliss supreme.

Yogini Circles, Human and Divine

Four yoginis in Nairātmyā's mandala assembly, or "yogini circle" (*yoginīcakra*), carry the names of socially marginal and even stigmatized groups in India. Śavarī, "Tribal Woman," makes reference to tribal groups who live in remote rural and forested areas. Because their clothing, way of life, and religious practices are so distinct from those of the mainstream and especially Brahmanical cultural norms, Śavaras appear in literature and art to represent not only kinship with nature but also barbarism and primitivism. Ḍombī hails from the Ḍom caste, one of whose hereditary occupations is to prepare corpses for cremation, a livelihood that renders them ritually impure by bringing them into ongoing contact with the polluting by-products of death. Pukkasī derives her name from a despised caste thought to have its origins in tribal hunters who were inducted into the Brahmanical social system in menial and defiling occupations. Caṇḍālī represents the lowest of the "untouchable" groups in India, also tribal in origin, consigned to such reviled employments as cleaning the streets, performing executions, transporting dead bodies, and tending cremation grounds.[32]

The inclusion of such groups in Nairātmyā's mandala assembly by all evidence reflects the actual constituency of Tantric circles. The hagiographic literature of Indian Buddhist Tantra celebrates adepts, both male and female, of markedly lowly social origins and even outcasts. Thus, one finds among the ranks of the enlightened *mahāsiddhas*, or "great perfected ones," many who engaged in despised and ritually polluting vocations, such as hunters, birdcatchers, ragpickers, leatherworkers, ropemakers, arrowsmiths, blacksmiths, gamblers, and beggars, practicing alongside their social superiors and even serving as gurus to aristocrats and royalty. This pattern of open association without regard for class background accords with an egalitarian ethos stemming from the belief that all beings possess a seed or spark of Buddhahood and hence share the same essence. The *Hevajra Tantra* professes that "all beings are Buddhas," from the gods in the heavens to the denizens of hell.[33] No human being, then, should be debarred from Tantric practice, for "even Caṇḍālas and other low-caste wretches and those whose minds are set on slaughter . . . may gain perfection, there is no doubt."[34] Therefore, the low-caste figures in the mandala retinue evoke the egalitarianism promoted in Tantric circles.

The presence of low-caste yoginis also helps delineate the mandala as a metaphor for purity of consciousness. A mandala, or mansion of enlightened consciousness, is by definition an image of divine perfection and beauty. Thus, the inclusion of that which is ritually impure within the sacred sphere of the mandala dramatizes the radical Tantric view that everything is pure for one who has pure vision. According to the *Hevajra Tantra*, one who sees truly knows everything to be equal and does not distinguish between highborn and low or engage in other false judgments based on personal preference and social convention.[35] One who moves beyond the mindstates of acceptance and rejection, which yield myriad forms of suffering, can experience reality as it is—the goal of all Buddhist practice—and blissfully engage in the compassionate art of liberating sentient beings. Moreover, enlightened awareness reveals the perfection of the world, and Nairātmyā's mandala portrays a perfect world as one in which humans of all ranks are valued for their inherent spirituality and potential for liberation.

The mandala is also a blueprint for ritual practice, namely, the esoteric rite of *cakra-pūjā*, "worship in a circle," so named because its celebrants gather in a circle to engage in sacramental feasting, sacred dance and song, and other Tantric practices. The assembly is patterned on the mandala, with human women taking the part of the retinue of divine yoginis and the sole male role of Nairātmyā's consort, Hevajra, assumed by a male yogi. The *Hevajra Tantra* sets forth two ways this process might proceed. One sends a male practitioner through the countryside in search of gatherings of yoginis, armed with knowledge of times and places they are likely to meet. The yogi is tutored beforehand in the secret signs the yoginis may use to communicate with him and the gestures he should use in reply. Having approached such a ritual gathering and requested admission using the appropriate gestures,

> If (the yoginis) show garlands in their hands,
> They are indicating that you should join them there.
> Motioning with their garlands means,
> "O holder of Tantric vows,
> Stay and take part in this assembly."
> At that place of assembly,
> He should remain in the sacred circle and
> Do all that the yoginis command.[36]

In this passage, the "circle of yoginis" (*yoginī-cakra*) is a group of women who have gathered to perform Tantric ritual. The fortunate yogi gains admission to their company and participates at their invitation.[37]

In another scenario described in the same *tantra*, the practitioner stages the ritual, patterned in this case on the shared mandala of Nairātmyā and Hevajra, which also has a circle of eight yoginis. He begins by drawing the mandala on the ground with colored powder made from gemstones, rice powder, or charcoal from a cremation ground, using symbols to represent the eight yoginis. He then invites eight "blissful *vidyā*s," that is, females versed in magic or yoga, to assume the places of the eight yoginis. Taking the part of Hevajra himself, he worships the women with kisses and embraces, and they regale him with dance and song. They may also engage in sacred union, generating the bliss and joy of enlightenment.[38]

Thus, the *Hevajra Tantra* evinces that the "circle of yoginis" made reference to gatherings of female Tantrics and to rituals in which human women played the role of their divine counterparts, confirming that the mandala has a performative dimension, in addition to mapping a process of psychological transformation.

Tibet and Nepal

The independent practice and mandalas of Nairātmyā were transmitted to Tibet and preserved in canonical sources.[39] In the Gelug and Kagyu sects, it appears that Nairātmyā is primarily envisioned with her consort Hevajra in the mandala they share, rarely figuring as an object of individual portrayal or meditation. The practice of Nairātmyā has, however, been important in the Sakya sect, which traces its Hevajra lineage to Virūpa, the Indian adept whose authority is grounded in his revelations from Nairātmyā. Therefore, Sakya representations of the goddess often appear in association with those of Virūpa.

One such composition shows Nairātmyā elevated beside Virūpa as he gazes up at her with eyes open wide in wonderment.[40] A painting in the Shelley and Donald Rubin Collection shows the adept and Nairātmyā seated side by side, their eyes locked in intimate communion, while the four-armed epiphany of the goddess dances in the space above them and another hierophany in the cross-legged meditative pose looks on (Fig. 19.3).[41] Nairātmyā may appear directly above Virūpa in painted portraits of the latter, recognizing her role as the divine source of his teachings.[42] Similarly, the two may be juxtaposed at the top of portraits of Sakya hierarchs and lineage holders, signaling that the transmission of teachings from Nairātmyā to Virūpa marks the origins of the Sakya curriculum.[43]

This type of composition introduces a variation on the iconography of Nairātmyā. She is shown, in the usual manner, as a dark blue ḍākinī with her customary attributes, but she is depicted in a seated pose, with her right heel pressed into her pelvis. Her left foot is extended slightly forward in a seated version of *ardhaparyaṅka*, which simply stipulates that one leg be drawn up and the other extended and thus may be interpreted as a seated or dancing pose.[44] Indeed, Nairātmyā is often depicted in a seated posture in artistic representations of Sakya provenance. One such painting is the first of a series devoted to Sakya tutelaries and luminaries, recognizing her as the sect's main divine patron.[45] Another Sakya composition shows the goddess seated amidst her retinue of yoginis, shown in their customary dancing pose, and surrounded by an array of hierarchs whose eyes are fixed on her.[46]

A number of metal votive images also depict Nairātmyā in a seated pose, generally enthroned on an upward-facing corpse and lotus pedestal (Pl. 13). Several are inscribed, confirming identification.[47] Although the inscriptions do not reveal sectarian affiliation, stylistic considerations and the distinctive iconography suggest a Sakya provenance. These exquisite statuary, such as the superb bronze held by the Los Angeles County Museum of Art, illustrated here, are cast in copper, a costly medium, and enhanced with gilding, painted details, and inlaid gemstones, rendering lavish honor to the divine patron of the lineage.

In Nepal, Nairātmyā retained independent significance and became a preeminent female Buddha of the Newar pantheon. She is identified with Guhyeśvarī, the primordial goddess of the Kathmandu Valley, who plays an

19.3 Nairātmyā and Virūpa, Tibet, Sakya lineage, sixteenth century. Thang-ka, detail. Mineral pigment and gold on cotton, 18.5 × 12.5 in. (47 × 31.75 cm). Shelley and Donald Rubin Collection, P1994.1.1. Photo: Shelley and Donald Rubin Collection. *The adept Virūpa in visionary communion with Nairātmyā, receiving revelations.*

important role in the Buddhist origin account of the valley and its Tantric tradition. Guhyeśvarī/Nairātmyā has two main temples, built over the openings of subterranean springs whose waters convey her nectarine essence of bliss.[48]

Dancing in Infinity

By virtue of her iconography and associated metaphysical themes, Nairātmyā is a cosmic figure, infinite in expanse and understanding. The same is true of all Buddhas, although each elicits a different aspect of this principle. The blue female Buddha evokes the spaciousness that Buddhists envision as enveloping and permeating phenomenal reality. Nairātmyā, as her name indicates, embodies the Buddhist verity of selflessness (*nirātman*), the absence of concrete, independently real persons and phenomena. The correlate of this truth is the Buddhist vision of reality as a vast web of interdependence and interconnectedness. Her cerulean body is a translucent shell inscribed on the face of reality, proclaiming that all bodies and all phenomenal appearances hover in empty space. Nairātmyā, having realized this truth, responds to the illusory nature of phenomena by rejoicing and dancing to liberate others.

Femaleness is consistently attributed to generative phenomena in Buddhist symbology, including womblike space, the nurturing earth, the letters of the alphabet, and mantras. The earth, which gives rise to all the life upon it, is personified as a goddess. Space, as the generative matrix of heavenly bodies and of all matter, is associated with female deities. Sound, the alphabet, and language, conceived as subtle layers of reality that underlie and shape phenomena, are commonly envisioned as feminine in Indian metaphysics and in Buddhism as well. Through her identification with the letter "A," the primal sound, the primordial vibration of space and consciousness, Nairātmyā personifies the origin of all phenomena and mindstates. She also represents the force of their dissolution, as the heat of yogic fire and the principle of emptiness.

As the source of phenomenal reality, Nairātmyā encompasses the universe within her being. All reality is contained within her, as are the processes of arising and dissolution. Therefore, to contemplate Nairātmyā is to behold "the essence of ultimate reality."[49] "Ultimate reality," dharmadhātu, all that exists, is the totality of existence. Nairātmyā is what is known in the broader Indic perspective as a world mother, source of all that is, designated in that context as Ādi Śakti (primordial female energy) and as Mahādevī, goddess supreme. Buddhist writings express that ultimacy in terms of emptiness and bliss, space and consciousness. To those unfamiliar with the tradition, "emptiness" may have a negative resonance, implying an absence of purpose or meaning. In the Buddhist context, however, emptiness is an exhilarating and inspiring concept, a liberating principle of ontological openness and existential freedom. Thus, as the "Lady of Emptiness," Nairātmyā is supremely blissful, embodying the transcendent happiness enjoyed by those who realize the truth of emptiness. There is no greater joy than discovering that suffering is an illusion and no greater pleasure than dancing in infinity.

CHAPTER 20

CHINNAMUṆḌĀ

Severed-Headed Goddess

The holy, adamantine Yogini, yellow with a red luster,
Has cut off her own head with a chopper and
Bears the head aloft in her left hand. . . .
She lunges with her right foot forward,
Crowned by skulls, naked, with freely flowing hair.
Envision the Buddhaḍākinī in the center,
Her body draped with five bone ornaments;
From the neck of her severed head,
A stream of blood gushes upward into her own mouth
And into the mouths of two yoginis at her sides.

—Meditation manual by Lakṣmīṅkarā[1]

Chinnamuṇḍā (pronounced *chee nah* MOON DAH), the "Severed-Headed Goddess," offers a startling, even shocking, portrait of ultimate liberation. Her youthful body, golden yellow with a roseate luster, is charmingly adorned by bone jewelry. She lunges forward in a spirited and vigorous manner, her arms poised dancelike in midair. Yet her head has been severed from her body, cut off by her own hand, and blood streams from her headless neck. The sight of Chinnamuṇḍā confronts the viewer with a paradox. She should be lifeless, but she is overflowing with vitality as she feeds herself and two female companions with the liquid that flows from her body. The inherent contradiction posed by the image of Chinnamuṇḍā points to a realm of awareness that defies ordinary logic and conventional concepts, including the seemingly ineradicable duality of life and death. Her image conveys the truth that when the illusory self, the false ego, dies, new modes of awareness and action become possible. One who masters the yoga of Chinnamuṇḍā literally transcends death and attains the Buddhist equivalent of immortality, namely, the deathless state wherein, no longer subject to the laws of karma and rebirth, one is free to re-create oneself eternally, in innumerable times, places, and bodily forms, out of compassion, to lead others to the same state of liberation.

Chinnamuṇḍā is a female Buddha, which means that, as a fully enlightened being, she occupies the vantage point of ultimate truth. She is a Buddhaḍākinī, or "Fully Enlightened Ḍākinī."[2] She is in fact regarded as a manifestation of Vajrayoginī/Vajravārāhī. The three figures are ultimately equated with one another but are understood to appear in different bodily forms to manifest different nuances of enlightenment. Because of their underlying unity, they may be invoked by the same mantra, which conveys the energy essence of a deity in sonic form: *Oṃ oṃ oṃ sarvabuddhaḍākinīye vajravarṇanīye vajravairocanīye hūṃ hūṃ hūṃ phaṭ phaṭ svāhā.*[3] Although the names Vajravairocanī and Vajravarṇanī appear in the mantra, they figure only in the visualization of Chinnamuṇḍā, as described below.

In many respects, Chinnamuṇḍā resembles the other forms of Vajrayoginī. She wears bone ornaments and a crown of five skulls that represent the five aspects of enlightened wisdom. Apart from these Tantric adornments she is naked, her long hair unbound, and she brandishes a ḍākinī chopper. However, her iconography also differs in significant ways. Whereas most forms of Vajrayoginī are red, Chinnamuṇḍā is often envisioned as yellow, perhaps in allusion to the golden radiance of transcendent wisdom (*prajñā*). In her left hand, in place of the usual skull bowl, she displays her own severed head, waving it aloft with a triumphant flourish (Fig. 20.1, Pl. 14).

Chinnamuṇḍā is accompanied by two divine yoginis: green Vajravarṇanī ("Adamantine Hue") on her left and yellow Vajravairocanī ("Adamantine Brilliance") on her right. The companion yoginis, too, are naked, with bone ornaments and loosely flowing hair, but their heads are intact and they bear skull bowls and small choppers in their hands. The dramatic focal point of the image is the three streams of blood that arch from the headless neck of the central female Buddha into her own mouth and the mouths of the yoginis at her sides. The three figures are envisioned in the midst of a fearsome cremation ground.[4] The epithet Trikāya-Vajrayoginī, "Three-Bodied Vajrayoginī," refers to the fact that three figures are integral to the iconography.[5]

Chinnamuṇḍā takes her place among a range of Indian divinities who drink blood, receive offerings of severed heads, or dismember themselves as a salvific act. Chinnamuṇḍā (along with her Hindu counterpart, Chinnamastā) is distinctive in that the blood she drinks is her own, the severed head is her own, and she does not die in an act of sacrificing herself to nourish others. She also stands apart from a tradition of Buddhist figures who offer their mortal body as the supreme gesture of selfless generosity.[6] Thus, although her iconography may have been informed by those motifs, it differs significantly and demands its own

20.1 Chinnamuṇḍā, Amrit Karmacharya, Patan, Nepal, last decade of twentieth century. Paubhā, detail. Pigment and gold on cotton, 21.5 × 16.75 in. (54.6 × 42.5 cm). Author's collection. *Severed-headed Chinnamuṇḍā nourishes herself and her companions with the elixir of nondual awareness and immortality. (See Pl. 14)*

interpretation. Elisabeth Benard's comprehensive study of Chinnamuṇḍā locates the primary significance of the self-beheading motif in its reference to internal yogic practices, attributing its mysterious, awe-inspiring quality in part to the fact that it is a "magnified depiction of something invisible to ordinary vision."[7]

Allegory for Inner Yoga Practices

Chinnamuṇḍā and the two yoginis who accompany her offer a visual allegory for advanced yogic meditations known in Buddhist terminology as perfection stage yoga (*utpanna-krama*) and in the Hindu context as *kuṇḍalinī-yoga*. This inner yoga, which comes at the end of a long course of meditative training and esoteric initiations, involves the movement and concentration of psychic energies within the subtle yogic anatomy of the body. The central energy pathway traverses the body along the spine and continues around the crown of the head to the forehead. Two ancillary channels run parallel to it. The channel on the right is known as *rasanā*, the one on the left is termed *lalanā*, and the main, central pathway is the *avadhūtī*. The two side channels coil around the avadhūtī at four main junctures, or chakras, at the navel, heart, throat, and forehead. The psychic energies or winds (*prāṇa*) which carry a person's thoughts and emotions normally course throughout the body in a network of seventy-two thousand psychic veins and in the two side channels. The dispersion of the energy corresponds to the myriad thought processes that mire the mind in worldly existence. Underlying the seemingly infinite variety of dualistic thoughts, however, is the fundamental division of the world into self and other, or subject and object. The right channel and subsidiary branching veins support the subjective portion of experience; the left channel and veins carry thought constructions pertaining to external objects.[8]

The winds do not ordinarily enter the central channel of their own accord. The goal of inner yoga is to gather all the energy into the central channel, use it to open and untie the knots at the chakras, and direct it in specific ways to generate subtle realizations and states of bliss. When the energies abide in the central channel, they no longer support dualistic thought. Conceptuality, deprived of its foundation, automatically disappears, baring the natural essence of the mind and restoring its capacity for direct, intuitive wisdom.[9] Geshe Kelsang Gyatso explains that when the energies are gathered in the central channel, "the dualistic conceptualizing mind—the source of cyclic existence—will no longer have any foundation and will therefore disappear. . . . The myriad of negative thoughts powered by the dualistic view will all vanish automatically, without effort."[10] Normally all the energies enter the central channel and dissolve into the heart chakra only at the moment of death, giving rise to a fleeting experience of illumination and a vision of the clear light. Inner yoga practitioners seek to replicate this process during life and to integrate the resultant nondual wisdom into daily, waking consciousness.[11]

In the yogic interpretation of her iconography, Chinnamuṇḍā embodies the central energy pathway of the body, or avadhūtī. The companion yoginis represent the two side channels: Vajravarṇanī on her left corresponds to lalanā, while Vajravairocanī on her right personifies rasanā. Several stages of the inner yoga are represented by the image, for the nature of the exchange among the three yoginis changes as the meditation unfolds.

The practitioner first envisions the triad on a red or multihued lotus at the navel, where the side channels intersect the central channel. Initially envisioning the three goddesses at the navel chakra draws the energy from the two halves of the body to the place where the three channels meet, in preparation for bringing the energy into the central channel.[12]

In the next stage of the meditation, the energy is concentrated into three luminous drops (*bindu*) at the lower ends of the three channels: a red drop on the right, a white drop on the left, and a blue drop in the center. The two outer yoginis are envisioned as exhaling into the central channel. Their breath pushes the red and white drops into the blue one, accomplishing the transfer of energy into the avadhūtī. The unified drop is then drawn up the central channel and absorbed into the heart chakra, where nondual awareness dawns:

> The two goddesses exhale, which makes
> The left and right drops dissolve into the middle one. . . .
> Envision it merging into the HŪṂ at the heart.
> That (heart drop) is clear and stainless,
> A nondual drop of intrinsic awareness,
> Free from all happiness and suffering—
> Pure awareness, emptied of worldly appearances.
> How wonderful!
> Practice yoga—attain nondual wisdom![13]

This is not the end of the meditation, however. The next step is to kindle an inner fire of psychic heat at the navel that melts the drop at the heart, generating a stream of blissful nectar. The nectarine fluid is then directed in various ways to generate further nuances of insight and bliss. The highest states of transcendent bliss are produced by its upward movement along the central channel, culminating at the crown of the head.[14]

At this stage of the visualization, the central font of blood that streams upward from Chinnamuṇḍā's neck assumes a primary role. The liquid that flows into her own mouth represents the melting drops that rise in the central channel and flood the crown chakra, giving rise to supreme bliss.[15] Life-giving blood is an apt metaphor for the yogic nectar in which the life essence is concentrated. The term "nectar" (*amṛta*) applies here in both of its meanings, as the ambrosia of bliss and elixir of immortality. Flooding the crown chakra, in essence "feeding oneself" with the nectarine drops, is the psychophysiological basis of transcendent bliss, as well as a source of profound regeneration and renewal. In this respect, the severed head borne aloft in her left hand corresponds to the skull bowl displayed by other female Buddhas. Both attributes reflect mastery of the inner yogic practice in which the concentrated life energy is brought into the crown chakra, turning it into a veritable cranial chalice, overflowing with radiant nectar of bliss and immortality.

Physical Renewal and Spiritual Rebirth

Following this interpretation, the streams of liquid that feed the companion yoginis may refer to a subsequent stage of the meditation, when the energy accumulated in the central channel is spread outward again to purify the right and left channels and peripheral veins throughout the body. The practitioner consciously directs the energy to remove blockages in the network of subtle veins, repair them where they are broken, restore them where they have shriveled or become brittle, and render them smooth and supple. The diffusion of the energy regenerates the body, restoring youthfulness and bestowing perfect health.[16] This yogic purification process accomplishes a profound healing on the metaphysical level, which underlies organic sickness and health. At this final stage of the inner yoga, the crimson liquid that pours from Chinnamuṇḍā's headless neck is a Tantric fountain of eternal youth.

Thus, the image of self-decapitation, perhaps seemingly gruesome, is actually a dramatic image of regeneration and spiritual rebirth. The associated yogic practice bestows youthful vigor and flexibility on the body and restores the original purity of the heart and mind. One who becomes adept at this yoga is also prepared for a conscious, enlightening death experience. Persons who experience the clear light of mind for the first time at death are not prepared to merge into its engulfing brilliance. The force of egoic attachment compels them to revert to individuated consciousness and continue on the afterdeath journey through realms of terrifying and enticing psychological apparition, until settling in a womb or egg for their next rebirth. A meditator who has undergone this psychic dissolution during life, however, can merge fully into the clear light and experience visionary encounters with enlightened beings in the afterlife, as well as choose the next form of embodiment that he or she will adopt.

Chinnamuṇḍā's headless condition may be interpreted as a symbol of the introspective and self-sufficient state of consciousness that prevails during this process of yogic purification, as the mind is withdrawn from sense objects and worldly appearances and immersed in its intrinsic luminosity and blissfulness. Even breath may be suspended during this state, as the entire psychophysical organism becomes self-sustaining.[17] Thus, the dissevered body of Chinnamuṇḍā is really an image of wholeness, proclaiming the possibility of tapping an infinite stream of energy within oneself. She holds her head at arm's length because she requires and receives nothing from outside herself. Liberated from worldly experiences, sense impressions, and even respiration, she drinks perpetually from an inner wellspring of joy and knowledge, the nectar of bliss and wisdom, the elixir of eternal life.

Chinnamuṇḍā portrays the paradox inherent in the process of spiritual awakening. It is at once a psychic death, insofar as experience of oneself as an individual, permanent self with fixed boundaries is eradicated, and a spiritual rebirth, the dawning of universal awareness and infinite expansiveness of being. The cremation ground in which Chinnamuṇḍā is envisioned dramatizes the death of selfhood at the heart of this transformation. The site of the combustion of the physical body is a fitting symbol for the yogic dissolution of the psyche into its purest form as luminous, blissful consciousness. The cremation pyres symbolize the flames of wisdom, kindled within as a yogic fire that incinerates the states of mind that feed the ego. Thus, Chinnamuṇḍā's stand upon the charnel ground represents the victory of one who has undergone psychic death and emerged, triumphant, on the other side.

Revelation and Transmission

The worship of Chinnamuṇḍā was introduced by Lakṣmīṅkarā, a female mahāsiddha, or "great perfected one," who may have lived in the ninth century. Lakṣmīṅkarā's biography traces her journey to enlightenment, explaining how she attained the level of visionary insight necessary to receive and impart a revelation of deity. Lakṣmīṅkarā was a princess by birth and a native of Uḍḍiyāna, an important Tantric center in northwestern India. She had received training in Sanskrit, philosophy, meditation, and esoteric yoga before leaving home to marry the prince of Laṅka. Lakṣmīṅkarā felt revulsion for her fiancé when she saw him return from a hunting expedition with piles of slaughtered animals, so she gave away her dowry, escaped to a cremation ground, and fended off search parties by feigning insanity. Lakṣmīṅkarā spent seven years in deep meditation in her self-imposed exile. Her efforts as a solitary yogini were crowned with full enlightenment and a state of visionary attunement in which she could see and receive instruction directly from Buddhas and bodhisattvas.

Lakṣmīṅkarā remained in the forest, residing in a cave, and began to attract and train disciples. One day the king, Jalendra, chanced upon her cave during a hunting expedition. Peering inside, he saw that her body was aglow, filling the cave with light, and that she was surrounded by celestial maidens who were worshipping and making offerings to her. The king returned the next day and requested her to be his guru. The forest-dwelling yogini knew she was not destined to be his teacher and imparted that he should instead receive initiation from one of her disciples, a low-caste sweeper who was a servant in the king's own palace. The ruler, following her guidance, became a disciple of his menial hireling. Eventually, Lakṣmīṅkarā and the sweeper traveled through the countryside, teaching and displaying miracles. When Lakṣmīṅkarā died, she ascended bodily into Khecara, Ḍākinī Paradise.[18]

Two meditation manuals authored by Lakṣmīṅkarā are preserved in the Tibetan canon.[19] Her portrayal with a sword in one hand and a head in the other also refers to her association with Chinnamuṇḍā.[20]

Lakṣmīṅkarā's biography records that she taught the visualization and inner yogas of Vajravārāhī but does not specify the severed-headed form of the goddess. When the core texts on Lakṣmīṅkarā's meditational system were circulated in Tibet, they were designated as "the six treatises on Vajravārāhī."[21] Similarly, lines of transmission recorded in Tibet place Lakṣmīṅkarā at the head of "Vajravārāhī" lineages.[22] This is unsurprising, for Chinnamuṇḍā is not regarded a distinct goddess but rather as a form of Vajrayoginī and Vajravārāhī, synonymous epithets for the supreme Tantric female Buddha. Therefore, the earliest writings, including those of Lakṣmīṅkarā herself, refer to Chinnamuṇḍā as Vajrayoginī, Trikāya-Vajrayoginī, Chinnamuṇḍā-Vajrayoginī, Vajravārāhī, and Chinnamuṇḍā-Vajravārāhī.[23] Accordingly, the earliest known artistic representation of Chinnamuṇḍā appears in a circa early thirteenth-century painting from Khara Khoto that centers on Vajravārāhī, casting Chinnamuṇḍā as one of her manifestations.[24]

Lakṣmīṅkarā's compositions include a song that the princess-adept used to usher her disciples into the realm of nondual wisdom. Tantric teachers generally composed such songs spontaneously for their inner circle of disciples, often in the course of a ritual feast, to transmit esoteric teachings. The poetic imagery, like Chinnamuṇḍā's iconography, defies interpretation from the standpoint of ordinary logic. The opening verse uses the motif of self-beheading to introduce the theme, developed in the rest of the song, that it is necessary to sever dualistic thinking at the root if one is to reach a level of direct knowing beyond conceptual dualities:

> Lay your head on a block of butter and chop—
> Break the blade of the axe!
> The woodcutter laughs!

A frog swallows an elephant!
It's amazing, Mekhalā,
Do not doubt.
If it confounds you, adept,
Drop concepts now!

My teacher didn't tell me,
I didn't understand—
Flowers blossomed in the sky!
It's marvelous, Mekhalā,
Have no doubt!
If you're incredulous, adept,
Drop your doubts!

A barren woman gives birth!
A chair dances!
Because cotton is expensive,
The naked weep!
. . . .
Amazing! An elephant sits on a throne
Held up by two bees!
Incredible! The sightless lead,
The mute speak!
. . . .
Amazing! A mouse chases a cat!
An elephant flees from a crazed donkey!

It's miraculous, Mekhalā,
Do not doubt!
If you're stunned, adept,
Drop your doubts!

Amazing! A hungry monkey eats rocks!
Wonderful! The experience of the mind—
Who can express it?[25]

The preceding verses confirm that for Lakṣmīṅkarā, severing the head signifies freedom from conceptuality and its limitations. The tool of this liberation is the blade of wisdom. The wielder of the blade laughs, perhaps with astonished joy, as the burden of ego is lifted. A small creature, a frog, swallows something ponderous, an elephant, just as the realization of nonduality consumes the entire edifice of self and world constructed by dualistic thought.

Lakṣmīṅkarā challenges her listeners with seemingly impossible scenarios—a chair dancing, bees lifting an elephant, a monkey eating rocks—offering a series of riddles that the logical mind cannot unravel. The only way to solve the riddles is to "drop concepts now!" Her song offers a tantalizing taste of the exhilarating freedom of nondual awareness that blossoms miraculously, like flowers in the sky, when one passes through the veil of illusion and enters the realm of miracles, magic, and infinite possibilities.

Other early teachers and formulators of the practice were direct disciples of Lakṣmīṅkarā or students of her disciples. Lakṣmīṅkarā's closest disciple was probably the low-caste sweeper who is the only protégé mentioned (albeit not by name) in her biography and who spent many years with her as companion and consort. The sweeper was authorized to confer initiation and transmit her teachings, as he did to King Jalendra, but he does not figure in her disciplic lineage. Instead, Virūpa is recognized as her immediate successor.[26] Virūpa wrote several texts on Chinnamuṇḍā[27] and was a key figure in the transmission of the practice to Tibet.

The sisters Mekhalā and Kanakhalā, who undertook Tantric practice and attained enlightenment together, are important for their formulation of the inner yoga of Chinnamuṇḍā. The guru who taught them the practice was Kāṅha, who may have learned it from his guru, Jālandhari, who in turn had studied with Lakṣmīṅkarā.[28] There is also evidence that the sisters received instruction directly from Lakṣmīṅkarā. Mekhalā is addressed by name in the song translated above, and the sisters are designated in the colophon as its transmitters.[29]

According to their shared biography, Mekhalā and Kanakhalā fell into disgrace when the family of the brothers to whom they were betrothed abruptly terminated the engagement. The girls decided that, instead of succumbing to despair, they would undertake spiritual practice together. The yogi Kāṅha passed through their village and taught the sisters how to meditate on Chinnamuṇḍā. Mekhalā and Kanakhalā remained unmarried and devoted themselves to the practice for the next twelve years. After attaining enlightenment, they visited Kāṅha in his hermitage to render homage and gratitude.

The guru pretended not to recognize them, prompting them to relate their story. He then demanded their heads as payment for his teachings. The sisters produced swords out of their mouths and beheaded themselves without hesitation, singing:

> We have blended creative and fulfillment meditation,
> We have destroyed all distinction between samsara and nirvana,
> We have united vision and action in perfect harmony
> We know no distinction between acceptance and rejection.

Dwelling in the blessed unity of vast space and pure awareness,
We know no separation between self and others.[30]

The "enlightenment song" of Mekhalā and Kanakhalā expresses their nondual wisdom by evoking the dualities whose underlying unity they have perceived: worldly life and liberation, acceptance and rejection, self and other. In this respect, severing their heads demonstrated that they had indeed transcended the dualities of ordinary awareness, which would hold such an act to be impossible.

Fantastic as it may seem, in the Tantric context the self-beheading of Mekhalā and Kanakhalā would not be regarded simply as a metaphor for nondual awareness. Rather, the sisters' stunning feat would be understood as a magical display, a natural result of their meditative mastery and yogic attainments. Supernormal powers are commonly attributed to inner yoga adepts, for the opening of the central channel, untying of the chakra knots, and purification of the network of subtle veins are regarded as the bodily basis for clairvoyant vision and extraordinary powers.[31] The sisters displayed other supernatural talents as well, such as the ability to pass through solid objects, control people and objects with a gaze, and transport physical objects through space. When some Hindu yogis were heckling the sisters, they solved the problem with ease, simply relocating the yogis' huts to a safe distance.[32] In view of the expectation that magical powers accompany success in Tantric practice, the guru's shocking and seemingly bizarre request that the sisters behead themselves was actually a challenge to prove their yogic mastery.

After their successful demonstration, Kāṅha restored their heads, acknowledged their level of realization, and authorized them to become teachers themselves. The sisters danced away and devoted the rest of their lives to liberating others. When they died, they ascended bodily to Khecara, the paradisal realm of the female Buddha, leaving behind no corporeal remains.[33]

Mekhalā and Kanakhalā are usually portrayed with swords, either dancing with the sabers held aloft or in the act of cutting off their heads, illustrating their miraculous display of self-beheading.[34] Indeed, after they performed this marvelous deed, people began to refer to them as "severed-headed yoginis."[35] This iconography also alludes to their achievement of unity with Chinnamuṇḍā and their role as teachers of the related inner yoga practice. Their teachings on the topic are preserved in the Tibetan canon.[36]

Later Interpretations

From India, Chinnamuṇḍā practice spread to Nepal and Tibet.[37] The practice may have transmitted to Nepal by Varendraruci, a Newar pundit, in the late eleventh or twelfth century, for he cotranslated two Chinnamuṇḍā texts (one by Lakṣmīṅkarā, the other by Virūpa) in the Tibetan canon.[38] One of the earliest known artistic representations of Chinnamuṇḍā appears in a fourteenth-century painting from Nepal, in which composition she is a subsidiary figure, appearing as an emanation of Vajravārāhī.[39] It is not clear to what degree her practice flourished in that country. I have not encountered a Newar text relating to the goddess, and one finds little evidence of the practice of Chinnamuṇḍā in Nepal today, although other forms of Vajrayoginī play a prominent role in Newar Tantrism.

In Tibet, Chinnamuṇḍā appeared in multiple sectarian contexts, including the Nyingma repertoire.[40] Practice of the goddess in her yellow, severed-headed form is maintained in the Sakya sect, which traces its origins to Virūpa.[41] Apart from this, she seems virtually to have vanished from the active Tibetan pantheon. However, a range of texts and works of art featuring the goddess suggest her ongoing presence in varying sectarian settings through the centuries. In these sources, the goddess is red and appears in diverse of epiphanies. There is an Indic precedent for envisioning Chinnamuṇḍā as red,[42] but these Tibetan sources evince novel iconographic configurations.

A nineteenth-century Tibetan painting portrays Chinnamuṇḍā as red, displaying her severed head in a skull cup. A mystical staff (*khaṭvāṅga*) is positioned so that it crosses her headless neck, as if to seal the energy within the central channel. Absent are the streams of blood and two companion yoginis.[43] This depiction introduces features common to other forms of Vajrayoginī, namely, a leftward-facing lunge, mystical staff, and skull bowl. A fascinating vision of Chinnamuṇḍā appears in a mandala centering on the goddess in a dancing rather than lunging pose, accompanied by her green and yellow companions. All three are beheaded and hold their dissevered heads in their left hand while raising a chopper aloft in the right.[44]

An interesting meditation practice recorded by Tāranātha (sixteenth century) evokes Chinnamuṇḍā in a sequential visualization. In the initial stage, the practitioner envisions the Nāroḍākinī form of Vajrayoginī (Pl. 11). In the second phase, Chinnamuṇḍā appears with a severed head, two companion goddesses, and streams of blood issuing into their mouths. In the third and final step, her head is restored to her body.[45]

These works of art and Tāranātha's progressive evocation indicate that Chinnamuṇḍā had retained a sufficiently vital presence in the Tibetan pantheon to inspire new visualizations and iconographic forms, but for some reason the severed-headed form of the goddess did not compel the same interest as other forms of Vajrayoginī. The practice of Chinnamuṇḍā was perhaps displaced by that of Chöd, which also features a motif of self-beheading.

Parallel Figures and Practices

Chinnamuṇḍā has a Hindu counterpart in the goddess Chinnamastā, whose name similarly means "Severed-Headed Goddess."[46] Chinnamastā, like Chinnamuṇḍā, occupies an important but arcane niche in her tradition. There are few images and temples in active worship, and these are sought out primarily by Tantric practitioners in pursuit of occult powers and yogic perfection.[47]

The iconography of Chinnamastā closely corresponds to that of her Buddhist counterpart. Chinnamastā is sometimes said to be "bright as millions of suns," suggesting a white or golden radiance, but in other cases is described and portrayed as red. The blood issuing from her headless neck streams into the mouths of two companion yoginis, who are variously blue, white, or red. Chinnamastā sits or stands on Kāmadeva and Rati, personifications of erotic desire, who recline beneath her in sexual union. Apart from these divergent details, the Hindu and Buddhist goddess triads are virtually indistinguishable iconographically.[48]

Chinnamastā figures among a group of ten Tantric goddesses known as the Mahāvidyās and, like Chinnamuṇḍā, is associated with esoteric yogic practices.[49] These techniques, designated in the Hindu context as *kuṇḍalinī-yoga*, are closely akin to the Buddhist inner yogas, as seen in the following description by David Kinsley:

> The blood spurting from Chinnamastā's severed throat represents the upward-flowing *kuṇḍalinī* that has broken through all the knots (*granthis*) of the *chakras* and has cleared the central passage, the *suṣumnā nāḍī*. . . . The power of the upward-flowing *kuṇḍalinī*, the power of the rising spiritual consciousness, hits the topmost *chakra*, the thousand-petaled lotus, with such force that it blows her head right off, that is, it transforms all conventional, habitual, limited mental structures.[50]

The similarity of the two goddesses, both in appearance and the practices associated with them, naturally raises the question of shared origins or borrowing. Differing views have been advanced, but there is substantive evidence that the Buddhist goddess is the earlier figure and that Chinnamastā was patterned after her. Extant texts and images of Chinnamuṇḍā predate those of Chinnamastā, and Buddhist terms (notably, *vajra*) appear in some of the Hindu mantras.[51] The possibility of an earlier, mutual source cannot be ruled out, but if that is the case it appears that all traces of the prototype have disappeared.

The motif of using one's own body to nourish others, seen in the visualization practices of both severed-headed goddesses, is rooted in female biological experience and thus arguably has a special resonance for women. Adelheid

Herrmann-Pfandt endorses the psychological appeal of the imagery for women by contrasting the motif with the pattern of self-sacrifice associated with the Hindu goddess Durgā. In one strand of Durgā worship, a male devotee offers himself to the goddess through a symbolic or ritual self-decapitation. In this scenario, the relationship of the sacrificer (the man) and sacrifice (the man) to the recipient deity (the goddess) is a male-to-female relationship. Herrmann-Pfandt suggests that the practice of Chinnamuṇḍā was especially appropriate for women because she "personifies in both of her roles as slayer and sacrifice a female-to-female relationship" in which "not only the goddess but also the ego is feminine," so that "a woman identifies directly with both aspects."[52] This dual identification accords with the Tantric emphasis on relinquishing one's ego, or ordinary self, while affirming one's enlightened essence by visualizing oneself as a deity.

There is evidence that Chinnamastā may have had a special resonance for women as well. The *Tantrasāra* offers the intriguing observation that "if any woman takes this mantra she not only becomes a *ḍākinī* along with other *ḍākinīs* but, shedding her husband and son, becomes a perfected yogini who can move about at will."[53] Although men as well as women have been counted among Chinnamastā's votaries over the centuries, this passage speaks to the possibility that her practice, too, has a distinctive significance for women.

The motif of self-decapitation associated with Chinnamuṇḍā invites comparison with the Tibetan practice of Chöd. Both entail a visualization in which one uses one's own dissevered body to feed and nourish others. In Chöd practice, the meditator envisions himself or herself as Vajrayoginī and proceeds to dissect, cook, and serve his or her entire body to a host of hungry, bloodthirsting spirits. Whereas Chinnamuṇḍā is envisioned in a cremation ground, Chöd is actually performed in that fearsome setting. Just as Chinnamuṇḍā encompasses the offerer, offering, and recipient, Chöd texts underscore the unity of the giver, gift, and receiver. In both practices the act of self-sacrifice, although envisioned differently, is a method for overcoming the illusion of separate selfhood and cultivating nondual wisdom.[54] The practice of Chöd, like that of Chinnamuṇḍā, was introduced by a woman, Machig Labdron. The importance of Chöd in contemporary Tibetan Buddhism and the virtual disappearance of Chinnamuṇḍā practice raise an interesting but perhaps unanswerable question of whether the Chöd visualization presently occupies the same niche, psychologically-cum-religiously, once filled by Chinnamuṇḍā.

The Paradox of Enlightenment

The bodily manifestation of every Buddha reveals profound truths about the supreme state of liberation. Chinnamuṇḍā's complex image operates on several symbolic levels. The reference to esoteric inner yogic visualizations would be relevant for those pursuing these advanced techniques. Her image also conveys a deeper truth, however, at the very heart of the mystery of ultimate liberation. Chinnamuṇḍā brims with vitality in a scene of death and destruction, confronting the viewer with the most seemingly irreducible opposition in human experience, the polarity of life and death. Dancing blissfully amidst the cremation flames, she proclaims that death is essential to transformation. Death is to be understood not as the decease of the physical body but rather the demise of the illusion of separate, egoic existence and passage into a greater reality that lies beyond and yet within the self. Seeing her image may empower others to cross the ultimate threshold and join her on the other side.

In Tantric soteriology, the realization beyond the death of the self is Buddhahood, the state of consummate happiness and universal awareness, attended by an ability to awaken others to their own inner freedom and capacity for liberation. This state of spiritual perfection is modeled by the severed-headed female Buddha, who feeds herself and others with her own vital essence. Herein we discover the ultimate significance of Chinnamuṇḍā's shocking iconography. As she takes her triumphal stand amid the cremation flames, her body flows with the elixir of eternal life—the nondual wisdom of Buddhahood, the ultimate form of nourishment in the universe.

CHAPTER 21

SIṂHAMUKHĀ

Lion-Faced Female Buddha

Homage to you, Siṃhamukhā!
Your lion face is shocking and black as a storm cloud;
You strike terror with your bared teeth shining, tongue lashing, and glare so violent
As you wield a knife and skull cup in the midst of your dance;
I praise and revere the one who burns with fiery wisdom.

Wearing dry skulls, snakes, and a tiger skin around your waist,
Draped with bone ornaments, with a complete retinue of enlightened females,
Gleeful executioner of all obstructers and destroyers,
I praise and honor the one who holds fast to the fortunate.

Your raging body terrifies the host of detractors;
Your shout, HŪṂ! PHAṬ! KILL! DESTROY! terrifies from afar;
Your diamondlike mind penetrates ultimate reality.
I praise and render homage to you, powerful ḍākinī!

—Sakya ritual prayer[1]

The female Buddha Siṃhamukhā (pronounced *SEEM hah MOO KAH*) has the face of a lioness and the body of a woman. Her leonine visage shines with the startling awakeness of enlightened awareness. Her mouth is drawn in a perpetual roar of untamable fury and exultant laughter. Her vibrant body surges with waves of pure, primal power. Siṃhamukhā manifests the elemental vitality of a lioness on the prowl or racing toward her prey. She embodies a torrent of energy that is unstoppable by any external force and can level anything in its path. Her fiery, feral persona conveys the intensity required of those who would experience ultimate reality. Her supernal rage is not a selfish drive to protect or destroy but rather a ruthless intolerance of anything that would block the flow

21.1 Siṃhamukhā, Tibet, late sixteenth century. Bronze, painted with cold gold and colored pigments, height 8.25 in. (21 cm). The State Hermitage, Leningrad, Prince Ukhtomsky Collection. Photo copyright John Bigelow Taylor. *Siṃhamukhā and her attendants, Tiger Face and Bear Face, form a feral female trinity.*

of spiritual growth and awakening. The lion-faced female Buddha is accompanied by two attendants with animal heads (Fig. 21.1), proclaiming that she communes with every living being and is kin to all that is sovereign, wild, and free.

Embodiment of Nondual Wisdom and Supreme Bliss

Siṃhamukhā, whose name means "Lion-Faced Lady,"[2] is a fully enlightened being. She has attained Buddhahood, the state of ultimate wisdom and supreme bliss. Her mind flows in a pure, nonconceptual stream, free from distortion and conceptual overlay. Thus, she is said to be a "wisdom ḍākinī," "wisdom-bestowing female," "great victorious mother," "female who delights in highest knowledge," and "enlightened being whose nature is primordial wisdom and ultimate reality."[3] Because her mind is completely purified, every experience arising in her mental stream has the quintessential "taste" (*rasa*) of supernal joy, and she enjoys a continuous flow of "spontaneously arising supreme bliss."[4] Her bliss is spontaneous because it is not dependent on external objects; it is supreme because it can never be diminished or destroyed. It is the primordial nature of the mind, an intrinsic quality of being that naturally arises when all the attachments that cause suffering have been severed.

One who has attained this realization is said to dwell in the realm of bliss. This "realm" is not an otherworldly paradise or afterlife destination, but rather the very world we live in, experienced with enlightened awareness. In Tantric parlance, the world itself becomes a mandala mansion—a palatial abode of shimmering perfection—for one who beholds it with pure vision. Siṃhamukhā's joyous demeanor and zestful dance bespeak this sublime enjoyment. Because her mind dwells in absolute freedom and her experiential stream is a river of bliss, her mode of being in the world is one of transcendent playfulness:

> In the center of an ocean of blood and fat
> Is the spontaneously wise ḍākinī,
> Playfully dancing amidst appearances and emptiness,
> Here in her pure mansion, the world of ordinary appearances.[5]

Even her choice of a lion's head expresses this humorous delight, for her bodily form is her artistic medium, to be shaped at will as she molds phenomenal reality to create astonishing, liberating illusions.

Although enlightenment is the same nondual, transcendent state for everyone who attains it, the expression of enlightenment has a creative dimension, for different beings will manifest it in varying ways and adopt novel bodily forms in order to reveal differing facets of supreme state. Numerous images and methods are required to liberate the diverse beings who inhabit the universe, with their varying temperaments and spiritual capacities. Therefore, although Siṃhamukhā dwells in the ultimate sphere of nondual reality, "she created a body out of love and compassion" to lead others to liberation.[6] The following passage from a Sakya liturgy emphasizes the concomitantly noumenal and phenomenal aspects of her divine embodiment:

> Your nature is spontaneously arising supreme bliss, (but)
> In order to guide heroes and ḍākinīs,
> You arise wondrously, playing,
> Your mind free from the clouds of conceptual elaboration;
> You are like a magical illusion that appears but doesn't exist.[7]

Because Siṃhamukhā has attained nondual wisdom, she is attached neither to form nor to formlessness. She dances in the visionary realm of magical fluidity that opens in the space between appearances and emptiness. Thus, while her mind "sports in the expanse of ultimate reality,"[8] she manifests in a divine body in order to transform sentient beings and to be for them a "source of Buddhahood,"[9] through a process of meditative identification with her that leads to the ultimate goal she herself has attained.

Goddess of Transcendent Anger

The practice of Siṃhamukhā is predicated on the Tantric principle that the emotions are irreducible aspects of the psyche. In the Tantric view, enlightenment is not a passionless state, devoid of mental and emotional content, for it is impossible to sustain a condition wherein thoughts and feelings do not occur.[10] Rather than striving to eliminate them, a practitioner on the Tantric path seeks to remove the attendant suffering by learning to observe each emotion as it arises and to refrain from adding conceptual overlay. Regardless of how agonizing an emotion may be, it is possible to achieve clarity in its midst, pinpoint the attachment that is causing the pain, and deconstruct the illusions fueling the attachment. For one who successfully practices this art, the emotion, formerly viewed as solid and unavoidably painful, dissolves into a luminous dance of energy. This process leads beyond such superficial and trivially distracting emotions as resentment, boredom, sadness, loneliness, impatience, guilt, and shame to the primal passions blazing at the core of the psyche, such as anger, lust, and envy. When the suffering associated with ego attachment is eliminated, the practitioner can tap the emotions as a source of energy for meditative transformation.

Tantric practice is recommended for those with an intensely passionate nature, because such persons have plentiful emotional energy at their command.

Meditation on Siṃhamukhā is especially appropriate for those with abundant anger, for she represents the enlightened essence of that incendiary energy. She primarily symbolizes the transformation of anger from a source of suffering into the clarity of mirrorlike wisdom. She exhibits the quality of anger in its ultimate purity; her "consciousness has been transformed into pure anger."[11]

The term that is translated here as "anger" (*dveśa* or *krodha*; Tib. *zhe-sdang*) encompasses hatred, aggression, and the drive to destroy something that is perceived as a threat or constraint. This propensity, although motivated by a desire to alleviate suffering, generally leads to behavior that intensifies misery for self and others. When the delusory elements have been removed, however, the result is "pure anger," or "transcendent anger," devoid of neurotic attachments and reaction patterns. Anger then becomes a potent resource, an energy source of tremendous magnitude, sufficient to overcome mental, emotional, and psychic obstacles to enlightenment.

Visualization and Inner Yoga

The practice of Siṃhamukhā centers on deity yoga (*deva-yoga*), a methodology common to all Highest Yoga Tantric deities. The initial stage involves developing a clear mental image of the goddess. The visualization of the deity is created from an intensely concentrated kernel of light. Paintings and statues may serve as points of reference, and meditation manuals delineate the deity's iconographic attributes to guide the process. A practitioner repeats the visualization until a vivid and detailed image emerges and the goddess herself appears, translucent, sparkling, and vibrant. Ultimately, a dynamic, three-dimensional, and sensorially rich experience of the deity becomes possible for one who masters the practice.

The meditator then envisions himself or herself as the deity, with the same appearance, ornaments, and divine qualities, as a means of awakening his or her indwelling Buddha nature. In this process, known as the "generation stage" (*utpatti-krama*) of imagining oneself as a deity, the practitioner first dissolves his or her physical body into light particles and disperses the light into empty space, breaking attachment to the physical body and the conventional reality it inhabits. When identifying with Siṃhamukhā, the meditator must detach not only from his or her ordinary body but also from the desire to possess a human form. Shedding one's former identity and donning a divine body in its place is a way to enter the experiential sphere of the deity, which consists not of solid objects but of luminous, flowing, interconnected energy patterns.

In a yet deeper level of the practice, known as the "perfection stage" (*utpanna-krama*), or yoga of the "veins and winds" (Tib. *rtsa-rlung*), the meditator proceeds from visualizing himself or herself as having the outward appearance of the deity to having the deity's internal yogic anatomy. This involves the visualization of a network of subtle veins, or nerves (*nāḍī*), that carry the life force (*prāṇa*). The goal of this yoga is to concentrate energy in the central channel (*avadhūtī*) that traverses the body vertically and to fan a yogic fire in the abdomen that will consume all karmic impurities and dualistic clinging.[12] Siṃhamukhā herself embodies this attainment, for her "totally pure body blazes with the heat of yogic fire."[13] The final stage of the process is to merge with the enlightened mind essence of the deity, to experience the complete fruition of bliss and emptiness. Thus, the successful completion of Siṃhamukhā's yoga is the attainment of Buddhahood.

All Tibetan sects include the practice of Siṃhamukhā in their advanced Tantric curriculum, both as a Highest Yoga Tantra meditational deity and as a protector, a being whose energies may be directed against obstacles on the path. Her protection may be invoked by ritual means, but one who would work with her subjugational powers in this way must first become adept at her visualization and yoga.[14]

Divine Forms and Mandalas

The form in which Siṃhamukhā is envisioned is quite consistent among the Tibetan practice lineages. Her dancing stance, ornaments, and implements remain the same, although her bodily hue varies. Her prevalent epiphany is dark blue with a white face (Pl. 15).[15] Blue befits her as the color associated with anger and its transformation into stable wisdom and mirrorlike clarity in Tantric symbology.

The following song of praise, from a Sakya meditation manual, offers both iconographic description and poetic evocation of the blue hierophany:

> Your body rises like a dark-blue mountain,
> Your lion face glows like moon-crystal,
> Your tongue is the vermilion hue of the dawn sky
> Amidst the light-garland of your terrifying fangs.
> Your laughter resounds from afar: HŪṂ! PHAṬ! PHEṂ!
> Your black iron hair hangs down,
> Your bone ornaments tinkle musically,
> You dance wondrously, in a heroic mood.
>
> Terrifying female of intensely burning wrath,
> With a sharp copper knife in your right hand . . .
> And a skull bowl in your left,

Supping the heart-blood of the worst evildoers,
You are a female who delights in highest knowledge;
Your favorite consort is supremely blissful Heruka,
Embraced in the form of a mystical staff.[16]

Siṃhamukhā displays many of the attributes common to wrathful deities, such as an angry visage, tiger-skin skirt, and bone ornaments. Her dancing pose, curved knife, and skull bowl are characteristic of female Tantric Buddhas.

On one level of interpretation, these accoutrements connote overcoming negativity. Following this line of analysis, Siṃhamukhā dances in triumph on negative forces and opposition she has overcome, personified by the prostrate corpse beneath her feet. Her knife "shatters the hearts and heads of those with horrible karma," sending them quickly to a higher state, and from her skull bowl she drinks "the heart-blood of the worst evildoers."[17] Her roaring laughter terrifies and repels those who approach to do harm.

On a deeper level of significance, her ḍākinī attributes allude to her attainment of bliss and wisdom. She brandishes her knife to cut off dualistic thinking at the root, while she raises her skull cup to drink deeply of the nectar of supreme bliss. Her laughter proclaims her victorious joy as she dances on the corpse of ego. She is encircled by the purifying flames of wisdom that incinerate all falsehood and illusion. Her mystical staff (*khaṭvāṅga*) signifies the traversal of all the stages leading to Buddhahood and also betokens that she is not celibate. At times she enjoys a consort, a male Buddha who is equal in attainment to herself and is, like her, "supremely blissful" yet appears in wrathful guise. Siṃhamukhā is envisioned in a cremation ground and is specifically associated with So-sa-gling cremation ground in Uḍḍiyāna, a major Tantric center.[18] The charnel field accords with her fearsome nature and may refer to the setting in which her practice was originally, and is ideally, undertaken.

Siṃhamukhā may be attended by a pair of theriomorphic females named Vyāghravaktrā ("Tiger Face") and Ṛkṣavaktrā ("Bear Face").[19] It is not surprising to find divine ḍākinīs with the heads of wild, fearsome creatures serving as her companions and emissaries, joining in her mission to destroy egoic forces and beings who would harm and place obstacles in the path of Dharma practitioners. One finds painted portrayals of the triad (Pl. 15) as well as ambitious, multicast sculptural renditions (see Fig. 21.1).

Siṃhamukhā also appears as red in color.[20] Red has multiple resonances in Tantric symbolism, connoting compassion as well as powers of attraction and conquest. Thus, Red Siṃhamukhā is less overtly wrathful in persona. A Sakya work describes her as "cheerful in demeanor, happy . . . with cheerful smile," as she reveals the path to liberation, but nonetheless as "roaring fierce mantras" and "doing fierce deeds protecting the Buddha's doctrine, diligent in averting obstructions to practice."[21]

The simplest mandala consists of five lion-faced goddesses in the colors of the five Buddha-wisdoms. Blue Siṃhamukhā in the center is surrounded by white, yellow, red, and green emanations, representing the totality of realizations constituting Buddhahood.[22] A Sakya meditation manual assigns each of the retinue deities with performing one of the four modes of enlightened activity: the white goddess in the east pacifies all illness and disease-inciting demons, the yellow one in the south increases life and merit, the red one in the west subjugates and overpowers, and the green one in the north destroys enemies and obstacles.[23]

A more elaborate mandala, introduced by the Nyingma yogini Ayu Khandro, consists of twenty-five female divinities. Blue Siṃhamukhā in the center is encircled by four lion-faced goddesses in the colors of their respective Buddha-wisdoms (white, yellow, red, and green). The next tier of the retinue contains sixteen fierce goddesses, eight with human faces and eight with the faces of a lion, tiger, hyena, wolf, vulture, crane, raven, and owl. The four gate guardianesses are white with a cuckoo head, yellow with a goat head, maroon with a lion head, and green with the head of a snake.[24] The fearsome females of Siṃhamukhā's entourage display and feast on charnel remains—blood, skin, entrails, hearts, and entire corpses—while dancing with abandon amid cremation flames on mats of human skin. Their gruesome attributes and diet betoken the obliteration of karma, mental obscurations, and emotional impurities, while their affinity for the burning ground signals the conflagration of ego in their enlightening company.

Siṃhamukhā's most distinctive iconographic attribute is her lion head. She is not, however, the only lion-headed goddess in the Tantric Buddhist pantheon. Goddesses of leonine visage appear in the trains of Siṃhamukhā, Palden Lhamo, and Gurgi Gonpo and in the mandala retinues of Nairātmyā, Kurukullā, and Jñānaḍākinī.[25] They are generally designated as Siṃhinī (Seng-ge-mo), Siṃhavaktrā, or Siṃhāsyā. These worldly, albeit supernaturally gifted beings, variously designated as *ma-mos* or "worldly ḍākinīs" (*jig-rten-pa'i mkha'-'gro-ma*), help carry out the activities of their leader and are not to be confused with Siṃhamukhā, a fully enlightened being. The ancillary lion-headed females exert a protective influence at the perimeter of the sacred space and represent psychological insights that must be mastered at the point of passage into the sphere of enlightened awareness. In contrast, Siṃhamukhā occupies the center of the mandala as its sovereign and personifies the ultimate realizations at the culmination of the spiritual journey.

Roots in Ritual Dance and Shamanic Trance

The concept of a goddess with a lion head is not unique to Buddhism, nor is her retinue of animal-headed divine females. The other contexts in which such figures occur may represent currents of Indian culture that fed into Vajrayāna iconography and practice. The most direct parallel is found in a strand of Hindu Tantra whose pantheons are cast in stone in several ninth- to eleventh-century yogini temples in Orissa and Madhya Pradesh. These architecturally unique monuments are characterized by a round, roofless construction with an unadorned exterior. Worshippers pass through a small doorway into an open-air sanctuary. The circular inner wall is divided into niches that frame carved reliefs of dancing yoginis with animal heads and other zoomorphic features. The animals represented include lionesses (Fig. 21.2), tigresses, she-bears, boars, snakes, and many varieties of birds.[26] These divine yoginis constitute the mandala retinue of Kālī and Bhairava in Kaula Tantric iconography.[27]

The remote settings of these temples, in jungles and on hilltops, accords with the secret nature of the practices apparently performed there. Kaula texts describe nocturnal rites in which participants partake of wine, meat, and other sacramental substances to induce a visionary state in which the awesome yoginis can be encountered directly. The female divinities (variously termed *yoginī*, *mātṛkā*, and *ḍākinī*) are invoked by mantra recitation and bodied forth by human women, who dance in an ecstatic state of trance-identification with the animal-headed yoginis. The protean yoginis undergo transfiguration before all present, taking on the appearance and movements of their divine counterparts.[28] As such a scene is described in a Kaula text, the enraptured women, ornamented as deities, flushed by dancing, and glowing with heightened awareness, could then receive worship, bestow blessings, and confer magical powers.[29]

Buddhist Tantrics held concourse with such groups, and there was considerable mutual influence among them. The motif of the lion-headed goddess, found in the company of other animal-headed females, was probably adopted into Buddhism from the Hindu tradition, which has a longer history of theriomorphic deities. It is possible that rituals and dances of ecstatic communion centering on the divine yoginis, akin to the Kaula practices, were current in Buddhist circles as well, for all the component elements were present. Buddhist Tantrics held similar feasts in cremation grounds and engaged in ritual worship of women as embodiments of divine yoginis.[30] Sacred dance figured in deity yoga, sacramental feasts (*gaṇa-cakra*), and ritual mandala enactments. In the latter practice, as described in Tantric literature, yoga practitioners donned ritual regalia, sat in the configuration of the mandala they were enacting, and

21.2 Divine Yogini, Hirapur, Puri District, Orissa, India, tenth century. Gray chlorite, height ca. 24 in. (61 cm). Photo: Archaeological Survey of India. *The lion-headed divine yogini recurs in the pantheon of Hindu Kaula Tantra.*

performed dance and song in order to body forth the deities of the mandala. In the classical pattern reflected in Tantric texts and still observed by Newar Buddhists in Nepal, men enact the part of male deities and women take the role of female deities.[31]

If Siṃhamukhā's mandala were ritually staged in this way, women would most naturally embody the deities of her all-female mandala. Such a scenario is not inconceivable, for female Tantrics gathered in cremation grounds and wilderness areas and assembled in a circle to engage in sacramental feasting and other yogic practices. Yogis who gained admittance to one of these yogini circles (*yoginī-cakra*) might attain initiation from and also worship the women.[32] Since all the constituent practices were present in Tantric Buddhism, Siṃhamukhā's mandala may have been ritually enacted in this way, with women mediating the presence of the animal-headed yoginis, just as they did in Kaula sects. Direct evidence of this is lacking, however, for the early forms of Siṃhamukhā practice in India are not well documented.[33]

Siṃhamukhā and the lion-headed yoginis of the Kaula pantheon in turn evince continuities with an even deeper stratum of Indian culture. One of India's earliest bodies of religious imagery, found on the carved steatite seals produced at the height of the Indus civilization (ca. 2600–1900 B.C.E.), includes an image of a woman positioned between a tree and a tiger in a dynamic pose suggestive of a dance movement (Fig. 21.3). The woman has undergone a zoomorphic transformation in which her hands have metamorphosed into claws, her feet have become hooves or claws, and she has sprouted a tail and horns. The woman's posture echoes the arch of the tiger's body as it rises on its hind legs in a position parallel to her own. One of the woman's clawlike hands rests on the shoulder of the tiger, which rotates its head to face her.

The religious practice portrayed on this protohistorical seal appears to fall broadly into the category of shamanic trance, in which the woman, acting perhaps as priestess or trance medium, has dissociated from her human status and is communing with and taking on the traits of a wild feline. The purpose of her sacred dance could be to channel elemental forces for healing or oracular work, to provide an object of worship in her altered state, or to gain the heightened awareness and powers of the trance itself. Regardless of its specific objective, which remains conjectural, the exercise clearly involves a woman and a wild feline communing and identifying with one another and possibly dancing together, the woman's zoomorphic transformation, and the implication that this practice confers special powers on her.

The presence of such an image in India's earliest religious iconography suggests that Siṃhamukhā, the female Buddha with a lion's face, represents the culmination of a long journey of this motif from an archaic shamanic context into the

21.3 Seal, Mohenjo-Daro, Pakistan, Mature Harappā period, ca. 2600–1900 B.C.E. Steatite, height ca. .8–1.5 in. (2–4 cm). National Museum, New Delhi. Used by permission. Photo: The Huntington Archive, The Ohio State University. *This protohistorical seal may portray a shamanic trance, as woman and wild feline commune and possibly dance with one another.*

more formally ritualistic and contemplative setting of Tantric Buddhism. What remained intact in the course of the migration was the theme of a woman acquiring feline traits as an expression of her heightened awareness, her ability to channel elemental powers and undergo bodily transformation, and her acquisition thereby of a numinous quality and divine status. As the lion-faced goddess surfaced in the Buddhist context, however, she lost some of the associations she carried in other settings and acquired new doctrinal significance, while the dynamic trance and ecstatic dance methodologies were largely replaced by internal visualizations and more sedate rituals performed by seated hierophants.

Buddhist Significance of the Lion

In Indus religiosity, it seems likely that identification with the animal was seen as the source of the knowledge, experience, or power that was sought. In the Buddhist context, however, the lion is primarily metaphorical in import. The purpose of Siṃhamukhā's bodily form, as a female Buddha, is to manifest the state of full enlightenment. With this in view, her lion face is not as radical a departure from tradition as it may seem.

The lion has a long-standing association with Buddhahood that dates to the earliest layers of the tradition. The aristocratic lineage into which the historical Buddha was born was the Śākya clan, whose insignia was the lion. The lion, too, was a favored symbol for the character of the Buddha. For example, before enlightenment, the sage faced the demonic hordes of Māra "like a lion, without distress or fear, terror or weakness, without dejection, without confusion, without agitation, without dread."[34] After his attainment of enlightenment, the Buddha's proclamations of truth were likened to a "lion's roar" (*siṃha-nāda*). The lion often appears as one of the emblems on his throne, which is known as the "lion seat" (*siṃha-āsana*). Having a jaw like a lion (*siṃha-hanu*) is one of the Buddha's thirty-two marks of perfection. His effortless activity of liberating beings is likened to "lion's play" (*siṃha-vikrīḍita*) and a "lion's yawn" (*siṃha-vijṛmbhita*). The posture that the Buddha adopted on his deathbed, lying on his right side for his final meditation, is termed the "lion's repose" (*siṃha-śayyā*).[35]

Many traits recommend this majestic creature as a symbol for the supreme spiritual state. The regal lion reigns supreme in the forest, just as a Buddha is sovereign in the world. A lion sustains a one-pointed focus and sensory alertness suggestive of the immediacy of enlightened awareness. The lion, by virtue of its wild, undomesticated nature, roams beyond the bounds of human structures and restrictions, just as enlightenment represents an unfettered mode of being that transcends all humanly constructed and hence artificial distinctions, whether cultural, conceptual, linguistic, or psychological. The behavior of a lion, and indeed of any wild creature, is unpremeditated and instinctive. This spontaneity is consonant with the Buddhist view that the highest mode of enlightened activity is a direct response to every situation as it arises, unencumbered by the preconceptions, self-projections, and arbitrary moral principles that cloud the ability to perceive clearly and respond skillfully.

The wildness of the lion also has a positive connotation in the Tantric context, for the ideal lifestyle of Tantric practitioners is one of radical freedom from social conventions, akin to a lion roving free and untamed. A lion may be held in captivity but can never be fully domesticated or rendered subservient to any purposes other than its own. This accords with the ferocious intensity and undeterrable focus of purpose required of those who would traverse the Tantric path, which demands intensive training and practice and an unwillingness to subordinate one's spiritual aspirations to any lesser goal.

The lion's fearlessness is another trait valued in the Tantric ethos, which insists on an unflinching confrontation of every aspect of the psyche and all that threatens to be painful, repulsive, or terrifying.[36] The regal comportment and self-possession of a lion suggest the leonine sense of pride that must be cultivated on the Tantric path. The lioness is known to be more ferocious and starkly predatory than the male of the species, so Siṃhamukhā's female gender may denote the presence of these qualities to a superlative degree.

Clearly, the magnificent lion, whose visage Siṃhamukhā shares, serves as an evocative symbol of many ideals of the Tantric path and the sovereign state of Buddhahood to which it leads, reinforced by the lion's significance in Indic culture as a symbol of excellence of every kind. The symbolic resonances evoked by the lion-faced female Buddha were enriched by a well-established association of the lion with Shakyamuni in particular and enlightenment in general, as well as by ecstatic practices centering on animal-headed yoginis in other religious systems.

The result of this rich nexus of associations is a dramatic image of Buddhahood in female form. Her persona integrates the brute strength and natural ferocity of the lion with the consummate refinement of a supremely wise and blissful being, conveying the paradox at the heart of "pure anger," that is, the supernal rage of one who has sublimated the instinct for self-preservation. Siṃhamukhā's leonine face and dancing body personify a mode of being undiluted by self-centered anger. Ignited by the incandescent blaze of transcendent fury, grounded in emotional self-mastery, she revels in the ultimate form of power: the ability to liberate oneself and others.

CHAPTER 22

KURUKULLĀ

Red Enchantress with Flowered Bow

HRĪḤ!
From the expanse of ultimate reality,
Your supremely blissful body emerges,
The color of love and passion,
Resplendent as a dazzling lotus . . .

Your compassion is boundless and unchangeable;
Your four arms brandish a hook that summons,
Noose that flings to the unexcelled realm, and
Bow and arrow of wisdom and artful liberation.
Praises to you, beautiful goddess!

—Nyingma ritual prayer[1]

Kurukullā (pronounced *koo roo koo LAH*) is a goddess with unlimited powers of enchantment. Her voluptuous body is bright, glowing red, the hue of passion and amorous desire. Glistening with ruby radiance, mistress of the art of seduction, Kurukullā displays the tools of her magical craft: the flowered bow and arrow with which she pierces the hearts of those she would enchant, the noose with which she binds them, and the elephant goad with which she draws them into her sphere of liberation. Kurukullā's weaponry is adorned with red lotus blossoms that send forth swarms of fierce red bees. The targets of her magic do not feel suffering. They are intoxicated by the fragrance of the lotuses, mesmerized by the buzzing of the bees, and bewildered by crimson clouds of rapture. Thus enraptured, they are susceptible to Kurukullā's transcendent sorcery. A reprobate can be won over to a life of religious aspiration; a reluctant object of desire can become an ardent lover; a wealthy person can become a patron; an enemy can become a friend. Kurukullā's magic has the power to soften the hardest heart, dissolve disharmony, and bestow the highest bliss.

Kurukullā's status in the Buddhist pantheon rose over time. She was introduced as a dhāraṇī goddess who presides over rites of love magic, subjugation, and bewitchment (*vaśīkaraṇa*). These rituals belong to the incantational and ceremonial strand of Mahayana practice later classed in the Action Tantra category. However, Kurukullā was eventually elevated to the level of a fully enlightened being, a female Buddha. As such, she also figures as a meditational deity in the highest and most esoteric division of Tantric practices, the Highest Yoga Tantra class, whose goal is the attainment of Buddhahood in the present lifetime.[2] In this status, she is a "female Tathāgata" (*de-bzhin gshegs-ma*), a primordial mother, the equal of Samantabhadrī and Vajravārāhī.[3]

Origin Account

Kurukullā represents the absorption into Buddhism of a popular genre of pan-Indian love magic. The following origin account reflects this derivation. The story opens with the dilemma of a senior queen who had lost the affections of her husband. The king had ceased to visit her quarters in the palace, so the lovelorn queen sent her maidservant into the marketplace in search of a magical elixir to reawaken his ardor. In the market, a woman with a reddish cast to her skin gave the servant some food over which mantras had been pronounced and instructed that it should be given to the person whose attentions were sought. The queen decided that the lowly repast would not be suitable for the king and disposed of it in a nearby lake. A serpent king ingested it and became enamored of the queen. Drawn to her bed by the power of the mantra, they enjoyed union and she became pregnant.

The ruler intended to punish his wife, knowing that the child could not be his. When the queen explained what had transpired, however, the king instead sent for the woman from the bazaar. When the red sorceress was brought into his presence, the king immediately recognized her to be an extraordinary personage. He bowed before her and requested her blessings. She taught him the mantra of Kurukullā, by which the king attained supernatural powers and earned the Dharma name Sahajavajra.[4]

Although the Buddhist account reveals the miracle-working heroine to be an emanation (*nirmāṇa-kāya*) of Kurukullā, the narrative clearly links her practice to a popular tradition of love potions and magical spells that were (and still are) dispensed by local folk practitioners who might be found in marketplaces and village squares and who need no credentials beyond their charisma and reputation. This form of sorcery has ancient roots in India's past. The *Atharva Veda*, a first-millennium B.C.E. compendium of ritual arts, anthologizes many recitations and rites of love magic, including an incantation to pierce the heart of a chosen lover with an arrow, arousing the heat of desire and passionate love.[5] There are different spells for men and women, indicating that this brand of sympathetic magic was the preserve of both genders and that each had its own methods for winning its objects of desire.[6]

Magical Subjugation as a Buddhist Art

The interests originally served by Kurukullā are admittedly doctrinally alien to Buddhism, with its emphasis on cultivating detachment and freedom from desire. Moreover, Buddhists could not fail to notice that the coercive rites of Kurukullā merit little justification in their ethical system. However, her magical offices were integral to the imaginal, mythic world that Indian Buddhists inhabited. Therefore, the incorporation of a figure such as Kurukullā was a natural development, yet it was also inevitable that her roles should be refined and redefined over time to align them more directly with Buddhist soteriology.

As Kurukullā rose in the pantheon, her sphere of influence expanded from the compulsion of love objects to the conquest of conceptual thought, Buddhist teachings, and primordial awareness itself. Surprising, then, is that the goddess never completely shed her original function and continued to preside over unvarnished rites of subjugation that, in Stephan Beyer's words, go "beyond defense into the darker realms of offense" and would surely be condemned in a non-Buddhist context.[7] That her rites have potential to harm is offset by the Mahayana desideratum of compassionate motivation and the meditative and ethical training required to command her energies. Currently, both dimensions of Kurukullā's character are integrated in her vocation as a female Buddha whose power of enchantment is her special art of liberation.[8]

Because Kurukullā is a fully enlightened being, there is no limit to her mastery. She is known as Wangdukyi Lhamo ("Overpowering Goddess") and as Trailokyavaśakāriṇī ("Subjugator of the Three Realms"), expressing her dominion over all that is below, on, and above the earth. At the most worldly end of the spectrum, where her rituals are continuous with the Indian folk magic in which they find their roots, she holds sway over humans, spirit beings, gods, rulers, countries, food, clothing, wealth, and fame. With the requisite number of mantra recitations—as few as one hundred or as many as one million—her noose can be made to rein in all beings, realms, and treasures of worldly existence.[9] Based on his fieldwork in Tibetan communities, Stephan Beyer reports that Kurukullā is often invoked to remove human and demonic obstacles to new ventures and building projects and by traders, students, and hopeful lovers seeking success.[10]

Although all of these benefits may be pursued for personal gain, they can also be sought with higher goals in mind. Most notably, Kurukullā's powers of attraction may be invoked by a religious teacher who wishes to enhance his or her ability to teach the Dharma and to create a setting—whether a small retreat center or large monastic university—where others can pursue spiritual training. A Nyingma text advises a practitioner with this aim to call on Kurukullā for the necessary instruction, swift understanding, retentive memory, teaching skill, victory in disputation, numerous disciples, materials for offerings and sacramental feasts, artfulness in liberative activities, and supernatural powers and signs of yogic accomplishment to inspire faith in others.[11] It was with this intention that the Fifth Dalai Lama meditated on Kurukullā during his dying hours, as he prayed to magnify his religious influence and accomplishments in his next life. He passed away with her mantra on his lips and her vision before him, assured of the fulfillment of his aspiration.[12]

Ultimately, Kurukullā's powers can be directed to the highest goal envisioned by the Buddhist tradition, namely, the transformation of consciousness. Thus, Kurukullā may be chosen as a meditation deity (*yi-dam*) by an advanced meditator who seeks to master all phenomena, thoughts, and perceptions; his or her own body, speech, and mind; and supreme peace, ultimate reality, and primordial awareness.[13] The final goal to be won through the practice of Kurukullā is enlightenment itself. At this most spiritual end of the spectrum, Kurukullā accomplishes the ultimate form of magic, the transformation of conventional awareness into the transcendent bliss and nondual wisdom of a fully enlightened Buddha.

Divine Forms and Symbolic Attributes

Kurukullā's iconography, as befits the mistress of enchantment, emphasizes the theme of passion. Her characteristic color is red, signifying her ardent nature, for red is associated with passion in Indian culture. The Sanskrit word for red (*rāga*) also denotes inflammation and feelings of attachment, love, and desire.[14] Red predominates in her iconography as the favored color of her aureole, silken garments, lotus pedestal, handheld lotus, floral adornments, and divine entourage. Her implements, moreover, are trimmed with red lotuses.[15] The lotus is associated with female sexuality and symbolizes, among other things, the female genitalia. The abundance of red lotuses in Kurukullā's iconography signifies her ability to arouse passion and her own possession of that quality in refined form. As one text explains, "the incomparable red lotus in her left hand, peerless and graceful, is the very seat of passion."[16]

Kurukullā's mood, as reflected in her facial expression (Pl. 16), is generally characterized as the "amorous sentiment," for hers is the "essence of sweet desire."[17] Her countenance should convey that she is "overwhelmed by desire" and has a "passionate heart," but she is also said to be loving as well as ardorous, for compassion and passion both stem from a deep capacity for sympathy and attachment.[18] This emotional quality can blossom into an impersonal yet devoted affection that anchors an enlightened being in the phenomenal realm, among those who still suffer, to serve their needs with tenderness, empathy, and fervent commitment. Thus, a divinity who is free from personal desire may nonetheless be said to be "attached" to living beings, that is, devoted to their welfare.

Kurukullā's implements reflect her roles in both ritual subjugation and meditative transformation. Her bow and arrow, appropriate implements for a goddess of enchantment, are used to pierce the hearts of the targets of her magic. The arrow moreover has a long-standing association with the infliction of lust. The *Atharva Veda* speaks of "arrows of desire."[19] In Buddhist lore, the demon king Māra sought to impassion Shakyamuni with flower-tipped arrows of desire in order to disrupt his meditation.[20] Thus, this classical weapon of emotional ensnarement is artfully wielded by Kurukullā both to captivate and to liberate. She uses her noose, often clasped with a threatening gesture, to snare and hurl and her elephant goad to hook and pull. If the aim is to gain a lover, her arrow inflicts the coveted love object with desire, her noose binds them with passion, and her hook draws the captive to the waiting paramour.[21] In other cases, her arrow inflicts someone who is sought as a friend or devotee with geniality, goodwill, and devotion, in a practice that may be used to win over an adversary, placate someone who is angry, or gain a political or military ally. Even the flowers play a role in her arsenal, for "worldly problems are trampled by the light-rays of her red lotus-missile."[22]

At a subtler level of activity, her implements can effect a change in consciousness, transmuting passion into wisdom. She uses her flowery bow and arrow to penetrate the minds of her targets and subjugate their selfish desire and dualistic thought, the hook to summon them into her blissful presence, and the noose to fling her fortunate captives into a higher realm of consciousness.[23]

Images of Kurukullā fall into two categories. One displays classical Mahayana iconographic traits; the other reflects Tantric interpretations. The Mahayana forms bear a family resemblance to the other dhāraṇī goddesses. In these manifestations, Kurukullā is seated, has a peaceful countenance, wears silken raiment, and is adorned with ornaments made of precious metals, gemstones, and pearls. Her crown, sometimes graced with flowers, may bear the image of Amitābha Buddha or the five Jina Buddhas. The Mahayana forms of Kurukullā may have four, six, or eight arms. In the four-armed versions, her upper pair of hands hold a bow and arrow, her identifying insignia. She is shown in the active

22.1 Kurukullā, Kurkihār, Gaya District, Bihar, India, Pāla period, ca. tenth century. Bronze, height 3 in. (7.5 cm). Patna Museum, 9688. Photo: American Institute of Indian Studies. *Kurukullā wields a bow, arrow, and red aśoka flower as her tools of enchantment.*

pose of shooting the arrow or drawing the arrow from her quiver (Fig. 22.1). Her lower right hand may rest on her knee in the gesture of granting blessings, as illustrated here, or be raised in the gesture of granting freedom from fear. Her left hand grasps the stem of a lotus or red aśoka blossom. She sits in a cross-legged meditation posture atop a solar disc and red lotus. Her lotus pedestal is said to rest on Kāmadeva and Rati, a divine couple that presides over love magic in the Hindu context, although I have not encountered this motif in artistic representations.[24] The four-armed epiphany prevails among extant Indic effigies.[25]

When Kurukullā has six or eight arms, the central pair of hands are typically held in front of her heart, crossed at the wrist with palms outward, displaying a vajra and bell in the gesture of "victory over the three realms" (*trailokyavijaya mudrā*).[26] The eight-armed form of Kurukullā has a mandala retinue of twelve deities. The goddesses in her entourage have Mahayana features, and several—Cundā, Aparājitā, and Ekajaṭā—are drawn from the dhāraṇī pantheon.[27]

Several white manifestations of Kurukullā are attested in the Mahayana grouping.[28] These specialize in the cure of snakebite and poisoning and the subjugation of supernatural nāgas (serpents), a sphere of mastery reflected in the origin story related above, where the Kurukullā mantra asserted magical control over a nāga king.[29] The white forms of the goddess wear eight nāga kings as ornaments, reflecting this specialty. One white epiphany even has the mythical bird Garuḍa, enemy of snakes, as her mount (*tārkṣyāsanā*).[30]

Two lengthy texts devoted to white Kurukullā in the *Sādhanamālā* indicate that this aspect of the goddess garnered considerable interest at one time. These works are replete with magical formulas, herbal recipes, and instructions for preparing amulets to neutralize poison, cure snakebite, and attract nāga maidens. Some of these techniques have little overt Buddhist content, whereas others, such as snakebite poultices, have no discernible religious purport.[31] Just as red Kurukullā provided a pretext for incorporating into Buddhism assorted love spells, white Kurukullā served as an entrée for sundry serpent lore.

In contrast to these lengthy textual treatments of Kurukullā's white forms, few artistic representations have been documented, nor is there much evidence of their inclusion in the active pantheons of Tibet or Nepal.[32] Their specialization was apparently taken over by other deities, such as Tārā, who includes protection from snakes in her extensive resumé. The associated procedures, too, may have been replaced by other propitiatory and medicinal methodologies. Moreover, the white forms lack Kurukullā's most distinctive attributes, the red coloration and flowered bow and arrow that became her hallmarks over time.

Tantric Epiphanies as a Female Buddha

The Tantric epiphanies of Kurukullā were introduced in India and now prevail in Tibet. The Tantric manifestations are red and display the abundance of red

22.2 Kurukullā, Amrit Karmacharya, Patan, Nepal, last decade of twentieth century. Paubhā, detail. Pigment and gold on cloth, 21 × 16.8 in. (53 × 42.7 cm). Author's collection. *Kurukullā in Tantric form is envisioned as a dancing female Buddha bearing her flowery tools of transformation. (See Pl. 16)*

flowers and lotuses seen in her Mahayana iconography, as well as her emblematic bow and arrow. They also exhibit attributes shared with other female Buddhas: a dancing pose, intense or impassioned countenance, upward-flaming hair, tiara of skulls, tiger-skin skirt, garland of severed heads, and ornaments of carved bone (Fig. 22.2, Pl. 16).

The following passage from the *Sādhanamālā* powerfully evokes the Tantric persona of the goddess in a widely practiced four-armed form:

She is the quintessence of sweet eros,
Glorious with the beauty of infinite fiery brilliance,
With full breasts and buttocks,
Terrible with fangs flashing in the light
Shooting from her three, leftward-rolling red eyes.
In her boundlessly brilliant gaping mouth,
Her broad tongue lashes its curling tip.
She is as bright as all fires. . . .
Her body is heavy with the weight of her full buttocks,
Draped with a capacious tiger hide,
With a garland of human heads dripping blood across her chest.
Her swaying bow and arrow, adorned by two large red lotuses,
Are never at rest.
She nurtures the three realms
By dragging them with her terrible goad;
The red lotus in her left hand, graceful and peerless,
Is the very seat of passion.
The skulls atop her fivefold crown
Mock the splendor of the radiance of the brilliant moon.
Her limbs are graced with five bone ornaments,
Holding the essence of the five victorious wisdoms.[33]

The amorous mood and sensuous body befitting a goddess of love are augmented in the Tantric conception by wrathful traits appropriate for the "subjugator of the three realms." The corpse or united couple upon which she dances and the severed heads garlanding her body represent persons, situations, and objects she has conquered, as well as mental states she can help the meditator bring under control. The five-pointed crown and bone jewelry signify her possession of the five transcendent insights of a Buddha: immovable concentration, impartial generosity, universal compassion, unimpeded liberative activity, and the ability to mirror reality without distortion.

The name of this iconographic form, "Kurukullā Originating in Uḍḍiyāna," links it to an important Tantric center.[34] This manifestation is also known as Hevajra-krama ("Hevajra System") Kurukullā, because it finds mention in the *Hevajra Tantra*.[35] The lotus she bears in her lower left hand may have a root that curls into a noose or be replaced by a noose of red or blue lotuses, but this variation reflects slightly different interpretations of the same emblem rather than distinct epiphanies of the goddess. This Tantric form is frequently encountered in Tibetan art and in Newar art produced for Tibetan patrons (see Fig. 22.2).[36] Paintings of Kurukullā may be rendered with gold and black or all golden lines on a vibrant red ground.[37] This dramatic mode of representation, known as the "red" style (*mtshal-thang*, "vermilion ground," or *mtshal-thang gser-bris*, "gold on red"), is not reserved for Kurukullā but offers an ideal medium for portraying the red enchantress.

Tantric hierophanies of Kurukullā include a six-armed manifestation that bears, along with the implements described above, a flaying knife and a skull bowl in the central pair of hands (Fig. 22.3).[38] The cranial cup and ḍākinī knife are characteristic insignia of Tantric ḍākinīs in general and female Buddhas in particular. Together they signify the union of bliss (skull cup) and emptiness (knife) that is the goal of Tantric practice.

Such implements reflect an increasingly Tantric interpretation of Kurukullā and her eventual elevation to the ranks of the Highest Yoga Tantra deities. It was, in fact, inevitable that the curved knife and skull bowl should be added to her iconography, for female Tantric Buddhas rarely appear without them. One might expect that her other implements would have been eliminated and replaced by the traditional Tantric accoutrements, but it is likely that her other weaponry—particularly her flowery bow and arrow—are so essential to her subjugating and enchanting activities that they could not be eliminated without significant redefinition of her modus operandi. Thus, Kurukullā is a rarity among female Buddhas, being one of the few to appear with more than two arms, a feature that in my view records her evolution from a dhāraṇī deity. Her lack of association with a male consort and appearance without the mystical staff (*khaṭvaṅga*) that signifies such a relationship also reflect her distinctive genesis.

Several mandalas are devoted to the Tantric forms of Kurukullā. The simplest in design center on Kurukullā atop a red lotus surrounded by four or eight goddesses identical to herself.[39] The eight retinue figures may alternately be represented by symbolic attributes.[40] There are also fifteen-, seventeen-, and twenty-three-deity versions of her mandala. Apart from the gate guardians, the retinues consist of emanated replicas of Kurukullā that she sends forth to accomplish her purposes.[41] In a notable variation on her fivefold mandala, the four retinue ḍākinīs have the standard directional colors of white, yellow, red, and green and bear a small drum (*ḍamaru*), skull bowl, and mystical staff.[42]

Kāmadeva and Lalitā as Divine Prototypes

Just as the practices of Kurukullā have roots in Indian love magic, her attributes reflect the influence of deities associated with the broader Indic tradition. She

22.3 Kurukullā, Tibet, Late Kadam school, ca. early eighteenth century. Thang-ka, detail. Gouache on silk, 44.5 × 29.5 in. (113 × 75 cm). The Parrish Art Museum, Southampton, N.Y. Photo: The Parrish Art Museum, Southampton, N.Y. *Six-armed Tantric Kurukullā displays a skull bowl and flaying knife in addition to her usual attributes.*

shares several striking similarities with Kāmadeva, the Hindu god of love, who provokes overpowering lust with his flower-tipped arrow and sugarcane bow strung with bees. His epithets include Puṣpadhanvā, "Holder of the Flowered Bow," and Puṣpaśara, or Kusumabāṇa, "Flower-Arrowed God," as well as Kusumāyudha, "Possessor of Flowery Weapons." The association of the floral bow and arrow with a well-known love deity surely figured in their bestowal on the Buddhist "goddess of love." Kāmadeva's bowstring made of bees finds resonance in Kurukullā's arsenal of bees. Interestingly, Kāmadeva, too, is seen as a powerful subjugator, as well as a cupid figure, purveyor of sweet amour. It is telling that several hierophanies of Kurukullā are envisioned as sitting or standing on Kāmadeva, a motif that expresses the superiority of her powers but implicitly recognizes the commonalities between them.

Kurukullā in her four-armed Tantric manifestation bears an intriguing resemblance to Lalitā (a.k.a. Tripurā and Tripurasundarī), the great goddess (Mahādevī) of the Śrīvidyā school of Hindu Tantra. Lalitā is envisioned as red in color, armed with a noose, hook, bow, and arrows, as seen in the following invocation:

> Homage to the one who
> Shines like a thousand rising suns,
> Endowed with four arms,
> Wielding a noose of love
> And flashing goad of anger,
> A sugarcane bow of mind
> And five arrows of the five subtle elements,
> Flooding the universe with her dawn-red splendor,
> With *campaka*, *aśoka*, and *punnāga* flowers
> Adorning her fragrant, shining tresses,
> Whose crown is glorious with rubies . . .
> Who is enchanting, her ears adorned with clusters
> of *kadamba* blossoms.[43]

The striking convergence between Kurukullā and Lalitā in their red coloration, handheld attributes, and floral adornments introduces the possibility that the Tantric iconography of Kurukullā was patterned on that of her Hindu counterpart. Lalitā is a regal, seated figure, akin to Kurukullā in her Mahayana manifestations, whereas the Tantric epiphany of Kurukullā evincing these specific attributes (the noose and goad, along with the bow and arrow) is a dancing ḍākinī. Were the same attributes conferred on Kurukullā in seated form, she would be virtually indistinguishable from Lalitā. Therefore, one wonders whether an assimilation of features of Lalitā, goddess supreme for a significant school of Hindu Tantrics, had a role in Kurukullā's evolution in the Buddhist pantheon. That is, Kurukullā may have been endowed with attributes of Lalitā and at the same time re-envisioned as a dancing Tantric figure in part to introduce a readily apparent difference between the two.

Similarities between the two goddesses do not end there. Like Kurukullā, Lalitā is a captivatingly beautiful goddess, a "universal enchantress" (*sarva-mohinī*) who "brings everyone under her spell" (*aśeṣajana-mohinī*) and "wields dominion over all worlds" (*sarvaloka-vaśaṅkarī*). Lalitā, too, is a goddess of "ruby radiance," the color of passion, who, "overflowing with desire and pleasure" (*kāmakelita-raṅgitā*), embodies the fullness of erotic desire (*śṛṅgāra-rasa-saṃpūrṇā*) and the essence of womanly love (*lolākṣī kāma-rūpiṇī*). Her abode is variously said to be a mountain and a cave.[44] She is a "ḍākinī queen" (*ḍākinīśvarī*) and, most suggestively, has as one of her epithets Kurukullā.[45]

Although Lalitā claims a broad spectrum of qualities, in keeping with her cosmic status, these distinctive titles and traits precisely converge with those of Kurukullā. In view of the commonalities between them, in both iconography and persona, it seems likely that attributes of Lalitā left an imprint on conceptions of Kurukullā.[46] Lalitā's sovereignty in her own pantheon may also have prompted Kurukullā's ascension in hers, as Kurukullā was infused with the exalted aura of a goddess supreme.

Kurukullā's association with love magic and connections with Kāmadeva and especially Lalitā disclose that her character was profoundly shaped by non-Buddhist elements of Indian culture. Thus, Kurukullā was easily absorbed into Hindu Tantra after the demise of Buddhism in India.[47]

The etymological derivation of the name Kurukullā is unclear. Indic sources identify it as the name of her mountain dwelling. Early manuscript paintings depict her within a mountain grotto, and one of these illustrations is accompanied by an inscription identifying her as "Kurukullā of Kurukulla Mountain in Lāṭadeśa" (i.e., Gujarat).[48] She is elsewhere described as "dwelling on Kurukulla mountain" and as residing in a cave on said mountain.[49] It not uncommon in India and the Himalayas for a village or topographical feature such as a lake or mountain to be both residence and manifestation of an eponymous goddess. Although "Kurukulla" does not appear among documented Indic toponyms, the name may formerly have been in usage, and Buddhists may have recognized the peak as a sacred site.

Because the name Kurukullā does not yield to translation, Tibetans often retain the Sanskrit nomen, sometimes modified to Kurukulle. The Tibetan version of her name, Rigjayma, "Mistress of Magic," or "Mistress of Knowledge," is not a literal rendition of the Sanskrit, as would usually be the case.[50] Interestingly, however, a direct Sanskrit rendering of Rigjayma would be Vidyā, an epithet suggestively recalling Lalitā, supreme goddess of the Śrīvidyā school, who is known as Vidyā, Ādividyā ("Primordial Knowledge"), and Mahāvidyā ("Great Knowledge").

Ritual Procedures

One genre of rite that falls within the purview of Kurukullā is that known in the broader Indian magical corpus as *strī-vaśīkaraṇa*, "bewitchment of women" or "compulsion of women." By performing such a ritual, a male practitioner can draw the object of his desire from a long distance away, and she will suddenly find herself in his presence and under his power. Such a procedure might be used to procure a lover, reconcile with an estranged spouse, or obtain a Tantric partner. According to one work in the *Sādhanamālā*, a male practitioner who wishes to attract a yogic consort should recite, day and night: "*Oṃ kurukulle hrīḥ*! Bring (insert name or description) under my control, *svāhā*!" The text promises:

> Then, overpowered, impelled by mantra, she will arrive with disheveled hair, naked, benumbed, and stricken by love. Having obtained her, he should worship the Buddha mandala and gain irreversible success in his yogic objectives.[51]

The same compendium celebrates Kurukullā as a "giver of success in . . . love magic that is unequaled in the world," through whose rites the hierophant may even enjoy the vinelike embrace of goddesses from heaven.[52]

This type of rite, a Buddhist rendition of popular Indic folk magic, also figures in the Tibetan ritual repertoire centering on Kurukullā, which encompasses a broad range of magical procedures, both simple and complex. The most rudimentary consist simply in the invocation of Kurukullā, incantation of her mantra, and envisionment of the object of desire. For example, intoning her mantra seven times in the presence of an angry person or opponent will calm the person and make him or her a devoted follower. Drinking water over which her mantra has been pronounced will attract food; rinsing one's face with the water will bestow beauty. Holding the hem of one's garment while incanting the mantra twenty-one times will grant mellifluence and oratorical power.[53]

A relatively simple visualization is prescribed for use with someone who is hostile to religious pursuits. The meditator envisions both himself or herself and the other person as Kurukullā. She or he then repeatedly imagines the other person dissolving into emptiness. Through the sympathetic resonance established between the two minds, the less evolved person comes vicariously into contact with higher states of awareness and becomes a devoted spiritual practitioner.[54] There are even intricate visualizations that deploy fierce red bees—each marked with a mantra syllable—to create a psychic link among Kurukullā, meditator, and subject to be spellbound.[55]

The color red predominates not only in the iconography but also in the rites of Kurukullā. The ritualist is customarily instructed to don red garments and flowers, use a rosary of red sandalwood, and practice in a place with red soil or beneath a red-blossomed aśoka tree. The ceremonial vessel, preferably of copper, is to be covered with red cloth and flowers. The ritual diagram should be drawn with red vermilion powder or the practitioner's own blood on red cloth or fabric dyed with menstrual blood. Talismans are to be tied with red thread spun by a woman.[56] A red arrow with a copper tip may also figure in the rites.[57] In the attendant meditation process, the vision of Kurukullā is generated from the red light radiating from her seed syllable, HRĪḤ. Characteristic is the case of the ninefold mandala of Kurukullā, in which she dances on the corolla of an eight-petaled red lotus, surrounded by eight red lotus ḍākinīs, identical to her in appearance, who send forth red, hooked light rays from their hearts to strike the hearts of those they wish to enchant or compel. The meditator then envisions the objects of the ritual dissolving into the hearts of the goddesses and thus brought under submission.[58]

The ritual repertoire associated with Kurukullā is indeed extensive and warrants further investigation if the full panoply of rites is to be documented.[59]

Status in Contemporary Pantheons

The large number of texts devoted to Kurukullā in the *Sādhanamālā* and Tibetan canon indicate her importance in late Indian Buddhism and the large number of practices transmitted to Tibet.[60] Tantric forms of the goddess now prevail in Tibetan Buddhism. She is important for all the Tibetan sects but has greater prominence in the Sakya school as a patron deity.[61] In this role, she figures as one of the Marpo Korsum, "Red Trinity," along with Red Gaṇapati and Red Ṭakkirāja. Painted representations of the triad may center on Kurukullā.[62]

Kurukullā has played little discernible role in Newar Buddhism.[63] It is noteworthy, then, that fine paintings of the goddess have been produced in Nepal and figure in the current repertoire of Newar artists. Such paintings would originally have been produced for Tibetan patrons and in the contemporary setting are created for Tibetans and for general sale in the Kathmandu art market. The iconographic form most frequently encountered in these compositions is the Tantric epiphany that prevails in the Tibetan pantheon, namely, the four-armed, dancing form in which she holds a bow, arrow, red lotus (or goad), and floral noose.[64]

In her current status, Kurukullā is a fully enlightened being who accomplishes both ritual and meditative transformation. She specializes in the ability to attract and command, one of the four modes of enlightened activity. The secret of Kurukullā's power is that she wields the unconquerable, irresistible force of love. Her heart is a reservoir of this emotion in its most refined form. Her drawn arrow, poised in front of her heart, becomes saturated with her beauteous heart essence. To be pierced by her arrow is to be penetrated by her transcendent love and undergo a profound change of heart. Herein lies the power of the goddess to subdue, impassion, and incite to higher love and awareness.

There would appear to be a potential for misuse of Kurukullā's rites to harm others, but those who would invoke her in ritual and meditation must never call on her services for selfish ends. Kurukullā is motivated by wisdom and compassion; her roseate glow proclaims her bounteous affection; her divine beauty reflects her transcendent purity. She will never grant a vision of herself or perform her magic for those who seek only to benefit themselves or inflict suffering on others. Kurukullā, like every Buddha, acts solely for the welfare, happiness, and liberation of all sentient beings.

Epilogue

Scholars have long recognized that reverence for female divinities has been a major force in Indian culture over the millennia. Thus, it should not be surprising that Buddhism, as a product of Indian soil, also evinces a rich and vital tradition of goddess veneration. Although Buddhism has not heretofore been examined from this perspective, an in-depth exploration of the female pantheon reveals a lively, long-standing, and profound engagement with the feminine divine. Readers have met on these pages the yakṣiṇīs, voluptuous nature spirits whose effigies adorn and protect the earliest Buddhist monuments. The radiant wisdom mother Prajñāpāramitā, golden and serene, represents the transcendent understanding of reality that crowns the spiritual quest. The green savioress Tārā, whose sparkling emerald complexion evokes the lushness of medicinal forests, nurtures beings to the full flowering of well-being and perfection. Vajrayoginī, a red female Buddha, dances in a ring of yogic fire that consumes all negativity and illusion. Nairātmyā, the blue female Buddha, soars in the infinite expanse of emptiness and bliss.

Moreover, Buddhism has exalted female deities to the pinnacle of the pantheon, to embody the loftiest principles of the tradition. The first goddess to occupy this supreme position was Prajñāpāramitā, "Mother of All Buddhas," who personifies the overarching cosmic reality and transcendent wisdom that gives birth to all enlightened ones. Centuries later, Tārā was enthroned at the summit of the pantheon as the ultimate savior and liberator, a worker of miracles and unfailing source of refuge and deliverance. Tārā was, moreover, the first female deity to be crowned with the title of Buddha. With the concept of female Buddhahood firmly in place, Tantric Buddhism advanced a number of female Buddhas who represent full enlightenment and preside over esoteric yogas and meditations whose goal is supreme liberation in the present lifetime.

Bringing the spectrum of goddesses together in a single work provides a favorable vantage point for identifying historical and thematic trends in the pantheon. The broad geographic and temporal scope of my study has made it possible to place the goddesses in relation to one another and to identify continuities and divergences among them. Further, the breadth of coverage clarifies the different types and statuses of figures that were advanced in accordance with the unfolding stages of Buddhist doctrine and practice.

The pantheon reflects the religious sentiments and ideals of the Buddhist populace over the centuries, including the forms of divine assistance they have sought and the types of beings in whom they have vested their hopes for blessings, protection, and guidance. My study of the pantheon has revealed some unanticipated themes in this regard. One is the surprising variety of goddesses associated with healing. The practice traditions of many of these figures include meditative and ritual healing methodologies. Another recurrent theme is an emphasis on protection from demonic spirits, a role shared by many goddesses in this work, disclosing an enduring preoccupation with harmful beings that generated a need for numerous ritual interventions.

My study also reveals that, for Buddhism, nature has a decidedly feminine face. The visual imagery and literary metaphors associated with many of these figures reflect a profound appreciation for nature as a repository of sacred energies and meaning. We find goddesses associated with such natural phenomena as the earth, trees, sacred groves, plant life, rice, fruit, flowers, lotuses, the dawn, the night sky, stars, planetary bodies, mountains, rivers, snakes, boars, bees, elephants, wild felines, and birds. However, the western dualism that assigns maleness to the cultural sphere while relegating femaleness to the natural realm is not operative here. The female pantheon includes figures that embody wisdom, knowledge, artistic inspiration, and rarefied yogic and spiritual realizations. Indeed, beginning with Prajñāpāramitā, the goddess of transcendent wisdom, we find a perennial association between female figures and wisdom in the tradition.

Another important theme that emerges here is the often close relationship between the Buddhist and the broader Indian pantheon of deities. Buddhists initially relegated the preexisting gods and goddesses of Indic cosmology to the status of worldly beings who had not attained the goal of liberation realized by Shakyamuni Buddha. Early Buddhist writers and iconographers incorporated a selection of such figures into their own pantheon in a supporting role, providing Shakyamuni with a host of supernatural allies to prosper and protect his followers. Thus, the cosmology of early Buddhist literature and art cannot be understood without reference to India's protohistorical iconography and Vedic and Upaniṣadic thought. Pṛthivī, the earth goddess, is a case in point. Buddhist narratives describe how the Buddha-to-be called on her as his witness at the critical moment of his confrontation with Māra but do not explain why she was thus chosen. The reason may be found in Vedic understandings of mother earth as an unfailing knower and speaker of truth. Furthermore, the full significance of the seat of enlightenment beneath the bodhi tree may be understood only with reference to the identification of this spot as the navel of mother earth, the throne of world sovereignty, which she grants only to one who is supremely virtuous.

The Mahayana pantheon evidences ongoing reference to the Hindu pantheon as a source of figural types and symbolic motifs. For example, Vasudhārā, the golden, grain-bearing goddess of abundance, has as her main prototype Pṛthivī, mother earth. Both Vasudhārā and Tārā inherited traits from Lakṣmī, the lotus lady. The original conception of Mārīcī was modeled on that of Uṣas, the Vedic goddess of the dawn. When Mārīcī was recast as a warrior goddess, her martial persona was patterned on that of Durgā in her demon-slaying mode. Parṇaśavarī, a healing goddess, exhibits the influence of Śītalā and other curers of fevers and epidemics. Jāṅgulī, protector against snakebite, is the Buddhist counterpart of Manasā, the Hindu snake goddess. Sarasvatī, a goddess of Vedic origins, was adopted whole cloth into the Mahayana pantheon, retaining her role as patroness of art and learning. Kurukullā in both her Mahayana and her Tantric guises shares significant commonalities with the Hindu deities Kāmadeva and Lalitā. Siṃhamukhā, with her leọnine visage, is the Buddhist analogue of divine yoginis of the Kaula pantheon. These and other shared motifs and figural types reveal the heretofore unrecognized extent to which the Buddhist pantheon developed in active dialogue with the Hindu theophany.

A work of this scope cannot be comprehensive in its treatment. Most of the goddesses represented here claim a complex textual, art historical, and religious history spanning many centuries, including multifaceted roles in contemporary Buddhist settings. I trust that my study will inspire deeper interest in these divinities and stimulate further research. Some of these figures would require several book-length studies to give full account of the historical, regional, and sectarian variations on their worship and interpretation.

Since I conceived this book, almost a decade ago, substantive new research on individual goddesses has begun to emerge, a trend that will surely continue. I envision many avenues for future research. For example, although my literary explorations were extensive, the literature devoted to each goddess merits further investigation. There are many unexamined Sanskrit texts in Indian and Newar archives that contain material relevant to these figures. The recent study by Elizabeth English on the Vajrayoginī practices compiled in the *Guhyasamaya Sādhanamālā* in the late twelfth century is indicative of the invaluable information that has yet to be discovered. Tibetan canonical and sectarian literature represents another significant resource. Realized masters and sectarian founders customarily author prayers, liturgies, practice manuals, and commentaries that become authoritative for their followers. Examining and analyzing the voluminous body of texts dispersed among the annals of the Dalai Lamas and other important teachers will yield increasingly nuanced historical and theological understandings of these figures and their differing roles and interpretations.[1]

Newly emerging archaeological and artistic evidence will augment or modify my findings. The discovery and excavation of Buddhist sites will continue to unearth images that shed further light on the iconographic evolution, popularity, and geographic purview of particular deities. The fund of art historical sources will expand as works of art dispersed in private, museum, temple, and monastery collections across the globe come to market or to publication. Moreover, ethnographic research among Buddhist populations in Tibet and Nepal and Tibetan Buddhists in diaspora will yield increasingly detailed documentation of contemporary ritual and performance traditions, social and institutional patterns, and popular and local practices.

The Indian pantheon traveled with Buddhism as the tradition spread into the Himalayas and Central, East, and Southeast Asia. My study has followed the trajectory of this core pantheon to Tibet and Nepal. However, further research remains to be done on the regions bordering those discussed in this volume. The pantheons of Kashmir, Ladakh, Bhutan, Sikkim, Dolpo, Mustang, and Central Asia display distinctive iconographies, novel practice traditions, local legendry, and indigenous sacred sites. Although progress has been made on all these fronts, further investigation of these unique regional pantheons will disclose new chapters in the historical transformations of the Indian pantheon.

This study also contributes to the ongoing inquiry into Buddhist constructions of gender. The female pantheon represents an important domain of gender discourse and ideology. Mapping this metaphorical terrain has implications for analysis of the inscription of human gender roles. Exploring the relationships between human and divine females will facilitate increasingly nuanced analyses of the varying status, roles, participation, and contributions of Buddhist women in different historical venues.

My documentation of the female pantheon also has ramifications for the history of the male pantheon. Some of the deities and related motifs documented here undoubtedly influenced the conception of male figures. Charting the recurrent themes of the female pantheon provides a basis of comparison so that the shared and divergent features of the male pantheon may be identified. Ultimately the male and female pantheons cannot fully be understood without reference to one another. Comparative analyses will in turn enhance our understanding of Buddhist constructions of gender in varying sociohistorical contexts.

Goddess studies have burgeoned on a number of fronts for the last several decades, significantly revising our understanding of many traditions by revealing female divinities of tremendous historical, social, and political significance in their respective geographic and cultural settings. Although the last decade has witnessed increasing scholarly attention to the female deities of Buddhism, the tradition is not yet one that immediately springs to mind when goddesses are under discussion. Nor do Buddhist figures—apart from the well-known Tārā, Prajñāpāramitā, and Vajrayoginī—find inclusion in cross-cultural goddess studies and anthologies. Buddhism has long been recognized for its intellectual achievements, psychological insights, and social vision of tolerance and harmony. However, in view of its extensive female pantheon, as documented in this volume, Buddhism may rightfully take a place among the world's goddess traditions.

Notes

Introduction

1. One group of goddesses that might rightfully have been included here, the Pañcarakṣā, are, because of their tremendous importance in Newar Buddhism, treated in another manuscript currently under preparation, *Buddhist Goddesses of Tibet and Nepal.*

2. It is difficult to find a term for "early Buddhism" before the appearance of specific, self-titled schools and movements. Readers will find various terms in use by other authors. For example, one finds the term "Hinayāna," coined in Mahayana texts to refer to earlier teachings but which no Buddhist movement has applied to itself. Some scholars identify early Buddhism as Nikāya Buddhism or Pali Buddhism, with reference to the genre and language of texts produced in that context. These terms, however, are not sufficiently standardized for adoption here. Some scholars use the term "Theravada" ("Teachings of the Elders"), the title embraced in Sri Lanka and Southeast Asia by those who adhered to the earlier discourses rather than to the later Mahayana revelations. To apply this term retrospectively to Indian developments, however, is somewhat anachronistic. Therefore, I have settled on the less technical but nonetheless descriptive "early Buddhism."

3. My threefold division of Indian Buddhism into early, Mahayana, and Tantric movements, or periods, does not designate movements around which clear-cut boundaries can be drawn. There is chronological overlap, and there are practical and doctrinal continuities among them, as well as further subdivisions within them. Western scholars of Buddhism recognize that this commonly invoked threefold scheme is useful and substantially descriptive but subject to qualifications if detailed account is to be given of the complexities of Indian Buddhist history.

4. Although *dhāraṇī* and "mantra" are closely synonymous, the term *dhāraṇī* is more consistently used in association with female divinities. Dhāraṇīs consist of strings of words, often of unknown lexical meaning, many in the feminine vocative case. According to Har Dayal, this grammatical feature underscores their feminine resonance and may figure in or stem from their original use to invoke female divinities; *Bodhisattva Doctrine*, p. 268.

5. In early Buddhism, enlightenment is framed as the attainment of *nirvāṇa* and, upon death, entrance into *parinirvāṇa*. In contrast, Mahayana envisions a series of ten or thirteen stages of spiritual progress, the *bodhisattva bhumis*. This series culminates in full Buddhahood, but even the first stage is a sufficiently lofty achievement to constitute a kind of "enlightenment." Upon reaching the seventh bhumi, the aspirant attains the ability to emanate multiple divine bodies throughout the universe. Upon achieving the tenth stage,

Buddhahood, a being may choose to emanate a divine form or forms other than that of a Buddha. Thus, to cite a familiar example, Avalokiteśvara, the great bodhisattva of compassion, could well have attained the tenth bhumi, the stage of Buddhahood. However, the fact remains that his appearance in the form of Avalokiteśvara is that of a bodhisattva, albeit one who is fully enlightened.

6. For a helpful guide to the history and nomenclature of Kriyā and Caryā Tantra in Tantric classificatory schemes: P. Williams and Tribe, *Buddhist Thought*, pp. 203–9.

7. I use here the term for the most esoteric Tantric practices and texts that finds wide adoption in western scholarship. Late Indian Buddhism introduced a range of terms, generally subdividing the esoteric yogas into a Yogottara, or Mahāyoga, class and a Yoganirutta, or Yogānuttara, or Yoginī class; P. Williams and Tribe, *Buddhist Thought*, pp. 203–4, 210–16.

8. This latter term is introduced in Gross, *Buddhism after Patriarchy*, pp. 94, 140, 175.

9. Simmer-Brown, *Dakini's Warm Breath*, pp. 149–50.

10. Klein, *Meeting the Great Bliss Queen*, p. 22.

11. Bokar Rinpoche, *Tara*, p. 12.

12. Ibid., p. 22 and quote on p. 15.

13. Ibid., pp. 12, 22–24.

14. Ibid., p. 12.

15. Ibid., pp. 11–13.

Chapter 1
Pṛthivī: Mother Earth

1. Bays, trans., *Voice of the Buddha*, p. 482.

2. *Ṛg Veda* 6.51.5: *pṛthivī mātar adhrug.*

3. *Atharva Veda* 14.1.1: *satyena uttabhitā bhūmiḥ*; 12.1.1, 12.1.17: *pṛthivīṃ dharmaṇā dhṛtām.*

4. *Śatapatha Brāhmaṇa* passage cited in Tucci, "Earth in India," p. 538.

5. Tucci, "Earth in India," p. 536.

6. *Ṛg Veda* 10.63.10; *Atharva Veda* 12.1.14, 12.1.32, 12.1.41, 12.1.47, 12.1.49–50.

7. *Atharva Veda* 5.19.11, 12.1.18.

8. Enthoven, *Folklore of Bombay*, pp. 80–81.

9. Horner, "Earth as a Swallower," pp. 152–58. See also jātaka no. 457; Cowell, ed., *Jātaka*, vol. 4, pp. 64, 66.

10. T. Rhys Davids, trans., *Buddhist Birth-Stories*, pp. 195–96.

11. Jones, trans., *Mahāvastu*, vol. 2, pp. 312–15, 366–67.

12. Bays, trans., *Voice of the Buddha*, pp. 480–509; quotes on pp. 480, 509.

13. Variations of *pṛthivī-nābhi* appear in the *Ṛg Veda*, while *paṭhavī-nābhi* appears in the *Mahābodhivaṃśa*; Coomaraswamy, *Elements of Buddhist Iconography*, p. 80 n. 94. The term *nābhir vasudhā-tala* is used in the *Buddhacarita*; *bodhi-maṇḍa* is favored in the *Nidānakathā* and *Lalitavistara*, although the latter work also employs the term *dhāraṇī-maṇḍa.*

14. Coomaraswamy, *Elements of Buddhist Iconography*, pp. 27, 80 n. 94.

15. T. Rhys Davids, trans., *Buddhist Birth-Stories*, pp. 188–90.

16. Jātaka no. 479; Cowell, ed., *Jātaka*, vol. 4, p. 146 and quote on p. 143.

17. Bays, trans., *Voice of the Buddha*, p. 554; see also p. 424.

18. Li Rongxi, trans., *Great Tang Dynasty Record*, p. 244.

19. *Buddhacarita* 13.68; Johnston trans., p. 201.

20. *Buddhacarita* 13.70–71; Johnston trans., p. 201. The throne figures similarly in the Southeast Asian version, wherein the Buddha states, before invoking mother earth, "This throne is mine, what need of another witness?"; Duroiselle, "Wathundaye," p. 145.

21. Bloss, "Taming of Māra," p. 157.

22. T. Rhys Davids, trans., *Buddhist Birth-Stories*, p. 194.

23. Jones, trans., *Mahāvastu*, vol. 2, pp. 299–300, 363. For the same motif in the *Nidānakathā*, see T. Rhys Davids, trans., *Buddhist Birth-Stories*, p. 175.

24. Jones, trans., *Mahāvastu*, vol. 2, pp. 301–2.

25. Bloss, "Taming of Māra," pp. 161–62. Most relevant is Shakyamuni's previous lifetime as a prince who demonstrated supreme generosity; see *Vessantara Jātaka* (no. 547); Cowell, ed., *Jātaka*, vol. 6, pp. 247–50.

26. Bloss, "Taming of Māra," p. 161.

27. T. Rhys Davids, trans., *Buddhist Birth-Stories*, pp. 197–98. For the blossoming of nature at the conception of the Buddha, see pp. 151–52, and following the birth of the Bodhisattva, *Buddhacarita* 1.21–26, 2.7–8, in Johnston trans., pp. 6–7, 21.

28. Bloss, "Taming of Māra," pp. 157, 162.

29. Indian Museum, Calcutta, G18; American Institute of Indian Studies neg. no. 245.45.

30. Two examples: Ingholt, *Gandhāran Art*, no. 62; Majumdar, *Sculptures in the Indian Museum*, pt. 2, pl. 8b.

31. Ingholt, *Gandhāran Art*, no. 346.

32. In an Amarāvatī relief of the scene, the hands do not appear; Sivaramamurti, *Amaravati Sculptures*, pl. 63.4.c.

33. M. Srivastava, *Mother Goddess in Indian Art*, p. 127. See, e.g., the Pallava relief in Sivaramamurti, *Śrī Lakshmī*, fig. 129.

34. Ratnagiri examples: D. Mitra, *Ratnagiri*, pls. 83A–B. Ellora examples: Malandra, *Unfolding a Maṇḍala*, figs. 170–71, 227, 255. Examples from Sārnāth and Bodhgayā: Leoshko, "Case of the Two Witnesses," figs. 8, 10; J. Williams, "Sārnāth Gupta Steles," figs. 5, 10.

35. Sārnāth reliefs in which a kneeling Pṛthivī holds a vessel: J. Williams, "Sārnāth Gupta Steles," fig. 2; Leoshko, "Case of the Two Witnesses," fig. 6. Pāla reliefs: Leoshko, figs. 9, 12, 14; Gangoly, "Earth-Goddess," fig. 3; Huntington and Huntington, *Leaves from the Bodhi Tree*, no. 31.

36. Leoshko, "Case of the Two Witnesses," p. 50.

37. Bosch, *Golden Germ*, p. 112.

38. *Atharva Veda* 12.1.44–45; Griffith trans., vol. 2, pp. 99–100.

39. Jones, trans., *Mahāvastu*, vol. 1, p. 78; Snellgrove, *Hevajra Tantra*, pt. 1, p. 89, v. 2.1.12.

40. *Padma Purāṇa* 6.229.72–74; Deshpande trans., vol. 9, p. 3168. *Viṣṇudharmottara Purāṇa* 61.1–3, cited in B. Srivastava, *Iconography of Śakti*, pp. 104, 109 n. 24. Similarly, the *Śrītattvanidhi* prescribes a full treasure vase (*nidhi-kumbha*) by her left foot; pp. 104, 109 n. 24, 165.

41. Cleary, trans., *Realm of Reality*, p. 159.

42. Gangoly, "Earth-Goddess," pp. 4, 5n.

43. Textual sources of this version are translated and discussed in Duroiselle, "Wathundaye"; Gangoly, "Earth-Goddess," pp. 4, 5n; Guillon, "Version mône inédite," pp. 143, 158–61.

44. Leoshko, "Case of the Two Witnesses," pp. 42, 44, 46, 48. For the suggestion that this figure is Māra's minion Meghakālī, see J. Williams, "Sārnāth Gupta Steles," pp. 180–81.

45. Beal, trans., *Si-yu-ki*, vol. 2, p. 121, cited in Leoshko, "Case of the Two Witnesses," p. 44. Note that earth "goddess" becomes "god" in Li Rongxi's translation, *Great Tang Dynasty Record*, p. 248.

46. See the fifth- and sixth-century Sārnāth and Bodhgayā steles in Leoshko, "Case of the Two Witnesses," figs. 5, 7, 8, 9.

47. This would be analogous to earlier reliefs in which Māra appears twice to illustrate different moments of the episode; see Malandra, "Māra's Army," pp. 122–23, 125–26, 129. In general, synoptic compositions are not uncommon in representations of the Buddha's life.

48. Bays, trans., *Voice of the Buddha*, pp. 480–509.

49. For a detailed, illustrated account of this iconographic evolution, see Leoshko, "Case of the Two Witnesses," pp. 40–48.

50. Ibid., p. 50 and fig. 14.

51. D. Mitra, *Ratnagiri*, pl. 83A.

52. Literary and artistic references to Māra's elephant mount and elephant-headed minion are compiled in Malandra, "Māra's Army," pp. 122–23, 126–28.

53. Aparājitā is commonly described as *gaṇapati-samākrāntā*, which can be construed as "trampling a gaṇapati" or "trampling Gaṇapati," leaving open the question of whether a generic gaṇapati demon or Gaṇeśa-Gaṇapati is intended.

54. G. Bhattacharya, "Dual Role of Ganesh," pp. 72, 75–76.

55. Skt. *aśeṣa-māra-nirdalinī*; *Sādhanamālā* no. 204. The text also describes her left hand as "gripping a noose with a threatening gesture" (*tarjanī-pāśa*), although the noose does not consistently appear in sculptural representations.

56. She is said to destroy or crush all māras (*bdud*) in Derge Tōh. nos. 3259 and 3593 and to pulverize (*rlag-pa*) all demons (*gdon*) in no. 3249.

57. For tenth-century images from Nālandā: Saraswati, *Tantrayāna Art*, nos. 184–87. For images from a range of dates and sites: M. Mitra, "Buddhist Goddess Aparājitā" and "Four Images"; Sahu, *Buddhism in Orissa*, p. 193 and fig. 24; A. Sengupta, "Note on a Buddhist Female Deity"; G. Bhattacharya, "Dual Role of Ganesh," figs. 8–10. A rare seated effigy: D. Mitra, *Ratnagiri*, pl. 24C.

58. Rahul Sankṛtyāyana, *Vinaya Tripiṭaka* (Sarnath, 1965), p. 279, cited in Shākya, *Vasundharā Devī*, pp. 6–7 of the Newar portion of the book.

59. This Vinaya tradition was related to me by Yvonne Rand, who received it as part of her Zen monastic ordination; I have not located a textual reference.

60. Emmerick, trans., *Sūtra of Golden Light*, pp. 51–52; see also p. 55.

61. Ibid., p. 52, translation slightly amended.

62. Ibid., p. 53.

63. Ibid., p. 52.

64. Skorupski, trans., *Sarvadurgatipariśodhana Tantra*, p. 98. Snellgrove, *Hevajra Tantra*, pt. 1, p. 89; see p. 108 for another brief invocation.

65. Chandra, *Buddhist Iconography*, nos. 397, 2482; Clark, ed., *Two Lamaistic Pantheons*, vol. 2, pp. 179–80, nos. 5B44–45.

66. Béguin, *Peintures du bouddhisme tibétain*, no. 41; Bays, trans., *Voice of the Buddha*, pl. 15.

67. Ferguson, "Great Goddess Today," p. 286; Guillon, "Version mône inédite," pp. 144, 149–53; Gangoly, "Earth-Goddess," pp. 6–8 and figs. 5–8; Appel, "Buddhist Goddess Vasundharā," pls. 3.13, 3.15–18.

68. Saram discusses and publishes many such effigies, largely in Thailand and Laos, in "Earth Goddess."

Chapter 2
Māyādevī: The Buddha's Wondrous Mother and Her Sacred Grove

1. Bays, trans., *Voice of the Buddha*, p. 85.

2. See jātaka nos. 7, 156, 163, 201, 276, 428, 455, 461, 505, 509, 538–39, 542–43, 545–47. King Śuddhodana is generally his father. In some instances, the king and queen are not named but referred to as "the royal family." The *Vessantara Jātaka* (no. 547) also delves into Māyādevī's past lives; Cowell, ed., *Jātaka*, vol. 6, pp. 247–50.

3. My main sources here are the major biographical accounts that took shape in the first and second centuries C.E., which offer relatively detailed accounts of the parturition. The scattered references to Māyādevī and Shakyamuni's birth in the voluminous Vinaya literature would lead too far afield in this context. For a comprehensive overview of biographical sources: Lamotte, *History of Indian Buddhism*, pp. 15 n. 14, 648–62.

4. Bays, trans., *Voice of the Buddha*, pp. 95–99. According to the *Nidānakathā*, the gods transported her to the Himalayas for this event; T. Rhys Davids, trans., *Buddhist Birth-Stories*, pp. 149–50. Lake Mānasarovar, near the base of Mount Kailash, is regarded as the site where the gods bathed Māyādevī on this occasion; Batchelor, *Tibet Guide*, p. 366. For further discussion and textual citations of Māyādevī's dream, see Young, *Dreaming in the Lotus*, pp. 21–24, 88.

5. Bays, trans., *Voice of the Buddha*, p. 108.

6. T. Rhys Davids, trans., *Buddhist Birth-Stories*, p. 152; Jones, trans., *Mahāvastu*, vol. 2, pp. 13–15; Bays, trans., *Voice of the Buddha*, pp. 102–3, 115, 118.

7. Jones, trans., *Mahāvastu*, vol. 1, pp. 117–18.

8. Ibid., vol. 1, p. 114, and vol. 2, p. 13; Bays, trans., *Voice of the Buddha*, pp. 113–14, 118.

9. Jones, trans., *Mahāvastu*, vol. 1, p. 116; vol. 2, pp. 14–15.

10. Bays, trans., *Voice of the Buddha*, pp. 114–15, 117–18. For several textual traditions on the healing powers of the pregnant Māyādevī: Durt, "Pregnancy of Māyā," pp. 44, 46, 53–58. Her healing powers also find mention in the *Avataṃsaka Sūtra*; Cleary, trans., *Realm of Reality*, p. 266.

11. *Buddhacarita* 1.5–9.

12. Jones, trans., *Mahāvastu*, vol. 1, pp. 117–18; vol. 2, pp. 16–17, quote on p. 17.

13. T. Rhys Davids, trans., *Buddhist Birth-Stories*, pp. 153–54.

14. Bays, trans., *Voice of the Buddha*, pp. 126, 129.

15. Ibid., pp. 129–30.

16. Ibid., p. 130.

17. Ibid., p. 47.

18. Jones, trans., *Mahāvastu*, vol. 2, p. 19.

19. T. Rhys Davids, trans., *Buddhist Birth-Stories*, pp. 152–53.

20. Jones, trans., *Mahāvastu*, vol. 2, p. 18; see also *Buddhacarita* 1.3.

21. Jones, trans., *Mahāvastu*, vol. 2, pp. 16, 20, 117. See also the birth of Dīpaṃkara in vol. 1, p. 176, and Bays, trans., *Voice of the Buddha*, p. 144.

22. For detailed analysis of how the birth differed from an ordinary one according to Indian embryology and metaphysics, see Hara, "Buddha's Birth Story."

23. Jones, trans., *Mahāvastu*, vol. 2, p. 20; Johnston, trans., *Aśvaghoṣa's Buddhacarita*, pt. 2, p. 6; Bays, trans., *Voice of the Buddha*, p. 144.

24. Cleary, trans., *Realm of Reality*, p. 313.

25. Ibid., pp. 313–14.

26. Ibid., p. 315.

27. Ibid., pp. 312–13.

28. Ibid., p. 267.

29. The *Lalitavistara* does not state outright that she died at Lumbinī but reports her death and then describes the processional departure for Kapilavastu; Bays, trans., *Voice of the Buddha*, p. 147.

30. These traditions are cited in Rahula, *Critical Study of the Mahāvastu*, pp. 202, 395 nn. 181–82; R. L. Mitra, trans., *Lalita-vistara*, pp. 153–54. There is also a tradition that the consultation on the Bodhisattva's destiny took place at Lumbinī; R. L. Mitra, p. 147.

31. *Buddhacarita* 1.86–87, 2.18.

32. André Bareau speculates that Māyādevī died in childbirth and biographers timed the death seven days later as a pious apologia; "Jeunesse du Buddha," p. 208.

33. Johnston, trans., *Aśvaghoṣa's Buddhacarita*, pt. 2, p. 23; T. Rhys Davids, trans., *Buddhist Birth-Stories*, p. 152.

34. Bays, trans., *Voice of the Buddha*, p. 147.

35. Ibid.

36. T. Rhys Davids, trans., *Buddhist Birth-Stories*, p. 148.

37. Jones, trans., *Mahāvastu*, vol. 2, p. 3.

38. On the tradition that she was reborn in Tuṣita Heaven: Bareau, "Jeunesse du Buddha," pp. 208–9.

39. Bays, trans., *Voice of the Buddha*, pp. 385–86; cf. *Leaves of the Heaven Tree*, p. 136, for the event as recounted in Kṣemendra's *Avadāna Kalpalatā*.

40. This event is related by Hsuan-tsang; Li Rongxi, trans., *Great Tang Dynasty Record*, p. 255.

41. A beautiful stele of this scene: Elvehjem Museum, Madison, Wisconsin, 1972.24.

42. Burlingame, trans., *Buddhist Legends*, vol. 30, pp. 47–53. The descent is widely illustrated in Indic art. Chinese pilgrims frequently cite the sojourn in Trāyastriṃśa because it reflects Shakyamuni's filial piety; see, e.g., Fa-hsien's account in Legge, trans., *Record of Buddhistic Kingdoms*, pp. 48–50, 56, 68. In Southeast Asia, the Buddha's heavenly sojourn is commemorated by a three-month monastic retreat during the rainy season when rice crops are growing, brought to a close by a festival of lights that concomitantly celebrates the maturation of the rice crop. The agrarian associations of this observance shed interesting light on elements of the Buddhist legend that conform to a widespread mythic motif in which the child of mother earth leaves the surface of the earth, joins her in her realm (usually underground) for several months, and returns as crops ripen, an event typically enacted by an annual ritual. See Ferguson, "Great Goddess Today," pp. 290, 298–99 n. 16.

43. Li Rongxi, trans., *Great Tang Dynasty Record*, pp. 189–90; quote on p. 190.

44. For the Sāñcī relief, on the eastern gate of Stupa I: Karetzky, *Life of the Buddha*, fig. 6 (topmost register). The conception is not, however, as common a subject at Bhārhut and Sāñcī as formerly believed, for many reliefs identified as conception scenes by Alfred Foucher in *On the Iconography of the Buddha's Nativity* were subsequently recognized as images of Gaja-Lakṣmī.

45. This scene, reproduced in Karetzky, *Life of the Buddha*, fig. 6, includes Māyādevī seated on an elephant, shaded by a canopy and holding what appears to be a babe-in-arms.

46. Gāndhāran examples of the conception are widely published. See, e.g., Ingholt, *Gandhāran Art*, nos. 9–10; Zwalf, *Gandhāra Sculpture*, nos. 141–42. Fischer discusses iconographic variations of the scene and publishes two additional reliefs in "Queen Māyā's Dream." Reliefs of other scenes in which the queen appears include Ingholt, nos. 10–11; Zwalf, nos. 142–44; and Karetzky, *Life of the Buddha*, fig. 19.

47. Ingholt, *Gandhāran Art*, nos. 13–15, 18; Zwalf, *Gandhāra Sculpture*, nos. 145–47, 149–51.

48. Ingholt, *Gandhāran Art*, nos. 17–18, 148; Zwalf, *Gandhāra Sculpture*, nos. 152, 154–57.

49. Ingholt, *Gandhāran Art*, nos. 20–22; Zwalf, *Gandhāra Sculpture*, no. 158. On this event and literary sources on Māyādevī's presence at the consultation: Karetzky, *Life of the Buddha*, pp. 23–28.

50. Amarāvatī reliefs of the conception, consultation, and nativity: Stone, *Buddhist Art of Nāgārjunakoṇḍa*, figs. 84, 159, 161, 189–90; Nāgārjunakoṇḍa reliefs: figs. 41–42, 65, 83, 162, 188, 210.

51. Sivaramamurti, *Amaravati Sculptures*, pp. 164–65 and pl. 24.3. Sivaramamurti convincingly interprets this scene as Māyādevī's dream of lustration by goddesses before the white elephant entered her womb, as described in the *Nidānakathā*.

52. This event is related in the *Lalitavistara*; Bays, trans., *Voice of the Buddha*, p. 96. Reliefs of the scene: Sivaramamurti, *Amaravati Sculptures*, pp. 176–77 and pl. 27.1; Fergusson, *Tree and Serpent Worship*, pl. 63.3.

53. J. Williams, "Sārnāth Gupta Steles," pp. 171–73, 175–76, and figs. 1–5, 9.

54. For the nativity among these eight scenes: Huntington and Huntington, *Leaves from the Bodhi Tree*, pp. 103–4, 531, and pls. 14, 31, 58, 61–62; Menzies, ed., *Buddha*, nos. 34, 36.

55. For ninth- and tenth-century Bihari stelae: S. Huntington, *"Pāla-Sena" Schools*, pl. 128; Huntington and Huntington, *Leaves from the Bodhi Tree*, no. 11; Pal, *Arts of Nepal*, vol. 1, fig. 88; Menzies, ed., *Buddha*, no. 1. Bronzes: the ca. eighth-century image in Schroeder, *Buddhist Sculptures in Tibet*, vol. 1, no. 67B; the tenth-century image in Saraswati, *Tantrayāna Art*, no. 193.

56. Béguin, *Peintures du bouddhisme tibétain*, no. 38; Rhie and Thurman, *Worlds of Transformation*, no. 11.

57. For art historical analysis of this image: J. Huntington and Bangdel, *Circle of Bliss*, no. 1.

58. On architectural usage of the term *śālabhañjikā*: Vogel, "Woman and Tree."

59. For further discussion of this genre of artistic representation, see chap. 3.

60. Coomaraswamy, *Yakṣas*, p. 86; see also p. 12.

61. This pairing of Cintāmaṇi Lokeśvara and Māyādevī is discussed and illustrated by Dina Bangdel in J. Huntington and Bangdel, *Circle of Bliss*, no. 49.

62. Beal, trans., *Si-yu-ki*, vol. 2, pp. 14–15, 38, 130.

63. Mukherji, *Tour of Exploration*, p. 51.

64. Pradhan, *Lumbini-Kapilwastu-Dewadaha*, p. 68.

65. The earliest recensions of the work do not designate the actual locations of these events. André Bareau provides a detailed survey of canonical and postcanonical texts regarding the Buddha's birthplace, reporting that for many centuries most sources were vague or silent on the matter, occasionally naming Kapilavastu or Lumbinī, until the tradition virtually unanimously settled on Lumbinī by the 1st century C.E.; "Lumbinī et la naissance du futur Buddha," pp. 69–74. Bareau holds that the birth took place at the palace in Kapilavastu but that Aśoka's discovery of a yakṣiṇī chaitya (or stupa) and possible statue at the Lumbinī grove was decisive in the ultimate selection of this location; pp. 77–80. I am grateful to John Strong for drawing my attention to this important study.

66. Pradhan, *Lumbini-Kapilwastu-Dewadaha*, pp. 20–22, 39–41.

67. Legge, trans., *Record of Buddhistic Kingdoms*, p. 67; Li Rongxi, trans., *Great Tang Dynasty Record*, pp. 179–81. This pool, appearing for Māyādevī's use, was probably not for a purificatory after-birth ablution, as might be assumed, but rather for a postpartum rite of well worship, a widespread observance in India today, described in Chawla, *Child-Bearing and Culture*, pp. 63–68.

68. Pradhan, *Lumbini-Kapilwastu-Dewadaha*, pp. 26, 29.

69. Ibid., pp. 34, 37.

70. Ibid., pp. 41–45, 56. The stupas have since disappeared.

71. For descriptions and photographs of the site in the late nineteenth and early twentieth centuries: Mukherji, *Tour of Exploration*; Landon, *Nepal*, vol. 1, pp. 3–10.

72. Kosambi, *Myth and Reality*, p. 101.

73. Charpentier, "Note on the Padariya or Rummindei Inscription," p. 18. Charpentier reconstructs the evolution as Lumbinī → Luṃmini → Rummịn → Rummin-deī.

74. Kosambi, *Myth and Reality*, p. 106. The rendering of the name as Luṃmini in the Aśokan inscription allows for either possibility.

75. Landon, *Nepal*, vol. 1, pp. 6 n. 1, 9; Kosambi, *Myth and Reality*, p. 106.

76. Pradhan, *Lumbini-Kapilwastu-Dewadaha*, pp. 42, 44; Sugandha and Majupuria, *Lumbini*, p. 10.

77. Kosambi, *Myth and Reality*, p. 101; Pradhan, *Lumbini-Kapilwastu-Dewadaha*, pp. 43–44.

78. Pradhan, *Lumbini-Kapilwastu-Dewadaha*, pp. 45, 56.

79. Ibid., p. 44.

80. On this practice: Pramod Kumar, *Folk Icons and Rituals*, pp. 56, 58; Huyler, *Gifts of Earth*, pp. 115, 122. William Crooke also reports an Ojha Kumhār custom wherein a child worships a clay horse on the sixth day after birth; *Popular Religion and Folklore*, vol. 2, p. 208. On Bengali worship of Śītalā with burnt clay horses and elephants, for human fertility and other benefactions: S. K. Mukhopadhyay, *Cult of Goddess Sitala*, pp. 9, 38–39, 48, 65.

81. Brighenti, *Śakti Cult in Orissa*, p. 376 and pl. 28; on the horse and fertility, pp. 373–75.

82. Kosambi, *Myth and Reality*, p. 101.

83. *Buddhacarita* 1.7; Johnston, trans., *Aśvaghoṣa's Buddhacarita*, pt. 2, p. 3.

84. Suggestive in this regard is a tradition that the grove was named after Māyādevī's mother, found in the *Mūlasarvāstivāda Vinaya* (R. Gnoli, ed., *Gilgit Manuscripts of the Sanghabhedavastu*, vol. 1, p. 33); John Strong, personal communication, Dec. 2001. A Tibetan tradition to this effect is cited in Rahula, *Critical Study of the Mahāvastu*, p. 196.

85. Kosambi, *Myth and Reality*, pp. 91–92; Crooke, *Popular Religion and Folklore*, vol. 2, pp. 100–101.

86. *Buddhacarita* 1.8 states that she was accompanied to the grove by thousands of ladies-in-waiting. The *Lalitavistara* relates that the king ordered the palace women to adorn themselves for the procession and that, although they were escorted to the grove by men, Māyādevī entered the grove surrounded only "by the daughters of both men and gods"; Bays, trans., *Voice of the Buddha*, pp. 126–27, 129; quote on p. 129.

87. Kosambi, *Myth and Reality*, p. 92.

88. Jones, trans., *Mahāvastu*, vol. 2, pp. 139–40.

89. P. Vaidya, *Gaṇḍavyūhasūtra*, p. 285, lines 5–6.

90. Cleary, trans., *Realm of Reality*, pp. 259–73.

91. On this well-documented phenomenon: Enthoven, *Folklore of Bombay*, pp. 290–93; Maity, *Human Fertility Cults*, chap. 5. The theme also finds mention in Buddhist literature, e.g., in jātaka no. 509.

92. T. Rhys Davids, trans., *Buddhist Birth-Stories*, pp. 153–54; Roth, "Woman and Tree Motif," pp. 98 n. 24, 99.

93. Bays, trans., *Voice of the Buddha*, pp. 129–30.

94. Jones, trans., *Mahāvastu*, vol. 2, p. 16; this incident does not appear in the version in vol. 1, p. 119. On the use of leaves in birth customs: Randhawa, *Cult of Trees*, p. 62.

95. Artistic representations of the nativity in which the aśoka tree (*Saraca indica*) is clearly identifiable include a Nāgārjunakoṇḍa relief (Randhawa, *Cult of Trees*, fig. 43), an Amarāvatī relief (Coomaraswamy, *Yakṣas*, pl. 20), and a ca. twelfth-century manuscript painting (S. Huntington, *Art of Ancient India*, pl. 28). The tree is predictably identified as the aśoka in the *Aśoka Avadāna*; Strong, *Legend of King Aśoka*, pp. 245–46. Hsuan-tsang reported, on his pilgrimage to Lumbinī, that the tree he saw was an aśoka; Li Rongxi, trans., *Great Tang Dynasty Record*, p. 179.

96. Maity, *Human Fertility Cults*, pp. 179–80.

97. Coomaraswamy, *Yakṣas*, pp. 85–86.

98. Strong, *Legend of King Aśoka*, pp. 245–46, quote on p. 245; see also pp. 120–22.

99. Burgess, *Buddhist Stūpas*, pl. 32 (upper right-hand corner).

100. For this fourteenth-century Newar painting: Pal et al., *Himalayas*, no. 101.

101. See, e.g., the Indic manuscript illustrations in Zwalf, *Buddhism*, p. 116 and pl. 156 (uppermost leaf); Gorakshkar and Desai, "Illustrated Manuscript," pl. 3a.

102. Kosambi, *Myth and Reality*, p. 88; Crooke, *Popular Religion and Folklore*, vol. 1, pp. 264–65.

103. On the fig tree in worship of Ṣaṣṭhī: Maity, *Human Fertility Cults*, pp. 185–86. On two forest observances: Jayakar, *Earth Mother*, pp. 185–86.

104. Kosambi, *Myth and Reality*, p. 102.

105. Sugandha and Majupuria, *Lumbini*, p. 9 and photograph on p. 8. I am grateful to Paula Arai for her firsthand account of the disposition of the shrine as of February 2000.

106. On the U.N. proposal: Pradhan, *Lumbini-Kapilwastu-Dewadaha*, pp. 45–46, 74–78.

107. The symbolic resonances of her name are addressed briefly in Thurman, "Buddhist Views of Nature," p. 99. The symbolic aptness of both parents' names has given rise to speculation that they are purely fictional; Obeyesekere, "Goddess Pattini," p. 226. Kosambi, *Myth and Reality*, p. 108, favors the translation "mother love." *Māyā*, as "illusion," can also have negative connotations as a deluding force that binds humans to worldly

existence; however, this meaning came to the fore in later Hindu philosophies, such as Advaita Vedanta, and would unlikely be implicit in her name. The more general meaning of *māyā* is illusion in the sense of creative power, miracle, and magic; its positive connotation is seen in its reference to the binding force of mother love.

Chapter 3
Yakṣiṇīs: Voluptuous, Magical Nature Spirits

1. My translation; P. Vaidya, ed., *Āryamañjusrimūlakalpa*, p. 442, vv. 3–5. I have rendered "yakṣiṇī-chiefs" as "great yakṣiṇīs" in the service of the syntax of the excerpt.

2. Coomaraswamy, *Yakṣas*, p. 85; S. Shukla, "Kāmukha Female Figures," p. 21.

3. V. Agrawala, *Studies in Indian Art*, pp. 16, 80.

4. Use of the term *yakṣa* remains constant for the male spirits. The females may be designated as *yakṣī* or *yakṣiṇī*; both terms appear in the Buddhist sources I consulted, often used interchangeably within a single work.

5. It is variously suggested that the word derives from the verb *yaj*, "to worship, sacrifice"; the Vedic *yakṣ*, "to reveal, be revealed, move quickly, flash upon"; the Sanskrit *yakṣ* or *pra-yakṣ*, "to honor"; or *yakṣaṃ*, "magical power"; R. Misra, *Yaksha Cult*, pp. 9–11.

6. For Vedic citations, see Coomaraswamy, *Yakṣas*, pp. 9–11, 14–15; R. Misra, *Yaksha Cult*, pp. 11–23.

7. Coomaraswamy, *Yakṣas*, pp. 11, 62, 65, 71 n. 14. The structural types are classified in R. Misra, *Yaksha Cult*, p. 92.

8. Coomaraswamy, *Yakṣas*, pp. 56–57, 62; R. Misra, *Yaksha Cult*, pp. 91–93, 96–97.

9. Coomaraswamy, *Yakṣas*, pp. 16, 56–57.

10. R. Misra, *Yaksha Cult*, pp. 44, 97.

11. This topic has been treated at length elsewhere, most notably, Coomaraswamy's pioneering yet nonpareil *Yakṣas*, the densely documented volume by R. Misra, and the thematic and analytic study by Sutherland, *Disguises of the Demon*. For an extensive survey of characterizations of yakṣas and yakṣiṇīs in the jātakas and other Pali literature, see R. Misra, *Yaksha Cult*, pp. 24–26, 35–45, 147–60; on early Buddhist artistic representations of yakṣa narratives, pp. 135–37.

12. Coomaraswamy cites several such instances in *Yakṣas*, pp. 65, 68–69, 76. In addition, the *Mahāvastu* records that Shakyamuni was lodged and dined by two yakṣas in their abodes; Jones, trans., *Mahāvastu*, vol. 3, p. 319. The *Yakkha Suttas* place Shakyamuni at a series of yakṣa abodes; C. Rhys Davids, trans., *Kindred Sayings*, pp. 262, 264, 266, 275.

13. *Mahāparinibbāna Sutta* 1.4, cited in Coomaraswamy, *Yakṣas*, pp. 69, 73.

14. On the devotional cult of Hārītī in Indian Buddhism, see chap. 5 herein. On her worship in Nepal, see Shaw, *Buddhist Goddesses of Tibet and Nepal*, forthcoming.

15. *Divyāvadāna* legend cited in Cohen, "Nāga, Yakṣiṇī, Buddha," p. 380.

16. Ibid., pp. 380–81.

17. Coomaraswamy, *Yakṣas*, p. 69; R. Misra, *Yaksha Cult*, p. 42 and 42 nn. 11, 14; Burlingame, trans., *Buddhist Legends*, vol. 30, pp. 98–99.

18. Coomaraswamy, *Yakṣas*, pp. 62–64, 69, 76.

19. Cohen, "Nāga, Yakṣiṇī, Buddha," p. 380.

20. Vogel, "Woman and Tree," p. 217.

21. R. Misra, *Yaksha Cult*, p. 149; Ryder, trans., *Shakuntala*, p. 198.

22. Ryder, trans., *Shakuntala,* pp. 198, 200–201, 204, 206.

23. In Pali texts one also finds the terms *rukkha-devatā* and *vana-devatā,* which are not gender-specific and may refer to a yakṣa or yakṣiṇī, but the Sanskrit terms *vṛkṣa-devatā, vṛkṣakā,* and *vana-devatā* are primarily feminine in usage. These terms are virtually but not strictly synonymous with *yakṣiṇī,* since a nāga or other type of spirit might inhabit a tree.

24. Roth, "Woman and Tree Motif," p. 110.

25. Coomaraswamy, *Yakṣas,* pp. 83, 87 n. 5. The simile appeared in *Atharva Veda* 6.8.1.

26. V. Agrawala, *Indian Art,* pp. 226, 229, citing Aśvaghoṣa's reference to this practice, termed *viśeṣakaracanā.* A later Bhūteśvara image shows a yakṣiṇī on a balcony applying just such markings to her face with cosmetics; see fig. 3.12, above. Susan Huntington alternately suggests that the face markings on the Bhārhut figures may be tattoos; *Art of Ancient India,* p. 69.

27. S. Huntington, *Art of Ancient India,* p. 69.

28. V. Agrawala, *Studies in Indian Art,* p. 86.

29. *Dīgha Nikāya* 3.202–203; Walshe, trans., *Long Discourses,* pp. 475–76.

30. Ryder, trans., *Shakuntala,* pp. 198–201.

31. On the crossed-ankle, or Praxitelean, pose: Cohn-Wiener, "Lady under the Tree," p. 28 and fig. on p. 26. Many of the images cited in the next note display this pose.

32. Gāndhāran yakṣiṇī images: Ingholt, *Gandhāran Art,* nos. 49, 61, 153, 359–62, 364; Zwalf, *Gandhāra Sculpture,* nos. 349–54. A yakṣiṇī carrying a child also appears in this corpus: Marshall, *Buddhist Art of Gandhāra,* p. 84 and fig. 112 (mislabeled). The female caryatids whose torsos emerge from acanthus leaves may also be yakṣiṇīs; Zwalf, nos. 346–48.

33. Stone, *Buddhist Art of Nāgārjunakoṇḍa,* pp. 38, 41, 62, 65, 69, and figs. 171, 186–87, 282. Stone notes that the largest stupa at the site may once have had a wooden railing (p. 41). Yakṣiṇīs also appear as framing figures in roundels.

34. Ibid., p. 41. On yakṣiṇīs in decorative reliefs of chaitya windows: Roy, *Śālabhañjikā,* pp. 45–46 and figs. 21–22.

35. Coomaraswamy, *Yakṣas,* p. 83.

36. *Avadānaśataka* no. 53; cited in Vogel, "Woman and Tree," pp. 201–2.

37. Vogel, "Woman and Tree," pp. 204–7, 218; on pp. 207–15 he cites a wide range of Sanskrit sources. Further analysis of the term may be found in Roth, "Woman and Tree Motif." For a fully illustrated monograph on the theme, see Roy, *Śālabhañjikā.*

38. Ridding, trans., *Kādambarī,* pp. 178, 194; Cowell and Thomas, trans., *Harṣa-carita,* p. 149. For additional references, see Roy, *Śālabhañjikā,* pp. 16–19; Pisharoti, "Dohada," pp. 110, 120–21, and, on the dating of the literary convention, p. 114.

39. *Mālavikāgnimitra,* act 3; quotations from Devadhar, *Mālavikāgnimitram,* pp. 64, 73. The episode is analyzed in Pisharoti, "Dohada," pp. 112–14.

40. Bloomfield, "Dohada or Craving of Pregnant Women," pp. 2–3.

41. Pal, *Hindu Religion and Iconology,* p. 20; Roth, "Woman and Tree Motif," pp. 104–5 n. 35.

42. In Gāndhāran reliefs, the supportive element is typically a vase of plenty, rendered in an obloid shape to meet compositional requirements. The lotiform support commonly appears at Bhārhut in the yakṣiṇī reliefs that span the upper half of the pillars between the central medallion and capital; Coomaraswamy, *Sculpture de Bhārhut,* figs. 1, 57–58, 104–7, 109. Additional photographs in which only the lotus and feet or lower body are visible (figs. 59, 67–68, 72–73, 78, 80, 83, 88, 108) further evince the motif's pervasiveness at the site. Similarly, the lotus commonly appears upbearing the smaller *vedikā* (railing) yakṣiṇī reliefs at Sāñcī.

43. Coomaraswamy, *Yakṣas*, pp. 98, 145–46.

44. Ryder, trans., *Shakuntala*, pp. 198–99.

45. For photographs of the Sanghol stupa pillars, see S. P. Gupta, ed., *Kushāṇa Sculptures from Sanghol*, and K. Srivastava, "Sculptures from Sanghol." For additional Bhūteśvara pillars not reproduced in my chapter, see Roy, *Śālabhañjikā*, pls. 50, 54, 59; P. Agrawala, *Mathura Railing Pillars*, pl. 27. Several additional motifs are found at a Jain stupa similar in date and style; see Smith, *Jain Stūpa*.

46. V. Agrawala, *Indian Art*, p. 226.

47. Roy, *Śālabhañjikā*, pp. 65–67; R. Misra, *Yaksha Cult*, pp. 125–26.

48. Boner and Śarmā, trans., *Śilpa Prakāśa*, p. x; see also p. 29. The gelaba-nārī was also foreshadowed at Sanghol, where one finds a figure apparently pulling a vine from a tree and another bearing a *vana-mālā* (forest garland); S. P. Gupta, ed., *Kushāṇa Sculptures from Sanghol*, figs. 17, 23.

49. Drawn from the sixteen major kanyā types of the nārī-bandha; see Boner and Śarmā, trans., *Śilpa Prakāśa*, pp. x–xi, 46–53, and pls. 21–27.

50. An extensive survey of terracotta female figurines for comparison may be found in Coomaraswamy, "Archaic Indian Terracottas." The reader is also directed to the large collection of early terracottas in the Allahabad Museum, well surveyed in Kala, *Terracottas in the Allahabad Museum*.

51. Donaldson, "Propitious-Apotropaic Eroticism," p. 89.

52. Ibid., p. 87.

53. *Śilpa Prakāśa* 1.392–93; Boner and Śarmā, trans., *Śilpa Prakāśa*, pp. lii, 46.

54. Boner and Śarmā, trans., *Śilpa Prakāśa*, p. liii.

55. Donaldson, "Propitious-Apotropaic Eroticism," p. 85.

56. Donaldson equates this imagery, symbolically, with other representations in which the legs of the figure are spread to display the *yoni*; ibid., pp. 87–88.

57. *Atharva Veda* 6.133.5.

58. On these auspicious motifs in yakṣiṇī adornments, see P. Agrawala, *Śrīvatsa*, pp. 1, 9, 13, 17–18 and accompanying illustrations; A. Srivastava, *Nandyāvarta*, pp. 62–63, 67.

59. Coomaraswamy, *Yakṣas*, pp. 56–57.

60. Donaldson, "Propitious-Apotropaic Eroticism," pp. 78, 93.

61. Skt. *sadā dṛḍha*; *Śilpa Prakāśa* 2.26–28; Boner and Śarmā, trans., *Śilpa Prakāśa*, p. 63.

62. Donaldson, "Propitious-Apotropaic Eroticism," p. 77.

63. Ibid., pp. 77, 86.

64. Ibid., pp. 78, 85.

65. Alice Boner discusses the significance of the directional orientation of monuments in this regard; Boner and Śarmā, trans., *Śilpa Prakāśa*, xxv, xxix, xxxi.

66. Donaldson, "Propitious-Apotropaic Eroticism," pp. 77, 96.

67. Coomaraswamy, *Yakṣas*, p. 99.

68. Donaldson, "Propitious-Apotropaic Eroticism," pp. 76–77, 85, 96.

69. Skilling, "Rakṣā Literature," p. 163.

70. Literary references to these practices may be found in Coomaraswamy, *Yakṣas*, pp. 57, 60, 66–67, 73–77, 80; R. Misra, *Yaksha Cult*, pp. 40, 98–100.

71. For jātakas that denounce blood offerings to spirit beings, see DeCaroli, *Haunting the Buddha*, pp. 24–25. Although bali offerings are morally illicit in this context, it is possible they were offered nonetheless, as they are at the Hārītī temple beside Svayambhū Stupa in Nepal.

72. Coomaraswamy, *Yakṣas*, pp. 74, 78–79; R. Misra, *Yaksha Cult*, pp. 100, 157–59.

73. Burlingame, trans., *Buddhist Legends*, vol. 28, pp. 170–75; R. Misra, *Yaksha Cult*, 99, 151.

74. Coomaraswamy, *Yakṣas*, pp. 74, 79, 98; R. Misra, *Yaksha Cult*, pp. 41, 152, 156–57.

75. R. Misra, *Yaksha Cult*, pp. 99, 151, 160.

76. Ibid., pp. 39, 156, 159–60.

77. The *Mahāmāyūrī* provides a lengthy list of yakṣas and yakṣiṇīs and their respective territories; see R. Misra, *Yaksha Cult*, pp. 159, 167–71.

78. The *Saṃyuktavastu*, cited in Coomaraswamy, *Yakṣas*, p. 56.

79. Skilling, "Rakṣā Literature," p. 163.

80. Walshe, trans., *Long Discourses*, pp. 471–78; quote on p. 478. At this stage of the tradition, the spells are called *paritta* rather than *dhāraṇī*, *vidyā*, or mantra.

81. Bays, trans., *Voice of the Buddha*, pp. 584–88.

82. Emmerick, trans., *Sūtra of Golden Light*, p. 68, with minor orthographic changes.

83. Skt. *svasti-gāthā* and *maṅgala-gāthā*; Skilling, "Rakṣā Literature," pp. 129–34.

84. Sutherland, *Disguises of the Demon*, p. 26; S. Shukla, "Kāmukha Female Figures," p. 21.

85. Lamotte, *History of Indian Buddhism*, pp. 620, 687, and quote on p. 637.

86. Literary treatment of this topic is vast and would entail a study in its own right. See, e.g., the narratives in Burlingame, trans., *Buddhist Legends*, vol. 28, p. 277; vol. 29, pp. 17–19, 211–14; vol. 30, pp. 182–83, 141–42, 207–10.

87. Dehejia, "Issues of Spectatorship," p. 5. I include here the figure inscribed as "Culakoka Devatā," who is portrayed in the classical manner of an arboreal yakṣiṇī; moreover, *devatā* is commonly synonymous with *yakkhi* in Pali literature.

88. For in-depth examination of the many ways in which spirit beings, including yakṣas, were integrated into Buddhist practice, thought, and institutional life, see Robert DeCaroli's excellent study, *Haunting the Buddha*, published as the present volume was going to press.

89. For relevant citations to Pali literature: R. Misra, *Yaksha Cult*, pp. 152–55, 160.

90. Sutherland draws this distinction between artistic and literary treatments in *Disguises of the Demon*, pp. 106–7, 137–38.

91. *Padakusalamāṇava Jātaka*, no. 432; Cowell, ed., *Jātaka*, vol. 3, pp. 298–300.

92. *Sakuṇa Jātaka*, no. 196; Cowell, ed., *Jātaka*, vol. 2, pp. 89–91.

93. *Telapatta Jātaka*, no. 96; trans. by Sutherland, *Disguises of the Demon*, p. 138.

94. For the entire story, see Cowell, ed., *Jātaka*, vol. 1, pp. 233–36.

95. *Mahāvaṃsa* chaps. 6–7; cited in Coomaraswamy, *Yakṣas*, p. 50.

96. Horner, trans., *Book of the Discipline*, vol. 1, pp. 48–49, 57–58.

97. Ibid., vol. 1, pp. 211–12, 215, 336–37; vol. 2, pp. 201–2, 206–7, 358; vol. 3, p. 19.

98. Sutherland, *Disguises of the Demon*, pp. 107–9, 119, 135.

99. On Tantric *yakṣiṇī-sādhana*, see chap. 5.

100. Grünwedel, *Buddhist Art in India*, p. 41 n. 1.

101. Vincent Smith as cited in Randhawa, *Cult of Trees*, p. 34; Vogel, "Woman and Tree," pp. 224–25. Both were speaking of the Mathurān corpus.

102. Lamotte, *History of Indian Buddhism*, p. 407.

103. S. Shukla, "Kāmukha Female Figures," pp. 19–21, 23. Vidya Dehejia critiques this view in "Issues of Spectatorship."

104. Roy, "Enchanting Beauties," quote repeated on pp. 65, 66.

Chapter 4
Śrī Lakṣmī: Glorious Good Fortune

1. R. E. Emmerick, trans., *Sūtra of Golden Light*, pp. 48–49, with minor emendation.

2. For overviews of the history and character of Lakṣmī, see Kinsley, *Hindu Goddesses*, chap. 2; Dhal, *Goddess Lakṣmī*. On associated agricultural festivals: Manna, *Mother Goddess Caṇḍī*, pp. 55–57.

3. The most comprehensive compilation of Vedic references to Śrī Lakṣmī remains that in Gonda, *Aspects of Early Viṣṇuism*, pp. 176–231. For a summary overview: P. Agrawala, *Goddesses in Ancient India*, pp. 92–98. Among Harappan figures that may represent early expressions of the archetype that later gave rise to Lakṣmī are the figurine with flowers in her hair and another that presses a hand to her breast; Kenoyer, *Ancient Cities*, figs. 1.7, 7.21. Coomaraswamy addresses her continuity with earlier terracotta figurines in "Early Indian Iconography," p. 181.

4. For Sāñcī examples of Lakṣmī grasping her sash: Marshall and Foucher, *Monuments of Sāñchī*, vol. 2, pls. 24, 56; vol. 3, pls. 74.1b, 76.12b, 76.15a, 78.21b, 78.22a, 87.71a. I haven't found an explanation of this widespread, clearly symbolic gesture, seen also in yakṣiṇi iconography. That the gesture intimates fertility is suggested by its positioning in the hip area and usage in association with Hārītī (Ingholt, *Gandhāran Art*, no. 340) and Ṣaṣṭhī (Joshi, *Mātṛkās*, figs. 41–43, 45, 46), divine patrons of childbirth.

5. Additional reliefs: Coomaraswamy, *Sculpture de Bhārhut*, fig. 123; Marshall and Foucher, *Monuments of Sāñchī*, vol. 2, pl. 13; vol.3, pl. 87.71a. Quotation from Gonda, *Aspects of Early Viṣṇuism*, p. 244.

6. One of at least two such Bhārhut examples is published in Coomaraswamy, *Sculpture de Bhārhut*, fig. 124. The unusual squatting, or yogic, pose she displays in this relief is discussed in O. Singh, *Iconography of Gaja-Lakshmī*, pp. 26–27.

7. Two-thirds of the Sāñcī reliefs portray the Gaja-Lakṣmī hierophany; see Marshall and Foucher, *Monuments of Sāñchī*, vol. 2, pls. 11, 13, 24, 25, 28, 41, 44, 56; vol. 3, pls. 74.1b, 83.49a, 87.71a, 88.76b, 90.85a, 91.i, 98, 102. Gaja-Lakṣmī was initially identified as a birth scene by Alfred Foucher in *On the Iconography of the Buddha's Nativity* and is mislabeled as such in his publications and other works. Ananda Coomaraswamy wrote "Early Indian Iconography" largely to rectify that misidentification; p. 187 and passim.

8. Marshall and Foucher, *Monuments of Sāñchī*, vol. 3, pl. 78.22d.

9. Dhal, *Goddess Lakṣmī*, pp. 49–52; Scheftelowitz, *Apokryphen*, pp. 72–73, 77–78.

10. For second- and first-century B.C.E. coins depicting Lakṣmī, see in Allan, *Coins of Ancient India*, the coinage of rulers of Ayodhyā: pp. 131, 133, and pls. 16.14–16, 17.8, 43.5; of the Rājanya tribe: pp. 211–12 and pls. 29.13, 29.20–21; of the Kulinda ruler Amoghabhūti (last half first century B.C.E.): pp. ci, 159–62, and pls. 22.1–8, 22.14–16; of Mathurā rulers of ca. 200–40 B.C.E.: pp. 170–71, 173–84, and pls. 24.1–18, 25.1–7, 25.12–26, 26.1–5, 44.9–10; and of Mathurā rulers of ca. 40–10 B.C.E.: pp. 187, 190–91, and pls. 26.12–18, 43.15–17. For third-century B.C.E. Kauśāmbī coins depicting Lakṣmī, see p. 149 and pl. 20.15; for third- and second-century tribal coins from Ujjayinī: pp. cxlv, 252, 256, and pls. 18.24, 36.4–5, 38.23–25.

11. The sandstone and terracotta images are difficult to date with precision. On the sandstone reliefs of Gaja-Lakṣmī from Kauśāmbī, one possibly dating from the Śuṅga period (second century B.C.E.), see O. Singh, *Iconography of Gaja-Lakshmī*, pp. 40–41. One of the reliefs appears on an architrave from a monument of unknown sectarian provenance.

For two terracotta plaques of Gaja-Lakṣmī from Kauśāmbī, possibly dating from the second and first centuries B.C.E., see Kala, *Terracottas in the Allahabad Museum*, p. 31 and figs. 69–70. For a Kauśāmbī plaque that may represent another conception of Lakṣmī, see P. Agrawala, "Unique Śuṅga Plaque."

12. Coomaraswamy, "Early Indian Iconography," p. 179; Coomaraswamy, *Yakṣas*, chaps. 11–12, especially pp. 98–99. For Vedic and Upaniṣadic references to water as the foundation and source of earth: Pintchman, *Rise of the Goddess*, pp. 28–29, 31–32, 46–47, 54–56.

13. Coomaraswamy, *Yakṣas*, p. 97.

14. Vajracharya advances this view in "Atmospheric Gestation," pt. 2.

15. See Coomaraswamy, *Yakṣas*, p. 155, and "Early Indian Iconography," pp. 178–79.

16. On Lakṣmī's ocean birth: Dhal, *Goddess Lakṣmī*, pp. 59, 84–88, 99–100, 102, 105, 108.

17. Vajracharya, "Atmospheric Gestation," pt. 2, p. 43.

18. Coomaraswamy, *Yakṣas*, p. 155. Contemporaneous yakṣiṇī figures may stand atop a lotus pedestal but are more commonly portrayed on other supports. See chap. 3, above.

19. Coomaraswamy, *Elements of Buddhist Iconography*, p. 22.

20. Dhal, *Goddess Lakṣmī*, p. 102.

21. Coomaraswamy, "Early Indian Iconography," p. 185. On the symbolism of the cloud elephant: Vajracharya, "Atmospheric Gestation," pt. 2, pp. 41–42, 47, 51 n. 10. On the inverted rain pot as cloud motif: Vajracharya, "Symbolism of Ashokan Pillars," pp. 55–57, 61.

22. O. Singh, *Iconography of Gaja-Lakshmī*, pp. 7–8, 10, 85, 91–92. The earth/female and rain/male pairing may allude to or prefigure the relationship between Lakṣmī and Indra (who is associated with rainfall, thunder, and elephants) in the *Mahābhārata* and other sources; Dhal, *Goddess Lakṣmī*, pp. 88–90.

23. On Lakṣmī and sovereignty: Bailly, "Śrī-Lakṣmī," and, on lustration, p. 142.

24. Zwalf, *Gandhāra Sculpture*, no. 95; Victoria and Albert Museum, IM.65-1911.

25. See Berkson, *Caves at Aurangabad*, pl. b on p. 113 and the topmost figure on p. 114; B. Misra, *Nālandā*, vol. 2, p. 75 and fig. 32; Brighenti, *Śakti Cult in Orissa*, pl. 33.

26. Boner and Śarmā, trans., *Śilpa Prakāśa*, pp. ix, li, 27–29, 92. The center of a lintel where her figure is carved is termed "Lakṣmī-sthala"; pp. 17, 151. Lakṣmī is also visualized in this location in a mandala mansion: *Lakṣmī Tantra* 37.45.

27. Boner and Śarmā, trans., *Śilpa Prakāśa*, pp. l–li.

28. *Agni Purāṇa* 41.8, cited in Dhal, *Goddess Lakṣmī*, p. 59.

29. Lamotte, *History of Indian Buddhism*, p. 637.

30. Dehejia, "Issues of Spectatorship," p. 5. On Bhārhut relief subjects correlated with their donors, see Dehejia, *Discourse in Early Buddhist Art*, pp. 277–80.

31. *Dhammapada Aṭṭhakathā* 2.17, cited in Sahai, *Iconography*, p. 162.

32. Jātaka no. 535; Cowell, ed., *Jātaka*, vol. 5, p. 213.

33. Jātaka no. 546; Cowell, ed., *Jātaka*, vol. 6, p. 181.

34. Jātaka no. 521; Cowell, ed., *Jātaka*, vol. 5, p. 61.

35. Jātaka no. 382; Cowell, ed., *Jātaka*, vol. 3, pp. 165–68.

36. Jātaka no. 284; Cowell, ed., *Jātaka*, vol. 2, p. 282. For additional references to Lakṣmī in Pali literature: Coomaraswamy, "Early Indian Iconography," p. 177; Haldar, *Early Buddhist Mythology*, pp. 106–10.

37. The story abbreviated here introduces *Khadiraṅgāra Jātaka* (no. 40) and is cited as the frame story of *Siri Jātaka* (no. 284); Cowell, ed., *Jātaka*, vol. 1, pp. 100–103, and vol. 2, p. 279.

38. Emmerick, trans., *Sūtra of Golden Light*, pp. 48–49.

39. Ibid.

40. Ibid.

41. For further discussion of Lakṣmī and Tārā, see chap. 17 below; on Lakṣmī and Vasudhārā, chap. 13.

42. My translation; P. Vaidya, ed., *Āryamañjusrimūlakalpa* [*sic*], p. 232, lines 12–14.

43. Derge Kanjur, rGyud section, Tōh. nos.: *Mahālakṣmī Sūtra* 740 (1 fol.); *Mahālakṣmī Sūtra* 1005 (2 fol.); *Ārya-śrīmahādevī Vyākaraṇa* 739 (10 fol.).

44. *Lha mo dpal chen mo'i sgrub thabs sgom lung man ngag dang bcas pa'i skor; sGrub thabs kun btus*, vol. 13, fol. 353–393; Chandra, *Buddhist Iconography*, no. 829; Willson and Brauen, eds., *Deities of Tibetan Buddhism*, no. 325.

45. Sakya scholar Ngawang Jorden, personal communication, July 1995.

46. Nebesky-Wojkowitz, *Oracles and Demons*, p. 77.

47. B. Bhattacharyya, ed., *Niṣpannayogāvalī*, pt. 1, pp. 70–71, 81–82.

48. Skorupski, trans., *Sarvadurgatipariśodhana Tantra*, p. 90.

49. Lakṣmī also appears thus at Gyantse in a Padmāntaka mandala and as a subsidiary figure in a mural of Sitātapatrā; Ricca and Lo Bue, *Great Stupa of Gyantse*, p. 84 and pl. 62 (lower right corner), and p. 101 and pl. 86.

Chapter 5
Hārītī: Goddess of Motherly Love

1. My translation; stotra by Bhavaratna in Pāṇḍeya, ed., *Bauddhastotrasaṃgraha*, p. 261, vv. 4, 6. The text spells her name Hāratī, the preferred rendering in Nepal.

2. "Hārītī" appears in the *Sādhanamālā*, "Hārītikā" in Kṣemendra's *Avadāna Kalpalatā*.

3. Pradhan, *Swayambhu*, p. 31.

4. These works, originally Sanskrit compositions in many cases, survive now primarily in Chinese and Tibetan. Peri, "Hārītī," provides a detailed survey of Chinese translations of works in which Hārītī is mentioned.

5. This narrative appears in *Saṃyuktavastu* chap. 31, in the *Bhikṣuṇī Vibhaṅga* of the *Mūlasarvāstivāda Vinaya*. Lamotte dates the compilation of this Vinaya to the fourth or fifth century (*History of Indian Buddhism*, p. 657), although portions of the work are earlier. I summarize here from Peri's French translation of the Chinese version, which dates from the eighth century, in "Hārītī," pp. 3–14. Her Sanskrit name is variously reconstructed from the Chinese as Abhirati, Nandinī, Nandikā, and Nandā. A briefer but quite similar version of the story appears in Kṣemendra's *Avadāna Kalpalatā* (eleventh century C.E.), translated in *Leaves of the Heaven Tree*, pp. 62–64.

6. This former life is recounted in Peri, "Hārītī," pp. 12–13, and in *Leaves of the Heaven Tree*, pp. 63–64.

7. Versions cited in Peri, "Hārītī," p. 22; R. Misra, *Yaksha Cult*, p. 73.

8. Peri, "Hārītī," pp. 16–20.

9. Ibid., pp. 20–21. Peri found no Sanskrit equivalent for the name "Tcheni."

10. Ibid., p. 30, from a biography translated into Chinese in the fifth century.

11. Ibid., p. 31, from the *Mahāmāyā Sūtra*.

12. Obeyesekere, *Cult of the Goddess Pattini*, pp. 62, 67; quote on p. 67.

13. Ibid., pp. 60, 66, 70.

14. Ibid., p. 59.

15. Ibid., pp. 57–59; quote on p. 59.

16. See, e.g., *Ayoghara Jātaka* in Cowell, ed., *Jātaka*, vol. 4, pp. 304–5, and *Jayadissa Jātaka* in vol. 5, pp. 11–12. On psychosocial dynamics of this pattern: Sutherland, *Disguises of the Demon*, pp. 144–45.

17. Burlingame, trans., *Buddhist Legends*, vol. 28, pp. 170–75; vol. 30, pp. 176–77.

18. Strong, *Legend and Cult of Upagupa*, pp. 34–36.

19. Foucher, *Beginnings of Buddhist Art*, p. 280.

20. For further discussion of "epidemic goddesses," see chap. 9 below.

21. *Leaves of the Heaven Tree*, p. 62.

22. For an excellent survey of these analogous figures: V. Agrawala, *Ancient Indian Folk Cults*, pp. 36, 79–94, 184.

23. My translation; stotra by Bhavaratna in Pāṇḍeya, *Bauddhastotrasaṃgraha*, p. 261, v. 5.

24. On yakṣiṇī worship at Buddhist stupas, see chap. 3.

25. Cohen, "Nāga, Yakṣiṇī, Buddha," pp. 381–83.

26. M. Mitra, "Hārītī in Buddhist Monasteries," p. 325.

27. Takakusu, trans., *Record of the Buddhist Religion*, p. 37.

28. Ibid.

29. Ibid., p. 38.

30. Ibid., p. 36.

31. E.g., Strong, *Legend and Cult of Upagupa*, p. 37; Cohen, "Nāga, Yakṣiṇī, Buddha," p. 389.

32. Murthy, *Sculptures of Vajrayāna Buddhism*, p. 54; M. Mitra, "Hārītī in Buddhist Monasteries," p. 323.

33. Beal, trans., *Si-yu-ki*, pp. 110–11 (reading "Po-lu-sha" as Peshawar).

34. Foucher, *Beginnings of Buddhist Art*, pp. 122, 282; Foucher, *Notes on the Ancient Geography of Gandhara*, pp. 17–19.

35. See chap. 3 on yakṣiṇī iconography.

36. For other important Gāndhāran effigies: Zwalf, *Gandhāra Sculpture*, no. 92; Dobbins, "Hāritī Image," fig. 1. A late (ca. fifth century, according to Tissot, "Site of Sahrī-Bāhlol," p. 605) Gāndhāran image from Sahrī Bāhlol (Peshawar Museum, no. 1773), commonly identified as Hārītī, would appear, rather, to be a Śaivite figure, perhaps a mātṛkā, created in a Buddhist context as a syncretic icon. For this widely published image—fanged, four-armed, bearing a wine cup, child, trident, and vessel, see Ingholt, *Gandhāran Art*, no. 341. The amended identification, suggested by Zwalf, p. 71, finds support in a slightly earlier (ca. fourth century) Gāndhāran image of Śiva bearing a similar trident and vessel; Taddei, "New Early Śaiva Image," fig. 1. Moreover, Hārītī is in no other known instance endowed with four arms.

37. Bivar, "Chronology of the Kuṣāṇas," p. 19 and, on the epidemic, pp. 19–21.

38. Lamotte, *History of Indian Buddhism*, p. 689.

39. *Mahāvaṃsa* 12.22, cited in Lamotte, *History of Indian Buddhism*, p. 336 (here Pāñcika's name appears as Paṇḍaka).

40. For additional discussion and images: Ingholt, *Gandhāran Art*, nos. 342–44.

41. For additional discussion of and citations on Pharro and Ardokhsho: Rosenfield, *Dynastic Arts of the Kushans*, pp. 246–47. For artistic representations: Rosenfield, fig. 78; Zwalf, *Gandhāra Sculpture*, no. 98. Separate images of Ardokhsho are also misidentified as Hārītī in many publications.

42. Rosenfield, *Dynastic Arts of the Kushans*, p. 247.

43. Joshi, *Mātṛkās*, p. 110 and fig. 16.

44. Possible examples: ibid., figs. 14, 15, 17, 18. A number of similar images are described but not reproduced in V. Agrawala, *Brahmanical Images of Mathura Art*, pp. 88–91. Several of the female figures bear a goblet or flower, attributes not demonstrably associated with Hārītī, but any or all of the child-cradling figures could well be Hārītī.

45. Coomaraswamy, *Yakṣas*, p. 239 and pls. 21c–e. See V. Agrawala, *Brahmanical Images of Mathura Art*, pp. 80–86, for descriptions of additional Kuṣāṇa and Gupta period images potentially identifiable as the couple.

46. Cohen analyzes and illustrates this shrine in detail; "Nāga, Yakṣiṇī, Buddha," pp. 381–91 and figs. 5–10.

47. For the Aurangabad relief, in Cave 7: Berkson, *Caves at Aurangabad*, pp. 115–18. For the Ellora relief, in Cave 8: Malandra, *Unfolding a Maṇḍala*, p. 104 and fig. 88.

48. Passage from the *Mantra Mahodadhi* (sixteenth century); Bühnemann, *Iconography of Hindu Tantric Deities*, p. 191.

49. D. Mitra, *Ratnagiri*, p. 168 and pls. 120A, 121A. One does find, on the right wall of the Hārītī chapels at Ajanta, two boys, perhaps sons of Hārītī, carrying roosters or chickens; Richard Cohen, personal communication, Aug. 2004. Thus, the association of the capon with Hārītī at Ratnagiri is not unique, but the vast distance between the Deccan and Orissa leaves open the possibility that the meaning of the motif differs in the two contexts.

50. S. Huntington, *"Pāla-Sena" Schools*, pp. 40, 195, and fig. 29.

51. Bhattasali, *Buddhist and Brahmanical Sculptures*, pp. 63, 67, and pl. 25.

52. For the iconography of Hārītī in Newar Buddhism, see Shaw, *Buddhist Goddesses of Tibet and Nepal*, forthcoming.

53. Waddell, *Tibetan Buddhism*, p. 219.

54. The prayer is translated in ibid., p. 216.

55. I learned of but did not witness this practice at the Sakya Thorig monastery, Bodhanath, Kathmandu.

56. For brief discussion of this painting: Béguin, *Peintures du bouddhisme tibétain*, no. 228. The mongoose is more commonly associated with Pāñcika/Kubera but as an attribute of Hārītī finds precedent in a Mathurān image of the couple in which both display the creature: V. Agrawala, *Brahmanical Images of Mathura Art*, p. 82, no. 244.

57. Willson and Brauen, eds., *Deities of Tibetan Buddhism*, no. 270.

58. Béguin, *Peintures du bouddhisme tibétain*, no. 60, vignette nos. 23–26.

59. A locus classicus of this motif is the *Āṭānāṭiya Sutta*, discussed in chap. 3.

60. Watson, trans., *Lotus Sutra*, pp. 309–11. Hārītī's name is rendered here, in literal translation from the Chinese, as "Mother of Devil Children."

61. Peri, "Hārītī," p. 27, citing a *Mahāmāyūrī Dhāraṇī* text.

62. *Sādhanamālā* no. 36, p. 82, last two lines; no. 48, p. 103, lines 9–11.

63. For the Chinese titles of these works: Peri, "Hārītī," pp. 83, 96.

64. On yakṣiṇī-sādhana, see Shaw, "Magical Lovers, Sisters, and Mothers."

65. My translation, from the French and Sanskrit in Peri, "Hārītī," pp. 84–85.

66. My translation, from ibid., p. 85.

67. My translation, from ibid., p. 86.

68. For these requirements, ibid., pp. 87, 91.

69. Ibid., pp. 87–88.

70. Ibid., pp. 91–92; quote on p. 92.

71. Ibid., pp. 96–97.

72. Both of these rites are described in ibid., p. 97.
73. Ibid., pp. 95, 96.
74. Foucher, *Beginnings of Buddhist Art*, p. 291.

Chapter 6
Female Buddhas: The Case of Gotamī

1. Translation from *Gotamī Apadāna* by Walters, "Gotamī's Story," p. 137.
2. The event is described with reference to Gotamī's virtuous qualities in *Buddhacarita* 2.2 and the *Lalitavistara* (Bays, trans., *Voice of the Buddha*, p. 149). For differing traditions on whether Gotamī was the younger or elder sister of Māyādevī, when she married Śuddhodana, and her selection as foster mother of the Bodhisattva, see Rahula, *Critical Study of the Mahāvastu*, pp. 210–11.
3. She appears in the *Lalitavistara* taking the Bodhisattva to a temple (Bays, trans., *Voice of the Buddha*, pp. 174, 182), on the eve of his great departure (pp. 304–6), and lamenting his absence (pp. 341–42, 344), but this attention is exceptional in my survey of literature in translation.
4. For textual sources and discussion of this much analyzed event: Sponberg, "Attitudes toward Women," pp. 13–16, 32 n. 14, 33 nn. 18–20, 34 nn. 21–22.
5. For other examples: Ingholt, *Gandhāran Art*, no. 105 (detail) and 162C; Zwalf, *Gandhāra Sculpture*, no. 207, as well as Zwalf's discussion of the relief illustrated here (no. 206 in his work) on pp. 187–88.
6. On the genre and performance of the *Gotamī Apadāna*: Walters, "Voice from the Silence," p. 368; Walters, "Gotamī's Story," pp. 114–15.
7. Walters, "Voice from the Silence," pp. 368, 371. On the historical context of the *Gotamī Apadāna*: Walters, "Stūpa, Story, and Empire."
8. Walters, "Gotamī's Story," p. 115.
9. Walters, "Voice from the Silence," pp. 372, 377; see also p. 358.
10. Ibid., pp. 368–69; see also pp. 377–79.
11. Ibid., p. 358.
12. Walters, "Gotamī's Story," pp. 118–38.
13. Li Rongxi, trans., *Great Tang Dynasty Record*, p. 211.
14. Walters, "Voice from the Silence," p. 375.
15. Ibid., pp. 373–75.
16. Ibid., p. 373.
17. Ibid., p. 375.
18. Ibid., pp. 375, 378.
19. Ibid., p. 378. For a contrasting interpretation of the biography that elicits themes of female oppression: Wilson, *Charming Cadavers*, pp. 30–31, 142–48.
20. This doctrine, stated once in both the *Majjhima-* and *Aṅguttara-nikāya*, is discussed in A. Sharma, "Female Buddha," pp. 74–75, and dates from between the late third and first centuries B.C.E., according to Kajiyama, "Women in Buddhism," pp. 56–58.
21. Walters, "Voice from the Silence," p. 379.
22. Sponberg, "Attitudes toward Women," pp. 13, 15–18.
23. On this Theravada controversy: A. Sharma, "Female Buddha," pp. 73–74, 76–77. It is possible, too, that the issue of female bodhisattvahood occupied the authors of the

Flower Ornament Scripture, wherein the goddesses discussed below (chap. 7), as well as women in the text, describe the series of almost exclusively female lifetimes in which they progressed on the Mahayana path toward Buddhahood.

Chapter 7
Goddesses in the *Flower Ornament Scripture*

1. Cleary, trans., *Realm of Reality*, pp. 189–90, elisions not noted.

2. I include Māyādevī among the twelve because of her status as a cosmic world mother in the text and because it refers to her explicitly as a goddess (e.g., as "goddess Māyā," *māyāyā devyāḥ*, p. 339, line 1, in P. Vaidya, *Gaṇḍavyūhasūtra*). The term *devī* primarily means "goddess" and secondarily "queen," both of which might apply to Māyādevī here; her exalted, supernal character in the text is most definitive in this regard. The other eleven are explicitly termed "goddess" (most often *devatā*, occasionally *devī*).

3. Cleary, trans., *Realm of Reality*, p. 160.

4. Ibid., p. 159.

5. This event is discussed in chap. 1, above.

6. Cleary, trans., *Realm of Reality*, pp. 159–60.

7. The night goddess may alternately be shown as white: Huntington and Huntington, *Leaves from the Bodhi Tree*, no. 89 (color plate).

8. On a range of such goddesses: P. Agrawala, *Goddesses in Ancient India*, pp. 89, 101–8. Buddhists apparently shared this conception, as seen in a *Lalitavistara* passage wherein most of the constellations and stars invoked by the Buddha are feminine in gender; Bays, trans., *Voice of the Buddha*, pp. 584–87. In the later Mahayana pantheon, too, the planets are personified by a female divinity, Grahamātṛkā, "Planet Mother."

9. Cleary, trans., *Realm of Reality*, pp. 160–71.

10. Kosambi, *Myth and Reality*, chap. 3, esp. pp. 82, 84–85, 95, 103, 108–9.

11. Cleary, trans., *Realm of Reality*, p. 161.

12. Ibid., p. 162.

13. *Ṛg Veda* 10.127.1–8; *Atharva Veda* 19.48.3.

14. Cleary, trans., *Realm of Reality*, pp. 170–71.

15. Ibid., pp. 171–259.

16. Ibid., pp. 265–66.

17. Ibid., p. 260.

18. Ibid., pp. 266–67.

19. Ibid., p. 267.

20. Ibid.

21. Ibid., p. 268.

22. Ibid., pp. 273–76.

23. Ibid., pp. 276–305.

24. *Nagara-devatā* is roughly synonymous with *grāma-devatā*, another commonly used term. On this genre of goddess: Kinsley, *Hindu Goddesses*, chap. 13.

25. Cleary, trans., *Realm of Reality*, pp. 306–7. The city goddess of Kapilavastu also appears on the occasion of Siddhartha's great departure from the city, asking him to look at "her" one last time before setting forth; Jones, trans., *Mahāvastu*, vol. 2, p. 159.

26. Cleary, trans., *Realm of Reality*, pp. 307–8.

27. Ibid., pp. 312–13.

28. Ibid., pp. 315–16.

29. The next most populous group is that of four monks. Three are Sudhana's first teachers, representing the point of departure of his journey; the goddesses appear much later and give more advanced teachings. The relegation of the male monastic voice is consistent with a broader Mahayana trend of shifting religious authority from the clerical faction to the more inclusive category of the bodhisattva.

30. This calculation is based on the Sanskrit edition of the *Gaṇḍavyūha Sūtra* by P. Vaidya. The 143 pages devoted to meetings with goddesses constitute 38 percent of the pilgrimage narrative and 33 percent of the entire text. The meetings constitute an identical proportion of Cleary's translation from the Chinese.

31. Cleary, trans., *Realm of Reality*, pp. 162, 182.

Chapter 8
Prajñāpāramitā: Luminous Mother of Perfect Wisdom

1. Translation by Lex Hixon, *Mother of the Buddhas*, p. 96; cf. Conze, trans., *Perfection of Wisdom*, p. 135.

2. Conze, "Development of Prajñāpāramitā Thought," p. 125. Joanna Macy contrasts Prajñāpāramitā and the other type of divinity; "Perfection of Wisdom," pp. 316, 326–29.

3. For insightful discussion of Prajñāpāramitā's concomitantly transcendent and gendered nature: Simmer-Brown, *Dakini's Warm Breath*, pp. 83, 86, 91–93, 112–15.

4. Conze, trans., *Perfection of Wisdom*, p. 31, with minor emendations.

5. Ibid., pp. 172–73; see also p. 105.

6. Hixon, *Mother of the Buddhas*, p. 76.

7. Conze, trans., *Perfection of Wisdom*, p. 172.

8. Ibid., p. 147.

9. Ibid., pp. 17–18, 111–12, 196, 236–37, and passim.

10. Ibid., p. 172.

11. Ibid., pp. 107, 138, and passim.

12. Ibid., p. 179.

13. Ibid., p. 268.

14. Ibid., p. 135.

15. Ibid., p. 107.

16. Ibid., p. 178.

17. Ibid., pp. 108, 111, 267; quote on p. 116.

18. Ibid., pp. 116–17, with orthographic changes and my rendition of *bhūtakoṭi* as "supreme reality," rather than "reality-limit."

19. Trans. by Hixon, *Mother of the Buddhas*, p. 74; cf. Conze, trans., *Perfection of Wisdom*, pp. 116–17.

20. Conze, trans., *Perfection of Wisdom*, pp. 107–8; see also p. 15.

21. Ibid., p. 105.

22. Ibid., pp. 17, 116.

23. Ibid., pp. 107–8, 116–17, 266–67.

24. Ibid., p. 299; see also pp. 15, 289.

25. Ibid., pp. 266–67, 300.

26. Ibid., p. 138, with minor emendations.

27. Ibid., p. 179.

28. On her identity with dharmas and hence presence in them, ibid., pp. 138, 145, 178, 297.

29. Conze, "Remarks on a Pāla Ms.," pp. 120–21.

30. See Schopen, "The Phrase *'sa pṛthivīpradeśaś caityabhūto bhavet.'*"

31. Fa-hsien, a Chinese pilgrim to India in the late fourth and early fifth centuries, recorded that he witnessed veneration of Prajñāpāramitā; Legge, trans., *Record of Buddhistic Kingdoms,* p. 46. Although it is widely accepted that Fa-hsien was referring to image worship, the object of worship was in all likelihood a manuscript, on the grounds that no images or iconographic descriptions of Prajñāpāramitā survive from that period.

32. Malandra, *Unfolding a Maṇḍala,* p. 58 and fig. 132.

33. Description from a Prajñāpāramitā commentary translated into Chinese in ca. 750 C.E.; Conze, "Iconography of the Prajñāpāramitā," pp. 247–48.

34. These nine descriptions are compiled and translated in D. Bhattacharyya, *Studies in Buddhist Iconography,* pp. 38–39, 41.

35. Skt. *pañca-tathāgata-mukuṭa*; *Sādhanamālā* no. 152, p. 312, lines 8–9; no. 159, p. 324, line 13.

36. For art historical treatment of my Fig. 8.1, see Huntington and Huntington, *Leaves from the Bodhi Tree,* no. 8. For detailed analysis of unique iconographic features of the image and an argument that "Prajñāpāramitā has *visually* displaced the Buddha in a most pointed way here," see Kinnard, *Imaging Wisdom,* pp. 135–41; quote on p. 141.

37. *Sādhanamālā* nos. 152, 154, 159. This manner of portraying the goddess is preferred over the two-armed form described in *Sādhanamālā* nos. 153, 157–58, which displays a single book-on-lotus, and in nos. 151, 155, which displays a lotus in one hand and a book in the other. I have not encountered an effigy that separates the book and lotus in this way.

38. Stone reliefs from Nālandā and Ratnagiri: D. Bhattacharyya, *Studies in Buddhist Iconography,* pl. 12; D. Mitra, *Ratnagiri,* pp. 316–17 and pl. 97B. A votive bronze: Saraswati, *Tantrayāna Art,* no. 142.

39. This configuration, with texts on both lotuses, is also attested in a ninth-century stone effigy in the Mahant Collection at Bodhgayā (Rick Asher, photograph no. A81-27-34). For a fifteenth-century Tibetan statue with this iconography, sans texts on the lotuses: Ashencaen and Leonov, *Visions of Perfect Worlds,* no. 9.

40. On the find-site of this image: Sahu, *Buddhism in Orissa,* p. 206.

41. For this two-armed configuration, see the manuscript illustration in Saraswati, *Tantrayāna Art,* no. 233; the fifteenth-century metal sculpture in Pal, *Arts of Nepal,* vol. 1, pl. 239. She is shown, rather exceptionally, with only the teaching gesture in Saraswati, *Tantrayāna Art,* no. 251.

42. White and yellow epiphanies with this iconography are described in the *Dharmakoṣa Saṃgraha,* a late Newar compendium; D. Bhattacharyya, *Studies in Buddhist Iconography,* pp. 40, 42. Newar artistic representations: Béguin, *Art ésotérique,* no. 9; Dehejia et al., *Devi,* no. 58; D. Bhattacharyya, *Studies in Buddhist Iconography,* pl. 4; Pal, *Arts of Nepal,* vol. 2, pl. 43; Stooke, "XI Century Illuminated Palm Leaf Ms," illus. on p. 8.

43. Saraswati, *Tantrayāna Art,* no. 143.

44. On this configuration: J. Huntington and Bangdel, *Circle of Bliss,* no. 23.

45. Chandra, *Buddhist Iconography,* nos. 699, 2361; Willson and Brauen, eds., *Deities of Tibetan Buddhism,* no. 190.

46. A Kashmiri statue exhibiting this feature, as well as vajra and rosary attributes: Pal, *Bronzes of Kashmir*, no. 67. A similar Tibetan statue, in which the rosary, text, and vajra are present but in different hands: Clark, ed., *Two Lamaistic Pantheons*, vol. 2, p. 206, no. 6A61. For this basic form, with rosary but sans vajra: Willson and Brauen, eds., *Deities of Tibetan Buddhism*, no. 191; *Sher phyin yi ge gcig ma'i gzhung gsal byed dang bcas pa bzhugs so* in *sGrub thabs kun btus*, vol. 6, fol. 135–148.

47. An Indic effigy incorporating the vajra: Pal, *Bronzes of Kashmir*, no. 67. Another Kashmiri bronze includes what appears to be a vajra, albeit not fully discernible in the photograph; Uhlig, *Tantrische Kunst*, pl. 15. Newar examples include a manuscript illumination published in Edou, *Machig Labdron*, following the table of contents, and drawings in late Newar iconographic guidebooks; Bühnemann, *Buddhist Deities of Nepal*, p. 55, fig. 40, and p. 101, fig. 54.

48. For four-armed examples with the teaching gesture: Chandra, *Buddhist Iconography*, no. 46; Rhie and Thurman, *Wisdom and Compassion*, pl. 122.2. For four-armed examples with meditation gesture: Chandra, *Buddhist Iconography*, no. 1083; Essen and Thingo, *Götter des Himalaya*, nos. 1-26, 2-84. The vajra appears in the depiction of a two-armed form in Willson and Brauen, eds., *Deities of Tibetan Buddhism*, no. 452, but not, interestingly, in the corresponding sādhana on p. 393, which stipulates a text where the vajra appears.

49. She has six arms when she appears in the Guhyamañjuvajra and Kālacakra mandala retinues, but as an independent figure only rarely: at the Sumtsek at Alchi (S. Huntington, *Art of Ancient India*, pp. 382–83 and pl. 19); on a Tibetan Prajñāpāramitā manuscript cover (J. Huntington and Bangdel, *Circle of Bliss*, no. 22). The six-armed form included in two late Newar iconographic sketchbooks (Bühnemann, *Buddhist Deities of Nepal*, p. 55, fig. 38, and p. 101, fig. 48) is also an obscure exception. According to Bühnemann, p. 17, the books include uncommon epiphanies possibly derived from written sādhanas such as the *Niṣpannayogāvalī*; thus, they may be forms in which divinities appear as attendants or mandala retinue figures.

50. See chap. 14 for more on the common confusion between Cundā and Prajñāpāramitā images.

51. Conze cites one Chinese and three Tibetan mandala texts in "Iconography of the Prajñāpāramitā," p. 257.

52. Lo Bue and Ricca, *Gyantse Revisited*, p. 144 and pl. 26; Tucci, *Gyantse*, pt. 1, p. 120 and figs. 31–32.

53. *Sādhanamālā* no. 159.

54. Mullin, *Female Buddhas*, p. 172 and see pl. on p. 173. The appearance of Prajñāpāramitā at the mandala's center has led some authors to misidentify it. The same is true when a text appears in the center of the mandala. As Mullin clarifies, this text is the *Root Medical Tantra*, not a Prajñāpāramitā scripture, as some have assumed.

55. Manuscript illuminations of Prajñāpāramitā: Saraswati, *Tantrayāna Art*, nos. 143, 233, 251, 270; Stooke, "XI Century Illuminated Palm Leaf Ms," p. 7. Surveys of images that appear in illuminated manuscripts: Stooke, p. 8; Conze, "Iconography of the Prajñāpāramitā," pp. 261–62; D. Bhattacharyya, *Studies in Buddhist Iconography*, pp. 53–54, 56.

56. On this spell: Conze, trans., *Buddhist Wisdom Books*, pp. 101–7; G. Gyatso, *Heart of Wisdom*, pp. 129–33.

57. Conze, trans., *Perfection of Wisdom*, pp. 103–5.

58. Ibid., pp. 109–10.

59. Ibid., pp. 149, 243, 250.

60. Ibid., p. 109.

61. See, e.g., ibid., p. 147; also p. 135.

62. G. Gyatso, *Heart of Wisdom*, p. 160.

63. Ibid., pp. 156–63; quote on p. 161.

64. For mantras appearing in various scriptures, see Conze, trans., *Perfect Wisdom*, pp. 146, 151, 158, 198, 201.

65. Lawson, "Dhāraṇī Sealings," p. 705. Lawson reproduces several such seals (figs. 9–12) and translates and discusses the mantra on pp. 709–14.

66. The Prajñāpāramitā liturgies in the *Sādhanamālā* are nos. 151–159.

67. Conze, trans., *Perfect Wisdom*, p. 146, slightly amended. The work was translated into Chinese in 900 C.E.; p. iii.

68. Ibid., p. 146.

69. On primordial wisdom as the fruit of the practice of Yeshe Tsogyal: Klein, *Meeting the Great Bliss Queen*, pp. 160–61, 165–66. On her womb as the source of reality and Buddhas: Klein, "Primordial Purity," p. 131.

70. J. Gyatso, "Development of the *Gcod* Tradition," pp. 324, 338, and, on Machig's role as founder and lineage holder, passim. The role of Prajñāpāramitā as divine emanator, or progenitor, of Chöd is further clarified in Edou, *Machig Labdron*, pp. 82–83, 86.

71. Trans. by Edou, *Machig Labdron*, pp. 151–52.

72. The text and rites devoted to it are described in Gellner, "'Perfection of Wisdom'"; quotes on p. 224.

73. Ibid., pp. 231–32; quote on p. 232.

74. Ibid., p. 230.

75. Prajwal Ratna Vajracharya, personal communication, July 2005.

76. On this Dharma mandala: Locke, *Karunamaya*, pp. 189–91, 193–95.

77. Wayman, trans., *Lion's Roar of Queen Śrīmālā*; Thurman, trans., *Holy Teaching of Vimalakīrti*, chap. 7.

78. Conze, trans., *Perfection of Wisdom*, p. 111.

79. Ibid., p. 61.

80. Ibid., p. 150.

81. Ibid., p. 17.

Chapter 9
Parṇaśavarī: Healing Goddess Clothed in Leaves

1. My translation; Chos-dbang blo-'gros, *sGrub thabs nor bu'i phreng ba'i lo rgyus*, fol. 18a.4–5.

2. sKal-bzang mkhyen-brtse, *Srad rgyud lugs kyi ri khrod ma rigs gsum gyi sgrub thabs*, fol. 35.2–3.

3. The *Atharva Veda* prescribes use of the *apāmārga* plant to "wipe" and "sweep" away diseases; see 4.17.6–8, 4.18.7, 4.19.4. *Śatapatha Brāhmaṇa* 5.2.4.a4 adduces use of the same plant for brushing away demons; Gonda, *Aspects of Early Viṣṇuism*, p. 12. For more recent examples: N. Bhattacharyya, *Indian Mother Goddess*, pp. 54–55; Crooke, *Popular Religion and Folklore*, vol. 1, pp. 129, 132; Abbott, *Indian Ritual*, pp. 318, 320–21.

4. Tib. *shing-lo gsar*; sKal-bzang mkhyen-brtse, *Srad rgyud lugs kyi ri khrod ma rigs gsum gyi sgrub thabs*, fol. 36.1, and *rJe btsun ri khrod ma ser mo'i sgrub thabs*, fol. 605.5, 606.1.

5. The six-armed forms, both green and yellow, prevalent in India are described in *Sādhanamālā* nos. 148–50. For English translations: B. Bhattacharyya, *Indian Buddhist Iconography*, pp. 196–97, 233.

6. In Chandra, *Buddhist Iconography*, for a red, two-armed form bearing a vajra and tarjanī mudrā, see no. 728; a blue, four-armed form holding an axe, lotus, branch or whisk, and noose, no. 729; a black, two-armed form holding peacock feathers and a bowl of medicines, no. 730; and an eight-armed form, no. 2368. For the same red form and slightly varying blue and black forms: Willson and Brauen, eds., *Deities of Tibetan Buddhism*, nos. 219–21. A green, two-armed form appears as a mandala retinue figure in *Niṣpannayogāvalī* no. 21.

7. *rJe btsun ri khrod ma ser mo'i sgrub thabs*, fol. 606.1–2.

8. My translation; ibid., fol. 626.5–627.3.

9. For a rare portrayal of the goddess in cross-legged pose: D. Mitra, *Ratnagiri*, pl. 76B. A cache of four-armed metal images in cross-legged posture, housed in the Patna Museum, have been identified as Parṇaśavarī in various sources; e.g., P. Gupta, ed., *Patna Museum Catalogue*, p. 151. I, however, identify these as Kurukullā; see chap. 22 n. 25.

10. Khokar, *Dancing for Themselves*, pp. 19 (no. 4), 97 on Nenaveli; p. 106 on Kar agam; pp. 19 (no. 1), 102, on third example, name of group and dance not given.

11. See, e.g., Enthoven, *Folklore of Bombay*, pp. 262, 272–73.

12. Additional examples: A. Gordon, *Iconography of Tibetan Lamaism*, pl. facing p. 73; Rhie and Thurman, *Worlds of Transformation*, no. 135 (upper left corner).

13. Artistic representations: Chandra, *Buddhist Iconography*, nos. 26, 727, 943; Ricca and Lo Bue, *Great Stupa of Gyantse*, pl. 84 and p. 232; Béguin, *Art ésotérique*, no. 23; Mullin, *Female Buddhas*, pl. on p. 117. Translated sādhanas and painted representations: Willson and Brauen, eds., *Deities of Tibetan Buddhism*, nos. 218, 441.

14. E.g., *rJe btsun ri khrod ma ser mo'i sgrub thabs*, fol. 606.2: *zhabs g.yas pa'i rting pas 'og gi phyogs brten cing*, referring to the pelvis obliquely as the "downward-facing," i.e., lower part, or door.

15. Clark, ed., *Two Lamaistic Pantheons*, vol. 2, pp. 207 (no. 6B3), 287 (nos. 249–50); Willson and Brauen, eds., *Deities of Tibetan Buddhism*, no. 222; Kreijger, *Tibetan Painting*, no. 14 (lower left corner).

16. For Parṇaśavarī amulet mantras, see the Newar manuscript in R. Mitra, *Sanskrit Buddhist Literature*, pp. 171–72. Parṇaśavarī does not presently have an active role in the Newar pantheon, but this manuscript and her appearance in the *Dhāraṇī Saṃgraha* evince her practice in Nepal, as does a Parṇaśavarī dhāraṇī text Daniel Wright collected in Nepal, now in the University Library of Cambridge (Wright, *History of Nepal*, p. 319). She is also included in the *Dharmakoṣa Saṃgraha* (D. Bhattacharyya, *Tantric Buddhist Iconographic Sources*, pp. 34–35) and *Saptavāra Dhāraṇī* (Grönbold, "'Saptavāra,'" pp. 369, 370 n. 7, 372, 374).

17. Instructions for compounding and consecrating these pills appear in sKal-bzang mkhyen-brtse, *Srad rgyud lugs kyi ri khrod ma rigs gsum gyi sgrub thabs*, fol. 44.2–5, 50.1.

18. Drikung Kagyu lama Sonam Jorphel Rinpoche, personal communication, 1995.

19. I attended one such ceremony led by Sakya Trizin in Kathmandu in 1995. Glenn Mullin reports that a major ceremony of this type was held every twelve years at Drikung Thel in Tibet; *Female Buddhas*, p. 116. I would expect that such ceremonies are held in Tibetan communities in India, although I did not have an opportunity to investigate this.

20. sKal-bzang mkhyen-brtse, *Srad rgyud lugs kyi ri khrod ma rigs gsum gyi sgrub thabs*, fol. 61.7–62.1.

21. Ibid., fol. 62.1–63.2, which describes this intricate visualization in greater detail.

22. *rJe btsun ri khrod ma ser mo'i sgrub thabs*, fol. 606.1, 662.5–7, 663.1–664.2.

23. This theme recurs in literary sources and was confirmed as part of her contemporary Tibetan conception by the Sakya lama Dezhung Rinpoche, personal communication, 1995, and the Drikung Kagyu lama Sonam Jorphel Rinpoche, personal communication, 1995.

24. Drikung Kagyu lama Sonam Jorphel Rinpoche, personal communication, 1995.

25. Oppert, *Original Inhabitants*, p. 476n; Fawcett, "On Some Festivals," pp. 264–65, 268, 273, 276–77, 279.

26. On contemporary worship of Salabai: Hardiman, *Coming of the Devi*, esp. chap. 2. On Māriyammān: Oppert, *Original Inhabitants*, pp. 471–85.

27. S. K. Mukhopadhyay, *Cult of Goddess Sitala*, pp. 15, 40–42, 55, 57.

28. Ibid., p. 55; Wadley, "Śītalā," pp. 56–57.

29. The Changu dance is a tradition of the Lodha Śavaras of southwestern Bengal; see S. K. Mukhopadhyay, *Cult of Goddess Sitala*, pp. 80–81, 108. On other Śavara dance traditions related to Śītalā, pp. v, 82–83; on women's songs and dances devoted to Śītalā in village Bengal, pp. 17–18, 27, 71–76.

30. G. Bhattacharya, "Dual Role of Ganesh," p. 73.

31. Bhattasali, *Buddhist and Brahmanical Sculptures*, pp. 60–61 and pls. 23a, 23b; the circular markings on the prostrate figures are not visible in the reproductions. A stele of a 6-armed figure in the Indian Museum, identified as Parṇaśavarī in B. Bhattacharyya, *Indian Buddhist Iconography*, p. 197 and fig. 140, has been identified as Aparājitā in G. Bhattacharya, "Dual Role of Ganesh," p. 76.

32. B. Bhattacharyya, *Introduction to Buddhist Esoterism*, p. 119; quote on p. 145. Also Bhattasali, *Buddhist and Brahmanical Sculptures*, p. 61. B. P. Sinha critiques the prevalent view that the trampling motif always expresses sectarian animosity and offers alternate interpretations in "Some Reflections on Indian Sculpture."

33. Wadley, "Śītalā"; Nicholas, "Goddess Śītalā and Epidemic Smallpox"; Marglin, "Smallpox in Two Systems of Knowledge," pp. 103, 115, 123, 125, 134–36.

34. Śavara (alternately spelled Śāvara, Śabara, Saora, Saura, Sawara) is used both as a generic term for tribal and mountain-dwelling peoples and in reference to a specific tribe with several subdivisions; Elwin, *Religion of an Indian Tribe*, pp. 1–10.

35. Śavaras presently wear woven or beaded skirts, but literary sources such as the *Kathāsaritsāgara* and recent writings report the wearing of leaf garments; Elwin, *Religion of an Indian Tribe*, pp. 16, 18, 20, 42.

36. *Skanda Purāṇa* 35.12–14, cited in D. Bhattacharyya, *Studies in Buddhist Iconography*, pp. 16–17, where he also notes a form of Durgā known as Parṇakairātī, or "Kirāta tribal woman dressed in leaves," described in the *Tantrasāra*.

37. On Śavareśvarī: Kinsley, *Tantric Visions of the Divine Feminine*, p. 219. On Śavarī: *Mantramahodadhi* 6.43–44; see Bühnemann, *Iconography of Hindu Tantric Deities*, p. 112 and fig. 25a.

38. For Āśavarī-rāginī paintings and discussion: Masselos et al., *Dancing to the Flute*, pp. 298, 300, 302, and pls. on pp. 175, 301.

39. Elwin, *Religion of an Indian Tribe*, chap. 5 and pp. 215–16.

40. Ibid., pp. 148, 161, 204–5, 207–8, 244.

41. Elwin, "Saora Priestess," p. 85.

42. Ibid.

43. I.e., the sculptures discussed herein and the *Sādhanamālā* (late eleventh or early twelfth century). Parṇaśavarī does not appear in the incipient Tantric iconography at Ellora; the date of her representation at Ratnagiri, possibly her earliest extant portrayal, is difficult to ascertain.

44. Kvaerne, *Buddhist Tantric Songs*, dohā no. 50.

45. Dohā no. 28, vv. 1–3; composite trans. drawn from Dasgupta, *Obscure Religious Cults*, pp. 105–6, and Kvaerne, *Buddhist Tantric Songs*, pp. 181–82.

46. Verse 4 refers to her as Nairāmaṇi, a possible reference to Nairātmyā; Kvaerne, *Buddhist Tantric Songs*, p. 184. Similarly, dohā no. 50, v. 1, mentions Nairāmaṇi, perhaps with reference to the Śavarī introduced in v. 5.

47. Shaw, *Passionate Enlightenment*, pp. 50–51 and fig. 6.

48. For Śavarī in the Hevajra mandala: Snellgrove, *Hevajra Tantra*, pt. 1, pp. 58, 74, 80. For the other two mandalas: *Niṣpannayogāvalī* nos. 6, 24.

49. D. Bhattacharyya, *Studies in Buddhist Iconography*, p. 16.

Chapter 10
Mārīcī: Lady of Sunrise Splendor

1. My translation; R. Mitra, *Sanskrit Buddhist Literature*, p. 170.

2. My translation; *'Phags ma 'od zer can ma'i sgrub thabs*, fol. 531.7–532.5.

3. Ibid., fol. 532.1–2, 532.6–533.3.

4. Bendall, trans., *Śikshā-samuccaya*, p. 139, with orthographic emendations.

5. *Sādhanamālā* no. 144.

6. My translation; *'Phags ma 'od zer can ma'i sgrub thabs*, fol. 527.3–5.

7. Bautze-Picron cites eighth-century evidence of this practice in "Between Śākyamuni and Vairocana," p. 264.

8. *Sādhanamālā* nos. 133, 141.

9. Maity, *Human Fertility Cults*, pp. 179–80; Randhawa, *Cult of Trees*, p. 34.

10. On the aśoka-dohada motif, see chap. 3.

11. The *aśokapuṣpa-pracāyikā* festival; Randhawa, *Cult of Trees*, pp. 36–37.

12. Strong, *Legend of King Aśoka*, pp. 128–29, 210.

13. For an example from the *Tārā Tantra*, see Willson, *In Praise of Tārā*, pp. 76–77. For use of the aśoka in rites of love magic associated with Kurukullā: Snellgrove, *Hevajra Tantra*, pt. 1, p. 54; *Sādhanamālā* no. 180, p. 367, and no. 188, p. 392.

14. P. Vaidya, ed., *Āryamañjusrimūlakalpa*, pp. 229, 231, 443.

15. See the Jain sūtra passage excerpted in Coomaraswamy, *Yakṣas*, pp. 66–67.

16. See chap. 2.

17. Randhawa, *Cult of Trees*, fig. 13.

18. Ibid., p. 34. For Mathurān examples, see figs. 32–33, 36 and Coomaraswamy, *Yakṣas*, pls. 6.2, 6.3.

19. R. Misra, *Yaksha Cult*, fig. 90; Randhawa, *Cult of Trees*, p. 32 and fig. 46.

20. S. P. Gupta, ed., *Kushāṇa Sculptures from Sanghol*, pls. 6–8, 11, 16B, 17–18, 23–24.

21. On the Buddhist Aśokā, see R. Misra, *Yaksha Cult*, p. 58; on the Jain, ibid., p. 174, and D. Mitra, *Bronzes from Achutrajpur*, p. 114.

22. Skt. *aśokacchaṭodbhavā*; *Sādhanamālā* no. 147.

23. D. Mitra, *Bronzes from Achutrajpur*, pl. 108; P. K. Mishra, *Archaeology of Mayūrbhañj*, pl. 32; and Rhie and Thurman, *Wisdom and Compassion*, no. 23, for a silk tapestry wherein standing beside a tree she is indistinguishable from a yakṣiṇī.

24. Aśokakāntā Mārīcī is usually paired with Ekajaṭā or, less often, Bhṛkuṭī, in this role. She may also attend or appear in a fourfold mandala retinue of Mahāśrī Tārā, Varada Tārā, and Mahattarī Tārā; M. Ghosh, *Buddhist Iconography*, pp. 46–49, 58–65.

25. Hock, "Sculpture of Ratnagiri," pp. 128, 159. Her appearances as an independent figure: D. Mitra, *Ratnagiri*, pls. 79A–B, and additional example in Donaldson, "Orissan Images of Aṣṭabhujāpīta Mārīcī," p. 35 and fig. 24. Her appearance as an attendant: D. Mitra, *Ratnagiri*, pl. 337A.

26. She is named as an attendant of Khadiravaṇī Tārā in *Sādhanamālā* no. 89, of Mahāśrī Tārā in no. 116, of Varada Tārā in no. 91, of Sita Tārā in no. 104.

27. *Sādhanamālā* no. 144, partially translated in B. Bhattacharyya, *Indian Buddhist Iconography*, pp. 210–11.

28. The horse appears in D. Mitra, *Ratnagiri*, pls. 54A–B, 77C–D, 78A, 268B (pedestal only), and perhaps pl. 76D (effaced); Saraswati, *Tantrayāna Art*, no. 127; D. Bhattacharyya, *Studies in Buddhist Iconography*, pls. 7–8; and possibly D. Mitra, "Metal Image of Mārīcī," p. 144 and pl. 10.1.

29. For the six-armed form at Ratnagiri: D. Mitra, *Ratnagiri*, pls. 51B, 54A–D, 76C–D, 77A–D, 78A, 78C–D. On its prevalence at Bodhgayā: Leoshko, "Pilgrimage and the Evidence of Bodhgaya's Images," p. 50 and pl. 9. For a Bodhgayā relief in which two images of six-armed Mārīcī flank Shakyamuni: Leoshko, "Implications of Bodhgaya's Sūrya," p. 233 and fig. 5. For six-armed examples from Bihar: Huntington and Huntington, *Leaves from the Bodhi Tree*, no. 12; P. Gupta, ed., *Patna Museum Catalogue*, p. 65; D. Bhattacharyya, *Studies in Buddhist Iconography*, pl. 7. For examples from Nālandā and Sārnāth: Saraswati, *Tantrayāna Art*, nos. 126–29; Sahni, *Museum of Archaeology at Sārnāth*, p. 148 and pl. 17b. For Orissan examples: Donaldson, "Orissan Images of Aṣṭabhujāpīta Mārīcī," p. 38 and figs. 25, 29.

30. This six-armed form is absent from the Tibetan Tanjur, figuring only as the principal deity of a Mārīcī mandala described in *Niṣpannayogāvalī* no. 17. It also appears in Newar iconography; see n. 87, below.

31. *Sādhanamālā* nos. 134 and 142 (Kalpokta Mārīcī), 137 (Aṣṭabhujapīta Mārīcī), 144 (Mārīcī Picuvā), and 146 (Saṃkṣipta Mārīcī). The iconographic descriptions are compiled in Saraswati, *Tantrayāna Art*, pp. 42–44.

32. Donaldson, "Orissan Images of Aṣṭabhujāpīta Mārīcī," pp. 37, 43.

33. Derge Tōh. nos. 3228, 3230, 3341, 3395, 3524, 3527–28, 3532, 3536, 3661A.

34. Saraswati, *Tantrayāna Art*, nos. 116–29; D. Paul, *Art of Nālandā*, pl. 47; Sahu, *Buddhism in Orissa*, figs. 40, 64, 71, 74; Donaldson, "Orissan Images of Aṣṭabhujāpīta Mārīcī," pp. 38–42 and figs. 28–36; A. Sengupta, *Buddhist Art of Bengal*, pl. 27.

35. Two examples in the Indian Museum, Calcutta: D. Paul, *Art of Nālandā*, pl. 68; M. Mitra, "Images of Mārīcī," pp. 345–46 and pl. 44. See also Schroeder, *Buddhist Sculptures in Tibet*, vol. 1, no. 93C, and additional examples cited in Bautze-Picron, "Between Śākyamuni and Vairocana," p. 289 and fig. 16.

36. A four-armed image from Udalā is reported but not reproduced in Sahu, *Buddhism in Orissa*, p. 222. A white, ten-armed form with four legs is described in *Sādhanamālā* nos. 132 and 135; I have not located representations of this epiphany. A red, sixteen-armed form with two sow faces protruding on the right and left of the main face is described in

Sādhanamālā no. 145. A painted example that approximates this, except for its possession of fourteen rather than sixteen arms, appears at the top of a nineteenth-century Bhutanese Drugpa Kagyu painting; Kreijger, *Tibetan Painting*, pl. on p. 131.

37. Skt. *caityagarbha-sthitā*, *caityaguhagarbhe*, and *caitya-alaṅkṛta-mūrdhajā*; e.g., *Sādhanamālā* no. 134, p. 276, line 11; B. Bhattacharyya, ed., *Niṣpannayogāvalī*, pt. 2, p. 40, lines 2–3.

38. Leoshko, "Pilgrimage and the Evidence of Bodhgaya's Images," p. 50. Leoshko further discusses the association of Mārīcī with the dawning of enlightenment in "Implications of Bodhgaya's Sūrya," pp. 232–33.

39. Willson and Brauen, eds., *Deities of Tibetan Buddhism*, nos. 195–96, and p. 291 on the respective roles of the Vajrāsana deities.

40. B. Bhattacharyya, ed., *Niṣpannayogāvalī*, pt. 2, p. 40, lines 4–5.

41. Lokesh Chandra adduces the role of the pig, an early-morning scavenger, as a herald of the dawn; preface of Tucci, *Gyantse*, pt. 1, p. xxiii. D. C. Bhattacharyya proposes that the pig signals welcome into Buddhist congregations of socially ostracized castes that domesticate the animal; *Studies in Buddhist Iconography*, pp. 21–22.

42. Gonda, *Aspects of Early Viṣṇuism*, p. 140.

43. Vārāhī appears in most of the standard groupings of "seven mothers" (*sapta-mātṛkā*) and "eight mothers" (*aṣṭa-mātṛkā*); see, e.g., Mani, *Saptamātṛkas*, pp. 19, 108–9, and figs. 12, 24, 40, 46, 49, 51, 53.

44. E.g., the boar-headed archer yogini at Hirapur, Orissa; Dehejia, *Yoginī Cult*, p. 98.

45. Skt. *śūkarākrāntavighnām*; *Sādhanamālā* no. 138, p. 284, line 4.

46. *Sādhanamālā* no. 132, p. 274, lines 18–19; no. 135, p. 279, lines 11–12.

47. *Ṛg Veda* 1.114.5.

48. Banerjea, *Development of Hindu Iconography*, pp. 432–33.

49. Stipulated in *Sādhanamālā* nos. 134, 137, 142, 146. For stelae in which Rāhu is depicted: Saraswati, *Tantrayāna Art*, nos. 117–21, 124–26. Rāhu is alternately shown beneath the chariot, in which location Bautze-Picron proposes that Rāhu is being vanquished; "Between Śākyamuni and Vairocana," pp. 280–81, 283.

50. She is so described in *Sādhanamālā* nos. 132, 135. Bautze-Picron cites images in which they appear; "Between Śākyamuni and Vairocana," p. 280 and figs. 12, 19.

51. Banerjea, *Development of Hindu Iconography*, pp. 429, 443.

52. The red, twelve-armed Tantric forms of Mārīcī are described in *Sādhanamālā* nos. 138–40 (Oḍiyāna Mārīcī), no. 136 (Vajradhātvīśvarī Mārīcī), no. 143 (Mārīcī), and no. 145 (Ubhayavarāhānana Mārīcī). The iconographic descriptions are compiled in Saraswati, *Tantrayāna Art*, pp. 44–45, 89–91.

53. *Sādhanamālā* no. 138, cited in the previous note, also gives a longer version of her name as Dvādaśabhuja-raktavarṇa-oḍiyāna Mārīcī, which no. 140 lenghtens to Dvādaśabhuja-raktavarṇa-oḍiyāna-svādhiṣṭhāna-krama Mārīcī. The name Oḍḍiyāna-udbhava Mārīcī ("Mārīcī Arising in Oḍḍiyāna") appears in the title of Derge Tōh. no. 3231.

54. Manuscript paintings: Saraswati, *Tantrayāna Art*, nos. 257–58. Stone statuary: Bautze-Picron, "Between Śākyamuni and Vairocana," p. 271 and fig. 9; Donaldson, "Orissan Images of Vārāhī," p. 180 and fig. 17; and Donaldson, "Oḍḍiyāna Mārīcī Image," which examines and illustrates the Mārīcīpur image in detail.

55. *Sādhanamālā* no. 136.

56. Vairocana is paired with Tārā in *Sādhanamālā* no. 26, Cakravartiṇī in *Niṣpannayogāvalī* no. 12, and an unnamed consort (*prajñā*) in *Niṣpannayogāvalī* nos. 1, 15.

57. This mandala, widely depicted on late Indic stelae of eight-armed Mārīcī, is described in *Sādhanamālā* nos. 134, 137, 142, 147. No. 134 is translated in Saraswati, *Tantrayāna Art*, p. 42.

58. Donaldson, "Orissan Images of Vārāhī," pp. 180–81 and fig. 20.

59. *Niṣpannayogāvalī* no. 17. For the same mandala, from the *Vajrāvalī*, see Vira and Chandra, *Tibetan Maṇḍalas*, pp. 58–59, and, without description of the retinue, in Willson and Brauen, eds., *Deities of Tibetan Buddhism*, no. 502.

60. For analysis of the names of the retinue deities, see the preface by Lokesh Chandra in Tucci, *Gyantse*, pt. 1, pp. xxiv–xxv.

61. Suggested perhaps first by B. Bhattacharyya in *Indian Buddhist Iconography*, p. 207, and repeated in numerous sources. D. C. Bhattacharyya also conjectures that she was patterned after a solar manifestation of Caṇḍī; *Studies in Buddhist Iconography*, pp. 19–20.

62. *Ṛg Veda* 1.92.4, 1.92.6, 6.64.1–2, 7.77.1–2, 7.80.1.

63. *Ṛg Veda* 1.92.1, 7.79.2.

64. *Ṛg Veda* 1.48.8, 1.48.15, 1.92.5, 1.92.15, 4.52.4, 7.75.6, 7.78.2–4, 7.81.6.

65. *Ṛg Veda* 6.64.3.

66. It is also possible that the horse-drawn chariot was informed by the iconography of Sūrya, whose vehicle is drawn by seven horses.

67. The raised sword is included in numerous tenth- and eleventh-century images from Nālandā and vicinity: D. Paul, *Art of Nālandā*, p. 61 and pl. 47; Saraswati, *Tantrayāna Art*, nos. 120, 122–26 (in no. 126, Mārīcī lunges to her left, the manner in which Durgā is most commonly depicted); Bautze-Picron, "Between Śākyamuni and Vairocana," figs. 6, 14, 15. Although the sword serves as a Buddhist symbol for wisdom (*prajñā*), which makes it a fitting attribute of Mārīcī, as Bautze-Picron notes (pp. 275–77), I hold that the reason for its adoption as an *āyudha* of Mārīcī was to draw an explicit analogy with Durgā.

68. These implements are held in varying combinations by Mārīcī's ten-, twelve-, and sixteen-armed forms. The sword is typically included in the iconographic descriptions, whereas the shield, not mentioned in the sādhanas, may appear in artistic images.

69. *Sādhanamālā* nos. 139, 145, discussed in B. Bhattacharyya, *Indian Buddhist Iconography*, pp. 212–13.

70. *Devī Māhātmya* 12.22–28.

71. See, e.g., *'Phags ma 'od zer can ma'i sgrub thabs*, fol. 532.6–533.3. This list includes the standard "eight great fears" (*aṣṭa-mahābhaya*) from which Tārā and other deities offer deliverance; it is the correspondence in both form and function that is significant here.

72. Chandra, *Buddhist Iconography*, nos. 25, 776, 1004 (six-armed), 2366 (eight-armed). At Gyantse, one finds wall murals of Mārīcī in two-, six-, and eight-armed forms; Ricca and Lo Bue, *Great Stupa of Gyantse*, pp. 101–2, 227, and pls. 87–89. She is typically seated in statuary and when she appears as a subsidiary deity in paintings of other deities; e.g., Kreijger, *Tibetan Painting*, pl. on p. 131 (to right of central figure).

73. Derge Tōh. nos. 3226, 3342, 3522, 3525.

74. Numerous works in the Tanjur are devoted to these forms: Derge Tōh. nos. 3229, 3231–33, 3340, 3344–45, 3529–30, 3533. A wall painting of red, twelve-armed Oḍḍiyāna Mārīcī at Gyantse is reported but not reproduced in Ricca and Lo Bue, *Great Stupa of Gyantse*, p. 227. A statue is published in Clark, ed., *Two Lamaistic Pantheons*, vol. 2, p. 207, no. 6B2. In view of the rarity of Tantric Mārīcī effigies in the Tibetan corpus, it is fascinating to find three twelve-armed Tantric epiphanies at the top of a nineteenth-century Drugpa Kagyu painting from Bhutan; Kreijger, *Tibetan Painting*, pl. on p. 131.

75. Willson and Brauen, eds., *Deities of Tibetan Buddhism*, nos. 196, 430; Chandra, *Buddhist Iconography*, nos. 656, 705, 793, 932, 2165. The Aśokakāntā form is also favored in monastery murals.

76. E.g., Getty, *Gods of Northern Buddhism*, pl. 41a, and Schroeder, *Indo-Tibetan Bronzes*, fig. 138E, as described in *Sādhanamālā* nos. 133, 141. I have also encountered the motif in contemporary metal statuary of Newar manufacture for Tibetan patrons.

77. Another example is held by the Field Museum in Chicago, inv. no. 122153.

78. *Sādhanamālā* no. 147 (Ārya Mārīcī); Chandra, *Buddhist Iconography*, no. 704; Willson and Brauen, eds., *Deities of Tibetan Buddhism*, no. 195, quotation on p. 291.

79. Willson and Brauen, eds., *Deities of Tibetan Buddhism*, no. 267; Chandra, *Buddhist Iconography*, no. 776.

80. The horse-drawn effigies are cited in n. 28, above.

81. This conclusion is based on interviews of Sakya and Kagyu lamas. Interestingly, protection from thieves reasserts the single role assigned to the goddess in the earliest known literary reference: Bendall, trans., *Śikshā-samuccaya*, p. 139.

82. Waddell, *Tibetan Buddhism*, p. 218, orthography amended in quotation.

83. Decleer, "Tibetan Translation of the *Svayambhū-purāṇa*," typescript, p. 23.

84. Saraswati, *Tantrayāna Art*, nos. 257 (twelve-armed) and 258 (ten-armed).

85. On the dating and role of this sevenfold group: Grönbold, "'Saptavāra.'"

86. I determined this from an examination of several *Dhāraṇī Saṃgraha* manuscripts in the collection of Ratnakaji Vajracharya of Kathmandu. For a published illustration from an eighteenth-century manuscript: D. Bhattacharyya, *Studies in Buddhist Iconography*, pl. 9.

87. Her six-armed form appears in the nineteenth-century *Dharmakoṣa Saṃgraha* (D. Bhattacharyya, *Tantric Buddhist Iconographic Sources*, p. 34) and a manuscript leaf (dated 773 N.S.) noted in Regmi, *Medieval Nepal*, vol. 2, pp. 980–81. The eight-armed form appears in the manuscript illustration cited in the previous note and one described in Grönbold, "'Saptavāra,'" p. 374.

Chapter 11
Jāṅgulī: The Buddhist Snake Goddess

1. My translation; *Sādhanamālā* no. 117, p. 246, lines 3–13.

2. These spells, termed *parittu* in Pali, are legion. See, e.g., *Khandavatta Jātaka* (no. 203 in Cowell ed.), and the *Khandaparitta* and *Upasena-sūtra*, discussed in Schmithausen, *Maitrī and Magic*, esp. pp. 11–23, 67. On the theme of friendliness, see pp. 35–44. For a later text of spells Shakyamuni revealed to snake kings for their use and to humans to invoke snakes to regulate rainfall and promote crops, see Bendall, "Megha-Sūtra."

3. On these snake goddesses, see Rawson, "Iconography of the Goddess Manasā"; A. Bhattacharya, "Concept of Tārā as a Serpent Deity."

4. Dehejia, *Yoginī Cult*, pp. 109, 158; H. Das, "Brahmanical Tantric Art," illus. facing p. 89.

5. Monier-Williams, *Sanskrit-English Dictionary*, p. 417a–b. The jungle reference is a later accretion to the meaning of the root.

6. Maity, *Human Fertility Cults*, pp. 78–81.

7. E.g., *Sādhanamālā* no. 120, p. 249, line 2 (*āśīviṣa-cumbhanikā* [emended from *cumbharikā*], *dṛṣṭi-viṣavat*); *Sādhanamālā* no. 117, p. 246, line 9 (*viṣa-puṣpakā*).

8. Strickmann, *Chinese Magical Medicine*, pp. 152, 154.

9. Davidson, *Indian Esoteric Buddhism*, p. 231.

10. Bendall, trans., *Śikshā-samuccaya*, p. 139. Bendall construes Jāṅgulyā as "snake charmer," but as a feminine singular instrumental noun it is also translatable as "by Jāṅgulī." "Jāṅgulyā" could also be an alternate spelling of Jāṅgulī here as in sundry Tibetan text titles. The same mantra is associated with Jāṅgulī in *Sādhanamālā* no. 120, p. 250. Another mantra against poison and snakebite, given without reference to Jāṅgulī (Bendall, p. 138) approximates her mantra in *Sādhanamālā* no. 118, p. 247, lines 1–5, and in slightly expanded and altered form in no. 120, p. 249, lines 7–11.

11. My translation; *Sādhanamālā* no. 120, pp. 248–50. I am grateful to Abhijit Ghose of Jadavpur University, Calcutta, for deciphering the grammatical inconsistencies of this passage.

12. See, e.g., the kumārī-pūjā texts in the *Śāktapramoda*, pp. 385–402.

13. Skilling, "Rakṣā Literature," pp. 144–47.

14. Ibid., pp. 148–49.

15. See, e.g., Watson, trans., *Lotus Sutra*, p. 310; Snellgrove, *Hevajra Tantra*, pt. 1, p. 52.

16. No Indian or Tibetan Jāṅgulī sādhana known to me describes her in two-armed form. She appears with two arms in a Chinese sādhana, said to be a translation of an Indic work, wherein her iconography displays, rather, Taoist elements; Strickmann, *Chinese Magical Medicine*, pp. 151–52.

17. See Bhattasali, *Buddhist and Brahmanical Sculptures*, pl. 22b. Other examples are noted in Hock, "Sculpture of Ratnagiri," p. 159; A. Bhattacharya, "Concept of Tārā as a Serpent Deity," p. 159. Jāṅgulī also appears thus in a Tibetan painting; Pal et al., *Himalayas*, no. 116.

18. *Sādhanamālā* no. 116 names Mahāśrī Tārā's entourage; the other members are Aśokakāntā Mārīcī, Ekajaṭā, and Mahāmāyūrī. Jāṅgulī appears amid such a retinue, displaying a snake and varada mudrā, as specified in this sādhana, at Ratnagiri, although the central Tārā is not the Mahāśrī form; D. Mitra, *Ratnagiri*, pp. 443–44 and pl. 337A. *Sādhanamālā* no. 91 relates Varada Tārā's retinue; the attendants are the same as those above. Jāṅgulī is depicted with two arms, holding a fly whisk and snake, in a late Tibetan print; Chandra, *Buddhist Iconography*, no. 2384. This rendition appears to be an effort to reconstruct her iconography in the absence of an active practice tradition in Tibet. Although the source of this iconography is unclear, it suggestively dovetails with her description as an attendant of Varada Tārā but adds a fly whisk.

19. *Sādhanamālā* nos. 106, 122. A posited link between Jāṅgulī and Sarasvatī, the lute-playing muse attributed with poison-destroying powers in the *Atharva Veda*, is refuted in Maity, *Cult of the Goddess Manasā*, pp. 227–29.

20. See *Mārkaṇḍeya Purāṇa* 23.50–61; Pargiter trans., pp. 130–32.

21. *Sādhanamālā* no. 121.

22. *Sādhanamālā* no. 119. The same iconographic configuration, body color unspecified, is described in no. 117, excerpted at the beginning of this chapter. A Tibetan statue replicating this iconography is published in Schroeder, *Buddhist Sculptures in Tibet*, vol. 2, no. 262A.

23. This passage is translated in Davidson, *Indian Esoteric Buddhism*, p. 231.

24. Malandra, *Unfolding a Maṇḍala*, fig. 246a. On Jāṅgulī in the *Niṣpannayogāvalī* set of twelve dhāraṇī goddesses: B. Bhattacharyya, *Indian Buddhist Iconography*, pp. 339–40.

25. Vasu, *Archaeological Survey*, vol. 1, intro., pp. 87–88 and pl. 47.

26. A. Ghosh, *Nālandā*, pl. 8B.

27. Evidence of her transmission to Tibet can be found in canonical texts (Derge Tōh. nos. 571, 990, 993, 3206, 3245, 3365–66, 3499, 3508–13) and occasional artistic representations: Clark, ed., *Two Lamaistic Pantheons*, vol. 2, pp. 204 (no. 6A53), 283 (no. 236); Schroeder, *Buddhist Sculptures in Tibet*, vol. 2, no. 262A.

28. Beyer, *Cult of Tārā*, p. xiii.

29. Mullin, trans., *Six Texts*, p. 22.

30. *Twenty-One Praises of Tārā*, vv. 18, 25–26; see trans. in Willson, *In Praise of Tārā*, pp. 115–16.

31. Pal et al., *Himalayas*, no. 116.

Chapter 12
Sarasvatī: Divine Muse

1. Trans. by Mullin, *Meditations on the Lower Tantras*, p. 127, with minor emendations.

2. On Vedic conceptions of Sarasvatī: Chatterjee, "Some Aspects of Sarasvatī", Tkatschow, "Sarasvatī," pp. 75–78; Kinsley, *Hindu Goddesses*, pp. 10–11, 55–57; Airi, *Concept of Sarasvati*.

3. *Ṛg Veda* 1.3.11–12; Griffith, trans., *Hymns of the Rigveda*, vol. 1, p. 5.

4. For Purāṇic conceptions of Sarasvatī: Kinsley, *Hindu Goddesses*, pp. 57–63; Tkatschow, "Sarasvatī," p. 77; M. Mukhopadhyay, "Lakṣmī and Sarasvatī in Sanskrit Inscriptions," p. 108. For her transmission of music to the nāgas: *Mārkaṇḍeya Purāṇa* 23.30–56; Pargiter trans., pp. 127–32.

5. For metaphorical dimensions of Sarasvatī as "Queen of Waters," see the *Sarasvatī Rahasya Upaniṣad* in Warrier, *Śākta Upaniṣads*, pp. 41–53.

6. Iconographic descriptions from the *Matsya*, *Agni*, *Vāyu*, *Viṣṇudharmottara*, and *Skanda Purāṇas* are surveyed in Kinsley, *Hindu Goddesses*, pp. 60–62; Khan, *Sarasvatī in Sanskrit Literature*, pp. 118–19, 130–32.

7. Kinsley, *Hindu Goddesses*, p. 63.

8. *Sādhanamālā* nos. 168 (Sarasvatī) and 151, 153 (Prajñāpāramitā).

9. Epithets compiled from Wayman, "Goddess Sarasvatī," pp. 247–48; Mullin, *Meditations on the Lower Tantras*, p. 122; S. C. Das, *Tibetan-English Dictionary*, p. 913b. For comparable Purāṇic epithets: A. Gupta, "Conception of Sarasvatī," pp. 68–69.

10. Tib. *rgya gar du phyi pa dang nang pa'i paṇḍita thams cad kyi rtsod pa med pa lha mo*; Chos-dbang blo-'gros, *sGrub thabs nor bu'i phreng ba'i lo rgyus*, fol. 20a.5. The term *rtsod pa med pa*, rendered here as "without contention," also means "without dispute," "authentic."

11. Arènes, *Déesse sGrol-ma*, p. 71.

12. E.g., R. Singh, *Hindu Iconography*, p. 16 and pl. 1.1. The earliest known inscribed effigy of Sarasvatī is a second-century C.E. Jain image; Smith, *Jain Stūpa*, pp. 56–57 and pl. 99.

13. Marshall, *Buddhist Art of Gandhāra*, fig. 65; Ingholt, *Gandhāran Art*, no. 363 (earlier misidentified as Sarasvatī in Grünwedel, *Buddhist Art in India*, pp. 105–6).

14. *Buddhacarita* 1.42; Johnston trans., pt. 2, p. 9.

15. Emmerick, trans., *Sūtra of Golden Light*, pp. 1, 2, 33, 37, 67–68, 101.

16. Ibid., p. 47.

17. Ibid., pp. 43–44.

18. Ibid., p. 46.

19. Ibid., pp. 43–46. The eight-armed form mentioned in the work (p. 47) is popular in Japan (p. 47 n. 44) but gained no currency in India.

20. For characteristic descriptions of her vina, see *Bram ze phur bu'i lugs kyi dbyangs can ma dkar mo'i sgrub thabs*, fol. 397.7, 413.4.

21. *Sādhanamālā* no. 165; Willson and Brauen, eds., *Deities of Tibetan Buddhism*, no. 8. A ninth-century metal sculpture of this hierophany survives from Nālandā; Khan, *Sarasvatī in Sanskrit Literature*, pl. 10. Tibetan images: Chandra, *Buddhist Iconography*, nos. 292, 518; Rhie and Thurman, *Wisdom and Compassion*, no. 27; Chandra, *Transcendental Art of Tibet*, p. 9.

22. My translation; *Bram ze phur bu' i lugs kyi dbyangs can ma dkar mo'i sgrub thabs*, fol. 397.6–398.3; cf. the similarly ornate description on fol. 413.3–6.

23. *Sādhanamālā* no. 162, trans. in B. Bhattacharyya, *Indian Buddhist Iconography*, p. 350.

24. The Nālandā image: Asher, *Art of Eastern India*, p. 82 and pl. 167. Ratnagiri examples: Hock, "Sculpture of Ratnagiri," pp. 162, 167–68. Sarasvatī has not been documented in Buddhist caves of Ellora.

25. Vajraśāradā, "Adamantine Autumnal Lady," in reference to the brightness of the autumn full moon, holds a manuscript in her left hand and a lotus in her right; *Sādhanamālā* no. 166. Another white, two-armed form, designated as Vajra Sarasvatī, holds a Prajñāpāramitā manuscript and red lotus; *Sādhanamālā* no. 168.

26. Chandra, *Buddhist Iconography*, no. 702; Willson and Brauen, eds., *Deities of Tibetan Buddhism*, no. 193.

27. E.g., the sixteenth-century Sikkimese statue reproduced in Kinsley, *Hindu Goddesses*, p. 61. The swan frequently appears in Newar portrayals, whereas the peacock, one of her vāhanas in Hindu settings, appears as her vehicle in East Asian Buddhism.

28. Chandra, *Buddhist Iconography*, no. 703; Willson and Brauen, eds., *Deities of Tibetan Buddhism*, no. 194. A practice manual on this form, transmitted from Kashmir, is *Dbyangs can ma dmar mo gsang sgrub kyi sgrub thabs rjes gnang dang bcas pa'i skor; sGrub thabs kun btus*, vol. 2, fol. 502–539.

29. This red, six-armed form may be seated or standing and bears a skull cup (or head of Brahmā), flaying knife, sword, Dharma wheel, lotus or lotus supporting a Prajñāpāramitā text, and vina or jewel. See *Sādhanamālā* nos. 161, 163–64, 167; 'Bri-gung Chos-kyi grags-pa, *sGrub thabs rgya mtsho*, fol. 17b.5–18a.1; Chandra, *Buddhist Iconography*, no. 944; Clark, ed., *Two Lamaistic Pantheons*, vol. 2, p. 203, no. 6A51, and p. 208, no. 6B5; Willson and Brauen, eds., *Deities of Tibetan Buddhism*, no. 442 (described as red but pictured as white).

30. Wayman, "Goddess Sarasvatī," p. 251, from *Bo dong lugs kyi dbyangs can ma dmar mo gsang sgrub lha lnga'i sgrub thabs*, fol. 542. For a blue form of Sarasvatī as Mañjuśrī's consort: Willson and Brauen, eds., *Deities of Tibetan Buddhism*, no. 188.

31. This view, stated, e.g., in Chos-dbang blo-'gros, *sGrub thabs nor bu'i phreng ba'i lo rgyus*, fol. 20a.2, 21a.1, 21b.2, is widely held among the Tibetan sects, according to Tucci, *Tibetan Painted Scrolls*, p. 590.

32. This widely occurring motif appears in paintings of diverse sectarian sources: Olson, *Tantric Buddhist Art*, pl. 44; Béguin, *Peintures du bouddhisme tibétain*, nos. 170–71; Chakraverty, *Sacred Buddhist Painting*, pl. on p. 39.

33. Pintchman, *Rise of the Goddess*, p. 118; Ludvik, "Benzaiten à huit bras," pp. 322, 325–36.

34. Ludvik, "Benzaiten à huit bras," esp. pp. 318–19.

35. On the influence of the *Mārkaṇḍeya Purāṇa* on the legendry and iconography of Palden Lhamo, see Shaw, *Buddhist Goddesses of Tibet and Nepal*, forthcoming.

36. My translation; Chos-dbang blo-'gros, *sGrub thabs nor bu'i phreng ba'i lo rgyus*, fol. 20a.5–20b.5.

37. Sakya master Khenpo Abbe, interview, Kathmandu, Nov. 1995.

38. My translation; Chos-dbang blo-'gros, *sGrub thabs nor bu'i phreng ba'i lo rgyus*, fol. 21a.2–21b.1.

39. My translation; ibid., fol. 21b.4–5.

40. Interviews of Śridar Rana, Ngawang Jorden, and Jampa Losel, Aug.–Nov. 1995.

41. Ngawang Jorden, interview, July 1995. Strict dietary and ablutional observances are also associated with Sarasvatī in some Hindu contexts, as described in the *Brahmavaivarta Purāṇa* and *Sarasvatī Vrata*, in which the restrictions on eating stem from her association with the tongue; A. Gupta, "Conception of Sarasvatī," pp. 86–87.

42. Sakya scholar Jampa Losel, interview, Sept. 1995.

43. For textual references: Dhal, *Goddess Lakṣmī*, p. 113.

44. Trans. by Mullin, *Meditations on the Lower Tantras*, p. 125.

45. Tāranātha, *History of Buddhism in India*, pp. 109–10.

46. Mullin, *Selected Works of the Dalai Lama II*, p. 206.

47. Ngawang Jorden, personal communication, July 1995

48. E.g., Tāranātha, *History of Buddhism in India*, p. 226.

49. Mullin, *Meditations on the Lower Tantras*, p. 127.

50. Ngawang Jorden, personal communication, July 1995.

51. For this form, see n. 28, above.

52. On Vasant Pañcamī (a.k.a. Śrī Pañcamī) observances: Anderson, *Festivals of Nepal*, pp. 231–33; Levy, *Mesocosm*, pp. 426–27.

53. Prajwal Ratna Vajracharya, personal communication, Sept. 2003.

54. Slusser, *Nepal Mandala*, pp. 293–94, 321–22.

55. E.g., Sarasvatī Courtyard at Kwā Bāhā, Patan, houses a temple to Mañjuśrī; Gellner, *Monk, Householder, Tantric Priest*, p. 84.

56. Locke, *Buddhist Monasteries of Nepal*, pp. 249, 290, and fig. 206.

57. Prajwal Ratna Vajracharya, personal communication, Sept. 2003.

58. Slusser, *Nepal Mandala*, p. 322. Sarasvatī Kund, a Licchavi-period shrine complex, now abandoned, is reported in Slusser, pp. 156, 169. The two earliest inscribed Sarasvatī images, from the Sasukhel area of Patan, date to ca. Nepal Samrat 434 (1314 C.E.) and N.S. 567 (1447 C.E.); Regmi, *Medieval Nepal*, vol. 2, p. 597.

59. *Agni Purāṇa*, chap. 50, which describes this form, appears to be the source for this iconography. Widely encountered in Nepal, it is attested in a ca. 1800 Buddhist artist's sketchbook; Pal, *Art of Nepal*, p. 174, fig. D23. A rare gilt bronze of this form, ca. 1500: Pal et al., *Himalayas*, no. 41.

60. Poem by Lekhnāth Pauḍyāl; Hutt, trans., *Himalayan Voices*, p. 29.

Chapter 13
Vasudhārā: Lady Bountiful

1. My translation; *Lha mo nor rgyun ma ser mo'i sgrub thabs*, fol. 277.7–278.3.

2. I summarize here from the *Vasudhārā Dhāraṇī* (a.k.a. *Sucandra Gṛhapati Paripṛcchā*) translation by N. Ghosh, *Goddess of Abundance*, pp. 115–18; quotation on p. 117.

3. Ibid., p. 117.

4. Her name is typically rendered as Vasudhārā in Indic sources and Vasundharā in Newar sources. For ease of cross-reference I use a single spelling throughout this study.

5. Sanskrit epithets from the *Vasudhārānāma-dhāraṇī Stotram* in Pāṇḍeya, ed., *Bauddhastotrasaṃgraha*, pp. 220–21, and *Vasudhārā-stotra Śatanāma* in N. Ghosh, *Goddess of Abundance*, pp. 112–14.

6. For textual sources of these epithets, see preceding note.

7. Tāranātha, *History of Buddhism in India*, pp. 109–10, 278.

8. Ibid., p. 308; Chandra, *Buddhist Iconography*, no. 831; Willson and Brauen, eds., *Deities of Tibetan Buddhism*, no. 327. Yamāri's hymn is preserved in the Tanjur (Derge 3752); texts on his sādhana are found in the *sGrub thabs kun btus* (see n. 10, below).

9. *Sādhanamālā* nos. 213–15; no. 215 is translated in B. Bhattacharyya, *Indian Buddhist Iconography*, p. 245.

10. The fruit, designated as *picura* in Tāranātha, *History of Buddhism in India*, p. 308, transcribed into Tibetan as *pitsurya-phala* in Yamāri's visualization and associated ritual (*Paṇḍita Dzamāri'i lugs kyi 'phags ma nor rgyun ma ser mo'i sgrub thabs man ngag*, fol. 287.3, 288.2, 289.6–7), and described as "blue-red" (*sngo dmar*, fol. 289.7), is identified as *picula* in Willson and Brauen, eds., *Deities of Tibetan Buddhism*, pp. 485, 577.

11. See, e.g., the two dated images from Kurkihār (Patna Museum nos. 9738, 9741); S. Huntington, *"Pāla-Sena" Schools*, pp. 52–53, 214–15, and pls. 45–46. The straight, sticklike stem of grain is a Bihari stylistic convention. An Orissan image, too, includes a kneeling figure who appears to be holding a vessel to collect treasure; P. Mishra, *Archaeology of Mayūrbhañj*, pl. 25 (mislabeled as Tārā).

12. Epithets from the *Vasudhārānāma-dhāraṇī Stotram* in Pāṇḍeya, ed., *Bauddhastotrasaṃgraha*, p. 220.

13. This feature reflects regional stylistic trends. Bengali images depict the grain as a long stem; D. Mitra, *Bronzes from Bangladesh*, pls. 54–55, 88, 91–93. Orissan images favor a fanned or curved spray; D. Mitra, *Ratnagiri*, pls. 137A, 179A–B. The statues from Kurkihār favor a stylized stalk with a straight stem; see n. 11 above.

14. This attribute is identified as corn in sources too numerous to cite, apparently following B. Bhattacharyya, *Indian Buddhist Iconography*, pp. 202–3, 238, 245, despite the fact that the grain depicted rarely resembles an ear of corn and the attribute is described as a cluster or bunch (*mañjarī*) of grain or rice (*dhānya*). This misidentification is also puzzling given that corn is neither native to South Asia nor a major crop there.

15. Skt. *dhānyamañjarī-nānāratna-varṣa-ghaṭa*; *Sādhanamālā* no. 215, p. 422, and, slightly varying, in no. 214, p. 422. Tibetan sādhanas closely follow this wording, e.g., *'bras kyi snye ma mchog dang rin po che sna tshogs pa'i char 'bebs pa'i bum pa*; *Lha mo nor rgyun ma ser mo'i sgrub thabs*, fol. 249.4–5, and similar phrasing in Derge Tōh. nos. 3238, 3239, 3349, 3604, 3656.

16. Two among many examples in which the raining vessel appears below her pendant right foot are a small metal image from Nālandā in P. Gupta, ed., *Patna Museum Catalogue*, pl. 26, and another from Kurkihār described on p. 150.

17. On the symbolism of the rain vessel, also known as *varṣa-sthālī*, see Vajracharya, "Symbolism of Ashokan Pillars," pp. 55–56, 59, 61.

18. Sahni, *Museum of Archaeology at Sārnāth*, pls. 15A–B.

19. D. Mitra, *Ratnagiri*, pls. 79C–D; Sahni, *Museum of Archaeology at Sārnāth*, museum nos. Bf20 and Bf21, pp. 147–48.

20. A four-armed metal sculpture from Kurkihār in the Patna Museum (Arch 9664), inscribed to the twelfth century, is published in Shere, *Bronze Images in Patna Museum*,

pl. 30. The lower right hand is in varada mudrā; the upper left hand displays a vessel surmounted by plants and the lower left bears a lotus. The upper right hand, angled toward the shoulder, may display *tathāgata-vandana* (the gesture of "adoring the Buddha") but has an additional indistinct element, possibly a rosary. A. Ghosh partially describes a four-armed Vasudhārā in the Nalanda Museum (no. 1–1052) in *Nālandā*, p. 48. P. Gupta describes a metal image (Art 301) that he identifies as and may well be a four-armed Vasudhārā in *Patna Museum Catalogue*, p. 164.

21. For this Vredenberg Manuscript illustration: Zwalf, *Buddhism*, pl. 157.

22. Dina Bangdel, personal communication, Dec. 2003; she was present during the ceremony.

23. Of the ten Vasudhārā sādhanas in the Tanjur, nine describe a two-armed form (Derge Tōh. nos. 3237–39, 3349, 3603–5, 3656, 3752). Only one describes this six-armed form (no. 3700, fol. 334a.2–4).

24. Two examples from northern ateliers: Sahni, *Museum of Archaeology at Sārnāth*, pp. 135–36 and pl. 15A; Saraswati, *Tantrayāna Art*, no. 152. Three early Chola examples: Ramachandran, *Nāgapaṭṭinam*, p. 55 and pl. 10.3.

25. *Sādhanamālā* nos. 284–85, 289. The retinues vary slightly, mainly with respect to the directional disposition of the figures, while mandala nos. 285 and 289 include eight door guardians. For a comparative diagram of the three versions: Mallmann, *Iconographie du tântrisme bouddhique*, pp. 460–61. For a fragmentary Nālandā stele of their mandala: R. Misra, *Yaksha Cult*, pp. 72–73 and fig. 18.

26. *Sādhanamālā* nos. 286 and 297 describe Jambhala as embracing a female partner (*prajñā*), but Vasudhārā is not specified. Vasudhārā is, however, named as consort in a ninth- or tenth-century mandala diagram in mantric form; D. Mitra, *Ratnagiri*, pp. 230–31.

27. Pal, *Two Buddhist Paintings*, p. 13.

28. *Sādhanamālā* no. 213, translated in B. Bhattacharyya, *Indian Buddhist Iconography*, pp. 202–3.

29. Tucci, *Gyantse*, pt. 1, p. 194, citing as its source the *sGrub thabs rgya mtsho*. The mandala is beautifully delineated in a nineteenth-century painting produced for a Newar patron; Pal, "Bhīmaratha Rite," fig. 12.

30. For this widely reproduced image, see. e.g., D. Chattopadhyaya, *Lokāyata*, p. 293.

31. For variations of this motif, symbolic analysis, and further references: Bolon, *Goddess Lajjā Gaurī*. On its appearance at a Buddhist cave site: Brown, "Lajjā Gaurī."

32. *Mārkaṇḍeya Purāṇa* 91.43–44; Pargiter trans., p. 518.

33. Continuities between the two are discussed in Tucci, "Earth in India," pp. 537, 550; Pal, *Two Buddhist Paintings*, pp. 10–12, 14, 17; B. Shukla, "Iconography of Vasudhārā," pp. 163–64.

34. *Atharva Veda* 12.1.44–45; Griffith trans., vol. 2, pp. 99–100, slightly amended.

35. *Atharva Veda* 12.1.10, 12.1.36, 12.1.59.

36. *Atharva Veda* 12.1.7, 12.1.9, 12.1.45.

37. *Atharva Veda* 12.1.6, 12.1.8, 12.1.18, 12.1.26, 12.1.44.

38. *Atharva Veda* 12.1.4, 12.1.17, 12.1.29, 12.1.42, 12.1.57. *Oṣadhī* (or *oṣadhi*), generally construed as herbs or medicinal herbs, can also refer to plants in general.

39. For further discussion of this aspect of Pṛthivī, see chap. 1.

40. D. Bhattacharyya, *"Vajrāvalī-nāma-maṇḍalopāyika,"* p. 74.

41. *Lakṣmī Tantra* 9.36, 9.38.

42. On this aspect of Lakṣmī: Gonda, *Aspects of Early Viṣṇuism*, pp. 220–21, 224–25; Manna, *Mother Goddess Caṇḍī*, pp. 55–57.

43. In contemporary representations, Lakṣmī typically showers coins from her palm, a motif attested as early as the Gupta period; Banerjea, *Development of Hindu Iconography*, pp. 213–14. Vasudeva Agrawala attributes this aspect of Vasudhārā, however, to a widespread Indic concept of a "rain of gold" (*hiraṇya-varṣa*) or "shower of heavenly gold" (*divya-suvarṇa-vṛṣṭi*) that falls from heaven when the earth reaches its apogee of abundance (*mahā-abhyudaya*); *Studies in Indian Art*, p. 107.

44. These attributes appear in the iconography of Lakṣmī according to the *Viṣṇudharmottara Purāṇa* and *Śrītattvanidhi*; B. Srivastava, *Iconography of Śakti*, pp. 102–4.

45. This latter motif appears on a number of seals; Banerjea, *Hindu Iconography*, pp. 194–95.

46. Dhal, *Goddess Lakṣmī*, pp. 91–93.

47. Sakya Trizin, personal communication, 1995.

48. Interviews with Khenpo Abbe, Khorchag Rinpoche, and Jampa Losel in Kathmandu, 1995.

49. Chandra, *Buddhist Iconography*, nos. 830, 953; Willson and Brauen, eds., *Deities of Tibetan Buddhism*, nos. 326, 451. This is the epiphany I invariably observed in temple murals.

50. Chandra, *Buddhist Iconography*, no. 832; Willson and Brauen, eds., *Deities of Tibetan Buddhism*, no. 328.

51. Chandra, *Buddhist Iconography*, no. 833; Willson and Brauen, eds., *Deities of Tibetan Buddhism*, no. 329.

52. Chandra, *Buddhist Iconography*, no. 716; Willson and Brauen, eds., *Deities of Tibetan Buddhism*, no. 207. A sādhana of Rakta Vasudhārā is one of the Lha-gsum ("Three Deities") in *Gnyan lo tsa ba'i dbang gi lha gsum las; sGrub thabs kun btus*, vol. 8, fol. 608–644.

53. Chandra, *Buddhist Iconography*, no. 1006; Willson and Brauen, eds., *Deities of Tibetan Buddhism*, no. 504. Late Newar descriptions are excerpted in D. Bhattacharyya, *Tantric Buddhist Iconographic Sources*, pp. 35–36.

54. Rhie and Thurman, *Wisdom and Compassion*, no. 73. For a ca. late fifteenth-century Ngor painting of the mandala: Pal, *Divine Images, Human Visions*, pl. 93.

55. This painting incorporates three mandalas that do not appear in the earlier *Vajrāvalī* series compiled in India by Abhayākaragupta. *Vajrāvalī* texts contemporaneous with the painting do not include the supplementary mandalas, which were added to the written *Vajrāvalī* compilation by the lCang-skya Qutuqtu (late sixteenth or early seventeenth century), drawing from the *Vajrācārya-kriyā-samuccaya* by Jagaddarpaṇa, or Darpaṇācārya (Derge Tōh. no. 3305); Lo Bue, "Iconographic Sources," pp. 186–87.

56. For the nineteenfold mandala iconography: Pal, *Two Buddhist Paintings*, pp. 10, 35–36.

57. A rare painting of Vasudhārā inscribed as painted in Lhasa was commissioned there by a Newar merchant; Pal, "Paintings from Nepal," fig. 27.

58. E.g., the two portraits in Pal, *Art of Tibet* [1983], pl. 25 and fig. P18.

59. E.g., Schroeder, *Buddhist Sculptures in Tibet*, vol. 1, nos. 172C–D.

60. Ricca and Lo Bue, *Great Stupa of Gyantse*, pp. 89–90, 224, 237, and pl. 70.

61. This method is prescribed in *Sādhanamālā* no. 284, which states that Vasudhārā and her retinue are to be drawn on a golden "leaf" (writing surface), Jambhala and his yakṣa retinue are to be drawn on a second leaf in reverse order, and their combined mandala is created by placing one over the other (p. 561, lines 16–18).

62. G. Leonov in Rhie and Thurman, *Wisdom and Compassion*, p. 353 and pl. 144.1.

CHAPTER 14
CUNDĀ: SAVING GRACE

1. My translation; Chos-dbang blo-'gros, *sGrub thabs nor bu'i phreng ba'i lo rgyus*, fol. 15a.4–16a.2.

2. On East Asian worship of Cundā: Whitaker, "Buddhist Spell."

3. Tāranātha, *History of Buddhism in India*, pp. 257–58.

4. Variant spellings include Cuṇḍā, Cundrā, and Cuṇḍrā, but the spelling "Cundā" is most widely attested, e.g., in the *Śikṣasamuccaya*, *Sādhanamālā*, *Niṣpannayogāvalī*, an eleventh-century Prajñāpāramitā manuscript from Nepal, and Tāranāthā's *rGya gar chos 'byung*. On the etymological quandary posed by the name: Conze, "Iconography of the Prajñāpāramitā," pp. 254–55. Attempts to link her name to *candra*, "moon," are tenuous, even on the basis of her "moonlike" white hue, for "moonlike" is a stock simile in iconographic prose.

5. Bendall, trans., *Śikshā-samuccaya*, p. 169.

6. Whitaker, "Buddhist Spell," p. 15.

7. Chos-dbang blo-'gros, *sGrub thabs nor bu'i phreng ba'i lo rgyus*, fol. 15a.4–5, 15b.2–16a.2.

8. Ibid., fol. 15a.5–15b.1.

9. The Tibetan rendition of the name suggests the etymological derivation of Cundā from the Sanskrit root *cud*, "to inspire, impel, incite." If this derivation is intended, the etymology appears to be a false one, for *cud* declines with the stem *cod* rather than *cund*. This may be why some Tibetan texts simply transcribe Cundā as Tsun-da or some variation thereon rather than attempt a translation.

10. *Sādhanamālā* nos. 129–31, partially translated in B. Bhattacharyya, "Cundā Image," pp. 44–45. For a Tibetan print: Chandra, *Buddhist Iconography*, no. 2362; for a Tibetan bronze: A. Gordon, *Iconography of Tibetan Lamaism*, facing p. 76.

11. Ellora examples: Malandra, *Unfolding a Maṇḍala*, pp. 65, 79, 81–82, 88, 98, and figs. 148, 205, 244c; Hock, "Sculpture of Ratnagiri," p. 116 n. 27. Nālandā images: Saraswati, *Tantrayāna Art*, nos. 131–37. A ca. eighth- or ninth-century image, probably from Bihar: Asthana, "Rare Image of Cundā." Two examples at Bodhgayā are noted in Leoshko, "Buddhist Sculptures from Bodhgayā," p. 52. Maināmatī image: Asher, *Art of Eastern India*, pl. 250 (labeled as Tārā). Ratnagiri images: Hock, "Sculpture of Ratnagiri," pp. 115, 119–20, 122–23; D. Mitra, *Ratnagiri*, pls. 51, 80B–D, 81A, 98, 247. Achutrajpur images: D. Mitra, *Bronzes from Achutrajpur*, pp. 117–22 and pls. 110–13. A four-armed image from Amarāvatī, another eastern site, is noted in Malandra, *Unfolding a Maṇḍala*, p. 99

12. In the Buddhist context, see *Bhadraghaṭa Jātaka* (no. 291 in Cowell ed.), and the Tamil classic *Manimēkhalāi*, in which it is a prominent motif.

13. Saraswati, *Tantrayāna Art*, pl. 216. The bowl is also full, but not heaping, in Niyogi, "Cundā," fig. 2.

14. Against Benoytosh Bhattacharyya's assumption that the manuscript is a *Cundā Dhāraṇī* text, Edward Conze argues that the *Cundā Dhāraṇī* would be at most two leaves, whereas the text in question is a full-sized manuscript; "Iconography of the Prajñāpāramitā," p. 245. The text is specified as a Prajñāpāramitā manuscript in the *Niṣpannayogāvalī* description of a twenty-six-armed form of the goddess and in the Sakya sādhana cited in n. 24, below.

15. For a seated image of Bhṛkuṭī that could easily be mistaken for Cundā: M. Ghosh, *Buddhist Iconography*, pl. 51.

16. Ibid., pp. 156–58.

17. As a case in point, a number of four-armed Cundā images in the Patna Museum (Arch. 8355, 8356, 8441, 8442) are misidentified as Prajñāpāramitā in P. Gupta, ed., *Patna Museum Catalogue*, p. 122; D. Bhattacharyya, *Studies in Buddhist Iconography*, p. 59, pl. 20; J. Mishra, *History of Buddhist Iconography in Bihar*, pp. 122–23. Such misidentifications are legion.

18. Jacob Kinnard suggests that this confusion may not simply be a contemporary phenonenon. He argues that all Buddhists may not have been able to differentiate images of Cundā and Prajñāpāramitā and that the overlap or "ambiguity" between images of the two may have been intentional so that one image might represent both in differing contexts and to blur their identities as wisdom figures; *Imaging Wisdom*, pp. 136–37, 144–46.

19. D. Mitra, "Images of Chundā at Bodh-Gaya," p. 303 and pl. 42; A. Sengupta, *Buddhist Art of Bengal*, p. 152 and pl. 71; D. Mitra, *Bronzes from Achutrajpur*, pl. 114. The presence of the alms bowl unmistakably identifies this latter image as Cundā.

20. An eight-armed Orissan relief, some of whose attributes are eroded, appears to be Cundā; Pushpendra Kumar, *Tārā*, pl. 21 (not labeled as Cundā in text). The eight-armed forms found in Java may have been based on Indic prototypes; Niyogi, "Cundā," p. 302.

21. Saraswati, *Tantrayāna Art*, no. 139. Another twelve-armed image from Nālandā identified as Prajñāpāramitā in Conze, "Iconography of the Prajñāpāramitā," pp. 249–50, was later identified as Cundā by Lohuizen-de Leeuw, "Paṭṭikera Chundā," pp. 133–34, although the former misidentification continues to appear in recent publications.

22. B. Bhattacharyya, "Cundā Image," pp. 47–48.

23. For a detailed survey of extant eighteen-armed images: Lohuizen-de Leeuw, "Paṭṭikera Chundā," pp. 122–34, 139, and pls. 18–21. On eighteen-armed images at Bodhgayā: D. Mitra, "Images of Chundā at Bodh-Gaya," pp. 299–303 and pls. 40–41.

24. Chandra, *Buddhist Iconography*, no. 772; Willson and Brauen, eds., *Deities of Tibetan Buddhism*, no. 263.

25. A red, four-armed form appears in a Kurukullā mandala as described in *Sādhanamālā* no. 174; a white, four-armed form, coupled with Ṭakkirāja, is found in the Kālacakra mandala in *Niṣpannayogāvalī* no. 26. For a twenty-six-armed form in the Mañjuvajra mandala and a two-armed form in the Dharmadhātu Vāgīśvara mandala, see *Nispannayogāvalī* nos. 21, 20.

26. Saraswati, *Tantrayāna Art*, no. 246. The manuscript, dated 1015 C.E., is presently in the Cambridge University Library (no. 1643). A. Sengupta, *Buddhist Art of Bengal*, p. 153, also opines that Cundā may once have been important in Cuṇḍā village in Comilla District (in present-day Bangladesh).

27. Lohuizen-de Leeuw, "Paṭṭikera Chundā," pp. 119–21.

28. Foucher, *Étude sur l'iconographie bouddhique*, pp. 144–45, pl. 8.3.

29. See Derge Tanjur, Tōh. nos. 3246, 3346, 3519, 3520, 3521. For early statues (four- and eighteen-armed) housed in the Potala: Schroeder, *Buddhist Sculptures in Tibet*, vol. 1, nos. 68E–F, 153A–D, 154G–H.

30. See, e.g., her inclusion in Kreijger, *Tibetan Painting*, p. 131, to left of central figure, and a sixteenth-century Sakya painting, Pal, *Art of Tibet* (1983), no. 64 (bottom row, second from left).

31. Chos-dbang blo-'gros, *sGrub thabs nor bu'i phreng ba'i lo rgyus*, fol. 15a.2–3.

32. Willson and Brauen, eds., *Deities of Tibetan Buddhism*, no. 152.

Chapter 15
Sitātapatrā: Invincible Goddess with a Thousand Heads and Hands

1. Trans. by Roerich, *Tibetan Paintings*, pp. 67–68, slightly amended. Roerich identifies the author as Tsongkhapa but provides no textual citation.

2. Gonda, *Ancient Indian Kingship*, p. 37. An Indian king is known as "one entitled to the white umbrella"; p. 37 n. 257. The Buddha, as royal heir, is given the same title in *Buddhacarita* 19.47; Johnston trans., pt. 3, p. 47.

3. *Viṣṇu Smṛti* 99.12, cited in Gonda, *Ancient Indian Kingship*, p. 37.

4. A third epithet, *mahāpratyaṅgirā-dhāraṇī*, is more difficult to translate (and reference to the Pañcarakṣā goddess Mahāpratyaṅgirā seems unlikely in this context). These epithets ubiquitously appear in conjunction with the Sitātapatrā mantra.

5. S. Sengupta, "Usnisa-sitatapatra-pratyamgira," pp. 50–52.

6. *gTsug tor gdugs dkar mo can mchog tu grub pa'i gzungs bshugs so*, fol. 556.

7. Trans. in Waddell, "'Dharanī,'" pp. 49–51, quote on pp. 50–51. This widely circulated account is often told in brief at the beginning of her texts and sādhanas; e.g., Chos-dbang blo-'gros, *sGrub thabs nor bu'i phreng ba'i lo rgyus*, fol. 25b.2–4.

8. Waddell, "'Dharanī,'" pp. 51–52.

9. *Mahāunmagga Jātaka*, no. 546; Cowell, ed., *Jātaka*, vol. 6, pp. 156–246; esp. pp. 186–91, 197–98; quote on p. 197. The goddess of the parasol is designated as *chatte adhivattha-devatā* and *chatte nibbata-devatā*.

10. *Mūgapakkha Jātaka*, no. 538; Cowell, ed., *Jātaka*, vol. 6, pp. 3–8, 17–18. Here she is described as *chatte adhivatthā devatā*, "goddess indwelling the umbrella," but immediately beforehand the umbrella is described as a "white parasol" (*setacchatta*).

11. I have not encountered a technical term for this gesture. Images displaying the gesture: Chandra, *Buddhist Iconography*, no. 2365; A. Gordon, *Iconography of Tibetan Lamaism*, illus. facing p. 74; Clark, ed., *Two Lamaistic Pantheons*, vol. 2, p. 202, no. 6A47; Pal and Tseng, *Lamaist Art*, no. 47.

12. For the six-armed form, see *Sādhanamālā* no. 192, the sole text devoted to Sitātapatrā in this collection. As her role, the text cites only that she destroys all *grahas*, i.e., ill-omened astrological influences. For artistic renderings: S. Huntington, *"Pāla-Sena" Schools*, fig. 254; Chandra, *Buddhist Iconography*, no. 926; Willson and Brauen, eds., *Deities of Tibetan Buddhism*, no. 424. For the eight-armed form: Sipra Chakravarti, *Catalogue of Tibetan Thaṅkas*, pl. 9a. She appears in both six- and eight-armed forms at Gyantse; Ricca and Lo Bue, *Great Stupa of Gyantse*, pp. 100–101, 233, and pls. 85–86.

13. My translation; 'Jam-dbyangs bLo-gter-dbang-po, *gTsug tor gdugs dkar can gyi 'khor lo bri thabs rgyal mtshan 'dzugs pa'i cho ga*, fol. 29.4–7.

14. Rhie and Thurman, *Wisdom and Compassion*, no. 125; Béguin, *Peintures du bouddhisme tibétain*, nos. 135–36; Roerich, *Tibetan Paintings*, pl. 24; Tanaka, *Art of Thangka*, vol. 1, no. 76; Mullin, *Female Buddhas*, pl. on p. 113; Chakraverty, *Sacred Buddhist Painting*, p. 29. The Museum of Asian Art, San Francisco, also holds an exquisite piece; The Avery Brundage Collection, B76D10. Additional examples from the Rubin Museum of Art and other collections may be found at the Rubin website (*www.himalayanart.org*). Even a small-scale rendering, such as a *tsag-li* (initiation card), might approach iconographic completeness, as in Willson and Brauen, eds., *Deities of Tibetan Buddhism*, no. 217.

15. E.g., A. Gordon, *Iconography of Tibetan Lamaism*, illus. facing p. 78; Ashencaen and Leonov, *Mirror of Mind*, no. 29.

16. For seventeen-deity mandala: Vira and Chandra, *Tibetan Maṇḍalas*, p. 147; *Ngor Mandalas* no. 7; *De bzhin gshegs pa'i gtsug tor nas byung ba'i gdugs dkar po can ma'i dkyil 'khor du slob ma dbang bskur ba'i cho ga bdud rtsi'i chu rgyun* in *rGyud sde kun btus*, vol. 1, fol. 409–485. For twenty-seven-deity mandala: Vira and Chandra, *Tibetan Maṇḍalas*, p. 148; *Ngor Mandalas* no. 8.

17. Vira and Chandra, *Tibetan Maṇḍalas*, p. 92. For ritual and meditative instructions, see *bCom ldan 'das gtsug tor nas byung ba'i gdugs dkar mo can gyi sgrub dkyil dbang chog dang bcas pa ral gri'i 'khrul 'khor*; *rGyud sde kun btus*, vol. 1, fol. 486–586. A nineteenth-century mandala in the Musée Guimet (MG21232) has more than twenty-nine deities and thus does not conform to a sādhana known to me; Béguin, *Peintures du bouddhisme tibétain*, no. 137.

18. Béguin, *Peintures du bouddhisme tibétain*, nos. 133–34.

19. See, e.g., the Kanjur text translated in Waddell, "'Dharanī,'" pp. 52–54, and *gTsug tor gdugs dkar mo can mchog tu grub pa'i gzungs bshugs so*, fol. 531–532, 537–538, 557–558. Wayman, "Messengers," pp. 314–17, lists many classes of demons from which she offers protection.

20. *gTsug tor gdugs dkar mo can mchog tu grub pa'i gzungs bshugs so*, fol. 531.

21. Waddell, "'Dharanī,'" p. 52.

22. S. Sengupta, "Usnisa-sitatapatra-pratyamgira," p. 71. For a relatively rare Newar painting of Sitātapatrā, dated 1820 C.E.: Kreijger, *Kathmandu Valley Painting*, no. 27. For a Newar statue of her viśva-rūpa form: B. Bhattacharyya, *Indian Buddhist Iconography*, fig. 146 (misidentified in caption).

23. See Pañcarakṣā chap. in Shaw, *Buddhist Goddesses of Tibet and Nepal*, forthcoming.

24. In interviews with lamas of the four major sects, I was informed that Sitātapatrā was "especially" important for their sect. Thinley names various sectarian lineage holders in "Sitatapatra Sadhana," p. 17.

25. See, e.g., the sādhanas devoted to her thousand-armed form in Thinley, "Sitatapatra Sadhana," pp. 17, 19; Willson and Brauen, eds., *Deities of Tibetan Buddhism*, no. 217. For translations of sādhanas devoted to her six-armed form: Mullin, *Meditations on the Lower Tantras*, pp. 128–33; Willson and Brauen, no. 424.

26. Lalou, "Notes a propos d'une amulette," p. 149.

27. Waddell, "'Dharanī,'" p. 54.

28. *gTsug tor gdugs dkar mo can mchog tu grub pa'i gzungs bshugs so*, fol. 558.

29. Lalou, "Notes a propos d'une amulette," p. 142.

30. A stone stele dating from the seventh or eighth century is reported in P. Gupta, *Patna Museum Catalogue*, p. 66. For references to effigies dating from the eighth century and later, see chap. 1 n. 57.

31. This evolution is discussed in chap. 1, above.

32. Bautze-Picron also argues for the ascendance of Mārīcī over Aparājitā in the Bodhgayā region; "Between Śākyamuni and Vairocana," p. 285.

33. Tib. *sngags gyi rgyal-mo*.

Chapter 16
Uṣṇīṣavijayā: Bestower of Long Life and Immortality

1. My translation; *gTsug tor rnam par rgyal ma'i rtog pa'i ṭīkā sgrub thabs*, fol. 517.4–7.

2. 'Bri-gung Chos-kyi grags-pa, *sGrub thabs rgya mtsho*, fol. 24b.2–25a.4. For variants on the story, including revelation of the mantra by Amitāyus in Sukhāvatī, see Chandra, "Comparative Iconography," p. 128.

3. *gTsug tor rnam par rgyal ma'i rtog pa'i ṭīkā sgrub thabs*, fol. 485.7.

4. My translation; *Uṣṇīṣavijayā Dhāraṇī* excerpt in R. Mitra, *Sanskrit Buddhist Literature*, p. 264.

5. Willson and Brauen, eds., *Deities of Tibetan Buddhism*, p. 286, with a slightly different translation of the mantra.

6. *gTsug tor rnam par rgyal ma'i rtog pa'i ṭīkā sgrub thabs*, fol. 517.6–7.

7. Ibid., fol. 517.4–5.

8. Ibid., fol. 485.7.

9. Tāranātha, *History of Buddhism in India*, pp. 170, 172, 174–75.

10. *gTsug tor rnam par rgyal ma'i rtog pa'i ṭīkā sgrub thabs*, fol. 515.2–3.

11. In the *Sādhanamālā*, the figure is identified as a Buddha in no. 212, "Buddha-on-lotus" in no. 191, and Jina Amitābha in no. 211.

12. *Sādhanamālā* nos. 191, 211–12; Willson and Brauen, eds., *Deities of Tibetan Buddhism*, no. 183; Chandra, *Buddhist Iconography*, no. 1054.

13. *Sādhanamālā* nos. 191, 211.

14. D. Mitra, *Ratnagiri*, p. 307 and pl. 253.

15. Pal, *Bronzes of Kashmir*, no. 70.

16. Vira and Chandra, *Tibetan Maṇḍalas*, pp. 94, 269; *Ngor Mandalas*, no. 131. In an unusual rendition, its textual source unknown to me, the retinue is peaceful and Uṣṇīṣavijayā has six arms: Tulku, *Sacred Art of Tibet*, pl. 27.

17. *Sādhanamālā* nos. 211–212; Chandra, *Buddhist Iconography*, no. 927; Willson and Brauen, eds., *Deities of Tibetan Buddhism*, no. 425. One also finds this configuration integrated into a more standard mandalic format: Linrothe, "Ushnīshavijayā," p. 7 and fig. 9; Piotrovsky, ed., *Lost Empire*, no. 20.

18. See, e.g., Neumann, "Wall Paintings," pp. 81–82 and figs. 5, 11–13. The paintings cited in n. 25, below, center on this arrangement, although additional figures are present.

19. Willson and Brauen, eds., *Deities of Tibetan Buddhism*, no. 506. For paintings: Rhie and Thurman, *Wisdom and Compassion*, no. 73; Rossi and Rossi, *Tibetan Thangkas*, no. 6.

20. For an example with Uṣṇīṣavijayā as the main figure: Tanaka, *Art of Thangka*, vol. 2, no. 76.

21. Interviews, Lama Sonam Jorphel Rinpoche, and Jampa Losel of Thorig Gompa, Kathmandu, autumn 1995. Instructions for the rite may be found in *gTsug tor rnam par rgyal ma'i rtog pa'i ṭīkā sgrub thabs*.

22. Jampa Losel of Thorig Gompa, interview, Kathmandu, autumn 1995.

23. For a *thang-ka*, or scroll painting: Essen and Thingo, *Götter des Himalaya*, no. 1-46. For statuary: Rhie and Thurman, *Wisdom and Compassion*, no. 124; Heller, *Tibetan Art*, no. 105; Pal and Tseng, *Lamaist Art*, no. 46.

24. For a print: Chandra, *Buddhist Iconography*, no. 771. For the sādhana, see *Shākya rakṣita'i lugs kyi lha mo rnam rgyal ma dkar mo'i sgrub thabs rjes gnang dang bcas pa bshugs so*; *sGrub thabs kun btus*, vol. 7, fol. 448–459.

25. For additional painted representations of the theme: Béguin, *Art ésotérique*, no. 22; Pal and Tseng, *Lamaist Art*, no. 19.

26. For a variety of sculpted versions, some with solid domes and some with Uṣṇīṣavijayā within the dome: Ricca and Lo Bue, *Great Stupa of Gyantse*, p. 228; Trungpa,

Visual Dharma, no. 51; Pal, *Art of the Himalayas*, no. 71; Ashencaen and Leonov, *Mirror of Mind*, no. 18; Essen and Thingo, *Götter des Himalaya*, nos. 1-20, 2-45, 2-50.

27. In this role, Uṣṇīṣavijayā was one of seven goddesses whose dhāraṇīs were recited on their respective days of the week to invoke their usual benefactions. On these goddesses and *Saptavāra Dhāraṇī* texts: Grönbold, "'Saptavāra.'"

28. The ritual is also called Bhīmarathārohaṇa in Sanskrit. In Newar, for a man, Buḍa Jaṃko; for a woman, Buḍi Jaṃko; and for both, Buḍabuḍi Jaṃko.

29. This description is based on interviews in Kathmandu, autumn 1994, of Ratnakaji Vajracharya, who performed the rite many times, supplemented by information from Levy, *Mesocosm*, pp. 676–77.

30. Pal, "Bhīmaratha Rite," p. 185.

31. For a survey and discussion of fifteenth- to nineteenth-century paintings of this theme: Pal, "Bhīmaratha Rite." For additional examples: Kreijger, *Kathmandu Valley Painting*, no. 28; Pal, *Arts of Nepal*, vol. 2, fig. 118; Van Kooij, *Religion in Nepal*, pl. 44; Waldschmidt and Waldschmidt, *Nepal*, p. 76.

32. This explanation of the horses was related to me by Ratnakaji Vajracharya in Kathmandu, May 1998. For other examples of the motif: Pal, *Art of Nepal*, no. S66; Essen and Thingo, *Götter des Himalaya*, no. 1-22; Shelley and Donald Rubin Collection, P2000.34.2, viewable at *www.himalayanart.org*, no. 700095.

33. For the earliest known example dated by inscription (1387/88 C.E.), in the John and Berthe Ford Collection: Pal, *Desire and Devotion*, no. 125. For an example datable on stylistic grounds to the second half of the fourteenth century: Béguin, *Art ésotérique*, no. 10. For sixteenth-century examples: Pal, *Arts of Nepal*, vol. 2, fig. 100; Shyamalkanti Chakravarti, "Three Dated Nepalese Paṭas," pp. 124–29 and figs. 1–2. This compositional type, with larger stupas in the background, is also attested in Tibet but appears to be a later development in that context. A ca. seventeenth-century example is held by the Southern Alleghenies Museum of Art, viewable at *www.himalayanart.org*, no. 90540.

34. The painting, dated 1808 C.E., held by the Museum of Asian Art, San Francisco, is analyzed by Dina Bangdel in J. Huntington and Bangdel, *Circle of Bliss*, no. 20, which includes detailed discussion of the Lakṣachaitya Vrata.

35. This motive is supplied by the inscription of a fourteenth-century painting dedicated to the "supreme wisdom" of the donor couple and their descendants; Pal, *Desire and Devotion*, no. 125 and p. 329.

Chapter 17
Tārā: Mahayana Buddha, Universal Savior

1. Selective compilation of the "108 praises" (*aṣṭaśata-stotra-nāma*), drawn from vv. 13, 15, 17, 27–28, 30, 33, 37, 49, based on trans. by Conze, *Buddhist Texts*, pp. 197–200; cf. Willson, *In Praise of Tārā*, pp. 101–2, vv. 27–39.

2. Waddell, "Indian Buddhist Cult of Avalokita and His Consort Tara" (1894); Blonay, *Matériaux pour servir à l'histoire de la déesse buddhique Tārā* (1895).

3. For textual citations: Arènes, *Déesse sGrol-ma*, pp. 145–52, 154–55.

4. Origin story as related by the First Dalai Lama; Mullin, trans., *Six Texts*, pp. 10–11.

5. Waddell, "Indian Buddhist Cult," p. 64, citing an oral tradition.

6. Summarized from the translation by Beyer, *Cult of Tārā*, pp. 64–65. Cf. Willson, *In Praise of Tārā*, pp. 33–35; Tāranātha, *Origin of the Tara Tantra*, pp. 11–14.

7. Arènes, *Déesse sGrol-ma*, pp. 152, 155–57, 161.

8. Beyer, *Cult of Tārā*, p. 231.

9. Ibid.

10. *Ārya-tārā-sragdharā Stotra*; Willson, *In Praise of Tārā*, pp. 258–70, vv. 10–12, 16, 19, 21.

11. Hymn by Candragomin; Willson, *In Praise of Tārā*, pp. 230–31, vv. 35–37.

12. Mullin, trans., *Six Texts*, p. 12.

13. Willson, *In Praise of Tārā*, pp. 259–61, vv. 3–4, 7–9.

14. Ibid., pp. 318–19 (Lodro Gyatso).

15. Beyer, *Cult of Tārā*, pp. 60–63.

16. For an English trans.: Willson, *In Praise of Tārā*, pp. 179–205.

17. See accounts in Bokar Rinpoche, *Tara*, pp. 26, 27, 30; Tāranātha, *History of Buddhism in India*, pp. 215–16; Willson, *In Praise of Tārā*, pp. 181, 185; Beyer, *Cult of Tārā*, p. 59.

18. For stories of these and other supernatural powers (*ṛddhi-siddhi*) from the *Golden Rosary*: Willson, *In Praise of Tārā*, pp. 194–96, 199–205.

19. Tāranātha, *Origin of the Tara Tantra*, pp. 31 and 18–19, respectively.

20. Roerich, trans., *Blue Annals*, pp. 1050–51.

21. Tāranātha, *Origin of the Tara Tantra*, p. 31.

22. Willson, *In Praise of Tārā*, p. 223.

23. Ibid., pp. 186, 192; Beyer, *Cult of Tārā*, pp. 237, 240.

24. Accounts in Bokar Rinpoche, *Tara*, p. 8; Beyer, *Cult of Tārā*, pp. 238–40; on the Pharping image, Galland, *Longing for Darkness*, pp. 60–65.

25. See, e.g., Willson, *In Praise of Tārā*, pp. 183, 186, 187; Beyer, *Cult of Tārā*, pp. 59, 237; Bokar Rinpoche, *Tara*, p. 38; Landaw and Weber, *Images of Enlightenment*, p. 86; Surya Das, *Snow Lion's Turquoise Mane*, pp. 193–94.

26. Beyer, *Cult of Tārā*, p. 237.

27. For recent accounts, see Bokar Rinpoche, *Tara*, pp. 34–35.

28. Ricca and Lo Bue, *Great Stupa of Gyantse*, p. 96.

29. M. Ghosh, *Buddhist Iconography*, pp. 17–21.

30. Ibid., pp. 54–57 and pls. 24–25.

31. Ibid., pp. 53–54 and pls. 22–23.

32. Wayman, "Twenty-One Praises"; Klieger, "Tārā," pp. 46–48; M. Ghosh, *Buddhist Iconography*, p. 20.

33. M. Ghosh, *Buddhist Iconography*, pp. 23, 30, 40, and pls. 3, 6.

34. On Cave 7: S. Huntington, *Art of Ancient India*, pp. 265–67 and fig. 12.30. On Cave 9: Pushpendra Kumar, *Tārā*, p. 136.

35. On the ca. 630 Cave 4 at Ellora: Malandra, *Unfolding a Maṇḍala*, p. 42 and fig. 85. On the dating and identification of the relief on the Nālandā main stupa: Malandra, p. 93, and the reproduction of the relief in M. Ghosh, *Buddhist Iconography*, pl. 5.

36. For their appearance in the retinue of Avalokiteśvara in chap. 2 of the *Mañjuśrīmūlakalpa*, portions of which date from the seventh and eighth centuries, see Snellgrove, *Indo-Tibetan Buddhism*, pp. 150–51. The *Mahāvairocana Sūtra*, widely dated to the seventh century, has Tārā and Bhṛkuṭī immediately flanking Avalokiteśvara in 2.81–83; Wayman, *Enlightenment of Vairocana*, pp. 11, 89.

37. P. Vaidya, ed., *Āryamañjusrimūlakalpa*, p. 45.

38. Ibid., p. 486, v. 506.

39. Trans. by Wayman, *Enlightenment of Vairocana*, p. 123.

40. For Tārā's appearance at Ellora in contexts other than attendance on Avalokiteśvara: Malandra, *Unfolding a Maṇḍala*, p. 49 and fig. 102, p. 71 and fig. 182, p. 79 and fig. 200, p. 81 and fig. 204, p. 82 and fig. 213, p. 84 and fig. 220.

41. Ibid., p. 72 and fig. 188.

42. I am grateful to Susan Landesman for sharing this material from her forthcoming study with me via personal communications in March 2005. For a brief précis of the *Tārāmūlakalpa*, see Lalou, "Mañjuśrimūlakalpa et Tārāmūlakalpa."

43. Willson, *In Praise of Tārā*, pp. 32, v. 6; 274, v. 4.

44. For comprehensive discussion of the Buddhahood of Tārā: Arènes, *Déesse sGrol-ma*, pp. 177–239.

45. Sūryagupta, in Willson, *In Praise of Tārā*, p. 248, v. 39; the preceding thirty-two verses provide an epithet and praise for each of the thirty-two marks. Beyer notes an apparently anomalous reference to the "thirty" marks of Tārā (*Cult of Tārā*, p. 182), which he attributes to her lack of a "recessed *liṅga*," reading *liṅga* as "male sexual organ." Other Buddhist authors apparently did not find a need to eliminate this Buddha trait, perhaps construing *liṅga* in its more general meaning as "sexual organ," in which case Tārā, as a female, would have no difficulty in having one that is "recessed."

46. Willson, *In Praise of Tārā*, pp. 226–27, 229, 337 (Candragomin); p. 274 (Akṣobhyavajra).

47. Stories of such interventions abound. Accounts in which she takes the appearance of an ordinary woman: Willson, *In Praise of Tārā*, pp. 179, 183, 197; Beyer, *Cult of Tārā*, p. 241; Tāranātha, *History of Buddhism in India*, pp. 192, 281. For a biography of a woman who manifested Tārā's presence in the world, see Drolma, *Delog*, and my discussion below.

48. Willson, *In Praise of Tārā*, pp. 269, v. 34; 227, v. 13; 275, v. 9.

49. Ibid., pp. 274–75, vv. 4–6, 10–14; 286, vv. 1, 6.

50. Ibid., pp. 243, v. 6 (Sūryagupta); 275–76, vv. 9, 16–17, 19–20 (Akṣobhyavajra).

51. Ibid., p. 269, v. 32 (Sarvajñamitra).

52. Ibid., pp. 274–75, vv. 6, 10, 12–14 (Akṣobhyavajra); 227, v. 15 (Candragomin).

53. Ibid., p. 274, v. 7.

54. Ibid., p. 286, v. 3; Mullin, trans., *Meditations on the Lower Tantras*, p. 97.

55. Beyer, *Cult of Tārā*, pp. 62–63.

56. Willson, *In Praise of Tārā*, pp. 226, v. 1; 227, v. 13; 244, v. 16; 246, v. 27.

57. Ibid., p. 228, vv. 19–20.

58. Ibid., pp. 245, v. 18; 247, v. 30; 229, v. 31.

59. Ibid., p. 228, v. 17.

60. Snellgrove, *Indo-Tibetan Buddhism*, pp. 150–51.

61. Skt.: 1) *siṃha*, lion, 2) *hastī*, elephant, 3) *agni*, fire, 4) *sarpa*, snake, 5) *taskara* or *cora-upadrava*, "attack by thieves," encompassing theft, bodily harm, and murder, 6) *jalārṇava* or *augha-vegāvarta*, designating violent water, whose dangers include floods, drowning, and shipwreck, 7) *nigaḍa* or *śṛṅkhala*, referring to shackles or imprisonment, 8) *piśāca*, a type of demon that here metonymizes all evil spirits.

62. D. Mitra, "Ashṭamahābhaya-Tārā," pp. 20–22 and pls. 2–3.

63. Candragomin wrote several hymns to Tārā as savior from the eight fears, translated in Beyer, *Cult of Tārā*, pp. 229–30; Willson, *In Praise of Tārā*, pp. 232–37. See also the

late seventh- or early eighth-century hymn by Sarvajñamitra; Willson, pp. 261–63, vv. 10–17.

64. R. Sengupta, "Sculptural Representation," pp. 12, 15.

65. D. Mitra, "Ashṭamahābhaya-Tārā," p. 22.

66. Relevant passages, cited and discussed: M. Ghosh, *Buddhist Iconography*, pp. 19–20.

67. Willson, *In Praise of Tārā*, pp. 301–6, vv. 20–27; cf. Mullin, trans., *Six Texts*, pp. 32–33.

68. Trans. by Willson, *In Praise of Tārā*, p. 305, vv. 22, 25.

69. The smaller effigies are simply described as "forms of Tārā" (*tārā-rūpinī*) in *Sādhanamālā* no. 99, a visualization formulated by, or attributed to, Candragomin.

70. For this panel: D. Mitra, *Ratnagiri*, pp. 428–29 and pl. 325B.

71. For late Indic images of Aṣṭamahābhaya Tārā in seated pose: M. Ghosh, *Buddhist Iconography*, pp. 23–24, 40–47, and pls. 11–15; Saraswati, *Tantrayāna Art*, no. 102. For a repoussé medallion crafted in India to adorn a Tibetan wooden text cover, fascinating for its inclusion of the perils in miniature: Singer, "Early Tibetan Painting Revisited," p. 69 and fig. 3a.

72. The seventh-century hymns by Candragomin describe her as green; Willson, *In Praise of Tārā*, pp. 234–35, 337–42. In the longer composition, he endows her with four attendants (Mārīcī, Bhṛkutī, Pratisarā, an orange sow-headed goddess) and eight emanations. An important ca. eleventh-century painting approximating this configuration is analyzed in Kossak and Singer, *Sacred Visions*, no. 3. She is also depicted as green in a Newar manuscript illustration dated 1015 C.E.; Saraswati, *Tantrayāna Art*, no. 256. She is described as white in *Sādhanamālā* no. 99, translated in M. Ghosh, *Buddhist Iconography*, pp. 39–40.

73. This development may have taken place in Tibet and is seen, for example, in a song by the First Dalai Lama; Willson, *In Praise of Tārā*, pp. 301–6. Mallar Ghosh explains that the previous identification of a late Pāla stele of Aṣṭamahābhaya Tārā as Khadiravaṇī was based on misidentification of one of her attendants; *Buddhist Iconography*, pp. 42–43 and pl. 11.

74. The late Indic version: Allinger, "Green Tara as Saviouress," p. 40 and fig. 2; Linrothe, "Murals at Mangyu," fig. 12. The Sakya version of Aṣṭabhujā Tārā, which shares only two attributes with the earlier conception: Willson and Brauen, eds., *Deities of Tibetan Buddhism*, no. 150; Ricca and Lo Bue, *Great Stupa of Gyantse*, pl. 79; Heller, *Tibetan Art*, no. 67.

75. Allinger translates and discusses this passage; "Green Tara as Saviouress," pp. 43–44.

76. See Tucci, *Temples of Western Tibet*, pt. 2, pp. 156, 161–62, and pls. 142–43; Chandra, *Buddhist Iconography*, nos. 2169–76.

77. See, e.g., the intricate treatments of the theme in Rhie and Thurman, *Worlds of Transformation*, nos. 37–38; Chandra, *Transcendental Art of Tibet*, pl. on p. 207.

78. E.g., Mullin, *Female Buddhas*, pp. 82–97; the unnumbered plates in Willson, *In Praise of Tārā*, listed on p. 7.

79. Stone reliefs: Schroeder, *Buddhist Sculptures in Tibet*, vol. 1, nos. 127A–C; wooden shrine: Pal, *Tibet*, pl. 64b.

80. On *gau* that invoke Tārā's protection: Beyer, *Cult of Tārā*, pp. 288–89.

81. Ashencaen and Leonov, *Mirror of Mind*, no. 23.

82. Arènes, *Déesse sGrol-ma*, pp. 34–35, 46–47, 58–61.

83. Susan Landesman, personal communication, March 2005.

84. Arènes, *Déesse sGrol-ma*, p. 48; see also pp. 50, 201.

85. Pal, *Tibet*, p. 129.

86. See the assertions to this effect, without documentation or argument, in Waddell, "Indian Buddhist Cult," pp. 58, 64, 66–67. The assertion is sufficiently ubiquitous in subsequent literature not to warrant citation.

87. I have never encountered such a reference. Arènes reports the same from his much more extensive literary survey; *Déesse sGrol-ma*, p. 100.

88. The earliest definitively identifiable occurrence of the triad is cited in n. 35, above. Subsequent examples are too numerous to cite.

89. R. Paul, *Tibetan Symbolic World*, pp. 63–64; Snellgrove, *Indo-Tibetan Buddhism*, p. 151; Arènes, *Déesse sGrol-ma*, pp. 61, 100–102. Paul and Snellgrove also adduce the asexual, celibate persona of Avalokiteśvara in the Mahayana context.

90. E.g., Tārā is paired with Hayagrīva in attendance on Lokanātha Avalokiteśvara; *Sādhanamālā* nos. 8, 18–19, 41. When Tārā and Bhṛkuṭī flank Khasarpaṇa Avalokiteśvara, Tārā is paired with Sudhanakumāra and Bhṛkuṭī is paired with Hayagrīva; *Sādhanamālā* nos. 13–16, 24, 26. For a corresponding relief sculpture: M. Ghosh, *Buddhist Iconography*, pl. 50.

91. He is paired with Pāṇḍaravāsinī in *Sādhanamālā* no. 30 (B. Bhattacharyya, *Indian Buddhist Iconography*, p. 134), the Guhyavajravilāsinī form of Vajrayoginī in the *Guhyasamaya Sādhanamālā* (English, *Vajrayoginī*, pp. 86–94, 360–62), and Guhyajñānā in a practice current in Tibetan Sarma schools (Shaw, *Passionate Enlightenment*, pp. 123–25).

92. *Niṣpannayogāvalī* no. 24.

93. On Tārā in the Pañca Jina mandala: Mallmann, *Iconographie du tântrisme bouddhique*, pp. 374–76; M. Ghosh, *Buddhist Iconography*, chap. 4.

94. J. Huntington and Bangdel, *Circle of Bliss*, no. 123.

95. Wangpo, *Appearing Aglow with Active Awareness*, p. 7; Vira and Chandra, *Tibetan Maṇḍalas*, pp. 138, 270.

96. Pushpendra Kumar, *Tārā*, pls. 22, 25, 27, 32; Huntington and Huntington, *Leaves from the Bodhi Tree*, no. 6.

97. *Sādhanamālā* no. 98, trans. in Gomez, "Two Tantric Meditations," pp. 321–27. "Śyāma Tārā" also does not designate other green epiphanies of Tārā in the *Sādhanamālā*, all of which have specific names, as discussed below.

98. For sādhanas in translation: Mullin, *Meditations on the Lower Tantras*, pp. 104–7; Willson and Brauen, eds., *Deities of Tibetan Buddhism*, nos. 9, 133–34, 439.

99. In a fivefold mandala stemming from Nāgārjuna and Atīśa, her retinue is golden Mārīcī, white Pratisarā, red Vārāhī, and blue Ekajaṭā; Willson and Brauen, eds., *Deities of Tibetan Buddhism*, nos. 145–49.

100. Trans. by Gomez, "Two Tantric Meditations," p. 325; see also Beyer, *Cult of Tārā*, p. 60.

101. The earliest hymn may be that attributed to Nāgārjuna but is difficult to date because of the complexity of dating Nāgārjuna himself. Most scholars accept the early ninth century as the terminus ad quem; Willson, *In Praise of Tārā*, pp. 279–81 and the hymn on pp. 282–85.

102. The brief sādhana dedicated to her in the *Sādhanamālā*, no. 89, mentions her requisite attendants but summarily describes her appearance and does not specify a posture. The earliest reliefs: Pushpendra Kumar, *Tārā*, pls. 24, 29, 31; Uhlig, *Tantrische Kunst*, no. 18; G. Bhattacharya, "Donors of a Few Tārā Images," fig. 9; Huntington and Huntington, *Leaves from the Bodhi Tree*, no. 7. Later Pāla examples: M. Ghosh, *Buddhist Iconography*, pp. 68–74 and pls. 27–29.

103. Béguin, *Peintures du bouddhisme tibétain*, no. 127; Olson, *Catalogue of the Tibetan Collection*, no. 44; Mullin, *Female Buddhas*, pl. on p. 67.

104. For passages on this theme in the *Tārā Tantra*: Willson, *In Praise of Tārā*, pp. 75–80.

105. D. Bhattacharyya, "Of Colour in Tantric Buddhist Art," p. 29.

106. For a helpful overview of the worship and ritual uses of trees and plant life: Manna, *Mother Goddess Caṇḍī*, pp. 44–49.

107. Gonda, *Aspects of Early Viṣṇuism*, pp. 11–14, 45, 217. For an array of magical practices (*abhicāra*) centering on the *āsurī* plant-as-goddess in an appendix to the *Atharva Veda*, see Magoun, "Āsurī-Kalpa."

108. Jayakar, *Earth Mother*, pp. 182–83; see also pp. 134, 179–82, 187–88.

109. *Khadiravaṇī Tārā Stotra* vv. 1–3; trans. by Willson, *In Praise of Tārā*, p. 282, slightly amended. Willson discusses Nāgārjuna's association with Tārā and the dating of this stotra on pp. 279–81.

110. Willson, *In Praise of Tārā*, pp. 284–85, vv. 10, 11, 13, 16.

111. Ibid., p. 98, vv. 1–3.

112. Ibid., pp. 259, 268 (Sarvajñamitra).

113. Ibid., p. 229, v. 30 (Candragomin).

114. Ibid., p. 301.

115. Ibid., p. 41, slightly amended.

116. See, e.g., the widely published Tārā in the Cleveland Museum of Art, painted by the Newar artist Aniko for a Tibetan patron, substantively discussed in Huntington and Huntington, *Leaves from the Bodhi Tree*, no. 113; Kossak and Singer, *Sacred Visions*, no. 37. Although these creatures recur on Buddhist throne backs and carry symbolic significance, I draw attention here to their visual impact rather than doctrinal associations.

117. Kossak and Singer, *Sacred Visions*, no. 3; quotes on pp. 56, 57.

118. Arènes, *Déesse sGrol-ma*, pp. 132–33, refuting Willson, *In Praise of Tārā*, pp. 17–18.

119. R. Paul, *Tibetan Symbolic World*, p. 99.

120. On Buddhist worship and images of Lakṣmī, see chap. 4, above.

121. Waddell, "Indian Buddhist Cult," pp. 64–65.

122. E.g., Willson, *In Praise of Tārā*, pp. 226, v. 4; 243, v. 10; 244, v. 12; 284, v. 11.

123. Mullin, trans., *Six Texts*, p. 31.

124. Willson and Brauen, eds., *Deities of Tibetan Buddhism*, nos. 206, 325.

125. Chandra, *Transcendental Art of Tibet*, pp. 40–41.

126. *Sādhanamālā* nos. 102–3, 112, in which liturgies she has a sixfold retinue; in *Sādhanamālā* no. 96, attributed to Nāgārjuna, she is designated as Vajra Tāra and appears sans retinue. No. 109 also describes a white, two-armed form but does not specify the handheld attributes.

127. Paintings of the triad centering on White Tārā: Essen and Thingo, *Götter des Himalaya*, no. 1–47; Mullin, *Female Buddhas*, pl. on p. 103.

128. Vessantara, *Meeting the Buddhas*, p. 186, citing Vagīśvarakīrti.

129. Mullin, *Female Buddhas*, p. 101, trans. slightly amended. For the entire text by the First Dalai Lama: Mullin, trans., *Six Texts*, pp. 35–45.

130. Mullin, *Meditations on the Lower Tantras*, pp. 103–4.

131. Beyer, *Cult of Tārā*, p. 394.

132. Atīśa, Gampopa, and the First Dalai Lama are among the prominent lineage holders. For some of these lineages: Beyer, *Cult of Tārā*, pp. 15, 387, 417–19; Vessantara, *Meeting the Buddhas*, pp. 184–85. For Atīśa's sādhana: Willson, *In Praise of Tārā*, pp. 345–49.

133. Willson and Brauen, eds., *Deities of Tibetan Buddhism*, nos. 4–7.

134. Trans. by Beyer, *Cult of Tārā*, p. 448.

135. For English translations of different versions of this practice, see that of the Seventh Dalai Lama in Mullin, *Meditations on the Lower Tantras*, pp. 95–104, and the Karma Kagyu version in Nyinje, *White Tara Who Saves One from Death*. Preliminary and subsidiary rites are compiled in Beyer, *Cult of Tārā*, pp. 375–467; on the circles of protection, see pp. 381–83, 456–57.

136. Beyer, *Cult of Tārā*, p. 456; Mullin, *Meditations on the Lower Tantras*, p. 103.

137. Landaw and Weber, *Images of Enlightenment*, pp. 89–90.

138. Beyer, *Cult of Tārā*, pp. 458–60.

139. Bokar Rinpoche, *Tara*, p. 41; Landaw and Weber, *Images of Enlightenment*, p. 90.

140. Trans. by Willson, *In Praise of Tārā*, pp. 268–69, vv. 30–31, 33, with minor emendations.

141. Ibid., pp. 268–69, vv. 30, 32–33.

142. *Sādhanamālā* no. 90; iconography and images are discussed in M. Ghosh, *Buddhist Iconography*, pp. 48–53, 64.

143. *Sādhanamālā* no. 91; her attendants are Aśokakāntā Mārīcī, Mahāmāyūrī, Ekajaṭā, and Jāṅgulī.

144. *Sādhanamālā* no. 92.

145. Willson and Brauen, eds., *Deities of Tibetan Buddhism*, no. 151. The name given in this Tibetan sādhana is Kāpali, a spelling unattested in Sanskrit. The author may have intended Kapālī, "Skull Bearer," or Kāpālī, "Garlanded in Skulls," although neither feature appears in her iconography, so my emendation is tentative.

146. Mahāśrī Tārā has the same fourfold retinue as Varada Tārā (see n. 143, above). See *Sādhanamālā* no. 116; Saraswati, *Tantrayāna Art*, nos. 231–32; M. Ghosh, *Buddhist Iconography*, pp. 57–63; Asthana, "Mahāśrī Tārā."

147. *Sādhanamālā* no. 111; M. Ghosh, *Buddhist Iconography*, pp. 54–57 and pls. 24–25.

148. *Sādhanamālā* no. 107; Chandra, *Buddhist Iconography*, no. 649; Willson and Brauen, eds., *Deities of Tibetan Buddhism*, no. 140.

149. Pal, *Bronzes of Kashmir*, no. 69; see also no. 68.

150. *Sādhanamālā* no. 104, trans. in B. Bhattacharyya, *Indian Buddhist Iconography*, p. 232.

151. *Sādhanamālā* no. 105. For a translation and line drawings, see B. Bhattacharyya, *Indian Buddhist Iconography*, p. 230 and fig. 171; Clark, *Two Lamaistic Pantheons*, vol. 2, p. 282.

152. Willson and Brauen, eds., *Deities of Tibetan Buddhism*, no. 144.

153. Young, *Dreaming in the Lotus*, pp. 143–45, quote on p. 143.

154. *Sādhanamālā* no. 308; the description is unclear regarding whether the lotus appears in one or both hands. She may be the manifestation known as "Yellow Tārā" (Pīta Tārā; sGrol-ma ser-mo) in Tibet; Chandra, *Buddhist Iconography*, no. 650.

155. Willson and Brauen, eds., *Deities of Tibetan Buddhism*, no. 138.

156. *Sādhanamālā* nos. 93–95, 97, 110. (Note that no. 96 addresses a white, two-armed form also called Vajra Tārā.) For iconographic variations and associated practices: M. Ghosh, *Buddhist Iconography*, pp. 74–90 and pls. 30–32B; Sahu, *Buddhism in Orissa*, pp. 210–11 and fig. 67; Willson and Brauen, eds., *Deities of Tibetan Buddhism*, no. 469. Additional artistic representations: Béguin, *Peintures du bouddhisme tibétain*, no. 131; Pal and Tseng, *Lamaist Art*, no. 45; Uhlig, *Tantrische Kunst*, nos. 28, 31.

157. *Niṣpannayogāvalī* no. 16; Vira and Chandra, *Tibetan Maṇḍalas*, pp. 56–57.

158. Chandra, *Buddhist Iconography*, no. 648; Willson and Brauen, eds., *Deities of Tibetan Buddhism*, no. 139; *rJe btsun sa skya pa'i man ngag dbang gi sgrol ma dmar mo'i sgrub thabs rjes gnang las tshogs dang bcas pa'i skor* in *sGrub thabs kun btus*, vol. 8, fol. 654–690.

159. Tromge, comp., *Red Tara Commentary*, pp. 3–7, 28, 32, 36–39, 62, 82.

160. *Sādhanamālā* nos. 100–101 (in which she is also designated as Mahācīnakrama Tārā); 124–26. Further discussion of Ekajaṭā: Bühnemann, "Goddess Mahācīnakrama-Tārā."

161. *Sādhanamālā* no. 114, translated in B. Bhattacharyya, *Indian Buddhist Iconography*, pp. 249–50, quotes on p. 250. Artistic representations: Ricca and Lo Bue, *Great Stupa of Gyantse*, pl. 81; Schroeder, *Indo-Tibetan Bronzes*, no. 128F.

162. *Sādhanamālā* nos. 310–11; Chandra, *Buddhist Iconography*, no. 646; Willson and Brauen, eds., *Deities of Tibetan Buddhism*, no. 137; Mallmann, *Iconographie du tântrisme bouddhique*, pp. 373–74. On the origins of this epiphany: Shaw, *Passionate Enlightenment*, pp. 87, 105–7.

163. Chandra, *Buddhist Iconography*, no. 645; Willson and Brauen, eds., *Deities of Tibetan Buddhism*, no. 136; *rJe btsun sgrol ma nyin zhi mtshan khro'i sgrub thabs rjes gnang las tshogs dang bcas pa'i skor* in *sGrub thabs kun btus*, vol. 3, fol. 519–540.

164. D. Bhattacharyya, *Studies in Buddhist Iconography*, pp. 12–14, discussed at more length by the same author in "Unknown Form of Tārā."

165. Beyer, *Cult of Tārā*, p. 292; Huber and Rigzin, "Tibetan Guide for Pilgrimage," p. 135.

166. For a painting showing 108 emanations, see Lipton and Ragnubs, *Treasures of Tibetan Art*, no. 44. For two paintings that include 201 and 200 miniature Tārās, respectively, see Béguin, *Peintures du bouddhisme tibétain*, nos. 123–24.

167. The triptych format: Chandra, *Transcendental Art of Tibet*, pp. 204–5. The five hundred-fold format: Lipton and Ragnubs, *Treasures of Tibetan Art*, no. 43.

168. E.g., D. Bhattacharyya, in *Studies in Buddhist Iconography*, chap. 2, and *Tantric Buddhist Iconographic Sources*, chap. 3; Getty, *Gods of Northern Buddhism*, pp. 119–27.

169. Song of Candrakīrti; Willson, *In Praise of Tārā*, pp. 286–87.

170. Sarvajñamitra's hymn; ibid., p. 268, v. 32.

171. Skt. *Bhagavatyāryatārādevyā namaskāraikaviṃśati-stotraṃ guṇa-hita-sahitam*. Recent translations: Beyer, *Cult of Tārā*, pp. 211–13; Willson, *In Praise of Tārā*, pp. 113–16, 353–66; Lopez, "Prayer Flag," pp. 551–52. Willson compiles commentaries on the verses; *In Praise of Tārā*, pp. 117, 120–66. For the commentary by the First Dalai Lama: Mullin, trans., *Six Texts*, pp. 7–24.

172. Beyer, *Cult of Tārā*, p. 211.

173. Ibid., pp. 231–32, 241.

174. Ibid., pp. 211, v. 1; 212, v. 3; 213, v. 15.

175. Ibid., pp. 211–13, vv. 2, 5, 10, 14.

176. Ibid., p. 214, and quote on p. 213.

177. Ibid., p. 469 n. 11. Although called "Twenty-One Tārās," there are twenty-five deities in the series. The basic Green Tārā appears first as the "root" form, while Khadiravaṇī Tārā and her attendants (Ekajaṭā and Aśokakāntā Mārīcī) are inserted before the ninth Tārā. For Sūryagupta's list of Tārās and their attributes: Tucci, *Temples of Western Tibet*, pt. 2, pp. 158–60; Willson and Brauen, eds., *Deities of Tibetan Buddhism*, nos. 275–299, accompanied by painted *tsag-li* of the series. Willson has compiled a commentary on Sūryagupta's system, along with illustrations; *In Praise of Tārā*, pp. 120–66. For prints:

Chandra, *Buddhist Iconography*, nos. 784–805 (note that the numbers 792–94 are repeated for insertion of Khadiravaṇī and her attendants); Clark, ed., *Two Lamaistic Pantheons*, vol. 2, pp. 276–81, nos. 206–26 (with some numerical and iconographic discrepancies).

178. Beyer, *Cult of Tārā*, pp. xiii, 333–35, 470. For paintings following this iconographic system, see n. 180, below. I have seen the mantras in a typescript sādhana but not in a published source known to me.

179. This system derives from the *kLong chen snying thig* of Longchenpa; Beyer, *Cult of Tārā*, pp. 118–19, 470. Khadiravaṇī appears as the ninth of the series proper. Xylographic prints: Chandra, *Buddhist Iconography*, nos. 2145–65.

180. Paintings of the entire series based on the iconography stemming from Nāgārjuna and Atīśa: Béguin, *Peintures du bouddhisme tibétain*, no. 122; Tucci, *Tibetan Painted Scrolls*, pl. 167; Tanaka, *Art of Thangka*, vol. 1, no. 23; Rhie and Thurman, *Worlds of Transformation*, no. 36 (see also nos. 34–35, canvases devoted to individual figures in series). A single canvas of the Sūryagupta version: Tanaka, *Art of Thangka*, vol. 2, no. 74. Nine paintings from a Sūryagupta series: Kreijger, *Tibetan Painting*, no. 15.

181. Rhie and Thurman, *Wisdom and Compassion*, no. 22.

182. E.g., Béguin, *Peintures du bouddhisme tibétain*, no. 132.

183. Batchelor, *Tibet Guide*, pp. 216–18.

184. Beyer, *Cult of Tārā*, p. 3.

185. Day, "Twenty-One Tārās," pp. 83, 85.

186. A. Chattopadhyaya, *Atīśa and Tibet*, pp. 178, 357, 380–81, 388, 417–18.

187. Beyer, *Cult of Tārā*, pp. 3–5, 8, 10–11, quotation on p. 11.

188. Ibid., pp. 13–15, 171.

189. Ibid., p. 4.

190. Substantive analyses of and Tibetan sources on the divine identities and historical roles of the princesses: Beyer, *Cult of Tārā*, pp. 5–6, 8–10; Tucci, "Wives of Srong btsan sgam po"; Shakya, *Life and Contribution of the Nepalese Princess*; Benard, "Transformations of Wen Cheng Kongjo."

191. Beyer, *Cult of Tārā*, pp. 55, 231; see also Waddell, "Indian Buddhist Cult," pp. 64–65.

192. Beyer, *Cult of Tārā*, p. 3.

193. Ibid., pp. 232, 241.

194. Lopez, "Prayer Flag."

195. Beyer, *Cult of Tārā*, p. 232.

196. Ibid., pp. 55–59. One such drama in translation: Allione, *Women of Wisdom*, pp. 221–79.

197. Havnevik, *Tibetan Buddhist Nuns*, pp. 122–23, 175–76, 199; quote on p. 175.

198. The lineages, texts, and sacerdotal and public/lay aspects of the ritual are detailed in Beyer, *Cult of Tārā*, pp. 63, 170–226.

199. Ibid., pp. 234, 289–90.

200. Willson, *In Praise of Tārā*, p. 229.

201. Beyer, *Cult of Tārā*, p. 407.

202. Willson, *In Praise of Tārā*, p. 222.

203. Surya Das, *Snow Lion's Turquoise Mane*, pp. 119–20.

204. Drolma, *Delog*, pp. 115–16.

205. Ibid., pp. 116, 118.

206. Ibid., pp. 120–23; quotes on p. 123.

207. For Tārā's oft-told interventions in Atīśa's life: Bokar Rinpoche, *Tara*, pp. 56–59.

208. Pal discusses possible evidence of Tārā in Licchavi Nepal; *Buddhist Art in Licchavi Nepal*, p. 36. She definitively appears in early ninth-century manuscripts (Regmi, *Medieval Nepal*, vol. 2, p. 583) and artistic sources from perhaps the tenth century (Pal, *Art of Nepal*, fig. S12 and p. 45).

209. Prajwal Ratna Vajracharya, personal communication, June 2003.

210. K. Vaidya, *Buddhist Traditions*, pp. 140–41, supplemented by ritual details related by Prajwal Ratna Vajracharya, personal communication, July 2003.

211. Lewis, "Mahāyāna *Vratas*," p. 119.

212. Ibid.

213. I did not witness a Tārā Vrata; this description was provided by Prajwal Ratna Vajracharya, personal communication, June 2003. The ritual manual is translated in Lewis, "Mahāyāna *Vratas*," pp. 119–26.

214. Locke, *Buddhist Monasteries of Nepal*, pp. 288, 290, fig. 205; K. Vaidya, *Buddhist Traditions*, p. 145.

215. Summarized from the translation in Lewis, "Mahāyāna *Vratas*," pp. 127–29. For another legend related to Tārā Tīrtha, see Zanen, "Goddess Vajrayoginī," pp. 132–33.

Chapter 18
Vajrayoginī: Her Dance Is Total Freedom

1. My translation, from a manuscript version of the song published, with several misprints, in Vajrācārya, ed., *Cacā-Munā*, vol. 1, p. 53.

2. This statement pertains to what the goddesses manifest; it does not describe their attainments per se. Whether a given divinity is fully enlightened is a theological nicety. However, by definition, a dhāraṇī deity does not *manifest* full enlightenment but rather a particular quality or power. This issue is discussed in my introduction.

3. This aspect of Tārā is discussed in chap. 17.

4. On the massive topic of the ḍākinī, I refer the reader to Simmer-Brown's comprehensive study, *Dakini's Warm Breath*, and extensive bibliography. For comparison of the yakṣiṇī and ḍākinī figural types: Shaw, "Magical Lovers, Sisters, and Mothers," forthcoming.

5. Skt. *pañcajñānātmikāṃ sahajānanda-svabhāvāṃ*; *Sādhanamālā* no. 217, p. 425.

6. The *trikāya* theme is common in Vajrayoginī literature. For a clear explication, see Tharchin, *Kechara Paradise*, pp. 288–91, wherein they are termed "wisdom," "enjoyment," and "emanation" bodies. Moreover, many of the practices described in his volume are framed in terms of attainment of one of the three Buddha-bodies of Vajrayoginī.

7. Skt. *mahārāga-svabhāvāṃ*; *Sādhanamālā* no. 236, p. 456.

8. Trungpa, "Sacred Outlook," pp. 236, 238.

9. Willson and Brauen, eds., *Deities of Tibetan Buddhism*, p. 258; see also p. 257.

10. See, e.g., Trungpa, "Sacred Outlook," p. 238.

11. D. Chattopadhyaya, *Lokāyata*, pp. 300–305.

12. For a range of dharmodayā (also spelled *dharmodaya*) designs and practice applications: English, *Vajrayoginī*, pp. 53, 95, 96, 97, 100, 216, 237, 361, 497 n. 518.

13. In a single triangle, all three corners will be marked with bliss whorls (*nandyāvarta*, Tib. *dga'-dkyil*). In interlocking triangles, as this motif was standardized, four corners are so marked in the dharmodayā of Nāroḍākinī and all six in that of Vajravārāhī.

14. G. Gyatso, *Dakini Land*, p. 396.

15. Schmidt, trans., *Vajra Yogini*, p. 6.

16. Tharchin, *Kechara Paradise*, p. 288. This accords with the general Buddhist principle that all phenomena proceed from and are reducible to states of consciousness.

17. For insightful discussion of the integration of the doctrine of emptiness with womb symbolism: Klein, "Nondualism and the Great Bliss Queen," pp. 90–92.

18. Exegesis based on that in Trungpa, "Sacred Outlook," p. 236, to which I've added the implicit allusion to blood.

19. My translation; *Sādhanamālā* no. 236, pp. 456–57.

20. On these benefits of the inner yogas: G. Gyatso, *Clear Light of Bliss*, pp. 46–48, 64–65. The phenomenon of physical youthfulness is readily observable in living adepts and widespread in biographical literature. For one such example, of a female adept who looked like a teenager when she died at age 115, see Havnevik, *Tibetan Buddhist Nuns*, p. 68.

21. *Sādhanamālā* nos. 217, 226–227 (Vajravārāhī), 233 (Vajrayoginī). English analyzes the previously unexamined *Guhyasamaya Sādhanamālā* in depth in *Vajrayoginī*, reporting the epiphany under discussion, designated as Vajravārāhī, to be the most prevalent among the twenty forms described the compendium (p. 36) and the focus of the longest sādhana, which English analyzes in chap. 3 and translates on pp. 225–313.

22. *Sādhanamālā* no. 217; see English, *Vajrayoginī*, p. 239, for a similar iconographic description in translation.

23. Hindu statuary of divine yoginis drinking from or displaying a skull cup: Dehejia, *Yoginī Cult*, pls. on pp. 100, 102, 107.

24. *Sādhanamālā* no. 226, p. 440, line 10; no. 227, p. 442, lines 15–16. The bell ornaments and anklets find mention in *Sādhanamālā* no. 233 (and no. 236, on another epiphany) and English, *Vajrayoginī*, p. 239.

25. Iconographic sources for Nāroḍākinī: *Sādhanamālā* no. 236; Willson and Brauen, eds., *Deities of Tibetan Buddhism*, nos. 77, 87. For an artistic rendering of the three-dimensionality of her dharmodayā: Rhie and Thurman, *Worlds of Transformation*, no. 194.

26. On the general significance of such hair: Lang, "Shaven Heads and Loose Hair," p. 33. For Buddhist exegesis: G. Gyatso, *Dakini Land*, p. 122.

27. These exegeses appear in Eleven Yoga sādhanas; see, e.g., G. Gyatso, *Dakini Land*, pp. 120–22. The number of bone ornaments is given as five (*pañca-mudrā*) or six (*ṣaṇ-mudrā*) in Sanskrit sādhanas of various forms of Vajrayoginī but appears eventually to have been standardized as five, possibly in the Tibetan context, on the principle that the female body itself represents wisdom, according to Gyatso, p. 121.

28. Beer, *Encyclopedia of Tibetan Symbols*, pp. 252–56.

29. Exegesis given in G. Gyatso, *Dakini Land*, p. 121. See also Beer, *Encyclopedia of Tibetan Symbols*, p. 256 and pl. 115, leftmost staff.

30. This conclusion, derived from my limited textual survey, is confirmed by Adelheid Herrmann-Pfandt in *Ḍākinīs*, p. 243, on the basis of her much more extensive textual study.

31. The Indian textual basis for the link between Nāroḍākinī and Nāropā is tenuous. The single brief sādhana in the *Sādhanamālā* describing this form (no. 236) makes no mention of Nāropā, whereas the short (one folio) text on Vajrayoginī by Nāropā in the Tanjur (Derge Tōh. no. 1579) describes her as "dancing" and in any case does not foretell the massive textual tradition that arose in Tibet. For the major foundational Tibetan authors and texts, see Herrmann-Pfandt, *Ḍākinīs*, pp. 242–43.

32. Tharchin, *Kechara Paradise*, p. 122.

33. For a detailed sectarian history of the practice: English, *Vajrayoginī*, pp. xxiv–xxv, and, on their derivation from Nāropā, G. Gyatso, *Dakini Land*, p. 4.

34. *Sādhanamālā* no. 225, p. 439, line 8.

35. *Sādhanamālā* no. 226, p. 440, line 10; no. 227, p. 442, line 16.

36. Tharchin, *Kechara Paradise*, p. 162.

37. This explanation of Vajrayoginī's wrathful aspect is drawn from ibid., pp. 212–15; quote on p. 215.

38. Donaldson, "Orissan Images of Vārāhī," p. 157.

39. For sādhanas in translation, see Willson and Brauen, eds., *Deities of Tibetan Buddhism*, no. 76, and the sādhana excerpted and analyzed in Trungpa, "Sacred Outlook." For Buddhist exegeses of her iconography, see the same Trungpa essay and Dawa-Samdup, ed., *Śrī-Cakraśaṃvara-tantra*, pp. 99–100.

40. These uninscribed images are datable on stylistic grounds: Huntington and Huntington, *Leaves from the Bodhi Tree*, nos. 60 (lower left image in color plate) and 130; Pal, *Tibet*, no. 65; Pal, *Art of the Himalayas*, no. 80. The first is a manuscript illustration of Eastern Indic or Newar provenance; the others are Tibetan representations. The twelfth-century examples in Schroeder, *Buddhist Sculptures in Tibet*, vol. 1, nos. 125C–E, may be of Indic provenance, although they also resemble Tibetan carvings in the Pāla-based Sharmthun style, per comparison with Huntington and Huntington, no. 130. The boar-head motif was standard by the thirteenth century, appearing in Kadam paintings of that date: Pal, *Tibetan Paintings*, fig. 9 and pl. 16; Kossak and Singer, *Sacred Visions*, nos. 20–21.

41. See, e.g., Tharchin, *Kechara Paradise*, p. 211, for this oft-expressed view, based on use of the boar as a symbol of ignorance at the center of the "wheel of existence" (*bhavacakra*).

42. English, *Vajrayoginī*, pp. 54–59 (twelve-armed), 62–65 (six-armed), 73–74 (four-armed).

43. Ibid., pp. 82–84. This appears to be the figure codified as Maitrīḍākinī.

44. Ibid., pp. 84–86, and, for the two "reverse *yab-yum*" forms, pp. 60–62, 86–94.

45. The sādhana corresponding to my illustration is quite brief and names the partners simply as Vajrayoginī and Saṃvara; Willson and Brauen, eds., *Deities of Tibetan Buddhism*, no. 88. For additional "reverse" forms: Chandra, *Buddhist Iconography*, nos. 268–69.

46. English, *Vajrayoginī*, p. 107.

47. Chandra, *Buddhist Iconography*, no. 596; Willson and Brauen, eds., *Deities of Tibetan Buddhism*, no. 86.

48. Willson and Brauen, eds., *Deities of Tibetan Buddhism*, no. 80; quote on p. 259. See also Chandra, *Buddhist Iconography*, no. 590, and English, *Vajrayoginī*, pp. 66–68, for an Indic sādhana. The same iconography appears in *Sādhanamālā* no. 224 but without the boar head.

49. Willson and Brauen, eds., *Deities of Tibetan Buddhism*, no. 84.

50. For practices and artistic representations: *Sādhanamālā* no. 218; Chandra, *Buddhist Iconography*, no. 41; Pal and Meech-Pekarik, *Buddhist Book Illuminations*, pl. 11; Willson and Brauen, eds., *Deities of Tibetan Buddhism*, nos. 98–99; *rDo rje phag mo dkar mo shes rab gsal byed kyi sgrub thabs byin rlabs dang bcas pa'i skor in sGrub thabs kun btus*, vol. 2, fol. 574–605.

51. Mullin, *Selected Works of the Dalai Lama II*, pp. 183–91.

52. Willson and Brauen, eds., *Deities of Tibetan Buddhism*, no. 79; Chandra, *Buddhist Iconography*, no. 589. For an Indraḍākinī mandala: Leidy and Thurman, *Mandala*, no. 32.

53. Willson and Brauen, eds., *Deities of Tibetan Buddhism*, no. 78.

54. Chandra, *Buddhist Iconography*, nos. 10, 588.

55. For this epiphany, bearing a knife: Lohia, *Lalitavajra's Manual*, p. 55, fig. 13, and the paintings cited in n. 57 below. For the same epiphany, bearing a vajra: Ashencaen and Leonov, *Mirror of Mind*, no. 22, and the Indic sādhana in English, *Vajrayoginī*, pp. 79–81, under the name Vidyādharī Vajrayoginī.

56. See, e.g., *sGrub thabs kun btus*, vol. 4, wherein their texts are serialized on fol. 57–111 (Nāroḍākinī), fol. 112–130 (Indraḍākinī), and fol. 131–164 (Maitrīḍākinī).

57. We find two such compositions in the National Gallery of Canada; Pal, *Divine Images, Human Visions*, nos. 96, 97.

58. Willson and Brauen, eds., *Deities of Tibetan Buddhism*, nos. 89–97, a series that includes her eightfold retinue. For painted representations and additional commentary: Uhlig, *Tantrische Kunst*, pl. 101; Mullin, *Female Buddhas*, pl. on p. 161; Linrothe and Watt, *Demonic Divine*, no. 58. The associated practices as transmitted by Phadampa Sangyay are described in *Khros ma nag mo gsang sgrub kyi gtor dbang dngos grub dpal ster; sGrub thabs kun btus*, vol. 4, fol. 216–227. For a Nyingma Chöd practice centering on this epiphany, translated into English: P. Rinpoche, *Kunzang Lama'i Shelung*, pp. 298–302.

59. Willson and Brauen, eds., *Deities of Tibetan Buddhism*, p. 262.

60. Edou, *Machig Labdron*, p. 152.

61. I use this title, as standard in English-language scholarship, for the Sanskrit *Śrī-heruka-abhidhāna-tantra* and Tibetan *rGyud gyi rgyal po dpal bde mchog nyung ngu*. An English translation by David Gray will soon be released under the title *Discourse of Śrī Heruka*.

62. E.g., for these four (in four-armed form) as the retinue of Nāroḍākinī, see Béguin, *Peintures du bouddhisme tibétain*, no. 162. In Cakrasaṃvara-Vajravārāhī mandalas, the four are typically four-armed; see, e.g., Dawa-Samdup, *Śrī-Cakraśaṃvara-tantra*, p. 101.

63. In the set of six "armor yoginis" (*kavaca-yoginī*), or "armor heroines" (Tib. *go-cha'i dpa'-mo*), the red yogini has six arms and the two additional yoginis are white and "smoke-colored." For their names and iconography: Chandra, *Buddhist Iconography*, nos. 572–77; Willson and Brauen, eds., *Deities of Tibetan Buddhism*, nos. 62–67. For early paintings in which Vajravārāhī is immediately encircled by the six armor yoginis: Rhie and Thurman, *Wisdom and Compassion*, no. 93; Kossak and Singer, *Sacred Visions*, no. 21. One finds this, too, in a Newar context; Kramrisch, *Art of Nepal*, no. 98.

64. For this configuration centering on dancing Vajravārāhī: Vira and Chandra, *Tibetan Maṇḍalas*, p. 206; *Ngor Mandalas* no. 67; Béguin, *Peintures du bouddhisme tibétain*, no. 160; Rhie and Thurman, *Worlds of Transformation*, no. 118. This configuration finds a possible source in the so-called "five-deity Cakrasaṃvara mandala" (counting the central couple as a single figure) introduced by Ghaṇṭāpa, in which the four ḍākiṇīs replicate the iconography of Vajravārāhī except for their bodily hue.

65. For the thirteen-deity mandala: Vira and Chandra, *Tibetan Maṇḍalas*, pp. 204, 211, 213, 215, 222, and discussion in English, *Vajrayoginī*, pp. 186–87.

66. For the thirty-seven-fold mandala: Vira and Chandra, *Tibetan Maṇḍalas*, p. 207; *Ngor Mandalas* no. 68; English, *Vajrayoginī*, pp. 188–204.

67. This mandala is examined in Shaw, *Buddhist Goddesses of Tibet and Nepal*, forthcoming.

68. Tharchin, *Kechara Paradise*, pp. xviii, 123.

69. The massive study by Elizabeth English, *Vajrayoginī*, is a major contribution on the history of Vajrayoginī iconography and practices in India and beyond.

70. G. Gyatso, *Dakini Land*, p. 392.

71. On the body mandala (*lus-dkyil*) visualization and deities: Tharchin, *Kechara Paradise*, pp. 177–91. For the thirty-seven-deity mandala, see n. 66 above.

72. For these epithets: Tharchin, *Kechara Paradise*, pp. 257, 266, 280, 283.

73. For a sample of such prayers and statements of aspiration: Tharchin, *Kechara Paradise*, pp. 264, 266, 279, 283; G. Gyatso, *Dakini Land*, p. 205.

74. G. Gyatso, *Dakini Land*, p. 121.

75. Additional examples: Rhie and Thurman, *Worlds of Transformation*, no. 194; English, *Vajrayoginī*, pl. 14; Tanaka, *Art of Thangka*, vol. 2, no. 60.

76. *Cakrasaṃvara Tantra*, fol. 246a.4–5, using the term "mKha'-spyod-gnas," *gnas* meaning "place" or "land."

77. See the biographies as translated in Dowman, *Masters of Mahāmudrā*. Only biographies 1, 5, 9, 10, 16, 18, 64, 76, and 84 do not end with ascent to Khecara.

78. I follow here the terminology preferred by Tibetan translators for the terms more literally translated as "lesser Khecara" (mKha'-spyod chung-ngu) and "great Khecara" (mKha'-spyod chen-po). "Lesser Khecara" is also designated as the "place Khecara," or "land of Khecara" (mKha'-spyod-gnas), as well as mKha'-spyod rig-'dzin, or Vidyādhara Khecara, with reference to the Vidyādhara status of those who attain it.

79. Dhargyey, *Vajrayogini Sadhana and Commentary*, pp. 36–37, 59.

80. Ibid., pp. 54–59; quote on p. 58. This yoga is supplemental to the standard Eleven Yogas.

81. G. Gyatso, *Dakini Land*, p. 22.

82. Ibid., p. 23.

83. See Shaw, *Passionate Enlightenment*, chaps. 4, 5, 7.

Chapter 19
Nairātmyā: Her Body Is the Sky

1. My translation; *Hevajra Tantra* 2.4.45–47. Verse citations in this chapter refer to Snellgrove's edition.

2. Skt. *mahāsukhā divyayoginī, sukhaṃdadā, tatsukhaṃ kāminī, sahajānandakāriṇī, mahāmudrāsukhaṃdadā, mahāsukhakarā*; see, e.g., *Hevajra Tantra* 1.8.50, 2.4.42–43, 2.4.45, 2.5.40, and *Sādhanamālā* no. 228, p. 448, line 5.

3. *Hevajra Tantra* 2.4.42.

4. Trans. by Snellgrove, *Hevajra Tantra*, pt. 1, pp. 77–78, slightly amended.

5. *Hevajra Tantra* 1.8.50.

6. Skt. *dharmadhātu-svabhāva*; *Hevajra Tantra* 2.4.47.

7. This description characterizes Indic and Tibetan writings, appearing with little variation in *Sādhanamālā* nos. 228–31 and Derge Tanjur Tōh. nos. 3293–94, 3640, as well as the Sakya sādhana in Willson and Brauen, eds., *Deities of Tibetan Buddhism*, no. 466. Two Indic statues of Nairātmyā are published in M. Mitra, "Nairātmā in Vajrayāna Buddhism," pls. 1–2, as are translations of several iconographic descriptions. For one of the earliest known painted representations: Newman, "Vajrayāna Deities," p. 132 (lower figure).

8. Snellgrove, *Hevajra Tantra*, pt. 1, pp. 74, 129; *Sādhanamālā* no 128, p. 447.

9. Beer, *Encyclopedia of Tibetan Symbols*, p. 150.

10. Snellgrove, *Hevajra Tantra*, pt. 1, p. 75 and 75 n. 1.

11. Exegesis in *Hevajra Tantra* 1.8.20.

12. For detailed analysis of khaṭvāṅga symbolism: Beer, *Encyclopedia of Tibetan Symbols*, pp. 146, 252–58.

13. *Sādhanamālā* no. 231, lines 4–5.

14. This fifteenfold mandala, as described in *Hevajra Tantra* 1.9 and *Sādhanamālā* no. 228, is illustrated in Vira and Chandra, *Tibetan Maṇḍalas*, nos. 106, 108; *Ngor Mandalas* nos. 106, 108; Kramrisch, *Art of Nepal*, no. 87; Rossi and Rossi, *Tibetan Thangkas*, no. 8.

15. E.g., the name Vajra Nairātmyā is used in the Sakya *rGyud sde kun btus*; most of vol. 19 of the printed edition is devoted to this mandala and related rituals.

16. Snellgrove, *Hevajra Tantra*, pt. 1, pp. 74–75, 129.

17. *Nispannayogāvalī* no. 6, diagrammed in Vira and Chandra, *Tibetan Maṇḍalas*, pp. 34–35; see also Willson and Brauen, eds., *Deities of Tibetan Buddhism*, no. 466. For painted representations: Pal, *Tibet*, no. 70; Rossi and Rossi, *Tibetan Thangkas*, no. 5. For a painted twenty-one-deity version, perhaps omitting the apex and nadir yoginis: Essen and Thingo, *Götter des Himalaya*, no. 2-355.

18. Skt. *svasaṃvedyātmikā śuddhir... vimucyate*; *Hevajra Tantra* 1.9.3.

19. These correspondences appear in *Hevajra Tantra* 1.9 and *Sādhanamālā* no. 228, pp. 446–47, citing the *Hevajra Tantra* as its source (p. 443). Since two goddesses named Gaurī occur in the mandala, the one in the inner circle is sometimes designated as Guptagaurī ("Hidden Gaurī"), as in *Hevajra Tantra* 1.9.17b.

20. *Hevajra Tantra* 1.8.48–53 and 2.5.68.

21. Trans. by Snellgrove, *Hevajra Tantra*, pt. 1, p. 81.

22. Skt. *svabhāvena viśuddham*; *Hevajra Tantra* 1.9.1.

23. *Hevajra Tantra* 1.9.7; pt. 1, p. 79.

24. *Hevajra Tantra* 1.9.3.

25. See Snellgrove, *Hevajra Tantra*, pt. 1, pp. 36, 103–6.

26. *Sādhanamālā* no. 228, p. 447, lines 14–15; no. 230, p. 451, lines 8–9.

27. *Sādhanamālā* no. 231, p. 452, lines 2–3; Derge Tōh. nos. 3293–94, 3640. For the fifteen yoginis and correlate vowels, see Snellgrove, *Hevajra Tantra*, pt. 1, p. 103.

28. Snellgrove, *Hevajra Tantra*, pt. 1, p. 109.

29. *Sādhanamālā* no. 228, p. 448, lines 5–6; epithet Caṇḍālī from *Hevajra Tantra* 1.1.31.

30. Trans. by Snellgrove, *Hevajra Tantra*, pt. 1, p. 94; see also p. 91.

31. Ibid., pt. 1, p. 50.

32. R. S. Sharma, *Śūdras in Ancient India*, pp. 138–41, 146, 226, 228, 291.

33. Snellgrove, *Hevajra Tantra*, pt. 1, p. 107.

34. Ibid., pt. 1, p. 107, slightly amended; see pp. 65, 72, 90, 98, 119 for similar statements.

35. See ibid., pt. 1, pp. 65, 72, 98.

36. My translation; *Hevajra Tantra* 1.7.8–9. For the secret signs and times and places to seek out yogini gatherings: Snellgrove, *Hevajra Tantra*, pt. 1, pp. 66–71.

37. Shaw, *Passionate Enlightenment*, pp. 81–84.

38. Snellgrove, *Hevajra Tantra*, pt. 1, p. 113.

39. Sādhana and stotra texts in the Tanjur include Derge Tōh. nos. 1305–9, 1311–13, 3293–94, 3393, 3640, 4619.

40. Pal, *Divine Images, Human Visions*, fig. 106.

41. For the full painting and discussion: Mullin, *Female Buddhas*, pp. 156–57.

42. E.g., Rhie and Thurman, *Worlds of Transformation*, no. 189.

43. E.g., J. Huntington and Bangdel, *Circle of Bliss*, no. 34; Tanaka, *Art of Thangka*, vol. 1, no. 42.

44. *Sādhanamālā* no. 230 stipulates the "dancing" version (*ardhaparyaṅka-nāṭhita-sthitāṃ*); nos. 228 and 231 do not specify a stance. Tibetan texts I have examined omit the posture or simply designate the ardhaparyaṅka. On the many interpretations of this pose: Willson and Brauen, eds., *Deities of Tibetan Buddhism*, pp. 486–87.

45. See Pal, *Tibetan Paintings*, p. 72 and pl. 39.

46. Li Jicheng, *Realm of Tibetan Buddhism*, pls. 99–100 (mislabeled).

47. Inscribed images: Weldon and Singer, *Sculptural Heritage of Tibet*, no. 28; Essen and Thingo, *Götter des Himalaya*, no. 2-332; Pal, *Tibet*, no. 66 (in a cross-legged meditation posture).

48. On Nairātmyā in Nepal, see the Guhyeśvarī chapter in Shaw, *Buddhist Goddesses of Tibet and Nepal*, forthcoming.

49. Skt. *svarūpaṃ dharmadhātukaṃ*; *Hevajra Tantra* 2.4.47.

Chapter 20
Chinnamuṇḍā: Severed-Headed Goddess

1. My translation; Lakṣmīṅkarā, *rDo rje phag mo dbu bcad ma'i sgrub thabs*, fol. 205a.3–6.

2. See previous note for citation. In some contexts, "Buddha" may be prefixed to "ḍākiṇī" or "yoginī" to designate a female deity of the Buddha family in a five-family mandala, but here the term serves as a title rather than a name, without reference to that fivefold scheme.

3. The same mantra appears in *Sādhanamālā* no. 232 for Chinnamuṇḍā, no. 233 for Vajrayoginī, and in slightly abbreviated forms in nos. 225 and 226 for Vajravārāhī. Adelheid Herrmann-Pfandt encountered the same phenomenon in Tanjur texts; personal communication, April 2000.

4. See *Sādhanamālā* no. 232. No. 234 is an abbreviated version that omits mention of the severed head and cremation ground; no. 238 simply relates mantras. No. 232 is translated in Benard, *Chinnamastā*, p. 85. Additional sādhanas are cited below. See also English, *Vajrayoginī*, pp. 94–102, for newly discovered sādhana texts.

5. The term *trikāya* generally refers to three Buddha-bodies, but its differing meaning here is explained in Virūpa's sādhana; Nihom, "Goddess with the Severed Head," pp. 230–31.

6. Edou's explanation of the difference between self-sacrifice as a bodhisattva practice and the Chöd bodily offering is applicable here; *Machig Labdron*, pp. 53–55. Because Chinnamuṇḍā remains alive throughout the visualization, and in some cases her head is restored, one must discount K. Mukherjee's otherwise appealing suggestion that "the underlying sentiment is *karuṇā* or universal compassion which inspires her to sustain the life of her attendants even at the cost of her own life" ("Vajrayoginī and Mahākāla," p. 210).

7. Benard, *Chinnamastā*, p. 119.

8. Ibid., pp. 104–5.

9. G. Gyatso, *Clear Light of Bliss*, pp. 18–21, 24, 29–30.

10. Ibid., pp. 65–66.

11. Benard, *Chinnamastā*, pp. 88–89, 118.

12. On technical aspects of this chakra in the visualization: ibid., pp. 88, 119; G. Gyatso, *Clear Light of Bliss*, pp. 29, 43.

13. My translation; Mekhalā and Kanakhalā, *gYung drung 'khyil ba gsum gyi zhal gdams*, fol. 35a.2–3.

14. G. Gyatso, *Clear Light of Bliss*, p. 95. Other inner yoga systems envision this process differently.

15. Benard, *Chinnamastā*, pp. 102–3.

16. G. Gyatso, *Clear Light of Bliss*, pp. 46–48, 64–65.

17. Ibid., pp. 69–70.

18. Biography summarized from Robinson, trans., *Buddha's Lions*, pp. 250–53; Kazi, *Tibet House Museum*, pp. 60–61; R. Mishra, *Advayasiddhi*, pp. 17–18, 89. See also Shaw, *Passionate Enlightenment*, pp. 110–12. A Nyingma account includes an episode in which Lakṣmīṅkarā beheads herself as a magical display; Benard, *Chinnamastā*, p. 11.

19. *rNal 'byor ma'i sgrub pa'i thabs*, Derge Tōh. no. 1547; *rDo rje phag mo dbu bcad ma'i sgrub thabs*, Derge Tōh. no. 1554. The latter, excerpted at the beginning of this chapter, is translated in Benard, *Chinnamastā*, pp. 72–74.

20. E.g., Chandra, *Buddhist Iconography*, no. 1183.

21. The author of the *Blue Annals* uses the term Phag-mo gzhung-drug, "six treatises of Vajravārāhī," with reference to Derge Tōh. nos. 1551–1556; Roerich, trans., p. 390.

22. Benard, compiling the lineages (*guru-paramparā*) as recorded by Bu-ston, Tāranātha, and the *sGrub thabs kun btus*, rectifies the recurrent claim in western scholarship that Chinnamuṇḍā was introduced by Śavara; *Chinnamastā*, pp. 13–16.

23. For literary citations: Nihom, "Goddess with the Severed Head," pp. 222–23. Chinnamuṇḍā-Vajrayoginī, not noted by Nihom, appears in a range of contexts, including a text cited in Benard, *Chinnamastā*, p. 14.

24. Pal, *Tibetan Paintings*, pl. 16 (lower left corner of main register).

25. My translation; *Sems nyid kyi rtog pa 'joms pa'i lta ba*, fol. 47b.5–48a.3.

26. See transmission lineages cited in n. 22 above. Clearly some selectivity is involved in tracing Chinnamuṇḍā practice only to Virūpa, as in Nihom, "Goddess with the Severed Head," pp. 223–25.

27. *dbU bcad ma'i sgrub thabs*, Derge Tōh. no. 1555, and stotra translated in Benard, *Chinnamastā*, pp. 74–75.

28. Tāranātha, *Seven Instruction Lineages*, p. 36.

29. On the colophon: Shaw, "Ecstatic Song by Lakṣmīṅkarā," p. 55.

30. Trans. by Dowman, *Masters of Enchantment*, p. 188.

31. G. Gyatso, *Clear Light of Bliss*, p. 65.

32. Shaw, *Passionate Enlightenment*, p. 79.

33. Tāranātha, *Tāranātha's Life of Kṛṣṇācārya*, pp. 62–63; Robinson, trans., *Buddha's Lions*, pp. 211–13.

34. Kazi, *Tibet House Museum*, pl. 14. I have seen similar portrayals in unpublished paintings and xylographic prints.

35. Dowman, *Masters of Mahāmudrā*, p. 318. Tāranātha even suggests that Vajravārāhī got the idea of a headless form from them; *Life of Kṛṣṇācārya*, p. 63.

36. *gYung drung 'khyil ba gsum gyi zhal gdams*, discussed in Shaw, *Passionate Enlightenment*, pp. 114–17.

37. Roerich, trans., *Blue Annals*, pp. 390–97, details the transmission of the practice to Nepal and Tibet.

38. Benard, *Chinnamastā*, p. 14.

39. Pal, *Nepal*, pp. 62–63, 82.

40. For the Nyingma citation: Benard, *Chinnamastā*, pp. 15–16.

41. *dPyal lugs phag mo skor gsum gyi sgrub thabs*; for iconographic description and mantra, see fol. 166.3–5. For a sādhana in translation: Willson and Brauen, eds., *Deities of Tibetan Buddhism*, nos. 81–83. A seventeenth-century painting of a Cakrasaṃvara mandala, possibly a Sakya work, includes the Chinnamuṇḍā triad in the lower register; Kreijger, *Tibetan Painting*, no. 64.

42. See English, *Vajrayoginī*, pp. 95–97, on a red form without a severed head.

43. Herrmann-Pfandt, *Ḍākinīs*, pl. on p. 265.

44. Meisezahl, *Geist und Ikonographie*, pp. 51–53 and pl. 1. Since a Gelug lama appears at the top of this painting, a search of Gelug sources might yield a corresponding sādhana.

45. Herrmann-Pfandt, *Ḍākinīs*, pp. 264, 267, 267 nn. 24–25. Tāranātha denotes the practice as that of Chinnamuṇḍā-Vajravārāhī rather than of Nāroḍākinī; p. 274.

46. Elizabeth English notes that the name "Chinnamastā" appears in a Buddhist context in the scribal insertions and marginalia of several texts anthologized in the *Guhyasamaya Sādhanamālā* but that the name Chinnamuṇḍā invariably appears in the texts themselves; *Vajrayoginī*, pp. 422–23 n. 206.

47. For temple locations: Benard, *Chinnamastā*, pp. 145–47; Kinsley, *Tantric Visions of the Divine Feminine*, pp. 164–65.

48. For iconographic descriptions of Chinnamastā: Pal, *Hindu Religion and Iconology*, pp. 79–81, 83; Benard, *Chinnamastā*, pp. 33–34, 41–42, 86. Their iconographic proximity has led to misidentification of artistic images. Gudrun Bühnemann contrasts their iconography and surveys images and misidentifications in *Iconography of Hindu Tantric Deities*, pp. 108–12.

49. For detailed discussion of Chinnamastā: Kinsley, *Tantric Visions of the Divine Feminine*, pp. 144–66. For practices in translation: Benard, *Chinnamastā*, pp. 22–46.

50. Kinsley, *Tantric Visions of the Divine Feminine*, p. 160.

51. B. Bhattacharyya, *Introduction to Buddhist Esoterism*, pp. 159–61, compares the texts, dates, and mantras and convincingly establishes the precedence of the Buddhist goddess. For additional Chinnamastā mantras that support his argument: K. Mukherjee, "Vajrayoginī and Mahākāla," p. 209. Benard cites two arguments for Hindu origins in *Chinnamastā*, p. 16.

52. Herrmann-Pfandt, *Ḍākinīs*, pp. 271–72.

53. Trans. by Pal, *Hindu Religion and Iconology*, p. 82, with minor emendation.

54. The philosophical dimension of Chöd as a means of cultivating nondual wisdom is highlighted in Orofino, "Great Wisdom Mother."

Chapter 21
Siṃhamukhā: Lion-Faced Female Buddha

1. My translation; *mKha' 'gro seng ge'i gdong pa can gyi man ngag*, fol. 288.2–5.

2. Alternately, in Sanskrit, Siṃhavaktrā.

3. Epithets from *mKha' 'gro seng ge'i gdong pa can gyi man ngag*: *ye-shes kyi mkha' 'gro ma*, fol. 269.1, 284.7; *rgyal ba'i yum chen*, fol. 286.4; *shes phyin ma*, fol. 286.4; *shes rab dga' ma*, fol. 286.7; *chos d.byings ye shes rang bzhin bcom ldan 'das*, fol. 288.1–2. The term "wisdom ḍākinī" refers to fully enlightened ḍākinīs.

4. Ibid., fol. 286.7.

5. My translation; ibid., fol. 286.2–3.

6. Ibid., fol. 286.1.

7. My translation; ibid., fol. 286.7–287.1.

8. Tib. *chos nyid ngang du rol*; ibid., fol. 286.4.

9. Ibid., fol. 285.7–286.1.

10. Buddhism recognizes a state of consciousness, or yogic concentration, that has no content. Termed *nirodha-samāpatti*, it is not permanent nor regarded as enlightenment.

11. Tib. *zhe sdang rnam dag rnam shes gnas gyur pa*; *mKha' 'gro seng ge'i gdong pa can gyi man ngag*, fol. 288.1.

12. This inner yoga is described in more detail in chap. 20.

13. *mKha' 'gro seng ge'i gdong pa can gyi man ngag*, fol. 286.4.

14. On Siṃhamukhā as a protector: Loseries-Leick, "Kālī in Tibetan Buddhism," p. 428. For her visualization within a longer subjugation ritual: Beyer, *Cult of Tārā*, pp. 314–16.

15. Chandra, *Buddhist Iconography*, no. 743; Willson and Brauen, eds., *Deities of Tibetan Buddhism*, no. 234; Essen and Thingo, *Götter des Himalaya*, no. 1-111.

16. My translation; *mKha' 'gro seng ge'i gdong pa can gyi man ngag*, fol. 286.5–7.

17. Ibid., fol. 286.6–7.

18. Ibid., fol. 285.7.

19. For a sādhana focusing on this triad, see *Seng gdong sngon mo gtso 'khor gsum ma'i sgrub thabs*. In this system, Siṃhamukhā is blue with a white face, Tiger Face is blue with a red face, and Bear Face is blue with a dark blue or black face; fol. 333.1–2. For artistic representations of the triad: Rhie and Thurman, *Wisdom and Compassion*, no. 117; Kreijger, *Tibetan Painting*, no. 44.

20. Chandra, *Buddhist Iconography*, no. 744; Willson and Brauen, eds., *Deities of Tibetan Buddhism*, no. 235. For a detailed ritual text on this form: *Seng gdong ma dmar mo'i sgrub thabs rjes gnang las tshogs dang bcas pa mkha' 'gro dgyes pa'i dbyangs snyan*. See n. 22 below for the fourfold mandala of the red epiphany. Siṃhamukhā does not play a discernible role in Newar Buddhism, perhaps because in that setting the lion-faced Siṃhinī holds prominence as an attendant of Vajrayoginī. The Newar song that describes Siṃhamukhā as red with a white face (Vajrācārya, ed., *Cacā-Munā*, vol. 1, pp. 76–77) is a recent composition, penned at my request by Ratnakaji Vajracharya under the nom de plume Kuliśācārya.

21. Trans. by Willson and Brauen in *Deities of Tibetan Buddhism*, p. 305.

22. E.g., in *Seng gdong rigs lnga'i sgrub thabs rjes gnang las tshogs dang bcas pa phrin las rnam rol*, according to the system of Jamyang Khyentse Wangpo, the deity in the center, Siṃhamukhā, is blue; in the east, white; in the south, yellow; in the west, red; and in the north, green (fol. 347.4–5), reproducing the standard directional colors of the five Buddha families. There is also a version centering on red Siṃhamukhā; see the eighteenth-century thang-ka in Béguin, *Peintures du bouddhisme tibétain*, no. 165, and the Nyingma painting in the Rubin Museum of Art, F1997.4.2.

23. *dPal sa skya pa'i gser chos mkha' 'gro seng gdong ma'i rjes gnang*, fol. 330.4–5.

24. Allione, trans., "Profound Essence of Simhamukha," p. 5.

25. Nebesky-Wojkowitz, *Oracles and Demons*, pp. 25, 29, 51; Vira and Chandra, *Tibetan Maṇḍalas*, pp. 28–29, 34–37.

26. The niches may number 42, 64, or 81. For an iconographic survey of these temples, see Dehejia, *Yoginī Cult*, and the images of lion-headed yoginis on pp. 34, 56, 170.

27. *Kaulajñānanirṇaya*, chap. 23, holds that the yoginis move on the earth and appear among mortals in the form of animals, "playing" in the guise of female vultures, hawks, swans, turtledoves, cuckoos, jackals, she-goats, tigresses, female cats and camels, snakes, horses, scorpions, mice, frogs, dogs, deer, elephants, and human beings and should be worshipped when they appear in those forms. See Bagchi ed., pp. 115–17.

28. Sanderson, "Purity and Power," pp. 201, 213 n. 94.

29. Pāṇḍeya, ed., *Gorakṣasaṃhitā*, p. 227–34.

30. On cremation ground feasting in a Buddhist context, see Snellgrove, *Hevajra Tantra*, pt. 1, pp. 115–16. On ritual "worship of women" (*strīpūjā*): Shaw, "Worship of Women."

31. I document this phenomenon in a book manuscript in progress on dance in Tantric Buddhism and Newar Vajrayāna, tentatively titled *Tantric Buddhist Dance of Nepal.*

32. On evidence for such practices: Shaw, *Passionate Enlightenment*, pp. 82–84.

33. Although Siṃhamukhā is clearly rooted in an Indian cultural context, she is conspicuously absent from extant Indic sources. There are no meditation manuals devoted to her in the *Sādhanamālā* or Tanjur, references in the biographies of Indian adepts, or Indic artistic representations of which I am aware. Tibetan sources trace her practice lineages to the Indian master Ratnākaragupta (a.k.a. rDo-rje gdan-pa), who transmitted the practice to Bari Lotsawa, abbot of Sakya Monastery 1102–10; see, e.g., *dPal sa skya pa'i gser chos mkha' 'gro seng gdong ma'i rjes gnang*, fol. 322, 328.7–329.1. The absence of a Siṃhamukhā sādhana among the numerous texts that Bari Lotsawa collected and translated for the Tanjur is thus puzzling. Pending the discovery of Indic images or texts, it is reasonable to surmise that her practice was formulated in Tibet, although it carries a strong imprint of Indic themes and motifs.

34. *Lalitavistara* passage; Bays, trans., *Voice of the Buddha*, p. 481, with minor emendation.

35. For textual citations of these terms: T. Rhys Davids and Stede, *Pali Text Society's Pali-English Dictionary*, s.v. *sīha*, and Edgerton, *Buddhist Hybrid Sanskrit*, pp. 594–95.

36. Snellgrove, *Hevajra Tantra*, pt. 1, p. 66: "Whatever demon should appear before him, even though it be the peer of Indra, he would have no fear, for he wanders like a lion."

Chapter 22
Kurukullā: Red Enchantress with Flowered Bow

1. My translation, from Tibetan text in Schmidt, *Kurukulle*, pp. 30–30b.

2. E.g., she appears in Anuttara Yoga Tantra sections in Chandra, *Buddhist Iconography*, no. 12; *Ngor Mandalas* no. 92.

3. E.g., Schmidt, trans., *Kurukulle*, p. 31.

4. Chos-dbang blo-'gros, *sGrub thabs nor bu'i phreng ba'i lo rgyus*, fol. 22b–23a; *rJe btsun ku ru kulle'i sgrub thabs*, fol. 539.2–540.2.

5. *Atharva Veda* 3.25.

6. For men's love spells, see *Atharva Veda* 1.34, 2.30, 3.25, 6.8–9, 6.82, 6.102; for women's, 2.36, 6.60, 6.89, 6.130–32, 6.139, 7.37–38.

7. Beyer, *Cult of Tārā*, p. 301; on safeguards against misuse, see pp. 303–4.

8. Technically, she specializes in "overpowering" (*dbang*), one of the four modes of enlightened activity. The other three are pacification, enrichment, and destruction.

9. Snellgrove, *Hevajra Tantra*, pt. 1, p. 87, vv. 1.11.12, 1.11.14–15; Schmidt, trans., *Kurukulle*, pp. 19b, 32b, 40b.

10. Beyer, *Cult of Tārā*, p. 302.

11. Schmidt, trans., *Kurukulle*, pp. 6, 12, 19–19b, 32–33.

12. *Nyingma School*, vol. 1, p. 824.

13. Schmidt, trans., *Kurukulle*, pp. 19–19b, 25, 26, 32b, 36b–37.

14. Monier-Williams, *Sanskrit-English Dictionary*, p. 872, s.v. *rāga*.

15. Beer, *Encyclopedia of Tibetan Symbols*, p. 276 and pl. 122.

16. *Sādhanamālā* no. 187, p. 390, last line.

17. Skt. *śṛṅgāra-rasa* (Tib. *chags-pa*); see, e.g., *Sādhanamālā* no. 180, p. 362, line 20; no. 187, p. 390, lines 12–13.

18. "Overwhelmed by desire": Skt. *kāma-vihvalā*; *Sādhanamālā* no. 171, p. 347, line 6. "Passionate heart": Tib. *chag–thugs*, from Tibetan text in Schmidt, trans., *Kurukulle*, p. 41. *rJe btsun ma ku ru kulle'i gsang sgrub*, fol. 560.7, describes her as *brtse bas rjes chags*, "loving and passionate."

19. Skt. *kāma-iṣavaḥ*; *Atharva Veda* 3.26.2.

20. E.g., *Buddhacarita* 8.7–19.

21. In one version of this practice, the iron hook draws a female captive by the vagina and a male by the "heart" (see, e.g., Beyer, *Cult of Tārā*, p. 306), the term "heart" perhaps used here in accord with its common Tantric reference to the male sexual organ.

22. *Sādhanamālā* no. 187, p. 389, line 8.

23. Schmidt, trans., *Kurukulle*, p. 30b; Trungpa, *Visual Dharma*, pp. 106, 108.

24. These only slightly varying four-armed forms are described in *Sādhanamālā* nos. 171–72, 177–78, 184, 188.

25. For painted representations: Saraswati, *Tantrayāna Art*, nos. 215, 249. For reliefs at Udayagiri and Ratnagiri: Sahu, *Buddhism in Orissa*, fig. 21; D. Mitra, *Ratnagiri*, pls. 75D, 76A. A twelfth-century votive bronze from Kurkihār in the Patna Museum (Arch. 9684) is published in Shere, *Bronze Images*, pl. 32 (mislabeled as Parṇaśavarī). Five similar images in the Patna Museum (Arch. 9668, 9688, 9691, 9695, 9970), described and misidentified as Parṇaśavarī in P. Gupta, ed., *Patna Museum Catalogue*, p. 151, also depict Kurukullā, conforming precisely to her four-armed iconography as described in the *Sādhanamālā*. I have confirmed this identification on the basis of photographs of the images in the American Institute of Indian Studies archive.

26. On this mudrā: Liebert, *Iconographic Dictionary*, pp. 300, 321. For the red, six-armed, seated form, which bears in addition to the trailokyavijaya mudrā a bow, arrow, goad, and red lotus, see *Sādhanamālā* nos. 173, 182.

27. The eight-armed form (Aṣṭabhuja Kurukullā), as transmitted by Indrabhūti, bears a bow, arrow, goad, noose, varada mudrā, lotus, and trailokyavijaya mudrā; *Sādhanamālā* no. 174, partially translated in B. Bhattacharyya, *Indian Buddhist Iconography*, pp. 150–51. For the mandala iconography: Mallmann, *Iconographie du tântrisme bouddhique*, p. 76. This mandala is depicted in a Gyantse mural; Ricca and Lo Bue, *Great Stupa of Gyantse*, p. 253.

28. A two-armed form of Śukla Kurukullā, holding a rosary in her right hand and a vase of lotus nectar in her right, is described in *Sādhanamālā* no. 180. A four-armed white form is described in *Sādhanamālā* no. 185. A six-armed white form known as Māyājālakrama Kurukullā is described in *Sādhanamālā* no. 181 as displaying a bow, arrow, rosary, white kunda flower, treasure vase, and *abhaya mudrā*, the gesture granting freedom from fear.

29. On her control over nāgas, see also Tāranātha, *History of Buddhism in India*, pp. 147–48.

30. *Sādhanamālā* no. 181, p. 372, line 14.

31. E.g., *Sādhanamālā* no. 180 includes instructions for a mixture of butter and herbs to be applied to a snakebite wound or ingested as a poison antidote (p. 366) and visualizations of nāga kings and Garuḍa, rather than Buddhist figures (p. 370). *Sādhanamālā* no. 181 recommends administration of water to a snakebite victim (p. 377) and other peripherally religious therapies (passim).

32. For depictions of white, six-armed Māyājālakrama Kurukullā: Ricca and Lo Bue, *Great Stupa of Gyantse*, pl. 82; Pal, *Tibetan Paintings*, pl. 49, both of Sakya provenance. Their iconography varies slightly from each other and the description in *Sādhanamālā* no. 181.

33. My translation; *Sādhanamālā* no. 187, pp. 390–91.

34. *Sādhanamālā* no. 179 (Uḍḍiyāna-vinirgata Kurukullā); Derge Tōh. no. 3370. For a rare Indic sculpture of this form: D. Mitra, *Bronzes from Achutrajpur*, p. 116 and pl. 107. Tibetan portrayals: Chandra, *Buddhist Iconography*, no. 12; Trungpa, *Visual Dharma*, no. 41; Béguin, *Peintures du bouddhisme tibétain*, no. 163.

35. Snellgrove, *Hevajra Tantra*, pt. 1, p. 87, v. 1.11.13; *Sādhanamālā* nos. 183, 186–87; Derge Tōh. nos. 1314–16, 1368; Willson and Brauen, eds., *Deities of Tibetan Buddhism*, nos. 10, 468. A stotra by Ḍombīheruka, a Hevajra lineage holder, is translated in Beyer, *Cult of Tārā*, pp. 302–3.

36. Example with lotus: Pal, *Nepal*, no. 48. Examples that feature the noose: *rJe btsun ku ru kulle' i sgrub thabs*, fol. 530.5–531.3; Chandra, *Buddhist Iconography*, nos. 520, 710, 970; Tarthang Tulku, *Sacred Art of Tibet*, pl. 21; Béguin, *Peintures du bouddhisme tibétain*, no. 164 (in this case, a cord noose); Eracle, *Thanka de L'Himalaya*, no. 61. Silk appliqués: Chandra, *Transcendental Art of Tibet*, p. 211; Pal, *Art of the Himalayas*, no. 118.

37. E.g., Mullin, *Female Buddhas*, pl. on p. 123.

38. I have not located a textual source for this form.

39. For the five-deity *Tantrasamuccaya* mandala: Vira and Chandra, *Tibetan Maṇḍalas*, p. 231; *Ngor Mandalas* no. 92. For the nine-deity mandala: Schmidt, trans., *Kurukulle*, p. 16b.

40. Essen and Thingo, *Götter des Himalaya*, no. 1-352.

41. A painting of a fifteen-deity version for which I have found no textual source: Klimburg-Salter, ed., *Silk Route*, pl. 125. A seventeen-deity mandala revealed by *gter-ston* (treasure revealer) mChog-gyur gLing-pa (nineteenth century): Schmidt, trans., *Kurukulle*, pp. 12b–13b. The twenty-three-deity mandala in the *Vajrāvalī* series: Vira and Chandra, *Tibetan Maṇḍalas*, no. 6b, p. 37.

42. *rJe btsun ma ku ru kulle'i gsang sgrub*, fol. 559.5–7; Willson and Brauen, eds., *Deities of Tibetan Buddhism*, nos. 201–5. The fifth color, blue, is not represented because Kurukullā in the center is red, as is the retinue figure in the traditionally red western sector.

43. My translation; *Lalitāsahasranāma* vv. 6–14, 21 from the Sanskrit edition in Tapasyananda, *Śrī Lalitā Sahasranāma*, pp. 89–92. For similar iconographic descriptions, see the classical sādhana, pp. 47–50; *Tripuropaniṣad* v. 13 in Brooks, *Secret of the Three Cities*, p. 98 and frontispiece; *Devī Upaniṣad* vv. 15, 24 in Warrier, trans., *Śākta Upaniṣads*, pp. 80, 82; *Saundaryalaharī* v. 7. I am grateful to Francesca Fremantle for directing my attention to Lalitā and the relevant textual sources.

44. *Lalitāsahasranāma* vv. 248, 336, 376, 454, 458, 697, 703, 706, 863, and *śloka* in Tapasyananda, *Śrī Lalitā Sahasranāma*, p. 49.

45. *Lalitāsahasranāma* vv. 438, 484; *Bhāvanopaniṣad* v. 4 in Warrier, trans., *Śākta Upaniṣads*, p. 67.

46. That Lalitā influenced Buddhist iconographers is confirmed by a form of Vajrayoginī that also bears her imprint; see English, *Vajrayoginī*, pp. 90–91.

47. Tucci, "Oriental Notes," pp. 151–52.

48. Saraswati, *Tantrayāna Art*, no. 249.

49. Skt. *kurukulla-parvata-sthitā* and *kurukullādriguhāntasthā*; e.g., *Sādhanamālā* no. 171, p. 343, line 8, and p. 345, line 7; no. 172, p. 347, last line; no. 188, p. 392, lines 4–5. A later painting that shows her in such a grotto: Pal, *Nepal*, fig. 48.

50. Tib. *rig*, "knowledge," especially knowledge and mastery of magic, directly translates *vidyā* in Sanskrit. As a homonym of *rigs*, which translates *kula*, or family, this rendition of the name preserves some reference, albeit indirect, to the Sanskrit.

51. My translation; *Sādhanamālā* no. 179, p. 361.

52. My translation; *Sādhanamālā* no. 187, p. 389, lines 3–4.

53. These practices are drawn from manuals by Amoghavajra, Dharmabhadra, and Kong-sprul as compiled in Beyer, *Cult of Tārā*, pp. 308–11.

54. Ibid., p. 308. An idiosyncratic Kurukullā rite was revealed to Piṇḍopa in a dream. As directed, he fashioned an image of the goddess from coral and placed it in the mouth of a female corpse that he then used as a meditation mat. After seven days, the corpse revived and became his servant; Roerich, trans., *Blue Annals*, pp. 757–58.

55. *Sādhanamālā* no. 179, pp. 360–61. For an English translation of the same practice from a Tibetan text: Beyer, *Cult of Tārā*, pp. 306–7.

56. Beyer, *Cult of Tārā*, pp. 305–6, 309–10; Schmidt, trans., *Kurukulle*, pp. 11–11b. The red-flowering aśoka finds mention in *Sādhanamālā* no. 180, p. 367, lines 1–2, and no. 188, p. 392, line 8, along with other red accoutrements in the aforementioned sources.

57. Chandra, *Transcendental Art of Tibet*, p. 210. For one such ritual arrow, iron with copper inlay: Ashencaen and Leonov, *Visions of Perfect Worlds*, no. 41.

58. Schmidt, trans., *Kurukulle*, p. 16b.

59. As this volume was going to press, an edited volume of Kurukullā rites (Pāṇḍeya, ed., *Kurukullākalpaḥ*) came to my attention. I refer the reader to this compendium, which provides both Sanskrit and Tibetan versions, for further research.

60. Many forms and practices of Kurukullā are represented in the Tanjur, including what I have characterized above as her Mahayana and Tantric forms. See Derge Tōh. nos. 1315–20A, 1368, 3208–9, 3212–18, 3367–70, 3561, 3563–67, 3569–79, 3657, 4621, 4623–26.

61. Beyer, *Cult of Tārā*, p. 14.

62. Essen and Thingo, *Götter des Himalaya*, nos. 2-341, 2-342. Related sādhanas: Willson and Brauen, eds., *Deities of Tibetan Buddhism*, nos. 10–12.

63. I have located no Newar historical references to or texts on the goddess. However, a four-armed Mahayana epiphany in the lower register of a ca. 1100 Newar painting evinces that she was once known in that context; Leidy and Thurman, *Mandala*, no. 13.

64. There are numerous historical and contemporary painted representations of this form in Nepal: e.g., Kramrisch, *Art of Nepal*, pl. 54; Pal, *Arts of Nepal*, vol. 1, pl. 286. An esoteric song describing this form, penned by Ratnakaji Vajracharya (under the name Kuliśā Ratna) at my request (Vajrācārya, ed., *Cacā-Munā*, vol. 1, p. 72), used artistic representations as a point of reference in the absence of Newar textual sources.

Epilogue

1. A major project of this type has been undertaken by Jeff Watt, who has been investigating the iconographic forms and practice lineages of Tibetan Buddhist deities in a vast range of literary sources. The results of his research are gradually being made available through the Rubin Foundation website, *www.himalayanart.org*.

Glossary of Tibetan

Aparājitā	gZan-gyis mi-thub-ma
Ayu Khandro	A yo mKha'-'gro
Bhṛkuṭī	Khro-gnyer can-ma, Khro-gnyer-ma
Blue She-Wolf	lCe-sbyang sngon-mo
Bodong	Pho-dong
Chinnamuṇḍā	dbU-bcad-ma
Chöd	gCod
Cundā	bsKul-byed-ma, Tsun-da
ḍākinī	mkha'-'gro-ma
Dakpa Khachö	Dag-pa mKha'-spyod
Darmdra	Dar-ma-grags
delog	'das-log
Derge	sDe-dge
Dhanada Tārā	sGrol-ma Nor-sbyin-ma
Drikung	'Bri-gung
Drogma	Phrog-ma
Drolkar	sGrol-dkar
Drolkar Yishinkorlo	sGrol-dkar Yid-bzhin 'khor-lo
Drolma	sGrol-ma
Drolma Karmo	sGrol-ma dkar-mo, sGrol-dkar
Drolma Marmo	sGrol-ma dmar-mo
Drolmala	sGrol-ma La
Dukselma	Dug-sel-ma
Gampopa	sGam-po-pa
Gelug	dGe-lugs
Go Lotsawa	'Gos Lo-tsa-ba
Gopāla Vasudhārā	Nor-rgyun-ma Ba-lang-rdzi
Gotsangpa	rGod-tshang-pa
Green Tara	sGrol-ma ljang-khu, sGrol-ljang-ma, sGrol-ljang
Gurgi Gonpo	Gyur-gi mGon-po

Gyantse	rGyal-tse
Hārītī	Yid-phrog-ma, Phrog-ma
Jamgon Kongtrul	'Jam-mgon Kong-sprul
Jamyang Khyentse Wangpo	'Jam-dbyangs mKhyen-brtse'i dbang-po
Jāṅgulī	Dug-sel-ma
Kagyu	bKa'-brgyud
Kanjur	bKa'-'gyur
Khachö	mKha'-spyod
Khachö Korsum	mKha'-spyod skor-gsum
Khadiravaṇī Tārā	Seng-ldeng-nags kyi sGrol-ma
Kulchayma	bsKul-byed-ma
Kurukullā	Rig-byed-ma
lama	bla-ma
Long-Life Trinity	Tshe-lha rnam gsum
Longchenpa	kLong-chen-pa, gLong-chen Rab-byams-pa
Lozang Tenpai Jetsun	bLo-bzang bsTan-pa'i rJe-btsun
Machig Labdron	Ma-chig Lab-sgron
Manoharā Vasudhārā	Yid-'phrog Nor-rgyun-ma
Mārīcī	'Od-zer can-ma
Marpo Korsum	dMar-po skor-gsum
Nairātmyā	bDag-med-ma
Namgyal Chorten	rNam-rgyal mchod-rten
Nāro Khachöma	Nāro mkha'-spyod-ma
Neljor Chuchig	rNal-'byor bcu-gcig
Nyingma	rNying-ma
Palden Lhamo	dPal-ldan Lha-mo
Pakmo Trönak	Phag-mo Khros-nag
Parṇaśavarī	Ri-khrod lo-ma g.yon-ma
Phadampa Sangyay	Pha-dam-pa Sangs-rgyas
Pīṭheśvarī	gNas-kyi dBang-phyug-ma
Prajñāpāramitā	Shes-rab-kyi pha-rol-tu phyin-ma, Yum-chen-mo
Pṛthivī	Sa'i lha-mo
Rakta Vasudhārā	Nor-rgyun-ma dmar-mo
Rigjayma	Rig-byed-ma
Sakya	Sa-skya
Sarasvatī	dByangs-can-ma
Sarma	gSar-ma
Serchö	gSer-chos
Sherchinma	Shes-phyin-ma
Siṃhamukhā	Seng-gdong-ma, Seng-ge'i gdong-ma, Seng-ge'i gdong-pa can, Seng-gdong-can

Sitātapatrā	gDugs-dkar-mo, gDugs-dkar-can, gDugs-can-ma
Songtsen Gampo	Srong-btsan sGam-po
*Śyāma Tārā	sGrol-ljang-ma
Tanjur	bsTan-'gyur
Tārā	sGrol-ma
Tröma Nakmo	Khros-ma Nag-mo
Tseringma	Tshe-ring-ma
Uḍḍiyāna Tārā	U-rgyan sGrol-ma
Uṣṇīṣasitātapatrā	gTsug-tor gdugs-dkar-mo
Uṣṇīṣavijayā	gTsug-tor rnam-par rgyal-ma, rNam-par rgyal-ma, rNam-rgyal-ma
Vaiśravaṇa	rNam-thos-sras
Vajrayoginī	rDo-rje rnal-'byor-ma
Vajravārāhī	rDo-rje Phag-mo
Vasudhārā	Nor-rgyun-ma
Wangdukyi Lhamo	dBang-sdud kyi lha-mo
White Tārā	sGrol-ma dkar-mo, sGrol-dkar
yakṣiṇī	gnod-sbyin-mo, 'byung-mo
Yangchenma	dByangs-can-ma
Yellow Tārā	sGrol-ma ser-mo
Yeshe Tsogyal	Ye-shes mTsho-rgyal
Yidrogma	Yid-phrog-ma
Yuloku	g.Yu-lo bkod
Yum Chenmo	Yum-chen-mo

Bibliography

Tibetan Sources

In Tibetan alphabetical order. Sanskrit names of Indian authors, when known or when reconstruction is generally agreed upon, are used.

bKa' srung nag mo'i rgyud bzhugs so. Rin chen gter mdzod chen mo, vol. 38 (NYI), fol. 1–13.

sKal-bzang mkhyen-brtse. *Srad rgyud lugs kyi ri khrod ma rigs gsum gyi sgrub thabs las tshogs rjes gnang dang bcas pa. sGrub thabs kun btus*, vol. 13, fol. 34–65.

mKha' 'gro seng ge'i gdong pa can gyi man ngag zab mo rnams. sGrub thabs kun btus, vol. 8, fol. 268–318.

rGyud sde kun btus: Texts Explaining the Significance, Techniques, and Initiations of a Collection of One Hundred and Thirty Two Mandalas of the Sa-skya-pa Tradition. Ed. 'Jam-dbyangs Blo-gter-dbang-po. Reproduction of sDe-dge edition belonging to Thartse Rimpoche of Ngor. 23 vols. Delhi: N. Lungtok and N. Gyaltsan, 1971.

sGrub thabs kun btus: A Collection of Sādhanas and Related Texts of the Vajrayāna Traditions in Tibet. Ed. 'Jam-dbyangs mKhyen-brtse'i-dbang-po and 'Jam-dbyangs Blo-gter-dbang-po. Reproduction of sDe-dge xylograph edition of 1902. 14 vols. Dehra Dun: G. T. K. Lodoy, N. Gyaltsen, and N. Lungtok, 1970.

rJe btsun ku ru kulle'i sgrub thabs rjes gnang dang bcas pa. sGrub thabs kun btus, vol. 8, fol. 528–555.

rJe btsun ma ku ru kulle'i gsang sgrub lha lnga'i byin rlabs kyi cho ga gsal ba'i sgron me. sGrub thabs kun btus, vol. 8, fol. 556–568.

rJe btsun ri khrod ma ser mo'i sgrub thabs rje gnang las tshogs dang bcas pa'i skor. sGrub thabs kun btus, vol. 6, fol. 603–667.

'Jam-dbyangs bLo-gter-dbang-po. *gTsug tor gdugs dkar can gyi 'khor lo bri thabs rgyal mtshan 'dzugs pa'i cho ga dang bcas pa rig sngags grub pa nor bu'i snying po. sGrub thabs kun btus*, vol. 11, fol. 1–62.

Cakrasaṃvara Tantra. rGyud gyi rgyal po dpal bde mchog nyung ngu. sDe-dge bKa'-'gyur, rGyud, KA, fol. 213a–246b.

bCom ldan 'das ma gtsug tor gdugs dkar mo'i sgrub thabs rjes gnang gzungs bklag thabs dang bcas pa bzhags so. sGrub thabs kun btus, vol. 8, fol. 427–437.

Chos-dbang blo-'gros. *sGrub thabs nor bu'i phreng ba'i lo rgyus dad pa'i myu gu zhes bya ba bzhugs so*. Reprint of a late eighteenth-century text. Tibet: n.p., n.d.

dPyal lugs phag mo skor gsum gyi sgrub thabs byin rlabs man ngag dang bcas pa'i skor. sGrub thabs kun btus, vol. 4, fol. 165–206.

Paṇ chen zla ba gzhon nu'i lugs kyi dbyangs can ma dkar mo phyag bzhi ma'i sgrub thabs man ngag dang bcas pa. sGrub thabs kun btus, vol. 7, fol. 515–527.

Paṇḍita Dzamāri'i lugs kyi 'phags ma nor rgyun ma ser mo'i sgrub thabs man ngag bcas pa bzhugs so. sGrub thabs kun btus, vol. 9, fol. 286–291.

dPal sa skya pa'i gser chos mkha' 'gro seng gdong ma'i rjes gnang las tshogs mngon rtogs shin tu zab pa'i gdams pa. sGrub thabs kun btus, vol. 8, fol. 319–330.

'Phags ma 'od zer can ma'i sgrub thabs rjes gnang man ngag dang cas pa. sGrub thabs kun btus, vol. 5, fol. 521–545.

Bo dong lugs kyi dbyangs can ma dmar mo gsang sgrub lha lnga'i sgrub thabs rjes gnang las tshogs dang bcas pa 'jigs bral dgyes pa'i lam srol. sGrub thabs kun btus, vol. 2, fol. 540–546.

Bram ze phur bu'i lugs kyi dbyangs can ma dkar mo'i sgrub thabs rjes gnang las tshogs dang bcas pa'i skor. sGrub thabs kun btus, vol. 2, fol. 394–429.

'Bri-gung Chos-kyi grags-pa. *sGrub thabs rgya mtsho nas nye bar phyung ba'i sgrub thabs nor bu'i phreng ba zhes bya ba.* Reprint of a seventeenth-century text. Tibet: n.p., n.d.

Mekhalā and Kanakhalā. *gYung drung 'khyil ba gsum gyi zhal gdams kyi nyams len zhes bya ba.* sDe-dge bsTan-'gyur, rGyud, ZI, fol. 34a–35a.

gTsug tor gdugs dkar mo can mchog tu grub pa'i gzungs bshugs so. bKa'-'gyur text reprinted in *'Bri gung bka' brgyud kyi chos skyod rab gsal bshug so*, fol. 531–560.

gTsug tor rnam par rgyal ma'i rtog pa'i ṭīkā sgrub thabs stong mchod rjes gnang gi cho ga sogs chos skor tshang ba. sGrub thabs kun btus, vol. 1, fol. 481–534.

Lakṣmīṅkarā. *rDo rje phag mo dbu bcad ma'i sgrub thabs.* sDe-dge bsTan-'gyur, rGyud, ZA, fol. 205a–206a.

———. *rNal 'byor ma'i sgrub pa'i thabs.* sDe-dge bsTan-'gyur, rGyud, ZA, fol. 195b–196a.

———. *Sems nyid kyi rtog pa 'joms pa'i lta ba zhes bya ba.* sDe-dge bsTan-'gyur, rGyud, ZI, fol. 47b–48a.

Lha mo nor rgyun ma ser mo'i sgrub thabs rjes gnang les tshogs dang bcas pa bzhugs so. sGrub thabs kun btus, vol. 9, fol. 245–285.

Rin chen gter mdzod chen mo. Ed. 'Jam-mgon Kong-sprul bLo-gros mtha'-yas. 135 vols. New Delhi: Dilgo Kyentse, 1974.

Seng gdong sngon mo gtso 'khor gsum ma'i sgrub thabs rjes gnang las tshogs dang bcas pa rdo rje'i sprin char. sGrub thabs kun btus, vol. 8, fol. 331–345.

Seng gdong ma dmar mo'i sgrub thabs rjes gnang las tshogs dang bcas pa mkha' 'gro dgyes pa'i dbyangs snyan. sGrub thabs kun btus, vol. 8, fol. 410–426.

Seng gdong rigs lnga'i sgrub thabs rjes gnang las tshogs dang bcas pa phrin las rnam rol. sGrub thabs kun btus, vol. 8, fol. 346–365.

Western Language, Sanskrit, and Newar Sources

Abbott, J. *Indian Ritual and Belief: The Keys to Power.* 1932. Reprint. New Delhi: Manohar, 2000.

Agrawala, Prithvi Kumar. *Goddesses in Ancient India.* New Delhi: Abhinav, 1984.

———. *Mathura Railing Pillars.* Indian Civilisation Series, vol. 6. Varanasi: Prithivi Prakashan, 1966.

———. *Śrīvatsa: The Babe of Goddess Śrī.* Varanasi: Prithivi Prakashan, 1974.

———. "A Unique Śuṅga Plaque of Goddess Lakṣmī from Kosam." In Gouriswar Bhattacharya, ed., *Akṣayanīvī*, 62–66.

Agrawala, Vasudeva S. *Ancient Indian Folk Cults*. Varanasi: Prithivi Prakashan, 1970.

———. *A Catalogue of the Brahmanical Images of Mathura Art*. Lucknow: U. P. Historical Society, 1951.

———. *Indian Art (A History of Indian Art from the Earliest Times up to the Third Century A.D.)*. Varanasi: Prithivi Prakashan, 1965.

———. *Studies in Indian Art*. Varanasi: Vishwavidyalaya Prakashan, 1965.

Airi, Raghunath. *Concept of Sarasvati (in Vedic Literature)*. Delhi: Munshiram Manoharlal, 1977.

Allan, John. *Catalogue of the Coins of Ancient India*. 1936. Reprint. Oxford: Trustees of the British Museum, 1967.

Allinger, Eva. "The Green Tara as Saviouress from the Eight Dangers in the Sumtsek at Alchi." *Orientations* 30, no. 1 (Jan. 1999): 40–44.

Allione, Tsultrim. *Women of Wisdom*. 1984. Revised and enlarged ed. Ithaca: Snow Lion, 2000.

——, trans. "Profound Essence of Simhamukha, the Powerful Queen of the Dakinis: Mind Treasure of A-yu Khadro, Dorje Palden." Typescript, n.d.

Anderson, Mary M. *The Festivals of Nepal*. 1971. Reprint. Calcutta: Rupa, 1988.

Appel, Michaela. "The Buddhist Goddess Vasundharā." In *Cultural Interface of India with Asia: Religion, Art and Architecture*, ed. Anupa Pande and Parul Pandya Dhar, 54–71. New Delhi: D. K. Printworld, 2004.

Arènes, Pierre. *La Déesse sGrol-ma (Tārā): Recherches sur la nature et le statut d'une divinité du bouddhisme tibétain*. Louvain: Uitgeverij Peeters and Departement Oriëntalistiek, 1996.

Ashencaen, Deborah, and Gennady Leonov. *The Mirror of Mind: Art of Vajrayana Buddhism*. London: Spink and Son, 1995.

———. *Visions of Perfect Worlds: Buddhist Art from the Himalayas*. London: Spink and Son, 1999.

Asher, Frederick M. *The Art of Eastern India, 300–800 A.D.* Minneapolis: University of Minnesota Press, 1980.

Asthana, Shashi. "Mahāśrī Tārā with Her Companion Deities: A Stone Panel." *National Museum Bulletin* [New Delhi] 7–8 (1993): 29–42.

———. "A Rare Image of Cundā in the National Museum Collection." In Gouriswar Bhattacharya, ed., *Akṣayanīvī*, 269–73.

Atharva Veda. See Griffith, Ralph T. H., trans.; Whitney, William Dwight, trans.

Bagchi, P. C., ed. *Kaulajnana-nirnaya of the School of Matsyendranatha*. Trans. Michael Magee. Tantra Granthamala 12. Varanasi: Prachya Prakashan, 1986.

Bailly, Constantina Rhodes. "Śrī-Lakṣmī: Majesty of the Hindu King." In *Goddesses Who Rule*, ed. Elisabeth Benard and Beverly Moon, 133–45. Oxford: Oxford University Press, 2000.

Baker, Ian. *The Heart of the World: A Journey to the Last Secret Place*. New York: Penguin Press, 2005.

Banerjea, Jitendra Nath. *The Development of Hindu Iconography*. Rev. ed. 1956. Reprint. New Delhi: Munshiram Manoharlal, 1985.

Banerjee, P. "A Manuscript Dated in the Regnal Year 53 of Rāmapāla." *Indo-Asian Culture* 18, no. 1 (1969): 61–63.

Banerji, R. D. *History of Orissa: From the Earliest Times to the British Period.* 2 vols. Calcutta: R. Chatterjee, 1930.

Bareau, André. "Constellations et divinités protectrices des marchands das le bouddhisme ancien." *Journal Asiatique* 247 (1959): 303–9.

———. "La Jeunesse du Buddha dans les Sūtrapiṭaka et les Vinayapiṭaka Anciens." *Bulletin de l'École Française d'Extrême-Orient* 61 (1974): 199–274.

———. "Lumbinī et la naissance du futur Buddha." *Bulletin de l'École Française d'Extrême-Orient* 76 (1987): 69–81.

Batchelor, Stephen. *The Tibet Guide.* London: Wisdom, 1987.

Bautze-Picron, Claudine. "Between Śākyamuni and Vairocana: Mārīcī, Goddess of Light and Victory." *Silk Road Art and Archaeology* 7 (2000): 263–310.

Bays, Gwendolyn, trans. *The Voice of the Buddha: The Beauty of Compassion.* Berkeley: Dharma, 1983.

Beal, Samuel, trans. *Si-yu-ki: Buddhist Records of the Western World. Translated from the Chinese of Hiuen Tsiang (A.D. 629).* 2 vols. 1884. Reprint. New York: Paragon, 1968.

Beer, Robert. *The Encyclopedia of Tibetan Symbols and Motifs.* London: Serindia, 1999.

Béguin, Gilles. *Art ésotérique de l'Himâlaya: Catalogue de la donation Lionel Fournier.* Paris: Réunion des Musées Nationaux, 1991.

———. *Les Mandala Himâlayens du Musée Guimet.* Paris: Réunion des Musées Nationaux, 1981.

———. *Les Peintures du bouddhisme tibétain.* Paris: Réunion des Musées Nationaux, 1995.

Behrsing, Von Siegfried. "Mārīcī-Figuren des Berliner Völkerkunde Museums im Rahmen eines ikonographischen Versuchs." *Baessler Archiv* (Berlin) 25 (1943): 1–23.

Benard, Elisabeth. *Chinnamastā: The Aweful Buddhist and Hindu Tantric Goddess.* New Delhi: Motilal Banarsidass, 1994.

———. "Transformations of Wen Cheng Kongjo: The Tang Princess, Tibetan Queen, and Buddhist Goddess Tara." In *Goddesses Who Rule*, ed. Elisabeth Benard and Beverly Moon, 149–64. Oxford: Oxford University Press, 2000.

Bendall, Cecil. "The Megha-Sūtra." *Journal of the Royal Asiatic Society*, n.s., 12, pt. 2 (April 1880): 286–311.

———, trans. *Śikshā-samuccaya: A Compendium of Buddhist Doctrine Compiled by Śāntideva.* 1922. Reprint. Delhi: Motilal Banarsidass, 1971.

Berkson, Carmel. *The Caves at Aurangabad: Early Buddhist Tantric Art in India.* New York: Mapin International, 1986.

Beyer, Stephan. *The Cult of Tārā: Magic and Ritual in Tibet.* Berkeley: University of California Press, 1973.

Bhattacharya, A. K. "Concept of Tārā as a Serpent Deity and Its Jain Counterpart Padmāvatī." In *The Śakti Cult and Tārā*, ed. D. C. Sircar, 152–68. Calcutta: University of Calcutta, 1967.

Bhattacharya, Gouriswar. "Donors of a Few Tārā Images from Magadha or South Bihar." In *Festschrift Dieter Schlingloff*, ed. Friedrich Wilhelm, 1–28. Reinbek: Verlag für Fachpublikationen, 1996.

———. "The Dual Role of Ganesh in the Buddhist Art of South Asia." In *Ganesh the Benevolent*, ed. Pratapaditya Pal, 65–80. Bombay: Marg, 1995.

———, ed. *Akṣayanīvī: Essays Presented to Dr. Debala Mitra in Admiration of Her Scholarly Contributions.* Bibliotheca Indo-Buddhica 88. Delhi: Sri Satguru, 1991.

Bhattacharyya, Asutosh. "The Cult of Sasthi in Bengal." *Man in India* 28 (1948): 152–62.

Bhattacharyya, Benoytosh. "A Cundā Image in the Baroda Museum." *Bulletin of the Baroda State Museum and Picture Gallery* 3 (1945–47): 43–48.

———. *The Indian Buddhist Iconography: Mainly Based on the Sādhanamālā and Cognate Tāntric Texts of Rituals.* 1924. 2nd ed., revised and enlarged. 1958. Reprint. Calcutta: Firma K. L. Mukhopadhyay, 1968.

———. *An Introduction to Buddhist Esoterism.* Reprint. Delhi: Motilal Banarsidass, 1980.

———, ed. *Niṣpannayogāvalī of Mahāpaṇḍita Abhayākaragupta.* Gaekwad's Oriental Series 109. Baroda: Oriental Institute, 1972.

———. *Sādhanamālā.* Vol. 1, Gaekwad's Oriental Series 26. Vol. 2, Gaekwad's Oriental Series 41. Baroda: Oriental Institute, 1925, 1928.

Bhattacharyya, Dipak Chandra. "Of Colour in Tantric Buddhist Art." In *Dimensions of Indian Art: Pupul Jayakar Seventy,* ed. Lokesh Chandra and Jyotindra Jain, vol. 1, 27–34. Delhi: Agam Kala Prakashan, 1986.

———. *Studies in Buddhist Iconography.* New Delhi: Manohar Book Service, 1978.

———. *Tantric Buddhist Iconographic Sources.* Delhi: Munshiram Manoharlal, 1974.

———. "An Unknown Form of Tārā." In *The Śakti Cult and Tārā,* ed. D. C. Sircar, 134–42. Calcutta: University of Calcutta Press, 1967.

———. "The *Vajrāvalī-nāma-maṇḍalopāyika* of Abhayākaragupta." In *Tantric and Taoist Studies in Honour of R. A. Stein,* ed. Michel Strickmann, vol. 1, 70–95. Brussels: Institut Belge des Hautes Etudes Chinoises, 1981.

Bhattacharyya, Narendra Nath. "The Cult of Tārā in Historical Perspective." In Narendra Nath Bhattacharyya, ed., *Tantric Buddhism,* 190–207.

———. *The Indian Mother Goddess.* 1970. 2nd ed. New Delhi: Manohar, 1977.

———, ed. *Tantric Buddhism: Centennial Tribute to Dr. Benoytosh Bhattacharyya.* Delhi: Manohar, 1999.

Bhattacharyya, Parnasabari. "Parṇaśabarī: A Tantric Buddhist Goddess." In Narendra Nath Bhattacharyya, ed., *Tantric Buddhism,* 215–21.

Bhattasali, Nalini Kanta. *Iconography of Buddhist and Brahmanical Sculptures in the Dacca Museum.* Dacca: Dacca Museum Committee, 1929.

Bivar, A. D. H. "Hārītī and the Chronology of the Kuṣāṇas." *Bulletin of the School of Oriental and African Studies* 33, no. 1 (1970): 10–21.

Bloch, Theodor. *Supplementary Catalogue of the Archaeological Collection of the Indian Museum.* Calcutta: Baptist Mission Press, 1911.

Blonay, Godefroy de. *Matériaux pour servir à l'histoire de la déesse buddhique Tārā.* Paris: Librairie Émile Bouillon, 1895.

Bloomfield, Maurice. "The Dohada or Craving of Pregnant Women: A Motif of Hindu Fiction." *Journal of the American Oriental Society* 40 (Fall 1920): 1–24.

Bloss, Lowell W. "The Taming of Māra: Witnessing to the Buddha's Virtues." *History of Religions* 18, no. 2 (Nov. 1978): 156–76.

Boeles, J. J. "The Buddhist Tutelary Couple Hārītī and Pancika, Protectors of Children, from a Relief at the Khmer Sanctuary in Pimai." *Journal of the Siam Society* 56, pt. 2 (1968): 187–205.

Bolon, Carol Radcliffe. *Forms of the Goddess Lajjā Gaurī in Indian Art.* University Park: Pennsylvania State University Press, 1992.

Boner, Alice, and Sadāśiva Rath Śarmā, trans. *Śilpa Prakāśa: Medieval Orissan Sanskrit Text on Temple Architecture by Rāmacandra Kaulācāra.* Leiden: E. J. Brill, 1966.

Bosch, F. D. K. *The Golden Germ: An Introduction to Indian Symbolism*. 1960. Reprint. New Delhi: Munshiram Manoharlal, 1994.

Brighenti, Francesco. *Śakti Cult in Orissa*. New Delhi: D. K. Printworld, 2001.

Brooks, Douglas Renfrew. *The Secret of the Three Cities: An Introduction to Hindu Śākta Tantrism*. Chicago: University of Chicago Press, 1990.

Brown, Robert. "A Lajjā Gaurī in a Buddhist Context at Aurangabad." *Journal of the International Association of Buddhist Studies* 13, no. 2 (1990): 1–16.

Bühnemann, Gudrun. *Buddhist Deities of Nepal: Iconography of Two Sketchbooks*. Lumbini: Lumbini International Research Institute, 2003.

———. "The Goddess Mahācīnakrama-Tārā (Ugra-Tārā) in Buddhist and Hindu Tantrism." *Bulletin of the School of Oriental and African Studies* 59, no. 3 (1996): 472–93.

———. *The Iconography of Hindu Tantric Deities*. Vol. 1, *The Pantheon of the Mantramahodadhi*. Groningen: Egbert Forsten, 2000.

Burgess, James. *The Buddhist Stūpas of Amaravati and Jaggayyapeta*. 1887. Reprint. Varanasi: Indological Book House, 1970.

Burlingame, Eugene Watson, trans. *Buddhist Legends, Translated from the Original Pali Text of the Dhammapada Commentary*. 3 vols. 1921. Reprint. Harvard Oriental Series 28–30. London: Pali Text Society, 1979.

Cabezón, José Ignacio. "Mother Wisdom, Father Love: Gender-Based Imagery in Mahāyāna Buddhist Thought." In *Buddhism, Sexuality, and Gender*, ed. José Ignacio Cabezón, 181–99. Albany: State University of New York Press, 1992.

Catalogue of Buddhist Sculptures in Patna Museum. Patna: n.p., 1957.

Chakravarti, Shyamalkanti. "Three Dated Nepalese Paṭas in the Indian Museum." *Indian Museum Bulletin* 4, no. 2 (July 1969): 124–33.

Chakravarti, Sipra. *A Catalogue of Tibetan Thaṅkas in the Indian Museum*. Calcutta: Indian Museum, 1980.

Chakraverty, Anjan. *Sacred Buddhist Painting*. New Delhi: Lustre Press, 1998.

Chandra, Lokesh. *Buddhist Iconography*. Compact ed. New Delhi: International Academy of Indian Culture and Aditya Prakashan, 1987.

———. "Comparative Iconography of the Goddess Uṣṇīṣaviyajā." *Acta Orientalia* 34, nos. 1–3 (1980): 125–37.

———. *Dictionary of Buddhist Iconography*. New Delhi: International Academy of Indian Culture and Aditya Prakashan, 1999–.

———. "Iconography of the Goddess Uṣṇīṣaviyajā." *Journal of the Indian Society of Oriental Art*, n.s., 10 (1978–79): 17–29.

———. *Transcendental Art of Tibet*. New Delhi: International Academy of Indian Culture and Aditya Prakashan, 1996.

Charpentier, Jarl. "Note on the Padariya or Rummindei Inscription." *Indian Antiquary* 43 (March–April 1914): 17–20.

Chatterjee, A. K. "Some Aspects of Sarasvatī." In D. C. Sircar, ed., *Foreigners in Ancient India*, 148–53.

Chattopadhyaya, Alaka. *Atīśa and Tibet: Life and Works of Dīpaṅkara Śrījñāna in Relation to the History and Religion of Tibet*. 1967. Reprint. Delhi: Motilal Banarsidass, 1981.

Chattopadhyaya, Debiprasad. *Lokāyata: A Study in Ancient Indian Materialism*. 6th ed. Delhi: People's Publishing House, 1985.

Chawla, Janet. *Child-Bearing and Culture: Women Centered Revisioning of the Traditional Midwife: The Dai as a Ritual Practitioner*. New Delhi: Indian Social Institute, 1994.

Clark, Walter Eugene, ed. *Two Lamaistic Pantheons*. 1937. Reprint. 2 vols. bound as one. New York: Paragon Reprint Corp., 1965.

Cleary, Thomas, trans. *Entry into the Realm of Reality*. Vol. 3 of *The Flower Ornament Scripture: A Translation of the Avatamsaka Sutra*. Boston: Shambhala, 1987.

Cohen, Richard S. "Nāga, Yakṣiṇī, Buddha: Local Deities and Local Buddhism at Ajanta." *History of Religions* 37, no. 4 (May 1998): 360–400.

Cohn-Wiener, Ernst. "The Lady Under the Tree." *Parnassus* 11, no. 6 (Oct. 1939): 24–29.

Conze, Edward. "The Development of Prajñāpāramitā Thought." In *Thirty Years of Buddhist Studies: Selected Essays by Edward Conze*, 123–47. Oxford: Bruno Cassirer, 1967.

———. "The Iconography of the Prajñāpāramitā." In *Thirty Years of Buddhist Studies: Selected Essays by Edward Conze*, 243–68. Oxford: Bruno Cassirer, 1967.

———. "Remarks on a Pāla Ms. in the Bodleian Library." In *Further Buddhist Studies: Selected Essays by Edward Conze*, 116–24. Oxford: Bruno Cassirer, 1975.

———, ed. *Buddhist Texts through the Ages*. 1954. Reprint. New York: Harper and Row, 1964.

———, trans. *Buddhist Wisdom Books: The Diamond Sutra and the Heart Sutra*. 2nd ed. London: George Allen and Unwin, 1975.

———. *Perfect Wisdom: The Short Prajñāpāramitā Texts*. London: Luzac, 1973.

———. *The Perfection of Wisdom in Eight Thousand Lines and Its Verse Summary*. Bolinas, Calif.: Four Seasons Foundation, 1975.

Coomaraswamy, Ananda. "Archaic Indian Terracottas." *Ipek* 3 (1928): 64–76.

———. "Early Indian Iconography: II. Śrī Lakṣmī." *Eastern Art* 1 (1929): 175–89.

———. *Elements of Buddhist Iconography*. 1935. 3rd ed. New Delhi: Munshiram Manoharlal, 1979.

———. *La Sculpture de Bhārhut*. Trans. Jean Buhot. Paris: Vanoest, 1956.

———. *Yakṣas: Essays in the Water Cosmology*. 1931. Revised, enlarged ed. Ed. Paul Schroeder. Delhi: Indira Gandhi National Centre for the Arts, 1993.

Cowell, E. B., ed. *The Jātaka or Stories of the Buddha's Former Births*. 6 vols. 1895–1913. Reprint. Delhi: Munshiram Manoharlal, 1990.

Cowell, E. B., and F. W. Thomas, trans. *The Harṣa-carita of Bāṇa*. Oriental Translation Series, n.s., 2. London: Royal Asiatic Society, 1897.

Cozort, Daniel. *Highest Yoga Tantra: An Introduction to the Esoteric Buddhism of Tibet*. Ithaca: Snow Lion, 1986.

Crooke, William. *The Popular Religion and Folklore of Northern India*. 2 vols. 1896. Reprint. New Delhi: Munshiram Manoharlal, 1978.

Cunningham, Alexander. *The Stûpa of Bharhut: A Buddhist Monument Ornamented with Numerous Sculptures Illustrative of Buddhist Legend and History in the Third Century BC*. 1879. Reprint. Delhi: Munshiram Manoharlal, 1998.

Das, H. C. "Brahmanical Tantric Art in Orissa." In *Rangarekha (Silver Jubilee Publication)*, 85–93. Bhubaneswar: Orissa Lalit Kala Akademi, 1992.

———. *Iconography of Śākta Divinities*. 2 vols. Delhi: Pratibha Prakashan, 1997.

Das, Sarat Chandra. *Tibetan-English Dictionary*. 1902. Reprint. Kyoto: Rinsen, 1985.

Das, Surya. *The Snow Lion's Turquoise Mane: Wisdom Tales from Tibet*. San Francisco: Harper San Francisco, 1992.

Dasgupta, Shashibhusan. *Obscure Religious Cults*. Calcutta: Firma KLM, 1976.

Davidson, Ronald M. *Indian Esoteric Buddhism: A Social History of the Tantric Movement*. New York: Columbia University Press, 2001.

Dawa-Samdup, Kazi, ed. *Śrī-Cakraśaṃvara-tantra*. 1919 (under title *Shrīchakrasambhāra Tantra: A Buddhist Tantra*). Tantrik Texts 7. Reprint ed. New Delhi: Aditya Prakashan, 1987.

Day, Terence P. "The Twenty-One Tārās: Features of a Goddess-Pantheon in Mahāyāna Buddhism." In *Goddesses in Religions and Modern Debate*, ed. Larry Hurtado, 83–121. Atlanta: Scholars Press, 1990.

Dayal, Har. *The Bodhisattva Doctrine in Buddhist Sanskrit Literature*. 1932. Reprint. Delhi: Motilal Banarsidass, 1975.

DeCaroli, Robert. *Haunting the Buddha: Indian Popular Religions and the Formation of Buddhism*. Oxford: Oxford University Press, 2004.

Decleer, Hubert. "A Tibetan Translation of the *Svayambhū-purāṇa*." Typescript, n.d.

Dehejia, Vidya. *Discourse in Early Buddhist Art: Visual Narratives of India*. Delhi: Munshiram Manoharlal, 1997.

———. "Issues of Spectatorship and Representation." In *Representing the Body: Gender Issues in Indian Art*, ed. Vidya Dehejia, 1–21. Delhi: Kali for Women, 1997.

———. *Yoginī Cult and Temples: A Tantric Tradition*. New Delhi: National Museum, 1986.

Dehejia, Vidya, et al. *Devi: The Great Goddess, Female Divinity in South Asian Art*. Washington, D.C.: Smithsonian Institution, 1999.

Deshpande, N. A., trans. *The Padma-Purāṇa*. 10 vols. Delhi: Motilal Banarsidass, 1988–92.

Devadhar, C. R. *Mālavikāgnimitram of Kālidāsa, Critically Edited with Introduction, Translation, Notes and Useful Appendices*. 3rd ed. Delhi: Motilal Banarsidass, 1966.

Dhal, Upendra Nath. *Goddess Lakṣmī: Origin and Development*. 2nd ed. Delhi: Eastern Book Linker, 1995.

Dhargyey, Geshe Ngawang. *Vajrayogini Sadhana and Commentary*. Trans. Alan Wallace. Dharamsala: Library of Tibetan Works and Archives, 1992.

Dhirasekera, J. D. "Hāritī and Pāñcika: An Early Buddhist Legend of Many Lands." In *Malalasekera Commemoration Volume*, ed. O. H. deA. Wijesekera, 61–70. Colombo: Malalasekera Commemoration Volume Editorial Committee, 1976.

Dobbins, K. Walton. "A Note on the Hāritī Image from Skārah Ḍherī, Year 399." *East and West*, n.s., 17, nos. 3–4 (Sept.–Dec. 1967): 268–72.

Donaldson, Thomas. "An Oḍḍiyāna Mārīcī Image from Orissa." *Oriental Art*, n.s., 34, no. 3 (Autumn 1988): 213–17.

———. "Orissan Images of Aṣṭabhujāpīta Mārīcī." *Journal of the Orissa Research Society* 3 (Oct. 1985): 35–44.

———. "Orissan Images of Vārāhī, Oḍḍiyāna Mārīcī, and Related Sow-Faced Goddesses." *Artibus Asiae* 55, nos. 1–2 (1995): 155–82.

———. "Propitious-Apotropaic Eroticism in the Art of Orissa." *Artibus Asiae* 37, nos. 1–2 (1975): 75–100.

Dowman, Keith. *Masters of Enchantment: The Lives and Legends of the Mahasiddhas*. Rochester, Vt.: Inner Traditions, 1989.

———. *Masters of Mahāmudrā: Songs and Histories of the Eighty-Four Buddhist Siddhas*. Albany: State University of New York Press, 1985.

———. *Sky-Dancer: The Secret Life and Songs of the Lady Yeshe Tsogyel*. London: Routledge and Kegan Paul, 1984.

Drolma, Delog Dawa. *Delog: Journey to the Realms beyond Death*. Trans. Richard Barron. Junction City: Padma, 1995.

Duroiselle, Charles. "Wathundaye, the Earth-Goddess of Burma." *Archaeological Survey of India, Annual Report* (1921–22): 144–46.

Durt, Hubert. "The Pregnancy of Māyā: II. Māyā as Healer." *Journal of the International College for Advanced Buddhist Studies* 6 (2003): 43–62.

Dwivedi, Umesh Chandra. "Hariti in Literature and Art." In Chitta Ranjan Prasad Sinha, ed., *Studies in Indian Art*, 111–20.

———. "Prajñāpāramitā in Literature and Art." In *Facets of Indian Culture: Gustav Roth Felicitation Volume*, ed. Chitta Ranjan Prasad Sinha, 301–20. Patna: Bihar Puravid Parishad, 1998.

Edgerton, Franklin. *Buddhist Hybrid Sanskrit Grammar and Dictionary*. Vol. 2, *Dictionary*. New Haven: Yale University Press, 1953.

Edou, Jérôme. *Machig Labdron and the Foundations of Chöd*. Ithaca: Snow Lion, 1996.

Elwin, Verrier. *The Religion of an Indian Tribe*. London: Oxford University Press, 1955.

———. "The Saora Priestess." *Bulletin of the Department of Anthropology* [Calcutta] 1 (1952): 59–85.

Emmerick, R. E., trans. *The Sūtra of Golden Light: Being a Translation of the Suvarṇabhāsottamasūtra*. London: Pali Text Society, 1970.

English, Elizabeth. *Vajrayoginī: Her Visualizations, Rituals, and Forms*. Boston: Wisdom, 2002.

Enthoven, R. E. *The Folklore of Bombay*. Oxford: Clarendon Press, 1924.

Eracle, Jean. *Thanka de L'Himalaya: Images de la Sagesse*. Turin: Priula and Verlucca, 1993.

Essen, Gerd-Wolfgang, and Tsering Tashi Thingo. *Die Götter des Himalaya: Buddhistische Kunst Tibets, Die Sammlung Gerd-Wolfgang Essen*. 2 vols. Munich: Prestel-Verlag, 1989.

Fawcett, F. "On Some Festivals to Village Goddesses." *Journal of the Anthropological Society of Bombay* 2 (1890): 261–82.

Ferguson, John P. "The Great Goddess Today in Burma and Thailand: An Exploration of Her Symbolic Relevance to Monastic and Female Roles." In *Mother Worship: Theme and Variations*, ed. James J. Preston, 283–303. Chapel Hill: University of North Carolina Press, 1982.

Fergusson, James. *Tree and Serpent Worship: or Illustrations of Mythology and Art in India in the First and Fourth Centuries after Christ, from the Sculptures of the Buddhist Topes at Sanchi and Amravati*. 1868. Reprint. Delhi: Oriental Publishers, 1971.

Fischer, Klaus. "Two Gandhāra Reliefs Depicting Queen Māyā's Dream: Had They an Erotic Significance?" In *South Asian Archaeology 1981*, ed. Bridget Allchin, 250–53. Cambridge: Cambridge University Press, 1984.

Foucher, Alfred. *The Beginnings of Buddhist Art and Other Essays in Indian and Central-Asian Archaeology*. English ed. Varanasi: Indological Book House, 1972.

———. *Étude sur l'iconographie bouddhique de l'Inde d'après des documents nouveaux*. Paris: Ernest Leroux, 1900.

———. *Notes on the Ancient Geography of Gandhara (A Commentary on a Chapter of Hiuan Tsang)*. Trans. H. Hargreaves. Calcutta: Superintendent Government Printing, 1915.

———. *On the Iconography of the Buddha's Nativity*. Trans. H. Hargreaves. Memoirs of the Archaeological Survey of India 46. Delhi: Manager of Publications, 1934.

Galland, China. *Longing for Darkness: Tara and the Black Madonna*. New York: Viking, 1990.

Gangoly, O. C. "The Earth-Goddess in Buddhist Art." *Indian Historical Quarterly* 19, no. 1 (March 1943): 1–11.

Gellner, David N. *Monk, Householder, Tantric Priest: Newar Buddhism and Its Hierarchy of Ritual.* Cambridge: Cambridge University Press, 1992.

———. "'The Perfection of Wisdom'—A Text and Its Uses in Kwā Bahā, Lalitpur." In *Change and Continuity: Studies in the Nepalese Culture of the Kathmandu Valley*, ed. Siegfried Lienhard, 223–40. Turin: CESMEO, 1996.

Getty, Alice. *The Gods of Northern Buddhism: Their History, Iconography and Progressive Evolution through the Northern Buddhist Countries.* 2nd ed. 1928. Reprint. New Delhi: Munshiram Manoharlal, 1978.

Ghosh, Amalananda. *Nālandā.* 5th ed. (Earlier editions titled *A Guide to Nālandā.*) New Delhi: Director General of Archaeology in India, 1965.

Ghosh, Mallar. *Development of Buddhist Iconography in Eastern India: A Study of Tārā, Prajñās of Five Tathāgatas and Bhṛikuṭī.* New Delhi: Munshiram Manoharlal, 1980.

Ghosh, Niranjan. *Concept and Iconography of the Goddess of Abundance and Fortune in Three Religions of India.* Burdwan: University of Burdwan, 1979.

Gomez, Luis O. "Two Tantric Meditations: Visualizing the Deity." In *Buddhism in Practice*, ed. Donald S. Lopez, Jr., 318–27. Princeton: Princeton University Press, 1995.

Gonda, Jan. *Ancient Indian Kingship from the Religious Point of View.* Leiden: E. J. Brill, 1969.

———. *Aspects of Early Viṣṇuism.* 1954. Reprint. Delhi: Motilal Banarsidass, 1969.

Gorakshkar, Sadashiv, and Kalpana Desai. "An Illustrated Manuscript of *Ashṭasāhasrikā Prajñāpāramitā* in the Asiatic Society of Bombay." In *Orientalia Iosephi Tucci Memoriae Dicata*, vol. 2, ed. G. Gnoli and L. Lanciotti, 561–68. Serie Orientale Roma 56, pt. 2. Rome: Instituto Italiano per il Medio ed Estremo Oriente, 1987.

Gordon, Antoinette K. *The Iconography of Tibetan Lamaism.* 1914. Rev. ed. New Delhi: Munshiram Manoharlal, 1978.

Gordon, Douglas Hamilton. "The Mother-Goddess of Gandhara." *Antiquity* 11, no. 1 (March 1937): 70–79.

Gray, David B. *The Discourse of Śrī Heruka (Śrīherukābhidāna): A Study and Annotated Translation of the Cakrasaṃvara Tantra (Treasury of the Buddhist Sciences).* New York: American Institute of Buddhist Studies, 2006.

Griffith, Ralph T. H., trans. *The Hymns of the Atharva-Veda: Translated with a Popular Commentary.* 2 vols. 2nd ed. 1916. Reprint. Delhi: Low Price, 1995.

———. *The Hymns of the Rigveda: Translated with a Popular Commentary.* 2 vols. 2nd ed. Benares: E. J. Lazarus, 1896.

Grönbold, Günter. "'Saptavāra', A Dhāraṇī Collection from Nepal." In *Le Parole e i Marmi: Studi in onore di Raniero Gnoli nel suo 70th compleanno*, ed. Raffaele Torella, 369–75. Rome: Instituto Italiano per l'Africa e l'Oriente, 2001.

Gross, Rita. *Buddhism after Patriarchy: A Feminist History, Analysis, and Reconstruction of Buddhism.* Albany: State University of New York Press, 1993.

———. "I will never forget to visualize that Vajrayoginī is my body and mind." *Journal of Feminist Studies in Religion* 3, no. 1 (Spring 1987): 77–89.

Grünwedel, Albert. *Buddhist Art in India.* 1893. English trans. of revised ed., 1901. Reprint. New Delhi: Cosmo, 1985.

Guillon, Emmanuel. "A propos d'une version mône inédite de l'épisode de Vasundharā." *Journal Asiatique* 275, nos. 1–2 (1987): 142–62.

Gupta, Anand Swarup. "Conception of Sarasvatī in the Purāṇas." *Purāṇa* 4, no. 1 (1962): 55–95.

Gupta, Parameshwari Lal, ed. *Patna Museum Catalogue of Antiquities (Stone Sculptures, Metal Images, Terracottas and Minor Antiquities)*. Patna: Patna Museum, 1965.

Gupta, S. P., ed. *Kushāṇa Sculptures from Sanghol (1st-2nd Century A.D.): A Recent Discovery*. New Delhi: National Museum, 1985.

Gupta, Shakti M. *Plants in Indian Temple Art*. Delhi: B. R. Publishing, 1996.

Gupte, R. S. *Iconography of the Hindus, Buddhists and Jains*. Bombay: D. B. Taraporevala Sons, 1972.

Gyatso, Geshe Kelsang. *Clear Light of Bliss: Mahamudra in Vajrayana Buddhism*. London: Wisdom, 1982.

———. *Guide to Dakini Land: A Commentary to the Highest Yoga Tantra Practice of Vajrayogini*. London: Tharpa, 1991.

———. *Heart of Wisdom: A Commentary to the Heart Sutra*. London: Tharpa, 1986.

Gyatso, Janet. "The Development of the *Gcod* Tradition." In *Soundings in Tibetan Civilization*, ed. Barbara Nimri Aziz and Matthew Kapstein, 320–41. New Delhi: Manohar, 1985.

Haldar, Jnan Ranjan. *Early Buddhist Mythology*. Delhi: Manohar, 1977.

Hara, M. "A Note on the Buddha's Birth Story." In *Indianisme et bouddhisme: Mélanges offerts à Mgr Étienne Lamotte*, 145–57. Louvain-la-Neuve: Université Catholique de Louvain, 1980.

Hardiman, David. *The Coming of the Devi: Adivasi Assertion in Western India*. Oxford: Oxford University Press, 1987.

Hargreaves, H. *Handbook to the Sculptures in the Peshawar Museum*. 1909. Rev. ed. Calcutta: Government of India, 1930.

Havnevik, Hanna. *Tibetan Buddhist Nuns*. Oslo: Norwegian University Press, 1990.

Heller, Amy. *Tibetan Art: Tracing the Development of Spiritual Ideals and Art in Tibet 600–2000 A.D.* Milan: Jaca Book, Antique Collectors' Club, 1999.

Herrmann-Pfandt, Adelheid. *Ḍākinīs: Zur Stellung und Symbolik des Weiblichen im Tantrischen Buddhismus*. Indica et Tibetica 20. Bonn: Indica et Tibetica Verlag, 1992.

———. "Ḍākinīs in Indo-Tibetan Tantric Buddhism: Some Results of Recent Research." *Studies in Central and East Asian Religions* 5/6 (1992–93): 45–63.

———. "*Yab Yum* Iconography and the Role of Women in Tibetan Tantric Buddhism." *Tibet Journal* 22, no. 1 (Spring 1997): 12–34.

Hevajra Tantra. See Snellgrove, David L.

Hixon, Lex. *Mother of the Buddhas: Meditation on the Prajnaparamita Sutra*. Wheaton: Quest Books, 1993.

Hock, Nancy. "Buddhist Ideology and the Sculpture of Ratnagiri, Seventh through Thirteenth Centuries." Ph.D. thesis, University of California at Berkeley, 1987.

Horner, Isaline B. "The Earth as a Swallower." In *Essays Offered to G. H. Luce*, ed. Ba Shin, vol. 1, pp. 151–59. Ascona: Artibus Asiae, 1966.

———, trans. *The Book of the Discipline (Vinaya-Piṭaka)*. 6 vols. 1938–66. Reprint. London: Pali Text Society, 1992–96.

Huber, Toni, and Tsepak Rigzin. "A Tibetan Guide for Pilgrimage to Ti-se (Mount Kailas) and mTsho Ma-pham (Lake Manasarovar)." In *Sacred Spaces and Powerful Places in Tibetan Culture: A Collection of Essays*, ed. Toni Huber, 125–53. Dharamsala: Library of Tibetan Works and Archives, 1999.

Huntington, John C., and Dina Bangdel. *The Circle of Bliss: Buddhist Meditational Art*. Contributing ed., Miranda Shaw. Columbus: Columbus Museum of Art and Serindia, n.d. [2003].

Huntington, Susan L. *The Art of Ancient India: Buddhist, Hindu, Jain*. With contributions by John C. Huntington. New York: Weatherhill, 1985.

———. *The "Pāla-Sena" Schools of Sculpture*. Studies in South Asian Culture 10. Leiden: E. J. Brill, 1984.

Huntington, Susan L., and John C. Huntington. *Leaves from the Bodhi Tree: The Art of Pāla India (8th–12th Centuries) and Its International Legacy*. Seattle: The Dayton Art Institute and University of Washington Press, 1990.

Hutt, Michael James, trans. and ed. *Himalayan Voices: An Introduction to Modern Nepali Literature*. 1991. Indian ed. Delhi: Motilal Banarsidass, 1993.

Huyler, Stephen P. *Gifts of Earth: Terracottas and Clay Sculptures of India*. New Delhi: Indira Gandhi National Centre for the Arts, 1996.

Ingholt, Harald. *Gandhāran Art in Pakistan*. Hamden: Connecticut Academy of Arts and Sciences, 1957.

Jash, Pranabananda. "Iconography and Relation: A Case Study of Hariti." In Chitta Ranjan Prasad Sinha, ed., *Studies in Indian Art*, 106–10.

Jayakar, Pupul. *The Earth Mother: Legends, Ritual Arts, and Goddesses of India*. 1980 (under title *The Earthen Drum*). Rev. ed. San Francisco: Harper and Row, 1990.

Johnston, E. H., trans. *Aśvaghoṣa's Buddhacarita or Acts of the Buddha*. 1936. New enlarged ed. Delhi: Motilal Banarsidass, 1984.

Jones, J. J., trans. *The Mahāvastu*. 3 vols. 1949–56. Reprint. London: Pali Text Society, 1976–87.

Joshi, N. P. *Mātṛkās: Mothers in Kuṣāṇa Art*. New Delhi: Kanak, 1986.

Joshi, N. P., and R. C. Sharma. *Catalogue of Gandhāra Sculptures in The State Museum, Lucknow*. Lucknow: The State Museum, 1969.

Kajiyama, Yuichi. "Women in Buddhism." *Eastern Buddhist* 15, no. 2 (Autumn 1982): 53–70.

Kala, Satish Chandra. *Terracottas in the Allahabad Museum*. New Delhi: Abhinav, 1980.

Kalff, Martin M. "Ḍākinīs in the Cakrasaṃvara Tradition." In *Tibetan Studies Presented at the Seminar of Young Tibetologists, Zürich, June 26–July 1, 1977*, ed. Martin Brauen and Per Kvaerne, 149–62. Zurich: Völkerkundemuseum der Universität Zürich, 1978.

Karetzky, Patricia Eichenbaum. *The Life of the Buddha: Ancient Scriptural and Pictorial Traditions*. Lanham: University Press of America, 1992.

Katz, Nathan. "Anima and mKha'-'gro-ma: A Critical Comparative Study of Jung and Tibetan Buddhism." *Tibet Journal* 2, no. 3 (Autumn 1977): 13–43.

Kazi, Sonam Tobgay. *Tibet House Museum: Catalogue Inaugural Exhibition*. New Delhi: Tibet House Museum, 1965.

Kenoyer, Jonathan Mark. *Ancient Cities of the Indus Valley Civilization*. Oxford: Oxford University Press and American Institute of Pakistan Studies, 1998.

Khan, Mohammad Israil. *Sarasvatī in Sanskrit Literature*. Ghaziabad: Crescent, 1978.

Khokar, Mohan. *Dancing for Themselves: Folk, Tribal and Ritual Dance in India*. New Delhi: Himalayan Books, 1987.

Khosla, Sarla. *Lalitavistara and the Evolution of Buddha Legend*. New Delhi: Galaxy, 1991.

Kinnard, Jacob N. *Imaging Wisdom: Seeing and Knowing in the Art of Indian Buddhism*. 1999. Indian ed. Delhi: Motilal Banarsidass, 2001.

Kinsley, David. *Hindu Goddesses: Visions of the Divine Feminine in the Hindu Religious Tradition*. Berkeley: University of California Press, 1986.

———. *Tantric Visions of the Divine Feminine: The Ten Mahāvidyās*. Berkeley: University of California Press, 1997.

Klein, Anne C. *Meeting the Great Bliss Queen: Buddhism, Feminism, and the Art of the Self.* Boston: Beacon Press, 1994.

———. "Nondualism and the Great Bliss Queen: A Study in Tibetan Buddhist Ontology and Symbolism." *Journal of Feminist Studies in Religion* 1, no. 1 (Spring 1985): 73–98.

———. "Primordial Purity and Everyday Life: Exalted Female Symbols and the Women of Tibet." In *Immaculate and Powerful: The Female in Sacred Image and Social Reality,* ed. Clarissa W. Atkinson et al., 111–38. Boston: Beacon Press, 1985.

Klieger, P. Christiaan. "Tārā—An Example of Buddhist-Hindu Syncretism." *Tibet Journal* 7, no. 3 (Autumn 1982): 46–52.

Klimburg-Salter, Deborah, ed. *The Silk Route and the Diamond Path: Esoteric Buddhist Art on the Trans-Himalayan Trade Routes.* Los Angeles: UCLA Art Council, 1982.

Kosambi, Damodar Dharmanand. *Myth and Reality: Studies in the Formation of Indian Culture.* 1962. Reprint. Bombay: Popular Prakashan, 1983.

Kossak, Steven M., and Jane Casey Singer. *Sacred Visions: Early Paintings from Central Tibet.* New York: Metropolitan Museum of Art, 1998.

Kramrisch, Stella. *The Art of Nepal.* New York: Asia Society, 1964.

Kreijger, Hugo E. *Kathmandu Valley Painting: The Jucker Collection.* Boston: Shambhala, 1999.

———. *Tibetan Painting: The Jucker Collection.* Boston: Shambhala, 2001.

Kumar, Pramod. *Folk Icons and Rituals in Tribal Life.* New Delhi: Abhinav, 1984.

Kumar, Pushpendra. *Tārā: The Supreme Goddess.* Delhi: Bharatiya Vidya Prakashan, 1992.

Kvaerne, Per. *An Anthology of Buddhist Tantric Songs: A Study of the Caryāgīti.* Oslo: Universitetsforlaget, 1977.

Lakṣmī Tantra: A Pāñcarātra Text. Trans. Sanjukta Gupta. Leiden: E. J. Brill, 1972.

Lalitavistara. See Bays, Gwendolyn, trans.

Lalou, Marcelle. "Mañjuśrīmūlakalpa et Tārāmūlakalpa." *Harvard Journal of Asiatic Studies* 1 (1936): 327–49.

———. "Notes a propos d'une amulette de Touen-houang: Les Litanies de Tārā et la *Sitātapatrādhāraṇī.*" *Melanges Chinois et Bouddhiques* 4 (1936): 135–49.

Lamotte, Étienne. *History of Indian Buddhism: From the Origins to the Śaka Era.* 1958. Trans. Sara Webb-Boin. Louvain-la-Neuve: Université Catholique de Louvain, 1988.

Landaw, Jonathan, and Andy Weber. *Images of Enlightenment: Tibetan Art in Practice.* Ithaca: Snow Lion, 1993.

Landesman, Susan. *The Great Secret of Tārā.* Delhi: Motilal Banarsidass, forthcoming.

Landon, Perceval. *Nepal.* 2 vols. 1928. Reprint. New Delhi: Asian Educational Services, 1993.

Lang, Karen. "Shaven Heads and Loose Hair: Buddhist Attitudes toward Hair and Sexuality." In *Off With Her Head! The Denial of Women's Identity in Myth, Religion, and Culture,* ed. Howard Eilberg-Schwartz and Wendy Doniger, 32–52. Berkeley: University of California Press, 1995.

Lawson, Simon. "Dhāraṇī Sealings in British Collections." In *South Asian Archaeology 1983,* ed. Janine Schotsmans and Maurizio Taddei, 703–17.

Leaves of the Heaven Tree: The Great Compassion of the Buddha. Based on Kṣemendra's *Bodhisattvāvadānakalpalatā.* Trans. Deborah Black. Berkeley: Dharma, 1997.

Legge, James, trans. *A Record of Buddhistic Kingdoms, Being an Account by the Chinese Monk Fâ-hien of his Travels in Indian and Ceylon (A.D. 399–414) in Search of the Buddhist Books of Discipline.* 1886. Reprint. New York: Dover, 1965.

Leidy, Denise Patry, and Robert A. F. Thurman. *Mandala: The Architecture of Enlightenment.* New York: Asia Society Galleries and Tibet House, 1997.

Leoshko, Janice. "Buddhist Sculptures from Bodhgayā." In *Bodhgaya: The Site of Enlightenment,* ed. Janice Leoshko, 46–60. Bombay: Marg, 1988.

———. "The Case of the Two Witnesses to the Buddha's Enlightenment." In *A Pot-Pourri of Indian Art,* ed. Pratapaditya Pal, 39–52. Bombay: Marg, 1988.

———. "The Implications of Bodhgaya's Sūrya as a Symbol of Enlightenment." In Gouriswar Bhattacharya, ed., *Akṣayanīvī,* 230–34.

———. "Pilgrimage and the Evidence of Bodhgaya's Images." In *Function and Meaning in Buddhist Art,* ed. K. R. Van Kooij and H. van der Veere, 45–57. Groningen: Egbert Forsten, 1995.

Lessing, Ferdinand D. *Yung Ho Kung: An Iconography of the Lamaist Cathedral in Peking with Notes on Lamaist Mythology and Cult.* Stockholm: Eegers, 1942.

Lévi, Sylvain. "Le catalogue géographique des Yakṣas dans la Mahāmāyūrī." *Journal Asiatique* 1 (Jan.–Feb. 1915): 19–138.

Levy, Robert. *Mesocosm: The Organization of a Hindu Newar City in Nepal.* Berkeley: University of California Press, 1992.

Lewis, Todd T. "Mahāyāna *Vratas* in Newar Buddhism." *Journal of the International Association of Buddhist Studies* 12, no. 1 (1989): 109–38.

———. *Popular Buddhist Texts from Nepal: Narratives and Rituals of Newar Buddhism.* Translations in collaboration with Subarna Man Tuladhar and Labh Ratna Tuladhar. Albany: State University of New York Press, 2000.

Li Jicheng. *The Realm of Tibetan Buddhism.* 1985. Indian ed. New Delhi: UBSPD, 1986.

Li Rongxi, trans. *The Great Tang Dynasty Record of the Western Regions.* Berkeley: Numata Center for Buddhist Translation and Research, 1996.

Liebert, Gösta. *Iconographic Dictionary of the Indian Religions: Hinduism, Buddhism, Jainism.* Asian Arts and Archaeology Series 5. 2nd ed. Delhi: Sri Satguru, 1986.

Linrothe, Robert. "The Murals at Mangyu: A Distillation of Mature Buddhist Iconography." *Orientations* 25, no. 11 (Nov. 1994): 92–102.

———. *Ruthless Compassion: Wrathful Deities in Early Indo-Tibetan Esoteric Buddhist Art.* Boston: Shambhala, 1999.

———. "Ushnīshavijayā and the Tangut Cult of the Stūpa at Yü Lin Cave 3." *National Palace Museum Bulletin* 31, nos. 4–5 (1996): 1–25.

Linrothe, Robert, and Jeff Watt. *Demonic Divine: Himalayan Art and Beyond.* New York: Rubin Museum of Art and Serindia, 2004.

Lipton, Barbara, and Nima Dorjee Ragnubs. *Treasures of Tibetan Art: Collections of the Jacques Marchais Museum of Tibetan Art.* New York: Jacques Marchais Museum of Tibetan Art and Oxford University Press, 1996.

Lo Bue, Erberto. "Iconographic Sources and Iconometric Literature in Tibetan and Himalayan Art." In *Indo-Tibetan Studies: Papers in Honour and Appreciation of Professor David L. Snellgrove's Contribution to Indo-Tibetan Studies,* ed. Tadeusz Skorupski, 171–97. Tring, United Kingdom: Institute of Buddhist Studies, 1990.

———. "The Newar Artists of the Nepal Valley: An Historical Account of Their Activities in Neighboring Areas with Particular Reference to Tibet. I." *Oriental Art,* n.s., 31, no. 3 (Autumn 1985): 262–77.

Lo Bue, Erberto, and Franco Ricca. *Gyantse Revisited.* Turin: Casa Editrice Le Lettere, 1990.

Locke, John K. *Buddhist Monasteries of Nepal: A Survey of the Bāhās and Bahīs of the Kathmandu Valley*. Kathmandu: Sahayogi Press, 1985.

———. *Karunamaya: The Cult of Avalokitesvara-Matsyendranath in the Valley of Nepal*. Kathmandu: Satyogi, 1980.

Lohia, Sushama. *Lalitavajra's Manual of Buddhist Iconography*. New Delhi: International Academy of Indian Culture and Aditya Prakashan, 1994.

Lohuizen-de Leeuw, J. E. van. "The Paṭṭikera Chundā and Variations of Her Image." In *Nalini Kanta Bhattasali Commemoration Volume*, ed. A. B. M. Habibullah, 119–43. Dacca: Dacca Museum, 1966.

Lopez, Donald S., Jr. "A Prayer Flag for Tara." In *Religions of Tibet in Practice*, ed. Donald S. Lopez, Jr., 548–52. Princeton: Princeton University Press, 1997.

Loseries-Leick, Andrea. "Kālī in Tibetan Buddhism." In *Wild Goddesses in India and Nepal: Proceedings of an International Symposium, Bern and Zurich, November 1994*, ed. Axel Michaels, Cornelia Vogelsanger, and Annette Wilke, 417–36. Studia Religiosa Helvetica Jahrbuch 2. Bern: Peter Lang, 1996.

Losty, Jeremiah P. "Bengal, Bihar, Nepal? Problems of Provenance in 12th-Century Illuminated Buddhist Manuscripts." 2 pts. *Oriental Art*, n.s., 35, no. 2 (Summer 1989): 86–96, and no. 3 (Autumn 1989): 140–49.

Ludvik, Catherine. "La Benzaiten à huit bras: Durgā déesse guerrière sous l'apparence de Sarasvatī." *Cahiers d'Extrême-Asie* 11 (1999–2000): 293–338.

Macdonald, A. W., and Anne Vergati Stahl. *Newar Art: Nepalese Art during the Malla Period*. New Delhi: Vikas, 1979.

Macy, Joanna. "Perfection of Wisdom: Mother of All Buddhas." In *Beyond Androcentrism: New Essays on Women and Religion*, ed. Rita M. Gross, 315–34. Missoula: Scholars Press, 1977.

Magoun, H. W. "The Āsurī-Kalpa: A Witchcraft Practice of the Atharva-Veda." *American Journal of Philology* 10 (1889): 165–97.

Maity, Pradyot Kumar. *Historical Studies in the Cult of the Goddess Manasā (A Socio-Cultural Study)*. Calcutta: Punthi Pustak, 1966.

———. *Human Fertility Cults and Rituals of Bengal (A Comparative Study)*. Delhi: Abhinav, 1989.

Majumdar, N. G. *A Guide to the Sculptures in the Indian Museum*. Pt. 1, *Early Indian Schools*. Pt. 2, *The Graeco-Buddhist School of Gandhāra*. Delhi: Manager of Publications, 1937.

Malandra, Geri H. "Māra's Army: Text and Image in Early Indian Art." *East and West*, n.s., 31, nos. 1–4 (Dec. 1981): 121–30.

———. *Unfolding a Maṇḍala: The Buddhist Cave Temples at Ellora*. Albany: State University of New York Press, 1993.

Mallmann, Marie-Thérèse de. *Introduction à l'iconographie du tântrisme bouddhique*. Paris: Librairie Adrien-Maisonneuve, 1975.

———. "Notes d'iconographie tântrique, IV: A propos de Vajravārāhī." *Arts Asiatique* 20 (1969): 21–40.

Mani, V. R. *Saptamātṛkas in Indian Religion and Art*. New Delhi: Mittal, 1995.

Manna, Sibendu. *Mother Goddess Caṇḍī (Its Socio Ritual Impact on the Folk Life)*. Calcutta: Punthi Pustak, 1993.

Marglin, Frédérique Apffel. "Smallpox in Two Systems of Knowledge." In *Dominating Knowledge: Development, Culture, and Resistance*, ed. Frédérique Apffel Marglin and Stephen A. Marglin, 102–44. Oxford: Clarendon Press, 1990.

Marshall, John. *The Buddhist Art of Gandhāra: The Story of the Early School, Its Birth, Growth and Decline.* 1960. Reprint. New Delhi: Oriental Books Reprint Corp., 1980.

———. *Taxila: An Illustrated Account of the Archaeological Excavations Carried Out at Taxila under the Orders of the Government of India between the Years 1913 and 1934.* 3 vols. Cambridge: Cambridge University Press, 1951.

Marshall, John, and Alfred Foucher. *The Monuments of Sāñchī.* 3 vols. 1940. Reprint. Delhi: Swati, 1982.

Masselos, Jim, et al. *Dancing to the Flute: Music and Dance in Indian Art.* Ed. Pratapaditya Pal. Sydney: Art Gallery of New South Wales, 1997.

Mehta, R. N. "Kurukullā, Tārā and Vajreśī in Śrīpura." In Narendra Nath Bhattacharyya, ed., *Tantric Buddhism,* 277–83.

Meisezahl, Richard O. *Geist und Ikonographie des Vajrayāna-Buddhismus: Hommage à Marie-Thérèse de Mallmann.* Sangkt Augustin: VGH Wissenschaftsverlag, 1980.

———. "Die Göttin Vajravārāhī: Eine ikonographische Studie nach einem Sādhana-Text von Advayavajra." *Oriens* 18–19 (1965–66): 228–303.

Menzies, Jackie, ed. *Buddha: Radiant Awakening.* Sydney: Art Gallery of New South Wales, 2001.

Merz, Brigitte. "Wild Goddess and Mother of Us All: Some Preliminary Remarks on the Cult of the Goddess Hāratī in Nepal." In *Wild Goddesses in India and Nepal: Proceedings of an International Symposium, Bern and Zurich, November 1994,* ed. Axel Michaels, Cornelia Vogelsanger, and Annette Wilke, 343–54. Studia Religiosa Helvetica Jahrbuch 2. Bern: Peter Lang, 1996.

Mishra, Jayadeva. *A History of Buddhist Iconography in Bihar: A.D. 600–1200.* Patna: Prabhavati Prakashan, 1992.

Mishra, Prabodh Kumar. *Archaeology of Mayūrbhañj.* New Delhi: D. K. Printworld, 1997.

Mishra, Ramprasad. *Advayasiddhi: The Tāntric View of Lakṣmīnkarā.* Delhi: Kant, 1995.

Misra, B. N. *Nālandā.* 3 vols. Delhi: B. R. Publishing, 1998.

Misra, Ram Nath. *Yaksha Cult and Iconography.* New Delhi: Munshiram Manoharlal, 1981.

Mitra, Debala. "Ashṭamahābhaya-Tārā." *Journal of the Asiatic Society, Letters and Science* 23, no. 1 (1957): 19–22.

———. *Bronzes from Achutrajpur, Orissa.* Delhi: Agam Kala Prakashan, 1978.

———. *Bronzes from Bangladesh: A Study of Buddhist Images from District Chittagong.* Delhi: Agam Kala Prakashan, 1982.

———. "Images of Chundā at Bodh-Gaya." In *Historical Archaeology of India: A Dialogue between Archaeologists and Historians,* ed. Amita Ray and Samir Mukherjee, 299–305. New Delhi: Books and Books, 1990.

———. "A Metal Image of Mārīcī from Jagajjivanpur." *Journal of Bengal Art* 4 (1999): 141–46.

———. *Ratnagiri (1958–1961).* 2 vols. paginated consecutively. Memoirs of the Archaeological Survey of India 80. Delhi: Director General, Archaeological Survey of India, 1981, 1983.

Mitra, Mallar. "The Buddhist Goddess Aparājitā: Four-Armed Form." *Journal of Bengal Art* 1 (1996): 161–67.

———. "Four Images of the Buddhist Goddess Aparājitā." In *Studies in Hindu and Buddhist Art,* ed. P. K. Mishra, 95–99. New Delhi: Abhinav, 1999.

———. "Goddess Vajravārāhī: An Iconographic Study." In Narendra Nath Bhattacharyya, ed., *Tantric Buddhism,* 102–29.

———. "Hārītī in Buddhist Monasteries." In *Historical Archaeology of India: A Dialogue between Archaeologists and Historians*, ed. Amita Ray and Samir Mukherjee, 321–25. New Delhi: Books and Books, 1990.

———. "Images of Mārīchī Found in the Museums of Calcutta." In *Studies in Archaeology: Papers Presented in Memory of P. C. Dasgupta*, ed. Asok Kumar Datta, 343–54 and plates 43–50. New Delhi: Books and Books, 1991.

———. "Nairātmā in Vajrayāna Buddhism: An Iconographic Study." *Kalyan Bharati: Journal on Indian History and Culture* 3 (1999): 84–95.

Mitra, R. L., trans. *The Lalita-vistara: Memoirs of the Early Life of Sakya Sinha (Chs. 1–15)*. Delhi: Sri Satguru, 1998.

Mitra, Rājendralāla. *The Sanskrit Buddhist Literature of Nepal*. 1882. Reprint. Calcutta: Sanskrit Pustak Bhandar, 1971.

Monier-Williams, Monier. *A Sanskrit-English Dictionary*. 1899. Reprint. Tokyo: Oxford University Press, 1982.

Mukherjee, B. N. "The Skārah Ḍheri Hārītī." *National Museum Bulletin* [New Delhi] 7–8 (1993): 2–6.

Mukherjee, Kalpika. "Vajrayoginī and Mahākāla—Two Most Fearful Deities in the Buddhist Tantric Pantheon." In Narendra Nath Bhattacharyya, ed., *Tantric Buddhism*, 208–14.

Mukherji, Purna Chandra. *A Report on a Tour of Exploration of the Antiquities in the Tarai, Nepal, The Region of Kapilavastu; During February and March, 1899*. Archaeological Survey of India, Imperial Series, 26, pt. 1. Calcutta: Superintendent of Government Printing, 1901.

Mukhopadhyay, Manisha. "Lakṣmī and Sarasvatī in Sanskrit Inscriptions." In D. C. Sircar, ed., *Foreigners in Ancient India*, 106–11.

Mukhopadhyay, Somnath. *Caṇḍī in Art and Iconography*. Delhi: Agam Kala Prakashan, 1984.

Mukhopadhyay, Subrata Kumar. *Cult of Goddess Sitala in Bengal: An Enquiry into Folk Culture*. Calcutta: Firma KLM, 1994.

Mullin, Glenn H. *Female Buddhas: Women of Enlightenment in Tibetan Mystical Art*. Santa Fe: Clear Light, 2003.

———. *Meditations on the Lower Tantras, From the Collected Works of the Previous Dalai Lamas*. Dharamsala: Library of Tibetan Works and Archives, 1983.

———. *Selected Works of the Dalai Lama II: Tantric Yogas of Sister Niguma*. Ithaca: Snow Lion, 1985.

———, trans. *Six Texts Related to the Tara Tantra by Gyalwa Gendun Drub, the First Dalai Lama (1391–1471)*. New Delhi: Tibet House, 1980.

Murthy, K. Krishna. *Sculptures of Vajrayāna Buddhism*. Delhi: Classics India, 1989.

Nebesky-Wojkowitz, Réne de. *Oracles and Demons of Tibet: The Cult and Iconography of the Tibetan Protective Deities*. Netherlands: Mouton, 1956.

Neumann, Helmut F. "The Wall Paintings of the Lori Gonpa." *Orientations* 25, no. 11 (Nov. 1994): 79–91.

Newman, John. "Vajrayāna Deities in an Illustrated Indian Manuscript of the *Aṣṭasāhasrikā-prajñāpāramitā*." *Journal of the International Association of Buddhist Studies* 13, no. 2 (1990): 117–32.

Ngor Mandalas. See bSod nams rgya mtsho and Musashi Tachikawa.

Nicholas, Ralph. "The Goddess Śītalā and Epidemic Smallpox in Bengal." *Journal of Asian Studies* 41, no. 1 (Nov. 1981): 21–44.

Nihom, M. "The Goddess with the Severed Head: A Recension of Sādhanamālā 232, 234 and 238 Attributed to the Siddhācārya Virūpā." In *Ritual, State and History in South Asia: Essays in Honour of J. C. Heesterman*, ed. A. W. van den Hoek et al., 222–43. Leiden: E. J. Brill, 1992.

Nispannayogāvalī. See Bhattacharyya, Benoytosh, ed.

Niyogi, Puspa. *Buddhist Divinities*. Delhi: Munshiram Manoharlal, 2001.

———. "Cundā—A Popular Buddhist Goddess." *East and West*, n.s., 27, no. 4 (Dec. 1977): 299–310.

Nyingma School. See Rinpoche, Dudjom.

Nyinje, Tenpai. *White Tara Who Saves One from Death*. Trans. Jens Hansen. Kathmandu: Ka-Nying Shedrup Ling Monastery, 1995.

Obeyesekere, Gananath. "The Buddhist Pantheon in Ceylon and Its Extensions." In *Anthropological Studies in Theravada Buddhism*, ed. Manning Nash, 1–26. New Haven: Yale University Press, 1963.

———. *The Cult of the Goddess Pattini*. Chicago: University of Chicago Press, 1984.

———. "The Goddess Pattini and the Lord Buddha: Notes of the Myth of the Birth of the Deity." *Social Compass* 20, no. 2 (1973): 217–29.

———. "Social Change and the Deities: The Rise of the Kataragama Cult in Modern Sri Lanka." *Man*, n.s., 12, nos. 3–4 (Dec. 1977): 377–96.

Olschak, Blanche Christine, with Geshé Thupten Wangyal. *Mystic Art of Ancient Tibet*. Boston: Shambhala, 1987.

Olson, Eleanor. *Catalogue of the Tibetan Collection and Other Lamaist Material in the Newark Museum*. Vol. 3, *Images and Molds, Paintings, Writing and Printing Equipment, Books, Seals and Documents*. Newark: n.p., 1971.

———. *Tantric Buddhist Art*. New York: China Institute in America, 1974.

Oppert, Gustav. *On the Original Inhabitants of Bharatavarṣa or India*. Westminster: Archibald Constable, 1893.

Orofino, Giacomella. "The Great Wisdom Mother and the Gcod Tradition." In *Tantra in Practice*, ed. David Gordon White, 396–416. Princeton: Princeton University Press, 2000.

Padma, Sree. "From Village to City: Transforming Goddesses in Urban Andhra Pradesh." In *Seeking Mahādevī: Constructing the Identities of the Hindu Great Goddess*, ed. Tracy Pintchman, 115–43. Albany: State University of New York Press, 2001.

Pal, Pratapaditya. *Art of Nepal, A Catalogue of the Los Angeles County Museum of Art Collection*. Los Angeles: Los Angeles County Museum of Art and University of California Press, 1985.

———. *Art of the Himalayas: Treasures from Nepal and Tibet*. New York: Hudson Hills Press, 1991.

———. *The Art of Tibet*. New York: Asia Society, 1969.

———. *Art of Tibet: A Catalogue of the Los Angeles County Museum of Art Collection*. Los Angeles: Los Angeles County Museum of Art and University of California Press, 1983.

———. *The Arts of Nepal*. Vol. 1, *Sculpture*. Vol. 2, *Painting*. Leiden: E. J. Brill, 1978.

———. "The Bhīmaratha Rite and Nepali Art." *Oriental Art*, n.s., 23, no. 2 (Summer 1977): 176–89.

———. *Bronzes of Kashmir*. New Delhi: Munshiram Manoharlal, 1975.

———. *Buddhist Art in Licchavi Nepal*. Bombay: Marg, 1974.

———. *Desire and Devotion: Art from India, Nepal, and Tibet in the John and Berthe Ford Collection*. London: Walters Art Gallery and Philip Wilson, 2001.

———. *Divine Images, Human Visions: The Max Tanenbaum Collection of South Asian and Himalayan Art in the National Gallery of Canada*. Ottawa: National Gallery of Canada, 1997.

———. *Hindu Religion and Iconology According to the Tantrasāra*. Los Angeles: Vichitra Press, 1981.

———. *Nepal: Where the Gods Are Young*. N.p.: The Asia Society, 1975.

———. "Paintings from Nepal in the Prince of Wales Museum." *Bulletin of the Prince of Wales Museum of Western India* 10 (1967): 1–26.

———. *Tibet: Tradition and Change*. Albuquerque: The Albuquerque Museum, 1997.

———. *Tibetan Paintings: A Study of Tibetan Thankas Eleventh to Nineteenth Centuries*. Basel: Ravi Kumar and Sotheby, 1984.

———. *Two Buddhist Paintings from Nepal*. Amsterdam: Museum van Aziatische Kunst, 1967.

Pal, Pratapaditya, and Hsien-ch'i Tseng. *Lamaist Art: The Aesthetics of Harmony*. Boston: Museum of Fine Arts, n.d. [1971].

Pal, Pratapaditya, and Julia Meech-Pekarik. *Buddhist Book Illuminations*. New York: Ravi Kumar, 1988.

Pal, Pratapaditya, et al. *Himalayas: An Aesthetic Adventure*. With contributions by Amy Heller, Oskar von Hinüber, and Gautama V. Vajracharya. Berkeley: University of California Press, 2003.

Pāṇḍeya, Janārdana, ed. *Bauddhastotrasaṃgraha*. Delhi: Motilal Banarsidass, 1994.

———. *Gorakṣasaṃhitā*. Vol. 1. Sarasvatībhavana-Granthamālā 110. Varanasi: Sampurnanand Sanskrit Vishvavidyalaya, 1976.

———. *Kurukullākalpah*. Rare Buddhist Text Series 24. Sarnath: Central Institute for Higher Tibetan Studies, 2001.

Pargiter, F. Eden, trans. *The Mārkaṇḍeya Purāṇa, Translated with Notes*. n.d. Reprint. Varanasi: Indological Book House, 1981.

Parimoo, Ratan. *Life of Buddha in Indian Sculpture (Ashta-Maha-Pratiharya): An Iconological Analysis*. New Delhi: Kanak, 1982.

Paul, Debjani. *The Art of Nālandā: Development of Buddhist Sculpture AD 600–1200*. 1987. Reprint. Delhi: Munshiram Manoharlal, 1995.

Paul, Robert A. *The Tibetan Symbolic World*. Chicago: Chicago University Press, 1982.

Peri, Noel. "Hārītī, le mère des démons." *Bulletin de l'École Française d'Extrême-Orient* 17, pt. 3 (1917): 1–102.

Petech, Luciano. *Medieval History of Nepal (c. 750–1482 A.D.)*. Serie Orientale Roma 54. 1958. 2nd ed. Rome: Instituto Italiano per il Medio ed Estremo Oriente, 1984.

Pintchman, Tracy. *The Rise of the Goddess in the Hindu Tradition*. Albany: State University of New York Press, 1994.

Piotrovsky, Mikhail, ed. *Lost Empire of the Silk Road: Buddhist Art from Khara Khoto (X-XIIIth century)*. Milan: Thyssen-Bornemisza Foundation, 1993.

Pisharoti, K. Rama. "Dohada or the Woman and Tree Motif." *Journal of the Indian Society of Oriental Art* 3, no. 2 (Dec. 1935): 110–24.

Pradhan, Bhuwan Lal. *Lumbini-Kapilwastu-Dewadaha*. Kirtipur, Kathmandu: Tribhuvan University, 1979.

———. *Swayambhu*. Kathmandu: New Printing Press, 1984.

Rahula, Bhikkhu Telwatte. *A Critical Study of the Mahāvastu*. Delhi: Motilal Banarsidass, 1978.

Ram, Rajendra. "Heretic Motifs in Mārīchī: The Sun Goddess of Buddhism, A.D. 700–1400." *Journal of the Bihar Research Society, Platinum Jubilee Volume*, 76–78 (1990–92): 231–38.

Ramachandran, T. N. *The Nāgapaṭṭinam and Other Buddhist Bronzes in the Madras Museum*. 1954. Reprint. Madras: Director of Museums, 1992.

———. "Prajnaparamita in Buddhist Iconography." *Triveni* 4, no. 6 (1931): 17–25.

Randhawa, M. S. *The Cult of Trees and Tree-Worship in Buddhist-Hindu Sculpture*. New Delhi: All India Fine Arts and Crafts Society, 1964.

Rawson, Phillip. "The Iconography of the Goddess Manasā." *Oriental Art*, n.s., 1, no. 4 (Winter 1955): 151–58.

Regmi, Dilli Raman. *Medieval Nepal*. Vol. 1, *Early Medieval Period, 750–1530 A.D.* Vol. 2, *A History of the Three Kingdoms, 1520 A.D. to 1768 A.D.* Calcutta: Firma K. L. Mukhopadhyay, 1965–66.

Rhie, Marylin M., and Robert A. F. Thurman. *Wisdom and Compassion: The Sacred Art of Tibet*. New York: Harry N. Abrams, 1991.

———. *Worlds of Transformation: Tibetan Art of Wisdom and Compassion*. New York: Tibet House, 1999.

Rhys Davids, C. A. F., trans. *The Book of the Kindred Sayings (Saṅyutta-Nikāya) or Grouped Suttas*. Vol. 1 of 5. 1917. Reprint. Oxford: Pali Text Society, 1996.

Rhys Davids, T. W., trans. *Buddhist Birth-Stories (Jataka Tales): The Commentarial Introduction Entitled Nidāna-Kathā, The Story of the Lineage*. Rev. ed. London: George Routledge and Sons, 1925.

Rhys Davids, T. W., and William Stede. *The Pali Text Society's Pali-English Dictionary*. London: Luzac, 1949.

Ricca, Franco, and Erberto Lo Bue. *The Great Stupa of Gyantse: A Complete Tibetan Pantheon of the Fifteenth Century*. London: Serindia, 1993.

Ridding, C. M., trans. *The Kādambarī of Bāṇa*. 1895. Reprint. New Delhi: Oriental Books Reprint Corp., 1974.

Rinpoche, Bokar. *Tara: The Feminine Divine*. San Francisco: ClearPoint Press, 1999.

Rinpoche, Dudjom. *The Nyingma School of Tibetan Buddhism: Its Fundamentals and History*. 2 vols. Trans. and ed. Gyurme Dorje with Matthew Kapstein. Boston: Wisdom, 1991.

Rinpoche, Patrul. *Kunzang Lama'i Shelung: The Words of My Perfect Teacher*. Trans. Padmakara Translation Group. 1994. 2nd ed. Boston: Shambhala, 1998.

Robinson, James B., trans. *Buddha's Lions: The Lives of the Eighty-Four Siddhas (A Translation of the Caturaśīti-siddha-pravṛtti by Abhayadatta)*. Berkeley: Dharma, 1979.

Roerich, George. *Tibetan Paintings*. 1925. Reprint. New Delhi: Gyan, 1997.

———, trans. *The Blue Annals*, by 'Gos Lo-tsa-ba gZhon-nu-dpal. 1949. 2nd ed. Delhi: Motilal Banarsidass, 1976.

Rosenfield, John. *The Dynastic Arts of the Kushans*. Berkeley: University of California Press, 1967.

Rossi, Anna Maria, and Fabio Rossi. *Tibetan Thangkas: Buddhist Paintings from the 11th to the 18th Century*. Entries by Jane Casey Singer. London: n.p., 2001.

Roth, Gustav. "The Woman and Tree Motif: *Śālabhañjikā—Dālamālikā* in Prakrit and Sanskrit Texts with Special Reference to Śilpaśāstras Including Notes on *Dohada*." *Journal of the Asiatic Society, Letters and Science* 23, no. 1 (1957): 91–116.

Roy, Udai Narain. "Enchanting Beauties in the Early Buddhist Art—A Symbological Investigation (3rd Century B.C.–3rd Century A.D.)." In Chitta Ranjan Prasad Sinha, ed., *Studies in Indian Art*, 62–68.

———. *Śālabhañjikā (In Art, Philosophy and Literature)*. Allahabad: Lokbharti, 1979.

Ryder, Arthur W., trans. *Shakuntala and Other Writings by Kalidasa*. Paperback ed. New York: E. P. Dutton, 1959.

Sādhanamālā. See Bhattacharyya, Benoytosh, ed.

Sahai, Bhagwant. "Bronze Images of Prajñāpāramitā in Bihar. In *K. P. Jayaswal Commemoration Volume*, ed. J. S. Jha, 162–65. Patna: K. P. Jayaswal Research Institute, 1981.

———. *Iconography of Minor Hindu and Buddhist Deities*. Delhi: Abhinav, 1975.

Sahni, Daya Ram. *Catalogue of the Museum of Archaeology at Sārnāth*. Calcutta: Superintendent Government Printing, India, 1914.

Sahu, Nabin Kumar. *Buddhism in Orissa*. Cuttack: Utkal University, 1958.

Śāktapramoda. Compiled by Devānandasiṃha. Bombay: Śrī Venkaṭeśvara Sṭīm Press, 1984.

Sanderson, Alexis. "Purity and Power among the Brahmans of Kashmir." In *The Category of the Person: Anthropology, Philosophy, and History*, ed. Michael Carrithers et al., 190–216. Cambridge: Cambridge University Press, 1985.

Sankalia, Hasmukh Dhirajlal. "A Unique Wooden Image of the Buddhist Goddess Tara from the Kanheri Caves." *Marg* 36 (1984): 84.

Sankarnarayan, K. "Goddess Sarasvatī and Benzai-ten." In *Cultural Interface of India with Asia: Religion, Art and Architecture*, ed. Anupa Pande and Parul Pandya Dhar, 341–49. New Delhi: D. K. Printworld, 2004.

Saram, Amila Joseph de. "The Earth Goddess in the Art and Culture of Burma, Thailand, and Laos." M.A. thesis, Ohio State University, 2002.

Saraswati, S. K. *Tantrayāna Art: An Album*. Calcutta: Asiatic Society, 1977.

Scheftelowitz, Isidor. *Die Apokryphen des Ṛgveda*. 1906. Reprint. Hildesheim: Georg Olms Verlagsbuchhandlung, 1966.

Schmidt, Erik Hein, trans. *Kurukulle: The Practice of the Lotus Dakini According to the Terma Revealed by Chokgyur Lingpa*. 1990. 3rd ed. Kathmandu: Rangjung Yeshe, 1994.

———. *Vajra Yogini: A Concise Daily Practice*. 1985. Kathmandu: Rangjung Yeshe, 1994.

Schmithausen, Lambert. *Maitrī and Magic: Aspects of the Buddhist Attitude toward the Dangerous in Nature*. Vienna: Verlag der Österreichischen Akademie der Wissenschaften, 1997.

Schopen, Gregory. "The Phrase *'sa pṛthivīpradeśaś caityabhūto bhavet'* in the *Vajracchedikā*: Notes on the Cult of the Book in the Mahāyāna." *Indo-Iranian Journal* 27 (1975): 147–81.

Schotsmans, Janine, and Maurizio Taddei, eds. *South Asian Archaeology 1983: Papers from the Seventh International Conference of the Association of South Asian Archaeologists in Western Europe*. 2 vols. Naples: Instituto Universitario Orientale, 1985.

Schroeder, Ulrich von. *Buddhist Sculptures in Tibet*. Vol. 1, *India and Nepal*. Vol. 2, *Tibet*. Zurich: Visual Dharma, 2001.

———. *Indo-Tibetan Bronzes*. Hong Kong: Visual Dharma, 1981.

Sengupta, Anasua [Anusua]. *Buddhist Art of Bengal (From the 3rd Century B.C. to the 13th Century A.D.)*. Delhi: Rahul, 1993.

———. "Note on a Buddhist Female Deity." *Indian Museum Bulletin* 26 (1991): 26–27.

Sengupta, R. "A Sculptural Representation of the Buddhist Litany to Tārā at Ellora." *Bulletin of the Prince of Wales Museum of Western India* 5 (1955–57): 12–15.

Sengupta, Sudha. "A Note on Usnisa-sitatapatra-pratyamgira . . . Dharani." *Buddhist Studies* (Dept. of Buddhist Studies, University of Delhi), March 1974, pp. 68–75. Article republished in *Studies in Hindu and Buddhist Art*, ed. P. K. Mishra, 49–56. New Delhi: Abhinav, 1999.

Seth, Ved. *Study of Biographies of the Buddha Based on Pāli and Sanskrit Sources*. New Delhi: Akay, 1992.

Shākya, Mahendraratna. *Vasundharā Devī Chagū Adhyayana*. (Newar) Lalitpur: Lotus Research Centre, 1994.

Shakya, Min Bahadur. *The Life and Contribution of the Nepalese Princess Bhrikuti Devi to Tibetan History*. Delhi: Book Faith India, 1997.

Sharma, Arvind. "Can There Be a Female Buddha in Theravada Buddhism?" *Bucknell Review* 24, no. 1 (Spring 1978): 72–79.

Sharma, R. C. *Bharhut Sculptures*. New Delhi: Abhinav, 1994.

Sharma, Ram Sharan. *Śūdras in Ancient India: A Social History of the Lower Order down to Circa A.D. 600*. 2nd ed. Delhi: Motilal Banarsidass, 1980.

Shaw, Miranda. *Buddhist Goddesses of Tibet and Nepal*. Forthcoming.

———. "An Ecstatic Song by Lakṣmīṅkarā." In *Feminine Ground: Essays on Women and Tibet*, ed. Janice Willis, 52–56. Ithaca: Snow Lion, 1989.

———. "Is Vajrayogini a Feminist? A Tantric Buddhist Case Study." In *Is the Goddess a Feminist? The Politics of South Asian Goddesses*, ed. Alf Hiltebeitl and Kathleen Erndl, 166–180. Sheffield: Sheffield Academic Press, 2000.

———. "Magical Lovers, Sisters, and Mothers: *Yakṣiṇī-Sādhana* in Tantric Buddhism." In *Breaking Boundaries with the Goddess: New Directions in the Study of Śaktism, Essays in Honor of Narendra Nath Bhattacharyya*, ed. Cynthia Hume and Rachel Fell McDermott. New Delhi: Manohar, forthcoming.

———. "The Mystery of the Headless Goddess: Tantric Symbol of Spiritual Rebirth." *Parabola: Myth, Tradition, and the Search for Meaning* 25, no. 2 (May 2000): 22–27.

———. *Passionate Enlightenment: Women in Tantric Buddhism*. Princeton: Princeton University Press, 1994.

———. "Worship of Women in Tantric Buddhism: Male Is to Female as Devotee Is to Goddess." In *Women and Goddess Traditions: In Antiquity and Today*, ed. Karen King, 111–36. Minneapolis: Augsburg Fortress Press, 1997.

Shere, S. A. *Bronze Images in Patna Museum, Patna*. Calcutta: Sree Saraswaty Press, 1961.

Shukla, Bhawani Shankar. "Iconography of Vasudhārā." In *Indian Art and Culture*, ed. Govind Chandra Pande et al., 163–72. Allahabad: Raka Prakashan, 1994.

Shukla, S. P. "Kāmukha Female Figures in Kushana Art and Their Bearing on the Buddhist Ideology." *National Museum Bulletin* [New Delhi] 7–8 (1993): 19–28.

Simmer-Brown, Judith. *Dakini's Warm Breath: The Feminine Principle in Tibetan Buddhism*. Boston: Shambhala, 2001.

Singer, Jane Casey. "An Early Tibetan Painting Revisited: The Ashtamahabhaya Tara in the Ford Collection." *Orientations* 29, no. 9 (Sept. 1998): 65–73.

Singh, O. P. *Iconography of Gaja-Lakshmī*. Varanasi: Bharati Prakashan, 1983.

Singh, R. S. *Hindu Iconography in Tantrayāna Buddhism*. New Delhi: Ramanand Vidya Bhawan, 1993.

Singhal, Sudarshana Devi. "Iconography of Cundā." In *The Art and Culture of South-East Asia*, ed. Lokesh Chandra, 385–410. Śata-Pitaka Series, Indo-Asian Literatures, vol. 364. New Delhi: International Academy of Indian Culture and Aditya Prakashan, 1991.

Sinha, B. P. "Some Reflections on Indian Sculpture (Stone or Bronze) of Buddhist Deities Trampling on Hindu Deities." In *Dr. Satkari Mookerji Felicitation Volume*, ed. B. P. Sinha et al., 97–107. Varanasi: Chowkhamba Sanskrit Series Office, 1969.

Sinha, Chitta Ranjan Prasad, ed. *Studies in Indian Art (Dr. Bhagwant Sahai Felicitation Volume)*. New Delhi: Ramanand Vidya Bhawan, 1998.

Sircar, D. C., ed. *Foreigners in Ancient India and Lakṣmī and Sarasvatī in Art and Literature*. Calcutta: University of Calcutta, 1970.

Sivaramamurti, C. *Amaravati Sculptures in the Madras Government Museum*. 1942. Reprint. Madras: Superintendent, Government Press, 1956.

———. *Śrī Lakshmī in Indian Art and Thought*. New Delhi: Kanak, 1982.

Skilling, Peter. "The Rakṣā Literature of the Śrāvakayāna." *Journal of the Pali Text Society* 16 (1992): 109–82.

Skorupski, Tadeusz, trans. *The Sarvadurgatipariśodhana Tantra: Elimination of All Evil Destinies*. Delhi: Motilal Banarsidass, 1983.

Slusser, Mary Shephard. *Nepal Mandala: A Cultural Study of the Kathmandu Valley*. 2 vols. Princeton: Princeton University Press, 1982.

Smith, Vincent A. *The Jain Stūpa and Other Antiquities of Mathurā*. 1901. Reprint. Varanasi: Indological Book House, 1969.

Snellgrove, David L. *The Hevajra Tantra: A Critical Study*. 2 pts. London Oriental Series, vol. 6. London: Oxford University Press, 1959.

———. *Indo-Tibetan Buddhism: Indian Buddhists and Their Tibetan Successors*. London: Serindia, 1987.

bSod nams rgya mtsho and Musashi Tachikawa. *The Ngor Mandalas of Tibet: Plates*. Tokyo: Centre for East Asian Cultural Studies, 1989.

Sponberg, Alan. "Attitudes toward Women and the Feminine in Early Buddhism." In *Buddhism, Sexuality, and Gender*, ed. José Ignacio Cabezón, 3–36. Albany: State University of New York Press, 1992.

Srivastava, A. L. *Nandyāvarta: An Auspicious Symbol in Indian Art*. Allahabad: Kitab Mahal, 1991.

Srivastava, Balram. "Buddhist Goddesses in Orissan Imagery." In *Buddhist Iconography*, 129–137. New Delhi: Tibet House, 1989.

———. *Iconography of Śakti: A Study Based on the Śrītattvanidhi*. Varanasi: Chaukhambha Orientalia, 1978.

Srivastava, K. M. "Sculptures from Sanghol: A Monumental Discovery." *Arts of Asia* 20, no. 1 (Jan.–Feb. 1990): 79–91.

Srivastava, M. C. P. *Mother Goddess in Indian Art, Archaeology and Literature*. Delhi: Agam Kala Prakashan, 1979.

Stone, Elizabeth Rosen. *The Buddhist Art of Nāgārjunakoṇḍa*. Delhi: Motilal Banarsidass, 1994.

Stooke, H. J. "An XI Century Illuminated Palm Leaf Ms." *Oriental Art* 1, no. 1 (Summer 1948): 5–8.

Strickmann, Michel. *Chinese Magical Medicine*. Ed. Bernard Faure. Stanford: Stanford University Press, 2001.

Strong, John S. *The Legend and Cult of Upagupta: Sanskrit Buddhism in North India and Southeast Asia*. Princeton: Princeton University Press, 1992.

———. *The Legend of King Aśoka: A Study and Translation of the Aśokāvadāna*. Princeton: Princeton University Press, 1983.

Sugandha, Bhikkhu, and T. C. Majupuria. *Lumbini: The Birth Place of Buddha (Past, Present and Future)*. (Pamphlet) Bangkok: Craftsman Press, n.d.

Sutherland, Gail Hinich. *The Disguises of the Demon: The Development of the Yakṣa in Hinduism and Buddhism*. Albany: State University of New York Press, 1991.

Taddei, Maurizio. "A New Early Śaiva Image from Gandhāra." In Janine Schotsmans and Maurizio Taddei, eds., *South Asian Archaeology 1983*, 615–28.

Takakusu, J., trans. *A Record of the Buddhist Religion as Practised in India and the Malay Archipelago (A.D. 671–695), by I-Tsing*. 1896. Reprint. Delhi: Munshiram Manoharlal, 1998.

Tanaka, Kimiaki. *Art of Thangka: A Catalogue of the Hahn Foundation for Museum*. 3 vols. Seoul: Hahn Foundation for Museum, 1998–2001.

Tapasyananda, Swami. *Śrī Lalitā Sahasranāma*. Madras: Sri Ramakrishna Math, n.d.

Tāranātha. *History of Buddhism in India*. Trans. Lama Chimpa and Alaka Chattopadhyaya. Ed. Debiprasad Chattopadhyaya. Atlantic Highlands, N.J.: Humanities Press, 1981.

———. *The Origin of the Tara Tantra*. Trans. David Templeman. Dharamsala: Library of Tibetan Works and Archives, 1981.

———. *The Seven Instruction Lineages: Tāranātha's bKa'.babs.bdun.ldan*. Trans. and ed. David Templeman. Dharamsala: Library of Tibetan Works and Archives, 1983.

———. *Tāranātha's Life of Kṛṣṇācārya/Kāṇha*. Trans. David Templeman. Dharamsala: Library of Tibetan Works and Archives, 1989.

Thaplyal, Kiran. "Gajalakṣmī on Seals." In D. C. Sircar, ed., *Foreigners in Ancient India*, 112–25.

Tharchin, Sermey Khensur Lobsang. *Sublime Path to Kechara Paradise: Vajrayogini's Eleven Yogas of Generation Stage Practice as Revealed by the Glorious Naropa*. Howell, N.J.: Mahayana Sutra and Tantra Press, 1997.

Thinley, Karma. "Sitatapatra Sadhana." *Buddhist Himalaya* 6, nos. 1–2 (1994–95): 17–20.

Thurman, Robert A. F. "Buddhist Views of Nature: Variations on the Theme of Mother-Father Harmony." In *On Nature*, ed. Leroy Rouner, 96–112. Notre Dame: University of Notre Dame Press, 1984.

———, trans. *The Holy Teaching of Vimalakīrti*. University Park: Pennsylvania State University Press, 1976.

Tissot, Francine. "The Site of Sahrī-Bāhlol in Gandhāra." In *South Asian Archaeology 1983*, ed. Janine Schotsmans and Maurizio Taddei, 567–614.

Tkatschow, Dwight. "Sarasvatī: Observations on the Iconography of an Ancient Indian Goddess." In *Mother Goddess and Other Goddesses*, ed. V. Subramaniam, 75–97. Delhi: Ajanta, 1993.

Tripathi, L. K. "Srī Laksmī in Early Indian Literature and Art." In D. C. Sircar, ed., *Foreigners in Ancient India*, 158–62.

Tromge, Jane. *Red Tara Commentary: Instructions for the Concise Practice Known as "Red Tara: An Open Door to Bliss and Ultimate Awareness."* Compiled from the teachings of Chagdud Tulku. Junction City, Calif.: Padma, 1994.

Trungpa, Chögyam. "Sacred Outlook: The Vajrayoginī Shrine and Practice." In Deborah Klimburg-Salter, ed. *Silk Route and the Diamond Path*, 226–41.

———. *Visual Dharma: The Buddhist Art of Tibet.* Berkeley: Shambhala, 1975.

Tucci, Giuseppe. "Earth in India and Tibet," in *Opera Minora,* vol. 2, pp. 532–67. Rome: Dott. Giovanni Bardi Editore, 1971.

———. *Gyantse and Its Monasteries.* 3 pts. *Indo-Tibetica* 4. 1941. English ed. New Delhi: Aditya Prakashan, 1989.

———. "Oriental Notes II: An Image of a Devi Discovered in Swat and Some Connected Problems." *East and West,* n.s., 14, nos. 3–4 (Sept.–Dec. 1963): 146–82.

———. *The Temples of Western Tibet and Their Artistic Symbolism.* 2 pts. *Indo-Tibetica* 3. 1935. English ed. New Delhi: Aditya Prakashan, 1989.

———. *Tibetan Painted Scrolls.* 1949. Reprint (without plates). Kyoto: Rinsen, 1980.

———. "The Wives of Srong btsan sgam po." *Oriens Extremus* 9 (1962): 121–30.

Tulku, Tarthang. *Sacred Art of Tibet.* 1972. 2nd ed. Berkeley: Dharma, 1974.

Uhlig, Helmut. *On the Path to Enlightenment: The Berti Aschmann Foundation of Tibetan Art at the Museum Rietberg Zürich.* Zurich: Museum Rietberg, 1995.

———. *Tantrische Kunst des Buddhismus.* Berlin: Safari bei Ullstein, 1981.

Vaidya, Karunakar. *Buddhist Traditions and Culture of the Kathmandu Valley.* Kathmandu: Shajha Prakashan, 1986.

Vaidya, P. L., ed. *Āryamañjusrimūlakalpa* [*sic*]. *Mahāyāna Sūtrasaṃgraha,* pt. 2. Buddhist Sanskrit Texts 18. Darbhanga: Mithila Institute, 1964.

———. *The Gaṇḍavyūhasūtra.* Buddhist Sanskrit Texts 5. Darbhanga: Mithila Institute, 1960.

Vajrācārya, Ratnakājī, ed. *Cacā-Munā.* (Newar) 2 vols. Kathmandu: Vṛddhimān Śākya and Vadṛīmān Śākya, 1996, 1999.

Vajracharya, Gautama V. "Atmospheric Gestation: Deciphering Ajanta Ceiling Paintings and Other Related Works." 2 pts. *Marg* 55, no. 2 (Dec. 2003): 41–57; *Marg* 55, no. 3 (March 2004): 40–51.

———. "Symbolism of Ashokan Pillars: A Reappraisal in Light of Textual and Visual Evidence." *Marg* 51, no. 2 (Dec. 1999): 53–78.

Van Kooij, K. R. *Religion in Nepal.* Leiden: E. J. Brill, 1978.

Vasu, Nagendranāth. *The Archaeological Survey of Mayurabhanja.* 2 vols. Calcutta: Mayurabhanja State, 1912.

Vessantara. *Meeting the Buddhas: A Guide to Buddhas, Bodhisattvas and Tantric Deities.* Glaskow: Windhorse, 1993.

Vira, Raghu, and Lokesh Chandra. *Tibetan Maṇḍalas (Vajrāvalī and Tantra-samuccaya).* New Delhi: International Academy of Indian Culture, 1995.

Vogel, Jean Phillippe. "The Woman and Tree or *śālabhañjikā* in Indian Literature and Art." *Acta Orientalia* 7 (1929): 201–31.

Waddell, L. Austine. "The 'Dhāraṇī' Cult in Buddhism, Its Origin, Deified Literature and Images." *Ostasiatische Zeitschrift* 2 (July 1912): 155–95.

———. " 'Dharanī' or Indian Buddhist Protective Spells." *Indian Antiquary* 43 (March–April 1914): 37–42, 49–54.

———. "Evolution of the Buddhist Cult, Its Gods, Images, and Art: A Study in Buddhist Iconography, with Reference to the Guardian Gods of the World and Hārītī, 'The Buddhist Madonna.' " *Asiatic Quarterly Review* 33 (Jan.–April 1912): 104–60.

———. "The Indian Buddhist Cult of Avalokita and His Consort Tara 'the Savioress,' Illustrated from the Remains in Magadha." *Journal of the Royal Asiatic Society* (1894): 51–89.

———. *Tibetan Buddhism: With Its Mystic Cults, Symbolism and Mythology*. 1895 (under title *The Buddhism of Tibet, or Lamaism*). Reprint. New York: Dover, 1972.

Wadley, Susan S. "Śītalā: The Cool One." *Asian Folklore Studies* 39, no. 1 (1980): 33–62.

Waldschmidt, Ernst, and Rose Waldschmidt. *Nepal: Art Treasures from the Himalayas*. Trans. David Wilson. Calcutta: Oxford and IBH, 1969.

Walshe, Maurice, trans. *The Long Discourses of the Buddha: A Translation of the Dīgha Nikāya*. 1987. Reprint. Boston: Wisdom, 1995.

Walters, Jonathan S. "Gotamī's Story." In *Religions of India in Practice*, ed. Donald S. Lopez, Jr., 113–38. Princeton: Princeton University Press, 1995.

———. "Stūpa, Story, and Empire: Constructions of the Buddha Biography in Early Post-Aśokan India." In *Sacred Biography in the Buddhist Traditions of South and Southeast Asia*, ed. Juliane Schober, 160–92. Honolulu: University of Hawaii Press, 1997.

———. "A Voice from the Silence: The Buddha's Mother's Story." *History of Religions* 33, no. 4 (May 1994): 358–79.

Wangchuk, Jamyang Khyentse. *The Vajrayogini Teaching According to the Ultimate Secret Yoga in the Naro-Khachod Tradition*. Singapore: Singapore Buddha Sasana Society, 1986.

Wangpo, Jamyang Khyentse. *Appearing Aglow with Active Awareness: The Long Sadhana of White Tara with Consort from the Chi-me Pak-ma Nying-tik Cycle*. (Booklet) Trans. James Rutke. N.p.: Wish-Granting Press, 1989.

Warrier, A. G. Krishna, trans. *The Śākta Upaniṣads*. 1967. Reprint. Madras: Adyar Library and Research Centre, 1975.

Watson, Burton, trans. *The Lotus Sutra*. New York: Columbia University Press, 1993.

Wayman, Alex. *The Enlightenment of Vairocana*. Delhi: Motilal Banarsidass, 1992.

———. "The Goddess Sarasvatī—from India to Tibet." *Kailash: A Journal of Himalayan Studies* 5 (1977): 245–51.

———. "Messengers, What Bring Ye?" In *Indo-Tibetan Studies: Papers in Honour and Appreciation of Professor David L. Snellgrove's Contribution to Indo-Tibetan Studies*, ed. Tadeusz Skorupski, 305–22. Tring, United Kingdom: Institute of Buddhist Studies, 1990.

———. "The Twenty-One Praises of Tārā: A Syncretism of Śaivism and Buddhism." *Journal of the Bihar Research Society* 45 (1959): 36–43.

Wayman, Alex, trans. *The Lion's Roar of Queen Śrīmālā: A Buddhist Scripture on the Tathāgatagarbha Theory*. New York: Columbia University Press, 1974.

Weldon, David, and Jane Casey Singer. *The Sculptural Heritage of Tibet: Buddhist Art in the Nyingjei Lam Collection*. London: Laurence King, 1999.

Whitaker, K. P. K. "A Buddhist Spell." *Asia Major*, n.s., 10, no. 1 (1963): 9–22.

Whitney, William Dwight, trans. *Atharva-Veda-Saṃhitā*. Rev. and ed. Nag Sharan Singh. 2 vols. Delhi: Nag, 1987.

Williams, Joanna. "Sārnāth Gupta Steles of the Buddha's Life." *Ars Orientalis* 10 (1975): 171–92.

Williams, Paul, and Anthony Tribe. *Buddhist Thought: A Complete Introduction to the Indian Tradition*. London: Routledge, 2000.

Willson, Martin. *In Praise of Tārā: Songs to the Saviouress*. London: Wisdom, 1986.

Willson, Martin, and Martin Brauen, eds. *Deities of Tibetan Buddhism: The Zürich Paintings of the Icons Worthwhile to See (Bris sku mthoṅ ba don ldan)*. Boston: Wisdom, 2000.

Wilson, Liz. *Charming Cadavers: Horrific Figurations of the Feminine in Indian Buddhist Hagiographic Literature*. Chicago: University of Chicago Press, 1996.

Wright, Daniel. *History of Nepal: With an Introductory Sketch of the Country and People of Nepal.* 1877. Reprint. Delhi: Asian Educational Services, 1993.

Yeshe, Lama. *Vajra Yogini*. London: Wisdom, 1979.

Young, Serinity. *Dreaming in the Lotus: Buddhist Dream Narrative, Imagery, and Practice.* Boston: Wisdom, 1999.

Zanen, M. "The Goddess Vajrayoginī and the Kingdom of Sankhu (Nepal)." In *L'Espace du temple*, vol. 2, *Les Sanctuaires dans le royaume*, ed. Jean-Claude Galey, 125–66. Paris: Éditions de l'École des Hautes Études en Sciences Sociales, 1986.

Zwalf, W. *Buddhism: Art and Faith*. New York: Macmillan, 1985.

———. *A Catalogue of the Gandhāra Sculpture in the British Museum*. Vol. 1, *Text*. Vol. 2, *Plates*. London: British Museum Press, 1996.

Index

Note: Page numbers in bold italics indicate illustrations.